NAPOLEON

Books by André Castelot

NAPOLEON

JOSEPHINE

THE TURBULENT CITY: PARIS

KING OF ROME

QUEEN OF FRANCE

NAPOLEON

By ANDRÉ CASTELOT

Translated from the French by Guy Daniels

1817

HARPER & ROW, PUBLISHERS

NEW YORK, EVANSTON, SAN FRANCISCO,

LONDON

DC
203
.C2713

FIRST EDITION

STANDARD BOOK NUMBER: 06-010678-6

LIBRARY OF CONGRESS CATALOG CARD NUMBER: 70-83587

CONTENTS

Illustrations follow page 182

INTRODUCTION

What a novel my life has been!

In order to make Napoleon live again, I have made a special effort to find unpublished or forgotten texts, so that I might enrich the narrative with details not yet generally known. Above all, however, I have tried to re-create the setting of the most unusual life story of all time. In so doing, I have retraced the Emperor's route from the pyramids to Moscow, from the Great St. Bernard to Austerlitz, and from one to another of those islands that cast their sorcerer's spell over Napoleon's life: Corsica, where he was born; Elba, where he ruled after falling from the pinnacle of power; Aix, where he made the gravest decision of his lifetime; and, finally, St. Helena, where he breathed his last.

Having completed such a voyage and laid by one's harvest of images, one is first of all confronted by a problem of selection. The enormous mass of archival materials, memoirs, and recollections is overwhelming. In particular, one is soon inundated by the terrible afflux of the correspondence kept up by this demon of a man, and by the thousands and thousands of orders he issued during those twenty years between Vendémiaire, when he stepped onto the stage of history, and Waterloo, when he left it to go off and die, a prisoner in chains, on an extinct volcano.

For the whole prodigious epic did not even last twenty years!

A.C.

NAPOLEON

I

NABULIO

My success, and everything good
that I have done, I owe to my mother.

NAPOLEON

ON MAY 9, 1769, about a hundred Corsican patriots were climbing
the paths of Monte Rotondo, in flight from the victorious French
troops. Among them was a young woman of nineteen, "pretty as a
picture," leaning on the arm of her husband. As they moved along
the path, their steps dislodging loose rocks, she was heard to say over
and over: "He will be the avenger of Corsica!"

It was her son that she meant: her son who was not yet born
(though she had no doubt that she would give birth to a boy); her son
who, all during that terrible retreat, "thrashed about violently" inside her.

On May 15 of the year before, Louis XV had acquired from the
Republic of Genoa, for a few million francs, the rights to Corsica. On
August 15—one year to the day before the birth of Napoleon—the
King proclaimed the island's "reunion" with France. But the real
work of conquering the acquired territory still remained to be done,
because the Corsicans were by no means in agreement with all this.
Although theoretically under the rule of the Genoese, they had been
more or less free. When, without anyone's asking for their opinion,
they became the subjects of the King of France, it was as if a rope
had been put around their necks.

The patriot Pasquale di Paoli (they called him the "Babbo") had
called an assembly of Corsican communes at Corte and issued a
formal protest against the landing of Louis XV's troops. With war
declared, the King had sent an expeditionary force to take possession

of Corsica. It had been defeated, and the survivors thrown into the
sea. "That little island will astonish the world!" Jean Jacques Rousseau
had exclaimed in admiration. But on May 9 the Corsican patriots,
commanded by Paoli, had been defeated at Ponte Nuovo. Louis XV
had in fact provided the requisite "thrust" by sending 20,000 men
under the command of the Comte de Vaux.

Only about a hundred of the defeated Corsicans had managed to
escape disaster and retreat to Monte Rotondo. Among them was a
small landowner, Carlo Maria Buonaparte, and his wife, nee Letizia
Ramolino, from a family of the petty nobility. Both were of Italian
extraction. He had married her on June 2, 1764, when she was only
fourteen.

Now, on this ninth day of May, 1769, he was gently helping her
along the path, as she repeated: "He will be the avenger of Corsica!"
And the pretty Letizia, "the little marvel" with the Greek profile,
continued to climb the steep slope of the mountain without once
complaining. As Napoleon said later: "She bore up under everything.
Losses, deprivations, fatigue—nothing made her lose courage. She
had a man's head on a woman's body. She was a woman from the
mountains of Corsica."

In a raging storm, the little band of patriots struggled across the
mountain, exhausted. Finally they took shelter in a grotto. (It still
exists, and is still called the Refugees' Grotto.) It was there that Carlo
Maria Buonaparte received the emissaries sent by the Comte de
Vaux to make a peace offer.

Any further resistance would have been futile. As the Emperor
was to say at a later date: "I was born as my country was dying."

Corsica accepted its new masters. Carlo Maria and Letizia, giving
up the role of Robinson Crusoe patriots, went back to their big yellow
stucco house in Ajaccio on the Strada Malerba, or Weed Street—aptly
named, it would seem. They lived on the ground floor and the second
floor, which at that time were infinitely less elegantly furnished than
they are today. The fine balcony that astounds the tourists of our day
had not yet been added. Likewise, the little tree-shaded plaza in
front of the house was laid out later, under the Consulate.

It was not the first time that little Letizia was about to give birth.
Before Giuseppe—the future King Joseph, born in 1768—she had had
a boy and a girl, both of whom died in infancy.

On August 15, 1769, Ajaccio (which at that time was only a small market town) was simultaneously celebrating the Assumption of Our Lady and—with forced enthusiasm—the first anniversary of the treaty annexing Corsica to France. Hardly had the High Mass begun at the cathedral, when Letizia Buonaparte felt her first labor pains. Helped by her sister-in-law, Gertruda Paravicini, she went quickly back to her home on the nearby Strada Malerba. When she got there (at about noon), she didn't have time to reach her bedroom. Instead, she went into the salon and lay down on a sofa covered with green silk, and almost immediately—with the help of Gertruda as midwife —was delivered of a boy who was "born in a caul," if we can take Napoleon's word for it.

Others maintain that Letizia gave birth to the future Emperor on the tile flooring of the salon. Stendhal even claimed that the delivery took place on one of the "antique rugs with great figures of heroes from mythology or the *Iliad*." This version is poetic but absolutely false.

Mme. Letizia set things straight: "The idea that he was born on the head of Caesar is a myth: he didn't have need of that. . . . We didn't have rugs in our houses in Corsica, and even less so in summer than in the winter."

That same day, as soon as the festival of the Blessed Virgin allowed it, Letizia's uncle, the Archdeacon Luciano, sent a priest to the Buonaparte home to give private baptism to the newborn baby.

"What is his Christian name to be?"

"Napoleone." (So long, in point of time, as the future Emperor writes his name Napoleone Buonaparte, we shall follow his example.)

Letizia, who pronounced it "Napollioné," has given the reason for this strange choice: "My uncle Napoleone died several weeks before the Battle of Ponte Nuovo, but he had come to Corsica to fight. It was in memory of that hero that I gave his Christian name to my second son."

Napoleon (which is how he spelled his name by then) was right when he said, "That name was endowed with a strength *(vertu)* at once virile, poetic, and overabundant."

But during his first few years he was called Nabulio or Nabulione. And because of his quarrelsome disposition, the family nicknamed him Rabulione, meaning "the one who never minds his own business." Despite the size of his head—it was so big that for a long time the child could not keep his balance—the baby Napoleone was puny. His face was pointed and his lips were thin. Mme. Letizia nursed the newborn herself, but also had the help of a robust peasant woman.

Of the thirteen children borne by Letizia in nineteen years, eight were to survive—eight children who one day would share thrones and principalities. All of them, that is, but one: Lucien (Luciano), who was not on good terms with his brother and had to content himself with the title of a papal prince.

Nabulio's mother went to the cathedral where she had very nearly given birth to Napoleone and made the customary offering of a candle, a coin, and a roll. The young Buonaparte's formal baptism was postponed until July, 1771, when a younger sister was to be born. (She died later that same year.) At about the same time, the father —who now went by the French name of Charles rather than Carlo Maria—was named assessor of the royal jurisdiction of Ajaccio. His salary was rather small: 900 livres. Henceforth, feeling that he had not been paid what he was worth, he concentrated all his efforts on one major aim: to see to it that the Kingdom of France assumed responsibility for the free education of his sons.

Meantime, Nabulio was developing into a fierce little fellow. As Napoleon was to say to his own son, the King of Rome: "You're a lazy one! At your age I was already thrashing Joseph! I was a mean one, always spoiling for a fight," he would say. "Nothing overawed me. I wasn't afraid of anybody. I would pummel one boy and scratch another. They were all afraid of me."

After two centuries, it is very hard to distinguish fact from fiction in the many stories of this kind. Is it true that the young Napoleone preferred games of war to all other child's games? It has been said that almost every evening he would go to the citadel to watch the maneuvers. And is it true that he trained a gang of street urchins outside of the town, where they fought with the *borghigiani*—the boys from the faubourg? It is certainly so reported.

When Nabulio left for school in the morning, he would take along a loaf of white bread that his mother had given him for lunch. One day Mme. Buonaparte learned that he often traded this loaf to a soldier for a piece of army ration bread. The story goes that when his mother reproached him for this, the boy replied: "I'm going to be a soldier some day, so I might as well get used to eating this bread."

It was Charles's plan to make his older son, Joseph, an ecclesiastic, and the younger one a soldier. In order to obtain scholarships for them, he had to prove "four degrees (generations) of nobility." But he had no difficulty in garnering proofs of his gentility; and the young Napoleone—along with Joseph, the future King of Spain—was sent off to the Collège d'Autun.

There, the same teachers and schoolmates who were so charmed by Joseph's gentle disposition were astonished by "the young Buonaparte's" untidy dress and bad manners. They didn't know what to make of his odd physique, his sallow complexion, and his accent. They taunted him, but he wasn't long in making himself respected. When one of his schoolmates derided the Corsican troops, he retorted: "If the French had been four against one, they would never have taken Corsica. But they were ten against one!"

The word "homesick" is a weak one to describe the confusion of the young Nabulio, who was not yet ten years old. Everything was different from Corsica: the climate, the food, the way of life, and especially the language. When he first came to Autun he spoke virtually no French. But as one of his teachers said, "He had a great deal of aptitude: he understood and learned easily." Nonetheless, Nabulio continued to think "in the Corsican dialect"; and despite all the lessons given him by Father Chardon, his conversational French remained distinctly poor.

Charles, meantime, with his consummate skill, was intriguing at both Versailles and Paris for his son "the young Buonaparte." The situation was favorable, because of the general eagerness to please the Corsican nobility who had come over to the side of France; and before long the clever petitioner received the following letter, dated March 28, 1779, and signed by the Prince de Montbarrey, the Minister of War:

> The Intendant of Corsica, Monsieur, has no doubt informed you that the King has consented to place your son, Napoleone de Buonaparte, as a student in one of His military schools. His Majesty has just decreed that he should be admitted to the school at Brienne.

One evening in the month of May, 1779, the abbé Hamey d'Auberive, vicar general of the Bishop of Autun, opened the creaky little wrought-iron gate of the modest (Military Academy of Brienne,

which had been in existence for only two years. Before him was a
short, tree-shaded walk leading to the main building. (That *allée* is
still there, but the branches of the eight linden trees have been
trimmed so often that they are now all twisted and knotted.) He
opened the folding door of the main building and, after passing down
a flagstoned corridor, entered a paneled room with two large windows. This was the parlor, which one can still see today. There he was
greeted by the Superior of the school, Father Leleu.

The abbé stepped aside. Behind him, terribly intimidated, stood
a little ten-year-old Corsican, puny and with disheveled hair.

"What is your name?"

"Napollioné dé Buonaparté."

It was thus that the future Emperor pronounced his name. And
a bit later, when he first met his young schoolmates, they burst out
laughing at him, as they repeated: "Napollioné? *La paille au nez*"—
Straw in the Nose! The name stuck.

For those who love the past, it is very moving to wander through
what remains of the little military school at Brienne where the "arrière-cadet Buonaparte," as he now signed his letters, passed from
childhood into youth.

(The school had formerly been a monastery; and the sole remaining building—a tumbledown structure whose tiled roof is overgrown
with moss—is touchingly reminiscent of an abandoned presbytery)
One can imagine the cadet in his uniform (light-blue coat with red
cuffs, white buttons bearing the school insignia, blue or black
breeches) daydreaming under the linden trees, or bounding up the
stairway (which still exists, worn and rickety) to the monastic cells
which served the students as a dormitory.

The young Napoleone was placed in the *classe de septième*. He
was ill at ease in his new surroundings, and still felt like a stranger.
His fellow cadets belonged to the nobility of France and were even
more quick than the little bourgeois of Autun to mock and laugh at
this tight-lipped savage.

He was certainly the most arrogant student at the school—perhaps because his fellow cadets, whose families bore high-sounding
titles, were condescending toward him as the son of a small Corsican
landowner. One day a supervisor, by way of punishing the boy for
some breach of deportment, ordered that he must wear rough serge
clothing (one of the punishments employed at the school) and take

his dinner while kneeling at the door of the refectory.

With everyone watching him, Napoleone entered the dining hall. He was pale and tense, with staring eyes.

"Down on your knees, Monsieur!"

At this, the boy was seized "with a sudden fit of vomiting and a violent nervous attack." He stamped his feet and screamed, "I'll eat standing up, Monsieur, and not on my knees. In my family, we kneel only before God!"

The supervisor decided to go ahead and use force. Napoleone threw himself to the floor, writhing, and screamed through his sobs: "Isn't that right, Mamma? Before God! Before God!"

The Superior had to be called. He put an end to the scene, and saved the cadet from his torture.

The cadet got his revenge for this and other humiliations during a particularly harsh winter. Deep snow covered the yard. Athletic games were out of the question, and the students had to be satisfied with marching back and forth in one of the rooms of the school building. One day Napoleone explained to his fellow cadets that (as one of the students later reported):

> They could have a lot more fun if they would shovel tunnels through the snow in the yard, dig trenches, and build parapets.
>
> "Once the first part of the work is done," he said, "we can form platoons, and mount a kind of siege. As the inventor of this new amusement, I'll lead the attacks."
>
> This plan was enthusiastically adopted by the excited boys, and put into effect. Our little simulated war went on for two weeks. It came to an end only when quite a few of the cadets—both besieged and besieging—were rather seriously hurt because of the gravel and stones mixed into the snowballs. I remember that I was one of those who suffered most from this bombardment.

(These words were written by L. A. F. de Bourrienne, who one day would become the secretary of General Bonaparte, and then of the First Consul.) "Between the two of us," he said, "there was the kind of camaraderie that is quickly established."

What Nabulio wanted above all was to learn correct French so that he would no longer be ridiculed. His teacher, the vice-principal

Dupuis, quickly obtained good results—except in spelling. For that matter, the young cadet's bad spelling was hard to detect, from his first days at school on through to the last, because his writing was illegible. In the words of a fellow cadet, Alexandre des Mazis: "His teachers couldn't decipher his compositions, and he himself had trouble rereading what he had written. Not only that, but this handwriting of his—carelessness that became a habit—became more and more illegible."

Many years later, under the Empire, an old man came to the royal residence at St.-Cloud and managed to get a private interview with the Emperor. Napoleon didn't give him time to open his mouth: before he could do so, questions came raining down on him:

"Who are you? Where are you from? What do you want?"

"Sire," the visitor stammered, "Sire, I was the one . . . yes, I was the one who had the honor to give Your Majesty, at Brienne, for fifteen months, lessons in penmanship—"

The Emperor interrupted him with a laugh. "Ah! So it's you? So you were the one! Well, you don't have much to brag about. Your teaching certainly turned out a fine product, I must say! Congratulations!"

But this didn't prevent him from granting a pension of 1,200 francs to the miserable teacher.

At Brienne, Napoleone took a dim view of Latin, and was "repelled and disgusted" when he had to translate it into French, or vice versa. On the other hand, his flair for mathematics was well manifested.

The religious instruction given by the priests revolted him. As he said later: "I would hear a sermon in which the preacher would say that Cato and Caesar were damned. I was eleven years old. I was shocked to learn that the most virtuous men of antiquity would be burned eternally because they hadn't followed a religion that they hadn't even heard of. . . . From that time on, I had no more religion."

He worked so hard—sometimes spending the whole night "going over the lessons of the day before"—that he grew thin. He looked ill —so ill that in 1782 when Mme. Letizia, going to the take the water cure at Bourbon, stopped by at Brienne to see her son, she didn't at first recognize him.

Later on he would say, "My temperament was such that I couldn't abide the idea of not being first in my class—right away."

His academic success paid off when, at the prize-giving ceremony in 1781, his prize was awarded him by Mme. de Montesson, who was accompanied by the Duc d'Orléans. (The father of Philippe-Égalité, having failed in his attempt to make Mme. de Montesson the Duchesse d'Orléans, was wedded to her in a morganatic marriage, and had since lived—by his own decision—as "Monsieur de Montesson.")

And there was another balm for the *amour-propre* of the young Corsican: the annual visit, on the day of the *fête du roi*, to the splendid château which overlooked the little town as it still does today. The cadet Buonaparte was dazzled by the white and gold salons of M. de Brienne's château—those great halls, with parquet or marble-tiled floors; the theater; the library; and especially, the salon that forms the center of the main building and looks out upon both the park and the *cour d'honneur*.

Buonaparte and his fellow cadets, preceded by lackeys in uniforms trimmed in silver, entered the "royal suite" dominated by the bed reserved for the sovereign just in case he took a fancy to spending the night at Brienne. That night the Duc d'Orléans would sleep in this bed beneath a canopy of blue velvet adorned with white plumes—the same bed in which, in 1805, the Emperor Napoleon would sleep on his way to be consecrated King of Italy.

Final examinations were near. Would Napoleone be judged worthy of entering the École Militaire de Paris? Earlier, the former inspector of this school, Brigadier General Keralio (Chevalier de Keralio), had made his appraisal in these terms:

> M. de Buonaparte (Napoleone), born August 15, 1769, height five feet three inches, has completed his *quatrième*. Good constitution, excellent health, obedient. He is honest and grateful, and his deportment is very good. He has always distinguished himself by his diligence in mathematics. He knows history and geography quite well. He is very poor in social accomplishments. He will make an excellent naval officer.

Another examiner, perhaps more perceptive, noted: "Domineering, imperious, and stubborn."

The new inspector, Reynaud des Monts, did not arrive at Brienne until September 22. After having questioned the students, he found that the cadet Buonaparte possessed the requisite abilities to enter the royal military school at Paris—the school founded by Louis XV at the request of the young Marquise de Pompadour. Napoleone, who had just turned fifteen, was beside himself with joy.

On October 17, 1784, "M. Napoleone de Buonaparte, Esq., son of the nobleman Charles-Marie de Buonaparte," left Brienne by mail coach with the four other cadets who had been accepted along with him. Father Berton accompanied them to Paris.

On St. Helena, Napoleon recalled: "The first night was very trying. The atmosphere was different. The classes were commanded by four officers of the Order of Saint-Louis, and eight sergeants of strict military bearing who barked out their commands."

A veteran named Champeaux (he was to die from wounds received at Marengo) was put in charge of teaching the manual of arms to his young cohorts. In this respect Buonaparte was a deplorably bad soldier: his mind was always elsewhere—as was plain to see. One day when his absent-mindedness was carried to excess, Champeaux rapped the future Emperor's fingers with a ramrod. Then he leaped backward: Napoleone had thrown his rifle at his head.

Instead of having the young man sent to the guardhouse to improve his character, the captain in charge of instruction merely asked one of the other students, Alexandre des Mazis, to try to civilize "this dangerous islander." This was the beginning of their friendship.

Actually, the two young men were much more concerned with exchanging their daydreams than with discovering the hidden charms of the manual of arms. Often, in the course of a drill, Major de Lannoy would give the command, "Order arms!" and everyone would see a rifle still sticking up in the air from the second rank, in a ridiculous fashion.

It was Napoleone de Buonaparte, daydreaming. Des Mazis, standing next to him on the right, would give him a quick jab with his elbow, whereupon the recalcitrant rifle would come to the ground with a sound all too clearly heard in the general silence. It was a very unmilitary sound, and it made Major de Lannoy shudder.

"Monsieur Buonaparte," the distressed instructor would shout, "wake up! You're always spoiling the drill!"

The new student was now wearing the natty uniform of the school: blue coat with red collar, white lining, and silver bands; jacket and breeches of blue serge; a pair of gloves (those students who rode horseback owned three pairs); and a cap embroidered in silver or trimmed in mohair.

He was good in mathematics, average in history, and in general got lower marks than at Brienne. Later, he would say: "They put me in the artillery class right away. I was the next to the last one admitted."

Buonaparte was not well liked at school; and the same scenes he had lived through at Brienne were repeated at Paris. This sullen, unsociable islander found fault with everything, voicing his criticisms in his harsh accent and "in a sharp tone of voice." He rebuffed his instructors, who therefore considered him an "ill-tempered young man," and they were shocked by the way he talked about Corsica. One of them, M. Valfort, told him once: "Monsieur, you are one of the King's students. You must bear that in mind, and moderate your love for Corsica—which, after all, is a part of France!"

Being very sensitive to the jokes of his fellow cadets, Napoleone was often humiliated and insulted; and he magnified all this in his imagination. If he saw the least smile on the face of someone mocking him, he would put up his fists and go after him. "Oh, the punches I gave them in those days!" he recalled. And the little country squire, the "King's scholar," gave those "punches" to people with names like Rohan, Broglie, and Montmorency-Laval.

When away from the military school on a pass, Napoleone stayed with his Paris acquaintances, the Permons, friends of the Buonaparte family, who lived at the Hôtel de Sillery, 13, Place de Conti. Supposedly he slept in the fourth-floor garret, the window of which looked out on the corner of the Place Conti and the Impasse Conti. It was here that Mme. Permon's younger daughter, Laure, who was to become Mme. Junot and, later, the Duchesse d'Abrantès, made the acquaintance of the future Emperor.

She wrote of him:

> The charming thing about Napoleon when he became a young man was his look—especially the gentle expression he could impart to it in a moment of kindness. But his anger was frightful; and however inured I was, I never looked at that adorable face—even in anger, when it was animated—without feeling a *frisson*. His smile was equally captivating, as the disdainful twist of his mouth made you tremble.

But of all that—the head which would wear the crowns of a
world, those hands of which the most coquettish of women would
have been proud, and whose soft white skin covered muscles of
steel and bones of diamond—of all that nothing could be discerned in him as a child. It only asserted itself when he became
a young man.

One day Laure's mother and her uncle, Démétrius Commène,
went with Napoleone to St.-Cyr to see his sister, Maria Anna Buonaparte. As soon as the visitors arrived, the girl started to weep. One
of her schoolmates, Mlle. de Montluc, was to leave the Convent of
Saint-Louis in a few days. A farewell tea party had been planned for
the occasion, and Napoleone's sister didn't have so much as one franc
to help pay the expenses.

The cadet's first reaction was to reach into his pocket. But "realizing, on second thought, that he wouldn't find what he wanted," he
reddened and stamped his foot. Whereupon Mme. Permon proffered
the ten or twelve francs needed to relieve the distress of Maria Anna.

When the visitors got back into their carriage, Napoleone exploded, cursing the management of such establishments as St.-Cyr
and the École Militaire, which he called "detestable."

As Laure reported the incident later:

> It was plain to see that his sister's humiliation was painful to
> him. My uncle finally grew impatient with the bitterness of his
> talk, and told him just that—rather dryly. Napoleone fell silent
> immediately. . . . But he was too overwrought. Before long he had
> brought the conversation back to the same subject, and finally his
> expressions became so offensive that my uncle said: "Be quiet!
> You have no right to talk like that, considering that you're being
> educated thanks to the King's charity."

The word "charity" made the cadet redden so violently that
Mme. Permon thought he was going to choke. When he could finally
speak, he said in a voice trembling with emotion: "As a student, I
don't belong to the King—I belong to the State."

Let it be noted that the "King's charity" amounted to an annual
expenditure, for each cadet, of 4,282 livres, or five million old French
francs. M. de Commène quite understandably shouted: "I won't let
you talk to me like that about your benefactor!"

"I won't say anything more to arouse your displeasure," the cadet replied. "But just let me add that if I were in charge of making the regulations, they would be drawn up very differently—and for the good of all."

If I were in charge!

On March 23, 1785, Buonaparte learned that his father had died a month earlier, on February 24, at Montpellier.

In accordance with the custom, one of the priests at the school wanted to take Napoleone to the dispensary so that he could be alone "in the first moments of grief." He refused to go, saying grimly: "I'm strong enough to bear this pain without anyone's taking the trouble to console me."

And yet, he was deeply affected, and said he was haunted by the fact that his father had died "a hundred leagues away from his own country, in a foreign land that was indifferent to his existence, far removed from all that was most dear to him."

It was not until a week later that he wrote to his mother: "By now, time has somewhat calmed my first pangs of grief, and I hasten to assure you of the gratitude I feel for the kindness you have always displayed toward me."

Since he now felt himself head of the family (though this role belonged to Joseph), he ordered:

Be consoled, Mother: the circumstances demand it. We shall redouble our solicitude and our gratitude. And we shall be happy if, through our obedience, we can assuage somewhat your inestimable loss of a beloved husband.

In closing, dear Mother, I beg of you to quiet your grief. My own compels me to this request.

Early the following year, Napoleone and his classmates were informed that in 1785 there would be no examinations for the Navy. Should he stay twelve months more at the royal military school when his only thoughts were of seeing Ajaccio again? He refused. And, like most of his fellow cadets who had been affected by this cancellation, the young Corsican (who had continued to be one of the best in the mathematics class) chose the Artillery.

The month of September—a time when all of France was in an uproar over "the Affair of the Diamond Necklace," which made headlines on August 15—marked the opening of the competition in which the graduates of all the royal schools in France participated. One of the two instructors in mathematics at the École Militaire de Paris had written the following evaluation:

> Napoleone de Buonaparte. Reserved and diligent. Prefers study to any kind of amusement. Likes to read good authors. Very much given to the abstract sciences. Has little curiosity about others. (Knows mathematics and geography extremely well) Taciturn; loves solitude; capricious, haughty, very egotistical; close-mouthed, but vigorous in his rejoinders. Has a good deal of *amour-propre*. Ambitious and aspires toward everything. This young man is worthy of sponsorship.

On September 28, the promotions were made public. Napoleone was ranked forty-second out of fifty-six students commissioned as second lieutenants. He said later of his pleasure at the promotion, "I was an officer at the age of sixteen years and fifteen days."

His commission, signed by Louis XVI at St.-Cloud, was in fact predated—as of September 1. The following month, Second Lieutenant Buonaparte and his friend Des Mazis were assigned to the Régiment de la Fère, garrisoned at Valence.

On October 28, as soon as he had put on his new uniform and received his silver collar fastener and his sword, Buonaparte hurried off to Mme. Permon's to let the two young ladies of the house have a look at him. When they saw him in his gigantic boots, which virtually swallowed up his legs ("very thin at that time"), they burst out laughing, and the young officer was irked.

"Now that you are wearing a sword," said Cécile, the older sister, "you must be a cavalier for the ladies, and be glad when they joke with you."

"It's easy to see that you're nothing but a little schoolgirl," Napoleone replied disdainfully.

"And you're just a Puss-in-Boots!" the girl came back.

It was hard for him to control his anger. Notwithstanding, the next day the young officer of sixteen, delving into his meager savings, brought "the little schoolgirl" a handsome edition of *Puss-in-Boots*. And to Laure he gave a set of puppets representing Puss-in-Boots running in front of the carriage of his master, le Marquis de Carabas.

At eleven P.M. on October 30 Buonaparte and Des Mazis, escorted by a *bas-officer*, left the Champ de Mars. They went to the stagecoach office, where they dined and spent the night. The next morning, at five o'clock, they got into the stagecoach which was to take them via Sens, Auxerre, and Autun to Châlon-sur-Saône, where they would embark in the "water coach" in which they would travel to Lyons.

A short way beyond Fontainebleau, when horses had to pull the heavy stagecoach uphill at a walk, the two young men got out to go on foot. As they did, Des Mazis saw his friend break into a run, leaping and waving his arms like a madman, as he shouted: "I'm free! At last I'm free!"

II

CORSICAN OR FRENCH?

When I had the honor to be a second lieutenant,
I lunched on dry bread, but I never let on
to anyone that I was poor.

NAPOLEON

ON NOVEMBER 5, at Lyons, Buonaparte and Des Mazis missed the mail boat to Valence. While waiting for the next boat, they went into a bookstore and spent what was left of the 57 livres that each had received as expense money upon departure from the school. Had it not been for the generosity of an artillery officer who had been traveling with them since they left Paris, they would have had to go the rest of the way on foot.

The next morning, at dawn, they left Lyons on the mail boat, and arrived at Valence that same evening. When they had reported to their colonel, M. de Lance, they went to the town hall, where the clerk of the court issued them the following billet for lodgings:

> To Mademoiselle Claudine-Marie Bou at the corner of the Grande-Rue and the Rue du Croissant, at Valence (in Dauphiné).
> In the name of the King:
> "Mademoiselle Claudine-Marie Bou, proprietor of the Café-Cercle, is hereby called upon to provide lodgings for two second lieutenants of the Royal Artillery Régiment de la Fère, and to furnish them with what they require."

Mlle. Bou, an old maid nearing the age of fifty, had for a long time been a maker of mohair buttons, before becoming co-proprietor (with her father) of the Café-Cercle, otherwise known as a "literary café."

The thinnish, downy-cheeked officer with the deep, rumbling

voice and the long, straight hair won his hostess over completely. For eight livres and eight sols per month, he rented from her a little room on the third floor with a window looking out on the Grand'Rue. Directly opposite was the famous Maison des Têtes, dating from the Renaissance (it still exists). In it was located a bookshop with the portentous name of Pierre-Marc Aurel, where Buonaparte fell in love with the works of Rousseau.

"Oh, Rousseau!" he once lamented. "Why did you live only sixty years? In the interests of truth, you should have been immortal!" (Though later on, he would change his mind about that.)

Mlle. Bou took care of the young officer's laundry. But for his meals—which he took with Des Mazis—he went next door to an inn called Les Trois Pigeons. Although the food there was good, he ate quickly, scarcely spoke to the other guests, disdained the card games that followed the meals, and hurried back to his room to read.

Although he had been graduated from military school with the rank of second lieutenant, Napoleone still had to pass through what were called "the three grades": gunner, corporal, and sergeant. But it only took him two months and five days to become "qualified in the skills of his service and worthy of the rank of officer." Finally he could wear the uniform of an artillery officer of the Régiment de la Fère—"the handsomest in the world," he said of it. The coat was blue, with a turn-down collar lined with red. The breeches were blue too, and the epaulets were lozenged in gold and silk.

Wearing this uniform, he was occasionally invited to the homes of a few families of the local nobility. As he later told the historian Emmanuel Las Cases, one of those whose homes he visited was a certain Mme. du Colombier. She was a woman of fifty who "ruled the town and instantly took a strong liking to the young artillery officer." She invited him to her country place, Basseaux, and on one such occasion advised him to lead a less austere life.

"My mother already has too many burdens," he replied. "I musn't add to them through my own expenses—especially when they are imposed by the stupid follies of my fellow officers."

If he liked to "visit" Mme. du Colombier, it was chiefly because of his hostess's daughter, the pretty and lively Caroline. But this relationship never got beyond the first stages of tender affection. As the Emperor recalled it: "No one could have been more innocent than we were. We would imagine little trysts. But, believe it or not,

our happiness consisted in nothing more than eating cherries together."

After Mlle. du Colombier, it was a Mlle. de Saint-Germain, with
her lovely open countenance, who attracted Buonaparte. Her father,
Joseph de Saint-Germain, a tax farmer, had been royally cuckolded.
His wife had rapturously welcomed the attentions of King Louis XV,
and borne him a daughter. Her name was Louise Marie Adélaïde,
and it was she that the young Napeolone fell in love with.

He asked M. de Saint-Germain for her hand in marriage, but he
refused—no doubt convinced that this young lieutenant of artillery
had no future. So it was the the future Emperor almost became, "by
the left hand," the son-in-law of Louis XV. As for Louise Adélaïde,
she would later marry the Comte de Montalivet, whom the Emperor
would make his Minister of the Interior.

In his little room above the Café-Cercle, Napoleone was working
on a *Letter on Corsica*. He had not yet learned to love France, as can
be seen from the harsh words he wrote then:

> You French, not satisfied with having snatched from us every-
> thing we hold dear, have also corrupted our morals. The present
> state of my country, and the impossibility of changing it, is one
> more reason for fleeing this land where I am obliged, out of duty,
> to praise men whom, for reasons of virtue, I should hate.

On another occasion he added, in an almost threatening tone:
"The Corsicans, following all the laws of justice, managed to shake
off the Genoese yoke; and they can do the same with the French."

Or again, on the same subject: "I drew my first breath in Corsica
and, with it, a violent love for my unfortunate country and its independence."

On August 12, 1786, he was granted a leave of six months. He
decided to spend it in Corsica—that Corsica he had left at the age of
nine. Finally, after more than seven years of being away from it, he
would see again the sun-bathed town rising in tiers from its blue gulf
to its crown of mountains.

He reached Ajaccio in mid-September. What a joy it was for
Letizia to embrace her dear "little Nabulio" in his handsome blue
and red uniform, the first Corsican to become an officer of the King.

He saw for the first time his new brother and sister, those children who had been born during his long absence: Paolina (or Paoletta), the future Princess Pauline; Maria Annonciata (or Carolina), who one day would become Caroline, Queen of Naples; and Girolamo (Jérôme), then only two years old, who would become King of Westphalia.

The rest of the family proved to be as anti-French as he himself was, and the whole clan rallied together in an out-and-out hatred of the "French occupation."

The household of the Strada Malerba was in financial straits bordering on poverty. All that had come of Charles's enterprises, after his death, were debts. Letizia put the young officer in charge of defending the interests of the family. Consequently he requested, "for reasons of health," an extension of leave "for a period of five and one-half months, effective May 16, 1787—with pay, in view of limited finances and the cost of the course of treatment." This request was granted, for it was an era when officers spent as much time at home as with their units.

His most important task was to obtain an indemnity of 3,050 livres for some of the family property. But whenever he broached the subject to the intendant of Corsica, he found himself opposed by the force of inertia. Obviously, he would have to take the matter up with someone in Paris or Versailles. And so, on September 12, 1787, after a stay of one year in Corsica, Napoleone left Ajaccio. He took his time making the trip; it was not until November 9 that he reached Paris.

The young second lieutenant—his beardless face showing premature wrinkles, and his clothes hanging loosely on his thin body—might be seen at mealtimes going to a tavern on the Rue de Valois with a sign reading "The Three Milestones," or perhaps to another cheap eating place in the Passage des Petits Pères where the food cost five or six sous per serving. Embarrassed by the skimpy sum he was paying for his dinner, rather than leave it on the table he would wrap his coins in the paper on which his bill had been figured and take the money to the cashier without saying a word.

In the evening, by way of relaxation, he would sometimes go for a walk in the gardens of the Palais-Royal, which were quite near. On one such evening (Thursday, November 22) he met up with a prostitute. It was she who initiated him. He himself has given an account of the incident:

I had left the Boulevard des Italiens and was walking rapidly through the *allées* of the Palais-Royal. My soul being agitated by the vigorous feelings that characterize it, I was indifferent to the cold. But when my imaginings became less lively I grew aware of the rigors of the season, and headed for the galleries.

I was on the threshold, at the iron gates, when I noticed a young woman. The time of evening, her figure, and her extreme youthfulness convinced me that she was a prostitute.

I looked at her, and she stopped. Her manner was not the "grenadierish" one that the others had; rather, it was perfectly suited to appearance. That impressed me.

Her shyness encouraged me, and I spoke to her—I, who, most sensitive of all to the odiousness of a prostitute's situation, had always felt myself soiled by so much as a glance from one of them. . . . But her pàle complexion, her frail physique, and her gentle voice were such that I did not hesitate for a moment. I told myself that she was either a mere dolt or a person who would be useful in the reconnaissance that I wanted to make.

"You must be very cold," I said. "How can you bring yourself to walk through the park?"

"Ah, Monsieur! I'm spurred on by hope. I have to finish my evening's work."

The indifference with which she uttered those words—the phlegmatic nature of her reply—won me over, and I went with her.

"You seem to have a very weak constitution. I'm surprised that the job doesn't wear you out."

"Oh, it does, Monsieur! But I've got to do something for a living."

"That may well be. But isn't there some job that's better for your health?"

"No, Monsieur. I have to live."

I was enchanted to see that at least she was answering my questions. No such success had crowned all the attempts I had made previously.

"Since you can stand the cold so well, you must be from the north."

"I'm from Nantes, in Brittany."

"I know that part of the country. . . . Mademoiselle, you must do me the favor of telling me how you lost your virginity."

"I lost it to an officer."

"Are you angry about it?"

"Yes, I am! I certainly am." (Her voice took on a melting, unctuous quality that I had not noticed before.) "I certainly am! My sister is well set up in life now. Why couldn't I be the same?"

"How did you happen to come to Paris?"

"The officer who ruined me—the man I detest—abandoned me. I had to flee from my mother's wrath. Another officer took me to Paris and gave me over to still another one, his successor. I lived with him for three years. He's French, but he had to go to London on business. He's there now. . . . Let's go to your place."

"But what will we do there?"

"Come on along. We'll get warm, and you can take your pleasure."

I was far from becoming scrupulous. I had irritated her so that when she was close-pressed by the argument I was readying, she could not escape by feigning an honesty that I wanted to prove she did not possess. . . .

Buonaparte did not recount what followed.

After twenty months of extended leave, Lieutenant Buonaparte rejoined the Régiment de la Fère, garrisoned in the fortress of Auxonne. He was poorer than ever, since he was now trying to send his mother a few louis every month. In order to save money, he rented the humblest room he could find in the south pavilion where the junior officers were quartered. He first lived in Room 16, Stairway 1, then Room 10, Stairway 3, which was furnished with "a four-poster bed with its mattress and rods," a few cane chairs, an old armchair, and a small table. There were only two towels and one pair of sheets. (Today, the four walls of this room have been classified as a "historical monument.")

He was having as much trouble as ever in paying for his main meal—which he now took with Des Mazis at a tavern run by a certain Dumont. The meal was served at three o'clock. To sit down to eat at a fixed time, order the courses, and, especially, spend more than ten minutes at the table—this was too much to ask of Buonaparte. Quite often, being completely without money, he ate nothing more than the *gaudes*—a kind of porridge made from corn—that a local peasant woman made for him at a cost of a few sols. For breakfast, a chunk of bread sufficed.

He spent all his free time working without a letup, intent upon

making up for his many months of leave. Over and above his military
duties and the technical studies that he pursued well beyond what
was demanded of him, he used his leisure time to write his (*History
of Corsica* and a "Dissertation on Royal Authority") in which we find
the following sentence—rather amusing when read after the event:
"There are very few kings who have not deserved to be dethroned."

Another of his opuses was a "Dialogue on Love"—love being a
sentiment that he considered "harmful to society."

In a few months' time he devoured more than thirty volumes,
analyzing them and commenting on them: works of history, ancient
and classical, and treatises on economics and politics that he borrowed or (blessed day!) was sometimes able to buy. Thus the stay at
Auxonne was of considerable importance in his development, his
tastes, his ideas. He recounted later:

> In order not to stick out like a sore thumb among my fellow
> officers, I was unsociable as a bear: always alone in my little room
> with my books, my only friends. . . . When as a result of abstinence
> I had saved up two écus of six livres, I would go, happy as a child,
> to a bookseller's shop near the bishop's palace. Often enough, I
> went to look over his shelves, filled with the sin of covetousness.
> I "coveted" books for a long time before I had enough money to
> buy them. Such were the joys and debaucheries of my youth.

Just at that time, military science had been revolutionized by the
new tactical theories of Comte de Guilbert—rapidity, surprising the
enemy, numerical superiority at a prearranged point.

(The role of artillery became primary and underwent an entire
evolution. And Brigadier General Jean-Pierre du Teil, commandant
of the Artillery School and the fortress of Auxonne, who had been
impressed by the intelligence of Lieutenant Buonaparte, named him
to a committee charged with studying "the throwing of bombs by
cannon.") Napoleone was the youngest member of the committee,
and the only second lieutenant. The professor of mathematics at the
Auxonne Artillery School was astounded by the know-how of this
puny little officer who was not yet twenty years old.

Of course the detailed plans were not drawn by him. "He was no
good at it," Des Mazis has related. "A sergeant drew them, and he
signed them. He protested that it was as hard for him to draw lines
as to write in a legible hand." But the reports were written entirely

by him; and Du Teil, when he saw them, exclaimed, "No question about it—this officer will reach one of the highest posts in the royal artillery corps!"

His reputation extended beyond the walls of the barracks. On New Year's Day, 1789, his chambermaid "told him she hoped that he would become a general some day."

"A general?" was his response. "A general? Ah, my poor Thérèse, I'd be satisfied if I reached the rank of major. I wouldn't ask for anything more."

Before long, Du Teil had put 200 men under Buonaparte's orders and made him responsible for constructing, on the ordnance grounds, "several fortifications which demanded extensive calculations." As he wrote proudly to his uncle, Joseph Fesch: "This unprecedented mark of favor has made the captains a bit irritated with me. They claim that it is an injustice to them to make a lieutenant responsible for such an essential task. . . . My comrades are also showing some jealousy, but all this will fade away."

In Paris, the Revolution had begun to pave the way for the future Emperor with the taking of the Bastille. "The equality which was to elevate me seduced me," he said later. But liberty appeared seductive to him only if it could be put into the service of his homeland —"occupied" by the French.

For the moment (he is writing on July 15 to the archdeacon Lucien) the news he hears from Paris strikes him as "astounding and just the right kind of thing to throw people into a state of alarm." He condemns anarchy. As a disciplined soldier, he cannot approve insurrection—especially in the army. In such a case it is mutiny; and he had been troubled by the rebellion of the gunners of the Régiment de la Fère. They had protested the reductions made in the allocations to the regiment, and the Baron du Teil had had to compromise with the ringleaders. On the other hand, periods of disturbance and popular unrest are by no means an obstacle to promotion: "Revolutions," he writes, "are an opportune time for military men with brains and courage."

Although he disapproves of mutinies and favors repressions, he applauds the transformation of the Estates General into a National Assembly. He could not conceal his joy when he learned of the resolutions passed during the frenzied night of August 4: the abolish-

ment of privileges which, at the same time, annulled the decree
issued by the Ministry of War in 1780—a decree which barred commoners from a military career and confined the "petty nobles" to the
lower ranks. Thus the "petty noble" Buonaparte need no longer
place any limits on his hopes.)

But he had no intention of forging his career in France. All he
could think of was Corsica; and immediately upon obtaining his second leave of six months, he announced that he was going to Ajaccio.

He remained there until the end of January, 1791. By that time he
had already overstayed his leave for three months, and he had to get
back to his regiment if he did not want to be classified as a deserter
—or an émigré. By way of lessening Mme. Letizia's burdens he took
his younger brother, Louis (Luigi), now twelve years old, back with
him. Louis, with no great enthusiasm on his part, had been slated for
a military career; and Napoleone decided to take over his support
and his instruction.

Scrimping was the first thing on the young officer's agenda, and
the task of supporting Louis was onerous. Even more than before, he
was obliged to eliminate everything superfluous from his way of life
and to cut down on food. In the evening, in order to avoid the
expense of going out, he would offer the pretext that he had to take
care of his young brother and give him lessons. Then, once again, he
would "bolt the door" on his poverty. The two of them had to live
on three francs and fifty centimes a day. Sometimes they took a meal
at a tavern (its sign, decorated with bottles and glasses, has been
preserved), but for the most part they dined in their room. Napoleone himself put the pot on the stove and kept an eye on it while
working. (A few pathetic souvenirs, including the modest tables and
the two chairs used by the future Emperor and the future King of
Holland, have been preserved at the museum of Auxonne.) Sometimes when Napoleone was off duty, the two brothers would go out
for a drive or a walk and have a glass of milk at one of the nearby
farms or in a café which today is called the Café Bonaparte.

In the little Napoleonic Museum of Auxonne there is an ivory
token with a name awkwardly inscribed upon it: Manesca Pillet. This
is the name of a young lady with whom the second lieutenant was
very much taken. He asked for her hand in marriage, but was given
to understand that Manesca had hopes for something better! Buonaparte, so it is said, was heartbroken.

"Love drives me mad," he complained, "and yet I'll never find it. One is never cured of that malady."

Effective in early April, 1791, new army regulations came into force. The Régiment de la Fère was now known only by a number: it had become the First Artillery Regiment. But Buonaparte was soon to leave it. On the first of June he was transferred to the Fourth Artillery Regiment, which was stationed at Valence. He was promoted to first lieutenant, and his pay was raised to 100 livres instead of 93.

Two weeks later, accompanied by Louis this time, he set out again on the road through the Rhône Valley.

On 14 July, 1791, on the Champs de Mars at Auxonne, he swore the civic oath "to the Nation, the Law, and the King." It was an important event in the life of the future Chief of State. No longer did he hesitate to embrace the cause of the Revolution. Later he avowed:

> Up until then, if I had been ordered to turn my cannons against the people I have no doubt that habit, prejudice, education, and the name of the King would have made me obey. But once I had sworn the oath to the Nation, that was all over and done with: I would have recognized only the Nation. Then my natural inclinations were in harmony with my duties, and combined admirably with all the metaphysics of the Assembly.

Another visit to Corsica enabled him to classify his opinions. He became lieutenant general of the Corsican National Guard. He had completely forgotten that he was a lieutenant of the Fourth Artillery Regiment! He had, indeed, so far forgotten this fact that he stirred up a riot in order to launch a popular movement and seize the Citadel, which was held by royal troops.

Thanks to the anarchy reigning in the island, Buonaparte was not worried—although normally he would have been shot by a firing squad.

At the same time that he had become a rebel of sorts, he was running the risk of being called up before another tribunal for desertion. As a matter of fact, on January 1, 1792, when his regiment was reviewed at Valence, Lieutenant Buonaparte was reported absent without leave. Thus he was running a twofold risk: that of being cashiered from the army, and that of being put on the list of émigrés.

"It seems imperative that you go to France," his brother Joseph advised him. And so, lightly abandoning his battalion of Corsican volunteers, Napoleone decided not to go back to Valence, where he would run the risk of being arrested, but to get to Paris. He wanted to plead his case before the Minister of War.

On May 29, he wrote to Joseph:

> I got here yesterday. Paris is in the worst kind of convulsions. It is inundated with foreigners, and there are many malcontents. For three nights the lights have been kept on in the city. They have doubled the forces of the National Guard remaining at the Tuileries to protect the King. . . .

That same day (it was a kind of first lesson for the future Chief of State), he attended a session of the Legislative Assembly, where he came across an old friend, Bourrienne, his classmate at Brienne, who had come to seek a post in "Foreign Affairs." They renewed their friendship as if they had taken leave of each other only the day before. Neither was any better off than the other, and fortune seemed to have turned its back on the two of them.

On May 30 the two friends took up lodgings at the Hôtel de Metz on the Rue du Mail. At the time Buonaparte was taking his meals with a tavernkeeper named Justat, who despite the high cost of living charged him only six sous per meal.

Although he did not go so far as to predict the fall of the King, Buonaparte felt that upheavals were imminent. As he wrote to his brother Joseph: "This country is being torn apart by some very ferocious parties. It is hard to figure out what is going on among so many different factions. I don't know how things will come out, but they will take a very revolutionary turn."

On June 20, Buonaparte was not far from knowing "how things would come out." That morning, he and Bourrienne had arranged to meet at a restaurant on the Rue St.-Honoré, not far from the Palais-Royal. When they came out of the restaurant, they saw a body of men estimated by Napoleone at five to six thousand strong, coming from Les Halles and heading for the Tuileries. In Bourrienne's words: "They were ragged and ridiculously armed, yelling and shouting the crudest kind of provocations. . . . No doubt about it: they were the lowest and most abject kind of people to be found in the faubourgs."

"Let's follow that rabble," Buonaparte suggested to his friend.

They were able to get to the Tuileries before the mob, and took up positions on the terrace along the riverside. From there they witnessed the invasion of the palace by the people of the faubourgs. Buonaparte was "surprised and revolted." On that day, his leanings were pro-royalist. In Bourrienne's words:

> He was amazed by so much weakness and forbearance. And when the King showed himself at one of the windows overlooking the garden wearing the red cap that a commoner had put on him, Buonaparte's indignation knew no bounds. *"Che coglione!* Why did they ever let that rabble in? They should have blasted four or five hundred with cannon, and the rest would have taken to their heels."

Two onlookers were nearby. Napoleone came up to them and shouted: "If I were king, things like that wouldn't happen!"

One of the two was a lawyer named Lavaux. Later he wrote that he was surprised by the "soldierly tone and the bilious look" of the young officer, whose eyes were glittering in a strange way.

"Those in charge are weak men," Napoleone had written to his brother. Nonetheless, on July 10, Servan reassigned First Lieutenant Buonaparte to his regiment. (It was one of the last acts of Louis XVI's Minister of War.) Moreover, on July 30, he was awarded a captain's commission predated February 6—which enabled him to collect considerable back pay. And so, despite having fought against the soldiers of the King of France at Ajaccio, M. de Buonaparte was paid by that same King. The commission was signed "Louis"—surely one of the last signatures of the unfortunate sovereign—and it concerned his future successor.

It was not for nothing that Buonaparte was the son of his father: he had done a perfect job of finagling. Not only did he entirely escape censure for having drawn the sword against French troops, but he was recompensed for having been AWOL as of the preceding New Year's Day.

Was fortune finally going to smile on him?

At dawn on August 10, as soon as he heard the tocsin ringing, Napoleone dashed down the stairs of his hotel on the Rue du Mail and (as he told Las Cases much later) ran toward the Carrousel, the court behind the Tuileries where Bourrienne's brother was staying. Along the way, in the Rue des Petits-Champs, he encountered a "hideous" bunch of men carrying a head impaled on a pike. Since, apparently, Buonaparte struck them as having "the looks of a gentleman," they came up to him and demanded that he shout: "Vive la Nation!" He remarked: "I did so with no difficulty, as you can well imagine."

When he reached the Carrousel, Captain Buonaparte saw the palace being attacked by "the worst kind of rabble." If the King hadn't had his family with him he might perhaps have remained at the head of those who were going to die for him. "If Louis XVI had shown himself on horseback, he could have won the victory," Napoleone wrote that same evening to his brother Joseph. But he preferred to follow the advice of Pierre Louis Roederer and (ignobly, almost timorously) seek refuge with that same Assembly which, two days later, would hand him over to the Insurrectional Commune.

The battle was on now, and the pillage began. While the bodies of the Swiss Guards defending the palace were being thrown out of the windows, the young captain ventured into the garden. Later, he would say: "None of the battlefields on which I fought ever gave me such a forcible impression of large numbers of corpses as those masses of dead Swiss." On this last day of the monarchy Napoleone was disgusted when he saw "well-dressed women committing the worst kind of indecencies on the bodies of the Swiss." For the rest of his life, he would have such a horror of crowds gone berserk that when faced with them he would lose some of his capacity to act (19 Brumaire was one such occasion) and could even (as in 1814, on the roads of Provence) give the impression of knowing fear himself.

After the suspension of the King, Buonaparte, when he learned that a Convention would soon be nominated, was of the opinion that his brother had no right to let such an opportunity pass by: he should run for office in the future Assembly. But Joseph, facing his opponents alone, would not be capable of succeeding in his campaign. At any rate, such was Napoleon's estimate. Consequently, he deemed his own presence in Corsica once again indispensable—at a time when "the fatherland was in danger," the frontiers of France had been crossed by invaders, and the Coalitionists were marching on Paris!

M. de Buonaparte still did not consider himself a Frenchman. The bloody violence of the conquerors of the Tuileries nauseated him, and the revolutionary movement interested him only insofar as it enabled him to play a role in his home island. His ambition had not yet reached beyond the compass of his native city.

When he got back to Corsica, Buonaparte took command of the six companies of volunteers who were stationed at Corte but were hoping they would soon be in action. As a matter of fact, France had been at war "against the kings" since April 20, 1791. With Louis XVI imprisoned in the Temple, the provisory Executive Council had decided to carry out a diversionary action against King Victor Amadeus of Savoy and would land in Sardinia, where they would surely find livestock, grain, and wine.

Meantime, at the Place de la Révolution, Louis XVI's head rolled on the scaffold.

Paoli, who had hoped that the Revolution would bring freedom to Corsica, turned in disillusionment toward England. The Paolists, the champions of independence, and the Francophiles continued to battle one another. And this time Napoleone, committed to the Revolution, chose the French cause. With the help of the republican troops barracked in the Corsican capital, he tried—but in vain—to retake the Citadel, which was now held by the Paolists.

For the Paolists, Captain Buonaparte had become public enemy number one. On May 3, 1793, Napoleone had to leave the city in a hurry: the Paolists had mobbed him, shouting: "Death to the traitor of the *patria!*"

The "traitor" took refuge in a cave, and three days later reached Ajaccio, where he managed to conceal himself behind an alcove. In this way he slipped through the dragnet of the gendarmes, who had also become pro-Paoli and therefore anti-French.

On May 8 a gondola took him to Bastia, where, on the following day, he met with the commissioners of the Convention, Christopher Saliceti and Lacombe-Saint Michel, both of whom had been sent to Corsica to find out what Paoli was up to. Buonaparte brought them up to date on the situation, and it was decided to send French troops to attack Ajaccio.

On May 23, four hundred men and a few—very few—pieces of artillery were embarked on the brig *Le Hasard* and the sloop *La Belette*. At the very moment when the ships were setting sail from Bastia, the house on the Rue Malerba was being pillaged by Paolist peasants who had come down from the mountains. The house was looted and partly burned; the Buonapartes' vineyard and their herds of livestock on the outskirts of the city were destroyed. By unanimous vote, "those Buonapartes, engendered in the slime of despotism," were banished from the country.

On May 31, 1793, the sloop and the brig carrying the "expeditionary force" headed by the commissioners and Joseph Buonaparte entered the Gulf of Ajaccio under fire from the Citadel. Napoleone Buonaparte had preceded the flotilla. When he reached a point not far from Ajaccio, abreast of the tower of Capitello, he noticed on the shore a group of refugees who, at the sight of the tricolor flying above the poop deck, made distress signals. Napoleone, urged on by a kind of premonition, made for the shore and discovered that the refugees were Mme. Letizia and her children. They had been driven out of Ajaccio on May 23 and had been hiding in the countryside since.

At nightfall, Napoleone had them put aboard his xebec and gave orders that they be taken to Calvi. He himself joined the troops, who were about to attempt a landing.

The attempt was made the next day, and it failed. Only thirty republicans joined the commissioners of the Convention. On June 2, Napoleone reached Calvi, and decided to leave the island and go back to his regiment. In the course of seven and a half years of service, he had spent only thirty months on duty.

On June 3, with the whole of his family, he embarked for Toulon. He would not see Corsica again until his return from the Egyptian campaign.

This time—and for good—Napoleone had chosen France.

III

"CAPTAIN CANNON"

Even if this officer were not given
his due, he would make his mark
all on his own.

DUGOMMIER

WHEN HE REACHED TOULON on June 13, 1793, Buonaparte took a little house in the borough of La Valette for his mother, Louis, Jérôme, and his three sisters. The future princesses Élisa and Pauline had to go to the fountain to do their laundry, since the relief money granted to Corsican refugees plus Napoleone's meager pay was all the family had to live on. Fortunately, early the following month some friends in Marseille, the Clarys, took in the Buonapartes, and the young captain went back to his regiment.

Thanks to General Jean du Teil, brother of the former commandant of Auxonne, Captain Buonaparte was not considered as a deserter; and on September 15 he was transferred to the Army of Italy at Nice, where he was to organize the transportation of gunpowder. As he was passing through Beausset, seventeen kilometers from Toulon, he learned that Saliceti, with whom he had waged the "campaign" of the preceding month, was in Toulon. This representative was on a mission with Gasparin, his colleague at the Convention. The Republic was trying to retake Toulon, which on August 28, "threatened with execution" by the Convention, had preferred to open its gates to the English and the Spaniards.

Buonaparte arrived at an opportune moment.

The artillery of the besieging forces no longer had a commander. Captain E.A.C. de Dommartin, who had been in command, had been badly wounded at the taking of Ollioules. Saliceti had a good opinion of the Buonapartes: he had seen them at work. Moreover, the young officer, eager to oblige, "played up to him." Consequently, the representative felt that "chance had served him wonderfully well," and he offered to the "well-versed Captain Buonaparte" the command of the artillery of the forces besieging Toulon. Thus it was that opportunity knocked for the future Emperor.

On September 17, moving fast, the new commander went to the headquarters at Ollioules, where he made the acquaintance of the obstreperous J.F. Carteaux, a former house painter and former gendarme-turned-dragoon, who had picked up his general's stars in the street one night during a riot. He strutted about "covered with gold braid from head to foot." The "well-versed" Captain Buonaparte announced to him that he had just been assigned to direct, under Carteaux's orders, the artillery operations.

"A waste of effort," said the sans-culotte general, twirling his mustache. "We have all we need to take Toulon. But we're glad to have you, anyway. Tomorrow you can share in the glory of burning the city, even though you didn't do any of the work."

In the meantime, he invited Napoleone to "share" his dinner. Thirty persons were seated at the table, but only the general was "served like a prince." The others were meagerly served—a fact which, in this era of fraternity, shocked the new arrival.

The next morning Carteaux and Buonaparte got into a cabriolet "to go and admire the preparations for the attack." They stopped on the heights which overlook the harbor from a distance. The English fleet was occupying both the inner and the outer harbors and, as A.F.L.V. de Marmont, then a young lieutenant, put it, "complemented with its firepower this vast and magnificent defensive system." Such was the stronghold, well defended by an army, against which Carteaux had decided to essay his "incapacity and his complete but confident ignorance."

There were a few cannons vaguely protected by "earthworks." The general, with one hand on the mane of his horse (a magnificent beast from the stables of the Prince de Condé) and the other on his sword hilt—"as if posing for a portrait"—interrogated his aide-de-camp.

"Dupas," he asked proudly, "are those our batteries?"

"Yes, general."

"And our artillery park?"

"Over there, close by."

"And our heated shot?"

"Over there in the cottages, where two companies have been heating them up since early this morning."

"But how will we transport such glowing red heated shot?"

The general and his aide-de-camp could not solve this tricky problem. Finally, they asked the "artillery officer if, according to his principles, there wasn't some way to solve it."

Buonaparte at first thought it was a joke. But the two officers seemed to be very serious indeed. And so, with all the tact and seriousness he could summon up, he tried to make them understand that "before getting encumbered with heated shot" they should "fire some cold shot in order to see how far it carried."

The only way he could convince them was by using the technical expression "trial shot." This impressed both of them and obliged them to follow his advice. The "trial shot," which carried scarcely a third of the distance, showed that the batteries were positioned much too far from the target.

Naturally, Carteaux and Dupas accused "those bastards, the Marseillais" and the aristocrats of Toulon of having—maliciously, of course—"spoiled the gunpowder." And they vied with each other in shouting.

The arrival of the representative Gasparin put an end to this burlesque scene. Buonaparte (if his account is to be believed) held himself erect, "queried the representative, demanded that he be given absolute authority for the job to be done, demonstrated in no uncertain terms the ignorance of all the others, and as of that moment took over direction of the siege, of which he became from then on, the supreme commander."

On September 20, Buonaparte moved up his cannons. The Battery of the Sans-Culottes, positioned at Brégaillon, "right next to the chapel, at the seaside," kept part of the harbor under its fire, using the heated shot, and the enemy evacuated La Seyne. Was it on that day that the "well-versed captain" decided: "In both tactical systems and sieges, one must concentrate one's fire on a single point"?

A few days later, on September 29, Captain Buonaparte was nominated for promotion to the rank of major, a nomination that was confirmed on October 19.

Carteaux was replaced by General Jean-François Coquille du

Gommier, who signed his name in the manner then in style: Dugommier. At last a real soldier was in command. He was "completely
subject" to the influence of the new major, and approved Buonaparte's idea of positioning in front of the Petit Gibraltar Fort a battery called the Battery of the Convention, in order to "counterbat-
ter" the fort. His aim was to create a diversion. Already the young
commander knew how to handle his soldiers, and he named the
position the Battery of Fearless Men.

On November 30 the English made a vigorous attack on the
battery; but just when they were on the point of taking it, they were
thrown back with heavy losses, leaving many prisoners behind.

In the report that he sent to Paris that evening, Dugommier
named "Citizen Buonaparte" among those "who had most distinguished themselves"; and on December 1 he appointed him adjutant
general.

From December 11 to December 16, Napoleone's batteries poured
down a heavy bombardment on the narrows. Fort Mulgrave, the
imposing earthworks built by the British, was taken. Then came the
turn of Petit Gibraltar (today, Fort Napoleon). Marmont, at Buonaparte's orders, turned the English cannon back against the enemy.
Supported by the batteries positioned at Le Caire, the infantry then
attacked the two forts commanding the narrows. The enemy evacuated them without having had time to spike the cannons. Thanks
to this, the harbor, the port, and the city were under the fire of
Buonaparte's artillery.

After the burning of the ships and the armories, while the powder
magazines were crackling and exploding, the gates of Toulon finally
opened. But only a few inhabitants welcomed the victors. The troops
immediately ranged through the city. Pillage was authorized, and
the Reign of Terror felt at home there. "The national vengeance
is unfurled." All the inhabitants were ordered to assemble in the
public square and were asked who the enemies of the Republic were.
Everyone pointed out his personal enemies or his creditors, who
were immediately seized and put to death. "The Infamous City,"
three-quarters destroyed by 12,000 ditch diggers brought in from
neighboring *départements*, was henceforth called the "Port of the
Mountain."

On December 22, Buonaparte was promoted to the temporary
rank of brigadier general. He was undoubtedly a republican, and at

that time he couldn't find words strong enough to castigate the royalists; but he was nonetheless horrified by the sight of the "strenuous executions by firing squad and the massacre."

Everyone was talking about the young general. General du Teil wrote to the Minister of War:

I have no words to describe to you the worth of Buonaparte. A great deal of know-how, just as much intelligence, and too much courage—there you have a poor thumbnail sketch of the virtues of this rare officer. It is up to you, as Minister of War, to make use of him for the glory of the Republic.

"Even if this officer were not given his due, he would make his mark all on his own," declared Dugommier, with astounding prescience.

But he was given his due.

His "temporary" rank of brigadier general was confirmed; on December 26 he was made responsible for carrying out an inspection of the coast from Marseille to Nice. In four months he had moved from the rank of captain to that of general—even inspector general.

In order to secure such a rapid promotion he was obliged to fill out a questionnaire. This "Statement of the Services of Citizen Buonaparte" has been preserved in the Archives de la Guerre. In it "Napoleone Buonaparte" made himself a year older than he actually was.

But in order to be promoted to general at the age of twenty-four one had to do all kinds of things, especially when one was driven by ambition—an ambition that his superiors were already holding against him.

At this time Napoleone got to know the family of the merchant Clary, who the summer before had taken care of Letizia and her children. Joseph seemed to be rather taken with one of the girls: Désirée. She was a piquant, charming brunette with beautiful black eyes. Désirée's sister, Julie, served as chaperone.

At first, Napoleone merely provoked laughter in the two young ladies. The young general's sallow face with its prominent cheekbones was still framed by long black hair which apparently had never known a comb. His uniform hung loosely on his thin body, and his wrinkled, worn boots looked as though he had bought them from some dealer in secondhand clothes. But when he smiled, when he looked at one with his flashing eyes, his whole face lighted up and one no longer saw anything else. And Désirée soon discovered that at the mere mention of Napoleone's name, her heart began to beat a bit faster.

As soon as he came to Marseille, the young general felt that he was in a position of trust with regard to Joseph and the two young ladies. If Joseph was to marry the coquettish and expansive Désirée, it seemed likely that Napoleone would wed the rather solemn Julie.

Or so it seemed until the day when the future Emperor told the three others:

> In a well-run family, one person must always yield to another. You, Joseph, are a person who can never make up his mind, and the same is true of Désirée. Julie and I, on the other hand, know what we want. Therefore, you would do better to marry Julie. As for Désirée (he added, taking the young lady on his knees), she will be my wife.

"It was in this way," Désirée said later, "that I became the fiancée of Napoleon." Joseph yielded gracefully. A few months later, on August 1, he married Julie. (Incidentally, we know nothing of her reactions to this sentimental game of musical chairs.) As for the marriage of Désirée and Napoleone, no one yet dared to speak of it openly. No matter that Buonaparte had just been named artillery commander of the Army of Italy. No matter that several days later he received his brevet as a general officer. His status was still mediocre, and Désirée still bore in mind her mother's exclamation: "With one Buonaparte in the family, I have enough!"

A rather amusing exclamation, when one knows how the story turned out. As for Joseph, he seems hardly to have helped his brother throughout the course of this "business." In any case, things were still undecided between the two young people when Napoleone and his staff established their headquarters in the Château-Sallé, which he had luxuriously requisitioned for himself. It was a cottage—or, more exactly, a farmhouse—where he could bring the whole family. Thanks to his annual pay of 15,000 livres, and to his six rations, they were finally leading a pleasant life.

But Napoleone, although still holding down his job as inspector of the coasts, had to take up his position with the Army of Italy. And so, while his mother and his sisters remained at the Château-Sallé, he himself took lodgings in Nice, at 1 Rue de Villefranche (today, 6 Rue Bonaparte). He had rented an apartment at the home of Joseph Laurenti, a rich merchant.

When he was not reading or working (pending the resumption of hostilities against the King of Sardinia), the young general liked to take long walks in the Laurentis' vast formal garden (which was almost a park) with its orange trees and lemon trees. At his side trotted the young lady of the house, Émilie, a brunette with glowing eyes who was only fifteen. The future Emperor found her charming —so charming that his memories of Désirée began to fade away.

On April 5, the eve of the first limited Italian campaign, Augustin Robespierre, whose attention had been attracted to young Buonaparte, wrote to his brother Maximilien:

> To the list of patriots that I have already given you, I would like to add Citizen Buonaparte, Commanding General of the Artillery, a man *of surpassing merit.* He is a Corsican. The only guarantees he offers are that of a Corsican who has resisted the advances of Paoli, and one whose property has been ravaged by that traitor.

Ever since he had been assigned to the Army of Italy, Napoleone had been working on an operations plan which would "lay open the Piedmont to the armies of the Republic." The younger Robespierre and his colleague, Ricord, were enthusiastic about the plan; and the two deputies saw that it was accepted by the commanding general of the Army of Italy, P.J. Dumerbion.

The campaign was a short one, and did not extend beyond Ormea, so that Napoleone was soon on his way back to Nice. Once again, he took lodgings with the Laurenti family. He found Émilie so exquisite that one night when he was alone with Mme. Laurenti (whom he called *maman*) he summoned up all his courage and asked for the hand of her daughter in marriage.

Mme. Laurenti, very much upset by this unforeseen move, said that she would speak to her husband about it.

M. Laurenti was not enthusiastic. A little sans-culotte general? A protégé of those murderous men who were ruling France for the moment? A man who had no other income but his pay? It was out of the question!

You certainly have a fine command [he said to Buonaparte].
You are a professional military man, and one with a brilliant
future, it seems to me. But who can say whether you will return
safe and sound from the Italian campaign? It is too soon to make
so rapid a commitment about our daughter's future. Be reasonable enough to give up these plans for marriage. If you cling to
them, we can talk about it when you come back. In the meantime,
your position will become clearer to you. As for us, we shall have
the time to question Émilie and discover her tastes and prefer-
ences. I'm sure that you understand me.

Buonaparte did not understand at all, and he withdrew to his own
rooms very upset, without saying another word to the Laurenti
family.

He found consolation in leaving on a mission to Genoa. He came
back on July 27 with the information that he had been sent to get.
Two weeks before, Augustin Robespierre had gone back to Paris,
recalled by his brother, who may have sensed the mounting crisis.
July 27 corresponds, as a matter of fact, to 9 Thermidor. And at the
same moment when Napoleone, very pleased with having carried
out his mission successfully, returned to Nice, Maximilien was outlawed, and his brother voluntarily joined him. That same night,
Augustin threw himself from the top of a cornice on the Hôtel de
Ville and broke his hip. The next day, he was taken to the scaffold
and was the second of the batch to die.

On August 5, on the field of Sieg, Buonaparte learned the news
that deprived him of his protectors. The next day he wrote to Tilly,
the French chargé d'affaires at Genoa, a letter which was very much
in the style of the times: "I was somewhat upset by the catastrophe
of Robespierre, whom I liked and who I thought was pure. But even
if he had been my brother, I would have stabbed him myself if he
made a bid for tyranny." (Despite this, the Emperor Napoleon would
later grant a pension to the sister of the Robespierre brothers who
was poverty-stricken.)

Was Napoleone a "Robespierrist"? Certainly not. But he preferred republican liberty to "the yoke of the aristocrats." When he
came to Nice, chance had put him under the orders (and the protection) of the brother of the Incorruptible One. Although he did not
approve the Reign of Terror, current events (and his self-interest)
prompted him to embrace the extremist cause.

And now he was compromised. It was certain (Napoleon acknowledged it later) that he enjoyed great favor with the representatives on mission who were in office before Thermidor. Thus Augustin Robespierre made hardly any decisions concerning the Army of Italy without consulting the young general.

Without waiting for orders from the Committee, the commissioners, "in consideration of the fact that General Buonaparte has totally lost our confidence owing to behavior of the most suspicious kind, and especially owing to the trip he recently made to Genoa," decreed as follows:

> Brigadier General Buonaparte, Commander in Chief of Artillery, Army of Italy, is temporarily suspended from his duties. The Commanding General of the said Army is hereby made responsible for assuring that he is arrested and brought before the Committee of Public Safety, at Paris, under good and reliable escort. All papers and other effects are to be sealed. . . .

Buonaparte "was convinced he was finished." However, he was not taken to Fort Carré at Antibes, as has been affirmed for so many years. Laurenti (and we know this from his *Mémoires*) "took up his case" and offered "his bond," and the disgraced general was merely sentenced to "remain under arrest at the home of his hosts." With a sentinel at his door, he paced up and down in his room on the Rue de Villefranche, chafing at the bit. If only Émilie could be there, at least! But M. and Mme. Laurenti had prudently sent their daughter to their country house of St.-Martin, above Grasse.

What else could he do but write to the representatives? On August 12 he stated to them:

> I have been branded without having been heard. . . . I have voluntarily suffered banishment from Corsica. I have abandoned my property; I have lost everything for the Republic. Since then, I have served at Toulon with some distinction, and I have merited from the Army of Italy some of the laurels it has earned. Hear me! Deliver me from the oppression that surrounds me, and give back to me the esteem of the patriots! . . .

He was heard. The investigation cleared Buonaparte and freed him. Saliceti frankly acknowledged: "After examining his papers and all the information we had gathered, we realized that nothing positive could be accomplished by keeping him under arrest."

General Dumerbion approved his release. He needed the "skills

of this officer, which, we must admit, have become indispensable in
an army that he knows better than anyone else." Men of his worth
—as his chief acknowledged—were "very difficult to find."

While waiting for hostilities to resume, Napoleone often went
from Nice to Antibes, where he saw Désirée, who had come to visit
her sister, Mme. Joseph Buonaparte. Napoleone once again fell under her spell, and the flirtation was resumed. On September 5, he left
Nice with the headquarters staff, and Désirée went back to Marseille.
It was to Marseille that he addressed this first letter to her, written
from Oneille. (This correspondence was later discovered and published by M. Girod de l'Ain, great-grand-nephew of Désirée. Note
that Napoleon calls Désirée by her second Christian name: Eugénie.)

> The unchanging sweetness which characterizes you, and the
> pleasing frankness which is yours alone, good Eugénie, inspired
> friendship in me. And yet, absorbed by my duties, I was not
> entitled to believe that this feeling should receive [sic] any deeper
> scar in my soul. A stranger to tender passions, I should not have
> been wary of the pleasures of your company. The charm of your
> person, of your character, gradually won the heart of your lover.
> Since then, you have read it in my soul. . . .

Lover? In the eighteenth-century sense of the word, no doubt.

The second letter that he wrote to Désirée was hardly a loving
one. He advised her to devote herself to music, "which, of all talents,
is the one that has most to do with feeling," and recommended that
she do a great deal of reading, which would "furnish out her memory." He said nothing more of his love; and Désirée was quite entitled
to tell him, in her reply, that "the most sensitive of women loves the
coldest of men."

This time, touched to the quick, Buonaparte defended himself:

> If, Mademoiselle, you could be a witness to the feelings that
> your letter inspired in me, you would be convinced of the injus-
> tice of your reproaches. . . . There is no pleasure which I would
> care to enjoy without you. There is no dream that I don't share
> with you.

But then a slightly didactic tone reappears. He advises her to
"learn how to sing some scale or other." The letter comes to an end
with these three unexpected words: "Memory, gaiety, health."

In the spring of 1795, Napoleone saw Désirée again at Marseille and at Montredont, where the Clarys' cottage was located. This time the flirtation became an affair. The general seemed genuinely infatuated, but his duties obliged him to travel: he could not give to Désirée all the time he would have liked to give. All he could do was write to her; and this time the tone was very different:

> I have just received your letter, which caused me the greatest pleasure. In every one of your words I recognized my own feelings, my own thoughts. I never stop remembering you. Your portrait is engraved on my heart. I have never had any doubts about your love, my sweet Eugénie. Why should you think that I could ever stop loving you?
>
> Yours for life. . . .

In one of his future letters, Napoleone mentions "outings during which love united us without satisfying us." There is no doubt that Désirée granted her "friend" a few privileges. They had strolled in the woods in the moonlight. The future Emperor also mentions an "enchanting evening." Did he mean that evening when he found Désirée hidden under his bed, and the inevitable happened? This was the same evening that he mentioned at St. Helena, when unburdening himself to Grand Marshal Bertrand, in the following precise and unpoetic terms: "It was because I had got Désirée's maidenhead that I made Bernadotte a marshal, a prince, and a king."

And he further confided to his companion in exile: "I told her mother."

And so, on April 21, 1795, he was officially engaged to Désirée. But as yet there could be no question of fixing a date for the marriage. Buonaparte was without a command at the moment. Since there was an excess of artillery generals, he was subsequently given (the last on the list) a command against the "brigands" of the Vendée. But he had no intention of reporting for duty at his new post. Was he put out at the notion of waging war against insurgent Frenchmen at a time when the country was no longer under the Reign of Terror? This has been affirmed so often that the legend has come to be believed. Actually, he was not horrified at the idea of a civil war; but artillery could not be of any use in Vendée, in a war fought among hedgerows and in the woods. In all likelihood he would be offered the command of a brigade of infantry, but he had no wish to change to another branch of the service. Such a command would not bring him any fame of the kind useful to his ambition.

Such are the actual reasons for his attitude, which he intended to explain to the Minister of War viva voce. And that was why he decided to leave for Paris, accompanied by Louis and two aides-de-camp assigned to him on his own authority: Junot and Marmont.

When, on May 8, he got into his carriage, Désirée was heart-broken. She gave him a locket containing some strands of her hair. Then, sobbing, she rushed to her writing desk and wrote:

> Each instant pierces my soul, since it takes the dearest of friends farther away from me. But you are always in my heart. In my imagination, I see you in every street I walk along. The thought of you follows me everywhere, and will follow me to my grave. O my friend! May your promises be as sincere as mine, and may you love me as much as I love you! . . .

On the draft of this latter, which has been preserved, Désirée inscribed, over and over again, "B . . . B . . . B . . . B . . . ," meaning "Buonaparte . . . Buonaparte . . . Buonaparte. . . . "
And on the back of the page she added:

> The carriage has passed out of view. Each instant pierces my heart, since it takes you away from me. . . . It takes away from me my dearest friend . . . the friend who . . . but I am following you. I am going posthaste with you. . . . My imagination is racing along, and sees you on every road that you take. . . .

Napoleone wrote to Désirée on May 9:

> I reached Avignon feeling miserable at the idea of having to be so far away from you for such a long time. The trip was depress-ing. The only thing that can assuage my suffering and make my situation endurable is the hope that my sweet Eugénie will think often of her good friend and continue to have for him those affectionate sentiments that she promised. *Adieu*, my sweet and affectionate friend. *Souvenir et amour*, from him who is yours for life.

Buonaparte and his companions found Paris barely recovering from another of those tumultuous "historic days." The whole of the city was hungry. . . . To subsist for one day would soon require more "paper money" than the amount of specie that one formerly required to live for a year. The louis d'or would soon be increasing its value at a rate of 100 francs per hour. And so, five days before, the "Empty Bellies" had marched on the "Rotten Bellies"; that is, the deputies in session at the Tuileries.

The rioters had proscribed the last of the Jacobins, such as Ricord, Buonaparte's strongest supporter. Hence Napoleone paid a call on Aubry, the Minister of War. Before receiving him, Aubry undoubtedly consulted the file on "Buonaparte (commissioned)," and read these words: "He has a bit too much ambition, and he intrigues for his promotion." He felt that the advancement of this little protégé of Robespierre had been very rapid indeed; and pending his departure for the west, offered him nothing more than a vague function with the General Staff.

The Minister of War must have been delighted to keep in suspense this artillery general who was only twenty-five (and who, moreover, made "rather bad" mistakes in French), whereas he himself—likewise an artillery officer—was still a captain at the age of forty-eight.

"Citizen Deputy," Buonaparte said, "a man ages quickly on the field of battle, and that's where I have come from."

This "little Italian"—who, moreover, was a Jacobin; or at any rate was said to be one—made a very bad impression. He was thin and bony, with a sallow complexion. The future Duchesse d'Abrantès even went so far as to call him "ugly." His hands were "thin, long, and black." She would later remember that pathetic-looking silhouette walking "with a rather clumsy and uncertain step" across the courtyard of the Hôtel de la Tranquillité (where the Permons were living) with an "ugly round hat jammed down over his eyes; from under its brim protruded a pair of badly powdered ears that looked like those of a hound dog." He refused to wear gloves because they were, as he put it, "an unnecessary expense." His boots were badly cut and almost never polished. People smiled when they saw this former protégé of Robespierre badgering the bureaucrats, "knocking on every door," telling everyone about his plans, muttering insulting things about the Royalist fops, whom he called "bad Frenchmen," and recounting the injustices of which he claimed to have been a victim. He maintained that he was ill (for that matter, his sick leave expired on July 15), and in the meantime he kept trying to pull more and more strings to avoid reporting to his duty post.

"I am beating a retreat," he said, "satisfied that the injustice done in return for services rendered is sufficiently realized by those willing to appreciate them."

Even at the theater his taciturn manner remained unchanged. He had once again come across Bourrienne, who took him to the Théâtre-Français. Amid gales of laughter, Napoleone would maintain "a glacial silence."

An unknown young woman was the only one—or almost the only one—to have admired the "very handsome expression" of this general with the odd name who "grew lively when he talked." She thought this young provincial might have "some merit." If he had not been "thin to the point of looking sickly and making one feel sorry for him," she would recount later, "people would have noticed his very fine features. His mouth, especially, was most gracefully formed. A painter, a friend of David's, told me that his features were Greek in their form—which made me respect him."

He had a consolation: Désirée's letters.

I have received your two charming letters [he wrote her]. They refreshed my soul and gave me a moment of happiness. . . . I feel sure, however, that with the love of my sweetheart I cannot be unhappy. . . . I beg you: Don't let a day pass without writing me, without assuring me that you still love me.

In July he moved to the Hôtel du Cadran Bleu at 10, Rue de la Huchette, where for three francs a week he took a small room. He had very little money, being on half-pay; and even that little was further diminished by the amounts he felt obliged to send to assist his mother. He ate only one meal a day, which cost 25 francs.

For all his fiancée's assurances that she loved him, Buonaparte fell once again into a state of depression. His letters reflect that state. If Désirée loved another, she should not hesitate to abandon the poor little general without a brigade. She must not hamper her soul. She must not impose obligations upon herself.

Poor Désirée! She loved him spontaneously, openly, and purely. She could not understand the pessimistic reactions of her lover, and his dramas of conscience. And so she continued to swear to him that she loved him with all her heart. Unhappy at being so far away from him, she begged him to love her always as she loved him: "That is, as much as one can possibly love. . . . "

But these protestations did nothing to restore Napoleone's spirits. He wrote to Joseph to unburden himself. Declaring that he had "very little desire to live," he said he intended, if not to commit suicide, then at any rate (or so he declared) not to turn aside if he should find himself faced with death. "And if things go on like this, my friend, some day I'll simply fail to get out of the way of a passing carriage."

And yet he kept hoping that "in the perpetual movement of highly placed persons," someone would ultimately take an interest in him. This seemed all the more improbable when, on August 16, Napoleone received an actual summons to leave for the Vendée. Its tone was threatening:

> I have every reason to believe that you are able to travel, and I invite you to proceed, as soon as possible, to your post, where your presence is becoming more necessary with each passing day. If your health does not permit you to serve actively, inform me accordingly, and I shall propose to the Committee that you be replaced.

It was no doubt after having received this summons that, on August 18, 1795, he went to the Committee of Public Safety. Would his luck change? He succeeded in gaining an audience and explained how the Army of Italy could be employed if his plan were followed.

Doulcet de Pontécoulant, the new Minister of War, listened closely to his presentation and then stated: "General, your ideas are brilliant and bold, but they must be studied with the calm of reflection before we can consider putting them into execution. Therefore, please take your time and, after you've slept on it, draw up a report that I can submit to the Committee."

"Time?" exclaimed Buonaparte. "I don't need it. My plan is so well worked out in my head that I can develop all the details in half an hour. A pen and two sheets of paper is all that I ask you for."

On the Committee's conference table, he sketched out in a rapid hand (and of course a scarcely legible one) the entire plan for the Italian campaign—the plan he would carry out eight months later.

"We must take the Borghetto Line. It is short, well supported, and easy to defend."

"You will be placed at the disposal of the Committee so that you can contribute your zeal and skill to the elaboration of campaign plans and operations for the army."

The upshot was that he was assigned to the Topographic Bureau of the Committee of Public Safety. This wasn't at all to his liking, and he conveyed the news to his brother without any enthusiasm. He even considered becoming an expatriate and serving in Constantinople "as a general of artillery, sent by the government to organize the Sultan's artillery, with good pay and a very flattering envoy's title." In his mind's eye he could already see himself en route to the Sublime Porte. "I'll have you appointed consul," he promised Joseph.

But would Pontécoulant, who had seemed to value him, let him leave?

On August 30 he received another letter from Désirée: "Never believe that I am happy. Could I be, far away from you? The memory of our charming walks is constantly in my heart. Yes, and those woods, with their gloomy foreboding. . . ." She meant, no doubt, those woods where the engaged couple had spoken of the obstacles that would still, it seemed, prevent them from marrying. "Alas!" she continued. "It was only too well founded, since we have to be separated for such a long time. It was Fate that willed it. . . ."

The next day Napoleone replied to her:

> I have received your charming letter, dear girl, and it has brought me the pleasure that the memory of you always inspires. Often, amid the raucous pleasures of this immense city, I think of my sweet Eugénie. My thought crosses the seas, braves the torments coupled with distance, and hurries to your side. . . .

He had resumed a social life of sorts, and was received at the home of Thérèsia Tallien, the notorious Notre-Dame de Thermidor. It was there, one evening, that he met one of Thérèsia's intimate friends; the pretty Rose de Beauharnais, who one day would be "the incomparable Josephine." Nee Tascher de la Pagerie in Trois-Ilets, a hamlet of Martinique, she was the widow of Alexandre de Beauharnais, by whom she had had two children: Hortense and Eugène. Her first husband, a boring fellow who had become a viscount on his own authority, had been elected president of Constituent Assembly before being guillotined by the same machine that he (like so many other sorcerer's apprentices) had helped to introduce.

Beauharnais' pretty, popular Creole wife had been imprisoned during the Reign of Terror, and since her release had been leading a rather loose life. She had had a close brush with death, and now she was carrying on in a giddy fashion, in order both to forget the nightmare and to find a protector who would help her in life. She no longer possessed the brilliant beauty that had been hers at twenty; but she was so skillful with make-up that she attracted the glances of far more men now than she had before. She knew how to walk and to sit down gracefully, how to recline in such a way as to bring out the suppleness of her body and her languorous natural grace, and just how to let her "irresistible" gaze fall on those she wanted to charm. Moreover, she had the elegant style of the Old Regime. But Buonaparte was not yet conquered, unless he dared to raise his eyes to that pseudo-viscountess who was perhaps already the mistress of Paul Barras, a member of the Directory. Was it on the eve of Vendémiaire or the day after that the liaison began between the merry widow and the "king of the rotten ones"? No one knows for sure.

Napoleone had good hopes of "arriving" thanks to his new acquaintances. When would his period of disfavor come to an end?

For many people, the death of Robespierre marked the end of the Revolution, since the blood of victims had ceased to be spilled. From now on, only the blood of murderers would be spilled. No doubt the hours that struck during the following years would not have the same echo of tragic grandeur; but the Revolution had not been brought to an end. It was the Terror that had died, not the Republic, which would still have to undergo its inevitable childhood illnesses, the last of which—the imperial one—would kill it.

To bring the Revolution to an end, to give it a meaning, to complete its work, there would have to be a dictatorship—both of the sword, since Europe was preparing to share the spoils, and of genius, since everything had to be accomplished, created, and built: a dictatorship all the more indispensable in that the France that reawakened on the morning of 9 Thermidor was not only chaos, disorder, and confusion but a country governed by an evil cohort of men "deep into debts and crimes," by horrible speculators, by those Thermidorians that Robespierre was fully entitled to regard with contempt.

Although the Convention had lost all its prestige, its longevity and the vigor it still displayed in its old age were amazing. How much it had shouted and discussed! How tenaciously it had perpetuated its work of self-destruction! But above all, had not that extraordinary

Assembly saved France, created a new universe, and worked as no
other parliamentary body had ever worked before? And it was from
its past accomplishments that it now drew the strength to utilize first
the extreme right, then the extreme left, each of which was alter-
nately rearing its head in the belief that its turn had come and the
hour of revenge was at hand.

In late September, 1795, the fermentation that Buonaparte had
mentioned had already been brewing for some time. The Convention, which had saved France on so many occasions, was now in its
death agony. Eleven of its members set to work, and on 5 Fructidor
(August 27, 1795) a new Constitution—that of the Year III—was
voted. The Directory was going to assume the power. But the Ther-
midorian deputies wanted to save their sinecures. They therefore
decided that two-thirds of the members of the Council of Five Hundred and the Council of the Ancients would be chosen from among
the deputies to the Convention. The royalist sections, who hoped to
see the surviving regicides disappear from power, demonstrated
against the decrees of the "Two-Thirds." Once again, Paris was like
the bridge of a ship when the decks are being cleared for action—
all the more so, since one had to vote either "for" or "against" the
new Constitution. There were so many abstentions—four-fifths of
those registered—that the new system of government was accepted.
What followed was only to be expected. At first they muttered it,
then they shouted it: the committees falsified the figures!

For several days young men with their hair cut long in the "Victory" style and wearing capes with the colors of the ultraroyalist
Comte d'Artois (later Charles X) had been running about the streets
shouting, "Down with the Two-Thirds!" The members of the Convention realized that, in their own phrase, "the revolutionary thunder had died out in their hands." Nonetheless, they declared
themselves to be "in permanent session," and entrusted their fate to
a general, Baron Jacques Menou, who had been a brigadier general
as far back as the Old Regime.

And Buonaparte?

On the morning of the twelfth—a very rainy morning—he had
dropped by at the Permons', where he ate a bunch of grapes and
drank a big cup of coffee.

"I had a late breakfast," he explained. "There was so much talk
of politics that I couldn't stand any more of it. I'm going out to pick

up some news. If I find out anything interesting, I'll come back and tell you."

By this time people were truly in motion. The royalist section of Filles St.-Thomas (or Le Pelletier) had assembled in arms, and was behaving in a threatening manner. General Menou got on horseback and, instead of sealing off that part of the city, massed his infantry and artillery in the Rue Vivienne. He parleyed, refusing to act vigorously.

Night fell—a sinister night. The weather was very bad, but neither the pouring rain nor the strong wind from the west prompted the demonstrators to go home. The drums of the rebellious sections were beating constantly, calling their men to arms against the Convention. The panicky deputies—"those blood-soaked terrorists," as the royalists called them—relieved General Menou of his command and named Barras commanding general of the Army of the Interior —the same Barras who, on 9 Thermidor, had marched on the Hôtel de Ville against Robespierre. Barras accepted, and declared to the deputies that he was ready to save the country from "the attack by the hirelings of the aristocracy." Such was the language of the age, and no one had any inclination to laugh.

"I am at my post," Barras declared. "Let every man do likewise."

The former sublieutenant of Louis XVI's colonial troops, realizing full well that he was merely an ad hoc general without the least experience, said he needed a general to assist him: a real general, and preferably an artillery officer.

"Buonaparte!" shouted an officer named Turreau.

Louis Fréron—the former Don Juan of the Terror, who was in love with Pauline Buonaparte—approved; and Barras, who had seen Napoleone at work during the siege of Toulon, accepted.

"Go and find him," he told Fréron.

After some difficulty, they found Buonaparte and brought him to Menou.

"How many troops do you have?" Napoleone asked.

"Five thousand."

"That's not many. And your artillery?"

"There are forty cannons."

"Where are they?"

"On the Plaine des Sablons."

Buonaparte called for a cavalry officer, and a "handsome young man" presented himself. It was Murat, who received the famous order: "Take two hundred horses, go immediately to the Plaine des Sablons, and bring back the forty cannons and the artillery park. We must have them here. Use your sabers, if you have to, but bring them here! You answer to me for it if you don't! Now get going!"

As A. C. Thiébault put it later, Buonaparte's "vigor, his absolutely imperative promptness and brevity of speech," at first surprised and then aroused enthusiasm in the garrison officers, who observed with astonishment the bustling activity of this "odd little chap whose penury was still evident in his disorderly dress, his long unkempt hair, and the antiquated look of his clothing."

It was six o'clock in the morning of 13 Vendémiaire, Year IV—October 5, 1795. The rainstorm had been followed by an unrelenting drizzle. The wind was still blowing.

What forces were in the field? Thirty thousand *sectionnaires* against 5,000 soldiers, 1,500 gendarmes and police, and 1,500 men forming a battalion called either "sacred" or "terrorist" according to one's opinion.

Buonaparte had also had 800 complete outfits of weapons brought for the deputies. As soon as the firing began, President Louis Legendre shouted: "Let us die with a courage fitting for the friends of liberty!" And, trembling somewhat, the deputies charged their guns with bullets.

Napoleone had positioned two eight-pounders in the Rue Neuve-St.-Roch, facing the church. As Thiébault recounted it later:

> Their fire enfiladed the street. When, in this way, the cannons had felled or blasted aside everything and everybody in view, a thousand men of the patriot battalion, followed by a battalion of infantry, emerged from the dead-end street and attacked those *sectionnaires* who still remained in front of the church and were occupying the Rue St.-Honoré. The shock was violent, and there was hand-to-hand fighting. But our troops gained ground, and six pieces of ordnance were immediately placed in battery, three to the right and three to the left of the dead-end street. They completed the routing of the *sectionnaires,* who fled toward the Place Vendôme and the Palais-Royal. . . .

The Convention had been saved.

The rain had stopped falling at eleven o'clock, but the sky was still overcast, and the wind did not stop blowing until evening. The Tuileries presented a sad spectacle. The vestibule and the ground floor were full of wounded men stretched out on straw. The surgeons were hard-pressed. Many of the deputies' wives had come to the palace to share the fate of their husbands or in flight from the fury of the *sectionnaires*. "Of this number," Baron Thiébault reported subsequently, "the oldest served as nurses while the youngest shredded linen. Thus it was at once a senate, a government, a headquarters, a hospital, a camp, and a bivouac."

Five days later the Convention, on a motion by Barras, commanding general of the Army of the Interior, appointed "General Buono-Parte" (as the *Moniteur* spelled his name) deputy commander; and on the sixteenth Napoleone was promoted to major general. On October 26, having become a director—one of the five kings of the new regime—Barras resigned his post and Buonaparte succeeded him as commanding general of the Army of the Interior.

It was a dazzling promotion which astonished everyone—everyone but him.

Several days before, he had moved out of the Hôtel du Cadran Bleu (which was perhaps too expensive for him) and was now living in a miserable, cheap hotel called A l'Enseigne de la Liberté on the Rue des Fossés-Montmartre, today the Rue d'Aboukir. Such were the lodgings from which he moved to the fine residence on the Rue des Capucines (the quarters he inherited along with his new command) which looked out on the Place des Piques—known up until the Revolution as the Place Vendôme, and earlier as the Place Louis-le-Grand —where one day Napoelon's new Trajan's Column would be raised.

In consequence of 13 Vendémiaire, an order of the day was promulgated which prohibited Parisians from keeping or carrying weapons, under penalty of death. Josephine's son, Eugène de Beauharnais, very much upset at the idea of having to give up the sword he had inherited from his father, came to see Buonaparte. Moved by the tears of the young officer and knowing that he was the son of a friend of Thérèsia Tallien and of Barras, Buonaparte let him keep his sword.

The next day, Josephine (who was then called Rose) paid a call on Napoleone to thank him. And the day after that, in all likelihood, the general in his turn paid a call to Mme. de Beauharnais at the new lodgings she had just taken on the Rue Chantereine. This first visit

to Eugène's mother was followed by others, though Buonaparte soon began to space them out, perhaps because the memory of Désirée was still holding him back.

The new military governor had a fine carriage and (says Bourrienne) "entertained at sumptuous lunches where ladies were sometimes present." He received petitioners and spoke with self-confidence—to everyone's amazement. "One wonders," said a contemporary, "where he comes from, what he has been, and what extraordinary services he has to his credit."

Apparently, he was in no way intoxicated with his power; and he even seems to have been perfectly aware of his incompetence as military governor and commanding general of the Army of the Interior. Thiébault, who saw him the day after 13 Vendémiaire, has described him entering his office at General Staff Headquarters with his little hat on top of which was "some sort of a plume" (rather awkwardly stuck in, for that matter), his tricolored sash tied worse than carelessly, his sloppy uniform, and a sword which "to tell the truth, hardly looked like the weapon that would make his fortune." He threw his hat on the big table in the middle of the room and walked up to an old general named Krieg, the author of a popular booklet titled *Manual for Republican Wars and Republican Soldiers.* He told the general to take a seat beside him and, pen in hand, began to question him on a host of matters relating to discipline and the service. "Some of his questions showed such a degree of ignorance that the other officers present could not conceal their smiles." Thiébault, struck by the number of these questions, and their order and rapidity, was especially fascinated at seeing a commanding general who, "with the greatest indifference, let his subordinates see how little he knew of professional matters that the least of them was supposed to know perfectly. This fact," he concludes, "made him grow a hundred cubits in my eyes."

Whether or not Buonaparte was thinking of Josephine, she at all events remembered him; and in December, 1795, she sent him a now famous note:

> You no longer come to see a friend who likes you. You have neglected her entirely. This is very wrong of you, because she is fond of you. Come to lunch with me tomorrow, Septidi [seventh day of the ten-day week on the Republican calendar]. I must see

you and talk with you about matters of business that concern you. Good night, my friend. I embrace you.

The Widow Beauharnais

What feelings prompted Mme. de Beauharnais to write that note? It may be that she had not forgotten what her friend Count Ségur had told her once: "That little general could well become a great man!"

There is no doubt that she had already yielded to the advances of Barras, whose mistress she now was, and who was already considered a great man. But on the other hand she was quite aware that the protection of this friend of hers was uncertain. She needed something better—someone who could cope with her expenses, which resembled the sieve of the Danaides. And besides, she found Buonaparte "droll."

In the belief that the Widow Beauharnais possessed a fortune, Buonaparte went—on that famous Septidi de Frimaire, Year IV—to the charming little town house located not far from the Chaussée d'Antin, on the Rue Chantereine—so-called because tree frogs (*reinettes*) used to croak there. Skillfully, Rose began by trying to persuade Napoleone that there was nothing but a good friendship between herself and Barras, that all the talk in Paris was pure slander. Buonaparte was ready to believe anything. Then he spoke of the "matters of business" concerning him—no doubt of the command of the Army of Italy that he still hoped to get, despite his newfound prestige.

He kept returning to the Rue Chantereine. The luxury he found there—the purely external luxury of a lady of easy virtue—dazzled him. He admired her exquisite way of saying to each person exactly what was necessary, and her tact in guiding a conversation. He had no suspicion that she had nothing but debts, that her servants were seldom paid and her tradesmen even less frequently. In the presence of this "lady" he was painfully aware that he was a decidedly petty provincial, and of decidedly petty nobility. He was not aware, at the time, that the title of viscountess with which the widow Beauharnais adorned herself was usurped. Buonaparte was under the spell of "the incomparable Josephine." For that was what he called her, since he was unwilling any longer to use her first name, Rose, which had been uttered by too many men.

She employed her coquettishness with a consummate art and skill. And he, devoid of experience, loved her as he had never loved anyone before. On St. Helena he acknowledged: "She was a real woman. . . . She had a *je ne sais quoi* that I liked."

She gave herself to him one January night—which cost her very little—and she was astonished, the next day, when she read his first letter:

> Seven o'clock in the morning: I woke up full of you. Your picture, and the memory of this intoxicating night, have given no rest to my senses. Sweet and incomparable Josephine! What a strange effect you have had on my heart! You are angry! Do I see you sad? Are you worried? My heart is broken with grief, and there is no repose for your friend. . . . But is there any more of it for me when, giving myself over to the deep feeling which overwhelms me, I take in—from your lips, from your heart—a flame that burns me? Ah! It was only last night that I realized that your portrait is not you! Darling, you leave at noon, and I shall see you in three hours. In the meantime, *mio dolce amor,* here are a thousand kisses for you. But don't give me any, because they set my blood on fire.

Now the question was: How was he going to get rid of his little fiancée from Marseille? Rather crudely, he wrote her that if she could not obtain her mother's and brother's consent for an immediate wedding, it would be preferable "to break off all relations" with her.

Désirée, crushed, responded:

> How can I begin to describe to you the frightful situation in which I have been placed by your letter? Ah! You have succeeded only too well! Yes, cruel man, you have reduced me to despair. The phrase "break off all relations" makes me tremble. I thought I had found in you a friend that I could love for the rest of my life. But no. I must leave off loving you, because I cannot conceive of any expedient that would make them consent to our marriage. I could never bring myself to speak of it to my family. . . .

Her attitude was that of a young lady of the eighteenth century —of that age when one either did not marry at all or one was married off by one's family. It was up to Napoleone to make the move. In asking Désirée to speak to her family on her own, he could not have received any other reply. But then that was just what Josephine's lover wanted.

His new love and his advancement were making a different man of him. His satisfied ego no longer ran the risk of being wounded; his sullen manner was no longer befitting. He became more expansive. His conversation "was always remarkable in one way or another, and even the ghost stories he sometimes told were interesting (or so he seemed to make them) because of his originality in recounting them." He was admired—and this was such a new experience for him!

Not that he had lost his hypersensitivity. One February evening, Josephine dared to accuse him of having sought her out for selfish reasons: perhaps in order to obtain that famous command of the Army of Italy. He took it very badly. Later, however, he was frank enough to acknowledge, apropos of his marriage to her: "For me, it was a good piece of business."

So he thought then, at any rate.

"She said she had one or two million francs in Martinique," he explained later. "But she only had five hundred thousand francs, that I never saw."

As soon as he got back home that night after their talk (a talk which certainly had its effect, since they would bring it up later on), he wrote her as follows:

And so you thought that I didn't love you for yourself alone! For whom, then? Ah, Madame! I would have had to change a lot! . . . I am still astonished by it, but even less than by the feelings which, when I awakened after my nap, made me humble myself before you again, without rancor and powerless to resist. . . . O incomparable Josephine, what is this power you possess? A single thought of yours poisons my life and causes my heart to be torn in two by the most contrary impulses. But an even stronger feeling, a less somber mood, takes hold of me and brings me back to you still guilty. I am convinced that if we argue, you should not take exception to my heart . . . to my conscience: you have brought them under your spell; they are still on your side. But, *mio dolce amor*, did you sleep well? Did you think of me even once? I give you three kisses: one on your heart, one on your mouth, and one on your eyes.

On March 2, 1796, Buonaparte was appointed commanding general of the Army of Italy. Was this a wedding gift from Barras? Napoleon, embarrassed at having been indebted for a favor to his wife's former lover, said later that he owed his appointment to Count Lazare Carnot, the "Organizer of Victory," who was now a Director: "He appreciated my great ability," he explained. Perhaps Carnot and Barras joined forces in order to convince their colleagues.

In March the marriage contract between Napoleone and Josephine was signed at the office of Maitre Raguideau, Mme. de Beauharnais' solicitor, who disapproved of the union between his client and a man who, he protested, had "only his cape and his sword." The sky was cloudless, but on the horizon a haze was beginning to dim the stars. At the town hall the former Rose de Beauharnais (in a chiffon dress with tricolored floral pattern), the witnesses (Barras, Tallien, and Calmelet, Josephine's confidential clerk), and the commissioner Collin-Lacombe (who, although not entitled to do so, had replaced the mayor, who had gone home to bed), had been waiting for the groom for two hours. Barras, worried, watching the clock; if Buonaparte changed his mind, Barras might have to pay the insanely big bills that the Creole had run up. Suddenly, they heard the clanking of a sword on the stone stairsteps. The door opened. It was Buonaparte, followed by his witness and aide-de-camp, Lemarois. Without taking the trouble to apologize for his delay, he rushed up to the commissioner and shook him awake: "Come on and marry us —quickly!"

Still half-asleep, Collin-Lacombe solemnized this marriage ceremony in which one of the witnesses (Lemarois) was not yet of age and hence could not be a witness; in which the mayor's substitute was in no way legally competent to join the pair in matrimony; and in which, finally, the groom added eighteen months to his actual age and the bride coquettishly subtracted four years from hers. Later, Napoleon told of the procedure employed: "The Empress Josephine used the birth certificate of her dead sister, who was three or four years younger, because she wanted to make herself younger."

As for him, what he did was out of gallantry vis-à-vis his wife. "Not having my birth certificate with me," he explained later, "I used the certificate of my older brother, who had come to Paris for the ceremony."

Five minutes later the members of the wedding party told one another good night on the sidewalk outside.

When he announced his marriage to the president of the Directory Buonaparte specified that he saw therein a new tie between himself and the nation: "It is one more warranty of my firm intention to seek my well-being only in the Republic."

Was it because the pretty viscountess had only recently been the mistress of one of the directors of the new government that she could be considered a "warranty" of her husband's republicanism? The "five kings"—and especially Barras—must have had a good laugh.

> And so you are married [Désirée wrote to Buonaparte]. Poor Eugénie no longer has the right to love you or to think of you. . . . You, married! I cannot get used to the idea. It crushes me. I can't stand it. I will show you that I am more faithful to my commitments than you are; and even though you have broken the ties that united us, I shall never become engaged to another. I shall never marry. . . . All I want is death. Life is sheer torture for me, since I can no longer dedicate it to you.

Sweet, affectionate Désirée, who wished for death and who would never marry. Two years and five months later, Désirée wed a French ambassador, the former Sergeant Bellejambe, otherwise known as General Bernadotte, whose career at the time looked as promising as that of Napoleone. They would eventually become the Prince and Princess de Pontecorvo, thanks to His Majesty Napoleon I. And one day they would be King and Queen of Sweden and Norway. It was a fine revenge for the abandoned girl.

IV

LOVE AND WAR

In love, the only victory is flight.

NAPOLEON

"BE PATIENT, MY DARLING. We'll have time to make love after the victory."

And then, his head bent down over the round table in the little salon (and dining room) of the town house on the Rue de Chantereine —a folding table of mahogany, a table covered with maps—Buonaparte sent his wife back to her trinkets and those countless mirrors that ornamented her rotunda-shaped boudoir. He was putting the finishing touches to the campaign plans that he had been mulling over for two years, ever since Augustin Robespierre had given him command of artillery in the Army of Italy: the plan he had conceived in March, 1794, which had aroused the enthusiasm of the deputy Ricord and the dictator's brother. Now that he was commanding general of the Army of Italy, Napoleone had no doubts that he could carry it out, even though (as he well knew) he had nothing better than an army without discipline, without food, and without shoes.

The Director had decided to extend a so-called diversionary war into the Piedmont and Lombardy for no other reason than to fill a desperately depleted treasury. As early as January 19, Carnot had written to B. L. J. Schérer, then commanding general of the Army of Italy: "We have no money. . . . You will have to find the means of getting along without it, or taking it where you can find it. . . . There is wealth behind a certain door that must be broken down. . . ." But when the "little Buonaparte's" plan was transmitted to Schérer, he replied: "Let the man who conceived it come and carry it out!"

They had taken him literally.

58

The expedition that Buonaparte had been called upon to carry out was thus one of plunder and pillage. He was by no means asked to "carry the torch of liberty" or to "go and frighten the crowned despots on the other side of the mountains." The government was in desperate straits—that was all there was to it.

On the evening of March 2, 1796, Buonaparte was informed that the post chaise was awaiting him at the end of the little driveway lined with lindens that led from his town house to the Rue Chantereine. Junot, his aide-de-camp, and Chauvet, paymaster of the Army of Italy, were already in the carriage. At the moment of parting from Josephine, Napoleone became anxious. Would she come and join him as soon as the situation in Italy made it possible? She quieted his fears. Of course. She would leave Paris whenever he asked her to come. Actually, however, the idea of giving up her life of pleasure to go off and live in an army camp far from her coiffeur, her couturier, and the tradesmen who provided her with frivolous things struck her as pure folly. And while Napoleone was setting out in the fog for the Italian front, Josephine retired to her bed of bronze-colored wood, no doubt murmuring as she was wont to do, in that Creole accent that so delighted her husband: "How *drolle* that Buonaparte is!"

But he, on his way toward the south of France, was preoccupied with her image and their shared memories. On the evening of March 14 he wrote to her from Chanceaux:

> Every instant is taking me farther away from you. I think of you constantly. My imagination exhausts itself trying to visualize what you are doing. If, in my mind's eye, I see you looking sad, my heart is torn and my grief deepens. Or if you are gay and behaving giddily with your friends, I reproach you with having so soon forgotten our painful separation of three days ago. Write me, my sweet, and at length. I send you the thousand and one kisses of a love most tender and true.

On the back of the envelope he wrote the name of "la Citoyenne Beauharnais." Was he afraid that the mail courier could not find the house of "la Citoyenne Buonaparte"?

When he reached Marseille on March 20 he went to see Mme.

Letizia, announced his marriage, gave her a letter from Josephine, and extracted from her a promise to write to the daughter-in-law he had imposed on her. And what a daughter-in-law! A viscountess! A woman of fashion! A widow six years older than Napoleon! A woman famous for her loose ways. It was even talked about in the newspapers! And a woman whose two children would have to be supported! At one stroke the clan had been increased by three persons who would absorb most of dear Nabulio's salary! And so, with evident ill humor, Mme. Letizia took more than a week to write to the new Citoyenne Buonaparte—or rather, to the Citoyenne Bonaparte, because Mme. Letizia's son had now decided to abandon the Italian spelling of his first and last names.

Four days later he passed through Toulon. A friend of his was there: Captain Decrès of the Navy, who would be promoted to rear admiral in 1798. Decrès had seen a good deal of Bonaparte at Paris, and thought he was on familiar terms with him. "Eagerly," he hurried to see him. The salon door opened, and Decrès was about to rush up to him, when Napoleon's "stance, his look, and the tone of his voice" stopped the unfortunate fellow in his tracks. Bonaparte was intent, immediately, upon showing the distance that separated that paltry beggar, "Captain Cannon," as he had been known, from the commanding general of one of the armies of the Republic who had just saved the regime and was beloved (at least so he believed) by one of the prettiest women in Paris.

On March 25 Napoleon reached Antibes, where he was greeted by Louis Alexandre Berthier, chief of staff of the Army of Italy. Berthier was a short, deformed individual, but in his huge head everything was methodically classified. Bonaparte, who apparently could gauge a man with one look, surmised that this indefatigable officer could handle all detail work for him.

He set up headquarters at Nice; and on March 27 he received André Masséna, J. M. P. Sérurier, A. E. F. Laharpe, and P. F. C. Augereau, all of them major generals, who looked down on this "puny fellow" twenty-six and a half years of age who had been foisted on them as their commander. A political officer! An intriguer! A cloakroom general! A "little puppet with unkempt hair" who thought he was going to wage war against the Austrian Empire and the Kingdom of Piedmont with 27,000 ragged men with no pay, empty stomachs, and shoes made of woven straw!

Masséna took Bonaparte's measure. In his words: "His short stature and his sickly-looking face did not incline us in his favor. The fact that he held in his hand a portrait of his wife, which he showed to everyone, and above all his extreme youth, persuaded us that his appointment was the result of an intrigue."

Which, for that matter, is rather accurate. Everything in the attitude of the four generals standing in front of their new commander showed they were perfectly aware that their troops were, in a sense, the general's wife's dowry. Scornfully, they kept their hats (adorned with tricolored plumes) on their heads. There is a story that Bonaparte, by taking off his own hat, compelled them to imitate him, after which he put his own hat back on—something the others dared not do. Whether this is legend or truth, one thing is certain: Masséna assures us that when Napoleon put his hat on again, he seemed "to grow two feet higher."

The major generals remained silent. But they were astonished when they heard Bonaparte question them with amazing competence "on the position of their divisions, their matériel, the morale of each unit, and how many combat-ready troops it had." Then he "traced out the direction that the different units were to take":

"Tomorrow, I shall inspect all units, and the day after tomorrow I shall march on the enemy."

This timetable was accurate, give or take three or four days.

After the officers, the men. At the time of his arrival at Nice, Bonaparte certainly knew that he would be commanding an army that lacked everything, but he was not completely aware of the real state of things, which was frightful. There was not a single franc. "We lived from hand to mouth. There were no means of transportation. Only the stage routes from the Rhône to the Var were supplied." In his memoirs the adjutant Dupin related that one day all he received as rations for the three officers and the quartermaster sergeant of his company was twenty-nine beans. He had counted them. In forty-eight hours the new commanding general succeeded in securing "six days' provisions of bread, meat, and brandy, plus 12,000 pairs of shoes." With some food on hand for the men, the next item was to establish discipline. "Either I will maintain order," wrote Bonaparte to the Directory, "or I will no longer command these brigands." Order was established, and those "brigands" became the best soldiers in the world. One battalion, which refused to leave Nice and go to its position before getting paid, was dissolved and split up among the other units. In Masséna's words: "This decisive move immediately inculcated in the troops a respect for the young general's authority."

In order to give his army a sense of identity, he reviewed the troops on the Place de la République. He moved here and there among the men, questioned them informally, and stimulated them by promising that they would soon be able to say with pride: "I was in the Army of Italy." Then, getting back on his horse, he addressed them in concise and vivid phrases that would become immortal:

Soldiers, you are naked and undernourished. The government owes you much, but can give you nothing. . . . Your patience in bearing all privations and your courage in facing all kinds of danger have won the admiration of France. She is a witness to your hardships. You have no shoes or coats or shirts, and almost no food. Our supply depots are empty, while the enemy's are stuffed with everything. It is up to you to capture them. You want to do it, and you can do it. Let's go!

Other republican commanders of course knew how to speak to their troops; but none of them had yet used the kind of language that stirred up real enthusiasm and echoed in men's memories.

"My men are evincing a trust in me that simply cannot be expressed," Napoleon wrote. Was it love that had given him such ardor? Was it the thought of Josephine, who was constantly on his mind? He wrote to her, this time addressing the letter to "Citoyenne Bonaparte, chez la Citoyenne Beauharnais": "Whether I am in the midst of business matters, leading the troops, or dashing through the camps, my adorable Josephine, and she alone, is in my heart, and occupies my mind and my thoughts."

Every night, he says, he dreams that he is holding her in his arms. "I have not so much as drunk a cup of tea without cursing the ambition and thirst for glory that keep me apart from the soul of my life."

He had reproached his wife for the coldness of her letters, and so she wrote to him, in her own blood (at least she claims it is hers), a few ardent, erotic lines. He replied:

What are you thinking of, my adorable darling—writing me things like that? Do you think my situation isn't cruel enough already, without increasing my sense of loss and convulsing my soul? What a style! What feelings you describe! They are fiery, and they burn my poor heart!

In his letter he tells her again that she is all that he thinks of. When he is bored by "the hustle and bustle of business matters," when people disgust him, when he is ready "to curse life," he puts his hand on his heart: "Your portrait lives there, and I look at it. . . ."

On April 2, 1796, with fanfare, the epic began: Bonaparte left Nice, taking the simple country road to la Corniche.

The Austrian general, J. P. Beaulieu, had, as a matter of fact, divided his forces, whereas the French army was positioned so that it could quickly merge into a single force and launch a massive attack against one of the enemy corps. This is what happened on April 12 at Montenotte—Night Mountain—located four leagues north of Savona.

"Keep a sharp eye on Montenotte," Bonaparte had ordered. "It's a case of vigilance versus boasting."

And, indeed, one of the Austrian corps was badly beaten and the other was compelled to retreat. The rout of the enemy was complete.

"Who were your forebears?" Napoleon was once asked.

"My nobility dates from Montenotte," he replied.

This first victory proved the soundness of his plan. It was now a matter of enlarging the breach thanks to the "wedge" that had been thrust in to the Austro-Sardinian troop disposition. The next day brought the Battle of Millesimo, which would open the way to Turin and Milan, and which preceded the victory of Mondovi.

On the evening of April 25, in a downpour of rain, Napoleon left for Cherasco where, the next day, he made his famous proclamation to the Army of Italy:

> Soldiers! Up to this time you have fought for nothing better than barren rocks—which, although made famous by your courage, are useless to the Fatherland. . . . Lacking everything, you have made up for everything you lacked. You have won battles without cannons, crossed rivers without bridges, made forced marches without boots, and bivouacked without brandy and often without bread. Only the republican phalanges—the soldiers of

liberty—could have endured what you have endured! For all this, my thanks. . . .

Then, after having reminded them of his request that they "respect" the "recently liberated peoples" and desist from looting (this being reserved for the government), he uttered those words which would be engraved upon men's memories:

> Soldiers! The Fatherland has the right to expect great things of you! Will you justify that expectation? . . . You still have battles to fight, cities to take, and rivers to cross. You have done nothing, since you still have everything to do. . . .

On the morning of April 27 the King of Sardinia sent a new proposal for an armistice to the conqueror, who was then at Cherasco, ten leagues from Turin. Bonaparte replied with an ultimatum into which he slipped a clause giving him the "right to cross the Po at Valenza" and guaranteeing his unobstructed passage across the states of the King of Sardinia—a route which would enable him to reach Lombardy and attack Austria. For the first time, Napoleon was about to become a statesman and have dealings, across the conference table, with gentlemen of the *ancien régime*.

The Sardinian emissaries (of Savoyard origin)—General Baron de la Tour, the Marquis Henry, and the young Colonel Marquis Costa de Beauregard, who was General Colli's chief of staff—came to Count Salmatoris' palace, where Bonaparte had his headquarters, at ten thirty that night. Beauregard wrote an account of that long evening. The three emissaries were surprised: there were no guards posted around the building, which was scarcely illuminated. A few soldiers, totally exhausted, were sleeping on the threshold and the front steps. In the immediate vicinity of the palace there was none of that activity typical of headquarters: no horses, no ammunition wagons, no pack mules. There weren't even any servants to receive the visitors, who wandered about until "a young man attached to the general staff" appeared.

This young man took the emissaries into a "reception room," where a big fire had been lighted. Berthier greeted them, questioned them as to the object of their mission, and then went to report to the commanding general. A half-hour later Bonaparte finally appeared. He was booted, but wore no sword. His bearing struck the Savoyards as solemn and cold. He listened in silence to General Baron de la Tour's preamble.

"Don't you have copies of the conditions that I proposed to the King?" replied Napoleon. "Has he accepted those conditions?"

At this point, the diplomats complained of the "harshness of those conditions."

"Since I offered them," Bonaparte answered dryly, "I have taken Cherasco, Fossano, and Alba. Yet I have added nothing to my first demands. You really should consider me moderate."

"We fear that His Majesty may perhaps be forced, vis-à-vis his current allies, to take certain measures which contravene his scruples and loyalty to his principles."

"God forbid that I should demand of you anything contrary to the laws of honor!"

Beauregard, La Tour, and Henry then tried to show him "how little advantage he would gain from some of the concessions he had demanded; in particular, the crossing of the Po at Valenza."

At this, Napoleon held his head high and, "with some sharpness," and in a louder tone of voice, declared: "My Republic, in entrusting me with the command of an army, believed I possessed enough discernment to judge what was right for her interests, without having recourse to the advice of the enemy."

At one o'clock in the morning, Bonaparte took out his watch and, seeing that the discussion was dragging on without producing anything decisive, spoke out: "Gentlemen, I hereby put you on notice that a general attack has been ordered for two o'clock. If I do not have the assurance that Coni will be in my hands before evening, this attack will not be postponed one minute. It may well chance that I shall lose battles, but I will never lose minutes through overconfidence or sloth."

How much he had changed in three months! He now spoke as the master.

The emissaries had to yield. They immediately set about writing the articles of the agreement, and the Chevalier de Seyssel left at a gallop to take the news of the truce to the King and to obtain his permission to hand over Coni and Tortona to the conqueror.

For his part, Bonaparte had Berthier countermand the attack. General Baron de la Tour then asked for coffee, and Bonaparte ordered some brought from the town. The emissaries watched as he

produced two porcelain cups from a little dressing case that was on
the sofa near his sword. Costa de Beauregard noticed with astonishment that the French general did not have any silver spoons. They
had to use "brass spoons of the kind used by soldiers."

When the truce was signed, Bonaparte introduced to the Savoyards generals Murat, Marmont, Despinoy, and two or three staff
officers. At dawn the emissaries went back to Turin, escorted by
French dragoons. In Costa's words:

> The light of dawn showed us the bivouacked troops of the
> French advance guard. Everything seemed to be in the greatest
> disarray: there were no cannons, and the horses were few in
> number, thin, and haggard. But the bearing of the soldiers ex-
> pressed a light-hearted, gay indifference. . . . Their awareness of
> victory made up for everything!

At his window, Bonaparte watched the diplomats leave. He had
difficulty concealing his joy: for the first time, he had won a civil
victory on top of a military one.

And yet Josephine's attitude, and her letters—"as cold as friendship"—dampened the victor's joy. On April 24 he had begged her to
set out for Italy. He had even requested it of Barras after the capture
of Mondovi—as if it were a matter of a reward.

"You're going to come, aren't you?" he wrote the next day to his
beloved Creole. "You're going to be here at my side, on my heart,
in my arms, on my mouth." And he closed with: "A kiss on the heart,
and another a little farther down—much farther down!"

Josephine was in no hurry to join her husband, who was the least
of her worries. She had other things on her mind, for she had fallen
hopelessly in love with a lieutenant, Hippolyte Charles, who was nine
years younger than she. She found him irresistible, and vastly amusing. Napoleon had never managed to amuse her. Well, sometimes,
perhaps, involuntarily. The memory of her husband didn't cause her
the slightest concern. The name of General Bonaparte was on everyone's lips but his wife's.

Marmont tells us that on May 6, at Tortona, "the glass on the
miniature of Napoleon's wife (which he always carried with him) was
shattered. He turned frightfully pale, and his reaction was extremely
painful.

" 'Marmont, my wife is either sick or unfaithful.' "

Then he plunged his spurs into his horse's sides.

But he was still filled with hope at the thought that he might soon hold Josephine close in his arms. As a matter of fact, they had agreed that she would set out for Italy accompanied by Murat. What would the unfaithful lady do? The future King of Naples, who was waiting for Mme. la Générale Bonaparte to make up her mind at last, grew impatient: he had to get back to his command. Josephine pondered. Should she abandon her beloved Hippolyte? Never! So she invented a pretext for not setting out.

"I'm pregnant!"

Bonaparte didn't doubt her word, so blinded was he by his memories of the little bedroom on the Rue Chantereine. For she had—with consummate art—persuaded him that it was he who had taught her her marvelous skills.

Indeed, when he received the news of her pregnancy, he wrote her, thoroughly bedazzled: "And so it is true that you are pregnant?" He was all tenderness. He was eager to see how she "carried children." His feelings can be discerned in these lines:

> Could it be possible that I might be deprived of the happiness of seeing you with your little belly? It must make you most attractive! You write me that you have changed a great deal. Your letter is short, sad, and written in a trembling hand. What is the matter, my adorable one? I thought I was jealous, but I swear to you that I'm not. Rather than to see you sad, I think I would furnish you with a lover myself. . . .

Why should she worry?

The Directory had not taken serious exception to the fact that Bonaparte, without consulting it, had dealt directly with the King of Sardinia. The Government could see only one thing: the "door" that had previously been mentioned to General Schérer had been "broken in," and the treasury was being filled. But Bonaparte could do even better. "Genoa," they suggested to him, "must not be more than forty-five leagues distant from Loreto. Would it not be possible to seize the Santa Casa and the immense treasures that superstition has been accumulating there for fifteen centuries?" And the directors had another suggestion for him. "It is the Milanese, above all, who should not be spared. Collect reparations in cash there immediately!"

In order to do that, the Imperial Austrian Army had to be destroyed. Bonaparte knew very well what he was doing when he demanded from the Piedmontese "the right to cross the Po at Valenza." The Austrian general, Beaulieu, had been completely fooled. Decoyed like a greenhorn of the general staff, he had gone off (rubbing his hands in self-congratulation) to take up a position across from Valenza, while Bonaparte, on May 7, having only two Austrian "squadrons" in his way, calmly crossed the river toward Piacenza—a maneuver that enabled the French to turn the enemy's flank with marvelous ease. On May 9, after having signed a truce with the Duke of Parma, Bonaparte was able to write the Directory: "If all goes well, I hope to be able to send you ten million or so." The next day he left the house at Casalpusterlengo where he had set up headquarters (the house still exists) and went off to launch the Battle of Lodi, which gave him all of Lombardy. That rich province fell like a ripe fruit.

Napoleon was beginning to create his fame.

"After Lodi," he said when he was at St. Helena, "I regarded myself no longer as a mere general but as a man destined to influence the fate of a people. It occurred to me that I could become a decisive actor on the political stage."

The Bridge of Lodi entered into legend—that bridge where the troops saw (or believed they saw) the commanding general, under a hail of bullets, "marching in front, carrying a banner." The Austrians, completely routed, fell back toward Oglio and Cremona. That same night the veteran soldiers of the army assembled and awarded a rank to their chief: that of corporal. Henceforth, he would be "the Little Corporal" and never "the Sergeant"—a rank awarded to him by the grenadiers after Castiglione.

The victory of Lodi opened to Napoleon the gates of Milan, from which the Archduke Ferdinand had left in a hurry, taking with him his gold and his collections.

On May 15, Whitsunday, Masséna, who had preceded his chief to Milan, welcomed him at the city gate—the "Porta Romana"—where the following words were emblazoned in Italian: "To the valorous French Army." To the dignitaries who came to greet Napoleon, he

said: "The Republic will do everything possible to make you happy."
The archbishop and the chief of the decurions were astonished when
they saw their conqueror, wearing a hat surmounted by a tricolored
plume, his half-powdered hair falling down over his shoulders like a
spaniel's ears. Napoleon got out of the carriage that had brought him
from Lodi and mounted a horse named Bijou. The bright sunshine
of the month of Floréal played over the scene. The Municipal Guard
lining the street presented arms. At the archducal palace, the conqueror presided over a banquet for 200 persons and, in Italian, promised the Milanese:

> You will be free! You will be free, and will be more sure of
> being so than the French. Milan will be your capital; the Oglio
> and the Serio will be your barriers. You will have 500 cannons and
> the eternal friendship of France. The Romagna will remain yours.
> You will embrace the two seas. You will have a fleet. No more
> regrets or quarrels. . . . The rich and the poor we shall always have
> with us. . . . But be wary of priests, and keep them away from
> public office. . . . If Austria were to attempt a new invasion, I
> would not abandon you.

The Milanese shouted enthusiastically. A delirious joy reigned in
the streets. People praised the name of the man who had snatched
Milan from the clutches of Austria. They shouted, they danced, they
lighted bonfires.

"Viva la liberta!"

And, once again, people started planting trees of liberty.

"Well, Marmont," Bonaparte asked as he was going to bed in the
archbishop's palace, "what do you think they are saying in Paris?"

"Their admiration must have reached a peak"

"They haven't seen anything yet. The future holds far greater
successes than those we have so far achieved. Fortune did not smile
upon me today merely so that I would disdain her favors. She is a
woman, and the more she does for me, the more I will demand of
her. In a few days we shall be on the Adige, and all Italy will be ours.
Then, perhaps, if the means put at my disposal are in proportion to
the scope of my plans, we shall promptly leave Italy to go farther. In
our day, no one has conceived anything great: it is up to me to set
the example."

"Already," as one eyewitness said later, "he had fixed his place and marked off the distances." He was armed with a glance "that went right through people," his friend Jean Jacques Cambacérès explained. Three months after his assumption of command, no one any longer dared to say that he was "the protégé of Barras, and of women."

On May 23 Bonaparte left for Lodi, where the army's general headquarters was located. He had scarcely arrived when he had to go back to Milan: violent riots had broken out. At Pavia, in the suburbs of Milan, and at Binasco as well, a rebellion had flared up. The Austrian and Piedmontese sympathizers had revolted, and the people had followed them. And with good reason. With their street-lamps extinguished, the Milanese had been bled white and subjected to crushing taxes and requisitions. The Monte di Pieta had been sequestered and—greatest of sacrileges—works of Da Vinci and Michelangelo had been sent to France. As Stendhal put it: "The good people of Milan did not realize that the presence of an army—even a liberating army—is always a catastrophe." This army, moreover, was as destitute as Job, and had been given the job of conquering Italy in order to loot the country and thereby fill the treasury of the French government.

The rebels were slaughtering soldiers who happened to stray off by themselves, and Bonaparte gave orders for reprisals: "Generals will send against the villages the necessary forces to repress them, to set them on fire, and to shoot all those found with weapons in their possession."

His troops carried out reprisals against several municipalities and burned the village of Binasco, where (as Jean Lannes admitted later) the rebellion was suppressed in a horrifying way. Before leaving Milan, Bonaparte assembled the municipal authorities and announced that they would pay with their heads for any new insurrection.

The next day he moved on to Pavia and set up headquarters. By way of punishment for the riots that had swept the city, he authorized looting for three hours. (Orders were given, however, to spare the homes of the biologist Lazzaro Spallanzani and the physicist Alessandro Volta.) And so the rebellion was put down with fire and blood. In Napoleon's words of a later date: "In the last analysis, one must be a military man in order to govern. It is only with boots and spurs that one can govern a horse."

At Brescia, Belmonte-Pignatelli, the emissary of the King of Naples, was waiting for Bonaparte. King "Nasone" (Big Nose) was, it turned out, ready to leave the coalition and wanted to sign a truce with France. There was little doubt that he would have to pay a heavy price for such a move.

As he dismounted, Napoleon was met by Miot, the Count of Melito, a statesman and writer, who had come to prepare the groundwork for the interview with the Neapolitan minister.

Very early in the talk, Napoleon mentioned Mantua, which was occupied by a powerful Austrian force.

> Nothing will have been really accomplished until we have Mantua. . . . Only then will I be able to call myself the master of Italy. Such a difficult siege will necessarily have to be very long; and for the moment I shall have to be satisfied with investing the fortress very closely. Austria is going to take its time assembling a relief army. Consequently, we have a month in which to advance to the center of Italy and make ourselves masters of it.

Emboldened, Miot then informed the commanding general that the Neapolitan prince Belmonte-Pignatelli was at Brescia.

Bonaparte replied: "I have no objection to discussing a truce."

"He used the word 'amnesty,' " Miot de Melito tells us, "and made the same error almost every time in the course of the conversation." (For that matter, he would go on making that same error all his life.)

Two hours later, the truce was signed.

Now it was the Holy See's turn. On June 22 the conqueror received Pius VI's emissaries at Bologna. Bonaparte was demanding at the outset of the talks, but finally unbent somewhat. Nevertheless, the conditions imposed upon the temporal sovereign of Rome were harsh:

> The ports of the Papal States will be closed to ships of the powers at war with the Republic, and open to French ships.
> The French Army will remain in possession of the legations of Bologna and Ferrara, but will evacuate the legation of Faenza. The Pope will turn over to the French Republic 100 paintings, vases, or statues . . . (in particular, the bronze bust of Junius Brutus

and the marble bust of Marcus Brutus) and 500 manuscripts. The Pope will pay the French Republic 21,000,000 livres in French money, including 15,500,000 in cash or bullion . . . and the remaining 5,500,000 in goods, merchandise, horses, and cattle. . . . The Pope will be required to authorize the transit of troops of the Republic. . . .

The Directory was enchanted. The "fiscal invasion," as Albert Sorel called it, was coming along very nicely. "Don't leave anything in Italy," the conqueror was told. The Italians must pay dearly for their freedom. It was no longer a war, but a razzia.

Napoleon had surmised that Josephine's pregnancy was a fabrication, and was suffering terribly. Why did his wife refuse to leave Paris? Perhaps he suspected her involvement with the handsome hussar.

I gather that you have made your choice, and that you know where to find a replacement for me. . . . As for you, I only hope that the memory of me is not hateful. My misfortune was to have known you only slightly. Yours was to have judged me in the same way as you judge the men around you.

But nothing could stir up any pity in Hippolyte's mistress. Her poor husband wrote to Joseph: *"Mon ami,* I am in a state of despair. My wife, who is everything in this world that I love, is ill. My mind is at the end of its tether. . . . I love her to the point of madness, and can no longer remain far away from her."

At this point Barras, alerted by Joseph, asked Carnot to calm Bonaparte by shifting the responsibility for Josephine's absence to the Directory and its "fear that the attentions her husband would lavish upon her would distract him from those which the glory and well-being of the nation demanded of him. . . . "

But, whatever the cost, the Creole had to make up her mind! Had not Bonaparte announced in his letters that if his wife was really ill he would hurry to Paris? And had he not declared that without Josephine he felt he could no longer be of any use in Italy? In short, he was ready to walk out on the diplomats (who were pleading for an armistice at the time) and abandon his army to whoever wanted to take it over. Thus the entire campaign of conquest depended upon whom Josephine would be sleeping with! To be sure, things had gone marvelously well so far; but there was the future to worry about. Were not the Austrians getting ready to reach out a hand to the invested city of Mantua? Meantime, nothing had yet been able to convince Josephine that she should give up her handsome, beloved Hippolyte, who could make her laugh to the point of tears and was so clever at sporting with her in her rotunda-shaped boudoir.

This time the five Directors got angry; and on June 24 they forced Josephine to get into her carriage and set out. "Profoundly unhappy, and all in tears," as a witness describes her, she finally left Paris. But no sooner was the carriage rolling·along on the road to Italy than she stopped weeping. For across from her, touching her knees, was Hippolyte. She had taken her lover along.

Finally, on July 13, a courier reached Milan and informed Bonaparte that "the incomparable Josephine" would be there in an hour.

Napoleon leaped on his horse and went to meet her. At the gates of Milan, he finally held her in his arms. He was so consumed with desire that he did not even notice the presence, at his wife's side, of Hippolyte Charles. Not only that, but during the first two days that he spent with her at Milan, he entertained her lover at dinner and in his salon.

One can feel nothing but a kind of uneasiness in reading the first letter he wrote to her after their new separation:

> A few days ago, I thought I loved you; but since I have seen you again, I feel that I love you a thousand times more. Since I have known you, I have adored you more every day.... Ah! I beg of you: Please let me see some of your defects. Be less beautiful, less gracious, less tender, less kind. And above all, never be jealous and never weep. Your tears drive me mad and set my blood on fire.... [Thus, by way of a switch, she had made him believe she was jealous.]
>
> Be sure to get plenty of rest. Try to regain your health quickly. Come to join me. And at least, before we die, we can say: "For so many days we were happy!"

Did he remember having written, in his days at Valence: "I believe unquestionably that love does more harm than good, and that it would be a favor on the part of a benign deity to rid us of it and liberate men from it"?

On July 15 Bonaparte left to rejoin the French troops which had been investing Mantua for a month. Before them was the expanse of water—the three lakes formed by the Mincio River—which partially protected the city. Napoleon had only 9,000 men. An equal number of Austrians were sheltered behind the walls of the old Lombard inner city. As early as July 17 Napoleon felt sure he could take Mantua "by a bold and happy stroke."

But Mantua continued to resist. Napoleon soon had enough of being bogged down in this manner (he loathed sieges), and on July 19 he left for his headquarters at Castiglione.

Immediately upon his arrival, however, he was called upon (between two battles and two passionate letters to Josephine) to settle some civil problems, since he regarded himself as the Proconsul of the new Italy. Certain commissioners of the Republic—especially Pierre Anselme Garreau, a former member of the Constitutional Assembly—were making the big merchants bear the burden of a harsh occupation. As Bonaparte wrote to the Directory: "They are being treated more harshly than you intended, and even more harshly than the English merchants are treated. This has alarmed all of the merchants in Italy, and makes us look like vandals in their eyes. . . ."

That was why, on the same day, he gave a severe dressing-down to Garreau: "When you were a representative of the people, you had unlimited powers: everyone thought it his duty to obey you. But today you are a commissioner of the Government. You are invested with great authority, but your duties have been defined by a specific directive. See that you abide by it!"

This masterful tone of voice will henceforth be his.

Beaulieu had been replaced by Marshal Wurmser, an Alsatian in the service of Austria. His army of 70,000 Austro-Hungarians came down from the mountains and infiltrated each side of Lake Garda, planning to close a vise upon the 40,000 French troops baffled by the resistance of Mantua.

At the same moment, on July 29, in Verona, Bonaparte was exulting: Josephine was with him. After having played hard to get for so long, she had deigned to leave Milan and come to join him. They were having coffee on the balcony of the modest house in which the Comte de Provence had lived: a balcony from which all the nearby

countryside could be surveyed. He held his languorous wife close to
him, and she laughed, repeating over and over again: "That's
enough, now, Bonaparte!"

The others present averted their glances in their embarrassment.
Suddenly one of them shouted: "The Austrians!"

Wurmser's "whitecoats," ordered to liberate Mantua, were in fact
coming down the mountainside in long lines. Masséna had been
ordered to guard the valleys commanding the Lombard and Venetian plains. But what had he done?

While Josephine, escorted by Junot, fled toward Desenzano,
Bonaparte received one dispatch rider after another. Before long he
had an overall view of the situation. It was far from promising. He
began issuing orders in torrents, trying to stop the enemy.

Then he went to Desenzano, where the narrow streets were
littered with corpses. There he learned that, not far from the peninsula of Sermione, the Austrians (whose boats were plying Lake
Garda) had fired on Josephine's carriage. "Wurmser will pay dearly
for the scare he just gave you," he told his wife.

There was no end of bad news. The road to Milan had been cut,
Brescia had been recaptured, Lannes and Murat had been taken
prisoner. After sending Josephine off to Florence with an escort of
dragoons, he called a council of war. Things were going badly, very
badly. There were those who already believed that the French had
lost Italy. And it was being rumored that the Neapolitans and
the Pope intended to break the truce and march toward the
north.

Bonaparte's plan was the Napoleonic strategy. Since the enemy
had divided his forces into two armies, he would defeat them one
after the other. As he explained later to Las Cases: "From that moment on, Wurmser's plan of attack was discernible. Alone against all
those forces, the French Army could do nothing: we were not even
one against three. But alone against each one of the enemy corps, we
were on even terms."

Consequently, that same evening from Roverbella he issued the
order to abandon Mantua temporarily. Sérurier was to spike his cannons. The counteroffensive was launched. With 42,000 men, he was
going to defeat 80,000.

General Quasdanovitch and his Austrians attacked Lonato. Napoleon, with Masséna's infantry and all of his dragoons that he had managed to salvage, marched on the town and cut the Austrian army into two pieces: one was thrown back to the Mincio, the other toward Lake Garda. Junot pursued the routed Austrian army as far as Salo. And Quasdanovitch had no recourse but to pull back the remains of his army to the north of Lake Garda. Bonaparte took 2,000 prisoners and was able to inform the Directory that "things were taking a satisfactory turn."

Now it was Wurmser's turn.

At six o'clock on the morning of August 5, at Castiglione, the two armies faced each other. Bonaparte fell back in order to lure the enemy toward him; and the Austrians, falling into the trap, attacked on their right, leaving their center vulnerable. Marmont, with twenty pieces of light artillery firing grapeshot in rapid bursts, captured a redoubt that the "whitecoats" had built in the middle of the plain. The cannonade redoubled, Wurmser's left flank fell back, and Augereau joined the festivities with a mettlesome spirit that would one day earn for him—the son of a greengrocer and a domestic—the duchy of Castiglione. Wurmser tried to hold his ground near the tower of Solferino, but was carried back by the rout of his troops and withdrew toward Trento. All of Lake Garda, a key position, was in the hands of Bonaparte.

"In war," he was to say later, "boldness is the best calculation of genius."

The victor returned to Verona and wrote proudly to the Directory: "The Austrian Army, which for six weeks has been threatening our invasion of Italy, has vanished like a dream, and the Italy that it was threatening is now peaceful. . . ."

In the same letter, he added: "At Castelnuovo, in Venetian territory, a volunteer was assassinated. I had the house burned, and on the site of its ruins I had a sign posted: 'A Frenchman was assassinated here.'"

The wings that Bonaparte was growing were still causing annoyance to certain members of the Government who, without admitting it, would like to see them clipped. Doesn't he seem, they insinuated, to be ambitious to conquer Italy much more for the purpose of playing the role of dictator and conqueror than for the glory of the Republic?

Bonaparte was aware of them. On August 9 he wrote to Carnot: "I have the impression that lots of people want to wrong me, and that all kinds of intrigue are being employed to lend credence to rumors as stupid as they are malicious. . . ."

And so, in order to have a free hand, he threatened once again to resign his command: "The heat here is excessive. My health is not so good. If, in all of France, there is one man of integrity and good faith capable of suspecting my intentions and throwing doubt on my campaign, I will immediately forfeit the happiness of serving my country."

When Napoleon was winning his first victories, when his popularity began to grow, and when he first spoke out in the voice of a leader, the directors realized that this "puppet-like fellow with the unkempt hair" might well become their master. From that point on they were obsessed by one idea: keeping him away from the capital. And so, for three and a half years, by threatening them with the specter of his presence in Paris, Bonaparte got everything he wanted from the Directory—even their agreement to the mad escapade of the Egyptian campaign.

"Take advantage of Fortune's gifts when her whims favor you," Napoleon would say one day. "And be fearful lest she change out of sheer vexation. For she is a woman."

And as a matter of fact, he had but a brief respite: a new campaign was about to begin at the end of this same month of August. On August 25 he left for Verona to "push the victory on to its final result": to drive Davidovitch's army back toward the Tyrol, while giving the *coup de grace* to Wurmser, whose army had apparently regrouped rapidly, with a hope that would be shattered.

Napoleon was heartsick because he had received no letters from the indifferent and brooding Josephine.

> This causes me no end of anxiety [he wrote her]. You were a bit ill when I left. I beg of you: Don't leave me in this state of anxiety. You promised you would be more thoughtful. And at the time, what you said was in full agreement with what you felt. . . . Think of me, live for me, be with me often, and remember that there is only one misfortune of which I am frightened: that of no longer being loved by my Josephine. A thousand kisses— very sweet, very tender, and very exclusive.

On September 1 he was at Peschiera. From there he drove toward
Trento, to where Wurmser had retreated. By September 5, it was all
over; and in announcing the capture of Trento to the Directory, he
added: "Citizen Directors, by the 22nd [of Fructidor] I will be at
Bassano. If the enemy is waiting for me there, a battle will take place
which will decide the fate of this entire country. . . ."

He had announced the impending battle. He had even given the
date and the name that it would have in history: Bassano, 22 Fructidor (September 8). He was so happy that for the first time he sent
Josephine (apart from two affectionate lines) only a bulletin of victory:

> Ma chère amie, the enemy has lost 18,000 prisoners; all the
> others are killed or wounded. Wurmser, with a column of 1,500
> horses and 5,000 infantry, has no recourse left but withdrawal to
> Mantua. Never before have we had such great and continuing
> successes: Italy, Friuli, and the Tyrol have been secured for the
> Republic. The Emperor will have to create another army. Artil-
> lery, pontoon equipment, and baggage—everything has been
> captured.

The occupation of Bassano—Bassano del Grappa—made it possible for Bonaparte to "close off" the retreat of the Austrian troops
toward Trento. As he had predicted, the latter were compelled to
seek refuge in Mantua, and the siege of that city began immediately.
Thus in three weeks the Austrians had lost 27,000 men; and Marmont
could leave for Paris taking twenty-two banners with him. On that
same day the cities of Ferrara, Bologna, Reggio, and Modena combined to form "la République Cispadane." Milan, where Bonaparte
spent two days with Josephine, was to become the capital of the
République Lombarde or République Transpadane, pending its des-
ignation as the Cisalpine Republic in commemoration of Caesar's
conquest of Gaul.

On September 26, Bonaparte issued a proclamation to the Italians:

> The time has come when Italy is going to make an honorable
> showing among the powerful nations. . . . Take up your arms! That
> part of Italy which is free is populous and rich. Discomfit the
> enemies of your rights and your freedom!

When they read it, the Directors were not pleased. This was *not* the policy that Paris had intended to pursue in Italy! Accordingly, a few days later (on October 8) Bonaparte wrote to the Government: "I have more honors than I need, and my health is so broken that I am going to find it necessary to ask you to appoint a successor."

This was a new threat—no doubt about it. Let Paris give him carte blanche, and he would fill the Government's treasury—since, for the Directory, that was the main thing. In this respect the "five kings" could not complain: since April, the Army of Italy had siphoned off "40 to 50 million" to the Republic.

On October 14 Napoleon once again left Verona, crossed the Adige, and reached the village of Ronco. From there, three roads led across the swamps. The middle one went past a town that was reached via a bridge over the Alpone. The town and the bridge were called Arcole, and their capture was of the utmost importance, since from there the French could attack the Austrian rear. But the bridge (which still exists) was strongly held by the enemy rear guard and had resisted all attacks.

Crossing the bridge was impossible—despite the French generals who raced to the head of their columns. Augereau, for example, seized a standard and managed to carry it as far as the end of the bridge, meanwhile shouting to his troops: "Cowards, are you that much afraid of death?"

Napoleon, "indignant at the hesitation of his soldiers" (so we are told by the inscription on the commemorative column at Arcole), then proceeded to seize a standard himself and plant it on the bridge. Now electrified, the grenadiers advanced, and had got as far as the middle of the bridge when they came under heavy fire from the flank. What happened then is far removed from the legend that describes Bonaparte seizing the flag under a deluge of grapeshot and bullets and advancing across the bridge, followed by the men with whom he would conquer the world. Napoleon himself set the record straight when he told Las Cases:

> The grenadiers at the head of the column, abandoned by those at the end, hesitated. They were caught up in the retreat, but they didn't want to leave their general behind. They grabbed him by the arms, the hair, by his clothes, and dragged him along in

their flight through the dead, the dying, and the smoke. The commanding general was thrown into a swamp. He sank down until he was half-submerged, among the enemy.

A great shouting was heard: "Forward, to save the general!"

Fished out of the swamp, and once again at the head of his troops, Bonaparte now rushed the enemy and forced him to evacuate the village. But the victory—the victory of Arcole—was not complete until two days later: Wednesday, November 17. It was only then that the French were able to fight free of those horrible swamps and defeat the enemy on the plain.

In Napoleon's own words, it was after the victory of Arcole that his "great ambition" was conceived. On the morning of November 15 he was merely the commander of an army in retreat. And if, on Monday, November 15, 1796, the bridge of Arcole entered into history, he himself entered into legend.

At a later day, Prometheus chained to his rock would sigh:

> Yes, I was happy when I was First Consul—at the time of my marriage [to Marie Louise], and when the King of Rome was born. And yet I felt out of sorts then. I suspect I was really happier after my victories in Italy. What enthusiasm! What cries of "Long live the Liberator of Italy!" And this at the age of twenty-seven! From then on, I foresaw what I could become. I could already see the world falling away beneath me, as if I were were borne on air. . . .

Found a dynasty? By no means! Thus far his only thoughts were of becoming "the Brutus of kings and the Caesar of the Republic." Everything seemed to be conspiring to make Bonaparte the happiest of men: everything but Josephine. The night of November 21, before retiring to his camp bed, he wrote her another passionate letter:

> Ma petite Josephine, I am going to bed with a heart full of your adorable image and very upset at having to be away from you for so long. But I hope that in a few days I will be luckier and will be able to give you, at leisure, proof of the ardent love that you have inspired in me. God, how happy I would be if I could be there to watch you at your dressing table: a little shoulder, a little white breast—elastic and very firm; and above them, a little face under a Creole snood—just delicious! . . . You know very well that I send a thousand kisses to the little black forest, and am eager to be

there. I vow everything to you. Life, happiness, and pleasure are
only what you make them.

To live in Josephine is to live in paradise. A kiss on the mouth,
on the eyes, on the shoulder, on the breast, everywhere—everywhere.

On November 29 his carriage drew near to Milan. He had difficulty restraining himself from leaning out the door and shouting:
"Faster! Faster!" Finally, after those six long weeks, he would be able
to hold her in his arms. The victor of Arcole would have his reward.

But upon his arrival he learned that she had left for Genoa—with
the hope of finding Charles there, no doubt. Was this what he was
thinking of when he later said: "Love is a stupidity *à deux*"?

With tightened throat and on the point of weeping, he wrote to
his unfaithful wife:

> I reached Milan and rushed to your lodgings. I had left every-
> thing so that I could see you and hold you tight in my arms.
> . . . But you weren't there. You go from city to city with the
> festivals. You get away from me when I show up. You don't care
> any more for your dear Napoleon. It was a whim that made
> you love him, and inconstancy is making you indifferent to
> him. . . .

And in a fit of rage, he added: "Don't worry about me. Go on
chasing after pleasure: happiness is made for you. The whole world
is only too happy if it can please you; and only your husband is very,
very unhappy."

On that day, according to an eyewitness, he was "pale and emaciated, just skin and bones, his eyes burning with a constant fever."

The Directory became more anxious with each passing day. "You
are luckier than the French people," Bonaparte wrote on January 1,
1797, to the Italian deputies assembled at Ferrara. "You can achieve
freedom without revolutions and crimes."

One can imagine the reaction of the five Directors—all of them
regicides—upon reading these lines. The word "crime" would not go
down easily. Now they were sure of it: Bonaparte wanted to be the
master—the absolute master—even off the field of battle.

As early as October 8 he had used the words "very bad" to characterize the political system prescribed by the Directory for Italy. And

in order to avoid any ambiguity, he had further specified: "Whenever your general in Italy is not the center of everything, you will be running great risks. . . . This manner of speaking will surely not be attributed to ambition."

A week later he had somewhat appeased them by reminding them that the summer campaign alone had enabled him to send 20 million francs to Paris—"despite numerous deceptions on the part of the Treasury." Moreover, he dazzled them with the prospect of Italy's "producing twice that much" if they would give him a free hand.

The image of this source of wealth, past and future, by no means quieted the anxiety of the Directors. They concluded that nothing would serve better than peace to put an end to the dictatorship of the new proconsul. And so the reasons for the political independence demanded by the commanding general of the Army of Italy were disregarded. This is why the Government entrusted the elegant General H. J. G. Clarke with a double mission: first, to negotiate an armistice with Austria as soon as possible; second, to restrain the ambitions of the man who was frightening the "five kings" at the Palais du Luxembourg. But when Clarke reached Turin he had some difficulty in obtaining a passport which would enable him to go to Vienna; and he had no choice but to go to Milan, where the chief result of his sojourn was that he was able to "discover" Bonaparte.

He still thought of the latter as the little protégé of Barras who had emerged from the paving stones of Vendémiaire, and thus he had no very high opinion of this ambitious man. Suddenly Clarke found himself in the presence of a kind of Caesar who spoke of "his" army and "his" policy, who legislated between victories, organized his conquests, created sister republics, changed his plans with great alacrity "when unforeseen circumstances made it necessary," and dictated, in the midst of battle, thirty letters or orders every day. To the Directory's confidential agent he appeared no less extraordinary when giving orders to his clerks than when, sword in hand, he seemed to be dictating every last move made by the enemy. Clarke was amazed to find such versatility in one and the same man. But Napoleon could have explained this to him in the same words he uttered later: "What constitutes the strength of a general? His abilities in civil matters: the capacity to take in everything in a glance, skill in calculation, administrative know-how, eloquence, and finally, a knowledge of men. All that is in the civil domain!"

After a few days, Clarke, who was genuinely fascinated, began to understand the reasons for the admiration of the victorious general and his unusual ascendancy "over all the individuals making up the Republican Army." He was certainly the absolute master of all those around him. He was playing the role of proconsul—no doubt about that. But Clarke, although not much of a republican, nonetheless saw him as "the man of the Republic" who "had no other ambition than to preserve the glory he had earned."

The visitor was certainly wrong when he affirmed that Napoleon "would never be a threat to his nation" (i.e., to the regime): Brumaire would prove the contrary. But Clarke showed considerable insight when he remarked that Bonaparte could never become "a party man." Apparently, Napoleon belonged no more to the Royalists, who were slandering him, than to the Anarchists, who would perhaps have liked to make him their man, but who were scarcely liked by the former second lieutenant whom Louis XVI had appointed to that rank. He was "his own man." He had been formed in a special mold and could not be compared to anyone else. Clarke seems to have come very close to discovering Bonapartism. "Please do not conclude," the Directory's envoy wrote to his masters, "that I speak of him out of enthusiasm. I write this in a calm state of mind, and am guided by no other interest than to inform you of the facts: posterity will rank Bonaparte among the greatest men."

And so, for the first time, someone made a judgment about Napoleon that would be ratified by posterity.

The future Emperor completed his conquest of Clarke by demonstrating that it would be necessary to inflict a few more defeats on Austria before thinking of negotiating with her. In order to get a better peace he would have to pin both shoulders of the Hapsburgs to the ground. Thus far they were only down on one knee. But the time would soon come when they would have to beg for mercy.

The enemy's plan was simple. Wurmser was holed up in Mantua with 17,000 Austrians. Marshal Josef Alvinczy, with 80,000 men, was to come and liberate the old inner city, which was still being besieged by Bonaparte. Then, with those 100,000 men, nothing would be easier (or so Francis II thought) than to pulverize the French and retake Milan. The plan was all the more certain to succeed in that Bonaparte was known to be sick and "as sallow as one could possibly hope." The Austrians were even drinking toasts to "his imminent death."

He was in fact feverish, with circles under his eyes and hollow, wan cheeks. Nonetheless, on January 7, 1797, he climbed on a horse and set out for Verona, on the road that would take him to Rivoli. Needless to say, he had surmised the enemy's plan: to descend upon Mantua through the valley of the Adige; to "slip" from the north to the south—from Trento to Verona. Still racked by fever—which did not prevent him from riding so hard that three horses died under him from exhaustion—he positioned his troops to the north of Verona, from Lake Garda to the banks of the Adige, taking in the citadel of La Corona and Rivoli, which commanded the upper end of the valley.

How many strategists would, in days to come, study the Battle of Rivoli and try to explain how a sizable army of 80,000 men could have been defeated by a force less than half as large!

Actually, in the middle of the morning the French were in a bad way. The day before, General Barthélemy Joubert had been thrown back to the plateau of Rivoli, and the enemy now seemed ready to turn the flank of the French troops, and even to encircle them. As a matter of fact, when the French soldiers saw the crests of the mountains thick with Austrian troops who were applauding themselves with a great clapping of hands, so great was their anguish that they all turned their eyes toward Bonaparte. But he, after a glance at the avalanche which was about to overwhelm him, merely said in a calm tone of voice: "They're in our hands!"

It took all the blind confidence that his officers had in their commander not to wonder if the fever had not played a bad trick on their idol. The French army was surely going to be annihilated. They were hemmed in on all sides, and Bonaparte had with him only Joubert's and Masséna's divisions.

He didn't even notice the shot—fired from cannon on the other bank of the Adige—that was falling on the French position. Then, suddenly, a new column was seen approaching from the west. Now the encirclement would be complete.

Bonaparte merely repeated calmly: "They're in our hands!"

The column was French. It was the Eighteenth Half-Brigade. Its commander, General Mounier, when he saw the enemy slip in between his troops and Bonaparte, had taken it upon himself to attack the Austrian rear guard. Having overcome it, his troops were now debouching onto the main battlefield, their band in the van and their colors flying.

"Their arrival," an eyewitness reported, "produced the needed effect. It revived the morale of our troops and changed our situation to the point where, among most of us, discouragement was replaced by enthusiasm."

Bonaparte, "who could not but make the most of their arrival," immediately galloped over to the Eighteenth Half-Brigade.

"Bravo Eighteenth!" he shouted. "You yielded to a noble impulse! You have added to our glory! To complete it, by way of reward for your conduct, you will have the honor of being the first to attack the troops who were foolhardy enough to turn our flank!"

This was greeted with cries of *Viva!* And the Eighteenth Half-Brigade, in column of attack by battalions and accompanied by some other available troops, all of them firing "from bottom to top," drove toward the crests occupied by the enemy, in the rear of Bonaparte's positions. The attacking troops heard with joy the muffled boom of the French cannonballs as they passed over their heads. Panting for breath, they overran the Austrian positions, using their bayonets so enthusiastically that, as the future General Thiébault tells us, "the ground was strewn with corpses, and hundreds of the enemy were thrown into the chasms."

Murat galloped at the head of his squadrons, bore down on the enemy, and completed the victory. The next day, Wurmser capitulated, and Mantua opened its gates to the French.

At Paris, the news of the Battle of Rivoli and the fall of Mantua, coming on the heels of the dispatches from Lodi and Arcole, unleashed an immense enthusiasm. No matter that the Royalists showed their rancor by calling the victor of Arcole "that bastard of a bandit" and his victories "the glory of a mountebank." In vain did the agents of Louis XVIII repeat predictions that the "young hero" would bring about his own death by firing squad on the Place de la Révolution. The joy of the general public was beyond description, and was dampened only by the fear that Bonaparte would too often expose himself to enemy bullets. The newspapers placed Napoleon "higher than man"; and the Directory, no longer able to stem the flood, decided to go along with it. Now there could no longer be any question of keeping the conqueror of Italy under its thumb. From that time on, directives were addressed to him with infinite precautions. One of them stipulated: "Moreover, this is not an order that the executive Directory is giving you, but a wish it is expressing." The Directors even recommended to Clarke that he not listen to any Austrian proposals "without consulting Bonaparte."

Pending negotiations with Vienna, the power of Rome had to be destroyed.

On Wednesday, February 1—from Bologna, where Josephine had come to join him—Napoleon declared war on the Pope. The next day he marched on Faenza, a Roman possession which fell easily. A single division under Junot—after an artillery bombardment that was virtually symbolical—obtained the "docile" surrender of Pius VI's soldiers. Bonaparte was then free to march on Ancona—which, as he announced to Josephine—surrendered after "a little fusillade and a *coup de main.*"

On February 16 he went to Tolentino to meet with the three cardinals named by the Pope "to sign a treaty" which, Bonaparte declared, "would make the Holy Father long repent his armed revolt." In the austere Palazzo Parisani (today the Palazzo Bezzi) the public is still shown the *sala* and the *camera di Napoleone* where Bonaparte got down to work "with the priestly crew"—contriving, in his own phrase, a terrible mask and "the language of a bogeyman." The conditions he wanted to impose on the Pope were so harsh that Cardinal Mattei went down on his knees. Bonaparte yielded on those points that he had insisted on merely to terrify the envoys. Finally, he obtained the most important concessions: Bologna, Ferrara, the Romagna, Ancona, and the closing of the gates of Rome to the English—not to mention countless art objects and a pretty little pile of gold that would delight the Directors. He discussed the money in the letter he sent to the Luxembourg the next day explaining why he preferred not to march on the Eternal City. "For us, thirty million is worth ten times as much as Rome, from which we couldn't have taken out five million. . . . That old machine will go off the tracks all by itself."

He next went to Mantua, where he drew up the plans for his decisive campaign, the march on Vienna, which (he calculated) on top of Arcole and the fall of Mantua should bring the Austrian royal

house to Canossa and result in peace—both on the Rhine and in the
Alps. Thanks to the reinforcements brought up by Bernadotte, Bonaparte now had 74,000 men under his command. Opposing him was
the Austrian army commanded by an adversary of stature: the
Archduke Charles, the son of Leopold II and the nephew of Marie
Antoinette, who had been appointed a marshal following the campaign of 1793.

The new campaign was about to begin. There was no question,
this time, of behaving as in a conquered country. In advancing toward the center of the Austrian mosaic, the French would encounter
"a brave people crushed by the war it had fought against the Turks,
and by the current war." According to the commanding general, the
inhabitants of the Austrian states were the sad victims of the "blind-
ness" and the "arbitrary measures" of their government. In all seriousness, Bonaparte tried to make his men believe that there was not
a single subject of the Emperor Francis who was not convinced that
English gold had corrupted the Viennese ministers.

"You will respect their religion and their customs," he recommended to the conquerors of Italy. "You will protect their property.
It is liberty that you are bringing to the brave Hungarian nation!"

On March 12, in spite of the miserable weather, the army followed
its commander up the valley of the Piave. The river had overflowed
its banks and become a torrent. Bonaparte and his men crossed it in
water up to the armpits ("holding on to each other by the arm," the
adjutant Dupin tells us) and pursued the Archduke, who had with-
drawn toward Tagliamento. That river, which would soon give its
name to a Franco-Italian *département* with Treviso as its chief town,
was from 800 to 900 meters in breadth, and had reached the high-
water mark. Some of Bonaparte's aides-de-camp explored it and
found some fording points. Bernadotte's division was the first to cross
to the other side, urged on by the ardent voice of their commander:
"Soldiers of the Sambre and the Meuse—the Army of Italy is watching you!"

Thanks to Murat's cavalry, which overwhelmed the Austrian uh-
lans from the rear, the Archduke Charles was again obliged to pull
back, and recrossed the Isonzo. The way to Vienna was open.

The commanding general wrote to the Directory: "So far, Prince
Charles has maneuvered worse than Wurmser and Beaulieu. . . ."

At the same time that he was ordering his troops to continue their victorious march, he sent the Archduke the following message— worthy of the legend that he was weaving so skillfully:

> *Monsieur le général en chef,* our brave soldiers are waging war while desiring peace. . . . Have we not killed enough people and committed enough wrongs against suffering humanity? I should be prouder of the civil crown that I might deem myself to have deserved than of the melancholy glory to be gained from military successes.

This was wisdom. And it may have been what he was thinking of that day in the future when he exclaimed: "In heroic times, the general was the the strongest man; in civilized times, he is the most intelligent of the brave."

Nevertheless, he continued to advance, having beaten—and badly beaten—the Austrian Emperor's two armies. On April 6, he was 30 leagues from the Austrian capital. At Vienna, "on orders from the Court, enormous placards were circulated among all the important ministers and the leading hostesses, and in all the antechambers of the imperial family, with instructions to pack up immediately and be ready to leave." In view of this state of things, the Austrians decided to negotiate. And at midnight on April 7, a five-day truce was signed.

On April 13, at five o'clock in the afternoon, the first talks were held between Bonaparte and the Austrian generals, at Leoben. They took place in a "neutralized" summerhouse situated in a park surrounded with French bivouacs. A monument representing a Cupid blowing a trumpet still perpetuates the memory of that meeting; but it was reared only to the glory of the conquered.

Five days later, the famous "preliminaries" of the truce of Leoben were ready to sign. The text was reread for the last time. But Bonaparte frowned. At the beginning of the text, the Austrian advisers had placed the phrase: "The Emperor recognizes the French Republic."

"Delete that!" Napoleon exclaimed. "The existence of the Republic is as plain to see as the sun. Such an article is suitable only for blind men! We are masters in our own land, and are free to establish whatever government we please without anyone else's objecting."

Clarke explained to the Government: "The Emperor's ideas differed from those of the Directory. The Gordian knot had to be cut. The new Alexander did it with the intention of serving the Republic effectively."

On the day following the signing of the preliminaries to the truce between the French Republic and the Emperor and King, Bonaparte wrote to the Directory: "I am asking you for a period of rest, since I have gained more glory than one needs to be happy. . . . My civil career, like my military career, will be unique and simple."

Napoleon had taken a new step: this was certainly a scarcely concealed threat. In other words: Either you leave me in complete charge of administering our conquests and negotiating with the enemy, or I will come to take your place.

The Directors yielded, but not cheerfully—all the more so in that the hastily signed preliminaries left "a great many things unsettled."

How could it have been otherwise? Italy was in a state of revolt; Joubert, in the Tyrol, was in difficult circumstances; and the Pope was doing everything possible to prove that the "old machine" still existed. As for the Austrians, they could think of only one thing: gaining time and seeing that the French bayonets were kept away from the road to Vienna. In spite of all this haste, however, a conference had been scheduled (it would take place several months later in Friuli), and Austria had already acknowledged the principle of ceding the right bank of the Rhine and thereby recognizing the frontiers of the terrible republic. The Emperor, not without a sigh, also agreed to give up Lombardy; but he demanded compensations.

Compensations for having been defeated? Bonaparte merely promised him that the question would be taken up in the course of signing the peace treaty.

The last week in March, 1796, Napoleon had left Nice at the head of a ragged army. On April 7, at Albenga, he had decided to attack the passages where the Apennines break off from the Alps: the Italian campaign was beginning. On April 7, 1797, at Judenburg, with only the Semmering Mountains separating him from Vienna, he signed the truce that he had offered to the Austrians. In one year, the "General Vendémiaire" had become the master of all northern Italy; and he would reign there six months as a veritable proconsul.

V

THE EGYPTIAN MIRAGE

The Middle East is waiting for only one man.

BONAPARTE

AT THE CRIVELLI, not far from Milan, Bonaparte took two guests aside into the lovely park of the château of Mombello: one was Miot, Comte de Melito, the French minister to Tuscany; and the other was the Milanese count Gaetano Melzi. Both of them looked at him with profound admiration. As the diplomat said later: "He was no longer merely the general of a triumphant republic: he was a conqueror in his own right, imposing his laws on the conquered. . . ." By now, Napoleon was more than manifesting himself through the persona of Bonaparte. The man that the two counts had before them was already a chief of state—one who spoke for more than two hours with an astounding insight into things to come:

> What I have done so far is nothing. I am only at the beginning of the course I must run. Do you think I am triumphing in Italy merely to build up power for the lawyers of the Directory—for the likes of Carnot or Barras? Do you think I am doing it to found a republic? What foolishness! A republic of 30 million men? With our morals, our vices? How could that possibly be? It is a chimera that the French are infatuated with, but one that will pass, as so many others have. They have a need for glory—for the satisfactions of vanity. But when it comes to liberty, they understand nothing. Just look at the army! The victories we have won—our triumphs—have already allowed the French soldier's true character to reassert itself. I am everything to him. Just let the Directors take it into their heads to remove me from my command, and they will see who is the master. The nation needs a leader, a

leader illustrious by reason of glory—not theories by means of which the French understand nothing. Let them have rattles: that will suffice for them. They will be amused by them, and will let themselves be led—provided one skillfully dissimulates the goal toward which one makes them march.

Whether Bonaparte was already thinking of a possible reign or not, he believed in his star and was fully aware of his worth. In this royal residence, he played the role of sovereign with complete naturalness. He dined alone. The ministers of the French and Italian governments remained at a distance, standing. Even his officers had to wait until their commander deigned to speak to them—a favor they did not all obtain. During the meal—taken very quickly—the local inhabitants had the right to pass in front of him, as they used to do on the occasion of the Archduke's great banquets.

The Parisians were restless again. This time it was the Royalists who were threatening the Directory. No doubt Napoleon had begun to become a Bonapartist; but being frankly republican, he still detested the partisans of Louis XVIII, that "club de Vichy" that the monarchists formed; they had gone so far as to demand his removal and arrest. They already knew that he would not play the role of a Monck. Bonaparte was very much irritated by what he called "the audacity of the enemies of the Republic," although he had only contempt for the Directory—the present government of that Republic. He accused the Directors of "weakness, of hesitant and pusillanimous behavior, of embezzlement, and of persisting in a system that is vicious and degrading to the national glory."

On July 18 the situation deteriorated; the Directors, with chattering teeth, decided to summon Bonaparte to help them. But the future Emperor refused: he had no intention of having his brand-new glory tarnished in degrading street fighting. He was no longer the General Vendémiaire but the Republic's proconsul in Italy.

Favored by the insurrection, he could no doubt have become one of the five Directors—convinced, and with reason, that "he would soon become such all on his own." History would have been deprived of the Egyptian expedition, and Bonaparte would have been able to put on the imperial crown sooner. But Napoleon was too young to meet the age requirement for a Director. Could the Constitution of

the Year III be violated in his favor? He hesitated—although in fact
that constitution would be followed by many others. Moreover,
would one of the "five kings" of the Directory agree to yield his place
to him? Wouldn't that mean letting the wolf into the sheepfold?
Always provided, of course, that such a corrupt government could be
compared to a sheepfold: a stable would be a more apt metaphor.

But the Citizen Directors relegated that apprehension to the
background: they feared for their lives. The Royalists were becoming
ever more of a menace. Would the regime be consumed in the blaze
of Fructidor? Once more, the Directors asked Bonaparte to come
and put a stop to the disorders.

"By the time Bonaparte gets here," whimpered Barras, "all he
will be able to do is avenge us. He will find us hanged."

On August 7, it was not Bonaparte who debarked at Paris but one
of his men; Augereau, the mason's son, as brave as he was brutal, who
had been sent from Italy by his chief. As he set foot on land, he stated
calmly: "I have come to kill the Royalists."

Augereau employed the rhetoric of the age to calm the fears of
his chief: "Our purity and our courage will save the Republic from
the frightful precipice to which it has been brought by the agents of
the throne and the altar."

A short time later, on September 3 and 4 (17 and 18 Fructidor) the
change of course to the left succeeded perfectly. The conspirators
and those deputies who were enemies of the regime were condemned to death, shot by firing squads, or sent to forced labor. The
streets remained peaceful, so that La Révellière-Lépeaux was able to
declare rapturously: "Not one drop of blood has been spilled." Quite
possibly, the 160 persons who had been shot by firing squad on the
plain of Grenelle did not entirely share that estimate of the situation.
Unquestionably, the coup d'état had riddled the Royalist party with
so much lead that it would not recover. True, it did try to stir up
trouble during the Consulate—even throwing bombs and setting
up ambushes—but it took the fall of the Empire to bring it back to
life.

"*Mon général,*" Augereau wrote to Bonaparte, "my mission is
accomplished. . . . Paris is calm and is marveling at a crisis which
loomed up horribly but went off like a holiday celebration. . . ."
Except, of course, for the 329 deportees, of whom 160 would perish
at Cayenne.

Augereau was sent to Germany—the purpose being to calm him down, and also to oppose him, if need be, to Bonaparte.

On 27 August, having set out from Milan, Bonaparte reached Passeriano, where the talks with Austria were to take place.

The first confrontation between the two heads of delegations went off very badly. Francis II's ambassador, the big, ugly Cobenzl (Napoleon called him "the bear of the North") struck Bonaparte as "not very used to discussions, but very used to trying to have his own way." And he noted: "Such people have great pretensions." Thus it was that, without further delay, he recommended to the Directors that they hold themselves in readiness for possible action on the Rhine.

The "compensations" demanded by the Emperor Francis consisted in obtaining the territory of Venice up to the Adige.

That same evening, in the course of their next meeting, Bonaparte and Cobenzl had a conversation that lasted almost five hours. Taking an even harder line, Napoleon declared that "under no pretext and under no circumstances" could he consent to the Emperor's becoming master of Venice. The diplomat, who had assumed there would be no objection to this demand, was seized with genuine fright. After a long silence, having recovered his aplomb, he asked in a faint voice: "If you keep on doing that, how do you think we can negotiate at all?"

On October 6, the negotiations appeared "virtually broken off," and Napoleon predicted a resumption of hostilities within two weeks. Since the old Austrian diplomacy could not adapt itself to the new vogue, matters would have to be decided by artillery. On October 9 Bonaparte threatened the Austrians with the announcement that he was heading for Vienna, and let them infer that he had received an order from the Directory to march on the capital of the Empire. It was true. But Napoleon did not tell them that he had replied to Talleyrand: "I assure you that I will do everything possible to get a peace, considering that the season is very advanced and there is little hope of doing big things." In the course of the conversation Napoleon accidentally capsized a tray, breaking some porcelain ware, and (so legend has it) later declared that he had done it on purpose. "I will break you in the same way," he threatened.

Still horrified and shaken, Cobenzl reported to Vienna: "He

behaved like a madman." How could they discuss things with a man like him? This time, it was no longer even a question of discussing with modesty—and imprecision—the constitutional frontiers of France. The commanding general demanded "the entire left bank of the Rhine." And when the unfortunate Cobenzl, no longer having any idea what argument to employ, stated that the Austrian Emperor could not act "in the name of" the German Empire, Napoleon replied in a phrase that was to become famous: "The Empire is an old serving woman who is used to being raped by everybody."

When he could speak again, Cobenzl said: "In exchange for the left bank of the Rhine, couldn't Austria at least have Venice?"

The talks were souring. Both parties were using threats.

"You are forgetting that this talk of ours is taking place in the midst of my grenadiers!" Bonaparte exclaimed.

Meantime Cobenzl, who had recovered his equilibrium, replied: "The Emperor wants peace but does not fear war. For my part, I shall have had the satisfaction of having made the acquaintance of a man as famous as he is interesting."

On the morning of October 13, 1797, when Bourrienne came to awaken Napoleon, he reported to him that the mountains were covered with snow that had fallen during the night. Napoleon, incredulous, leaped out of bed and ran to the window: the evidence was irrefutable. "Snow before the middle of October! What a country! Come on—we have to make peace."

A march on Vienna had become impossible. As Napoleon said:

How could we resist all the Austrian forces that would come to the aid of Vienna? It would take more than a month for the armies of the Rhine to come and support me, and in two weeks the roads and corridors will be snowed in. There is nothing more for it: I will make peace. Venice will pay the costs of war and of the Rhine boundary. The Directors and the lawyers can say what they want to.

In the final settlement, Venice, Istria, and Dalmatia were given to the Emperor; the "Cisalpine Republic" was to extend to the Adige, Mantua, and Peschiera; and France would occupy Mainz and have the Rhine as a frontier. The old adage was accomplished: "Quand la

France boira le Rhin, toute la Gaule aura sa fin" (When France drinks the Rhine, all Gaul will come to an end).

In sum, Cobenzl had secured Venice, which for him was the main thing. Nonetheless, he fretted and fumed: "It seemed to me that it would be cruel if the carnage were to begin again, merely because Bonaparte got carried away. . . ."

On October 17, "one hour after midnight," the signatures were exchanged at Passeriano, but the treaty was datelined Campoformio, halfway between the two residences, where no one had set his foot.

In taking leave of Cobenzl, Bonaparte apologized for having conducted the negotiations in a manner that was hardly diplomatic. With a smile, he said: "I am a soldier and accustomed to risking my life every day; I am full of the fire of youth; I cannot act with the restraint of an accomplished diplomat."

And the two men embraced. They would meet again.

When, on October 26, the text of the treaty reached Paris, the Directors were furious. So Bonaparte had dared to sign without their authorization! And he had dared to exchange Venice, which had been conquered, for Milan, which had been taken from the Austrians! But what could they do? "If the Directors had refused ratification of the treaty," La Révellière explains, "they would have been ruined vis-à-vis public opinion." A few "details" would smooth out the rough spots. An "artistic commission" would send to Paris the famous Lion of Venice, whose origin was unknown except for the fact that in the twelfth century, in the Piazza di San Marco, it was placed atop a column brought from Syria. On the other hand, it was known that the celebrated bronze horses once adorned the imperial loggia at Byzantium. They had been seized by the crusaders in the course of the Fourth Crusade. Those horses would likewise be brought to Paris when the Arc de Triomphe on the Place du Carrousel was completed. And so one thing furnished consolation for another.

The Government, putting a good face on misfortune, proclaimed that the treaty "fulfilled all its wishes." And on that same day of October 26, anxious to get rid of Bonaparte, it placed him in command of the Army of England—an army whose mission it was to invade, some day, the British Isles! Then, in order to avoid hearing "the saber" clanking noisily on the parquets of the Palais du Luxembourg, the Directors wrote to Napoleon announcing that the Government was "granting him another reward": that of "putting the finishing touches, with his own hand, to the great work" that he had "carried so far forward." Thus he was named plenipotentiary to the Congress of Rastatt, and which was soon to ratify the decisions on the German Empire that had been datelined Campoformio.

In Paris, people were delirious with joy. The signer of the Treaty of Campoformio was compared to "one of the greatest men of antiquity"; and mathematician Gaspard Monge declared that France had not had such a hero since Vercingetorix.

Before setting out for Rastatt, Bonaparte, in his capacity as chief of state, offered the following advice to the people of the Cisalpine Republic:

> Join together! Put an end to your suspicions, forget the reasons you believe you have for breaking up into separate groups, and, working together, organize and consolidate your government. . . . In order to be worthy of your destiny, pass only wise and moderate laws. But have them enforced vigorously. . . . States may be compared to ships at sea, or to armies. What matters for them is a cool head, moderation, wisdom and reason in the conceiving of orders, commands, and laws, plus energy and vigor in their enforcement.

On the evening of November 26, in a carriage pulled by eight horses and "enveloped" by thirty hussars, Bonaparte reached Rastatt, halfway between Baden-Baden and Karlsruhe.

Two days later, the Austrian plenipotentiaries also reached Rastatt with Metternich, who was representing the Emperor of Austria. On the French side, the Directory had sent a former member of the Convention, Jean-Baptiste, the future Comte de Treilhard. At the time of his appointment as president of the Five Hundred he had sworn "hatred toward the royalty"; but this did not prevent him, toward the end of the Consulate, from being one of the most ardent supporters of the establishment of the Empire. In addition to him, the French delegation included the stern Bonnier d'Arco and, finally, Merlin, flanked by his spouse, who (as Bonaparte said later) "was the most bourgeois person imaginable. The only thing she talked to me about was the dishes she served; and she called her husband 'my smart little darling.' "

The representatives of the foreign powers made fun of the round hats of the French, and of their shoes tied with laces instead of ribbons. But, as Lavalette records, "they had to yield to the French Republic; and the jokes made at the expense of those gentlemen expired at their arrival."

On November 30 the agreement was signed, and it confirmed the decisions taken at Udine: Venice reverted to the Emperor Francis, and Mainz became French. The city which had been occupied by the French in 1644, 1688, and 1792 had been lost nine months later. It was returned to the French; and until 1814, Mainz would be the *chef-lieu* of the Département of Mont-Tonnerre.

There, in embryonic form, were all the causes of the Napoleonic wars. England would never agree to the French occupation of the left bank of the Rhine. Austria, driven out of the Low Countries, could never resign herself to being deprived of the biggest share of the Italian cake. So long as France was not muzzled within her natural boundaries, war would break out again and again. And all the more so when the Napoleonic empire advanced her "French" frontiers to the Elbe and the Ionian Sea.

Bonaparte returned to Paris on December 5.

On December 10, on the occasion of the presentation of the banners garnered in Italy, the five members of the Directory received him magnificently, taking care not to let the public know how he had irritated them by signing the Treaty of Campoformio without their authorization. In the rear of the courtyard a vast amphitheater had been constructed; here were gathered "ambassadors, ministers, generals, and high-ranking officers of the army and navy—everyone distinguished by rank, authority, fame, or worth." At the far end, facing the main vestibule, an "altar of the Fatherland," surmounted by statues of Liberty, Equality, and Peace, had been erected. In spite of the cold, women with extremely low-cut dresses, as the fashion demanded, looked out the windows. As one eyewitness said: "Despite this luxury, this affluence, the studied elegance of dress, the finery of the women, and the sumptuous attire of the Directors, it was a thin little man—pale, sallow, and simply dressed—who was the cynosure of all eyes and seemed to occupy all that space by himself."

The celebrations in his honor would continue. He breathed in all this incense, not with joy (Bourrienne tells us that he even seemed to be tortured) but with the feeling that the adulation rendered him was "one of the inconveniences of his position. . . . He knew that if he fell out of favor, he would soon be free of this scourge."

As Napoleon said, "I am indebted only to curiosity and novelty for all these official flatteries which are accorded to everybody, with only the date, the title, and the name being changed."

Only one reward brought him pleasure: he was elected to the Institute (the Physical Sciences and Mathematics section), since Carnot's chair had been declared vacant—not by reason of the occupant's death, but as a result of the coup d'état of Fructidor. Bonaparte had eleven competitors, but he was well out ahead of them.

On the evening of December 30, Bonaparte had a "most delicious" surprise. When he came home that night, he saw some workmen changing the name of the Rue Chantereine. Henceforth, it would be called Rue de la Victoire.

"What a change in our little house, which had been such a quiet place before!" recounted Josephine's daughter Hortense. "Now it was filled with generals and other officers. The soldiers on guard duty had a hard time keeping back the common people and the members of high society impatient and avid to see the conqueror of Italy."

Josephine had ordered costly renovations. The bedroom, situated on the second floor, had become a tent with striped fabric, decorated with *sièges-tambours*. The beds "in the antique style" could be brought together or separated by means of an ingenious spring. "Everything was 'new model' and done on purpose," Bonaparte was to say.

For that matter, the frivolous Creole had not yet returned home. She had left Italy after her husband, had seen to it that she was acclaimed all along the way, being addressed as a "virtuous spouse" —and on December 25, between Moulins and Nevers, she had rejoined her dear Hippolyte, with whom she henceforth dallied, putting off the time when she must go back to her conjugal domicile. Along with their billing and cooing, the two lovers set up an operation for military provisioning—the Compagnie Bodin—which enabled Josephine to indulge in her expenses, which were absolutely indispensable in her own eyes and absolutely useless in the eyes of her husband. It was not until January 2 that her traveling coach stopped in the new Rue de la Victoire.

The next day Bonaparte, dressed in the green uniform of the Institute, went to the party being given by Talleyrand at the Hôtel

Gallifet in honor of the wife of the commanding general of the Army of Italy. The decor, the service, the gambling tables, and the buffet dinner were worthy of the *ancien régime*. The poet Arnault, who had dined at the house on the Rue de la Victoire, accompanied Josephine and her husband.

"Give me your arm," Bonaparte said to her when they entered the ballroom. "I can see a lot of bothersome people ready to assail me. So long as we are together, they won't dare start up a conversation which would interrupt our talk. Let's circulate through the room. You can identify the masks for me, since you know everybody. . . ."

The crowd lined up on both sides of their passage, as for a pair of sovereigns. It was almost like being back at Versailles. Bonaparte was so thickly surrounded that the famous writer Mme. de Staël asked Arnault to help her approach the great man. Arnault succeeded.

"Madame de Staël insists that she needs some other recommendation to you than her own name," he told Bonaparte, "and she wants me to introduce her. Allow me, General, to obey her."

"The circle again tightened around us," Arnault reports, "since everyone was anxious to hear the conversation about to take place between two such interlocutors. . . ."

"Corinne" offered the conqueror a laurel branch.

Bonaparte refused coldly: "They should be left to the Muses," he said.

No question about it: this bluestocking called "Corinne" irritated him.

She persisted: "General, what woman do you love the most?"

"My wife."

"That's very simple. But what kind of woman do you have the highest regard for?"

"The kind that does the best job of taking care of her home and family."

"All right. But when all is said and done, what woman would you rank above all others?"

"The one who has the most children, Madame!"

During the supper, Bonaparte and Talleyrand stood behind Josephine's chair as if ready to wait on her. Stanislas de Girardin gave an account of the scene:

Her husband seemed to be giving her all his attention. It is even said that he is very amorous and excessively jealous. Bonaparte is not more than five feet tall. His face is pale, his cheeks are hollow, his eyes are small and lackluster. He has all the symptoms of consumption.

One other person made a mistaken judgment that evening—a badly mistaken one. This was Mallet du Pan, who declared: "That Scaramouch with the sulfurous head has had nothing more than a *succès de curiosité*. He is all washed up—definitely washed up!"

The incense with which the Parisians enveloped Napoleon did not go to his head. He was annoyed by the acclamations he received upon arriving at the theater. Quickly disabused, he confided to Bourrienne: "The Parisians don't preserve the memory of anything. If I stay here any length of time without doing something, I'll be finished. In this great Babylon, one reputation gives way to another. When they've seen me three times at the theater, they'll stop looking at me."

Was he entertaining notions of seizing power—or, at any rate, of sharing in it by demanding a waiver of the age requirement to become a Director? Barras (an untrustworthy witness) states that Napoleon spoke to him one evening, "with unusual vivacity, of the docility of the Italian peoples and the ascendancy he had over them": "They wanted to make me Duke of Milan and King of Italy."

"From the outset of this little speech," Barras continues, "I was scarcely master of my own feelings. Bonaparte, noticing with his incomparable alacrity that I was aware he was feeling me out, caught himself short and, ostensibly continuing what he had started to say, told me: 'But I have no such designs in any country.'"

Barras further relates that, after Rastatt, every time that Bonaparte went to the Directory

> . . . he seemed to be simmering, and would stamp his feet if he was made to wait a few minutes. Sometimes we even made him wait a little by way of deliberate mischief. Then, when he had entered and was attempting to take a seat "directorially" at our table, like a colleague, we would repulse his familiarity with an excess of politeness and give him a chair which was not one of ours.

One other idea was stirring in Napoleon.

As soon as he had returned from Germany, he got to work preparing the plans for the expedition against England, which he was to command. Without enthusiasm, he issued the necessary orders for the fleets to assemble at Brest.

He explained to his former classmate at Brienne: "Bourrienne, everything is going to waste here. I no longer have any glory: this little continent of Europe doesn't provide me with enough of it. I must go to the Orient: all the great glory comes from there."

In his view, an expedition to Egypt would "serve to maintain his fame and raise his prestige even higher."

But how could he convince the Directory that in order to defeat perfidious Albion it would be better to plant the French flag atop the minarets of Cairo than atop the Tower of London?

By way of a beginning, Talleyrand, at Bonaparte's request, submitted to the Directory a report recommending a French expedition to Egypt.

Egypt had declined a long way from its one-time splendor. In the seventh century the Arab invasion had inundated the venerable land of the pharaohs and enslaved the Coptic descendants of the ancient Egyptians. In the thirteenth century a sultan had been unwise enough to introduce 12,000 slaves—Georgians, Armenians, Circassians—into Egypt. By way of just retribution, these "bought men" or Mamelukes became the masters in their turn, and the Nile Valley recovered some of its magnificence. But the inevitable decadence set in; and early in the sixteenth century the Sublime Porte (otherwise known as Turkey) conquered Egypt and Syria from the Mamelukes —leaving them, however, some of their authority. Thus their chiefs, twenty-four in number, continued to manage the provinces with the title of bey. Their government, or divan, was presided over by a Turkish governor called "the pasha with nine tails" who represented the Sultan of Constantinople. But for almost a half-century now the authority of the Porte, which had fallen to the female line, consisted merely in having its representative received at Cairo with great pomp. For practical purposes the Mamelukes—10,000 to 12,000 men —were the sole masters of the country. Certainly there was a card to play by declaring that Napoleon was coming not as a conqueror but as a friend of the Sultan, in order to free the indigenous population from the yoke of the Mamelukes.

The project seemed to be a folly. But Bonaparte was by no means mad. "I measured my daydreams by the compass of my reasoning," he would say later.

What arguments could he employ to defend his project? First, there was the problem with the Mameluke beys, who were attempting to obstruct the French trade. (This was not the fault of the Turks, since Constantinople and Paris got along well.) Life was in fact becoming more and more precarious for the French merchants in Egypt. Next, the putative annexation of Egypt would make it possible to control the routes leading to Arabia and India, and would replace the colonies lost under the reign of Louis XV.

Initially, the Directors offered some timid observations: the extravagance of the project shocked some of them. But before long they could think of only one thing: *"éloigner le sabre"*: get Napoleon out of Paris. There is nothing more dangerous than "a hero out of work," as Christopher Herold has said. Once Napoleon had been sent, at his own request, thousands of kilometers away from France, his popularity would no longer give the government sleepless nights. And if the Austrians resumed hostilities? Well, what did it matter? Everything possible had to be done in order to drive away the specter of a military dictatorship!

On March 5—the second anniversary of Bonaparte's departure for Italy—the new commanding general of the Army of Egypt received "all authority to assemble 30,000 men at Toulon, and make up a fleet there for the transport and security of the expedition." But the destination of the expedition was to remain secret. Thus Bonaparte was given carte blanche to organize what people of common sense called his suicide: to take the best French army off to the ends of the earth in order to harass England—whose coast could be seen, on a clear night, from the cliffs along the French coast! As Bourrienne said, and with reason: "A victory on the Adige would have been more valuable than a victory on the Nile."

"It's as though the earth were scorching his feet," said one of the Directors. Napoleon threw himself into the preparations for the expedition with a passion. To read the orders he sent off in all directions is an extraordinary experience. The most minute details are provided for—even how many pairs of socks each man is to take with him.

On May 9, 1798, a man on horseback stopped in front of the guard on duty at the entrance to Toulon and ordered him to open the gates:

"I am the commanding general, Bonaparte!"

Awaiting him at Toulon were the army, the fleet, the scientists and scholars, and a part of the future Empire: Louis, Eugène Beauharnais, Murat, and the generals Berthier, Davout, Lannes, Marmont, Duroc, and Bessières. Also present were J. B. Kléber and L. C. A. Desaix.

At sea, the armada would cover from eight to ten square kilometers. When the units from Genoa, Cittavecchia, and Ajaccio joined the main fleet, the invasion forces would comprise 400 vessels—frigates, brigs, sloops, and transports—carrying 55,000 men, 1,026 cannons, 1,000 pieces of field artillery, 467 vehicles, and 1,000 horses; not to mention numerous women (in addition to the female sutlers) who had come aboard the ships more or less clandestinely.

An eyewitness who saw the fleet drop anchor before Alexandria claimed that, "seized with unimaginable terror," he could no longer see the ocean but "only ships and the sky." To take such a large fleet almost throughout the length of the Mediterranean was a dangerous operation. If Nelson's English fleet, already alerted, were to meet up with Bonaparte's fleet, the expedition might well be annihilated, or at any rate decimated. For that matter, could one even fight a sea battle with ships overloaded with nonsailors?

Immediately upon his arrival at Toulon, Bonaparte addressed his troops:

> I am now going to take you into a land where, by your future exploits, you will surpass those which up until today have astonished your admirers, and will perform for the nation those services she is entitled to expect from an invincible army. I promise each and every soldier that upon his return from this expedition he will have enough money at his disposal to buy nine acres of land.

"Vive la République immortelle!" the men shouted.

On May 19 Napoleon climbed the twenty-two rungs of the ladder leading to bridge of the *Orient*. He then wrote to the Directory: "It is seven o'clock in the morning. The light squadron has left the harbor, the convoy is under way, and we have fine weather as we hoist anchor."

When he had received this news, Barras noted, much relieved: "He has finally left. *Le sabre s'éloigne. . . .*"

Incredible as it may seem, only a few of Bonaparte's companions knew the real destination of the voyage. Some thought it was Sicily or Naples. Almost no one suspected an expedition to the Levant. For the moment, however, most of the passengers—seasick, crowded together, and poorly fed—were wishing they were back on land and trying to forget their hardships by making fun of the nine acres of land promised by the commanding general.

On June 9, after three weeks at sea, the *Orient* and the French fleet arrived at Malta, at the entrance to the harbor of La Valette. "Never before," reported an eyewitness, "has Malta seen such a big fleet in its waters. Far into the distance, the sea was covered with ships of all sizes whose masts resembled a huge forest."

The Knights of Malta, a military and religious order which raided Moslem shipping, numbered 332, of which 200 were French; and the 10,000 to 12,000 men of the Maltese garrison had no warlike spirit. Their artillery, consisting of 1,000 pieces, had not been used for a century. Bonaparte ordered the fleet to attack the outer defenses of La Valette. Most fortunately, fear made the Grand Master of Malta capitulate and Malta was ceded to France in return for pensions to be paid to the Grand Master and the Knights.

During the week that he spent at Malta, Bonaparte dictated 68 reports "with the impetuosity of a cyclone." He organized, legislated, took a hand in the reorganization of hospitals, religion, the national guard, taxes, the postal service, clothing regulations, the administration of justice, and pensions. He requisitioned money, arms, large ships, frigates, and the galleys of the Order, and sent the Knights back to the continent—except for thirty-four of them who joined the Army of Egypt.

On June 19 Bonaparte left Malta. Nelson was still pursuing him without having caught up with him. During the night of June 22–23 the English men-of-war, traveling at twice the speed of Bonaparte's ships, passed the French at a distance of several miles without seeing them. On June 29, with fourteen ships of the line, Nelson entered the harbor of Alexandria. The French fleet was not there. Embittered, he headed back toward Sicily.

He would return.

Two days later, at dawn, Bonaparte sighted the coast of Egypt. The vision of this flat, sun-scorched country gave rise to a soldiers' joke which soon became a classic: "Look! There's the nine acres of land they're giving you!"

Bonaparte, in a proclamation, recommended to his republican atheists—to those who not so long ago had hailed the Goddess of Reason—that they have regard, and even respect, for the Faithful:

> The peoples with whom we are going to live are Mohammedans. Their first article of faith is: There is no God but Allah, and Mohammed is his prophet. Do not contradict them. Behave with them as you have behaved with the Jews, with the Italians; respect their muftis and their imams as you have respected the rabbis and the bishops. Show the same tolerance toward the ceremonies prescribed by the Koran—and toward the mosques—that you have shown toward synagogues and convents, toward the religions of Moses and Jesus Christ. . . .

Things looked bad for the landing. There was a strong wind, and a heavy ocean swell. It took an entire night to reach shore, and many boats foundered on the reefs. Seasickness played its part, too; and the number of drownings was surely greater than what Bonaparte later reported.

At one o'clock in the morning of July 2 (12 Messidor Year VI) Napoleon set foot on Egypt, not far from the beach of Marabut. At three A.M. he reviewed 5,000 men.

Their morale was execrable. The whole army was in a state of "insurrection," Bonaparte stated subsequently. Nothing had been unloaded from the ships: no provisions, no matériel, no horses, no artillery. The wells were empty. There was not a drop of water to be found.

The news of the capture of Malta had caused anxiety and a great stir at Alexandria. Thus the Mamelukes—or, to be more precise, the two principal beys: Murad, commander of the army, and Ibrahim, chief of the administration—had had the call to arms sounded.

As the French army set out for the city, Bedouin warriors on horses swarmed along their flanks and the rear of the column. The stragglers, including quite a few women, were taken prisoner. Herold writes:

> When the prisoners were returned several days later, the stories they told spread through the whole army and squelched any urge to straggle on subsequent marches. The male prisoners, with

their soft, white skin, had provoked the admiration of their cap-
tors, lean but vigorous, who had raped them repeatedly. The
women had merely been beaten. The tastes of people who subsist
on camel's milk the year round are unpredictable.

At dawn, the rear guard reached Alexandria. Bonaparte was no
longer thinking of thirst: he had just seen, in the clear light of dawn,
the proud, red-granite column of Pompey. He ran up to it and
climbed up on the plinth. He gazed at the two obelisks of Cleopatra
and the Arab ramparts, from which minarets and cupolas emerged.
The East of his dreams was before him.

At the walls, they began to parley with the poorly armed defenders. "Suddenly," Lieutenant Desvernois tells us, "there burst forth a
terrible howling of men, women, and children, and a volley of artillery informed us of the Arabs' intentions."

At this point, Bonaparte gave orders to sound the charge, and the
howling redoubled. At 11 o'clock in the morning the sheiks and ulema
surrendered the city. Immediately upon entering Alexandria, "Bonaparte, member of the National Institute, and Commanding General," read to the Egyptians a solemn proclamation in which he very
cleverly stipulated:

> Peoples of Egypt, you will be told that I have come to destroy
> your religion. Do not believe it! Reply that I have come to restore
> your rights and to punish the usurpers, and that I respect God, his
> prophet, and the Koran more than the Mamelukes do. . . . Tell
> them that all men are equal before God; only wisdom, talents, and
> virtues differentiate them. But what wisdom, what talents, what
> virtues distinguish the Mamelukes, so that they have exclusive
> possession of everything that makes life sweet and enjoyable? Is
> there a fine piece of land? It belongs to the Mamelukes. Is there
> a beautiful slave girl, a fine horse, a handsome house? Those
> things, too, belong to the Mamelukes. If Egypt is their farm, let
> them show us the lease that God gave them on it. But God is just
> and merciful toward the people. . . .

As Napoleon would frankly acknowledge later, this was a form of
demagoguery called "charlatanism." And he would exclaim: "One
must be a charlatan! That's the way to succeed!"

He stayed in Alexandria until July 7, still unaware of the drama
that was being played out in the desert: Desaix's division, sent on

ahead as the advance guard, had headed across the plains of Beheira so as to reach Cairo via Damanhûr. The march, as the soldier François described it, was "through a countryside of sand—flat, barren, without trees or houses—and in intolerable heat that obliged us to consume, in a few hours, the little water we had been able to get."

Frightened, Desaix warned Bonaparte: "If the whole army does not cross the desert with the speed of lightning, it will perish."

Napoleon agreed. He never for a moment forgot the example of St. Louis, who faced with this same desert, "spent eight months in prayer, whereas he should have spent them in marching, fighting, and establishing himself in the country."

The Mameluke army had to be defeated quickly. After having organized the "base" of Alexandria, Bonaparte in his turn left for Damanhûr, where the advance guard was reforming. In that miserable little town the men had been able to buy flat cakes, not with money but with the buttons of their uniforms, because the Egyptians firmly believed that the Mamelukes would soon come and throw the invaders into the sea. What would happen when the future conquerors discovered, on the evidence of coins, that the merchants had done business with the French? But by showing buttons from uniforms, the Egyptians could affirm that they had massacred the Infidels.

Bonaparte forced the march to Cairo, an exhausting one under the scorching sun. En route entire villages were briskly massacred— "in order," the soldier François tells us, "to set a terrible example for that half-savage and barbarous country."

On July 19, Napoleon was at Wardan. Bourrienne, who was standing some distance away from his commander, saw Bonaparte speak first to Berthier, then to Julien, his aide-de-camp, and especially to Junot. Bonaparte was pale—paler than usual. "There was even something convulsive in his face," Bourrienne noted "and he had a lost look." He struck his head with his hand several times. Suddenly, his face pallid and twisted in wrath, Bonaparte came up to Bourrienne and exclaimed "in a failing voice":

> "You are not loyal to me! Women!... Josephine!... If you were loyal to me, you would have told me everything I have just learned from Junot. She has cuckolded me! She!... They'd better look out! I'll exterminate that race of puppies and pretty boys!

. . . And as for her, a divorce! . . . Yes, a divorce! A public, sensa-
tional divorce! . . . I must write . . . I know everything. . . . It's your
fault. You should have told me!"

But whatever his emotions at the time, Bonaparte had to repress
them and resume the pursuit of the Mamelukes.

In the dawn of July 21 (3 Thermidor, Year VI) the soldiers beheld
a tremendous spectacle: on the one hand, the pyramids—colossal and
majestic triangles which glittered in the sun; on the other, across the
Nile and behind the ramparts, the 350 minarets of Cairo and, towering above all this, the citadel of Saladin. Twelve thousand fellahs
occupied Embaba; several tens of thousands of soldiers were milling
about in the plain; and along the near bank of the river, occupied by
Ibrahim's gun emplacements, was a long line of 6,000 Mamelukes
with flashing arms, ready to charge. Did Bonaparte then say (as he
is reported to have said): "Soldiers, from the top of those pyramids,
forty centuries look down on you"?

In any case, since the army occupied a front of several kilometers,
the famous speech could certainly have been heard by only a few
units.

The officers ordered, "Fall in!" In an instant, the men formed into
squares six ranks deep. The Mamelukes charged, but at fifty paces,
they encountered a hail of grapeshot and bullets. The carnage was
frightful. Soon the fleeing Mamelukes were throwing themselves
into the Nile, where the horrible butchery was finished.

Those forty centuries could not have witnessed a more extravagant spectacle. A gigantic bazaar was established on the field of
battle. People looted, sold, and traded. As a witness reported: "Some
put on turbans still wet with blood; others proudly draped themselves in sable-lined pelisses or in gold-trimmed jackets."

In the immense fortress city of Cairo there was consternation.
Murad and Ibrahim had fled; and the Pasha Abu-Bakr, the pale representative of the Sultan of Constantinople, followed their example.
Hence the Arab sheiks and ulema decided to capitulate; and on July
24, Bonaparte made his entry into the city. He was on horseback. At
his side was General Kléber, a splendid soldier with the build of an
athlete who excited much more admiration from the Arabs than did
the puny little sallow-faced general.

Cairo rather disappointed him. How different it was from the decor of the *Thousand and One Nights* that he thought he would find in the famous city! "It is difficult," he wrote the Directory, "to find a land more fertile [he was of course speaking only of the narrow valley] and a people more impoverished, ignorant, and degraded." For him, the 300,000 inhabitants of Cairo were "the most wretched population in the world."

On August he left the city for Bilbeis, in pursuit of Ibrahim Bey. En route, he met up with a caravan going to Mecca, and the pilgrims called him the King of France. On the morning of August 14, at Bilbeis, north of the Sinai Desert, a peasant gave Lavalette a letter that had been entrusted to him by a French officer from Alexandria whose exhausted horse could go no farther. Napoleon's aide-de-camp paled when he read the note. It reported the disaster of Abukir: the entire French fleet, surprised at anchor by Nelson, had been destroyed or captured. Bonaparte himself read the note before going to the mess table.

"You know what it contains," he said to Lavalette. "Keep the secret."

The lunch was very gay. The troops had just seized all the booty that the Mamelukes had taken from a caravan. Bonaparte decided that the soldiers could sell the goods for their own profit as soon as they returned to Cairo. All the guests were smiling when, in the middle of the meal, he announced calmly: "You seem to get along well in this country. That is very fortunate, because we have no more fleet to take us back to Europe. . . ."

The consternation was general. Meantime, Bonaparte tried to make the situation seem less dramatic:

> Well, we now find ourselves obliged to do great things. And we will do them! To found a great empire. We will found it! Seas of which we are not the masters separate us from the Fatherland; but no sea separates us from Africa or Asia. We are strong in numbers, and we don't lack men to furnish our cadres. Nor do we lack munitions. We will have a lot of them. If necessary, Champ and Conté will manufacture them for us.

Of course they had lost their ships of the line, but the transports were still in the port of Alexandria. And besides, would not the French fleet of the Atlantic come to their aid? They should not let the disaster of Abukir make them forget the victories won by the army! Paris would get both news bulletins at the same time; and the prestigious names of the Pyramids, Cairo, and the Nile would eclipse the name of Abukir, which doesn't mean anything to anyone.

Nevertheless, Bonaparte and those he had brought along with him in this mad adventure were the prisoners of their conquest—a conquest which, for that matter, was far from being completed.

VI

SULTAN EL KEBIR

Mohammed's superiority consists
in having founded a religion without a hell.

NAPOLEON

BY STUDYING THE LIST of the "articles" that the commanding general asked the Directory to have sent to him, one can get an idea of
the army's needs. The "invaders" asked not only for soap, oil, sheets,
wine, and "the seeds of all kinds of vegetables" but also for surgeons,
physicians, pharmacists, dealers in wines and spirits, distillers, and
even dancing girls and puppeteers.

While waiting for the "deliveries," at the time of the inauguration
of the Institute of Egypt, the commanding general bombarded the
savants with questions: Could the ovens used by the army be im-
proved? If so, how? Could one make beer without hops (which did
not grow in Egypt)? What are the commonest methods for purifying
the water of the Nile? What type of mill is the most suitable for
construction at Cairo—water mills or windmills? Does Egypt possess
the resources for the manufacture of gunpowder?

In short, they lacked everything; and this situation did not make
for peace of mind. Disgust with the country, lassitude, and a desire
to go home: such was the mood of the troops, the officers, and even
the generals. In the course of a dinner given by General Duguas,
Bonaparte asked Murat: "How are you faring in Egypt?"

"Very well," replied the swashbuckler, who was quaking before
his commander.

"So much the better! I know that some of you are talking of
mutiny. Let them beware! The distance between me and a general
and me and a drummer is the same. If necessary, I would have one

shot as quickly as the other. As for you, Murat, if you falter, I'll see to it that you get a bullet in the head."

It is easier to give orders than to give up. Bonaparte did not want to waste any time looking backward; he was busy organizing things. He had excellent quarters in Cairo. The house of Mohammed Bey el Elfi, on Esbekieh Square, where he was living, was sumptuously laid out: a marble staircase, fountains, and mosaics. To aid in forgetting the unfaithful Josephine, he had a batch of Asian women sent to him. Their obesity, their "coarse extremities" (to use his expression), and especially their odor were such that he repeatedly sent them back without having used them. But he allowed one exception: the daughter of the Sheik El-Bekri, who was sixteen years old. After the departure of the French, she was arrested because of her brief affair with Bonaparte. "When she was questioned as to her conduct," a witness reports, "she answered that she had repented of it. They then asked her father for his opinion, and he said that he had disowned his daughter. They then proceeded to cut the unfortunate girl's throat."

Toward December 1, the commanding general became interested in the very young and very blond Pauline Fourès, the wife of a lieutenant in the artillery who had followed her husband to Egypt in masculine disguise. The husband was removed from the scene by the expedient of having him put on board the sloop *Chasseur*, which was to "put in at some port on the continent." Once rid of him, Bonaparte openly flirted with Pauline at a dinner party. Then he spilled a carafe of water on the young woman's dress, which made it possible for him to repair the damage in his private apartments. When, a bit later (on December 19), the British man-of-war *Lion* intercepted the *Chasseur*, the English, laughing up their sleeves, made haste to land the cuckolded husband on the Egyptian coast and wished him "good luck." He came back to Cairo, only to learn that the commanding general was living with his wife, whom the soldiers called "Bonaparte's Cleopatra" and the officers called "Bellilotte," after her maiden name of Bellisle.

Bonaparte succeeded in arranging for a divorce between M. and Mme. Fourès; and he even proposed marriage to his mistress, provided she would give him a child. Pauline was considered the *souveraine de l'Orient*, and there were many people who believed she would succeed Josephine. In any case, with this affair, Bonaparte seemed only too pleased to forget his role of cuckolded husband.

The women that their general had asked to be sent from France were slow in arriving, and the soldiers, many of whom had wives in France, "legally" took concubines, since the sheiks had decreed any marriage valid provided the husband declared: "There is no other God but Allah, and Mohammed is his prophet."

Napoleon's chief concern in Cairo was the administration of the conquered country. The day following his arrival in the city, he created his own "divan" or council of government. His aim was to make the French policy legal.

Although the French had brought the Egyptians certain inventions that they lacked—things as simple as the wheelbarrow and the windmill—there was no question of applying Western methods of government, and the hangmen did not go without work. "Every day I make five or six heads fall in the streets of Cairo," Bonaparte announced.

He chose as chief of police a flamboyant personage—a Christian Greek by the name of Barthélemy. With his wife riding at his side, at a gallop, and followed by a gang of flunkies and Janissaries, Barthélemy lopped off heads in great style. Augustin Belliard, a historian of the Egyptian campaign, said of him: "When you saw him marching toward the Citadel with his naked scimitar, followed by his garroted patients, it was a sight well calculated to suppress all evil intentions in a great many people."

But in spite of such terror tactics the Egyptians were apparently charmed by the interest Bonaparte took in their customs and their history. He stirred the emotions of the public by the way he presided over the feast celebrating the flooding of the Nile on August 18. Accompanied by all his generals, the general staff of the army, the Kiaya of the Pasha, the Aga of the Janissaries, and other Moslem notables, Bonaparte went at six o'clock in the morning to the junction of the Nile and the Khalidj Canal. A huge crowd was assembled on the hillocks along the edge of the Nile and the canal.

The cannon boomed, and a statue representing the fiancée of the Nile was thrown into the water. It was the signal for the ritual bathing. Even future shrouds were immersed in the river. Then the Arab poets chanted:

O great republican
With the legendary lock of hair,
You have brought light to Egypt—
Brilliant as a crystal lamp.
Ya Salaam!

Having been given the name of El Kebir ("the Great Sultan") by
the people, Napoleon felt it would be proper to wear a turban and
an Oriental robe. But such was the laughter of his general staff that
he wore his disguise only one day.

But along with his praiseworthy attempts at collaboration, certain
mosques were transformed into cafés—which enraged the Egyptians. Their chief reproach was that the French were the Infidel.
Thus, to massacre them was a work of piety that Allah would approve, a part of the Holy War.

The final signal for the revolt was given in the night of October
20–21. Nicholas the Turk, who was present, reported: "One fine day,
a sheik of El Azhar [the Cairo university and mosque] began to run
through the streets shouting, 'Let all those who believe that there is
but one God come to the Mosque El Azhar! Today is the day to fight
the Infidel.' "

At five o'clock in the morning, Bonaparte was awakened and
informed that General Dupuy, the commandant of Cairo, had been
killed by a lance thrust. The commanding general got on his horse,
and orders crackled:

> Order to General Bon to send a part of his division to bivouac
> on the Place du Château and another on Esbekieh Square.
> . . . Order to the commander of the 22nd at El Qobbeh to come
> and occupy the heights between Cairo and El Qobbeh. The
> movement that took place this morning makes it necessary to
> bring the troops closer together. . . . Order to General Dumas to
> get on horseback at dawn and make a patrol. . . . Order to General
> Bon to tear down the Great Mosque [El Azhar] during the night,
> breaking a few columns. . . .

Also, he sent Sulkowski, an aide-de-camp whom he particularly
valued, to take a message to General Dumas. In a suburb of Cairo the
officer's horse stumbled, and Sulkowski fell off. He was massacred,
and his body was thrown to the dogs.

The artillery joined in the fray and bombarded those parts of the city where the revolt was raging—especially the area around the Mosque El Azhar. Then calvarymen and infantrymen "mopped up" the terrain.

The revolt was finally quashed, and Bonaparte sent the following order to Berthier:

> Citizen General, you will please order the commandant of Cairo to have the heads cut off all those prisoners who were captured with arms in their possession. They will be taken to the edge of the Nile . . . and their headless bodies will be thrown into the river.

With peace restored, Bonaparte, haunted by the thought of the canal which formerly linked the Red Sea and the Mediterranean, decided to go to Suez, which General Bon had been occupying since December 7. Suez, moreover, was the only port that the English had not deigned to blockade.

When he left Cairo on December 24 he took with him as provisions only three roast chickens wrapped up in paper. To get to the Springs of Moses, he used the ford (crossable at low tide) that the Hebrews had used in times past. But on his return the tide had risen, and the commanding general and his escorts were almost drowned as the biblical pharaoh was.

On December 30 he discovered the remains of the Pharaohs' Canal. On two occasions he followed the bed of the canal at a gallop. His companions heard him exclaim: "It would be a great thing, but I could not accomplish it now!"

One day early in the time of the Second Empire, Ferdinand de Lesseps read Napoleon's sentence about the canal and began to dream. That dream resulted in the Suez Canal.

"A man named Bonaparte, who claims to be a French general, has carried the war into the Turkish province of Egypt." It was in these terms that Napoleon's landing at Alexandria and the capture of Cairo were announced at Constantinople by the Sultan Selim III. (Selim III had as his favorite a distant cousin of Josephine, also born in Martinique, who had been her friend at boarding school. Her name was Aimée du Buc de Riverny. Captured by pirates while en route to Europe, she had been offered to the Commander of the Faithful, who had created her the Sultana Valide.)

On December 5 the Sublime Porte, having concluded an alliance with Russia, became the ally of England and made ready to march on the French. Only one who did not know Bonaparte would imagine that he would peacefully await the Turks in the shade of the Pyramids. "A commanding general," he used to say, "should never give any rest to either the conqueror or the conquered."

Thus he decided to launch a bold counteroffensive and attack the Turks and the English beyond the Isthmus of Suez; that is, in Syria, which at that time was formed of five "pashaliks": Aleppo, Damascus, Tripoli, Acre, and Jerusalem. At the end of January he detached from his army the divisions of Kléber, Lannes, and Reynier, plus a part of Murat's cavalry, some 13,000 men, 400 of whom were soldiers mounted on Arabian camels. Besides these divisions there were also the physicians, commissaries, interpreters, and (since this was the East) a great retinue of servants.

On January 24, 1799, the first troops of the "Army of Syria" ("Army of Palestine" would have been more accurate) left Cairo. They encountered the same difficulties they had endured in crossing the barren deserts of Beheria: thirst became a great factor, and the siege guns sank down into the sand. They decided to take ship at Damietta and head for Acre.

On February 1, Bonaparte left Cairo, stating that he would return in one month. Actually, he would be absent for four months.

On March 3 the general staff reached the sun-bleached walls of Jaffa and laid siege to it. The Jaffa garrison held out for two days, and was then taken by assault. The pillage was horrible. The 2,000 men who had been defending the fortress were put to the bayonet. The "dromedary" François (to give him the appellation used by these knights of the desert) described the scene: "From every hand came the cries and wails of those who could not escape, some of whom were bayoneted in their turn." From 3,000 to 4,000 Albanians (or Arnauts, as they were called by the Turks) had taken refuge in the citadel. The victors surrounded them, and Napoleon sent two of his aides-de-camp—his stepson, Eugène Beauharnais, and Croisier—"to quiet the fury of the soldiers as much as possible." As soon as the men in the citadel saw the two officers carrying their white sash, they "shouted from the windows that they were willing to surrender if they were assured that their lives would be spared and they would escape the massacre to which the city had been doomed." Otherwise, they said, they would open fire.

Beauharnais and Croisier agreed to take them prisoner—"despite the decree of death that had been pronounced against the entire garrison of the captured city"—and they were taken to the French camp.

When Bonaparte saw so many men coming, he threw up his hands. "What do they expect me to do with them? Do I have the provisions to feed them? Or the ships to take them to Egypt or France? What in hell have they done to me?"

Eugène and Croisier tried to defend their decision. "There were just the two of us among a host of enemies. Besides, didn't you recommend a letup in the slaughter?"

"Well, yes," Bonaparte answered, "as regards women, children, old men, and noncombatants. But not armed soldiers. You should have let yourselves get killed rather than bring these wretches to me."

And he repeated emphatically: "What do you expect me to do with them?"

They made the prisoners sit down helter-skelter in front of the tents and gave them some biscuits and bread taken from the army provisions, which were already very short. Then they tied their hands behind their backs.

Bonaparte consulted with his division commanders. What could they do with these 3,000 to 4,000 men? Sending them to Egypt would require too large an escort; there were no ships on which to put them; releasing them was too risky.

Three days of discussion ensued. On the fourth day, Bonaparte made an iron decision: to massacre all of them except for 400 to 500 Egyptians and Turkish artillerymen whom he hoped to make a part of his own army.

Berthier tried to make his commander see the cruelty of this order. Had not the prisoners been granted a "kind of hospitality" in the French camp?

"I'll tell you what," said Bonaparte, pointing toward a Capuchin monastery. "Go on in there. And if you know what's good for you, never come out again!"

And he added: "Come, general! You have your orders—now carry them out, do you hear?"

What followed was a mass slaughter. They took the men, their

hands still bound, to the edge of the sea. That first day—March 8—
the executions were by means of shooting. "Some of them," Bourrienne tells us, "managed to swim out to some reefs far enough
offshore that the fusillade could not reach them. The soldiers laid
down their arms on the sand and, to get them to come back, made
the Egyptian gestures of reconciliation in use in the country. They
started to come back; but as they did, they met death and perished
in the water."

In the next three days, in order to save powder, bayonets were
employed to finish the job.

On March 11, the plague began its terrible ravages. Seven to eight
hundred men were to perish. On that same day, accompanied by his
general staff, Bonaparte inspected the hospitals. Napoleon was making sport of life and death. He was now risking his life with the same
sang-froid he had displayed, on the preceding days, in ordering the
atrocious carnage. "Finding himself in a small, crowded room he
helped to raise up the hideous corpse of a soldier whose ragged
uniform was befouled by the opening of an abscessed bubo." And
René Desgenettes, who reported this fact, was no stranger to heroism. This surgeon was unquestionably the hero of the medical corps
that accompanied Bonaparte. He braved all dangers; and his reputation for courage was so great that when he was taken prisoner during
the Russian campaign, the Czar set him free merely upon hearing his
name.

On 19 March, having crossed the Belus (now the Qishon), the
army finally encamped before Acre. In command of this miserable
"little pile of stones" were El Djezzar, Sir Sidney Smith, and a French
émigré, Louis Phélipeaux, Bonaparte's former youthful comrade at
the École Militaire de Paris. The same Phélipeaux whom the little
Corsican hadn't been able to bear in the old days, and whom he used
to kick furiously under the desk during lessons. It was Phélipeaux—
in command of the excellent Turkish troops of Djezzar Pasha and
supplied by the British fleet (200 sailors had disembarked)—who was
going to checkmate his former comrade.

While the army encamped on the small hills beyond the range of
Phélipeaux's cannons, Bonaparte positioned his artillery on the Butte
aux Poteries, Tel Harassim. From this hill one could see the interior
of the besieged town—those old Arab quarters whose features have
scarcely changed; today it is still dominated by the Mosque of Jazzar

where, in a damascined casket, a few hairs from Mohammed's beard are preserved.

The town that Bonaparte had in front of him had been built on a spit of land extending into the sea, and was encircled by crenellated ramparts blanked with towers and bristling with cannon. These fortifications had been built with materials taken from the strong, ancient walls which had been in ruins for centuries—ever since they had been raised there by the Crusaders. From the direction of the sea, which protected it on three sides, the town was impregnable. The fourth side faced the Butte aux Poteries. And it was against that side that Napoleon launched his first assault, on March 28.

The attack was repulsed. Two days later an enemy sortie was likewise repulsed, after which Djezzar the Butcher, imitating Bonaparte, has his prisoners strangled—apparently despite the protests of Phélipeaux and Sir Sidney Smith. Two hundred and fifty cannon, plus a few guns brought in by the English, were firing on the French. As for Bonaparte, all he had was his light campaign artillery. The heavy siege batteries, which were to have been brought by sea, had not yet arrived, and the commanding general was in a hurry.

Before long the French artillery had run out of ammunition. Bonaparte then told the soldiers to go and gather up the cannon balls fired by the enemy, "saying that they would be paid in accordance with the caliber: "13 sols for a 24-caliber cannonball, 9 for an 18-caliber, 8 for a 12-caliber, 6 for a 6-caliber, and 4 for a 4-caliber."

During Holy Week, the siege "settled down." While the artillery batteries continued their duel and the besieged garrison was receiving its own cannonballs back again, trenches were dug—but not deeply enough, it appears. And every day brought new cases of the plague. On April 1 the town was assaulted again, with no other result than Bonaparte's narrowly escaping death when a wall collapsed beside him. There were a great many dead and wounded. One week later, the besieged forces attempted another sortie, and were again repulsed. The corpses were piling up in front of the French positions —"those rotting corpses behind which we entrenched ourselves," as François wrote.

Just as at Mantua, Bonaparte could not stay in one place: he was too fond of movement and became terribly bored. And so, on April 15, he set off. He left Acre for several days in order to go and help Kléber, who with only 2,000 men was threatened by a counterattack

by the Pasha of Damascus in the plain of Esdraelon, dominated by
the heights of Mount Tabor. There were 35,000 Ottomans in the
field, and for ten hours Kléber had been combating a force that
outnumbered his seventeen to one. Suddenly, the soldiers heard
three cannon shots, and the shout rang out across the battlefield:
"Bonaparte!"

From the heights south of the battlefield, Napoleon had surmised
the situation and was making for Kléber's troops at full gallop.

In the words of Nicholas the Turk:

> When the Moslem troops saw that help had come for General
> Kléber, they realized they were themselves surrounded, and
> sought safety in flight. The French, seeing them run for the moun-
> tain, began to laugh at their fright. When their army had been
> dispersed in this way, the commanding general sought out Gen-
> eral Kléber, and the two of them embraced.

Then Bonaparte headed for Nazareth. He stopped near the Fountain of the Virgin and set up quarters in the Franciscan hostelry of
Casa Nova. The wounded were likewise cared for there; and today
it is a moving experience to examine the parochial registers giving
the names of a number of Bonaparte's soldiers who died there in
spite of the intensive care given them by the monks.

The soldiers of the Republic remembered that they were Christians. One of them who had had a finger torn off buried it with these
words: "I don't know what will happen to my corpse, but I'll always
have a finger buried in the Holy Land."

By April 18, Bonaparte was back at Acre, where the interminable
siege and the attacks continued.

Finally, the artillery was unloaded from the ships and immediately put into action, but without much more success. The fruitless
attacks began again. During the attack of May 8, Bourrienne tells us,
"victory was already being proclaimed. But the breach, recaptured
from the rear by the Turks, was thereafter approached only with
some hesitation, and the 200 men who had entered the town were
not reinforced."

> Yes, Bourrienne [Napoleon said the next day], I see now that
> this miserable shanty town has cost me a lot of men and time. But
> things have gone too far for me not to make a last try. If I succeed,
> as I think I will, the town will yield me the treasures of the pasha

and enough arms for 300,000 men. Then I will cause all Syria to revolt, and provide it with arms. . . . I will reach Constantinople with masses of soldiers. I will overthrow the Turkish Empire. I will found in the Orient a great, new empire that will fix my place in posterity; and perhaps I shall return to Paris via Adrianople or Vienna, after having destroyed the House of Austria!

The next day, this dream faded, as others had before it. The grenadiers threw themselves desperately into the breach; but they met up with murderous fire, and the attack (the eighth) failed.

Bonaparte had made his decision the day before. "If I don't succeed in the last attack that I am going to attempt, I shall leave immediately. Time is short. I won't be in Cairo before mid-June."

On May 11 he gave up the siege. Because of a miserable little fort, he had to turn back. Perhaps Kléber was right when he said with a sigh: "We are using Turkish methods to attack a fort defended by European methods."

The tragedy (comparable to the retreat from Russia) began with the abandoning of the victims of the plague. As the light infantryman Millet said: "This pierced the heart of the army, since we had to leave our unfortunate brothers in arms to the mercy of barbarians who would cut off their heads as soon as we had left. A number of these poor wretches followed us, shouting and begging us not to abandon them."

Some of them were given opium with which to poison themselves, but the results seem not to have been "satisfactory."

On May 21 the retreating (not to say routed) army reached Tantura. It was stiflingly hot. The men had nowhere to sleep "but on the arid and burning sands; on their right was the hostile and empty sea." The casualties in wounded and sick men were already high. As soon as his tent was put up, Bonaparte sent for Bourrienne to dictate a note to him: from this time on, every healthy person had to go on foot. "All the horses, pack mules, and camels will be given to the wounded, the sick, and the plague victims who have been brought along and who still show some signs of life."

By May 24 when they got back to Jaffa, full of plague victims, it was difficult for the general who had been defeated at Acre to go on believing in his lucky star. He again went to see the sick men, walking

rapidly through the rooms and lightly flicking the tops of his yellow
boots with his riding crop.

What was to be done with these poor fellows? As Bourrienne said,
"In the state they were in, to take them along with us meant con-
taminating the rest of the army with the plague." Was poison administered to these survivors? Some witnesses deny it, others say it was
done.

On May 28, strewing its path with corpses, the army left Jaffa for
Cairo. It wasn't until June 14 that Bonaparte regained "his" capital.
During this long march he had plenty of time to think about his
situation, which was not exactly splendid. Forty thousand men had
disembarked at Alexandria the year before, and only half of them
were left. Both victories and checkmates had cost a great many lives.

During the difficult march through the burning sand, he had to
face up to the fact: for the first time, he had been defeated. Later he
would say: "My imagination died at Acre." And he added: "Both my
plans and my dreams . . . England destroyed everything."

But this defeat would go almost unnoticed, thanks to the victorious general's visit to Nazareth—and to the victory at Mount Tabor,
where the past (and what a past!) came to life again under his footsteps. An epic tone would transform the defeat into a day of glory.
The soldiers of Rivoli would be compared to Godfrey of Bouillon's
crusaders, who had come to save "the holy places."

Phélipeaux died of the plague; and only the English believed Sir
Sidney Smith when he prophesied, writing to Nelson: "The plain of
Nazareth marks the extreme limit of the extraordinary career of
Bonaparte."

Soon after Bonaparte's return to Cairo a dispatch rider came to
inform him that from 9,000 to 10,000 Turks, reinforced by Sir Sidney
Smith's forces, were disembarking and had already occupied the fort
of Abukir, not far from Alexandria, having massacred the garrison.
Bonaparte immediately set out with an army of 10,000 men. On July
25, the two armies came face to face. They remained in that position
for two long hours—"in the calm before the storm," as Bonaparte
told it.

"This battle will decide the fate of the world," he announced to
Murat.

The French batteries were the first to fire. Surprised by the violence of the French barrage, the first wave of Turks faltered. Lannes charged in and threw the Ottomans into disorder, pushing them back to the plain, where the cavalry was waiting for them. In one hour, the first rank of Turks was thrown back to the sea. This left the second rank, the center of which occupied the fort of Mount Vizir with 17 guns. From the outset of the battle, the French artillery had been firing on the enemy's rear. Murat, with 600 cavalrymen, plunged into the opening made by the artillery and carried out a frightful massacre.

"Did the cavalry swear they would do everything today?" exclaimed Bonaparte.

The Eighteenth Line Regiment was fighting its hardest. But it had been overrun by Janissaries who, having been promised a silver plume for every Frenchman killed, were sabering furiously and not hesitating to finish off the wounded. Irritated by this sight, and urged on by the example of their general, the Sixty-ninth Line Regiment rushed to the aid of the Eighteenth and managed to penetrate into the fortress. At this point, Lannes' cavalry galloped toward the camp of Mustafa Pasha, the white-bearded Seraskier of Rumelia, who was fighting like a hero. Although badly wounded, he held out against the French; and at the moment of surrender, he wounded Murat in the jaw. The future brother-in-law of Napoleon riposted by cutting off two of the pasha's fingers with his saber; and it was Bonaparte himself who bandaged the loser's wound with his handkerchief.

The last stage of the battle was nothing more than a slaughter. As Napoleon told it later: "Floating in the water were thousands of turbans and sashes that the sea cast back upon the shore." Among the few survivors was the future khedive Mehemet Ali, founder of the last Egyptian dynasty. The French lost only 200 dead but in his letter to the Directory, Bonaparte admitted that this battle seemed to him "the most terrible" that he had seen.

After the battle, Bonaparte sent an officer to the English flagship to negotiate an exchange of prisoners. The English admiral gave the officer a copy of the *Gazette Française de Francfort* dated June 10, 1799. For ten months, Bonaparte had had no news of France. He read through the newspaper with feverish haste.

"*Eh bien,*" he told Bourrienne, "my forebodings have not deceived me. Italy is lost! The wretches! All the fruit of our victories has vanished. I must leave."

No doubt it was virtually impossible for Bonaparte to request a "leave" of the Ministry of War; but the fact remains that he decided to abandon his post and his army.

He returned to Cairo on August 11 and carefully concealed his plans for departure. He merely announced that he was leaving for an inspection in the delta. Not even Kléber, who was to take Bonaparte's place, was informed of his plans. But Napoleon made an exception for Pauline Fourès, whom he was not taking with him.

"I may be captured by the English," he explained to her on the eve of his departure. "You must have a care for my reputation. What wouldn't they say if they found a woman on board?"

On August 18 Bonaparte and his companions left Cairo, and on August 22 they stopped not far from Alexandria, where two frigates were anchored in the harbor. Admiral Ganteaume, who feared that the English ship sighted that morning sailing toward the west would come back, insisted that the embarkation take place at night. Only a few officers, the servants, and a detachment of guides came aboard the *Muiron* and the *Carrère*. In the meantime, Napoleon wrote to the Divan of Cairo; and in order to explain his flight, he invented a whole story.

> Having been informed that my squadron was ready and that a great army was embarked in it; convinced, as I have already told you several times, that so long as I do not strike a blow that will destroy all my enemies at once, I shall never be able to enjoy in peace and tranquillity the possession of Egypt, the most beautiful part of the world, I have decided to put myself at the head of my squadron, leaving my command, in my absence, in the hands of General Kléber, a man of distinguished merit. I have recommended to him that he have the same friendship as myself for the ulema and the sheiks.

Bonaparte did not even dare to face the "man of distinguished merit." Kléber was never notified. In a letter written in haste, Bonaparte announced to him his departure, prompted by "the fear that the English fleet may appear from one moment to the next," and he tried to explain his reasons as best he could. Likewise, he gave Kléber a piece of advice which, by itself, demonstrates the failure of the useless and indefensible conquest:

> If, as a result of incalculable events (all attempts having proven fruitless), by the month of May you have received no help or news

from France; and if, this year, despite all precautions, the plague strikes Egypt and you lose more than 1,500 men, I am of the opinion that you should not risk undertaking the next campaign, and you are authorized to conclude peace with the Sublime Porte, even if the evacuation of Egypt should be its principal condition.

When Kléber read these lines, he exploded.

"The man has gone off like a second lieutenant who leaves unceremoniously after having filled the cafés of the garrison with the noise of his humming and his debts."

The army, on the other hand, found this surreptitious departure very amusing. They admired the fabulous return voyage of the frigate that slipped through the English ships, and were happy to give their commanding general the name of General Bonattrape (General Catch-on-the-Fly).

Bonaparte was sailing toward the unknown. The news from France was already old—it dated from early June, and he wouldn't reach Paris before mid-October. Would he find the country invaded? Was it not possible that his presence, of itself, would be considered as a danger by those (known or unknown) who held power? Since "the sword" that Barras had mentioned was returning, would they not take advantage of the pretext of "desertion" and the failure of the Syrian campaign to put an end to the career of the candidate for the Directory? His companions, all of whom were as anxious as he (if Bonaparte were arrested they would ipso facto be more than compromised), hung on his every word. But "as yet nothing in what he said gave any notion as to what he was going to do," his aide-de-camp, Lavalette, said later, although "a few unguarded words, a bit of daydreaming out loud, and some indirect insinuations" gave them "a lot to think about." Nor did Napoleon become any more prolix when speaking of the government of the Directory. His disdain was total.

On 17 October the *Muiron* entered the port of Ajaccio. Very quickly, a crowd of people in boats gathered around the ship's stern excitedly. An old woman dressed in black raised her arms toward the general, crying: *"Caro figlio!"*

At last Bonaparte recognized her and shouted: *"Madre!"* It was the woman who had nursed him as a child.

For the last time in his life Napoleon spent several days in his

native town, staying with his entire staff in the beloved *casa,* which
had been renovated on orders from Mme. Letizia. He found his
house in the same state in which it can still be seen today: his small
room with the walnut bed, his Louis XVI night table, and the low
ceiling with the uncovered crossbeams. La Madre's salon had become almost sumptuous. The new gallery, with twelve windows giving onto the Rue du Poivre and the walls painted in blue and yellow
stripes, was inaugurated by a dinner for forty. The guests particularly
liked the wine from that year's vintage, already gathered. It was
excellent, and it sold for two sous a bottle in Ajaccio.

Bonaparte also went to the Milelli, in search of childhood memories. The view of the Gulf from there was extraordinarily beautiful.

The winds were not on Bonaparte's side: there was a dead calm.
It was not until October 8 that the breeze enabled the flotilla to put
out to sea. The next day they dropped anchor off St. Raphael. The
news of Bonaparte's return spread ashore, and the sea was soon
covered with boats.

According to regulations, all persons returning from the Middle
East were presumed to have been infected by the plague and had to
undergo the traditional quarantine. But, as one of Bonaparte's companions reported: "We tried to get the crowd to go away. But in vain.
They carried us off and put us ashore. And when we told the crowd
of men and women pressing around us what danger they were risking, they all shouted: 'We prefer the plague to the Austrians!' "

Of course there could be no question of Bonaparte's remaining on
the *Muiron* for forty days. As soon as he was informed of the situation
at home and abroad (the Austrians, the Russians, and the English
were retreating, or at any rate, no longer advancing, thanks to Brune
and Masséna), he set out for Paris.

The news of his return reached Paris on October 13. Thiébault,
who was walking in the Palais-Royal gardens that evening, has described the occasion:

  I had just entered by the main gate when, at the other end of
  the park, I saw a group form and grow in size; then men and
  women came running as fast as they could. . . . I decided they
  must be announcing an important piece of news: an uprising, a
  victory, or a defeat. To find out for sure, I hastened toward them.
  I even tried to question a few persons I met who were coming

from the group at a rapid pace. None of them stopped. But one man, while still running, shouted breathlessly to me: "General Bonaparte has just landed at Fréjus!"

Then I, too, felt the effect of the vertigo, and the first moment of stupor immobilized me for some seconds, with my eyes on the ground. Then I hurried to get back to my cabriolet, which I had left on the Rue du Lycée. . . . The news, which the Directory had had announced to the councils by a messenger preceded by a band, spread with the speed of electricity. . . . The bands from the garrisons of the capital were already marching through Paris, showing how joyous they felt. They were followed by a host of citizens and soldiers. When night fell, fireworks were improvised in all parts of the city, and Bonaparte's return—as longed for as it was unexpected—was announced in all the theaters with shouts of: "Vive la République! Vive Bonaparte!"

At the same moment, Josephine was already going to meet her husband, accompanied by her daughter Hortense. She was counting on the memory of their embraces to help avoid a divorce. But she took the Burgundy road, whereas Bonaparte had chosen the Bourbonnais.

Bonaparte, however, was speeding toward Paris with the firm intention of getting a divorce. And that intention was reinforced on October 16 when, arriving at six in the morning at the Rue de la Victoire in the cold Parisian fog, he found the house empty. He was told that Josephine had left to go and meet him, but to no effect. His wrath was deep and terrible. He was tortured by the idea that, once again, Charles might be traveling with her.

"The warriors of Egypt," he exclaimed, "are like those at the siege of Troy: their wives have been just about as faithful."

The evening of his arrival, while the fog still hung heavily over the city, he went to see Barras. And he went again on the afternoon of the next day. The Director talked to him about Egypt and France, and Bonaparte replied by bringing up his "domestic troubles." He talked, he narrated, he specified, giving "the most intimate details on his conjugal situation relative to his beauty's conduct during his absence."

"Be philosophical, then," Barras advised him.

"That's easy to say," Napoleon replied. There was scarcely any limit to his foul statements about his wife, as he made the worst of

her Creole libertinage—though perhaps Barras embroidered in reporting the scene:

> . . . even with the Army of Italy, when I sent for her so as to
> have her near me. Sometimes it would be a cavalry officer or an
> infantry officer. They were conscripts! And again, only recently,
> it was that little Charles. She squandered all kinds of money on
> him. She gave him huge sums, and even jewels, behaving like a
> prostitute!

The next day, Napoleon had all his wife's things left with the
concierge of their town house and ordered that *la belle* not be allowed in the building. But on the evening of the eighteenth, returning from her unsuccessful trip in a heavy fog, Josephine disregarded
the order, climbed the stairs, and banged on the closed door of the
bedroom. For several hours Bonaparte (as she still called him) heard
her weep, plead, pound on the door, and swear that everything he
had heard was false, that she loved only him, that the little Hippolyte
had never been anything more than a friend. She had no qualms
about calling the children, Eugène and Hortense, who came down
from their rooms and joined in their mother's weeping. He plugged
up his ears so as not to hear. And then, at last, he weakened. He
opened the door, took a look at her tear-stained face, and enfolded
her in his arms.

That night, for her too, he would be "General Bonattrape."

But he would never forget. Much later, when he had gone out one
morning for a walk with Duroc, a cabriolet "going very fast" passed
the two men on the boulevard. The Emperor had taken the arm of
his companion, and the Grand Marshal of the Palace felt the pressure
of Napoleon's wrist as he leaned against him with all his weight.
Napoleon was very pale. "It's nothing," he said. "Don't say anything."

Charles was riding in the cabriolet.

VII

BRUMAIRE, YEAR VIII

A revolution is an opinion
that has acquired some bayonets.

NAPOLEON

WHAT THE JOURNALISTS seem to have noticed first of all was the change in his hair style: "He is wearing his hair short and unpowdered."

Napoleon was beginning to show through Bonaparte.

As for the Directors, at first they remained undecided. What should they do? Should they treat Bonaparte as a rebel, a defeated general, or a victorious hero?

"Well," Sieyès said, quite undisturbed, "we have one more general. But the most important question is: Did that general have his government's permission to return?"

General Moulins, one of the Directors, wanted to have the commanding general of the Army of Egypt arrested and sentenced for desertion. He was made to listen to reason. Then the "five kings," fearing the crowd's reactions if they tarnished the image of their idol, grimaced and decided to receive the "glorious general" at a public session. On October 17, a misty day, Bonaparte made his appearance before them in a rather unusual getup, half military and half mufti. Moreover, his clothes reflected something Levantine. The "civilian" aspect was represented by his hat, a felt top hat of the kind then called *le chapeau rond*. Military dress was represented by his gray-green coat, and the Levantine note was struck by a Turkish scimitar hanging from his belt on a silk cord.

When he returned he told Bourrienne: "They offered me the choice of the army that I wished to command. I didn't attempt to refuse, but I asked for some time to get back my health."

Fight for "people like that" to save their "thrones"? He had better things to do! What a sorry state he had found the country in! The
"national mess" *(le margouillis national)* was evident everywhere.
France was filled with complaints. Cities like Lyons were in ruins.
The Republic seemed inert. Vice was in style. A police report noted:

> The depravity of morals is extreme, and the new generation
> is in a state of great disorder whose unfortunate results for future
> generations are incalculable. Sodomy and lesbianism are as bold-
> faced as prostitution, and are making deplorable progress.
>
> In Paris the newly rich—profiteers, suppliers, and speculators;
> disguised rather than properly dressed, and strolling arm in arm
> with women in transparent dresses and hoydenish ways—flaunt
> their luxuries in the eyes of those who can eat only from time to
> time.

The provinces imitated the capital. "Alas!" wrote Le Coz, the
constitutional bishop, "how depraved our society is! Fornication,
adultery, incest, poison, murder—such are the hideous fruits of phi-
losophism, even in the countryside. Justices of the peace tell me that
if this torrent of immorality is not stopped, many communes will soon
become uninhabitable."

Brigands, highwaymen, masked robbers of stagecoaches and
couriers, Vendéan bandits (who tortured their victims with fire),
frauds, marauders, and other criminals were marvelously organized
to kidnap, rob, and kill. Plundering was established as absolute sovereign, and highway robbery went unchecked. To go from Nice to
Marseilles without being robbed of one's baggage was an exploit. Not
even Bonaparte's baggage was respected when he crossed Provence.
Needless to say, the theft of public monies was considered by certain
individuals as a work of piety, and the administration, completely
impotent, did nothing to interfere—indeed, it tried to get some of
the crumbs from the table. As General Moncey put it: "The present
authorities, and especially the central administration, have become
a public calamity as a result of graft. Everything is stymied by the
administration's moves, everything is chilled by its insinuations—
even its presence." In ten years, France seemed to have returned to
a state of savagery.

Taxes were paid only in part—or else in paper money, which by this time had merely symbolic value. And, indeed, why should people pay taxes to enrich the men in power in the government?

On 18 Brumaire, a deputy named Cornet would be heard speaking of the "hands of vultures" who were "fighting over the unfleshed members of the skeleton of the Republic." True enough, it was an age that did not shrink from bold images. But it is nonetheless a fact that the gang of Thermidorians in power, all of whom were more or less regicides (there were so many nuances in the vote of January 21, 1793, that no one, not even they, knew exactly how he had wanted to vote), were out to live—and live well—at the expense of that so-called Republician regime which they claimed to have saved but which was actually nothing more than a corpse. For almost five years now, that oligarchy—revolutionary in name only—had managed to survive through coups d'état and switches in the majority, through shifting the rudder first to the right and then to the left. And this is not to mention the plots and mutinies that made it possible to change course once again and whip up the old jade of the Republic.

As for the people, they had been stuffed so full of illusory promises and big words stirring them up to street fighting that now, sobered up and disgusted with this revolution that had been so grand under the monarchy, they no longer believed in anything and scarcely dared to hope that they might some day believe in something—or someone. One report stated: "Our setbacks provoke neither joy nor anxiety. In reading the history of our battles, one seems to be reading the history of another people."

No doubt General Bonaparte did not bring the French that freedom they had been hoping for since the assembling of the Estates General. But he cannot be reproached with having wanted to twist the neck of freedom when he made his clean sweep of Brumaire. Freedom could not be strangled for the very good reason that it no longer existed—and that situation did not date from the day before. Freedom had become a word with no meaning. Morals were loose, and corruption was bold-faced, but entertainments were prohibited on Décadi (the last day of the ten-day revolutionary "week," corresponding to Sunday). "Where is our freedom," asked the inhabitants of the Département of Yonne, "if we can't dance when we want to?"

Without openly acknowledging it, France was ready to accept a dictatorship. It remained only for the despot to appear, and he would be greeted as a savior. "Everything is coming to an end," declared the peasants when they learned of Bonaparte's return. "We're going to have a king, and it's no use making the conscripts go off to the army."

Legend was already putting a halo around him. His brilliant victories in Italy, and even the useless expedition to Egypt (as it receded into the past and the sense of reality was blunted, that expedition began to take on the glamour of an epic), had made people forget the way the general had risen to prominence from the street fighting of Vendémiaire. The victory on land at Abukir made them forget the naval disaster of Abukir, just as the Pyramids had effaced the stinging defeat of Acre. For everyone, Bonaparte was the hero. When the French of late 1799 spoke of "the general," they meant only one leader.

What should he do? What plan should he choose? Should he try to become a member of the Directory? Or should he create a new government? He had to "choose what was most sure, to weigh everything, to master everything amid so many conflicting interests and passions—and all that in twenty-four hours!" Fouché was right when he said that to manage this required "great skill, a stubborn character, and promptness of decision."

But what door should he knock at first? At Barras' door, of course! It was the most attractive—at first glance, anyway. But the disdainful irony—almost the condescension—that this "plume of the Directory" displayed toward Bonaparte did not escape the latter. Besides, he quickly realized that Barras—too rotten, too much disgraced— had served too long (had served himself, especially) and had become unfit for use, though he considered himself indispensable.

But it was still necessary, if one wanted to seize power, to "organize the coup d'état from within," and hence to have one or two accomplices among those heading the government. The rather obtuse Louis Gohier, who had become infatuated with Josephine, might well follow orders, but he could never take command. And the same went for the insignificant Roger Ducos.

Beginning on October 23, Bonaparte paid calls on Director Moulins. This name means nothing to anyone today: it meant little more in 1799. Everyone was aware that he had obtained his rank only through politicking. But could he play a secondary role?

What we need [Bonaparte said to him] is a strong government that enjoys the confidence of all those interested in maintaining the Republic. And I am immodest enough to say that if I were in Sieyès' place, the Directory would regain, at one and the same time, the strength and the confidence it needs. Gohier, to whom I talked about this, would be glad to see me in that position. But he is restrained by one scruple: the Constitution requires that a member of the Directory be forty years old. . . .

Moulins, though of limited intelligence, was careful not to take the bait that had been offered to him. He couldn't change the Constitution, could he? Bonaparte did not meet the age requirement. All he had to do was wait a bit to get older. But Napoleon was not the man to let himself age. And there was a similar response from the graybeard Gohier. He, too, refused to understand—even at the thought that if Josephine's husband were to become a Director, *she* would come to live near him.

The only one left was Sieyès, a man Bonaparte did not like at all.

For some time, Sieyès, a former abbé, now a Director, had been looking for a "sword"—a strong man who could put an end to the situation. But he wanted a sword whose hilt he himself would grasp. And so he had given thought, in turn, to Jean Jourdan, Barthélemy Joubert, and then Jean Moreau. When Moreau learned of Bonaparte's arrival at St. Raphael, he said coldly to the former ecclesiastic: "There is your man. He will carry out your coup d'état much better than I could."

Bonaparte had decided to cross the Rubicon. And since he could not do it any other way, he decided to cross it—despite his repugnance—in the company of Sieyès. The "civil route" for seizing power having proved impracticable, he would take sword in hand. And the alliance with Sieyès would "prop him up" in the eyes of the public, who wanted no more of the corrupt Barras.

Seconded by Pierre Louis Roederer, who was very excited about what he called "a patriotic plot," and aided by Talleyrand, who thus initiated a beautiful series of betrayals in the trend of his convictions, Bonaparte had secret interviews with Sieyès at Palais du Luxembourg. The events followed a carefully elaborated scenario. The Minister of Foreign Affairs took the candidate for dictatorship to the Luxembourg, but left him in his carriage and went alone to see Sieyès. Having made sure that Sieyès was alone and was not expecting anyone, he sent word to Bonaparte that the way was clear. A few minutes later the conference among the three men began.

During their first interview, Bonaparte declared to Sieyès: "Citizen, we have no constitution. Or at any rate, we don't have the one we need. Your genius must provide us with one. You have been aware of my sentiments since my arrival. The time to act has come. Have all your steps been resolved upon?"

The abbé-turned-Director, who always had a constitution in his pocket, explained that they could set up a consulate consisting of three consuls, while Bonaparte would take care of the military power.

"I agree that the government should be reduced to three persons," Bonaparte said, "and since it is considered necessary, I consent to serve as one of the provisory consuls, along with you and your colleague, Roger Ducos."

So Bonaparte was demanding a place as consul! The abbé grimaced but gave in. When Bonaparte had left, he exclaimed: "The general seems as much at home in politics as on the field of battle. We must follow his advice. If he withdrew, all would be lost, whereas his acceptance of the provisory consulate guarantees success."

Now the plot was hatched, and the public began to suspect something.

Josephine had put her charm into the service of those who would be called the Brumaireans. She lured to the Rue de la Victoire various undecided individuals who had to be won over, arranged for people to meet one another, facilitated private talks, smoothed things out, and allayed the suspicions of those whose reactions might be feared (Gohier was one such). In the afternoons toward four o'clock she received her admirer and worked on him with smiles, lisping, and flirtation, always hoping to bring him over to the side of the plotters. But the Director surmised nothing at all. One day when Fouché came to the house on Rue de la Victoire, Gohier asked him: "What's new, Citizen Minister?"

"Nothing. Really nothing."

"Are you sure?"

"Still the same idle talk."

"How's that?"

"Still talking about a plot."

"A plot?" asked Josephine, pretending to be astounded.

"Yes, a plot," explained Fouché, laughing inwardly. "But I know what to believe and what not to believe. I see the whole situation clearly, Citizen Director. Trust me. It's not me they are attacking. If there had been a plot, by this time we would have had proofs of it on the Place de le Révolution or the Plaine de Grenelle."

Gohier smiled and attempted to calm Josephine, who had skill-fully affected a frightened expression. "The minister speaks as a man who knows his business. The fact that he says things like that in front of us, Madame Citizen, proves that there's no reason they should take place. Follow the example of the government, and don't let those rumors bother you. Sleep peacefully!"

By this time the plot was well under way. How should they pro-ceed? With the help of several deputies brought into the plot by Lucien, they would make the two assemblies believe that the Pari-sians were preparing an uprising. In order to be able to deliberate in security the Council of the Ancients and the Council of the Five Hundred, having entrusted Bonaparte with their protection, would vote for a transfer to St.-Cloud, the royal estate on the outskirts of Paris. There, they would arrange to trip up the regime. As had been provided since the outset of the affair, only two of the Directors would come into the new government: Sieyès and Ducos. In a pinch it was hoped that Gohier, thanks to Josephine, would enter into the plot. No one particularly cared about the insignificant General Mou-lins. As for Barras, a large amount of money would certainly quiet his scruples.

All this seemed very facile at first glance; but on second thought, the operation seemed to bristle with difficulties and unknown quanti-ties. Would the Directors who had been eliminated let themselves be dethroned all that easily? Of course Barras had no conscience, and many things would be made easy for him. But wouldn't he still try to hang on to his power? There was much to be feared!

In order to take the pulse of the deputies and, as Napoleon would say later, "to give them the time to convince themselves that I could do without them whatever I could do with them," Lucien conceived the idea of bringing them all together and having the Council of the Ancients organize a subscription banquet in honor of Bonaparte. Two hundred and fifty political personalities—including the "five kings" of the staggering Republic—agreed to pay 30 francs to go on November 6 (15 Brumaire) through an unending fine rain and take their places at an immense horseshoe-shaped table set up in the glacial church of Sulpice, transformed by the Revolution into a Temple of Victory. It was a bizarre banquet. With teeth chattering (from cold and fear), each guest watched his neighbor anxiously and suspiciously. In the words of Lavalette:

> I have never seen a more tongue-tied group—or one in which the guests showed less trust and good spirits. Scarcely a word was exchanged between people seated next to each other. And those who were in on the plot preferred silence to risking dangerous conversations with neighbors who might not be in on the secret.

Bonaparte had "so little trust in the government—or, rather, so much defiance toward it"—that without any attempt at concealment, he had a loaf of bread and a demi-bouteille of wine brought to him. When he had consumed this Spartan meal, he went (followed by Berthier and Bourrienne) from table to table, saying flattering things to some people and meaningless things to others. After some fifteen minutes, his companions heard him murmur: "I'm bored. Let's get out of here!"

Outside, it was getting colder and colder. It was even sleeting.

The plans of the plotters had leaked out to the public, and the three members of the Directory who were not on the favored side were more or less informed. Did they meet the next day? Did they tell one another of their anxieties? But what could they do? Could they give the order to arrest the future dictator? Where would they put him? Could they even have found jailers to keep him or judges to bring him under indictment and interrogate him? They remained inert. They had no idea that the plot would explode the next day, 18 Brumaire.

The evening of the seventeenth, Josephine—employing a "veritable ruse of a loose woman"—asked her son to take the following note to Gohier:

> My dear Gohier. Please come with your wife to take breakfast with me at eight o'clock in the morning. Don't fail me, because I have some very interesting things to discuss with you. Adieu, my dear Gohier. You may always count on my sincere friendship.
>
> La Pagerie-Bonaparte

As Bonaparte had said: "When it comes to plotting, everything is permitted." His aim was simple: to have Gohier under his control.

Beginning at seven o'clock the next morning, in weather that was fine but cold (the Observatoire had noted the first white frost of the season), the garden and the narrow little walk, 90 meters long, leading from the Rue de la Victoire to Napoleon's town house were full of officers in dress uniform. Seeing this assemblage, everyone understood: It will happen today!

General Lefebvre, in command of the garrison of Paris (including the National Guard of the Directory), was of course also invited. When he saw the crowd of officers, he seemed a bit surprised. But Bonaparte subdued him by offering him the sword he had worn in Egypt and referring disparagingly to those "lawyers who are the cause of all the trouble."

General Debelle appeared in mufti.

"What's this?" exclaimed a friend. "You're not in uniform?"

"I didn't know anything about it. But wait a minute. It won't take me long." Then, turning to a gunner, an officer's orderly, he said: "Give me your uniform, old fellow."

And right there in the street the two of them exchanged uniforms.

But what about Gohier? Why hadn't he come?

The Director, surprised at the early hour that Josephine had mentioned in her note (a breakfast at eight in the morning!) had preferred to delegate his wife. When Mme. Gohier arrived at the Rue de la Victoire and saw all the plumes and gold braid, she immediately understood the situation.

"What?" exclaimed Bonaparte when he greeted her. "Isn't the chairman coming?"

"No, General. He can't. He—"

Napoleon interrupted her. "He absolutely must come. Write him a note, Madame, and I'll have it taken to him."

"All right, General, I'll write him. But I have servants of my own here to take the letter."

Mme. Gohier wrote to her husband: "You did well not to come. From everything that is going on here, I can tell that the invitation was a trap. I shall rejoin you shortly."

It was now Josephine's turn to try to convince the stubborn lady. "Everything you see here, Madame, should make you realize what is going to happen inevitably. I can't tell you how sorry I am that Gohier did not come in response to my invitation, arranged with

Bonaparte, who wants the chairman of the Directory to be one of the members of the government that he proposes to form. The fact that I sent him my letter by my son showed the importance that I attached to it."

"I am going back to my husband, Madame," replied Mme. Gohier. "I shouldn't be here."

But that morning the Gohiers did not understand where their true interests lay—and Gohier remained at the Luxembourg. He had not even been surprised by the departure of the Directory's Guard, which under a pretext of maneuvers left the Luxembourg to the sound of drums and trumpets. And instead of going to the firing range, they set out for the Tuileries.

It was now past eight o'clock, and the decrees transferring the assemblies to St.-Cloud and naming Bonaparte commanding general had not yet been sent to the Rue de la Victoire. Several times, Napoleon sent messengers to inquire about them. Were the Conscript Fathers going to stall? All we know is that they had been in session for more than an hour.

But everything went off according to plan. The deputies, assembled at seven o'clock, had heard Régnier (one of the conspirators) exclaim: "The Republic is threatened by the anarchists and the party in league with the foreigners. We must take steps for public security. We are assured of General Bonaparte's support. In the shadow of his protective arm the councils will be able to deliberate on the changes necessitated by the public interest."

Where would they go under that "protective arm"? To St.-Cloud!

"There," continued Régnier, who had learned his lesson well, "sheltered from surprises and sudden attacks, you can consider in calm and security the means of eliminating the present perils."

The majority of the assembly then voted for the draft decree proposed by Régnier: the transfer to St.-Cloud and the appointment of Bonaparte.

Bearing this good news, Fouché rushed to the Rue de la Victoire and entered the small rotunda-shaped dining room which was serving as an antechamber. He told Bonaparte: "You can trust in my devotion and my zeal. I have just issued orders for closing the city barriers and stopping all couriers and stagecoaches."

"All that is quite unnecessary," said the new commanding general. "As you can see, the fact that so many citizens and soldiers have rallied around me makes it plain enough that I am acting with and for the nation. I will have no trouble seeing to it that the council's decree is respected and public order maintained."

A few moments later the inspectors of the Council of the Ancients arrived in great state to read the four decrees to Bonaparte:

Article 1. The legislative body is transferred to the commune of St.-Cloud. The two councils will hold sessions there, in the two wings of the palace.

Article 2. They will be there by noon tomorrow, 19 Brumaire. Any continuation of functions or deliberations elsewhere or before that time is prohibited.

Article 3. General Bonaparte is made responsible for carrying out the present decree. He will take all steps necessary for the security of the national assemblies.

Article 4. General Bonaparte is summoned to appear before the Council to receive a copy of the present decree, and to take an oath.

Thus he was supposed immediately to swear his loyalty to a system he was preparing to overthrow.

"Follow me!" he shouted, turning toward the officers around him. And, already on the run, he shouted to Bourrienne: "Gohier didn't come. Too bad for him!"

Napoleon jumped on a big black horse, a rather restive one with a white head, lent to him by Admiral Bruix. Followed by his generals and other officers, he went down the boulevard. The procession passed under the windows of the financier Gabriel Ouvrard, a supplier to the Navy, who lived at the corner of the Rue de Provence and the Chaussée d'Antin. Ouvrard realized the way the wind was going to blow. Leaving his window, he sat down at his desk to write to Admiral Bruix:

Citizen Admiral:

Having seen General Bonaparte pass by on his way to the Council of the Ancients, and having noticed some troop movements, I have a presentiment that a change in political affairs is imminent. This circumstance may necessitate a need for funds. Would you be so kind, my dear Admiral, as to convey notice of my offer to provide such funds. . . .

For the first time in his life, at the Council of the Ancients, Bonaparte had to speak before a group of legislators. He seemed ill at ease, and his delivery was jerky and hesitant: The Republic was perishing, he declared. "You realized it, and you passed a decree which is going to save it. . . . We want a Republic founded on liberty, on equality, on the sacred principles of national representation. And we shall have it—*I swear it!*"

The gallery applauded noisily, while General Bonaparte's staff shouted with vibrant voices: "We swear it!"

As for Fouché, he had gone from the Rue de le Victoire to the Luxembourg, where he announced to Chairman Gohier the decree transferring the sessions of the legislative bodies to the château of St.-Cloud.

The Directors Sieyès and Roger Ducos had already joined the Committee of Inspectors of the Council of the Ancients. Sieyès, indeed, after a last lesson in horseback riding, had left (on horseback) for the Tuileries, where Roger Ducos had joined him, under the pretext of "going to hear the news."

"The majority is at the Luxembourg," Gohier emphatically told Fouché, raising his voice. "And if the Directory has orders to issue, it will entrust their execution to men worthy of its confidence."

When Fouché had left, Gohier brought Moulins up to date, after which the two of them went to see Barras; he was in the bathtub and had a servant inform them that he could not receive them. When he emerged from his tub after an hour of soaking, the Vicomte carefully trimmed his beard, then declared he was ill and could not see his two colleagues, who were left dangling. He was hoping to receive a visit, if not from Bonaparte then from one of his emissaries, calling him to the Tuileries. But nobody came except his secretary, Bottot, who told him about the painful scene that had just taken place in the garden of the Tuileries.

Bonaparte had, in fact, left the assembly room of the Council of the Ancients and gone to the Tuileries Gardens, where he found himself facing the 10,000 men who were to recognize him as the supreme commander. It was then that he noticed Bottot, sent by Barras, who was trying to work his way through the crowd to Bonaparte. With his instinct as a stage director of history, Bonaparte instantly realized the use he could make of the unhappy Bottot's presence. Since the master was not there, it was the servant who would bear the brunt of the general's wrath. Bewildered, Bottot found himself being dragged up in front of the grenadiers. Then Bonaparte, holding him by the arm, with blazing eyes made his famous speech:

> What have you done with that France that I left to you in such splendid condition? I left you peace, and came back to find war! I left you victories, and I came back to find defeats! I left you the wealth of Italy, and I came back to find plundering laws and poverty everywhere! What have you done with the 100,000 Frenchmen that I commanded—my companions in glory? They are dead! This state of affairs cannot last! . . .

From a distance, the crowd watched the scene. The weather had become warmer: the thermometer showed six degrees, and a pale sun made the gold of the uniforms glitter. When they had got up that morning, the Parisians had read the white posters put on the walls by Roederer's and Regnault's men in the name of the *département*. The regime was on trial. Big letters spelled out: "They have fixed things so that"—and then, a bit lower down: "there is no more constitution."

At his command post in the Tuileries, Bonaparte received Gohier and Moulins, to whom he declared: "There is no more Directory."

Gohier exclaimed wrathfully: "There is no more Directory? You are mistaken, General. Moreover, you know that you agreed to dine today at the home of the chairman of that Directory. Could it be that you accepted that invitation—that you yourself even set the day and the hour—in order to conceal hostile plans?"

"My plans are in no way hostile. The Republic is in peril and must be saved. Such is my will! And it is only by means of vigorous measures that we can succeed. Sieyès and Ducos are resigning, and Barras has sent in his resignation. The two of you, left all alone, will certainly not refuse to hand in your own resignations!"

But the two Directors were still unwilling to give up the one-fifth of a throne that each held.

"Everything will be settled tomorrow!" exclaimed Gohier.

Bonaparte looked at him so hard that, two hours later, Gohier sent in his resignation. "Moulins," reports Mme. Reinhard, "who had never known why and how he had become a member of the Directory, followed the example of the person he had always trotted after."

And Barras? Despite the speech of which Bottot had informed him, he had not yet decided to act. He was still persuaded that Bonaparte would not dare touch him and would come looking for him. He was flabbergasted when, at noon, Bruix and Talleyrand came to see him in the name of the commanding general to "negotiate his retirement."

"If you offer the least resistance in order to thwart his plans, Bonaparte is determined to use against you all the means of force within his power."

Then Talleyrand proffered a previously prepared letter that Barras was supposed to address to the legislature "to notify it of his resolution to retire to private life."

He "retired to private life" all the more willingly in that Talleyrand and Bruix had taken the precaution to provide themselves with a very large sum of money—Ouvrard's money. A few minutes later, Bonaparte's dragoons served as an escort "of honor" for the ex-Director on his way to his château of Grosbois. M. le Vicomte de Barras, who had given Bonaparte a leg up into the saddle, was leaving history forever.

The conspirators agreed on the appointment, the next day, of three provisory consuls: Bonaparte, Roger Ducos, and Sieyès.

"Perhaps," suggested Sieyès, "we should have about forty of the opposition arrested."

This expedient struck Napoleon as premature. He felt there would be no opposition or resistance.

Sieyès was piqued. "You'll see tomorrow, at St.-Cloud," he said.

On the morning of November 10 (19 Brumaire), Bonaparte set out for St.-Cloud. It had stopped raining, and a west wind had cleared the sky of clouds, but it was cold and humid. Couture wrote later:

> I saw him—I still see him—in the Tuileries Gardens about to leave for St.-Cloud: his face sun-tanned, thin, and elongated; the hair laying flat and cut two inches above the ears; the little hat, the yellow trousers, with a large stain on the left thigh; the little uniform, the half-boots; and under him, a big horse whose housing was iron gray and whose head was white. . . .

The road from Paris to St.-Cloud was crowded with officers on horseback, onlookers, carriages full of deputies, functionaries, and journalists, and especially troops in battle dress. The cuirassiers (they were called the *gros talons* or "big heels") trotted heavily along, and the cannon—for such there were—made a horrible noise as they rolled along. They all went up the ramp which, today, leads onto the highway from the west. Following Bonaparte's orders, they took up positions around the château.

The onlookers watched Bonaparte as he, in his turn, went up the ramp. Once arrived in the courtyard, he started to gather information. What was the pulse of his adversaries and those who had promised to support him? The talks, it seems, were very animated. Most of the legislators were unaware of the plotters' plans. As for those in on the plot, they talked of it only vaguely. Some said the Republic was going to be saved; others, that it was going to be lost.

The assembly halls—the Grand Salon for the Council of the Ancients and the Orangerie for the Council of the Five Hundred—were not ready, alas! The deputies, meaning the two assemblies mixed together, initiated an uneasy congress in the open air. As they prattled away, they kept an anxious eye on the profusion of uniforms. The Ancients seemed the more resigned, whereas the Five Hundred spoke up loud and clear: "Ah! So he wants to be a Caesar, a Cromwell. . . . We'll see about that!"

The Ancients began to yield. Those who were in on the plot no longer dared to speak out so openly. A current of opposition was building up. Toward one o'clock (and this was announced to Bonaparte) the Council of the Ancients, preceded by its band playing the "Marseillaise," entered the Grand Salon. Those participating in the plot tried to talk the time away. Everyone knew that nothing would really begin until the Five Hundred were in session.

It was three o'clock before the Orangerie was finally ready. The members of the Five Hundred had put on their togas and their ample red cloaks. They took their places—and at once a storm broke out. The shouts became louder: "No dictatorship! We are free here! Bayonets won't frighten us!"

The presiding officer, Lucien Bonaparte, tried in vain to reestablish a semblance of order. Most fortunately, the gentlemen of the council, who took themselves to be Romans, had a predilection for "impressive scenes." One of them proposed that they swear loyalty to the Constitution of the Year III. Was this perhaps a way of infusing new blood into the dying Directory? Lucien yielded. In order to gain time, he was ready to swear fealty to the regime that he would soon overthrow to the benefit of his brother.

And so every deputy went up to the rostrum, extended his right arm with a pretty draping of his toga, took his oath, and went back to his seat. All the rites were scrupulously respected. At the rate they were going, they would be kept busy for a full five hours.

"It's time to haul up short!" exclaimed Bonaparte, striking the parquet floor with his riding crop.

Unless he intervened personally, all was lost. He decided to begin with the Council of the Ancients, hoping that they would carry the Five Hundred along with them.

He walked into the hall, and began by castigating the alleged plotters.

Shouts arose: "Let him name the plotters! Name them! Name them!"

"If a complete explanation has to be given," said Bonaparte, "if I must name names, I will. I will tell you that two of the directors, Barras and Moulins, proposed that I be put at the head of a party to overthrow all those who have liberal ideas."

"We must create a general committee to hear these revelations!" shouted some of the deputies.

"No! No!" shouted others. "No general committee. The plotters have just been named. France must hear everything!"

Then they asked Bonaparte to go into detail about the vague accusations he had just formulated against Barras and Moulins: "You mustn't hide anything any more!"

"It was then," Bourrienne continues, "that the interruptions, the attacks, and the interrogations upset him, and he thought he was done for."

He even stammered: "If I am a traitor, then all of you are Brutuses. . . . I hereby state that when all this is over, I shall be nothing more in the Republic than the arm that will uphold what you will have established!"

The Ancients were perfectly willing to be Brutuses; but they demanded names besides those of the two directors who had resigned. And how could Bonaparte give them those names when the alleged terrorist plot did not exist? He became confused. He felt ridiculous, and more and more distressed. His speech rapidly turned into a kind of unbridled conversation carried on by fits and starts with the presiding officer. Whereas the questions asked by the officer were clear and precise, Bonaparte's answers were "ambiguous and contorted." He talked of "volcanoes, secret disturbances, victories, the 18th of Fructidor, Caesar, Cromwell, and tyrants." Time and again he was heard to affirm, in the mounting tumult: "That is all I have to tell you."

"And he wasn't saying anything," observed the frantic Bourrienne. "Or, at any rate, not much."

Unable to understand, his hearers were reduced to guesswork: "Liberty, equality . . . hypocrites . . . intriguers . . . I'm not one of them . . . I will abdicate my power as soon as the danger threatening the Republic has passed. . . ."

> Without having been there [reported Bourrienne] one cannot really have an idea of what went on. It must be admitted that there was not the slightest semblance of order in all his incredible, incoherent stammerings. Bonaparte was anything but an orator. One may well suppose that he was more accustomed to the sound of battle than to that of discussions in the hustings. His rightful place was in front of a battery—not in front of the armchair of a presiding officer of an assembly.

Suddenly, Bonaparte stopped stammering: he seemed to have found a theme, and he began to threaten the deputies: "And if some orator in the pay of foreign powers speaks of 'outlawing' me, may the thunderbolt of war destroy him instantly! If he talks of 'outlawing' me, I will appeal to you, my brave comrades in arms!"

And he turned to the few grenadiers who had remained on the threshold of the hall: "To you—brave soldiers whom I have so often led to victory! To you—brave defenders of the Republic with whom I have shared so many dangers in order to proclaim liberty and equality! Remember that I march forward accompanied by the God of Victory and the God of Fortune."

This was a phrase that he had uttered with success before the Divan of Cairo; but at St.-Cloud the results it produced were considerably less impressive. Bourrienne took him by the sleeve and murmured (or so he tells us): "You'd better leave, General. You no longer know what you're saying."

Bonaparte stammered a few more words, then walked toward the door, calling out: "Let those who love me follow me!"

But the only ones who followed him were Bourrienne and Berthier.

At the Council of the Five Hundred, in spite of Lucien's presidency, it was much worse. As soon as Bonaparte entered, and before he had even said anything, his presence alone set off hostilities. The "hooligans" of the Mountain (the extreme left wing) rushed at him and pummeled him with their fists. Amid the furious shouts from the Five Hundred, one could make out: "Outlaw the dictator! Down with dictator!"

Or: "What? Bayonets, sabers, and armed men here?"

"Let us die at our post! Long live the Republic and the Constitution of the Year III!"

Lavalette writes: "He was squeezed so tightly among the deputies, his staff, and the grenadiers who had rushed into the hall that for a moment I thought he would be suffocated. There was no way to advance or to retreat. . . ."

Deputies, spectators, and soldiers were now fighting like ragpickers. One of the deputies caught his foot in his toga and fell flat on the floor. An incredible scene of violence was taking place just below the rostrum. The grenadiers were clearing a way for themselves to come and rescue their commander, who was being taken to task by the huge Destrem (the deputy with the flushed face) who bellowed at Napoleon: "Was it for this that you conquered?"

Destrem, of whom it was said that "a blow of his hand" was worth "a blow struck by somebody else's fist," had grabbed the puny Bonaparte by the shoulder. The general, half-fainting and no longer aware of what was happening, was finally pulled free and taken away by his soldiers.

Lucien tried to defend his brother, but a deputy interrupted him: "Bonaparte behaved like a king!"

"None of you," Lucien said, "could attribute plans for squelching freedom to the man who—"

A stentorian voice interrupted him: "Bonaparte has lost his glory! I doom him to disgrace—to the hatred of the Republicans!"

Shouts of approval arose from all the benches. One cry was heard above the tumult: "I demand that General Bonaparte be brought before the bar of justice to account for his conduct!"

Lucien exclaimed: "And I demand to leave the chair!" He abandoned his place below the rostrum, leaving the chairmanship to Chazal. But that didn't settle anything. The confusion increased, the shouts redoubled, and ultimately the same motion that had dethroned Robespierre was offered: "Moved, that General Bonaparte be outlawed!"

At this, Lucien left his deputy's seat, went back up to the rostrum, and in the kind of theatrical gesture that the age demanded, took off his toga as he declared: "There is no more freedom here! Since I can no longer be heard, you will at any rate see your presiding officer, as a sign of public mourning, lay down here the symbols of popular authority."

They begged him to stay on, and he yielded.

Bonaparte and Sieyès were still in the Grand Cabinet. When he learned that the apprentice dictator was now "outlawed," the abbé turned to Bonaparte.

"They are dreaming of '93," he said. "They are outlawing us! Well, General, indulge yourself in throwing them out of the hall."

Bonaparte unsheathed his sword, brandished it, opened the window, and shouted: "To arms!"

A moment later, the hero of Italy appeared in the courtyard, shouting: "My horse!"

When he saw his iron-gray mount kicking, pawing the ground, and prancing, Bonaparte (who had never been a brilliant horseman) was taken aback. Two men managed to keep the beast in hand, not without difficulty. After some trouble, the general mounted and tried to cut a noble figure as he rode. In his excited state, he scratched the pimples on his cheeks, bringing blood—which enabled him to claim that the Five Hundred had tried to assassinate him.

His soldiers seemed ready to "cross the Rubicon," but the grenadiers of the Corps Législatif hesitated. It was after five o'clock; darkness was setting in; a cold November fog was advancing over the park; and the sky was clouding over more and more. Things had to be settled before night fell.

Lucien had just sent his brother an anguished call for help: "Unless the session is interrupted within ten minutes, I am no longer responsible for anything."

Bonaparte finally gave precise orders.

A few moments later a platoon of grenadiers broke into the assembly hall. At first Lucien wondered if all was lost. Had his brother failed? Were they coming to arrest him or free him?

"You talk to me of reconciliation," he declaimed to the deputies, "and you have me arrested!"

But the grenadiers did nothing more than take Lucien to join Bonaparte and Sieyès. Meantime, in the courtyard of the château, General Sérurier was trying to galvanize his troops: "The Ancients have joined Bonaparte, while the Five Hundred tried to assassinate him!"

A matter for civilians! The grenadiers remained unmoved. Then Bonaparte explained to them: "I was going to show them how to save the Republic, and they tried to assassinate me!"

And turning to the grenadiers, he asked: "Soldiers, can I count on you? I'll bring the deputies to their senses!"

He was greeted by silence. But with the arrival of Lucien, everything changed, since "the appearance of legality" had come to join up with the plotters. More prompt to act than his brother, Lucien ordered: "A horse for me, General! A horse! And a rolling of drums!"

He jumped on his horse and cried:

> Citizens! Soldiers! The chairman of the Council of the Five Hundred declares to you that at this moment the immense majority of that council is terrorized by a few deputies of the journalistic fraternity who besiege the rostrum, threaten their colleagues with death, and throw together the most frightful resolutions. I declare to you that these bold brigands, no doubt in the pay of England, have rebelled against the Council of the Ancients and have dared to talk of "outlawing" the general responsible with carrying out its decrees, as if we were still in the frightful time of their reign when that single word "outlawed" was enough to make those whom the nation held dearest lose their heads. I declare that this small group of mad dogs have outlawed themselves by their attacks on the freedom of that council. . . .

A tremor ran through the ranks, and Bonaparte felt that his luck was reviving.

> Let them be thrown out by force! These brigands are no longer the representatives of the people but the representatives

of the dagger! May this title remain with them and follow them everywhere. . . . And when they dare to show themselves to the people, let every finger point to them as the bearers of this well-deserved name of representatives of the dagger. Vive la République!

However, despite the shouts of "Vive Bonaparte!" that followed this harangue, the troops still hesitated. The idea of turning their weapons against the representatives of the nation—even when described as "representatives of the dagger"—gave them pause. Besides, in the windows they could see several deputies who were pointing at Bonaparte and shouting, "Down with the dictator! Outlaw him!"

"Soldiers," cried Bonaparte, "I have led you to victory. Can I count on you?"

A few shouts—but not yet enough—were heard from here and there: "Oui! Oui! Vive le général! What is the order?"

"Soldiers, there was reason to believe that the Council of the Five Hundred would save the nation. But on the contrary, it is destroying it. Agitators are trying to stir the council up against me. Soldiers, can I count on you?"

"Oui! Vive Bonaparte!"

"Well, I'm going to bring them back to their senses. For too long now, the nation has been tormented, plundered, and pillaged. For too long now, its defenders have been vilified and immolated!"

Once again the troops shouted: "Vive Bonaparte!"

And he continued, frequently interrupted by shouts of "Vive Bonaparte!": "Three times, as you know, I have risked my life for my fatherland, but the enemy's weapons respected that life. I have just crossed the sea, risking my life for a fourth time—exposing it to new dangers. And now I find those dangers in the bosom of a senate composed of assassins!"

This time a clamorous shout of "Vive Bonaparte!" reached the ears of the Five Hundred, who shouted back: "Vive la République! Let's die for liberty! Outlaw the dictator! Long live the Constitution of the Year III!"

At this, Lucien unsheathed his sword and held it against his brother's breast, as he cried: "I swear to pierce the breast of my own brother if ever he undermines the liberty of the French!"

This gesture removed the last hesitation. The Guard applauded the speaker, and Bonaparte gave the order to march. The drums beat out a double-quick step. It was the knell of the regime. A few seconds later, General Leclerc entered the Orangerie. Bayonets glittered in the doorway. In a stentorian voice, Leclerc shouted: "Representatives, withdraw! The general has ordered it!"

Then, since the deputies seemed not to be ready to obey him, he cried: "Grenadiers, forward! Drummers, sound the charge!"

At the same time, Murat turned to his men and gave a less proper command: "Heave those people out of here!"

Then, speaking to the deputies: "Citizens, you are dissolved!"

The drummers beat their drums furiously. Colonel Dujardin and his grenadiers went through the "sanctuary of the laws" on the run. When they reached the other end of the hall, they turned around and began rushing at the assembly. Immediately, amid clouds of dust, there was a scramble for safety. The Five Hundred, looking ridiculous in their kilts and Roman costume, leaped out of windows and ran off into the park. A few stubborn deputies clung to their seats, but the soldiers seized them and put them out bodily. Those who resisted too strenuously felt the steel of bayonets at their backs.

Captain Coignet recalled: "We saw fat gentlemen crawling through windows. Coats, fine caps, and plumes were being scattered on the floor. The grenadiers tore the gold braid off those handsome costumes."

Outside, there was a rout—a desperate flight into the night that was falling on the groves and thickets. In order to be able to run faster, the "frightened factionists" (as Bonaparte called them) left some of their clothes in ditches and on lawns, making dark red patches in the mist.

To an expelled deputy wandering sadly through the park, the politician Réal called out: "The farce is over!"

It was because of this farce that the Ancients, who had almost been forgotten, regained some importance. "Embodying ipso facto all of the national representation" (as was affirmed by their presiding officer, who had been won over to the plot), they passed the following decree:

> The Council of the Ancients, in view of the retreat of the Council of the Five Hundred, decrees as follows: Four of the

members of the Directory having resigned, and the fifth being under surveillance, a temporary executive committee of three members will be named.

This was not yet a consulate. Wouldn't it be better to try to find a few of the Five Hundred, even without their kilts? The bailiffs went off to look for them. They checked the taverns in the vicinity, searched hither and yon, and soon rounded up a fairly large group of deputies who sat dozing on the benches of the Orangerie while waiting to submit to orders. They were ready to do anything, and to prove it they began by expressing their gratitude to Bonaparte and proclaimed that "he, Murat, Lefebvre, Gardanne and other generals had served their fatherland well."

On a motion by the lawyer Chazal, a former Girondin—who was saying exactly what he had been told to say by Bonaparte and Sieyès —the new rump parliament passed with total docility the final decree:

> The Corps Législatif creates temporarily a consular executive committee consisting of Citizens Sieyès and Roger Ducos (ex-Directors) and General Bonaparte, who will bear the titles of Consuls of the Republic.

It would be easier for the pill to go down if it were sugar-coated, so Chazal proposed that the deputies' salaries continue to be paid during the "enforced vacation." This proposal was no doubt accepted with enthusiasm.

Outside the door, Bonaparte was waiting impatiently. Fortunately, all that remained to be done was to have the three consuls enter, to a flourish of trumpets, and take an oath of "inviolable loyalty to the sovereignty of the people; to the French Republic—one and indivisible; to equality and liberty; and to the representational system."

Orderlies on horseback had brought to the Parisians in the cafés and the theaters a reassuring declaration drawn up by Fouché. Performances were halted, and in each theater an actor read the following proclamation to the audience:

> The councils were in session at St.-Cloud to deliberate on the interests of the Republic and of liberty when General Bonaparte,

who had entered the Council of the Five Hundred to denounce
"counterrevolutionary" intrigues, narrowly missed being killed
by an assassin. The genius of the Republic saved the general's life;
he is returning with his escort.

As he hurried back toward Paris with his "escort," Bonaparte
overtook hungry troops returning to their barracks in the rain that
fell for most of that night. They were singing the old revolutionary
songs.

The Revolution was nonetheless dead. When the supreme commander's bayonets got into the act to the rolling of drums—something that Mirabeau had foretold more than ten years before—they
finished off the regime.

The way was cleared for Bonaparte.

VIII

THE FIRST CONSUL

There is nothing so difficult
as harnessing a nation that has
shaken off its pack saddle.

NAPOLEON

THE NEXT DAY, Paris awoke under the Consulate.

The 20 Brumaire happened to be a Décadi (the Sunday of the revolutionary calendar); and since the weather was better than it had been the day before, the Parisians—between rain showers—were out strolling, reading the posted announcements, and commenting on the news. No doubt some of them remained defiant; but the majority wore radiant smiles, as though a load had been lifted from them. They could breathe again. And if we can believe newspapers like *l'Ami des Lois*, they "kissed one another in the public squares with an excitement that was almost delirious."

In Mme. Reinhard's words: "The people are ecstatic, and believe they have reconquered liberty."

That night, in spite of the rain and a rather strong wind, all Paris was illuminated. Processions of public officials (commissioners and justices of the peace) and troops, preceded by bands, wound their way through the city to read by torchlight the law that had been passed the night before, creating the Consulate. Speeches were interrupted by shouts of "Vive la République! Vive Bonaparte! Vive la Paix!"

At ten o'clock on the morning of November 11, Bonaparte, wearing civilian clothes (dark gray frock coat, black beaver cap) took his place in a very modest carriage escorted by only six dragoons. It was in this modest carriage that he went to the Luxembourg for his first act as Chief of State. As he neared the palace, a few onlookers cried: "Vive Bonaparte!" He seemed not to have heard them, and gave orders for his carriage to stop in front of the Petit Luxembourg, the residence of Sieyès.

Following Bonaparte's talk to the "abbé," the first meeting of the three consuls took place at noon. Roger Ducos, a former justice of the peace who was a bit surprised to find himself still a chief of state, declared with a bow to Bonaparte: "There's no point in voting on the chairmanship: it rightfully belongs to you."

Sieyès, displeased, said nothing. Cleverly, Bonaparte proposed a rotating chairmanship for periods of twenty-four hours. Alphabetical order enabled him immediately to take the chair for this historic session.

Gaudin, the new minister of finance who had been appointed just that day, found in the Treasury a sum of 67,000 francs in cash which had come from an advance of 300,000 francs made the day before. Meantime, the debt amounted to 64,000,000 francs—not to mention unpaid subscription bonds and unkept promises on government stock receipts. In order to meet the first expenses, the new minister decided he would utilize the sight drafts of persons awarded contracts for lumbering. Incidentally, those drafts would be protested, since no lumber deliveries had been made for three years.

Graft was everywhere. Bonaparte exploded: "What a fine bunch of people!" he exclaimed to Bourrienne. "What a government! What an administration! Can you imagine anything more pathetic than their financial system?"

When Napoleon wanted to send off a courier there wasn't the slightest amount available for his traveling expenses! Then the new consul attempted to ascertain "the exact size of the army." No one could tell him.

"But," he persisted, "you must have rosters at the Bureau of War?"

"What good would they be? There have been so many transfers that we couldn't keep track of."

"But you must at least have pay records that will give us the answer?"

"We haven't been paying them."

"How about the provisions lists?"

"We haven't been feeding them."

"And for the uniforms?"

"We haven't been issuing them."

During this first session Sieyès had heard Bonaparte talk knowledgeably of fiscal matters, of administration, of the army, politics, and laws. He came out of the meeting absolutely astounded, and kept repeating: "Gentlemen, you have a master! That man knows everything, wants everything, and can do everything!"

On November 15, by way of a first step toward the throne, Bonaparte established his living quarters in the Petit Luxembourg, which today is the residence of the presiding officer of the Senate. It was there that the three consuls and the three legislative committees met. The sessions began at nine in the evening and lasted until late at night.

The Consulate kept the right of originating legislation and created a Council of State in charge of developing and drawing up draft laws and the regulations for public administration. The chief thing yet remained: "It was known," said Fouché, "that the government planned by Sieyès was to have an apex, a kind of monarchical summit with a republican base. This was an idea he had been enamored of for a long time. With an attentive and even eager curiosity, we were waiting for him finally to unveil the capital of his constitutional edifice."

Anxious to get rid of the "sword," Sieyès proposed to Bonaparte that it be transformed into a "capital" (on a column); that is, that Napoleon be given the functions of a "Grand Elector" responsible for naming the two consuls, with an annual salary of 6,000,000 francs, a guard of 3,000 men, and Versailles as his residence.

Versailles? "I want to stay in Paris!" Bonaparte exclaimed violently. "This must not be! Rather than that, we'll be in blood up to our knees!"

At this point he could no longer contain himself. "Rising and letting out a burst of laughter, he took the document from Sieyès' hands and with one stroke of the pen demolished what he said in a loud voice were 'metaphysical stupidities.' "

"Do I understand you clearly? You are proposing for me a position in which I will appoint all those who have something to do, and I won't be able to take a hand in anything. . . . That's impossible! I will not play a ridiculous role! Rather nothing than to be ridiculous!"

And again: "How could you have believed, Citizen Sieyès, that a man of honor—a man of talent and some ability in public business— could ever consent to being nothing more than a hog being fattened up on few million francs in the royal château of Versailles?"

The "hog being fattened up" set off general laughter, and the position of Grand Elector was no more.

At the session of December 12 it was decided to create two figure-head consuls: they would be nothing more than the two arms of the First Consul's armchair.

Next came the formal election of the three consuls. A decaliter vessel used as a standard unit of measure took the place of the voting urn. During the voting, Bonaparte stood with his back to the fire-place, keeping warm. At the moment when the votes were to be counted he walked to the table, picked up the ballots, and said gravely to Sieyès: "Instead of counting them, let us once again dem-onstrate our gratitude to Citizen Sieyès by giving him the right to appoint the first three magistrates of the Republic. And let us agree that those he names will be presumed to be those-for whose election we have just voted."

The ballots were quickly burned. The Constitution of the Year VIII was determined. Sieyès eliminated himself (something Bona-parte would later regret); and Roger Ducos, realizing that he wasn't up to the job, resigned. Bonaparte, "appointed" by Sieyès, would himself choose his two satellite assessors.

His first appointment was Jean Jacques Cambacérès, who had been chairman of Public Safety and of whom it was said that he was the best one to add dignity to low dealings. Then Talleyrand advised Bonaparte to name Charles François Lebrun, who in a way stood for what was good from the past—"enlightened despotism" with Vol-tairian sauce.

While Lebrun led a petit-bourgeois kind of life, Cambacérès daz-zled his guests with his royal luxury. Fifty and sixty footmen in blue uniforms with gold braid hovered over him—not to mention numer-ous butlers in silk. An amusing rumor had it that the effeminate second magistrate of the Republic once said: "I used to go and visit the chippies like everyone else. But I never stayed long. As soon as I had finished, I would tell them: 'Adieu, Messieurs!' And I'd leave."

As for the "Citizen and the Citizeness Bonaparte," they lived very simply. There was no pomp and ceremony at the Petit Luxembourg. They were still camping out. The servants had neither uniforms nor gold braid. And there was only one butler—a surprising thing for that era.

Napoleon wanted everyone to get one idea into his head for good: that in these closing days of the eighteenth century he was the master—and the only master—of France.

For its part, *Le Diplomate* announced: "People are attributing to Bonaparte a new and bold revolutionary slogan, as follows: 'Positions are open to all Frenchmen, whatever their opinions, provided they have an education, ability, and virtues.' If this is true, and if he who said it keeps his promise, we are indeed at the end of the Revolution."

The temporary consulate was dissolved, and Bonaparte said the last words about that brief magistracy: "Citizens, the Revolution has been geared to the principles that began it: it is finished."

The brother of Louis XVI, who in his exile had taken the titles of Comte de Lille and Louis XVIII, wrote to the First Consul:

> Now that you have consolidated your power and your abilities, it is time for me to explain myself. It is time for me to tell you of the hopes I have founded on you. . . . If I were writing to anyone other than Bonaparte, I would offer and stipulate rewards. But a great man must himself decide upon his fate and that of his friends. Tell me what you want for yourself, and for them, and the moment of my restoration will be that when your wishes will be granted.

In giving the letter to his favorite, the Duc d'Avaray, "M. le Comte de Lille" had added with a sigh: "It's a high-priced ticket in a lottery that offers little hope."

Although d'Avaray did not succeed in getting the letter to its destination, a later message from Louis XVIII did reach Bonaparte, who answered:

> I have received your letter, Monsieur, and I thank you for the praiseworthy things you said to me. You must no longer hope for a return to France: you would have to walk over 100,000 corpses.

. . . Sacrifice your interests to the peace and happiness of France, and history will give you credit for it. I am not insensitive to the misfortunes of your family! . . . I would take pleasure in contributing to the agreeableness and tranquillity of your retirement.

"If I reinstate the Bourbons," he exclaimed, "they will raise up a statue to me and put my corpse under the pedestal!"

It had been suggested to him that in his capacity of consul he should wear a red cap. But he had replied—and this, too, was a profession of faith—"Neither a red cap nor red heels!" (Under the *ancien régime*, the aristocrats had worn red heels.)

He was the future, and nothing from the past could be suitable for him. Was he already thinking of putting on the crown? George Washington had just died on his beloved estate of Mount Vernon. That is what Bonaparte could become for France: a Washington. At any rate, some people thought so.

If I had been in America [he said later] I would have been glad to be a Washington, and I would have deserved something for it; because I don't see how it would have been reasonable to do otherwise. But if he had been in France, under the dissolution within and the invasion from the outside, I would have defied him to be himself. Or, if he had tried to be, he would merely have been a fool, and would only have perpetuated great misfortunes. As for me, I could only be a crowned Washington.

And it was too bad! Perhaps, for his glory, it might have been better if Bonaparte had never put on the crown. As France proved under the Consulate—which was a leftist government without narrow views—she could very well have lived under the command of an uncrowned Washington. In any case, there could be no question of the future Emperor's assuming the "leftist" crown at that time. In February, 1800, the death of George Washington merely enabled him to address "all the troops of the Republic" and to evoke liberty:·

Washington is dead. That great man fought against tyranny. He consolidated the liberty of his country. His memory will always be dear to the French people and to all free men of the two worlds—and especially to the French soldiers who, like him and the American soldiers, have fought for equality and liberty. Consequently, the First Consul orders that for ten days black crepe be hung on all the flags and pennants of the Republic.

Ten days later (on February 17) the mourning was ended, and Bonaparte—in his first step toward that "tyranny" evoked on the occasion of the death of the great American—decided to take up quarters in the Tuileries. Time and again he went through the château and ordered the whitewashing of the walls, which were covered with revolutionary graffiti and red caps. Bourrienne heard him tell Lecomte, who was then the architect of the Tuileries: "Get rid of all that! I don't want that kind of crap!"

"How melancholy it is here in the Tuileries, General!" Bourrienne remarked.

"Yes," he replied, "as melancholy as greatness."

On February 18, Murat, commanding the Guard of the Consuls, reviewed the troops who were to march on parade the next day for the ceremonies on the occasion of Bonaparte's formal installation in the Tuileries. The uniforms were new even though the men had not been paid for a month.

On that same day, wearing civilian clothes, Bonaparte strolled through Paris, followed by only two officers. At every intersection, to the accompaniment of trumpets and drums, they were announcing the results of the plebiscite approving the new constitution. In the Halles, the announcement was greeted with the revolutionary shout of "Ça ira!" In the more elegant parts of the city—like the Place Vendôme—some were heard to shout: "Long live the King!"

The next morning the sky was unfortunately overcast. In the courtyards of the Tuileries and the Carrousel, 3,000 troops were lined up. They were accompanied by their bands and were commanded by Lannes, Murat, and Bessières. The procession debouched into the Place du Carrousel, which at that time was relatively small and shapeless. Following a piquet of heavy cavalry came the councillors of state, crowded into hired carriages of the kind called *carrosses* by the newspapers of the day, the numbers on these hired hacks having been concealed by strips of paper. Then a military band consisting of 50 musicians, bedizened and decked out in gold braid, made its appearance. After it came the General Staff, on horseback, wearing plumes and tricolor sashes. Then came the ministers (who likewise rode in hired carriages), followed by Bonaparte's escort: cavalrymen wearing busbies and green pelisses with red shoulder knots. Roustam, on a prancing Arabian pony, preceded the consuls. Their carriage, surrounded by escorts and heralded by trumpets, was pulled

by six white horses—a gift sent by Emperor Francis after Campoformio.

A loud shout of "Vive Bonaparte!" resounded.

"As soon as the consul's carriage stopped," Bourrienne reported,
"Bonaparte jumped out and immediately climbed—or rather, leaped
—onto his horse, and reviewed the troops. . . ." After having reviewed the ranks, he took up his stand near the gate to the Tuileries.
When the consul saw, passing in front of him, those flags that were
no longer anything but a staff and a few rags pierced by bullets and
blackened by burned powder, he took off his hat and bowed. This
gesture was greeted by tremendous applause.

That same day—the command was symbolic—he ordered that
the numerous trees of liberty planted in the courtyard be uprooted,
under the pretext that they kept the sunlight from reaching the
living quarters. He also ordered the effacement of the inscription
which, up until that time, one could read on the roundhouse beside
the iron gates of the Carrousel: "On August 10, 1792, royalty was
abolished and will never be reestablished."

Remembering the applause that had greeted him that day, he
said: "The people's joy was genuine; and the people were right. For
that matter, take a look at the great thermometer of public opinion
—the stock market. On 17 Brumaire the high was 11 francs, on the
29th it was 16, and today it is 21! When things are like that, I can
let the Jacobins babble. But they'd better be careful not to talk too
loud!"

Then he added:

> Being in the Tuileries is not everything: what matters is to stay
> here. Just think of all the people who have lived there—brigands
> and *conventionnels* [members of the Constitutional Convention].
> Just look (he said to Bourrienne, looking out through a window of
> the palace), there is your brother's house. It was from there that
> I saw the Tuileries besieged and the good King Louis XVI carried
> off. But don't worry! Just let them come!

What a way he had come in a mere eight years!

The night of February 19th, the first time he went to bed in the
Tuileries, he couldn't resist evoking the past and telling Josephine:
"Come along, little Creole, and lie down in the bed of your masters!"

Those newspapers born of the Revolution affected a disdainful attitude toward the "consular pomp and ceremony," which they maintained was unworthy of a true republican. But there was not yet a court at the Tuileries. Elizabeth Petrovna Divow, a contemporary, wrote:

> When the door opened at ten o'clock and a tipstaff called out, "The First Consul!" I can assure you that if a fly had buzzed in the room it would have been heard. Everyone stood up to greet him, and it was at that moment that I was presented to him. He talked to me in a very amiable way for a few minutes, and then everyone went to the table.

The affair described was a *petit dîner* given in Josephine's apartments; but gatherings of 200 persons were held every ten days in the Galerie de Diane on the second floor. Little by little, Bonaparte got into the habit of going to the table first. Of course dinner was always served on the double-quick. Rarely did it last more than twenty minutes or half an hour.

"If you want to eat quickly," Bonaparte said at that time, "you should come to my apartments. If you want to eat well, go to the Second Consul's; and if you want to eat badly, go to the Third Consul's."

Following the official dinner, those personalities invited to remain afterward went into the salons, and boredom descended upon the Tuileries. A new review, new presentations, new banalities—Bonaparte himself was scarcely amiable. He did, however, take an interest in the dresses worn by his lady guests, but for political reasons. Hortense tells us:

> In order to encourage the manufactures of Lyons and eliminate the payment of any tribute to England, the First Consul prohibited our wearing chiffon and threw into the fire everything he thought was of English manufacture. When my mother and I entered sumptuously dressed, his first question was always: "Is that chiffon you are wearing?" Often we replied that it was linen from St. Quentin, but our smiles would betray us, and he would instantly rip apart the dress of foreign make. This disaster to our clothes happened several times, and we had to have recourse to satin and velvet.

Whether his wife was wearing English chiffon or French velvet, Bonaparte admired her. In her famous yellow salon she moved about gracefully, and she knew how to make his guests comfortable, including those government functionaries and their wives who were often ill at ease there. She was well versed in the hostess's art—that very difficult art she had learned long ago in another era when she was the wife of Alexandre de Beauharnais but separated from him. Bonaparte, who was not yet thinking of creating a dynasty, had given up the idea of separating from a valuable helper who held her own very well in his work of reconstruction. He wanted her to be a kind of queen for the new regime.

"I want you to be richly dressed and dazzlingly got up, do you understand?"

Certainly the "Consuless" didn't have to be asked to get herself up. She nonetheless exclaimed: "Yes, and then you'll make a scene. You'll shout, and you'll strike out the words 'payable' at the bottom of my bills."

And she began to pout, an eyewitness tells us, "like a little girl, making a charming face." At such times it would appear that she was irresistible, and he made no attempt to resist her.

"Yes," he answered, "I do sometimes strike out the words 'payable' because you often let yourself get taken so badly that it is a shame to authorize such abuses. Though I may ask you to be elegant on formal occasions, I am still very consistent. And since there must be a scale to weigh all interests, I use it with a hand that is equitable, although strict."

But it was becoming almost impossible to use that scale so far as his wife's expenses were concerned. At the time her bills amounted to 6,000,000 francs. It was Talleyrand who had spoken to the new master about the detestable impression that might be made on the public by the unpaid bills of France's First Lady. The First Consul's wrath was terrible. But it did not prevent Josephine—to whom Napoleon gave larger and larger sums every year—from continuing to run up staggering bills until her very death. And Fouché, in the mistaken notion that he could find out what was going on "within" the consular family, gave Josephine 1,000 francs a day to spy on her husband.

Bonaparte had not waited for the results of the plebiscite (they were unprecedented results, since the change of regime was approved by 3,012,569 Frenchmen as against only 1,562) to begin re-building France—which, as has been said, was nothing more than a heap of ruins.

As might be suspected, anarchy had by no means ceased with the fall of the Directory. Plunder and pillage frequently assumed the hideous aspect of civil war.

There was trouble, too, with the west of France. Before long, the Bretons and Normans were at bay. One of the Bretons, when he was surrounded, agreed to turn over his cannon and small arms to the First Consul. Bonaparte received this "fat Breton" (as he unjustifiably called him) and tried to win him over to the party of peace. Neither liked the other. "He was a fanatic," said Bonaparte later. "I moved him without succeeding in convincing him. After half an hour I had got no further than at the beginning. He wanted to keep his armed bands and his weapons. I told him that there could not be a state within a state."

Actually, the consul did not succeed in convincing the Chouan (royalist rebel) because the former cadet and gentleman, De Buonaparte, treated this carpenter's son so disdainfully that "Georges" (as everyone called him) was terribly embittered and henceforth could think of only one thing: to get revenge, to stir up the rebellion again, and especially to show what he meant by the words "the essential blow": the assassination of Napoleon. He fled Paris and went to London, later returning to France to give final shape to his plans.

Whereas the weakness of the Directory had obliged that defunct regime to govern by means of shifting the rudder first to the left and then to the right in order to lean on each of the opposing forces in turn, Bonaparte had to muzzle both Royalists and Jacobins almost simultaneously. "I treat politics like war," he would remark later. "I hoodwink one flank so as to trounce the other."

"Considering that most of the Parisian newspapers are in the hands of enemies of the Republic," Napoleon began by clamping down on the Royalist papers. At the outset, those on the extreme left were permitted freedom of action. But the Jacobins did not rest easy. Being former revolutionaries and terrorists whose "too red" past had excluded them from jobs (they were actually called *exclusifs*) they plotted energetically against the First Consul. They, too, were talking of assassinating Bonaparte.

According to a police report, "If on the one hand the Royalists are restless and trying to overthrow the government, it is a demonstrated fact that the anarchists are working toward the same goal by much more expeditious means."

And that was no small matter. The bad news received from the Army of Italy early in Germinal (Savona had been recaptured) enabled a few agitators on both sides to create an atmosphere of panic in Paris: there was talk of arrests of Royalists, of Jacobin plots, of a planned attempt on the life of the First Consul. The speculators were betting on a drop in the market. From improvised platforms put up at intersections, political mountebanks spread false rumors among the onlookers. Pamphlets circulated, their contents shouted out by hawkers. One of them went: "The past has deceived me, the present torments me, and the future terrifies me."

France seemed to have been put up for auction by those responsible for administering the country. And so Bonaparte dictated the following note to Lucien:

> Since 1790 the 26,000 communes in France have been 26,000 orphans—daughters abandoned and plundered by their municipal guardians. . . . In general, the change of mayors, deputy mayors, and councillors was merely a change from one kind of robbery to another. They have plundered the byways, the paths, the trees, the church, and the property of the commune. And they are still stealing under the mask of the municipal government.

The "guardian" of these "abandoned daughters"—the one responsible for putting an end to the robberies—would soon be named: he will be a prefect, he said, who "will inspect his communes at least twice a year."

The important thing was to broadcast, affirm, and repeat that everything would be better—that everything was already better. Bonaparte recommended it to them: "The only way to lead the people is to show them a future: a leader is a dealer in hope."

Little by little, Bonaparte discovered the extent of the disorder. A lack of unity appeared in the most unexpected areas. Although the inhabitants of towns and villages were obliged to observe Décadi as the republican day of rest, the peasants and other country dwellers (far from the gendarmes) preferred Sunday as their day of rest. Prefects everywhere were advised not to offend acquired habits and tastes.

"My policy," said Bonaparte, "is to govern men the way the greatest number want to be governed. That, I believe, is the way to recognize the sovereignty of the people."

And again: "A government should look for its point of support where it can actually be found."

He also needed another "point of support": healthy finances. It wasn't a question of their being in disorder: they simply didn't exist. Poverty evokes a semblance, however minimal, of property. But this was simply a void—and frightful deficit.

A report dated February 24 stated: "The First Consul requests the Minister of Finance to inform him as soon as possible as to who now has the 'Regent.' " This was the famous diamond, which been "mislaid" somewhere among the pawnbrokers of the Directory.

They were still depending on short-term loans at a high rate of interest to survive. They were selling lumber from the park at Versailles; they were converting the metal from bells into money. Bonaparte counted on renewed confidence to bring gold back into the treasury. (It is a well-known fact that gold—a kind of distrustful, timid, and fearful "personage"—hides at the sign of the least danger.) In order to reestablish confidence—in order to have a credit establishment that was quasi-official if not independent—Bonaparte created a Bank of France. (Or rather, he transformed the former Accounts Current Office into that institution.)

To achieve this resurrection—to go back to the undertakings of the first revolutionary assembly—he had to move prudently.

To Mathieu Dumas he explained: "Soon after I took over this job I learned that I had to be careful not to aspire toward all the good that I could accomplish: public opinion would get ahead of me; the underfed horse would soon jump the fence into the rich pasturelands and become unmanageable."

Naturally, the grass was not yet thick and succulent. But the "pasturage," which had been well sown, would sprout. They could already draw up a favorable balance sheet.

Often after eight o'clock in the evening, a stylishly dressed young man would visit the shops on the Rue de l'Arbre Sec or the Rue St.-Honoré (the stores remained open until late). Fingering one corner of his cravat, he would ask in an affected tone of voice: "Your shop seems to be very busy—do many people come here? Tell me: What do they say about that joker, Bonaparte?"

Sometimes the shopkeepers would throw the young man out. How dare he talk so cavalierly about the man who was saving France! And the young man would go away laughing. He seemed delighted —he *was* Bonaparte.

But there were serious matters as well. First Consul Bonaparte was frustrated by his inaction at a time when the war (a war he was not at all responsible for, since it was the heritage of the Revolution) had resumed violently in Italy and was on the point of breaking out again in Germany. On March 15 he wrote to Moreau:

> Today I am a kind of puppet who has lost his freedom and his happiness. Great honors are fine, but only when one imagines or remembers them. I envy your happy lot. Together with brave men, you are going to do admirable things. I would gladly trade my consulary purple for the epaulets of a *chef de brigade* under your orders. I very much hope that circumstances will permit me to come and give you some help.

Moreau, at the head of 100,000 men spread out from Strasbourg to Constance, was indeed in an enviable position. Imagine what Bonaparte could do with an army like that! Unfortunately, the Constitution of the Year VIII prohibited him from taking command of the army. His role was limited to "distributing the armed forces" and "regulating their direction." He could not take up the sword himself. So far as the generals were concerned, the First Consul was obliged to negotiate with them without being able to command them, even from a distance. And the "help" he had mentioned in his letter to Moreau was a piece of bait held out to his old rival. "It may very well come to pass," he had added, "that if things go well here I will be your guest for a few days." But Moreau, when he read those words, pretended to believe that he had been relieved of his command. And he exclaimed: "I don't want any little Louis XIV with my army!"

It was nonetheless agreed that Moreau would cross the Rhine and drive toward Ulm. Meantime Bonaparte, giving up his unsuitable enforced role of "puppet" according to the Constitution, would at the last moment put himself at the head of a reserve army at Dijon whose commander (officially) would be Berthier, replaced by Carnot as Minister of War. This army, the Army of Marengo (since it would be moving on Italy) would be reinforced with one-third of the right flank of Moreau's forces—the 30,000 men under Lecourbe.

The commander of the forces massed on the Rhine would have to yield (and he would even do it gracefully), since in "distributing" the forces of the Republic the First Consul was remaining within the limits of his authority.

Soon, however, the news Bonaparte was getting from Italy became bad. Masséna, opposed by the entire Austrian Army under Melas, had been compelled to abandon Savona and hole up in Genoa with half his forces while the rest of them retreated to Nice. Everything General Bonaparte had built up in Italy seemed lost.

For everyone except the First Consul.

On March 17 Bourrienne found him stretched out flat on a huge map of Italy, sticking his famous red pins into the places to which he would lead his troops. His plan was simple. By crossing the Great St. Bernard Pass, he could attack the enemy's rear. In stupidly "blundering" (as he put it) toward Genoa and Savona, the Austrians had opened the way to upper Italy. It was imperative to get there "at top speed." The reserve army must leave Dijon immediately and set out for Geneva and the Valais.

Unfortunately, Moreau had lost some time. Bonaparte (this was still one of his prerogatives) had vainly sent Berthier to Basel to set things up with the commander of the Army of the Rhine "to carry out the plan for the campaign." The man responsible for the admirable retreat on the Danube in 1796 dragged his feet; and Bonaparte had to have him reprimanded (prudently) by Carnot: "Make him realize that his delays are basically jeopardizing the security of the Republic."

The stubborn Moreau (he was not a Breton for nothing) finally crossed the Rhine. That same day the "impregnable" fortress of Hohenville capitulated; and on May 5, while Bonaparte was preparing to go to inspect "Berthier's army," the news of the victory of Stockach reached Paris. "I was about to leave for Geneva," the First Consul wrote to Moreau, "when the telegraph informed me of the victory you had won over the Austrian Army. Glory, and three times glory!"

That same evening Napoleon went to the Opera, where he had Moreau's victory telegram read aloud. He joined in the applause of the audience.

It was still impossible for the First Consul to admit that he was going to take command. And so, that evening, he told the members of the government: "Say that I am leaving for Dijon, where I am going to inspect the reserve army. You can add that I may perhaps go to Geneva, but say positively that I shall not be absent for more than two weeks."

Then he turned to the Second Consul: "If anything happens, I will return like a thunderbolt! To all of you I recommend the great interests of France. I hope they will soon be talking of me in Vienna and London."

Shortly before dawn, Bonaparte, with his consul's uniform under his long gray greatcoat, got into a black berlin pulled by post horses and set out for Burgundy—"which he had already traveled through so many times under very different circumstances," recalled Bourrienne, who was still with him. The sun was rising, the weather was fine, the sky was clear. Bonaparte, who at first seemed to be asleep, came awake and began to talk volubly. With Bourrienne, it was a heart-to-heart talk: the movement of the Austrians, the fate of Masséna's army, the weakness in numbers of the reserve army, the crossing of the Alps—so many subjects for anxiety.

He had lunch at Sens at eleven o'clock, and that evening he reached Avallon, having covered 208 kilometers in fifteen hours. An officer, Major Frenceschi, who had just come from Genoa, was waiting for Napoleon. On April 28 he had managed to leave the port (blockaded by an English cruiser) in a small boat.

He gave the First Consul a report on the situation as of nine days before: it was tragic. The 50,000 Austrians commanded by Melas had besieged Genoa, defended by 15,000 starving Frenchmen who had become veritable ghosts, while an enemy squadron prevented any supplies from reaching them by water.

By the time of Frenceschi's departure they were already making starch bread, and "mercenaries were pulling up the grass that had grown in the cemeteries to put it into the mortar with whitened bones." But Masséna still refused to consider capitulating.

Saddened and anxious, Bonaparte went to bed. Early in the morning of May 7 he left Avallon. The sights he saw along the road were hardly calculated to console him. For lack of transportation, laggards belonging to demi-brigades that were supposed to go to Dijon were stumbling along or stretched out by the roadside. At noon, when

Bonaparte reached the prefecture of Dijon, Berthier withdrew from his command and took up his functions as chief of staff.

At three o'clock in the morning of May 9 Bonaparte reached Geneva, which had become the *chef-lieu* of the Département du Leman, where he lodged with the son of the naturalist Horace Bénédict de Saussure. His host had a cold meal prepared for him, and he ate it "in a gay mood." But he was still anxious. He distrusted Moreau, being familiar with his delays, his jealousy, and his urge for independence, which would perhaps become more pronounced following his victory at Stockach. He was distinctly annoyed when he remembered how long it had taken Moreau to set his troops into motion.

Nor did Bonaparte have any confidence in Bernadotte, who had been given command of the Army of the West. The news from the Vendée was hardly good. The *département* of the Alpes-Maritimes had been invaded. The Austrians were occupying the Pass of Tende. As for Masséna, he did not dare think of the tragedy he was living through! And that was not all. Napoleon was well aware of the great number of enemies—Jacobins and Royalists, or mere intriguers—that he had left behind in Paris during his absence; and the weakness of his ministers and his two colleagues gave him reason for fear.

Nor was Bonaparte unaware of the way the Austrians were talking about his "reserve army." To wit: "The cavalry is riding mules; the infantry consists of crippled old men and children armed with sticks tipped by a bayonet; and the artillery consists of two one-pound blunderbusses."

He needed a victory! A victory on which he could pin everything: his own future and that of France.

Late in the afternoon of May 12 Bonaparte reached Lausanne. At six the next morning, near St. Maurice du Valais, he inspected Jean Lannes' infantry which, after the vanguard, was preparing to set out for St. Bernard. The rain that had been falling for a week had let up. The sun was shining.

He doubtless felt a twinge when he saw the equipment of the army which was about to assault the Alps. Some of its men were wearing wooden shoes; others had new shoes, issued at Dijon, which hurt so much they preferred not to wear them. So they had formed battalions of "barefoots" who, according to the custom, hoped to get shoes for themselves from the corpses as soon as the first battle took place. In the meantime they had to cross the Great St. Bernard.

When Bonaparte got back to Lausanne he was given word by an officer who had left Genoa on April 29 and had just arrived. Needless to say, the situation had worsened since the departure of Major Frenceschi: "Along the streets and boulevards, men staggered at each step. From one doorway to another, haggard women dragged themselves along, begging bread. In the light of the torches lighted in the evening, the corpses thrown onto the garbage heaps were an indescribable sight."

"Go back and tell Masséna," said Bonaparte, "that you saw me near St. Bernard. In a short time, Italy will be reconquered and Genoa will be liberated."

As the days went by, fear descended upon Paris. Bonaparte's absence created real anguish. Of course no one was deceived, and everyone knew that he had gone off "as fast as he could to bring help to the Army of Italy." But would he arrive in time to help Masséna? If he didn't, or if he was defeated, chaos would reign. The Royalists regained hope, rejoiced, and began to plot again in earnest. Alliances were already being formed. Former Thermidorians and malcontent Brumaireans (like Sieyès) were planning, each of them, for a "substitute government" in case "he" returned defeated. As intrigues multiplied, even Joseph Bonaparte refused to go to the Tuileries. He proclaimed himself "presumptive heir" and did not want to "work with the consuls." He was certain that Cambacérès and Lebrun were by no means qualified for their posts.

Balzac was on solid ground when later on, in *Une ténébreuse affaire,* he had one of his characters say, apropos of Bonaparte: "If he is a conqueror, we will adore him. If he is a loser, we will bury him."

IX

MARENGO, OR THE CONSECRATION

OF THE REGIME

Unavoidable wars are always just.

NAPOLEON

AT MARTIGNY, a little town ensconced in the valley of the Rhône at the foot of the range of the Great St. Bernard, the house of the Bernardins still exists—facing the apse of the parochial church, surrounded by chestnut trees. It is the residence of the Father Superior of the Congregation and a rest house for the monks of the famous hospice of the Pass, who struggle (with the help of their dogs) to save lost travelers. On the morning of May 17, 1800 Bonaparte was welcomed by monks in black cassocks decorated with a white cord derived from the surplice of regular monks.

He went up the four low steps that led to the narrow doorway, above which was a glassed-over impost in the form of a semicircle. The architecture was similar to that which Napoleon would see at the hospice: vaulted ceilings with ogival windows, thick walls, gray-blue flagstones.

The room where Bonaparte spent four days—a room with four windows looking out over the tree-shaded square—is still there, although it has been repainted and wainscoted. Today it serves as a refectory.

As soon as he was settled, Bonaparte laid out on a table the maps of the Valais and the Piedmont, and on them he arranged a large number of dice representing the positions of the demi-brigades and regiments. Bourrienne watched him mark out with heavy strokes of his blue pencil those obstacles—natural or artificial—that the troops would encounter before emerging onto the plain.

For two years a small French post had occupied the St. Bernard

Pass at a height of 2,472 meters. Two cannons were trained on the valley of Aosta, compelling the respect of the little Austro-Sardinian garrison. The troops were commanded by the Prince de Rohan. When it was learned that republican troops held the narrow part of the pass, the garrison moved up to occupy the village of St.-Rémy— the first village on the other side of the pass.

Lannes' advance guard, coming from the direction of Switzerland through icy blasts of wind and threatened avalanches, was already moving up toward the hospice.

"We are fighting against ice, snow, torrents, and avalanches. The Great St. Bernard, astonished at seeing so many men crossing it so abruptly, is putting up a few obstacles against us." It was in these terms that Bonaparte announced to his two figurehead colleagues the beginning of a new epic: his repetition of Hannibal's exploit. It was not done, however, on a prancing horse and almost balanced on a rock (as shown by David in his painting of the event), but—more modestly—on a mule.

At the hospice, the good monks had obtained from the two valleys an ample provision of cheese, bread, and wine. Tables were set up between the hospice and the road. Each soldier, as he passed by, drank a glass of wine, took some bread and cheese, and then quickly made room for the man following him.

In three days, 30,000 men—slipping, falling, and getting up again —would climb up these hopelessly bad roads, which above a certain altitude were filled in with snow. About 100 cannons and thousands of cases of provisions also had to be taken over the pass. And it was soon discovered that even when ten mules were hitched up in single file to one vehicle, the ice, the snow, and the overflowing torrents made the operation impossible. It was then that a peasant spoke up:

> "When I was a boy I heard from an old corporal who had fought many battles in Italy that in order to get a cannon across the mountain the first thing you had to do was take the whole thing apart. Then you get a thick pine tree trunk, and round off the ends so it won't stick in the ground. You hollow it out like a trough so you can put the cannon parts in it, and drive in spikes to fasten the ropes to. Then you hitch up men or burros, and it goes along just fine, they say."

And that is what they did.

The gun sponges, jacks, and accessories were likewise placed in trunks hollowed out like a trough and pulled by thirty men. The gun carriages required twenty men, while the wheels were carried on muleback or by the men themselves (ten for each wheel). It was a nightmare for the men and sheer torture for the beasts of burden; but the army and its equipment made it—through blizzards and blasts of icy wind.

Finally, on May 18, a courier brought good news to Martigny: Lannes, at the head of the vanguard, which had gone beyond the hospice, had occupied the town of Aosta, defended by a handful of Austrian Croats. Napoleon conveyed this news to Talleyrand, saying: "Not since Charlemagne had the Great St. Bernard seen such a big army. Above all, it wanted to oppose the crossing of our heavy field artillery. But at length half of our artillery is at Aosta."

But the "rush" of the vanguard was suddenly held up by the resistance of the Fort of Bard, which dominated the steep slopes of the Doire Valley from the summit of Mount Albaredo, and was manned by only 200 Austrians. This citadel, whose guns commanded the passage toward Ivrea and the plain, seemed impregnable. "Attempt the impossible, but get through!" Bonaparte ordered Berthier.

Today the highway, which has been cut through the stone, passes to the right of the huge rock on top of which the fort was built. The old highway (which still exists as a country road) goes through the village. It is bordered by two rows of gray houses that are crouched in a fault between the base of the rock and that of the mountain. It rejoins the present-day highway at Donnaz, the next village, three kilometers farther on.

It was over this road—littered with straw so they would not make noise and alert the enemy—that a small part of the artillery sneaked at night. Hearing the faintest of sounds, the Austrians (Croatian recruits) did indeed send down a hail of projectiles onto the village from the fort. And noticing the stratagem of the French, they illuminated the pass at night with flares. At this, the infantry climbed up Mount Albaredo—using a frightful path that rose straight up, or sometimes steps carved into the rock—to the mountain's summit overlooking the fort. But the greater part of the artillery and the cavalry were unable to get through.

At eight o'clock on the morning of May 20, wearing his gray

uniform coat, Bonaparte left the monastery of the Bernardins and set out on the road, which begins to climb the moment it leaves the village. Following him in a char-à-banc with Father Terretaz was an Alpinist and a learned botanist, Murith (he would later become provost, but was then canon of the hospice), who had come down from the pass the day before. They went along the Dranse, with its many rapids. When the gorge became narrower, the route crossed and recrossed the torrent via little wooden bridges.

At St.-Pierre they seemed to enter into another world: that of the summits. Ever thicker snow covered the ground. At one point Napoleon became impatient and urged his mule on too fast, with the result that he almost fell, mule and all, into the abyss of the Dranse. He was unseated; but fortunately the guide caught him in time and pulled him back into the saddle with a firm hand.

It began to grow cold and windy, and Bonaparte buttoned his coat up around his neck. The climb was hard going, and the dragoons got off their horses and walked, leading their mounts by the bridle. The road, which by this time was entirely covered with snow, was becoming narrower and narrower.

Bonaparte scarcely looked at the admirable landscape. He seemed sad and taciturn, astounded that no courier had come from the valley of Aosta to bring him news of the capture of Fort Bard, which was still holding up the vanguard in its march toward the plain.

Abruptly, the massive hospice came into view, nestled in the hollow of the pass and virtually wedged in between Switzerland and Italy. At that time it was a two-story building. It had been built on the site of an old temple of Jupiter, and some of the stone ruins of that temple may have been used in its construction.

Father Murith, urging on his mule, went ahead of Bonaparte and introduced the monks to him when he arrived. The Consul went up the few steps that had not yet been covered with snow and entered the hospice.

Bonaparte asked that a room be put at his disposal. It was a low, vaulted room with a wood fire crackling in the fireplace. He dictated a few orders after having had bad news from Berthier: the vanguard was still being held up by the fort at Bard. The Consul did not understand why. But he would, a few days later, when he himself saw how the fort blocked the valley with its great mass.

Toward six o'clock they started down the other side of the mountain, and by nine that night they were halfway down. In the morning they continued on toward Aosta. The valley was pleasant to gaze upon, and the trees were in blossom. The soldiers of the reserve army did not feel homesick: everyone in the valley spoke French, as they still do today.

The next day, while the rear guard was crossing the pass in its turn, Bonaparte reached the old town of Aosta and stayed at the bishop's palace. On the morning of May 25 he left to rejoin Berthier, who was at Verrès, some 40 kilometers away. The road to Turin now followed the valley bottom, which was intersected by rocky passes and covered with vines growing on trellises and supported by columns of stone or hewn wood. At Verrès, Bonaparte learned that the Fort of Bard was still holding out. The infantry, overcoming a thousand obstacles, had managed to take a path across the mountain and reach the valley on the other side of the pass. But the artillery was still immobilized in front of the fort. Intent upon seeing the situation for himself, the First Consul continued on his way.

Abruptly, the Fort of Bard loomed up before him: several thick, squat buildings of gray stone superimposed upon one another and pierced with loopholes, the whole crowning a huge rock that seemed to have tipped down from the summit of Mount Albaredo. With its towering bulk, it closed off the valley, forming an obstacle which even today seems impassable. Bonaparte ordered the few troops accompanying him to set out at a gallop for a little goat path to the left of the "wretched castle" that led to the top of Mount Albaredo. He climbed the path on foot. When he reached the plateau overlooking the fort from nearby, he concealed himself behind the brushwood to avoid being shot at by the besieged troops, and examined the fort very closely. The outworks, connected by underground galleries to advance batteries of which sixteen were of big caliber, were protected by enclosures, moats, drawbridges, towers, and roundhouses. In the fort, Captain Bernkopf commanded a garrison of 350 to 400 Sardinians and Croats.

It was imperative to reduce this fortress. Bonaparte chose a site for the emplacement of a new battery to bombard a precise point and "guaranteed that with the first salvoes from the cannons the fort would surrender."

But it was not that simple. The first three columns of grenadiers and riflemen who, with Bonaparte watching, rushed to assault the fort were repulsed with heavy losses. The batteries, however, were finally emplaced (under a cloudburst) at the site designated by Bonaparte; and the next day, by way of prelude to the imminent surrender, a terrible bombardment shook the fort.

Bonaparte left on June 1 for Novara. The next day abounded in good news. At Turbingo, he learned of the fall of Fort Bard. Then a courier sent by Murat reported that the citadel of Milan had capitulated. Napoleon immediately decided that his entry into the capital of Lombardy should be worthy of the event, which was a considerable one. He would make his appearance not as a general but as Chief of State.

An old dilapidated stagecoach that had belonged to the Marchese del Monte was discovered. It was repaired; six white horses were hitched up to it; and on June 2 the equipage drew up before the Hôtel de la Couronne de la France. Bonaparte got in, and the carriage set out for Milan. But a terrible rainstorm suddenly broke out, and they had to stop. As the rain came through the roof of the carriage, the occupants sought refuge in a farmhouse.

They got under way again when the rain lessened, but another downpour then came through the roof, meantime transforming into muddy water spaniels the troops of the escort and the gilded and plumed officers of the general staff who were following on horseback. When the Milanese saw this spectacle—so far removed from General Bonaparte's triumphal entry in 1797—they were hardly inclined to wax enthusiastic and acclaim the republicans: all the more so since they feared a victorious return of the Austrians. Kept in line by Murat's cavalrymen, the crowd remained mute; and when Napoleon reached the archducal palace, he did not bother to conceal his rage.

Gradually, however, confidence returned. The general staff organized a soiree at La Scala, where the applause was produced on command, together with the inevitable bouquet of flowers and the shouts of "Long live Bonaparte! Long live the liberator of Italy!" And the second *Bulletin* of the Reserve Army was able to announce: "The people of Milan seem very much inclined to resume the tone of gaiety they had during the time of the French. The commanding general, Berthier, and the First Consul attended a concert which, although improvised, was very pleasant. . . ."

This concert (on June 3) was all the more "pleasant" since it provided an opportunity for Bonaparte to hear the famous soprano Giuseppina Grassini, whom he had already met during his first stay at Milan. At that time, however, being still very much in love with Josephine, he had paid no attention to the singer's extraordinarily beautiful face. This time, he was so well disposed toward her that the diva was astonished and reminded him "that she had made her debut at precisely the same time as the first exploits of the general commanding the Army of Italy."

At that time [she told him] I was in the finest flush of my beauty and my talent. No one talked of anything but me in *The Virgin of the Sun*. I captivated everyone's eyes, I inflamed everyone's heart. You alone remained indifferent; and yet it was you alone that I was thinking of. How bizarre, and how odd! When I was worth something, when all Italy was at my feet, when I heroically disdained it for a single glance from you, I could not win that glance. And now you are showering glances on me—at a time when I am no longer worth the trouble, when I am no longer worthy of you!

Signorina Grassini underestimated her charms (she was twenty-seven years old): for the Consul, the soprano with the golden voice certainly was "worth the trouble." Indeed, when Berthier came into Bonaparte's room the next morning, he found the First Consul, all smiles, having breakfast with the prima donna, who was smiling too.

That same day, Napoleon called a meeting of 200 Milanese priests. In a state of stupefaction, they heard the First Consul of that French Republic, which was still considered atheistic, declare to them:

I wanted to see all of you gathered together here so that I might have the satisfaction of informing you personally of the feelings I have about the Catholic, Apostolic, and Roman religion. Being convinced that this religion is the only one that can secure true happiness for a well-ordered society and strengthen the foundations of good government, I assure you that I will bend my efforts to protect it and defend it at all times and by all means.

And the man who had just spent the night in the arms of Signorina Grassini added: "No society can exist without morality. Therefore, it is only religion which can provide a strong and enduring support for the State."

On the evening of June 6, Bonaparte was plunged into gloom by bad news brought by the young first lieutenant Marbot: Masséna had been compelled to capitulate. The son of General Marbot (who had just died of typhus at Genoa) gave Bonaparte a horrifying account of the last days of the siege: "Typhus had worked horrible ravages; the hospitals had become hideous charnel houses; misery was at its worst. Almost all the horses had been eaten. . . ." In short, Masséna had had to open the gates of the city. But the enemy—Admiral George Keith —had declared: "General, your defense has been too heroic for us to deny you anything!"

"It was therefore agreed," continued Marbot, "that the troops of the garrison would not be made prisoners; that they would keep their arms; that they would go to Nice; and that, the day following their arrival there, they might take part in the hostilities."

Actually, these conditions were not bad. Moreover, Piacenza had just been taken. But the First Consul, victorious in the north and beaten in the south, had to have a decisive victory. He was not unaware that in Paris the news of the entry into Milan would be eclipsed by the cruel loss of Genoa. He needed not only a victory but a speedy one, since the 20,000 troops who had been besieging Genoa would soon be swelling the forces of Melas.

June 12 was a red-letter day: Bonaparte's friend General Desaix arrived. The First Consul was closeted with him for three hours. When Bourrienne expressed his surprise at the length of the audience, Bonaparte replied: "Yes, I spent a long time with him, but you know I think highly of him. As soon as I get back to Paris, I shall make him Minister of War. He will always be my second-in-command. I would make him a prince if I could. To my way of thinking, he has a personality straight from antiquity."

The next day, Bonaparte entrusted Desaix with the command of two divisions. At ten o'clock that same morning, he reached San Giuliano and noticed, in the middle of the plain stretching out before Alessandria, the little village of Marengo. It was situated between the road to Tortona, lined with mulberry trees, and a stream: the Fanta-none. Bonaparte seemed perplexed. While the rain fell in torrents, he climbed to the top of the tower of San Giuliano to observe the countryside. There he realized that Marengo—the village after which the battle of the morrow would be named—was the key to the situation. After having shown surprise that the enemy had not provided for a better defense of the village, he came down from his observation post and had a brushwood fire started so that he could dry himself. Then he went to Torre-di-Galofoli to spend the night.

Before going to bed he sent a staff officer on a reconnoitering mission to find out whether the Austrians had thrown a bridge over the Bormida, which before debouching into the Tanaro, downstream from Alessandria, made many meanders between the city and Marengo. The aide-de-camp soon returned to report that there was no bridge. Freed of anxiety, Bonaparte fell asleep. But he had extended his forces too far: Desaix had headed for Novi and crossed back over the Po.

The next morning, Napoleon was awakened by a barrage: the Austrians had marched out of Alessandria, thrown two bridges over the Bormida, and were emerging onto the plain!

Bonaparte's wrath was frightful. He accused the unfortunate officer of cowardice: no doubt fear had prevented him from proceeding far enough to carry out his mission and discover the enemy's preparations. In great haste, Napoleon sent these lines to Desaix: "I thought I was going to attack the enemy, but he has moved first. In the name of God, come back—if you still can!"

Troubled, even anxious, he jumped on his horse. Certainly the situation was not promising. And on that June 14 he was going to risk everything! He had only 15 cannons, whereas Melas had got about 100 across the river by means of those damned bridges!

The battle was soon raging. The Austrian artillery was seven times stronger than that of Bonaparte. The French infantry soon had to retreat under the thrust of 40,000 Austrians. Ammunition ran short. Decimated, the French army had to fall back from the imperial forces. From the top of the bell tower of San Giuliano, affecting a serenity that was not in his heart, Bonaparte ordered the Consular Guard into the fray. The mounted grenadiers, in resplendent uniforms, charged at the gallop and threw the enemy cavalry into a rout. "Ah! That gave us a breather!" the grenadier Coignet recounted. "That gave us confidence for an hour!"

The Baron de Melas fought fiercely. He, too, was wagering his entire future. If he was beaten, he would have to capitulate! The Austrians showed themselves to be admirable (Napoleon would say so on St. Helena) and resumed the offensive vigorously. When the

brief respite was over, Coignet and his comrades were still retreating
—but in good order.

It was noon. Melas had already sent a herald of victory to Vienna.
Coignet recalled:

> Looking behind us we saw the Consul sitting on the levee
> beside the Alessandria road, holding his horse by the bridle and
> flicking little stones with his riding crop. He paid no attention to
> the shot falling on the road. When we drew near, he got on his
> horse and set off at a gallop behind our ranks. "Courage, soldiers!"
> he said. "Reinforcements are on the way. Hold fast!"
> The soldiers shouted "Vive Bonaparte!" But the plain was
> strewn with dead and wounded, since there hadn't been time to
> pick them up. We had to attack on all sectors. The echelon fire
> from the battalions in the rear had been holding them in check;
> but it was hard getting those damned cartridges into our rifle bar-
> rels. We had to piss in them first to clean them out, and that took
> time. "The battle is as good as lost," our officers said. . . .

Bonaparte's staff, which was then gathered around him, made no
attempt to conceal their anxiety. Even Desaix, who at that moment
reached the field of battle with 8,000 fresh troops, kept repeating:
"The battle is lost!" But he added: "It's only two o'clock. We still have
the time to win a battle today. Here I am. We are fresh, and if
necessary we'll get ourselves killed."

The Consul issued orders to Berthier that would hopefully enable
his troops to assume the offensive and transform the retreat into an
attack. The Austrians, sure of their victory, had already trimmed
their shakos with leaves and were advancing arm on shoulder "as if
on their way home." They no longer paid any attention to the
French, whom they thought to be in full retreat.

But Bonaparte's soldiers were in fact regaining their courage.
They had just seen the troops brought by Desaix, in serried ranks,
reach the battlefield. They were marching calmly, in no hurry, "like
a forest swayed by the wind," the artillery in the intervals between
the demi-brigades, and a regiment of heavy cavalry bringing up the
rear. The enemy, more and more assured, seemed to be trying to pass
them without noticing them, when (in Coignet's words), ". . . a thunderbolt struck the head of their column. . . . Grapeshot, shells, and
battalion fire rained down on them, and the charge was sounded

everywhere! Everybody about-faced and rushed ahead! Our men didn't shout—they roared. . . ."

At two o'clock, all had been desolation and anguish. It had seemed a defeat—and perhaps the end of Bonaparte and his good luck. At five, victory had "once again proven faithful to the flag of Arcole," making eyes sparkle and filling hearts with joy. Bonaparte had conquered Italy for the second time. But Desaix had disappeared. He had fallen near San Giuliano. Marching at the head of the Ninth Light Demi-Brigade, he had taken a bullet in the chest. If the legend is to be believed, he murmured: "Go and tell the First Consul that I die regretting that I did not do enough for posterity."

For a long time, the aide-de-camp Savary looked for his body among the dead. Finally, he recognized his general because of his long hair. He wrapped the body in a hussar's cloak and had it taken to headquarters.

Bonaparte, badly upset, was heard to sigh: "Why am I not allowed to weep for him?"

That same evening, he wrote to the other consuls: "I shall soon be in Paris. There is nothing more I can tell you right now. I am terribly afflicted by the death of the man I loved and esteemed above all others."

The next morning at four o'clock, some Austrian negotiators emerged from Alessandria and came to ask for an armistice. Bonaparte granted it, on condition that they immediately evacuate Mantua, the entire Piedmont, and Lombardy. And he specified that the artillery in the strongholds would have to be handed over as well.

"I hope the French people will be pleased with its army," Napoleon wrote from Milan. The good news came at a good time. The most pessimistic rumors had been bruited about the capital. There had been talk of a "terrible defeat" and the death of "a great leader." The government seemed overwhelmed. Mme. Danjou wrote to d'Avaray, the companion of Louis XVIII, to say that the consuls and ministers had met in order to determine who would replace Bonaparte if he was dead or captured—"which seemed very probable and synonymous."

The two other consuls were in "the greatest anxiety," and were wondering what kind of face they would wear on 2 Messidor (June 22), on the occasion of the bimonthly reception for the diplomatic corps. Happily, that same day, beginning at eleven o'clock, first one courier, then a second, then a third, arrived with the news of the brilliant victory of Marengo—which, as it happens, the *Moniteur* spelled "Maringo."

Delirious joy reigned. As a police report tells us:

> Beginning at noon, with the first salvo from the cannons, most of the workmen left their jobs and gathered in the streets and squares to listen avidly to the news. Crowds of them assembled to read the placards that the Prefect of Police (on orders from the government) had put up in the city, and especially in the faubourgs. Shouts of "Vive la République!" and "Vive Bonaparte!" were followed by some very racy remarks and some very gay jokes. In the faubourgs, they were struck by the government's frankness in reporting the number of men lost or taken prisoner. "It's not like the old days," they said. "Now, at any rate, we know everything."
>
> The cabarets were full until eleven o'clock at night. And not one glass of wine was drunk except to the Republic, the First Consul, and the armies.

On the morning of July 3, the cannon announced to the Parisians that the conqueror had come back to the Tuileries during the night. The crowd immediately went on a rampage. A human sea beat up against the château. They shouted for the First Consul, and he appeared on the balcony, while the Guard's band struck up the music. Long shouts of enthusiasm reached his ears. Bonaparte took Bourrienne by the arm: "Do you hear that? Those shouts are as sweet to me as Josephine's voice."

But his joy could have been more complete. It had been dampened when he learned that plans had been made for someone to succeed him, on the assumption that he had been killed in combat.

> *Eh bien*, they thought I was dead, and they tried the Committee of Public Safety business again! . . . I know everything! . . . And those were men I had saved—men I had spared! Do they think I'm a Louis XVI? Just let them dare, and they'll see! Let no one be mistaken: for me, a battle lost is a battle won . . . I fear nothing. I'll send all those ingrates and traitors back to the dust. . . . I'll save France despite the sedition-mongers and bunglers. . . .

Letizia Bonaparte; miniature by Bourgeois from the Musée Carnavalet, 1789. *Madame Mère* "that rare woman, and one can well say, of a character unique in France . . ." *Collection Plon-Perrin*

La Casa Bonaparte at Afaccio; painting by Alexandre Dalige de Fontenay, August, 1795. The second story was occupied by a cousin, Marie Bossi, the wife of Antonio Pozzo di Borgo. It was she who one day inadvertently threw dirty water from her window on Madame Letizia ——— which began a long, indeed perma-

Bonaparte; plaster medallion, 1794. One of the few portraits of the "learned captain" Bonaparte; an anonymous work done in 1793. *Collection Plon-Perrin*

Bonaparte and the Pasha of Cairo. Bonaparte wore the oriental robe which Bourrienne describes for only one day . . . but a watercolorist had the time to do this unexpected portrait of the future emperor whom the Egyptians called the Great Sultan, the sultan *El Kebir. Collection Josse Lalance*

Josephine; pencil drawing. "The dearest Victoria." *Collection Plon-Perrin*

Crossing the Grand St. Bernard Pass in May of 1800; from the Louvre. This picture illustrated a text written by Bonaparte: "A simple tree, hollowed out in the form of a trough, in which were laid eight pounders and howitzers; a hundred men yoked themselves to it, dragging it, and worked for two days to get it over the Saint Bernard Pass." *Collection Plon-Perrin*

Napoleon, a study for the Coronation by David, November, 1804, from the
Musée Frédéric Masson. This person, dressed only in a sword and crown of
laurels, represents Napoleon, drawn by David as a sketch for his famous
painting. The painter similarly undressed all the principal people of his
composition. *Collection Plon-Perrin*

Napoleon, arriving at the foot of Zuran hill which looked out over the future battlefield of Austerlitz, receives some Moravian peasants at the site of the Emperor's bivouac, December, 1805; painting by

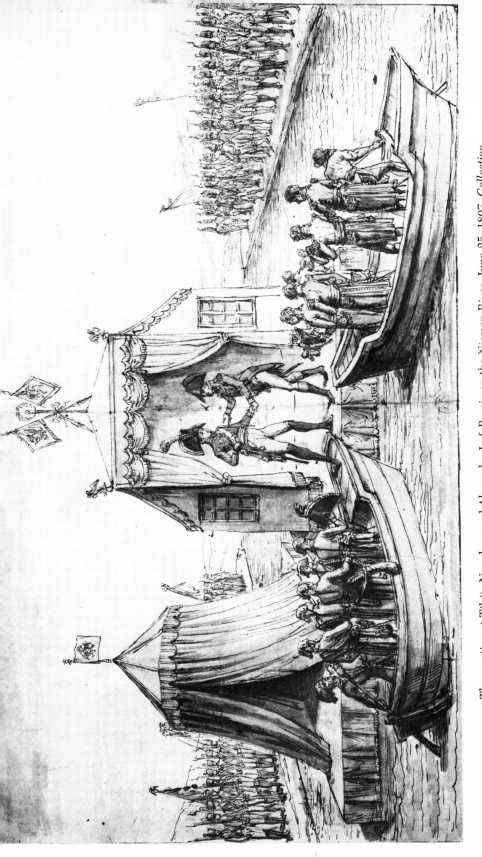

The meeting at Tilsit: Napoleon and Alexander I of Russia on the Nieman River, June 25, 1807. *Collection Plon-Perrin*

The Russian Campaign: a campsite at Ghyacz, September 2, 1812. *Collection Plon-Perrin*

Moscow burns and the fire threatens the Kremlin. Napoleon flees through a small gate leading over the Moscova; engraving by Schmidt after Oldendorp. *Collection Plon-Perrin*

His majesty, the King of Rome, on horseback; engraving, 1813. *Collection Plon-Perrin*

The baptism of Napoleon II, King of Rome; engraving by Alix after Rousseau, Château de Vois-Preaux. *Collection Josse Lalance*

Napoleon in the park at the château of Malmaison, the favorite residence of
the Emperor and Empress; after Isabey. *Collection Plon-Perrin*

Marie Walewska; portrait by David, 1814, from the collection of Comte d'Ornano. *Collection Josse Lalance*

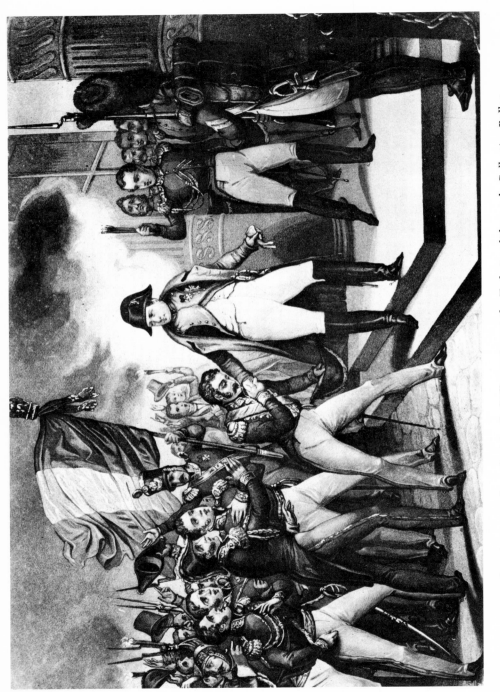

Napoleon, returning from the island of Elba, arrives at the Tuileries; lithograph. *Collection Bulloz*

Portrait of Napoleon toward the end of his life; a copy of this painting has been hung in a hall of Plantation-house, the residence of the governors of Saint Helena. *Collection Roger Viollet*

The Emperor's tomb at the Invalides; Napoleon lies with his head in the direction of Place Vauban; designed by Visconti. *Carte Postale Chantal, Editions Chantal*

The tone was no longer that of Bonaparte: it was already that of the Emperor.

Two days later, in the bright sunlight of Messidor, all Paris went to the Carrousel for the now-traditional military parade of Quintidi. Precisely at noon, Bonaparte appeared under the porch of the château, behind a Mameluke holding a bow. A tremendous ovation was heard. Simply dressed, in a gray uniform, he mounted a white horse caparisoned in orange-red velvet. Behind him was a splendid retinue of aides-de-camp in plumes and gold braid. "None of the portraits resemble him," wrote Charles Nodier, who saw him in this glory. "It is impossible to depict the character of his face, but it is overwhelming. . . . It is very long, with a stone-gray complexion, and the eyes are deep-set. . . ."

It was a fine day (64 degrees at noon), with only a few clouds in the blue sky. In accordance with the custom established since Ventôse, Bonaparte took his place across from the château, at the spot where the lesser Arc de Triomphe now stands. While the military band played its slow and solemn marches, the troops filed past—a symphony of blue uniforms, yellow buff belts, red epaulets, white leggings, vermilion plumes, and tall grenadier's caps. His gaze "glittering like crystal," Bonaparte watched these men with whom he was going to conquer Europe.

It was the night of July 14, after the games and entertainments, when Paris was given over to demonstrations of joy, illuminations, orchestras playing, and fireworks. In the Tuileries the First Consul raised his glass "to the 14th of July, to the French people, the sovereign of us all." And 500 guests responded in one voice: "Vive Bonaparte!"

Marengo had engendered a Caesar and a dictatorship. But it was a dictatorship that enabled Bonaparte to impose the Concordat and the Civil Code, to attract émigrés back to their country, to channel gold quite naturally toward the coffers of the state (from which it had strayed), and at the same time to re-create abundance.

Convalescence would lead to a cure. Trust was reborn. On August 13, to their great surprise, the rentiers—who since the Revolution had received only "papers"—were apprised of the following decree, which proved to them that Bonaparte's government kept its promises: "Dating from the second half of the Year VIII, the government bonds and pensions will be redeemed in cash."

Te Deums were heard all over France. The reports are unanimous: the provincial towns decked themselves out in flags and demonstrated their enthusiasm to the sound of salvoes of cannon. Even the Vendée seemed overjoyed by this event, which seemed pregnant with peace.

And yet it would not be true to say that the enthusiasm was universal: too many Royalists and Jacobins considered Marengo a catastrophe, since it consolidated the coup d'état of Brumaire. Although France was emerging from convalescence, the royalist drama had not yet been played out.

At the gates of Paris, it was not unusual to encounter citizens more or less well disguised and provided with false papers who were slipping into the capital clandestinely. These people were émigrés braving the terrible decree passed by the Directory in the days following the events of Fructidor—a decree which was still in effect and which condemned to death any émigré apprehended on the territory of the Republic.

Bonaparte studied the question—"one of the great wounds of the state," in his phrase. From now on, permission to reenter France would be granted to "relatives or heirs of émigrés, wives who had followed their husbands, artisans and farmers, and persons working for hire." Obviously, there was no question of restoring property to the "repatriates": those who had acquired national property could relax. Pending the amnesty of April 26, 1802, which permitted the return of all émigrés who desired it, more than 50,000 persons could reenter the country. Those returning from exile told of their fears—even their terror—upon drawing near to the first French post. How would the republicans receive the *ci-devant* (people of the Old Regime)? Mme. de Boigne, who came back to France a short time later, has told how, with pounding heart, she entered the customs office. She stood erect in front of the employee who, very slowly, was writing out a description of her. At this point the official in charge stepped up. "Just write 'Pretty as an angel.' That will make it shorter, and Madame won't get so tired."

Abruptly, Mme. De Boigne felt that she was back home.

The rebirth of the "ordered world" had begun. The "repatriates" looked fearfully at one another "like people who had escaped a shipwreck and found themselves on a desert island." Little by little, the First Consul's attitude restored their urge to live. Bonaparte by no means believed (as some of his enemies have declared) that France was born on 19 Brumaire.

The extremists, both Jacobin and Royalist, equally embittered when they saw the majority of the old revolutionaries and most of the émigrés bow before the new master, again took up their plan to kill Bonaparte. In the shadow of the Consulate, the assassins sought the most effective way: shooting Napoleon in the back with a pistol during a review at the Carrousel, or (a more daring undertaking) introducing a barrel of gunpowder into the cellars of the Tuileries. But the best way to get rid of the "tyrant" would, as it turned out, be suggested to the Chouans by their most implacable enemies, the republican extremists (the *exclusifs*), who haunted the cabarets near the city gates, ruminating their rancor and concocting plots around tables stained with wine. A group of these "anarchists," headed by the Jacobin Chevalier were planning to eliminate the First Consul by setting off, under his carriage, an infernal machine similar to the one invented by an Italian engineer in 1585, during the siege of Anvers. The device consisted of a barrel bound with iron hoops and filled with gunpowder, inflammable substances, and bullets. The explosion was to be set off by a gun from which the barrel had been sawed off, triggered from a distance by a string. Unfortunately for the *exclusifs*, Fouché's active police had sniffed out the plot; and on November 7, 1800, all the plotters were arrested.

At this point the Chouans decided to adapt the same plan to their own purposes. Acting upon instructions from two royalist plotters— the Chevalier de Limoëlan and his friend, Saint-Régent—a man named Carbon, who had formerly been in the service of Limoëlan, bought an old black mare and a wretched cart with light rails along the sides. On the cart the plotters placed a barrel full of gunpowder.

On the evening of December 24 (3 Nivôse, Year IX), as had been announced in the newspapers, the First Consul was to go to the Opera (which at that time was situated on the present-day Place Louvois) to hear Haydn's oratorio *The Creation*. Wouldn't it be best to profit from this nocturnal outing by placing the infernal machine somewhere along the route?

On Thursday, December 22, Saint-Régent hired a hackney coach and drove to the Place du Carrousel, just in front of the Hôtel de Longueville, opposite the Tuileries, which in 1800 served as the Consul's stables. At that time the Place du Carrousel was narrow, dark, and cramped. On either side of the entrance to the palace were two pavilions serving as guardhouses. As the cabman reported later, Saint-Régent looked at the long, gray façade and the dome atop the central pavilion, taking out his watch as he did so. Then, turning his back on the "governmental palace," he seemed to ponder. He was exactly on the corner of the Place du Carrousel and the Rue St.-Nicaise. This street ran parallel to the palace, crossing the Carrousel for a distance of a few dozen meters, and forming one end of it. It began at the gallery along the edge of the river, and after having crossed the site of the future wicket gates of Rohan, came to an end near the Rue St.-Honoré, more or less abreast of the present-day Place du Théâtre Français. The Rue de la Loi (today the Rue de Richelieu), which led to the Opera, was almost a continuation of it.

After some reflection, Saint-Régent found the site excellent. They would position the cart carrying the barrel in the Rue St.-Nicaise, toward the Rue St.-Honoré, some 20 meters from the Place du Carrousel. One of them would stand watch before the Hôtel de Longueville, at the far side of the square. Thus he would see the carriage when it left the Tuileries, and would be able to signal to the person who, with a long fuse, would ignite the bomb.

A few days earlier, Bonaparte had told Roederer: "If, three or four years from now, I were to die in my bed of a fever, and if by way of completing my life's work I were to draw up a testament, I would tell the nation to beware of a military government and choose a civil magistrate."

The evening of December 24, Paris was enveloped in a cold mist —a typical night for the month of Nivôse. While many Parisians were preparing for the traditional midnight repast on Christmas Eve (midnight Masses had not been reestablished, but ceremonies were tolerated in private churches), Bonaparte settled down in his wife's yellow salon. As he sat there by the fire, poking it as was his habit, he seemed reluctant to go out—even in order to hear Garat, "incomparable" singer that he was. He had in fact begun to drowse off on a settee when Josephine, who may have ordered a special dress for the occasion and wanted to show it off, came to awaken him.

"Allons, Bonaparte," she insisted. "It will take your mind off your worries. You work too hard."

But the Consul closed his eyes and murmured: "You can go on if you want. I'll stay here."

At length, after a considerable debate, he yielded and ordered the horses to be hitched up. He left first, preceded by an escort of cavalrymen from the Consular Guard. Lannes, Berthier, and Lauriston were riding with him. The nearby bell of St.-Roch was striking eight as the carriage, having crossed the Place du Carrousel, turned to the left and entered the Rue St.-Nicaise. Bonaparte was drowsing.

Suddenly a terrible explosion rent the air. The Consul started awake. The explosion broke the carriage windows. His reaction was that of a soldier: "We've been mined!"

The carriage stopped after turning into the Rue St.-Honoré, and the coachman asked for orders. Bonaparte decided to go ahead immediately, without losing one minute of which the enemy could take advantage to kill him, and without even ascertaining whether Josephine had been hurt in the attack. He had no idea how many plotters there were. Perhaps someone was watching him, waiting for a chance to kill him. And so he shouted: "To the Opera!"

Behind him, the scene was frightful. Although the machine had exploded in the interval between the two carriages, it had mowed down the rear guard (a dozen persons were killed, and twenty-eight were wounded) and damaged forty-six houses, some of them so badly that they had to be demolished. On every hand lay bodies and "scattered arms and legs."

After putting in a brief appearance at the Opera (where the news of his escape after the attempt on his life provoked a tremendous ovation), Bonaparte went back to the Tuileries. The salon on the ground floor, overlooking the terrace, was already full of officials come to get the news, first details of which had begun to circulate. There was considerable indignation when it was learned that the horse hitched to the cart had been held by a little girl of fourteen. (The investigation disclosed that her name was Pensol, and that she was the daughter of a woman who hawked vegetables on the Rue du Bac.) One of the assassins had given a dozen sous to the unfortunate child to hold the horse, while he himself slipped away after lighting the fuse. At any rate, such was the supposition. It could only be a supposition, since everything—the little girl, the cart, and the horse

—had disappeared in the explosion. There was no trace of the murderers. But everyone exclaimed in one voice: "It was the Jacobins who did it!" A barrel stuffed full of shot, placed on a cart, and exploded just when the head of the government was passing by—was not this the plan that the *exclusifs* had conceived? For that matter, the plotters of November 7 had not yet been brought up for trial; and in order to save them their accomplices would not hesitate to exterminate the master of France!

Nor did Bonaparte himself give any thought to the Chouans:

> This is the work of the Jacobins! [he exclaimed]. It was the Jacobins who tried to assassinate me! . . . No nobles, priests, or Chouans were involved in it. . . . I know the truth of it, and nobody can make me change my mind. It is those low scoundrels who have been in open revolt, in a constant conspiracy, in armed rebellion against all the governments that have followed one another. If they can't be put in chains, they must be annihilated. France must be purged of that vile scum. No pity for such villains! . . .

Fouché was one of the few to accuse the Chouans. Bonaparte looked at him contemptuously: it was only to be expected that the regicide, the man who had carried out the massacre of Lyons, wanted to save his friends of the old days.

Fouché took the abuse—imperturbable, saying nothing. But the next day he seized the opportunity and set about the careful preparation of a list of 130 *Septembriseurs* belonging to "that class of men who in the past ten years have committed all manner of crimes." (The future Duc d'Otrante was forgetting both the mass shootings at Lyons, of which he was one of the organizers, and the massacres at Toulon.) When he signed the list, he added, quite without irony: "Not all of these men were caught dagger in hand; but all of them are universally known as capable of sharpening the dagger and taking it up." And on 14 Nivôse—eleven days after the attempt—Bonaparte issued a decree deporting about 100 extremists to the Seychelles Islands.

But at the same time that he was getting rid of his embarrassing friends, Fouché continued his investigation. He had had some remnants of the black mare picked up from the Rue St.-Nicaise, and had summoned all the horse dealers in Paris. Only two days after Christmas, a seed merchant named Lambel recognized the black horse that he had sold to Carbon. A short time later, a man named Thomas, who hired out carriages, reported that the equipage had been kept in his stable; and a blacksmith stated that he had shod the mare. All these men gave a description of Carbon. It took very little time to identify him, since there was a description on file for every one of the Chouans. The oldest niece of Limoëlan's former servant was interrogated for a long time, and finally admitted that her uncle was hiding with some nuns on the Rue Notre-Dame-des-Champs. On January 18 Carbon was arrested. At first he denied everything, but later he squealed on Saint-Régent and Limoëlan. The leader of the conspiracy was not located. But Saint-Régent, who had been wandering about Paris without daring to ask for anyone's hospitality, was arrested on January 25 by a policeman who came across him by chance on the Rue du Four.

Before the criminal court, Carbon tried to save his life by proving that he had left his accomplices at the Place des Victoires more than an hour before the attempted assassination. In spite of this, he was condemned to death, along with Saint-Régent, who begged his judges to send him to the scaffold as soon as possible. They were executed on April 20 (30 Germinal, Year IX) to prolonged applause from the crowd. (Limoëlan succeeded in escaping from Paris and reaching the United States, where he entered the priesthood.)

The day after Fouché had come to Malmaison with proofs of the guilt of the Chouans and the innocence of the Jacobins, Bonaparte was heard to tell the Council of Ministers, apropos of other intransigents who had ostensibly come over to the regime: "Those twelve or fifteen people are metaphysicians who should be burned at the stake. . . . It's a mistake to think I would behave like Louis XVI and offer no resistance. I am a man of the people, and I would never let myself be insulted like a king."

That same week it was suggested to him that the Place Bellecour at Lyons be renamed Place Bonaparte. He refused, saying, "Such honors should not be accorded to a man who is still alive."

Austria had been coy about signing the armistice, and Bonaparte had had to threaten Vienna that he would resume hostilities in Italy and on the Rhine simultaneously.

When Austria had come around, England did the same: she

needed a period of rest, however short. But England considered this armistice as shameful and "more disadvantageous than war." To the English way of thinking, it could only be a cease-fire pending new hostilities.

On September 23, 1801, while he was at Malmaison, Napoleon learned of the preliminaries of the Peace of Amiens. Later he would say: "I believed in good faith that the fate of France, of Europe, and of myself had been settled at Amiens. As for me, I intended to devote myself solely to governing France, and I believe I would have accomplished miracles."

On November 10, he received Lord Cornwallis, who had represented England at Amiens. Bonaparte wanted to show—for the first time in ten years—that France again had a decor worthy of its past. The consuls were surrounded by a brilliant court. "Amid all these resplendent uniforms," Constant tells us, "his was remarkable for its simplicity. But the diamond called 'the Regent,' which the First Consul had taken out of pawn a few days before, glittered on his sword hilt."

One morning at Malmaison, those who made up the little court saw Bonaparte push his plate away after having scarcely eaten. He paced up and down, drank three cups of coffee, and then got on his horse and rode off for several hours.

Napoleon had just learned of the loss of Egypt. The big guns had been silenced on the edge of the Nile, and Kléber had been assassinated by a fanatic, Suleiman, whom the Turks called a patriot.

In the shadow of the Peace of Amiens, Bonaparte had to make the public swallow the Egyptian defeat:

> History, in any case, will not pass over what the French did to bring civilization and European science to Egypt. It will recount the effort they expended in conquering that country, and the wisdom and discipline they employed in keeping it for such a long time. And perhaps it will deplore its loss as a new calamity for mankind. . . .

Bonaparte wanted to put an end to the drama that had been stirred up in France by the "Civil Constitution" of the clergy. Actually, in dissipating this painful state of anarchy, he would be approved by the majority of the nation, who remained basically Catholic. Already, in most parts of the country, the *culte décadaire* had been abandoned in favor of the Catholic religion. Only the functionaries still followed (reluctantly) the official service: most of the faithful had gone back to their altars and their priests—preferably refractory priests.

A decree soon authorized freedom of religion. This was no doubt intended as a first step toward the reestablishment of the old order. Unfortunately—and this was not the result being sought—this first step gave rise to numerous schisms owing to the existence of "constitutional" or clandestine priests, and "unsworn" priests, both subdued and refractory. ("Unsworn" priests were those who had refused to take the oath of allegiance to the Revolution required by the Church Establishment Bill of July 12, 1790.) Religious collectives of diverse tendencies made their appearance.

Bonaparte was scarcely even a deist. Moreover, many things about the Catholic Church disturbed him. "I am certainly far from being an atheist," he affirmed, "but I can't accept everything they try to teach me without being false and hypocritical."

Bonaparte believed in God *par raison d'État*, and recognized the usefulness of religion—if only to help the disinherited to accept inequality. Above all, he did not want to destroy religion, but rather use it to his own advantage. To Roederer he confided: "I brought the war of the Vendée to an end by making myself a Catholic; I established myself in Egypt by making myself a Moslem; and I won over the people of Italy by making myself an ultramontanist. If I were governing a nation of Jews, I would restore the Temple of Solomon."

Shortly after Marengo, while stopping at Verceil, he had requested Cardinal Marciana to communicate to the Pope his desire to see the end of the actual schisms that were dividing the French clergy. Despite his victories, Bonaparte knew that he would not be able to reestablish peace and religious unity without the help of Rome. Only the Pope could put an end to the chaos.

The authority of the Pope, at the summit of the Catholic hierarchy, seemed to him to be indispensable: "If the Pope didn't exist, he would have to be created for this occasion, as the Roman consuls created a dictator when circumstances were difficult."

And he stated clearly: "The Pope will never be able to render me a greater service. He alone can reorganize the French Catholics under a republican allegiance—smoothly and without bloodshed. I have asked him to do it."

But it was easier to elaborate the groundwork for an agreement than to achieve its goal: the Concordat.

"How should I treat him?" Bonaparte's first envoy to Pius VII asked the First Consul.

"Treat him as if he had 200,000 men," he replied arrogantly.

Although he was sincere in wanting to reach an agreement, Bonaparte demanded—with unyielding obstinacy—a church that was more Gallican than Papist. He did not receive Cardinal Consalvi until June 22, 1801. "Let him come in the most 'cardinalesque' costume he can find," he recommended.

The next day, a commission was created and work on the Concordat was begun—not without difficulty. The negotiators agreed that henceforth Catholicism would be recognized "as the religion professed by the majority of the French"—a truism, to say the least. The "hierarchy of the Church" was also acknowledged by the State, which would appoint the new bishops, receive their oath of loyalty, and give them salaries, while the Pope would accord the canonical investiture.

"We have finished the novel of the Revolution," declared Bonaparte. "Now we must begin its history."

And he added: "The Concordat is not the victory of any one party but the consolidation of all."

Politically, Napoleon had sized things up accurately: ratification by the Holy See really crucified the future Louis XVIII: "If I, like Saint Louis, had my barons gathered together, I would nail up a protest on the doors of the Vatican. But I am without troops, without money, without asylum!"

It was Napoleon who (calling himself "the devoted son of His Holiness") announced to the Pope the promulgation of the Concordat for Easter Sunday, which fell on April 18, 1802—the same day chosen to celebrate the Peace of Amiens. That morning, the Parisians were awakened by the great bell of Notre Dame, which had been mute for ten years.

"The great bell!" exclaimed a worker. "I like that better than the alarm gun!"

The First Consul was likewise awakened early by the bells. Constant was getting him into his uniform of a colonel of the Consular Guard, when Joseph and Cambacérès entered the room.

"Eh bien!" Bonaparte said. "We're going to Mass. What do the Parisians think of that?"

"A lot of them," Cambacérès replied, "intend to go to the first performance and hiss the play if they don't find it amusing."

"If anybody tries to hiss me, I'll have him thrown out by the grenadiers of the Consular Guard!"

"But what if the grenadiers begin to hiss like the others?"

"I'm not worried about that. My veterans will go to Notre Dame here, just as they went to the mosque in Cairo. They'll watch what I do. And when they see their general behaving properly and with dignity, they'll do the same, saying: 'That's the order!' "

"I'm afraid," put in Joseph, "that the general officers won't be so accommodating. I've just left Augereau, and he is raging against what he calls your stupid sermons. He won't be so easy to bring back to the bosom of our Holy Mother Church. Nor will a few others be."

"Bah!" Bonaparte shrugged. "That's just the way Augereau is. He makes a lot of noise. But if he has some moronic little cousin on his hands, he'll place him in the seminary so I can make a chaplain of him."

France was to be once again the oldest daughter of the Church.

The sky above Paris was cloudy, and a wind was blowing. The day began with the traditional review on the Place du Carrousel. Then, as soon as he had put on his red First Consul's uniform, Bonaparte made ready to leave for Notre Dame. Preceded by a body of Mamelukes—a strange escort for anyone going to hear a Te Deum—the First Consul and his two colleagues took their places in a carriage drawn by eight splendid bay horses. They were a gift from the King of Spain—a Bourbon! The Mamelukes who were holding the horses by the bridle were dressed in green and gold, as were the outriders and footmen.

The day before, the clergy had inquired whether Bonaparte, Cambacérès, and Lebrun should be "incensed" at the same time. "No," the future Emperor had replied. "For my two colleagues, that smoke is still too solid."

An English eyewitness, Henry Redhead York, has described the occasion:

> Three thrones had been placed in front of the altar, for the consuls. Bonaparte's had been placed a bit in front of the others, but he moved it even farther in front before sitting down. He

remained in his armchair during the entire ceremony except for
the consecration of the host and communion, when he stood, and
at the moment of the host when, not content to stand, he crossed
himself devoutly.

Consul Lebrun was at his right and Cambacérès at his left.
Those two automatons remained completely indifferent during
all of the ceremony. When the High Mass was over, the bishops
approached by turns to take the oath of loyalty. Each time that
one of these mitered prelates kneeled before Bonaparte, he
would respond with an amiable nod of the head.

The consular court seemed dumfounded to be present at such an
occasion. The next day, Bonaparte asked Augereau how he had liked
the ceremony.

"It was fine," replied the general. "All it lacked was the million
men who gave their lives trying to destroy what we are reestablish-
ing."

But Bonaparte took very seriously his role as protector of the
Church. Talleyrand was to acknowledge later: "When, in 1802, Napoleon reestablished religion in France, he performed not only an act
of justice but also one of great cleverness. . . . The Napoleon of the
Concordat is the truly great Napoleon: enlightened and guided by his
genius. . . ."

Bonaparte's genius was manifested in matters other than religious
questions: the Civil Code is in fact one of its most evident manifesta-
tions. Napoleon would eventually disappear, and his empire would
eventually collapse, but his thought would continue to govern nations.

Upon his return from Marengo, Cambacérès had described to
Bonaparte the draft laws he had drawn up—the laws that had been
debated in the Convention years ago. Bonaparte had congratulated
him: "I've read them. They show a capacity for analysis that I like.
. . . Since you have already drawn up several codes, don't you think
it would be useful to recast them and submit to the Corps Législatif
a draft code in line with the ideas of the century and worthy of the
government?"

Justice would be only a meaningless word if the Consulate did not
provide it with a weapon: with laws. Animated by Bonaparte and
headed by Cambacérès, the commission began its tremendous un-

dertaking. One day, there would emerge from this work the Civil Code—which would become the Code Napoleon.

> Beginning with the very first session [Cambacérès tells us] Bonaparte expressed himself in positive terms on the necessity of putting more emphasis on paternal authority, on the usefulness of revising the divorce laws, on the right freely to dispose of property, on adoption. . . . Everything he said was well reasoned, and I did not fail to applaud.

Bonaparte presided over the sessions several times a week. B. de Molleville, who had been a minister under Louis XVI, acknowledged that he was astonished when he heard the First Consul discoursing. "Where in the devil did he learn all that?" he asked himself.

In the course of discussion of that article of the Code dealing with the wife's obedience to her husband, Bonaparte said: "This clause is a particularly good thing for Paris, where the women think they are entitled to do anything they want to. I'm not saying it will have an effect on all of them, but it will on some."

He was even more intensely interested in the sessions of the Council of State. A certain degree of ceremony marked his appearance at these sessions. His approach was heralded by a drummer stationed at the bottom of the steps of the Tuileries. He would then enter, followed by an aide-de-camp. (Later, he would be preceded by a chamberlain.) Sitting down in a chair whose arms were scarred from his stabbing them with a penknife during the discussions, he would place his snuffbox near him. (He took snuff frequently, and the chamberlain on duty always had to have a full box within easy reach).

As soon as the doors had been closed and locked, the session began. Bonaparte would listen closely and patiently. The questions he put were pithy, and he was not at all embarrassed when compelled to admit he knew nothing of certain problems. At such times he would ask numerous questions, requesting the definition and exact meaning of words unfamiliar to him. Then would come the contradictions, objections, and refutations, in open debate. (At this time he still permitted debate—something he would not tolerate a few years later.)

Sometimes he would say to one councillor: "Come now, you Jacobin. Give us your opinion."

Then turning to another member of the Council: "And you, as a Royalist, give us yours."

He knew how to soft-pedal his tendency to dominate, and remained very calm, "carrying even to excess his patient willingness to hear everything."

"Sometimes I'm a fox and sometimes a lion. The whole secret of governing consists in being one or the other, as the situation demands."

Every day he managed to hold several councils at which the problems of government, finance, and jurisprudence were discussed. Some sessions would last until five o'clock in the morning, since he refused to leave a question until he had formed a well-grounded opinion.

A few of his councillors and ministers found it very hard to keep up this frantic pace. "You're a bit lazy," he said to one of them. "We have to make haste. Everyone is complaining about us, saying we're not getting the job done fast enough."

And he added: "I realize it's a terrible skein to disentangle, but we have to get moving!"

Sometimes, after long hours of discussion, some of the exhausted councillors would doze off. But not for long; they would soon be awakened by the taunts of the First Consul: "Come, come, Citizen! Wake up! It's only two o'clock. You must earn the money that France is paying you!"

But it occasionally happened that he himself, after having worked all night, would go to sleep in the middle of a council meeting. For that matter, he did nothing to keep himself awake. Did he not, after all, "have sleep at his orders," as the politician Antoine Thibaudeau said? At such times the members of the council would withdraw noiselessly.

X

TOWARD THE THRONE

*Clever policy consists in making nations
believe they are free.*

NAPOLEON

DURING THE SUMMER Bonaparte went at the end of each *décade* to
the delightful château of Malmaison, purchased by Josephine during
the Egyptian campaign. During these "weekends" under the Consulate, the First Consul and his wife lived like bourgeois estate owners
entertaining their friends.

But his responsibilities as First Consul always took precedence
over everything else. As early as five or six in the morning, he would
get up and leave Josephine alone under the vast canopy of the bed.
(She was to die in this bedroom one day.)

"A happy marriage," he affirmed, "demands a continual exchange
of perspiration."

At St. Helena he recalled how much importance his wife attached
to the nuptial bed: "A woman who wants to exert influence over her
husband should always sleep with him."

Nonetheless, he eventually abandoned the conjugal bedroom at
Malmaison and took one at the other end of the château, directly
above the library, which was situated in the corner pavilion on the
south side. The decor of this library has not changed. One has the
feeling that the First Consul will soon appear and sit down at his huge
desk. Although he thought "that the room resembled a sacristy, he
was compelled to admit that it was difficult to do any better in such
an unsuitable location."

It was there that he and his secretary worked. The sessions attended by the consuls, councillors, or ministers coming from Paris

were held in the next room, done entirely in blue and white drill and decorated with war trophies.

When the weather was good, dinner would be served in the park: the table would be set up in front of the château on the left side of the lawn, "and a bit beyond the drive on the right."

On May 6, 1802, Chabot took his place at the speaker's rostrum.

"The Senate," he announced, "is invited to give the consuls a token of the national gratitude."

The idea was to give a more definitive character to the regime born in Brumaire, Year XIII. It was decided that the powers of the First Consul should be prorogued for ten years. Bonaparte had been hoping for more, and hence he thanked the deputation from the Tribunate with a few banal phrases. But he issued the following warning to the Council:

> Everything was destroyed, and we have to create it anew. There is a *gouvernment des pouvoirs*, but what is the rest of the nation? Just grains of sand. . . . We are diffuse, lacking a system, lacking assemblies, lacking contact. So long as I am in office, I shall be responsible for the Republic. But we must provide for the future. Do you believe that the Republic has been finally consolidated? If so, you are very wrong. We are equal to the task. But we do not have a Republic, and we shall not have one if we do not throw a few masses of granite on the soil of France.

The Senate seems not to have understood; or perhaps the senators were afraid of being crushed by the "mass of granite." In any case, they did nothing more than to ratify (on May 8, 1802) the vote of the Tribunate.

Bonaparte did not consider this gift to be adequate, since his ambition was to keep power until his death. He demanded that the people be consulted. And so, on May 10, the Council of State submitted to the First Consul the text of the two questions that were to be posed to the French people: *Primo:* Shall Napoleon Bonaparte be consul for life? *Secondo:* Shall he be empowered to designate his successor?

This was in effect a return to monarchy—the creation of a new dynasty. The word "successor" was spelled out plainly, and Napoleon would never again be able to say: "My heir is the French people."

The new dynasty would have its order of chivalry. On May 19, the *Moniteur* published the text of the decree establishing the Legion of Honor—"the knighthood of the Revolution," as the Royalists termed it ironically. For her part, the Duchesse d'Abrantès remarked: "This creation of an order of chivalry in a country where one moved only among republican institutions struck me at first as a kind of monstrosity in a Republic."

And Mme. de Staël exclaimed: "That Bonaparte who escaped from Egypt thinks he is a pharaoh!"

But it was the "pharaoh" who had the last word.

"It would be a mere bauble for your vanity," someone told him.

"Eh bien," he replied, "it's with baubles that mankind is led."

On July 29, 1802, the Senate announced the results of the plebiscite: "The French people and the Senate proclaim Napoleon Bonaparte First Consul for life." Out of 3,570,259 persons who voted, only 8,374 Frenchmen were unwilling to make Bonaparte a kind of king.

In Paris, 60,395 persons voted yes. Those opposed numbered only 60. And the Vendée? The vote from this Royalist département was eagerly awaited. It was 17,079 ayes against 6 nays!

Some of the voters conveyed their feelings along with their votes. Thus the residents of the Hôtel des Invalides, "who marched in a crowd to the town hall of the Tenth Arrondissement," declared quite naturally: "May Bonaparte be consul for life, and may God protect him!"

Napoleon's prestigious name was already appearing on coins; and August 15—the birthday of the new master—was decreed a national holiday. As Cobenzl wrote: "Where will it stop—this torrent which is more rapid and devastating in time of peace than in time of war?"

Napoleon had already been elected President of the Italian Republic. At the end of this same year, the deputies of the eighteen Swiss cantons conferred upon him the title of Mediator of the Swiss Confederation.

Even certain Royalists began to admire him—to find that there was something good in Bonaparte. "Who the devil would we put in the place of that little rascal?" exclaimed (reportedly) the Duc de

Laval, an émigré who had recently returned and yet had been banished to a place forty leagues from Paris by a *lettre de cachet* signed
by the "little rascal."

The Republic was already just a memory. Thus one day a man
from the old royal court, while chatting with Lucien Bonaparte,
referred to Normandy and the Languedoc as "the most beautiful
provinces of the kingdom." Then he added: "You must pardon me.
It's an old habit."

"Oh, you needn't beg my pardon," the First Consul's brother
replied wittily. "It's quite understandable. I sometimes surprise myself speaking of the Republic."

For Bonaparte, who already considered himself the equal of the
kings—until such time as he would become their master—France
was bound to recover her place in Europe as rapidly as possible. And
that place could only be the first.

Was Bonaparte going to take up residence at Versailles? He considered the château to be "a hideous monster." The ancient palace
seemed as outmoded in those days as the former entrances to the
Métropolitain seem to Parisians today. Hence Napoleon preferred
the château of St.-Cloud—certainly not "modern," but more on the
human scale. It was there that he would take his first steps as a
sovereign.

At that time there was a great influx of foreigners who, trembling
a bit at first, came to visit this new France whose borders had been
closed to them for ten years—this tempestuous daughter of Europe
who had dared to throw to the world the head of a king! The accounts
of those tourists are all the most valuable in that the foreigners
approached the France of the Consulate and her chief with somewhat the same mentality as an explorer discovering an unknown
tribe.

For a glimpse of how the master of France behaved when receiving guests at the palace of the Tuileries, here is a report by J. F.
Reichardt, the German composer:

> Once in the courtroom properly so called, the ministers of the
> different countries lined up, with their nationals behind them in
> order of precedence. . . . In accordance with the established
> protocol, the Prince of Baden, who was traveling incognito under

the name of the Count of Enerstein, found himself standing at the end of the room. But the clever Bonaparte nevertheless managed to give everyone his due, while yet respecting the established order: he simply began making his rounds from the other end. . . .

Later, Reichardt saw Napoleon leaving the chapel, "nodding and smiling, just like the king used to do at Versailles. . . ."

Napoleon's tyranny was exercised mainly against his own relatives. And yet it must be recognized that he was afflicted with an insatiable family, and that his brothers and sisters brought him only vexations and disappointments.

All of them, that is, but his dear Pauline. According to certain individuals, Bonaparte was, indeed, the lover of "la Paganetta" (the little pagan), as Pauline was called. Simonville, one of her short-term lovers, claimed that the First Consul's sister told him shortly after 18 Brumaire: "I am on very good terms with my brother. He has already slept with me twice."

Nothing that the nymphomaniacal and thoughtless Pauline might do is surprising. If *Napoleone caro mio* had asked her, why should she have refused? But at no time in his life did Bonaparte's rather undemanding senses seem to have prompted him to commit such an amoral act. His bedroom behavior, whether with Josephine or his mistresses, seems to have been that of a man little disposed toward erotic fantasies and complications.

And Hortense? A good many contemporaries maintained that Bonaparte's stepdaughter had been his mistress too. Of course there was no blood bond between them, and it is quite true that Hortense was much more sensual than Napoleon. But it is difficult to imagine her sporting with the husband of the mother she adored.

Although the First Consul was said to have more mistresses than was actually the case, his casual intimacies *were* frequent. And Josephine, if she wanted to avoid making a scene, had to close her eyes to her husband's infidelities.

"Love does not really exist," he said one day. "It is an artificial sentiment born of society. But then I may not be qualified to judge: I'm too reasonable."

But hadn't he once adored Josephine to the point of folly?

"It's true that I have gone for a week—or even two weeks—

without sleep because of a woman," he explained. "But that is not love. Whatever one says, love does not resist absence."

He seemed to be forgetting his despair at the time when the fickle Creole refused to see him or come to join him in Italy.

In the early days of the Consulate, he became interested in a young *pensionnaire* of the Théâtre-Français, Thérèse-Étiennette Bourgoin. She was a former dancer, and her physical make-up (like that of any adolescent girl) provided a piquant contrast with his "spiced amusements." J. A. Chaptal, the Minister of the Interior, was very fond of the young lady, who was called "the goddess of joy and pleasure," and "protected" her officially. No doubt he was unaware of the interest that Bonaparte had taken in his mistress, because one evening in 1804, when he was working with Napoleon (who had just recently put on the crown), he was dumfounded when he heard a caller announced: "Mlle. Bourgoin."

"Let her wait!" the master ordered.

Realizing what such a visit meant at this late hour, the minister picked up his portfolio and left. The next day he sent in his resignation—final this time.

Had the Emperor done this on purpose—to get rid of Chaptal, whom he called Papa Enema? In any case, Mlle. Bourgoin conceived a deadly rancor toward the master because of it.

Later he regretted not having given more time to women, if only to chat with them "on the sofa." In his words: "I would have learned lots of things. A woman is a river that needs water, and one must bring it to her."

The famous order "Let her wait!" was to be heard again.

This time the lady in question was another actress, Mlle. Duchesnois—Catherine-Joséphine Raquin—who was not at all pretty. She was afflicted with a nose "whose snorting," said Alexandre Dumas, "corresponded to its large size," and her face reminded you of "one of those porcelain lions that are placed on balustrades." But she had the figure of a Venus de Milo, and she made haste to show it and to give herself, in order to erase the first—and unpleasant—impression.

When he ordered her to wait, the First Consul, absorbed in his work, was no doubt thinking only of the nose and the snorting. But a little later he must have remembered her body, because upon learning that Mlle. Duchesnois was still there, he said: "Tell her to get undressed and get into bed!"

However, the nose must have had the last word. Because he continued to work and when he was reminded for the third time of the presence of Mlle. Duchesnois, Bonaparte ordered: "Tell her to get dressed again and go away!"

Mlle. George, who was the great enemy of Mlle. Duchesnois, did not have to fear such treatment. He first noticed her in 1802, at the Théâtre-Français playing the role of Clytemnestra in *Iphigenia in Aulis.*

At the time, she was sixteen years old. Already majestic, she brought to mind the statue of a young and noble Roman lady. She had begun her love life at fourteen, and she, too, was eager to unveil her splendid charms. Hers were of course *amours de théâtre:* she had made her amorous debut in the arms of an actor—her "beau Lafon," as she called him. When Bonaparte first took notice of her she was the mistress of a Polish noble, Prince Sapieha. But she was nonetheless a bit ruffled when, the same night as the performance of *Iphigenia,* Constant came to her home to ask her, on behalf of the First Consul, to come to St.-Cloud the following evening at eight o'clock.

"He wants to compliment you personally upon your success," the *valet de chambre* told her.

"Monsieur, tell the First Consul that I shall have the honor of going to St.-Cloud tomorrow. You can call for me at eight o'clock— but at the theater, not here." (This stipulation was no doubt made so that no one would fail to see what was happening.)

The next evening, wearing a loosely fitting white chiffon dress and a lace veil, with a cashmere scarf over her shoulders, she got into the carriage with Constant. When they arrived at the château, her heart was beating violently—or at any rate so she reported later. Preceded by Constant, she went through the Orangerie and passed through the French window giving onto the terrace, into the bedroom. Roustam was standing guard. "I'll go and notify the First Consul."

Now she was alone. A huge bed, a large divan—everything struck her as rather menacing.

Finally, he came in.

The Consul [she wrote later] was wearing silk hose, satiny white breeches, and a green uniform with red trimming and collar. He was carrying his hat under his arm. I rose. He came over to me, looked at me with that enchanting smile which was his alone, took me by the hand and sat me down in that enormous divan, then lifted my veil and threw it to the floor just like that. . . .

According to Mlle. George in her *Mémoires*—representing the coquetry of an old lady recording her reminiscences a half-century later—she stayed with the Consul until five o'clock in the morning and nothing happened. Nothing, that is, except that when Bonaparte learned that her veil was a gift from Prince Sapieha, he tore it "into a thousand little pieces." In order to replace it, Constant had to go and get "a white cashmere scarf and a large English lace veil"— presumably from Josephine's wardrobe.

Mlle. George, in describing her four nights at St.-Cloud, reported it was not until the third night that she became his mistress:

> Little by little he undid all my clothes. He played the role of *femme de chambre* with such gaiety, grace, and decency that one simply had to yield, willy-nilly. And indeed, how could one fail to be fascinated by that man, and attracted to him? He played the little boy and the child to please me. He was no longer the Consul. He was a man in love, perhaps, but it was a love in which violence and roughness had no part. . . .

Bonaparte, who loathed "crude extremities," as he put it, marveled at "Georgina's" little hands. They were "covered with dimples," Théophile Gautier said. "Truly royal hands made for the scepter." Her feet were less favored. It is said that when someone exclaimed, "She has the bearing of a queen!" a waggish fellow replied, "Yes, and the feet of a king."

> He was laughing [she continues], playing with me, and making me run after him. To avoid getting caught, he climbed up on the ladder used to get books from the shelves. Since the ladder was on rollers and very light, I pushed it the entire length of the study, while he laughed and shouted at me: "You're going to hurt yourself! Stop it, or I'll get angry!"

Georgina's whole life was brightened by this adventure. When she spoke of Napoleon, it was always with a quaver in her voice.

"He left me to become Emperor," she said.

One night he "stuffed into her bosom" a big bundle of bank notes: 40,000 francs.

"Why are you giving me all that?"

"I don't want my Georgina to lack for money while I'm away."

"Never once," she comments, "did the Emperor send money to me by someone else: it was always he who gave it to me. He was more tender that night than I had ever seen him. . . ."

Forty thousand francs. The figure should be multiplied by five, at the very least. And this was for an absence of a few weeks. Bonaparte had to leave, in fact, to inspect the camp at Boulogne and the coasts of the North Sea, since the war was about to resume.

Since December 28, 1802, relations with England had been strained. It was on that day that the First Consul, "surprised and hurt," learned that the Comte d'Artois, the brother of Louis XVI, had taken the liberty of wearing the orders of the old monarchy on his uniform while reviewing a regiment of British troops.

"That is an insult that the French people will never forget!" he fumed.

And he felt he was fully justified in instructing Talleyrand to let Lord Whitworth, the British ambassador to Paris, know that the two countries seemed to him "not to be at peace but merely in a state of temporary armistice."

One month later, Bonaparte decided that the time had come to put France on guard against "perfidious Albion." The Municipal Council of Orléans had asked if the city could reerect the statue in honor of Joan of Arc. The First Consul ordered that Citizen des Ormeaux, the mayor of Orléans, be informed by letter that this request was "much to his liking." And he explained: "The illustrious Joan of Arc proved that there is no miracle the French genius cannot produce under circumstances in which the national independence is threatened." Then he added: "Our neighbors, more calculating and more clever than we are, have taken advantage of the frankness and loyalty in our character constantly to sow among us those dissensions that have given rise to the calamities of this age and all the disasters recalled in our history."

By the terms of the Peace of Amiens, England was to have evacuated Malta by September, 1802. But five months later she had not even begun preparations for evacuating. Bonaparte looked upon

Malta as a second Gibraltar. And he felt that England's manifest intent to occupy these two key positions in the Mediterranean demonstrated conclusively her design to add the commerce of the Mediterranean to that of the Indies, of America, and of the Baltic. On February 15, 1803, the First Consul said, "Of all the calamities that could happen to the French people, none is comparable to that one."

The English position was simple. The French minister was told:

> The Piedmont has been annexed, and you are ready to decide the fate of Germany, Switzerland, and Holland. In spite of our decision not to interfere in any way with the affairs of the Continent, we are being implicated in them against our own wishes—both because of the complaints addressed to us and because of the public opinion being expressed here with unprecedented vigor.

For London, the fact that France had annexed the Piedmont in September, 1802—and the fact that she had not evacuated Holland —authorized Great Britain to keep Malta. To this specious argument, France could reply that the Peace of Amiens stipulated nothing at all with reference to Holland or the Piedmont. (These matters had been dealt with in the Treaty of Lunéville, which in a way had been replaced by the Peace of Amiens.)

On February 18, 1803, Bonaparte summoned Lord Whitworth and had a violent row with him that lasted almost two hours—in the presence of the diplomatic corps, "mute with astonishment and fear."

All the grievances that had been simmering for months boiled over. The First Consul thundered: "Do you want war? We have been fighting for fifteen years. That's far too much. But you want fifteen more years of war, and you are forcing me into it!"

Then, turning to the French and Spanish ambassadors, he explained: "The English want war. But if they are the first to draw the sword, I shall be the last to sheath it. They have no respect for treaties. From now on, treaties should be covered with black crepe."

Whitworth preferred to remain silent and let the storm pass.

"Why these armaments?" Bonaparte went on, raising his voice. "Against whom are these precautionary steps being taken? I do not have a single armed ship of the line in the ports of France. But if you arm, I'll do the same! You may be able to kill France, but you'll never be able to intimidate her!"

Without losing his equanimity, the British ambassador tried to get in a word, hoping that "an amicable explanation—"

But Bonaparte interrupted him. "There are no explanations to be given when the stipulations are so clear and positive as those of the Peace of Amiens."

Then, before leaving the room, he said: "We shall be fighting in two weeks—Malta or war!"

The English were unwilling to evacuate Malta and indeed they could not. And so, after fourteen months of peace, there would be war again—a war lasting twelve years.

When he returned to the embassy, Lord Whitworth wrote to his chief: "It seemed to me that I was listening to a captain of dragoons rather than to the head of one of the most powerful states of Europe."

"He must be mad!" Hawkesbury exclaimed. "We must be prepared for the possibility of an immediate severing of relations."

On May 1, Lord Whitworth made Talleyrand an "offer of agreements" concerning Malta. England was to keep it for ten years—and the French troops would evacuate Holland immediately. Moreover, His Majesty's Government would retain all rights to the island of Lampedusa, near Malta. Britain, he added, demanded a reply from France within seven days.

Napoleon was angered equally by the tone of the demand and the difference in treatment. Why should England occupy Malta for ten years, whereas France was supposed to abandon her conquest immediately?

"I don't want the conference to turn into a sharing of the spoils," he told Talleyrand. "Be chilly, aloof, and even a bit proud. If the note contains 'ultimatum,' make him understand that that word implies war—that his manner of negotiating is that of a superior with an inferior. If the note does not contain that word, see that he puts it in. Tell him we have to know how things stand—that we have had enough of this state of anxiety."

Of course the conference brought no detente. Following Bonaparte's instructions, Talleyrand tried to save the peace by proposing that the island of Malta be handed over to one of the powers guaranteeing the Peace of Amiens. But Lord Whitworth merely repeated England's earlier proposals.

On May 16, the First Consul said: "I am going to risk an undertaking that will be the most difficult ever conceived in the realm of policy—but also the most fecund in terrifying results. In three days' time, given some foggy weather and more or less favorable circumstances, I can become the master of London, Parliament, and the Bank. . . ."

Four days later, the annulment of the Peace of Amiens was announced to the assemblies. Bonaparte had decided on war "only with the greatest repugnance."

On June 12, after having attended a performance of *Esther*, he received the Russian ambassador at St.-Cloud. "I am going into this war," he told him, "with regrets and a feeling of horror. . . . Because, speaking as a European rather than a Frenchman, I would be as distressed as you yourself if, upon arising one morning, you were to learn that England no longer existed."

The First Consul redoubled his preparations. He even established a company of "guide-interpreters." He had the works at the camp of Boulogne reactivated, and issued orders that the soldiers be taught to swim, "relieving one another every three hours." And he ordered the construction of a flotilla of flat-bottomed boats which would make it possible to cross the Channel.

And yet he paid too little attention to the following article, which appeared in the *Journal des Débats* three days after his return:

> Tests have been completed on a new invention whose total and brilliant success will have the most useful results for France's commerce and internal navigation. For the past two or three months, a strange-looking boat has been on view, moored to the end of the quay used by the Chaillot fire engine. It appears bizarre because it is equipped with two large wheels placed on an axle as if for a chariot, and behind these wheels is a kind of big stove with a pipe said to be a little water pump intended to move the wheels and the boat. A few weeks ago, some malefactors sank this construction. But its inventor repaired the damage, and yesterday he obtained the most flattering recompense for his labors and his talents. At six o'clock in the evening, assisted by only three persons, he set his boat in motion, together with two others attached behind it. For an hour and a half he provided onlookers with the strange spectacle of a boat propelled by wheels, like a chariot, the wheels being equipped with paddles or flat oars, and themselves moved by a fire pump. As we followed it along the

quay, its speed against the current of the Seine seemed to be about the same as that of a hurried pedestrian; that is, about 2,400 *toises* per hour. Coming downstream, it was much greater. . . . The author of this brilliant invention is M. Fulton, an American and a famous mechanical engineer.

Of Fulton's abilities as a mechanical engineer there could be no doubt. In July, 1801, at Brest, he demonstrated his *Nautilus*, a genuine submarine 6.4 meters long. When on the surface, it was propelled by means of a sail, and when submerged (making only very little speed, no doubt), by means of a propeller turned by a sailor operating a crank. The boat submerged when water was pumped into its ballast tanks, and reached a depth of 7 meters. It carried a tank of air under pressure, making it possible to remain under water for six hours. And what was the purpose for which the *Nautilus* was designed? To place cases full of explosives under the sides of enemy ships!

When these two inventions were mentioned to the First Consul, he shrugged: "In all capital cities there are hordes of adventurers and schemers offering to all sovereigns various alleged miracles which exist only in their imaginations. They are nothing but charlatans and impostors, and this American is one of them. Don't tell me any more about him."

By the time he changed his mind, it was too late: Fulton had taken his inventions to America.

The English, now on a wartime footing, were waiting to hear the terrible shout: "They are coming!" Volunteers were signing up to repulse the invader, "Boney" (as they had nicknamed Napoleon). According to a secret agent's report circulated at Boulogne in August:

The most ridiculous thing is the volunteer cavalry [of the British]. Most of them have only hired horses that they use on those days when they are on duty, after which Monsieur le cavalier is on foot. . . . But there is one regiment that is not in this condition: the Dragoons of St. James. The richest young lords of England belong to it. . . . Every cavalryman has a retinue of five or six servants on horseback, one of them carrying the port wine, another the liqueur, and a third the civilian clothes of his master. Thus when Monsieur le dragoon de St. James wearies of being in formation, he can take off his uniform and become a private citizen again. . . .

But this didn't alter the fact that England, along with her 70,000 militiamen, could put into the field an army of 136,000 men—not to mention the crews of her ships.

England had not been invaded since the Battle of Hastings, and now she was beginning to tremble with fear. The new cabinet, headed by the famous Pitt, was putting its hope not only in the English coastal batteries but also in the vast conspiracy being set afoot in Paris. The Royalist conspirator Georges Cadoudal, his pockets bulging with English gold, had disembarked on the coast of Normandy on August 20, 1803, having been deposited by the brig *El Vencejo* at the foot of the cliffs of Biville. The terrible Georges had reached Paris; and by the time the new year of 1804 began, he had been there five months without a single police officer's having suspected it. Pitt rubbed his hands: with all the support that the Chouan had, the First Consul's power would certainly collapse. And this was without even taking into account the opposition of the aristocratic salons.

"France will perish if Bonaparte does not do so soon!" exclaimed Mme. de Staël. "I'll give my life and my fortune to the generous mortal who strikes down the tyrant. Why have I only one heart to offer him? I adore him. I will wed him!"

Wed the unbearable Corinne? The idea was enough to discourage the boldest man. It was not so much the candidates for the hand of Mme. de Staël that Bonaparte had to fear as Georges, who headed up a gang of desperadoes and had promised to arrange for the kidnapping of the "tyrant." Naturally, if the First Consul offered the least resistance to his abduction, they would have no trouble silencing him—for good. The British minister Wyndham put it plainly and confidently: "M. de Cadoudal possesses the natural ease and assurance which are the signs of a superior mind. More than all others known to me who are involved in Royalist affairs, he gives me the feeling that he was born to become great." This "man of superior mind" could not fail (or so the English thought) to put an end to the career of that accursed general who made it impossible for Pitt to sleep at night. As the Countess of Albany, an ultraroyalist, wrote at the time: "It is a terrible thing when a bit of a man sets the world topsy-turvy."

But the "bit of a man" had no intention of letting his enemies work their will.

On January 13 State Councillor François Réal, the police chief, came to Malmaison in a very excited state. The moment Bonaparte received him, he reported a serious development: "Pichegru is in Paris. Cadoudal had him come from London."

A captured Chouan, Quérelle, who had been sentenced to death, had revealed this information *in extremis* during a last interrogation, in the hope of saving his life.

The First Consul paled. If Pichegru had come to Paris, it was undoubtedly in order to take part in the homicidal plans of Georges Cadoudal and his gang of assassins.

Pichegru! Nothing could be more astonishing than the destiny of this peasant from the Arbois who in a dozen years had become a lieutenant general under the Revolution and commanding general of the Army of the North. He was a national hero who had conquered Holland in a magnificent campaign. In 1796, under the Directory, he had resigned from the army and become a member of the Council of the Five Hundred. He was involved in the coup d'état of 18 Fructidor, and had been deported to Cayennes. Less than a year later, he escaped from the prison colony, reached London, and offered his services to the British government. They engaged him and gave him a pension.

The peace of 1801 condemned him to idleness. He chafed at the bit more and more, conceived a grudge against his successful rival, Bonaparte, and ended up by loathing him. It was at this time that the Chouan Cadoudal appeared. He was only one of many plotters who had knocked at Pichegru's door. But he was at the head of a solid organization, and he offered Pichegru the role of moving spirit in the plot aimed at killing the First Consul. The general accepted—all the more willingly since General Moreau was one of the plotters. But a Chouan who had been arrested informed the police.

Immediately, the city was declared to be in a state of alert. The death sentence was decreed for anyone sheltering the "brigands," and the three leaders of the plot were soon in the hands of the authorities.

"Why did you come to Paris?" Cadoudal was asked.

"I came to assassinate the First Consul."

"Did you have a lot of men with you?"

"No, because I was not supposed to assassinate the First Consul until there was a prince in Paris, and so far there is none."

"And so the plan was conceived—and was to be carried out—in agreement with a French prince of the Old Regime?"

"Yes, Citizen Judge."

A French prince? A terrible deed was in the making. According to Bonaparte, the prince could only be Louis Antoine de Bourbon-Condé, the Duc d'Enghien, one of the commanders of the émigré army, who was living on Bavarian territory at Ettenheim, not far from the right bank of the Rhine. Actually, however, the plotters had been awaiting the arrival of the Prince de Polignac, who had no connection with the Bourbon family.

A gendarme, Sergeant Lamothe, was sent from Strasbourg disguised as a civilian. He put up at the Auberge du Soleil at Ettenheim, and he got the proprietor of the inn—loyal companion of the prince—to talking. The latter pronounced the name of the Marquis de Thumery with a German accent. In his mouth the *t* became a *d* and the last syllable was transformed into *riey*. Sergeant Lamothe, therefore, understood him to say "Dumouriez." Likewise, in his report the gendarme transformed the name Lieutenant Schmidt into "Smith."

When the report reached the Tuileries, on March 8, Bonaparte went into a terrible rage. So Dumouriez, that traitor to the Republic, that deserter who had gone over to the enemy, had joined up with the Duc d'Enghien! And Smith—no doubt the famous Spencer Smith, the English agent from Stuttgart—was also at Ettenheim! Like a bear in a cage, the First Consul paced back and forth in his study.

"Am I a dog that can be killed in the street while my murderers are sacrosanct? They are attacking me bodily. . . . I'll give it back to them in kind. . . . I won't fail to punish the plotters. The guilty man's head will be my recompense!"

Just at this time it was being rumored (the rumor was in fact false) that the Duc d'Enghien often crossed the Rhine to go to Strasbourg. Bonaparte's wrath knew no bounds:

> The Bourbons think they can spill my blood like that of the lowest beast! But my blood is as good as theirs! I'll give them back the same kind of terror they are trying to fill me with. I'll forgive Moreau his weakness and the fact that he was carried away by a

stupid jealousy. But the first of those princes who comes within my reach will be shot without mercy. . . . I'll teach them to know what kind of man they are dealing with. . . .

"May I suggest," Cambacérès put in, "that if some personage from the Bourbon family was in your place of power, rigor would not be carried to such a point?"

"What are you saying, Monsieur? Please be advised that I will not spare those who send assassins to get me."

The next day, at ten in the morning, the First Consul summoned his council to the Tuileries: Cambacérès, Lebrun, Réal, Murat, Chief Justice Régnier, Fouché, and Talleyrand. Fouché and Talleyrand would do everything possible—and it would not be difficult—to urge Bonaparte into creating an impassable chasm between the France of yesterday and the imperial France of tomorrow. Thus the future Emperor, who had not been involved in the Revolution, would become the accomplice of the *conventionnels* (members of the National Convention). Their calculation was accurate. And Bonaparte soon furnished them with proof of the fact. To the demi-regicide Cambacérès, who had opined that before violating a frontier one should perhaps gather complementary intelligence, he shouted: "These days, you're very sparing of Bourbon blood!"

But Cambacérès by no means considered himself defeated. When the council was over, he followed Bonaparte into his study and reminded him "even more emphatically of the consequences of the deed he was about to commit." The Second Consul spoke of violating the right of nations, of spilling the blood of kings, and of all Europe —which, after the abduction now being planned, might rise up against France.

"Up to this point," he said, "you have been a stranger to all the crimes of the Revolution. But now you are going to imitate us."

"In the eyes of the world," Bonaparte replied, "the death of the Duc d'Enghien will be nothing more than a just reprisal for what was attempted against me. The house of Bourbon must be taught that the blows they aim at others can return upon them! Death is the only way to force them to give up their abominable undertakings!"

Then he repeated the argument advanced by Talleyrand: "Once we've gone this far, there's no turning back!"

That same evening, Baron Méneval found Bonaparte hunched

over a huge mahogany table illuminated by torches. A big map of the Rhine region was spread out on it. The First Consul was calculating distances, and establishing timetables. Suddenly he got up and dictated an order to be sent to Berthier: "Citizen Minister, you will please order General Ordener to go by the night post to Strasbourg. The aim of this mission is to advance to Ettenheim, surround the city, and remove the Duc d'Enghien, Dumouriez, and an English colonel. . . ."

For a whole hour, while the rest of the palace slept, Bonaparte dictated, scrupulously preparing all the details of the ambush.

At Ettenheim, the Duc d'Enghien suspected nothing. Of course he was receiving a pension from London, and of course he had several times offered his sword to the British government to fight France. But there was nothing new in that. Had not the émigrés been in the pay of the Republic's enemies since 1792? The Duc d'Enghien had had no part in Cadoudal's plot. Indeed, he had at first believed that the plot was pure invention, though he had later recognized the truth of the matter when the first accomplices arrested by the consular police had confessed.

Napoleon was at Malmaison when he learned that the prince's arrest had been effected without difficulty. French troops had penetrated into foreign territory and, in violation of the right of nations, carried off the Duc d'Enghien. The First Consul received a report from Police Chief Major Charlot that is worth reading:

> General Dumouriez turns out to be the Marquis de Thumery, whom I arrested. I made inquiries to ascertain whether Dumouriez had been at Ettenheim, and was assured that he had not. I assume the only reason he was thought to be there was that his name had been confused with that of General Thumery. The Duc d'Enghien, with whom I talked of the matter, assured me that Dumouriez had never come to Ettenheim; that it was possible that the latter had been designated to bring him instructions from England, but that in any case he would not have received him, since it was beneath his rank to have dealings with such people; that he considered Bonaparte to be a great man, but that as a prince of the House of Bourbon he had sworn implacable hatred toward him, and toward the French, against whom he would wage war on every opportunity. . . .

Thus Bonaparte had evidence that Sergeant Lamothe had been seriously mistaken. The First Consul was still in a position where he could stop the entire proceedings; but he had been irritated by the last sentence in Major Charlot's report, and refused to be deterred by the sergeant's mistake. He made no change in his orders. Forty-eight hours later, while the Duc d'Enghien was on the way from Strasbourg to Paris, a second courier arrived at Malmaison with papers seized at Ettenheim. Some of the documents proved that the duke was at the head of an antirepublican network; a rather peaceably inclined organization, to be sure, but one with branches reaching as far as France. A copy of a letter he had written to his grandfather, the Prince de Condé, showed that he had been thinking of the possibility of Bonaparte's death: "It is very important for me to remain close to the border, since the way things stand now, the death of one man could bring a total change."

No doubt Enghien was thinking of the dictator's death on the field of battle, since he abhorred assassination; but all Bonaparte could see in this was an allusion to the success of Cadoudal's plans.

Finally, the last of the Condés was implicated by the rough draft of a long report he had prepared for transmittal to Sir Charles Stuart:

> The Duc d'Enghien beseeches His Britannic Majesty to kindly grant him the favor of considering employing his services, no matter how or in what military grade, against our implacable enemies by deigning to entrust him with the command of some auxiliary troops among whom he might place veteran loyal officers of his nation and the deserters who might join him. The number of such troops would be great at the present moment, when the Republic is beset with troubles. The Duc d'Enghien has been in a position to become convinced of this fact in a positive manner during a sojourn of two years on the borders of France.

When Josephine learned from her husband of his plans, she begged him not to stain his hands with the blood of the Condés. He replied:

> Women should not become involved in matters of this kind. My policy demands this move. By it, I will acquire the right to use clemency thereafter. Impunity would only encourage dissension; and I would be compelled to persecute, exile, and sentence people unceasingly, to undo all I have done for the émigrés, and to put myself in the hands of the Jacobins. The Royalists have already compromised me several times vis-à-vis the revolution-

aries. The execution of the Duc d'Enghien will free my hands
with respect to everyone.

That evening, Josephine insisted once again, and Bonaparte lost
patience with her: "Run along! You're a mere child!"

"Well, Bonaparte," she replied, "if you have your prisoner killed,
you will be guillotined yourself, like my first husband. And this time
I'll be with you!"

He shrugged his shoulders. Women understand nothing about
politics: it was a fixed idea of his.

Would Fouché have a better chance? He came to Malmaison at
nine o'clock in the morning. Bonaparte was walking in the park,
taking great strides. "I know what has brought you," he told Fouché.
"Today I am striking a great blow—one that is necessary."

> I then tried to tell him that if he did not produce irrefutable
> evidence that the duke was conspiring against his person at Et-
> tenheim, he would stir up both France and Europe against him.
> "What need is there for proof?" Bonaparte shouted. "Isn't he
> a Bourbon—and the most dangerous of them all?"

Fouché insisted, and set forth "political reasons sufficient to over-
ride state policy." But it was in vain. The First Consul finally told him
angrily:

> "Haven't you and your friends told me a hundred times that
> I would end up by being the General Monck of France and re-
> storing the Bourbons? Well, it is no longer possible to retreat.
> What stronger guarantee could I give to the Revolution than that
> you cemented with the blood of a king? And anyway, I have to
> get it over with. I'm surrounded by plots. I must instigate terror
> or perish."

While the Duc d'Enghien was on his way to Vincennes, and while
the military commission, very skittish about the role it had to play,
was becoming acquainted with the brief (consisting of five sheets of
paper containing nothing more than the questions to be posed to the
accused), Bonaparte wrote the following note to Police Chief Réal:

> Go immediately to Vincennes to have the prisoner interro-
> gated. Here are the questions you will have asked: "Have you
> borne arms against your country? Have you been in the pay of
> England? Have you tried to offer your services to England? Have

you not been heedless of all natural sentiment, to the point where you called the French people your most cruel enemy? Did you not propose levying a legion and encouraging desertion by the troops of the Republic, saying that your sojourn of two years near the border had enabled you to gather intelligence from the troops stationed on the Rhine?" And finally: "Do you have any knowledge of the plot devised by England with a view to overthrowing the Republic? And if the plot had succeeded, were you not supposed to enter Alsace or even go to Paris, depending upon the circumstances?"

Réal was sleeping peacefully at home. But at Vincennes, in a little room adjoining the "courtroom," a captain was interrogating the prisoner. Enghien told his life story, admitted that he had been receiving a pension from England (his property, after all, had been confiscated by the Republic), and stated he had never been in contact with Cadoudal or Dumouriez. He had not been involved in any plot; he fought openly.

When the interrogation was over, a pen was handed to him. "Before signing the present record of proceedings," he wrote, "I request most emphatically a private audience with the First Consul. My name, my rank, my way of thinking, and the horror of my situation give me hope that he will not refuse my request."

The judges deliberated. Should the trial not be postponed so that the prisoner's legitimate request might be conveyed to the First Consul? Réal should have been there that evening, but he was still sleeping. No doubt he would have transmitted the prince's request to the master. There is every likelihood that after this interview between the soldier of Rivoli and the soldier of Berstheim, blood would perhaps not have been spilled. But in the absence of Réal, Savary was in charge. The judges were there to "pass judgment on the spot."

The door of the salon opened. Several officers came up from the courtyard. Savary, standing behind the chair occupied by General Hulin, who was presiding, was warming himself at the fire. The prince, surrounded by gendarmes, entered the room. One can imagine the interest and curiosity felt by these officers—six or seven soldiers of the Republic—when they looked at this Bourbon with the long, light-brown hair, clear eyes, and aquiline nose: this last of the Condés, whom they were going to try without documents, and without even granting him counsel. It was not a trial; it was an assassination.

"Have you borne arms against France?"

"Look at me. I'm a Bourbon. It was you who used arms against me. I have maintained the rights of my family. A Condé cannot reenter France unarmed. My birth and my opinions make me the eternal enemy of your government."

According to Savary, in his *Mémoires,* Hulin then alluded to Cadoudal's plot:

> "You will never convince us that you were indifferent to events whose consequences for you would be great. . . ."
>
> "Monsieur," Enghien replied after a silence, "I understand you very well. It was not my intention to remain indifferent. I had asked the English whether I might serve in the British army, and they had replied that they could not arrange for such service, but that I should stay on the Rhine where I had a role to play immediately, and so I waited. Monsieur, I have nothing more to tell you."

If these were the words actually spoken by the prince, his quasi-admission might well have appeased the conscience of the judges and given them grounds for believing there was a degree of complicity with Georges.

"Take the accused away and clear the courtroom."

The deliberation was brief. Hulin dictated to the clerk: "The court-martial having deliberated behind closed doors, the presiding officer asked for a vote, beginning with the junior officer present. The presiding officer having cast his vote last, the court unanimously found the accused guilty and invoked. . . ."

The general stopped. By virtue of what law were they to sentence this cousin of Louis XVI who, in combating the regicide Republic, had tried to avenge his dead and recover what had been taken from him? Hulin hesitated, then plunged on ahead. They would fill in the blanks in the sentence later. ". . . and invoked Article———of the Law of———, in these terms———; and, in consequence, sentenced him to death. It is ordered that the present sentence be carried out immediately at the discretion of the captain serving as *rapporteur.* . . ."

Hulin then took up the pen to write to the First Consul, asking that he grant the audience requested by the condemned.

"What are you doing?" Savary demanded, when he saw the presiding officer begin his letter.

"I am writing to the First Consul."

The executioner cut off the discussion: "Your job is done. The rest concerns only me!"

Réal had not been awakened. The First Consul's letter was waiting there for him, in plain view, on his night table. He saw it when he awoke, and read it. In a panic, he rapidly put on his uniform of Councillor of State and set out on the road to Vincennes. At the city gate he met Savary, who asked where he was going.

"To Vincennes," he replied. "Last night I received orders to go there for the interrogation of the Duc d'Enghien."

Then, dumfounded, Réal heard Savary (likewise dumfounded) tell him that it was all over: the Duc d'Enghien had been shot. Réal, trembling for fear he would lose his position, went back home as Savary headed for Malmaison.

At eleven o'clock he was received by the First Consul, to whom he reported that the proceedings were completed. Bonaparte seemed surprised. All this haste astonished him (which may indicate that the order given to Murat the preceding evening is apocryphal). Savary told Bonaparte what had happened.

"There is something in this that is quite beyond me," Bonaparte said. "What we have here is a crime that serves no purpose, but tends to make me appear odious."

As he left the Consul's study, Savary met Josephine.

"Eh bien," she asked him, "is it over?"

"Oui, Madame. He died this morning—with a great deal of courage, I must admit. When he was dead, the gendarmes were told they could take his clothes, his watch, and all the money he had on him. But no one wanted to touch them."

Josephine, it is said, then rushed into Bonaparte's room, saying: "The Duc d'Enghien is dead! Ah, mon ami! What have you done?"

And the First Consul is supposed to have replied: "Those wretches were too quick about it."

He seems to have sincerely regretted the speed with which everything was done—done, that is, in accordance with his own wishes —but he was going to cover up for his subordinates. At dinner that evening everyone was silent. When he got up from the table, Bonaparte was furious and shouted: "At least they'll see what we are capable of! From now on, I hope they'll leave us in peace!"

Later, in the salon, where the heavy silence again reigned, he exclaimed: "I have spilled blood. But I had to do it, and I may do it again. If so, however, it will be without anger and simply because bloodletting is one of the procedures of political medicine. I am the man of the State. I am the French Revolution, and I will uphold it."

On March 24, in order to take the pulse of the capital, Bonaparte went to the Opera with Josephine. "Like a man walking into artillery fire," he advanced to the front of his box seat. There was a burst of applause. And so, as Chateaubriand put it, the wind had blown and all was over.

Ten days before he died, Napoleon added the following lines to the testament he had already completed:

> I had the Duc d'Enghien arrested and tried because it was necessary for the security, the interest, and the honor of the French people at a time when the Comte d'Artois, as he himself acknowledged, had 60 assassins in his pay in Paris. Under similar circumstances, I would still do the same thing.

After this admission, it would be puerile to reproach Savary for his too ferocious haste and Réal for sleeping too deeply. The night of Vincennes was the doing of Bonaparte. It was he and he alone who, in full awareness of what he was doing, turned the Duc d'Enghien "into dust before his time."

The shots fired by the execution squad at Vincennes were heard throughout Europe. The Russians were the most indignant. The same people who, four years earlier, with the approval of Alexander, had assassinated Czar Paul (and by horrible means), were now talking of "the most cowardly of usurpers—that veritable tiger who now governs France."

Czar Alexander, who had ordered his court to wear mourning·for Enghien (although he had no blood ties whatsoever with the Bourbons), was trying to drag Europe into a regular crusade against "the leader of the brigands—the monster lurking in his lair of the Tuileries." But Austria, although "disturbed by the news of the drama of Vincennes," dared not say anything. As Cobenzl admitted straight out, his country "was afraid of Bonaparte."

Yet the Czar still hoped that the Elector of Baden, whose territory had been violated, would be prompted by the German Diet to do more than send a weak letter of protest. But that was all he would do. At the mere mention of Bonaparte's name, the Elector quaked. As for the Bourbons of Spain, Naples, and Florence, they even avoided wearing mourning for their cousin.

Thus the "court of Petersburg" gained nothing at all from the effort put into its "folly," as Napoleon put it. And it was Talleyrand, laughing up his sleeve, who had the last word when he wrote to the Russian chancellor:

> One may well ask the following question. If, at the time when England was considering the assassination of Paul I, it had been learned that the authors of these plots were only one league from the border, would not the authorities have been in a great hurry to have them arrested?

All that remained to make a clean sweep was to try Moreau, Georges Cadoudal, and Pichegru. Pichegru committed suicide in prison, and Moreau was acquitted. Cadoudal was sentenced to death. He died as he had lived—as a man of wit. As he climbed up on the scaffold, he said: "We did more than we thought we would. We wanted to give Paris a king, and we gave it an emperor!"

For the Jacobins, Bonaparte could from now on be considered as having spilled the same blood that they had. "I'm delighted," exclaimed Curée, the "tested republican." "Bonaparte has joined up with the Convention."

Certainly there was no ground for the continuing fear that he would imitate General Monck. If he were offered the crown (about which he had been thinking for a year), he would keep it for himself! Napoleon was being impelled toward the throne not only by a few arriviste senators like Fontanes, but by the force of circumstances. From everywhere—and especially from the army—petitions came into the Tuileries demanding that the First Consul (the other two no longer existed) become emperor. Thibaudeau reports that the sailors of the Toulon fleet even demanded he divorce Josephine immediately so that he could remarry and found a dynasty. On every hand, people were talking of empire as "a certain means of stabilizing the peace and tranquillity of France."

It was Fouché, the mass murderer of Lyons, who offered his services to implement the wishes of the nation, to win over those who were hesitating, and to convert the opposition. A commission was created. And on March 27, only one week after the execution of the Duc d'Enghien, the Senate "invited" the First Consul to "complete his work by rendering it immortal, like his glory."

The corpse of the unfortunate man decaying in the moats of Vincennes was to serve as a stairstep to the new throne.

The Senate had also posed the question of hereditary power. Josephine on this eve of the regime demurred: "Bonaparte, don't make yourself a king!"

He shrugged. He had made his decision. In the meantime, he responded to the senators' request, inviting them to "inform him of all their thoughts on the matter."

On April 30, Curée—still the "tested republican"—took the floor at the Tribunate. He had been well prompted. He asked that the government of the Republic be entrusted to an emperor, and that the imperial power be made hereditary. After three hours of debate, the Tribunate passed the following resolution:

> *Primo.* That Napoleon Bonaparte be named Emperor, and that in this capacity he be made responsible for governing the French Republic.
> *Secundo.* That the title of Emperor and the imperial power be made hereditary in his family, from male to male, by primogeniture.
> *Tertio.* That in effecting the modifications of the organization of constituted authorities demanded by the establishment of hereditary power, equality, liberty, and the rights of the people be preserved in full.

On May 4 the Senate received a delegation from the Tribunate which informed them of the "resolution" that had been passed: the creation of a new monarchy. At this point the presiding officer of the upper chamber told them, in all seriousness: "For the first time, you are exercising vis-à-vis the Senate that republican and popular initiative assigned to you by the fundamental laws."

The Consulate was finished. In a few days, to the sound of cannon, the Senate would bring to Bonaparte the decree establishing his imperial dignity.

XI

THE EMPEROR OF THE REVOLUTION

One never climbs so high as when
he knows not where he is going.

NAPOLEON

(BONAPARTE WAS STAYING at St.-Cloud when, on May 10, 1804, the
Senate unanimously voted for the establishment of an imperial government "headed by Napoleon, since this is important for the interest of the French people.")

By the same proclamation, it was declared that the hereditary
power should pass "to the descendants of Napoleon Bonaparte and,
in the absence of offspring, to those of Joseph and Louis," who were
created imperial princes. What followed made Joseph wince, since
the *senatus consultum* stipulated that the Emperor could adopt as
his successor whichever of his nephews he designated, but only when
the fortunate party so chosen had reached the age of eighteen. For
the succeeding ages, adoption would be prohibited. Thus those future emperors of France who had no direct heir could not designate
their successors.

St.-Cloud was buzzing with anxious rumors. Everyone wondered
what his position and title would be. Since no decisions had yet been
made, the claimants besieged Talleyrand and Fouché, who were
supposed to be in on the secret. Joseph and Louis were more or less
calm: they would certainly become "Imperial Highnesses." But Mesdames Bacciochi and Murat—Élisa and Caroline—were more anxious. Their husbands seemed not to have been named princes,
meaning that they themselves would remain commoners! And this
at a time when those "strangers"—Julie and Hortense—would bear
the title of princess!

And the ministers? The former consuls? The high dignitaries? The military leaders? What would their fate be? Since an empire had been created, was not a titled and bedizened court indispensable?

On May 17 it was rumored that the next day would be "the great day." And indeed, beginning at dawn of the eighteenth, one salvo after another was heard. Soon, preceded by a regiment of cuirassiers, the senators arrived at the palace. Napoleon, wearing his uniform of a colonel of the Guards, was waiting for them in the Grand Salon. Surrounded by Councillors of State and generals, he was calm and seemed in perfect control of himself—although for the first time he would hear himself called "Sire" and "Your Majesty."

The solemn moment arrived. Cambacérès stepped forward, and after having addressed the new sovereign, finished his speech with these words: ("For the glory and happiness of the Republic, the Senate proclaims, from this moment, Napoleon Emperor of the French.")

> I accept [the Emperor replied]. I accept the title that you deem useful to the glory of the nation. I submit to the sanction of the people the law of heredity. I hope that France will never repent of the honors she will confer upon my family. In any case, from the very day that my descendants cease—if they should cease—to deserve the love and confidence of this great nation, my spirit will no longer be with them.

Loud shouts of "Vive l'Empereur!" punctuated his words and made the windows of the salon vibrate.

Then "Imperial Prince" Joseph was named Grand Elector, and "Imperial Prince" Louis was named Grand Constable. Obviously, there could be nothing for Lucien, who had found refuge in Rome and refused to get a divorce, or for Jérôme, who was not only a quasi-deserter but had dared to get married in the United States without having asked permission.

Of the two ex-consuls, Cambacérès and Lebrun, the former was made Arch-Chancellor of the Empire, and the latter, Arch-Treasurer. Then the senators went to call on Josephine, whom they "were glad to be the first to address" with the title of "Imperial Majesty."

Before the guests were seated at the table, Duroc announced to the court that henceforth the two former consuls would be called "Monseigneur," as would the high dignitaries. The ministers would have the title of "Excellency," and the sixteen new marshals that of "Monsieur le Maréchal."

It was plain to see that the Emperor, when he came into the salon, took a certain pleasure in calling his sisters-in-law "Princess Joseph" and "Princess Louis." Although Murat remained calm, since he feared his imperial brother-in-law, the same could not be said of his wife. Indeed, Caroline was a prey to the greatest despair. Mme. de Rémusat has described the scene for us:

> During the dinner, she was so lacking in self-control that on several occasions, when she heard the Emperor mention "Princess Louis," she could not hold back her tears. She drank glass after big glass of water, trying to get hold of herself and give the appearance of doing something; but the tears always won out. Everyone was embarrassed, and her brother wore a rather nasty smile. As for me, I experienced the greatest surprise—and, at the same time, what I might call a kind of disgust—at seeing this pretty young woman consumed by such petty feelings. At that time, Mme. Murat was twenty-two or twenty-three years old. Her dazzlingly fair complexion, her beautiful blond hair, the circlet of flowers on her head, and the pink dress she was wearing—all these things endowed her with something young, almost child-like, which contrasted unpleasantly with those feelings, proper only to someone much older, which plainly possessed her. One could have no pity for her tears; and I am sure they produced a most unpleasant impression on everyone—not just myself. Mme. Bacciochi, older and with more composure, was not at all moist-eyed. But she was abrupt and peremptory, and treated all of us with noticeable haughtiness.

The next day, in the Empress' salon, Mme. Murat gave the Emperor a frightful time. The officers on duty, chamberlains, and ladies of honor in the next room heard her shouts, her sobbing, and her moans.

"Why am I and my sisters condemned to obscurity, while strangers are heaped with honors and dignities?"

"I have the power," exclaimed the Emperor, "to confer honors as I see fit!"

When Caroline's screeches were redoubled, Napoleon remarked: "Indeed, to judge from your claims, mesdames, one would think we had received the crown from the hands of our late father, the king!"

Finding nothing she could say in reply to such a pertinent remark,
Mme.Murat decided to faint. Seeing his sister's body stretched out on
the rug, Napoleon was overcome by pity. Henceforth Mmes.Murat
and Bacciochi would be princesses and Imperial Highnesses. But
their husbands would remain—for the time being—commoners.

The news appeared in the *Moniteur* on May 20. It was a Sunday
—or, more precisely, Décadi, 30 Floréal, of the Year XII, since the
Revolutionary calendar was still in effect. Floréal was coming to an
end, and Prairial would begin in a few hours; but the weather was
nonetheless bad, and the main thoroughfares of Paris were deep in
mud.

This was most unfortunate on that particular day. For since morning, the scoffing Parisians crowded along the sidewalks (an innovation
of the Consulate) had been observing a strange spectacle. Preceded
by mounted buglers and drummers, a band on a float, and the dragoons of the gendarmerie, flanked by a cohort of plumed generals,
and followed by more buglers and drummers, from fifteen to twenty
mounted civilians in silk stockings and short breeches were trying
without much success to parade like cavalry officers. These gentlemen (the appellation "citizen" had gone out of use the day before)
—the mayors of Paris and the presiding officers and chancellors of the
Corps Législatif and the Senate—were making their way thus arranged to the main public squares of the capital to read the decree
proclaiming Bonaparte Emperor of the French. When the readings
were over, the masquerade (as it was called by Fontanes, presiding
officer of the Corps Législatif) departed to the strains of a fast march
that made the horses rear. Fontanes' own horse (he said later) almost
threw him in the mud time after time.

As the Parisians gazed upon this "Mardi Gras parade" (the expression is again from Fontanes), they of course applauded, but without
delirious enthusiasm. The majority was no doubt satisfied that the
"factions had been annihilated" and that "revolutionary fury was
only a memory," but the people were still a bit baffled by this return
to formulas they had thought were banished once and for all.

"He's only an ordinary man after all!" sighed Beethoven. And
with an angry stroke of the pen he deleted the subtitle of his Third
Symphony, *Bonaparte,* and wrote: *"Sinfonia eroica, composta per
festiggiare il sovvenire d'un grand'Uomo."* For Ludwig van Beethoven, the genius of the Revolution was dead.

The first holiday of the new empire took place on July 15. After the Te Deum at Notre Dame, Napoleon went to the Invalides to hear the oath sworn "to the Emperor" by the members of the Legion of Honor. The sky, which had been hazy that morning, was clouded over. At the gates the governor presented the keys to the building. In front of the church Cardinal de Belloy, in as loud a voice as his advanced age permitted him, addressed the Emperor and offered him holy water. "Napoleon," Stendhal tells us, "smiled a theatrical smile, in which one shows one's teeth while the eyes remain unsmiling." The Emperor reached his throne under the canopy. Everyone who had anything to do with the new State was there: the "monseigneurs" and the "excellencies," wearing plumes and gold braid, many of them surprised to see the old order of things so quickly restored. The Cardinal Legate began to say the Mass. After the reading from the Gospels, Lacépède launched into a flowery speech.

To the sound of cheers, Napoleon left the Invalides: by this time the sky was lowering with stormclouds. A fountain with a marvelous pedestal intended to show off to the Parisians the Lion of St. Mark's stolen from the Republic of Venice had been built in front of the church. Such things already seemed quite natural. As Napoleon would say one day: "I could marry the Madonna without shocking the Parisians."

That day, Napoleon had put on his already legendary uniform: that of a colonel of the Guards. Moreover, he was booted and spurred and was wearing his little hat. But he concluded (wrongly, as it happens) that henceforth he needed imperial regalia. And so three days later he decided to wear, on all solemn occasions, a white tunic edged in gold and a red velvet cape embroidered with golden bees. He would wear a golden crown in the form of entwined laurel leaves, hold a golden scepter and a golden staff, and gird on a sword whose golden hilt was studded with diamonds. Josephine, too, would wear a velvet cloak of "imperial purple" over a white silk dress embroidered in gold.

Only his anointment and coronation were now lacking. Napoleon was already thinking about it, and was waiting for the Pope's reply on this subject. Accordingly, he concluded the decree on imperial pomp with these words: "Everything relative to the ceremonies and festivities of the coronation will be determined subsequently."

Anyone observing Bonaparte at this time would never suspect
that he had once been the occupant of that miserable Room 9 at the
Hôtel de Cherbourg, and that he had taken meals costing six sous in
some cheap eating house in Les Halles. Now, upon arising, the Emperor took tea or orange-flower water in a silver cup. He resided in
the palace of Catherine de' Médicis, the mother of three French
kings. His bedroom on the ground floor of the Tuileries had two
windows with a view of the gardens: it was the former *chambre de
parade* of Louis XVI. His map room was the same in which the king
used to sleep, and where Catherine de' Médicis once worked. Did he
remember that not so long ago, on the eve of Vendémiaire, he himself had come into this room so poorly dressed, with breeches so worn
out, that he asked Mme. Tallien to get him, through her contacts,
some cloth for a uniform?

Every morning, in what had been Louis XVI's study, the Emperor
would soak in his bath, his head covered with a kerchief whose
corners hung down to his neck. So attired, he would have the dispatches and newspapers read to him. When he got out of his bath,
he would be given another kerchief, since the first one would always
have been soaked as a result of his constantly twisting, turning, and
splashing in the bathwater. In the summer, he would put on a white
piqué dressing gown and trousers. In the winter he wore heavy
flannel trousers and dressing gown. Those mornings when he did not
bathe, he would put on this same attire immediately upon getting up,
and sit down by the fireplace. (A fire was kept going almost all the
year round.) Then he would read the papers himself and throw them
on the floor when he was finished with them. It was the secretary's
job to pick them up and file them.

When his bath had been taken and the dispatches had been read,
Napoleon would go to his Athénienne of Sèvres porcelain and begin
his toilette.

> I used to shave him [Constant wrote] before I had taught him
> to shave himself. . . . When he had got the habit, he at first used
> a mirror attached to the window, as everyone else did. But he
> would get so close to it and lather his face so recklessly that he
> would inundate the mirror, the window and the curtains, the
> dressing table, and himself. In order to remedy this inconveni-
> ence, the servants held a council, and it was decided that Roustam

would hold the mirror. When the Emperor had shaved one side of his face, he would turn the other side to the light and make Roustam move from the left to the right, or vice versa, depending upon which side he had begun with.

When he had shaved, he would wash his face and hands, then do his nails carefully. "He had beautiful hands," Bourrienne tells us, "and he was very proud of them. So he took particularly good care of them; and sometimes, while talking, he would look at them with great satisfaction."

> Then [Constant continues] I would take off his flannel under-vest and his shirt, and go over his chest with a very soft silk brush. After this I would give him a rubdown with eau de Cologne, which he used in large amounts, since he was given this brushing and rubdown every day. It was in the Middle East that he had learned this hygienic habit, which was very good for him. . . . When all these preparations had been completed, I would put light flannel or cashmere slippers on his feet, white silk stockings (he never wore any other kind), underdrawers of very fine linen or fustian, and either white cashmere breeches with soft riding boots or tight-fitting trousers of the same material and color, with short English boots that came halfway up his calf. They were fitted with little silver spurs no more than six lignes in length. All his boots had that kind of spurs on them.
>
> Then I would put on him his flannel undervest and his shirt, a very slim chiffon cravat, and over that a black silk collar. Finally, a *gilet rond* of white piqué, and either a light cavalryman's uni-form or a grenadier's uniform—but most often the former. When he was dressed, he would be handed his handkerchief, his snuff-box, and a little tortoise-shell case full of licorice flavored with aniseed and cut very fine.
>
> One can see from the above that the Emperor had himself dressed from head to foot. He never put a hand to anything. He let himself be handled like a child, and during all this time he would be tending to business matters. Napoleon was born, so to speak, requiring *valets de chambre.* He had as many as three of them when he was a general, and he had himself looked after with as much luxury as when he was at the peak of his fortunes.

Unless he was getting ready to go hunting, he would go into his study immediately upon being dressed. That study, from which orders were sent to the four corners of the world, had a single window looking out upon the garden. Leaning down a little, one could see the banks of the Seine "covered with wash-houses." Opposite the window was a great, glassed-in bookcase in the middle of which a grandfather clock chimed the hours. The Emperor, his back to the fireplace, worked at a mahogany desk with gilded copper fixtures (*cuivres dorés*) that he had designed himself, in the form of a violin. Here in his study, too, he lacerated the arms of his chair with his penknife and dried his pen on the sleeves of his coat. Facing him was a console divided into pigeonholes for files. "The new books of the week" were ranged in type.

His private secretary, "silent as a piece of furniture," sat at a little table placed in the bay of the window. The torture would begin for the poor wretch. Napoleon would at first dictate seated at his desk. Then, as the ideas developed and his thoughts came in a rush (though without confusion), he would get up and begin his legendary pacing back and forth.

> This pacing [Méneval reports] continued throughout his dictation. His delivery was dignified and emphatic, but was never interrupted by a pause. As he got further into his subject, his inspiration would make itself felt. It would be manifested by a more lively tone and a kind of tic consisting in a movement of the right arm, which he twisted, pulling with his hand.

He dictated terribly fast. One had to catch his thoughts on the fly, skipping over words and replacing them with blanks to be filled in later. He would distort or transform all proper names: Salamanca would become "Smolensk," or the Ebre would become the "Elbe." "Take this down!"

He would skip from one subject to another. But each of his secretaries finally came to know his habits, his favorite expressions, and what Baron Fain calls "the dominant idea of the moment." It can be found in all his letters and conversations of the period in question.

> Napoleon rarely wrote with his own hand. Writing fatigued him: his hand could not follow the rapidity of his ideas. He took up the pen only when, by chance, he was alone and needed to commit to paper the first rush of an idea. But after a few lines he would stop and throw down the pen. . . . His writing was a hodgepodge of disconnected letters, and was quite illegible. Half the

letters were lacking in every word. He could not himself make out what he had written, or else he did not want to take the trouble. . . .

Sometimes, between two dictations, the Emperor would stretch out on the settee near the fireplace. He would close his eyes and meditate.

"When I meditate," he admitted, "I'm in a state of agitation that is really painful. I'm like a girl having a baby."

But outwardly, he would seem to be dozing.

"If I always seem to be ready for everything, to face up to anything," he explained to Roederer one day, "it is because I never undertake anything at all without first having meditated for a long time and foreseen what might happen. It is not a genie, but meditation, that suddenly reveals to me, in secret, what I must say and do under circumstances not anticipated by others."

When this first stint of work was finished, Napoleon would begin his daily life as a sovereign. Going out from what he called his "interior," he would enter his salon—formerly the boudoir of Queen Marie Thérèse, the wife of Louis XIV, then of Madame Royale, the daughter of Louis XVI. The *grandes entrées*—those who had been granted this right because of their position or by special favor—were admitted. Writing under the Restoration, the chamberlain Bausset reported: "Many people who today seem to have forgotten it placed a high value at that time upon the employment of such a distinction." The Emperor would speak to each one of them (something the kings had never done), and when he had made his rounds (by that time it would be nine thirty in the morning) he would retire to have breakfast. The prefect of the palace would precede him into the salon, where the breakfast would be served by the first butler. Like the King before him, the Emperor ate alone at a little mahogany cloth-covered table. Often his breakfast lasted no longer than eight minutes. But when he felt the need to "close the study," as he would say in announcing it, the meal might last a rather long time. "On these occasions," Bausset tells us, "nothing could equal the gentle gaiety and charm of his conversation. His expressions were rapid, positive, and picturesque. I owed the most pleasant hours of my life to this time of my service."

Sometimes, at Bausset's suggestion, he would receive savants and artists while having breakfast. But he never went so far as Louis XIV, who asked one of them to share his meal.

Napoleon would sometimes summon his nephews and nieces during mealtime. It was only they who (sometimes) sat down at his table. One day when Hortense's two sons were eating with him, a boiled egg was served to little Prince Louis, who was three and a half years old. Napoleon caused him to turn his head by pointing out a toy to him, and then stole his egg. When the child saw that his egg cup was empty, he picked up a knife and threatened the Emperor: "Give me back my egg or I'll kill you!"

"What, you rascal? You want to kill your uncle?"

"Give it back, or I'll kill you."

Napoleon complied, laughing, and said: "You'll be a strapping blade!"

On another occasion he said to the little Napoléone, Élisa's daughter: "Alors, Mademoiselle. I've just heard some fine news. You made peepee in the bed last night."

The five-year-old child—the future Comtesse Camerata—replied: "Mon oncle, if you can't say anything except stupidities, I shall leave."

He laughed about it all that day.

After breakfast, the real work began. Back in his study, Napoleon governed, received ministers and director generals, or presided over councils.

"Sire, here is a draft. . . ."

The requests rushed in upon him.

Apparently, his voice had a very special accent when he shouted: "That's not accurate!" And he would repeat the statement, each time substantiating it with new evidence. Sometime he would get up and go to consult his "tools"—his situation reports, which enabled him (although everything was classified in his head) to determine instantly the size or position of a regiment, or perhaps the financial statement of each ministry.

Early in his reign, an important problem was being discussed at the Council of State: What emblem would be engraved on the imperial seal?

"A lion!"

"An elephant!"

"A rooster!"

"A rooster is a farmyard creature," Napoleon remarked. "He's too weak."

They took a vote, and the rooster was elected, but Napoleon insisted: "The rooster has no strength: he cannot be the image of an empire like that of France. We must choose between the eagle and the lion. . . . We should choose the lion, stretched out on the map of France with one paw ready to reach over the Rhine. Woe to the man that argues with me!"

Although they seemed somewhat to be imitating Austria and Russia, it was the eagle that they finally chose.

Dinner was served at six o'clock. Napoleon did not like to interrupt his work, and he often made Josephine wait unconscionably. One day, twenty-three chickens were put into the oven, one after the other, so that there would always be a properly roasted fowl for the Emperor.

At the Tuileries and at St.-Cloud, Napoleon and Josephine dined alone except on Sundays, when the imperial family—all but Madame Mère, who had the right to sit in an armchair—took their places at the table. Dinner was served by pages, seconded by *valets de chambre*, butlers, and carvers, but never by liveried servants. On these occasions, the meal lasted some twenty minutes. The Emperor drank Chambertin wine diluted with water. One of his menus has been preserved:

Two soups	*Purée de marrons.*
	Macaroni.
Two removes	*Brochet à la Chambord.*
	Culotte de boeuf garni.
Four entrées	*Filets de perdreaux à la Monglas.*
	Filets de canard sauvage au fumet de gibier.
	Fricassée de poulet à la chevalière.
	Côtelettes de mouton à la Soubise.
Two roasts	*Chapon au cresson.*
	Quartier d'agneau.
Desserts	*Gelée d'orange moulée.*
	Crème à la française au café.

Génoise décorée.
Gaufres à l'allemande.

The courses, under silver dish covers, were set out on the table "cold collation" (everything served at once), and the Emperor took his choice. Often he ate only soup, one course, and dessert; and he sometimes began with the sweets.

After the meal, on those occasions when he did not go directly back to his study, Napoleon went to Josephine's quarters on the ground floor of the palace, in the former apartments of Marie Antoinette. Court society met in the salons of the second floor, looking out over the Place du Carrousel. There, the Emperor often showed himself to be clumsy and lacking in breeding.

Mme. de Rémusat remarked: "He knew neither how to enter nor how to leave. He had no idea of how to greet someone, how to get up, or how to sit down. He walked this way and that, not knowing what to do or to say."

He asked André Grétry, the composer, for the twentieth time: "What is your name?"

"Sire, it is still Grétry," Grétry sighed.

One evening at the Tuileries he asked the Duchesse de Fleury rather crudely: "Well, Madame, are you still so fond of men?"

But there were times when he performed his act as a charmer. Bausset says: "Nothing could equal the grace and amiability of Napoleon. Endowed with a lively wit, a superior intelligence, and extraordinary tact, he surprised and enchanted people the most in his moments of abandon and chatting." Like a consummate actor, he made good use of both his famous smile and his steely glance.

How many contrasts there were in him! And those contrasts were constant. He was the man who one day told Montalivet: "I do not ask people to love me, but to serve me well. . . . I am not a man, but a historical personage."

Yet this did not prevent him from weeping when recalling his sister Pauline's loose behavior; or, later, from breaking into sobs when he told Hortense of his decision to get a divorce, as he said to her: "I am sacrificing my own happiness and yours as well."

He knew himself very well: "There are two distinct persons in me: the man of the head and the man of the heart."

The man of the heart actually did exist in him, in spite of what people have said to the contrary. Napoleon never forgot those who helped him in his youth—like the great Carnot, whose republicanism had cost him his pension. The Emperor not only had it restored, but he granted him retirement pay as a former minister in the amount of 10,000 francs. Again, the Guard was ordered to present arms to the Marshal de Ségur, who in 1784 had countersigned his commission as an officer of the king. Nor did Napoleon forget General du Teil, who had perhaps been the first at Auxonne to realize the worth of the young second lieutenant. Mme. de Montesson, who had crowned him on the day of distribution of prizes at Brienne, was granted a pension of 160,000 francs.

His sensitivity was extreme; and of all his senses, that of smell seems to have been the most developed. It was painful to him to remain in a room that had been recently painted. "His perception was so acute," Méneval tells us, "that he could detect the presence of a tunnel, a basement, or a sewer a long way away—or of odors coming from distant places that none of those around him had suspected."

His great febrility was manifested when he took off his clothes: he would tear them off and throw them to the floor in a kind of rage. His nervousness provoked terrible outbursts of anger. Those around him—from his marshals and his family to the lowest footman—were told they were fools, incompetents, traitors, thieves, and cowards.

One day he shouted at Lucien: "I'll break you—like this watch!" And he threw the watch to the floor. His nostrils dilated, "swelled by an inward storm," and his eyes shot lightning.

At such times he appeared genuinely "terrible." But the next day, he would hardly remember the storm of yesterday.

Unquestionably, stupidity was what most revolted him.

"I make bold to hope," said Barbé-Marbois, from whom he had just removed the portfolio of Minister of Finance, "that Your Majesty will not accuse me of having been a thief."

Whereupon Napoleon exclaimed, implacably: "I would prefer it a hundred times more. Dishonesty has its limits, but stupidity has none."

Yet laziness could anger him too. Being himself indefatigable, he could not tolerate any lack of energy in others.

He worked his aides-de-camp mercilessly. "A man would have to be made of iron to stand up against the work we do," one of them sighed.

When he couldn't manage to sleep, he would ask Josephine to read to him. Or sometimes he would awaken at three in the morning and call out: "Ohé! Oh! Oh! Monsieur Constant!" And he would ask his *valet de chambre* to prepare a bath for him. Most often, he would send for Méneval and dictate to him until dawn. He would be surprised when he saw the young secretary fighting off sleep: "What's the matter with you, Méneval? You're sleeping on your feet!"

From Boulogne, on August 20, Napoleon wrote to Josephine (addressing her with *vous* rather than *tu*):

> In ten days I will be at Aachen. From there I will go with you to Cologne, Coblenz, Mainz, Trier, and Luxembourg. . . . You can wait for me there, unless you are afraid of being fatigued by such a long trip. . . . I am anxious to see you, to tell you everything you inspire in me, and to cover you with kisses. A bachelor's life is a miserable one, and nothing is worth so much as a good wife, beautiful and loving. . . .

Josephine left with part of her court for Aachen, where she waited for her husband, who seemed very frisky indeed.

On August 24 he wrote to her again:

> I may arrive at night, so let lovers beware! I would be most annoyed if it puts them to any inconvenience, but one must take the good things of life wherever they may be had. My health is good, and I am working quite a lot. But I am too well behaved. That has a bad effect on me. So I am anxious to see you and tell you all sorts of things to please you.

She was still his mistress and companion.

"A beautiful woman is a joy to the eyes," he said, "and a good woman is a joy to the heart. The former is a jewel, and the latter is a treasure."

For him, Josephine was still both.

On August 27 he left Boulogne with Eugène. That night he stopped at St.-Omer. He spent the entire day of the twenty-eighth there. Then he spent two nights at Arras, and another at the château of Laeken, just outside Brussels. On September 2 he reached Aachen, where he put up at the prefecture of the Ruhr. Josephine was so glad to see the Emperor again that she wept. Her joy was so great that she failed to notice that her husband had picked out one of her ladies-in-waiting, the pretty Elisabeth de Vaudey, as a favorite.

While still at Aachen, Napoleon ordered that the regalia that had been used for the anointment and coronation of Charlemagne be carried in a solemn procession: the crown, the sword, the staff, the imperial globe, the golden spurs. The skull and armbone of the Emperor of the West were exhibited. As he watched the ceremony, Napoleon must have been thinking of his own coronation, for as soon as he returned he discussed its details. How would the new sovereign be attired? The Council of State favored the pompous traditional costume. But this idea did not charm the Emperor, and it is much to be regretted that his first reaction was not taken as a guide:

> If you bundle me up in all those clothes [he protested] I'll look like a baboon. Imperial vestments will never impress the people of Paris, who go to the Opera where they see handsomer vestments on Laïs and Chéron, who wear them much better than I. Can't you just put that cloak on over my regular clothes?

Being very much taken up with their own costumes, the councillors refused. If the main personage of the ceremony did not wear splendid garments, how could they insist on garments of gold and silver for themselves?

The place of coronation was also debated. Why not Aachen? Twenty emperors had been crowned there. Napoleon favored this choice—"if only to make the Parisians see that one can govern without them."

He hated Paris and its *canaille*, rabble, as he called the Parisians.

"This city has always made things bad for France. Its inhabitants are ungrateful and frivolous. They have said horrible things about me."

At the council, no one undertook to defend Paris, and Napoleon put his case more strongly:

> So long as I have a drop of blood in my veins, I'll never let the Parisians make the laws. I don't need 200,000 men to bring Paris to its senses: 1,500 is enough. Sooner or later, I'll have those gentlemen seized and sent 200 leagues away. They're the kind of people that ought to be pissed on.

Several members protested that there was no longer any opposition in Paris. At this he exclaimed: "I should hope not! There couldn't be any!"

Someone murmured: "They are peaceable—"

"Because they can't budge," the Emperor concluded.

Nonetheless, Paris was chosen as the site of the coronation. But Napoleon had no illusions as to his popularity. The Parisians were muzzled, and if they offered any resistance they did so in silence. The question was whether the Pope would agree to come to Paris to attend the coronation of the man whom Louis XVIII, in his exile, was already calling Monsieur the Usurper.

At the outset, the master's plans met with some obstacles even in the Council of State. All the members, in agreement with the Protestants and the numerous atheists who were crying scandal, affirmed that if the Pope anointed the Emperor, it would in a way mean giving the Head of the Church the power of naming the sovereign. And wasn't that one of the prerogatives of the people? The Emperor found a ready answer for them by putting the question on the political plane:

Messieurs, you are deliberating in Paris, at the Tuileries. But suppose you were deliberating at London in the British cabinet. Suppose you were the ministers of the King of England, and you had just learned that the Pope was crossing the Alps to anoint the crown of the Emperor of the French. Would you consider that a victory for England or for France?

This argument had a certain weight—a fact that became very apparent when the reaction of the French émigrés was ascertained. For when they learned that the "son of the Revolution" wanted to be crowned by the Pope, the émigrés and Royalists wailed loudly. Joseph de Maistre, Sardinia's minister to St. Petersburg, considered the possible coronation as a "crime" or an "act of apostasy," and could find "no words to describe his sorrow."

How should the question be posed to Pius VII?

Napoleon had the Papal Legate, Cardinal Caprara, come to St.-Cloud. As the founder of the Fourth Dynasty, he told him, as if it were the most natural thing in the world:

All the authorities make me realize how glorious it would be if my anointment at the coronation were performed by the Pope, and how much it would benefit religion. For the moment I am not addressing a formal request to the Pope because I do not want to expose myself to a refusal. Please make overtures, therefore; and when you have transmitted the reply to me, I shall make, as I should, the necessary arrangements.

The cardinals resigned themselves to the crowning of the little Corsican by the Head of the Church; but they were unwilling that the Pope should leave Rome for that purpose. "M. de Buonaparte" had only to go to the Eternal City. Had not Charlemagne made the trip to Rome to have himself crowned by Leo III?

Pius VII was aware, as his legate had written him, that the new emperor "would consider it an insult if His Holiness raised obstacles." The possible refusal of the Pope seemed to frighten Caprara so much "that he dared not even imagine it." It was Talleyrand, a former bishop, who took on the job of arranging things. In a detailed note, he first emphasized "the extreme surprise of His Holiness." Then he went directly into the heart of the matter: should not Pius VII show his gratitude? Had not the new emperor done a good deal for the Church?

The note was a veritable balance sheet. Could it not be interpreted as proving to the Vatican that it might expect other advantages besides? By agreeing to come to Paris (a very long trip, to be sure, especially for a sick old man), would not Pius VII be able to hope for the modification of certain organic articles concerning the status of the French clergy, who were actually under subjection to the State? Would Napoleon perhaps (and here the Pope was again deceiving himself) show his gratitude by returning the legations to him?

One important point "caused great pain to the heart of His Holiness": on the day of his anointment and coronation, the new emperor was supposed to swear he would respect freedom of religion. As Consalvi informed Caprara, in this the Pope saw "an obstacle which, if it were not removed, would prevent him from carrying out his plans to go and perform in person the anointment and consecration of His Imperial Majesty. . . ."

Napoleon had not even envisaged the possiblity that the Pope might refuse to come to Paris because the Protestants and Jews were to be free to practice their own faiths. And so Talleyrand tried to demonstrate to the Holy See that taking an oath to respect the different religions of the French was not the same thing as approving them. Everyone knew that as a "docile son," the new emperor would encourage people "rather" to practice the Catholic religion. Had he not practiced it himself since his childhood?

With one obstacle removed, another was about to rear itself: the coronation. Although Napoleon considered the presence of the Pope indispensable at the consecration of the new emperor, and at his anointment, there should be no question of the Pope's crowning him. He did not intend to be treated as a vassal, even if the lord paramount was the Vicar of Christ. It was from the people, not from God, that he claimed to have derived his crown. At this point, some advisers suggested separating the two ceremonies completely, and making the coronation an exclusively civil ceremony. Joseph Fesch declared that only one thing counted: the anointment. He was not far from considering the coronation as a secondary act. "The Pope," Consalvi replied, "does not consider it in any way appropriate to his dignity that, after his having been invited to go to Paris for the express purpose of placing the imperial crown on the august head of His Majesty with his own hand, this ceremony be performed by another hand."

Another hand? That was the question, indeed! That other hand could only be the hand of the Emperor!

Napoleon informed Rome that he "wanted to take the crown to avoid any discussion among the great dignitaries of the empire, who would claim to be giving it to him in the name of the people." It was he who had restored the crown that the Bourbons had let fall from their incapable hands, and it was he who would crown himself. All the Pope had to do during this part of the ceremony was "say a prayer."

For that matter, what was the purpose of exchanging notes, proposals, and reports, since "the two halves of God" would soon see each other: "His Majesty will discuss these matters himself at Paris with His Holiness, and will do everything compatible with his position, the well-being of the State, and his duty, to satisfy him."

Without enthusiasm, and merely for the sake of peace and quiet, Pius VII yielded: he agreed to go to Paris on December 2. On All

Souls' Day, on the morrow of All Saints' Day, after having celebrated Mass, the Pope set out on the trip as if he were on his way to be tortured.

While Pius VII and his retinue of 108 persons were setting out on the road to Mont-Cenis, Napoleon was being racked by a dilemma. If Josephine was anointed by the Pope and crowned by her imperial husband, could she still be put aside? If he wanted to have an heir, should not the Emperor immediately repudiate his wife, and even remarry? Cruel as it was, Napoleon decided to pose the question to the chief interested party: Josephine herself.

As soon as her husband started to speak, the Creole broke into sobs. That didn't help things at all. In the face of his wife's weeping, he felt disarmed: "If you show too much grief, if you simply obey me, I feel I will never be strong enough to compel you to leave me. But I must say I am most desirous that you manage to resign yourself to the interests of my policy, and that you spare me all the embarrassment of this painful situation."

Advised by Mme. Rémusat, Josephine told Napoleon that she "would await his direct orders to come down off the throne where he had placed her."

In other words, she was willing to be repudiated, but not willing to be a heroine and herself request permission to leave him. The Bonaparte clan, convinced that the Empress was going to leave the Tuileries, noisily manifested their great pleasure without the least modesty. This time, at last, they were rid of those "Beauharnais" who had given them sleepless nights for nine years! Napoleon, enraged when he learned that his family had dared to "brag that they had brought him around to doing what they wanted," decided to keep Josephine and have her crowned.

My wife [he explained to Roederer] is a good woman who has never done them any harm. She is content to play the empress a bit—to have diamonds, beautiful dresses, and the miseries of her age. I never loved her blindly. If I make her Empress, it is only the just thing to do. I have a man's heart. Above all, I am a just man. If I had been thrown into prison instead of mounting the throne, she would have shared my misfortunes. It is right that she share in my grandeur. She will be crowned, even if it costs me 200,000 men. . . .

Faced with the threat of such a hecatomb, everyone was silent. Joseph, however, once again raised the problem of the imperial heredity and made much of his claims as the oldest. The *senatus consultum* permitting Napoleon to designate his successor from among any of his nephews gave Joseph no rest.

But on the advice of Roederer, he yielded, agreeing to get into line and go to make honorable amends at Fontainebleau, where Napoleon was waiting for the Pope. Napoleon indicated his satisfaction: "I have been called upon to change the face of the world—or so I believe. You would do well, therefore, to remain within a hereditary monarchical system that offers you so many advantages."

But there were also—also and especially—the women of the clan, whose anxieties were of a more earthly nature. Napoleon had to "put himself in battle array" (as he expressed it) to persuade his sisters and sisters-in-law to carry the Empress' train at Notre Dame and to follow her during the long procedure of the ceremony. Did not "Princess Joseph" claim that "such duties were painful to a virtuous woman"?

"During the six days that this quarrel has been going on," the Emperor told his brother, "I have not had one moment of rest. It has cost me my sleep."

The ladies got so excited that, by means of a subtle maneuver which appeased them, it was agreed that they would not "carry" the train but "support" it. Not only that, but each of them was offered a chamberlain to bear the train of her own dress.

The church where the ceremony was to take place had not yet been determined. The Church of the Invalides had been proposed; but since it had no choir loft, and a relatively narrow structure, this plan was abandoned in favor of Notre Dame, where (the Emperor affirmed) 20,000 persons could easily be accommodated.

The architects and decorators, however, were bothered by one fact: the Gothic style of Notre Dame was completely out of fashion. Orders were given to cover the exterior of the edifice with cardboard and to decorate the walls, the columns, and the capitals of the interior. While the costumiers, the tailors, and the shoemakers were letting their imaginations take flight toward the Renaissance, the master of the horse, the grand chamberlain, and the master of ceremonies were busy studying a delicate question. The canons of Notre Dame were demanding new vestments and objects of worship to be used in the ceremonies, "since, for the anointment and coronation of kings," they said, "the tradition is to buy everything new." More-over, the presence of the Pope and the fact that His Holiness would celebrate a Mass demanded the use of special materials and accesso-ries such as a bishop's throne, other thrones, flabella made of ostrich plumes, *faldistoires, scabelli.* Fortunately, the Pope gave up the idea of having himself carried to Notre Dame in the *Seda gestatoria* by the ostlers dressed in red damask when Napoleon informed him that "the honor had been delegated to Murat"—not to mention the God-dess of Reason who, some eleven years ago, had been set on a gar-landed armchair and carried by sans-culottes from Notre Dame to the Tuileries. Followed on her return trip by all of the deputies, she who had "dethroned the *ci-devant* Holy Virgin" had covered exactly the same route planned for the Holy Father.

The Roman pontifical rite was modified by using a hodgepodge of rites from Rome, Reims, Germany, and elsewhere. The Emperor was especially intent upon deleting or transforming, in the text to be read by the Pope, certain verbs that he considered displeasing, such as *eligimus* ("whom we have selected"). With respect to the trans-feral of the sword, *concessum* ("conferred") bothered him. It was to become *oblatum* ("presented").

As for the ornaments—the sword, the crowns, the rings, the scep-ter, the globe, the staff—considerable difficulty was encountered in locating the sword, the scepter, and the staff, which had been used in the anointment and coronation of kings for several centuries, but had been dispersed by the Revolution. Once found, they were newly decorated. The scepter no longer had a haft. It was replaced by a precentor's baton—a very old one found in the treasury of St.-Denis. The *main de justice* (staff) was also provided with a new haft. Here and there, jewels were added, so that the objects could figure worth-ily in the coronation parade under the name of *les honneurs de Charlemagne* (the regalia of Charlemagne). But the Emperor had the imperial ornaments made by his goldsmith, Biennais, whose shop had a sign reading "The Violet Monkey."

The difficulties were indeed piling up. What oil would be used for the anointing? The holy vial no longer existed, since during the Revolution Alexandre de Beauharnais, Josephine's first husband, had had it brought from Reims to Paris (such is the irony of history) to be burned on the Altar of the Nation. Consequently, they had to be content with the chrism reserved for bishops. Again, Napoleon rebelled when he was told he had to be given nine anointings, and they were limited to two applications of oil to the hands and the forehead.

On November 20 Napoleon wrote to the Pope: "I flatter myself that in the course of this week I shall have the honor of seeing Your Holiness and expressing the sentiments I entertain toward you. By going to my palace at Fontainebleau, which is on the way, I shall be able through this circumstance to have that pleasure one day earlier."

Actually, the purpose of the Emperor's going to Fontainebleau was not "to have the pleasure" of Pius VII's company a day earlier, but to avoid having to greet the Pope at the gates of Paris, and thus yielding the first place to him.

On Advent Sunday—since Pius VII of course refused to admit that it was Quartidi, 4 Frimaire, "the day of the medlars"—His Holiness reached his destination. A cold rain was falling when the papal cortege, consisting of about a hundred cardinals, prelates, abbés, and employees of all kinds, coming from the direction of Nemours, entered the forest of Fontainebleau via the long hillside of Bourron.

Pius VII was tired. Highwaymen had robbed him near Piacenza, and at Lyons Cardinal Borgia had died as the result of a cruel illness. His Holiness had left Rome twenty-three days before and had been upset by the pace of traveling: it was too fast, and incompatible with the dignity which should characterize the movements of the successor of St. Peter.

At the crossroads of Crois St.-Hérem, Napoleon, wearing a green huntsman's costume, made it appear that he had interrupted a wolf hunt when he saw the papal carriage climbing the hill. Immobile on his horse, he watched Pius VII's equipage come toward him; and he did not move toward His Holiness a minute earlier than the scheduled time. The Pope seemed to hesitate. There was a stretch of muddy ground between him and the Emperor, and the Holy Father had nothing but his white, gold-embroidered slippers on his feet. Finally, the Pope made the first move and, floundering through horrible mire, approached the Emperor. At this point Napoleon hurriedly dismounted and went to meet his guest and embrace him. But of course there could be no question, for him, of kneeling! Moreover, considering the condition of the ground, the Pope could not be shocked at this deviation from protocol. Then the carriage moved on, making it possible (by means of a maneuver likewise carefully worked out in advance) for the Emperor to get into the vehicle through the right-hand door, leaving the Holy Father on his left.

On the way from the Crois St.-Hérem to the palace, the Mamelukes preceded the imperial equipage; and it was under this rather impious escort that Pius VII made his entry into the horseshoe-shaped courtyard.

The cannon roared, the bells rang out, and at the bottom of the Louis XV stairway Maurice de Talleyrand-Périgord, the former Bishop of Autun, bowed. Then the Pope was requested to go and "pay his compliments" to Josephine.

At the Tuileries, on that same day of November 25, Isabey was explaining to each participant what he should do during the ceremonies. For this purpose he used little marionettes clothed in paper costumes of different colors, positioned on a floor plan of Notre Dame laid out on the Emperor's own desk. In the Salon de Diane, the rehearsals followed a plan sketched out in chalk on the floor. Among the other marionettes was the Emperor, one inch tall, wearing a red cloak.

The generals, high functionaries, and members of delegations and deputations invited to the coronation included many who had held posts under the Revolution. One can imagine their surprise when they received the following letter:

> Divine Providence and the Constitutions of the Empire having placed the imperial hereditary dignity in Our family, We have designated the fifth day of the month of Frimaire next for Our anointment and coronation. . . . We write you this letter so that you will not fail to present yourself at Paris before the first of Frimaire next, and to signify your arrival to Our Grand Master of Ceremonies. Until then we pray God that He will have you in His holy keeping.

On the eve of the coronation, it hailed. The sun was timidly glancing through the clouds when the Senate set out for the Tuileries to inform Napoleon of the results of the plebiscite. It had been a rather puerile sham: the figures had been falsified. The vote in favor of heredity had amounted to 2,959,891, with the opposition tallying 2,567. The votes from the army had not amounted to more than 120,302. With his own hand, imperturbable, Napoleon had struck out this number and written in 400,000. And the same went for the 16,224 votes of the commercial agencies, which became 50,000. All of this enabled the presiding officer of the Senate, on this day of December 1, to announce that 3,574,898 persons had voted for the adoption of the following proposal:

> The imperial dignity is hereditary in the direct, natural, legitimate, and adoptive descent of Napoleon Bonaparte, and in the direct, natural, and legitimate descent of Joseph Bonaparte and Louis Bonaparte.

Then the presiding officer, Neufchâteau, congratulated the Emperor upon having "brought the vessel of the Republic safely into port."

"Yes, Sire," he repeated, "of the Republic. This word might grate in the ears of an ordinary sovereign. But here the word is appropriate, in the presence of the one who has given us the enjoyment of the *res* in the sense in which the *res* can exist among a great nation."

That same Saturday, Napoleon learned to his great wrath that Josephine had thrown herself at the feet of the Pope and confessed that she had been married to Bonaparte only in a civil ceremony. What was to be performed the next day would thus be a sacrilege. His Holiness was preparing to bless the Emperor's concubine by giving the triple unction, with the chrism reserved to bishops, to a couple living in mortal sin. The Pope notified the Emperor that he would depart forthwith unless this grave fault done to the Church was corrected before the following morning. He was perfectly willing to anoint the Emperor, but he would not even tolerate Josephine's presence at Notre Dame.

Napoleon yielded, and the ceremony of marriage was performed at night, almost clandestinely. It was not the priest of the parish of the Tuileries—of St.-Germain-l'Auxerrois—but Fesch himself who, without witnesses, united "M. et Mme. Bonaparte." Hence there would be—or so Napoleon thought—two possible causes for appeal.

Everybody was watching the skies that morning. At the Observatory, the clerk recording "the state of the air" wrote in his log: "Sky very cloudy; wind from the north; fog; temperature 3.3 Centigrade." Was it going to snow?

Thousands of guests were heading for Notre Dame. But except for the corteges of the Pope, the Emperor, and the Arch-Chancellor, no equipage was allowed beyond the Palais de Justice. And onlookers laughed when they saw women in plunging necklines holding up their trains and the bottoms of their dresses as they ran toward Notre Dame through muddy streets in a glacial wind.

Amid indescribable disorder, the guests took their seats as best they could on benches placed in the nave, perpendicular to the altar. At the back of the church, masking the central portal and obstructing the name, was a gigantic cardboard structure on which was written in letters of gold: HONNEUR; PATRIE; and NAPOLEON EMPEREUR DES FRANÇAIS.

It was the imperial throne. At the top, on a platform reached by twenty-four rather steep steps, the Emperor's seat was perched. Just below it, and smaller, was the seat of the Empress. The diplomatic corps and the ministers were seated at the foot of this monument and around it, while the members of the Senate and the Corps Législatif, the magistrates, and the *grands officiers* of the Crown were seated midway between the throne and the altar. The first row, near the altar, was occupied by the ten archbishops and the forty bishops (who had had to dress at the Préfecture de Police). The delegations were massed in the aisles and transepts, and the guests crowded the galleries.

At eight thirty, when the Pope's equipage was just getting under way, a drama developed in front of the Pavillon de Flore. The cross-bearer, Monsignor Speroni, refused to take his place in a carriage. The pontifical ceremony demanded that he have a mule. But there weren't any in the imperial stables. He was offered a horse, and it was suggested that he walk. In vain. The outriders had to undertake a search. Finally they discovered a donkey belonging to a woman selling fruit on the Rue du Doyenné. For 67 francs, she agreed to rent them her beast. The donkey was decked out in a velvet caparison; Speroni was assured that it was actually an ill-favored mule; and the procession, led by dragoons, began. But the appearance of the cross-bearer, curiously topped by a three-cornered hat and mounted on the fruit vendor's donkey, unleashed gales of laughter.

Speroni seemed delighted and waved his cross in all directions. The laughter had scarcely quieted down when the heralds-at-arms appeared, followed by the Pope's carriage, upholstered in white velvet, surmounted with the pontifical tiara, and drawn by eight gray horses. When he arrived at the archbishop's palace, the Pope put on

an ample, heavy gold cope. Passing through a long *galerie de toile*,
he reached the basilica. Then he took his position on the throne that
had been set up for him in the choir loft, "in the expectation of a
Pontiff who meditates profoundly on the things of Heaven, and for
the happiness of the earth."

At the Tuileries the principal actors in the ceremony had put on
(not without some difficulty) the curious costumes designed by David
and Isabey—a kind of compromise between "the antique" and Henri
III. Although the women proved very flexible in these matters, some
of the veteran soldiers of the Year II got up as "minions" must have
hesitated a bit before stepping out into the street in those costumes.

Before leaving for Notre Dame the protagonists of the solemn
drama stopped in at Josephine's apartments; and they all gaped when
they saw the Empress "aglitter with diamonds, her hair done up in
a thousand curls as in the days of Louis XIV." She looked twenty-five.

It was eleven o'clock.

The cannon boomed, announcing the departure of the Emperor
and Empress from the Tuileries. It was still cold, and the sky remained cloudy, but the threat of snow seemed to have disappeared.
The sun, however, still shone only faintly through the mist. The
famous state carriage was drawn by eight gray horses richly caparisoned. On its top, as on the top of the Pope's carriage, was a golden
crown supported by four eagles with outstretched wings. The *Journal des Débats* reported:

> This carriage, remarkable for its elegance, its luxury, and the
> paints which adorned it, attracted as much attention as the pro-
> cession itself, whose magnificence is difficult to describe. Imagine
> 7,000 or 8,000 cavalrymen in the finest uniforms, interspersed
> with groups of musicians, moving in procession between two solid
> ranks of infantry more than a half-league long. Add to this the
> luxury of the numerous carriages, the beauty of the horses draw-
> ing them, plus the presence of 4,000 or 5,000 spectators, and one
> will still have only an imperfect idea of the spectacle offered by
> the procession alone.

As might be expected, that most reactionary of reactionaries, M.
de Frénilly, was not in agreement:

> All this pomp was nothing more than a masquerade in which
> everyone was trying out his clothes while the roles had not been

studied by anyone—from that fine mountebank, Murat, who had risen from his father's cabaret to the governorship of Paris, from which he was to step up and mount a throne; from the three imperial sisters who had left off washing their laundry at Marseilles to come, wearing plumes and covered with diamonds, to carry the train of Barras' former mistress; from that pack of flunkies—Montmorency, Cossé, La Trémoille, etc.—installed as *grands officiers* two weeks before; to that dumpy little has-been general of 13 Vendémiaire who appeared in his coronation carriage wearing a dalmatic and a white cloak. There was enough in these saturnalia to make one laugh or to make one weep, depending upon one's taste or character.

At the archbishop's palace, the Emperor and the Empress put on their "grand vestments," the two famous red velvet capes, which partly hid Napoleon's long robe *à l'antique* of white satin trimmed in gold, and Josephine's silver brocade dress. Just a short time ago, before the departure from the Tuileries, Isabey (so it was said) had helped her with her make-up; but she nonetheless took the time for a last "touching up." Finally, the procession started through the long gallery toward the basilica. As had been arranged, Napoleon's three sisters and his two sisters-in-law "supported" Josephine's cloak, while Joseph, Louis, and the two ex-consuls "carried" that of the Emperor. Then came the marshals designated to carry the "honors" or regalia, wearing blue velvet and white satin, all rustling with plumes. The former companions of General Bonaparte had divided up these regalia, consisting of the silver scepter, the pearl-decorated staff, and the *boule du monde*. All these marvels, as well as the laurel crown the Emperor had on his head, had been manufactured by the jeweler Biennais, whose bill came to 7,000 francs. Kellermann, Lefebvre, and Pérignon were carrying *les honneurs de Charlemagne*.

The moment the Emperor appeared in the nave, everyone present stood and shouted: "Vive l'Empereur!" "The Emperor's short body," Mme. de Rémusat reported, "virtually disappeared under that enormous ermine cloak. On his head was a simple crown of laurels; he resembled an antique medal. But he was extremely pale, genuinely moved, and the expression in his eyes was stern and a bit troubled."

The two orchestras struck up a military march and continued playing almost uninterruptedly throughout the long ceremony. It had been necessary to prepare 12,137 pages of scores for the musicians.

It was noon. The ceremony began in the choir, where the prayer stools of the Emperor and Empress had been placed. The audience could scarcely discern the actual movements involved in the anointing and coronation. Napoleon by no means wanted the former Jacobins to see him on his knees before the Pope, his face and hands covered with oil.

First came the religious oath: the Emperor swore "before God and His angels to make and preserve the law, the justice, and the peace of the Church." Then followed the prayers—the interminable litanies of the revised and expurgated text. The Duchesse d'Abrantés wrote:

> I cannot describe what I felt when the Emperor came down from his throne and approached the altar, where the Pope was waiting to anoint him. . . . Napoleon seemed very calm. I watched him closely to see whether his heart was pounding more violently under the imperial dalmatic than under his uniform of a colonel of the Guards; but I could see nothing, although I was only ten paces away from him. The length of the ceremony seemed only to bore him, and several times I saw him stifle a yawn. But he did everything he was told to, and always did it properly. When the Pope gave him triple unction on the head and hands, I noticed from the direction of his gaze that he was thinking about drying himself rather than anything else. I am certain of this, since I was very familiar with his way of looking about.

After having blessed the imperial ornaments—the sword, the imperial globe, the scepter, the *main de justice*, and the collar—Pius VII consecrated the two rings, the two cloaks, and the two crowns.

> Receive this ring [he said], which is the sign of the Holy Faith, the proof of the power and solidity of your empire, by means of which, thanks to its triumphant power, you will conquer your enemies, you will destroy heresies, you will keep your subjects in union, and you will remain perseveringly attached to the Catholic Faith.

"You will destroy heresies." This is what would be contradicted a short time later, by the Emperor's oath guaranteeing freedom of worship.

The great moment had arrived.

All eyes were on the red velvet cushion. Napoleon reached out his hand, grasped the glittering golden crown, casually turned his back on the Pope, looked out at the breathless crowd, then calmly put the crown on his head.

The most astonishing destiny in history was following its course: the former cadet, Napoleone Buonaparte, General Bonaparte, the lifetime consul of the Republic, had become Emperor Napoleon I.

Next he looked at Josephine. Shaken with emotion, she was coming toward him, the train of her sumptuous ermine cloak held by her daughter and her two sisters-in-law. The Empress' tears were falling on her clasped hands, "which she raised much more toward her husband than toward God," as Laure d'Abrantès said.

The Emperor was about to perform his first act as a sovereign. "With graceful slowness" he picked up his wife's crown, placed it on his own head for a moment, as if he wished to "imperialize" it, then put it "coquettishly" on the head of his dear Creole.

Josephine rose, and the two of them, followed by the Pope, went toward their thrones, curiously perched on top of the structure that had been erected in the middle of the nave for the occasion. Cheers resounded. Napoleon's gaze met that of Laure. Did he, at that moment, remember her uncontrollable laughter of that morning of October 28, 1785, when she had seen him as a brand-new officer in his top boots? Her "Puss-in-Boots," as she had then nicknamed him with a laugh that pained him, had become, on this December 2, 1804, Emperor of the French.

"His face alone reminded me of the past," Laure wrote, "without words, and without any intention—as a scent or a harmony reminds us of days gone by."

The Holy Father gave his accolade to the new emperor, and intoned: "Vivat Imperator in aeternum!"

"Vive l'Empereur! Vive l'Impératrice!" the audience responded in a long shout that resounded under the vaulted ceiling.

When the interminable Mass was concluded, the Pope went to the vestry. He preferred not to hear the civil oath which Napoleon, in a strong voice and with his hand on the Bible, was going to swear —and which, incidentally, he would be unable to keep:

I swear to maintain the integrity of the territory of the Republic; to respect, and cause to be respected, the laws of the Concordat and freedom of worship; to respect, and cause to be respected,
equality of rights, political and civil liberties, and the irrevocabil-
ity of conveyances of national property; to levy no taxes or duties
except in virtue of the law; to maintain the institution of the
Legion of Honor; and to govern with a view solely to the interests,
happiness, and glory of the French people.

Then the herald-at-arms proclaimed majestically: "The most
glorious and most august Napoleon, Emperor of the French, is
anointed, crowned, and enthroned!"

While His Holiness, at the archbishop's palace, "was permitting
the clergy of Paris to come and kiss his feet," Napoleon left Notre
Dame. The cannon began to fire a salvo of one hundred rounds.

Night was falling. The long procession, surrounded by five torch-
bearers, started back for the Tuileries, passing along the boulevards
and through the Place de la Concorde, brightly illuminated by col-
ored lights and Chinese lanterns. As they had on the way to Notre
Dame, clusters of pages dressed in gold and green were hanging on
to the front and rear of the carriage, a veritable reliquary heaped
with olive branches, laurel branches, eagles, palm fronds, armorial
bearings, crowns, allegorical figures, and bees. It was "a whole world
rolling along!" Trumpeters and kettle drummers preceded cuirassiers, mounted light cavalrymen, Mamelukes, and the interminable
procession of carriages containing the members of the imperial
family and the dignitaries.

Mme. Letizia had not come to Paris and was still pouting at Rome.
But this did not prevent David from "painting her in, like a sign-
board," in his famous picture—which, for that matter, represented
much more the coronation of Josephine than that of Napoleon.

"It will be nicer that way," the Creole had told the painter.

Once back at his apartments, the Emperor paraded in front of the
ladies of the court, still wearing the attire demanded by etiquette.

"Mesdames," he said, laughing, "you owe it to me that you are so
charming."

But to his eyes, the most charming was Josephine; and he asked
her to keep on her crown for dinner, with just the two of them
present.

During the entire month of December Paris was given over to

festivities and partying. Only the sky failed to join in: snow, rain, and winds succeeded one another. The weather did not even improve for the "Distribution of the Eagles" three days after the coronation, when icy blasts transformed the festivity into confusion. People were astounded and seemed almost surprised upon learning that Napoleon could not control the weather. Had he not, with a simple gesture, made St. Peter's successor come to Paris? Even the Royalists, who had been amazed, were quiet. And on December 27, at the opening of the legislative session, Napoleon could justly say: "Unless death surprises me in the midst of my undertakings, I hope to leave to posterity a memory which will forever serve as an example, or as a reproach, to my successors."

A few weeks later, the Senate unveiled the statue of *Napoleon I, as a Roman Emperor.* It was prudent to be thus specific, since the sovereign was represented stark naked. On September 26, 1791, the presiding officer of the Legislative Assembly, deeming that Louis XVI was merely "the first functionary of the Nation," had ordered that the henceforth useless throne be removed from the Salle des Séances. Now the throne had been brought back, and statues were being erected to the Emperor in his lifetime.

Italy was still a republic, of which Napoleon was president. The Emperor of the French considered this situation to be an anomaly that ought to be corrected as soon as possible. He first offered the throne to Joseph, stipulating that the future King of Italy would have to give up all claim to the crown of France. Joseph, who considered himself the son of "the Emperor, Charles Bonaparte," refused to renounce what he called, in all seriousness, "rights derived from the popular will." Napoleon then turned to Louis, and summoned him and Hortense to the Tuileries.

"My policy," he told them, "requires that I adopt your oldest son so that he can be named King of Italy."

The face of the pitiful Louis immediately darkened: "I will never agree to my son's being greater than I!"

Finally, Napoleon appealed to Lucien, offering him the Italian crown provided he would get a divorce. Lucien refused with dignity. And so Napoleon, enraged at the attitude of the clan, would be obliged to take the crown himself, making a viceroy of the faithful Eugène. But it was understood that Josephine's son should regard himself as a kind of prefect and take the fewest possible initiatives.

Napoleon wanted, however, to enjoy the pleasure of putting the crown of iron on his own head; and so he and Josephine left for Milan. At Troyes, he took temporary leave of Josephine and "most of the imperial baggage," and went to Brienne to relive some of his school-boy memories, giving himself two days of leave between two crowns.

Mme. de Brienne welcomed him at the château and took him into "the King's room," with the bed at which he had gaped with wonder when he was a cadet.

"Why don't you sell me your château?" he asked the lady of the house. "What can Brienne mean to you, as a childless widow? To me, it means a lot."

"For me, it is everything," she replied.

The next day, he wandered through the park and the buildings of the former school. Then, saddened by the abandoned state of things, he quickly mounted his Arabian pony and left Brienne, taking the road to Bar-sur-Aube. He dashed through the fields at a fast gallop, "like a schoolboy or an emperor let out to play." He wanted to revisit those places that "the arrière-cadet Buonaparte" had so often passed through in the old days.

Soon, he was out of sight. His retinue looked for him for some three hours. Finally a revolver shot fired in the air by Armand Caulaincourt, the master of the horse, brought Napoleon back to his officers. When he returned he was laughing, "happy that he, the master of 40 million persons, had been his own man for three hours!" His horse was dripping sweat, and blood was streaming from its nostrils and its mouth. The former crown scholar must have covered (or so Caulaincourt estimates) at least fifteen leagues. Where had he been? He himself hadn't the slightest idea! He had galloped through woods, crossed fields, and gone through villages. In the distance he had glimpsed the outlines of the château of Brienne, and this familiar image had "guided him on the way back."

Later the others learned that he had stopped in front of the hut of "la mère Marguerite," who used to sell eggs and milk to the students at the school. History—in this case, the *Mémoires* of Constant—tells us that Napoleon called to the farmer's wife: "Bonjour, la mère Marguerite! Aren't you curious to see the Emperor?"

"Si fait, mon bon monsieur. I'd be very curious. Nay, here is a little basket of fresh eggs I'm going to take to Madame. And then I'll stay at the château so as to try and see the Emperor. I won't make any trouble. I won't be able to see him as well now as I could in the old days, when he and his friends used to come to my house to drink milk—"

"Comment, mère Marguerite? You haven't forgotten Bonaparte?"

"Forgotten? Mon bon monsieur! Do you think a person could forget a young man like that? A young man who was well behaved, serious, and even sad sometimes, but always good to poor people. I'm only a peasant, but I could have told you he would make his way."

"He didn't do badly, n'est-ce pas?"

"Ah! dame! non!"

Apparently, la mère Marguerite recognized Napoleone when he asked her, using the same voice he had used in the old days: "Allons, la mère Marguerite! Give us some milk and some fresh eggs. We're dying of hunger!"

After the frugal meal, needless to say, the inevitable purse full of gold napoléons was dumped into the old lady's apron.

Toward noon, before getting back into his carriage, he looked at the plain stretching out toward La Rothière, and murmured: "What a fine battlefield this would be!"

He would have to wait another nine years before he would be back on this battlefield—and then he would have all Europe against him.

From April 24 through April 29 he stayed at Turin. On May 1, in a bit of flirtation with glory, he put on the uniform he had worn at Marengo—including the laced hat, already blackened with age, and the republican sword—and took Josephine to the battlefield, where a division performed, retrospectively, the movements executed by the army on June 14, 1800. A "shudder of pain" passed through the ranks when the Emperor, in a speech made to celebrate this pilgrimage, uttered the name of Desaix, whose body would soon be transported to the hospice in the Great St. Bernard.

On May 6, at Alessandria, he made ready to receive his brother Jérôme, with whom he was then on very bad terms.

Jérôme, youngest of the Bonapartes, was fifteen years younger than Napoleon. When he had reached the age of sixteen, his brother, who was then First Consul—had had him appointed midshipman. With this rank he embarked on the *Foudroyant*, which set sail for

Santo Domingo, where Jérôme watched the recapture of Port-au-Prince. For this he was promoted to ensign. But this uniform seemed too modest for Jérôme. And so, to the stupefaction of his admiral, he attired himself in the superb uniform of an officer of hussars of Berchiny: breeches, sky-blue dolman and pelisse, and scarlet vest. Women gasped with admiration when they saw him so attired—especially since he was anything but an ill-favored young man—and Napoleon promoted him to naval lieutenant.

When he was eighteen (at the time he was in the harbor of Fort-de-France, in Martinique), he was given the command of a brig. As master of his own vessel, he made haste (war having been declared between France and England) to send his ship into battle—after he had abandoned it to visit the United States, where he piled up considerable debts.

The brother of the First Consul was quite simply a deserter. He had not taken war seriously—this was the least one could say!—and he took an equally frivolous attitude toward his marriage. Without the authorization of either his brother or Mme. Letizia (he was still a minor), he married "the belle of Baltimore," a pretty girl named Elizabeth Patterson. And he unscrupulously borrowed thousands of dollars from the French agents.

Napoleon, who at that time was preparing to mount the throne, was enraged when he learned of Jérôme's latest prank. But what could he do? The Atlantic was between the two brothers.

But enticed by the imperial purple, M. et Mme. Jérôme Bonaparte disembarked at Lisbon in the spring of 1805. Following the master's instructions, the French chargé d'affaires told them that he had a passport ready for the brother of His Imperial Majesty, but that "the woman in his company" (such were the terms employed by the Emperor) was strictly prohibited from entering the territory of the empire.

> It is essential [Napoleon had further stipulated] that she not be allowed to disembark at Bordeaux, and that she be instructed to return to America. She must be called "Mademoiselle Patterson" with a meaning that will be made plain to her. You understand how much interest I take in this matter.

At this juncture, Jérôme decided to throw himself at the feet of his brother. He was convinced (he assured his wife) that he would be pardoned, and that their marriage would be recognized. The spouses kissed, swore eternal love, and separated. They would never see each other again.

Before Jérôme came to see him, the Emperor wrote him from Alessandria, emphasizing that he had done no wrong that a simple repentance would not wipe out, so far as Napoleon was concerned. But—and this was the basic question—how could that stupid marriage be cancelled out?

Napoleon was not embarrassed for all that: "Your union with Mlle. Patterson is null in the eyes of religion and in the eyes of the law as well. Write to Mlle. Patterson, telling her to return to America. I will grant her a pension of 60,000 francs for her lifetime, on the condition that in no case will she bear my name."

For ten days, the two brothers negotiated without seeing each other. Jérôme resisted—and to stand up to Napoleon for ten days was a notable performance. But the eleventh day, he yielded. He was finally received; and an hour later he emerged from the imperial study "visibly agitated," as an eyewitness said. Resigned to his fate, Jérôme gave up all hope of seeing his wife again—all the more so since the unfortunate woman, having been refused entry at all the European ports, sought refuge in England, where she gave birth to a son. For Napoleon's enemies, the child was living proof of the imperial despotism.

On June 2, by way of compensation, Jérôme was promoted to commander, and the Emperor gave him command of a squadron, writing him in all seriousness: "Do not trust too much in the name you bear: it is glorious to be beholden only to one's own merit."

But Jérôme deemed this compensation inadequate. On his own authority, he began wearing the uniform of a full captain and, in addition, gave himself the title of Imperial Highness. And he spent so much money that in that same year of 1805, Napoleon wrote: "If this pension does not suffice him, it is my intention to let him be imprisoned for his debts. It is inconceivable what that young man costs me, although he gives me trouble and is of no value to my system."

After nine months of sailing, which took him to the Antilles, Jérôme managed to capture eleven British merchantmen. His ship, the *Vétéran*, had succeeded in joining up with Concarneau despite the presence of four British frigates, and these feats of arms brought him the rank of rear admiral and the title of a French prince. Even better, the Emperor informed him that since his marriage was null and void, he would be engaged to Princess Catherine, the daughter of the King of Württemberg. But before consummating the marriage, he would have to cover himself with glory. And so the Emperor placed him (this was on the eve of the campaign of 1806) at the head of an army corps. Jérôme as general proved to be as audacious as Jérôme the admiral had been. He contented himself with making his entry into cities that his subordinates had captured, handing out appointments in the Legion of Honor to his friends, piling up debts, and chasing after women.

Napoleon's Italian coronation took place on May 26, 1805, in the Cathedral of Milan, which was draped in gauze and crepe, the Gothic style not being any more appreciated in the capital of Lombardy than at Paris. Josephine, who was not receiving a crown, watched the ceremony from a side seat. The Emperor used the gallery that had been constructed to enable him to go from the palace to the Cathedral of St. Ambrose. The floor was covered with multicolored carpets. The famous iron crown had been fetched from Monza, and the new King of Italy held it in his hand like a hat as he entered the Duomo. After him came the dignitaries, carrying *les honneurs de Charlemagne* as they had at Notre Dame. After the Archbishop of Milan had blessed the crown of Lombardy as it lay on the altar, Napoleon boldly "shoved it, rather than placed it, on his head," as he uttered the sacramental words: "Dio me l'ha data, guai a chi la toccherà!" (God gave it to me. Woe to him who touches it!)

"It would be difficult to imagine," says an eyewitness, "the expression on the Emperor's face at that moment: it was glowing with joy." Diplomats from Prussia, Spain, Bavaria, and Portugal then presented the orders of their respective countries to "His Majesty, the King of Italy."

That same evening, in Josephine's room, the windows of which looked out over the Duomo illuminated by a thousand lights, the Emperor was deliriously happy. He kept rubbing his hands and repeating with laughter: "God gave it to me. Woe to him who touches it!"

As Chateaubriand said, in describing those days in Milan: "A great, awakened nation opened its eyes for a moment. Italy was coming out of its sleep, and remembered its genius, like a divine dream." For the first time in centuries, it had a sovereign. He may have been a stranger; but he was of a race akin to its own, and spoke its language. Great nobles jostled one another trying to kiss his hands, and in the streets of Milan, Italians were seen to throw themselves flat on the ground before the carriage of "King Napoleone," hoping (or so the crowd shouted) they would be lucky enough to be crushed by it. Fortunately, there were no victims.

A few days later, at the request of its doge, the Senate of the Republic of Genoa asked (by a vote of 20 to 22) that it be annexed to the empire. When he heard this news, the Czar exclaimed: "The man is insatiable! His ambition knows no bounds. He is the scourge of the world. He wants war, he will get it—and the sooner the better!"

XII

THE SUN OF AUSTERLITZ

The only things a person does well
are those he does for himself.

NAPOLEON

EVEN BEFORE THE CORONATION, the Allies had jointly planned the
formation of a third coalition. Russia, taking the lead in diplomatic
operations, had sent emissaries to London, Berlin, Stockholm, and
Vienna. With the single exception of Prussia, which wanted to remain neutral (not out of preference but out of prudence), all of them
had promised subsidies or troops in order to grasp the new empire
by the throat. On November 6, 1804, Austria had signed a convention
with Czar Alexander, promising to put 235,000 men in the field.

With Napoleon crowned King of Italy, the Emperor Francis, who
had formerly been master of a part of the peninsula, had good cause
for alarm. France and Austria now had a common border. Vienna,
if she did not want to be devoured, would have to arm herself more
rapidly. England, for her part, had on April 11, 1805, bound herself by
a treaty of alliance to Russia. This treaty was the "cornerstone" of the
edifice which, as the Czar thought, was being erected to restore
peace to Europe. It was a question of erecting a barrier which would
check the French overflow. The prudent treaty signed by these powers left the frontier of the Moselle and the Rhine to France. (London
seemed to have resigned herself at that time to the loss of Anvers.)
On the other hand, it was stipulated that Italy, although it was a
kingdom governed by a "Napoleonide," should "never" be annexed
to France.

What pretext would Europe invoke to violate the peace?

On August 5, 1805, Semën Vorontsov, the Russian minister at Vienna, explained without circumlocutions:

> As for the motives and justification of a coalition against Bonaparte, the latter can be recognized as just and necessary only in view of his violation of the treaties of Amiens and Lunéville, his kingship of Italy, the usurpation of Genoa, and, finally, all that may be anticipated from his audacity and the enormous and gigantic power that has been formed, which threatens all of Europe.

For the moment, Napoleon was not overly disturbed by the sound of tramping feet coming from Russia and Austria. The defeat of England was his principal aim; and he hence attached capital importance to the movements of his fleets and the tasks assigned to them. "They will have a great influence on the fate of the world," he affirmed. And early in the year he sent his admirals an order to depart, "as soon as possible," with all their squadrons, for Martinique.

Altogether, the forces thus combined were supposed to form an armada of 40 to 50 ships of the line. Why send them, each force coming from a different direction, to rendezvous in the distant Caribbean Sea? The Emperor believed that in this way he could put the English off the track and wear out Nelson, who would take off in pursuit of Admiral Villeneuve, commanding the fleet of Toulon. Then, when the French squadrons had rendezvoused, they would return under the command of Admiral Ganteaume to Europe. They would attack whatever English ships might be opposite Ouessant, then force the crossing of the Channel, and lastly occupy the narrows of the Pas-de-Calais in order to cover the Imperial Army's landing in England.

Such was the plan brought to completion by Napoleon during the first months of 1805—a plan that today's naval strategists find less extravagant than some people have thought.

For Napoleon, crossing the Atlantic twice in sailing vessels was as simple as ordering a few light brigades to conceal themselves behind a small hill and surprise the enemy by rushing out upon the field of battle at just the right time. But the plan would be frustrated by the currents, the dead calm, and the tides, which seemed to disdain the imperial plans and obey the orders of the British Admiralty.

On July 6 Napoleon abruptly left Genoa for Paris. As he hurried along toward the capital he was obsessed by the movements that his squadrons were supposed to be executing, in obedience to orders borne by corvettes that the Emperor was surprised not to see frisking over the waves. Since he had to give up his plans for the regroupment at Martinique, the regrouping would have to take place off the French coast.

Admiral Villeneuve, with all his forces combined, would maneuver so as to overwhelm the 70 ships of the British fleet which remained on guard in the Channel. The ships formed a barrier which, seen from the camp at Boulogne, seemed insurmountable.

In sum, he repeated, the French fleet was to gain control of the Pas-de-Calais, if only for three, four, or five days. Those few days that Napoleon was almost begging of his admirals should allow him (or so he thought) finally to invade "perfidious Albion."

When the Emperor reached the charming little château of Pont-de-Briques on August 3, everything seemed ready for the invasion of the British Isles. Medals commemorating the landing in England had already been struck. The company from Vaudeville had received orders to embark, so that performances from the French repertory could be given in London. Some 20,000 cartridges were waiting to be divided among the troops of "the armies of the coasts of the Ocean." The cases to be carried by the sloops and the prams on "J Day" had been assembled. Napoleon had decided that the landing —on a front the length of some 200 ships—was to take place on the coast 13 kilometers from Dover, at the point where Julius Caesar had landed in the past. The destination was London, via Canterbury and Chatham. Perhaps (and this, too, had been foreseen, as Albert Chatelle tells us) the English would attempt "a last stand 10 kilometers from London, at Bleakheath, where Cromwell had once routed the troops of Charles I." The most extravagant plans were proposed. A member of the Academy of Sciences suggested in all seriousness to Marshal Davout the creation of a corps of mounted porpoises. He advised that each "rider" be provided with two swimming bladders, for use if the porpoise, attracted by a sardine, threw him off its back. Boulogne, like the rest of France, was afflicted by a fever: a "war fever," as the *Moniteur* called it. The Emperor informed his "good little Josephine": "I have some fine armies here, some fine flotillas, and everything that can make the time pass pleasantly for me. All I lack is my good Josephine, but I must not tell her that. For men to be loved, women must have doubts and fears as to the extent of their empire."

Since Napoleon had complained to Murat that all he saw at Boulogne were "faces with mustaches," Murat had made haste to suggest to his brother-in-law "a beautiful and witty Genoese lady" who was "most anxious to meet Your Majesty." Laughing, the Emperor agreed to see her privately. The young Genoese—perhaps a certain lady named Piatti, Pierre André Wimet has suggested—came to visit Napoleon four or five times in the paneled alcove of his room, on the first floor of the château.

But this was only a soldier's idle amusement: the Emperor was still entirely given over to his preparations. He informed the minister Décrès: "The English don't know what is hanging over their heads! Everything is going along well here, and if we have control of the situation during twelve hours of crossing, all will be over for England!"

If only Villeneuve could appear! Napoleon already saw himself disembarking, entering London; then, after having consolidated his conquest, rapidly executing a countermarch toward Germany in order to prevent the slow concentration of the Austro-Russian troops. For as a matter of fact, Napoleon was informed of everything that was happening behind the Inn River. He was counting on forestalling an attack by the new allies and reaching Vienna "before next November." At this time he was still under the illusion that the combined fleet and Admiral Ganteaume, who was at Brest, had been able to join up, and that their joint forces would reach Boulogne in time to participate in the great project. Unfortunately, on August 25 he was informed that Villeneuve, after cruising off the Spanish coast for thirteen days, had returned to Cadiz. The Emperor could not find words strong enough to describe such "infamous conduct." Henceforth, all was lost! How could he cross the Channel when he was opposed by the powerful and threatening British fleet?

Napoleon drew up a new plan. "As of this moment," he wrote to Talleyrand, "I am changing my plan of attack. I must gain twenty days and stop the Austrians from crossing the Inn, while I shall meantime cross the Rhine. They have no idea how rapidly I will make 200,000 men countermarch."

He left only 25,000 men at Boulogne—a large enough number to discourage any British notions of invasion. Needless to say, the Emperor practiced a bit of deceit and launched a rumor that only 30,000 men of the army on the Channel were being sent toward the Danube.

"When I have given a lesson to Austria," he said, "I'll get back to my original plans."

And the formidable "countermarch" was effected with mathematical precision. As Captain Aubry reported later, "the troops stationed at Boulogne, Ambleteuse, Amiens, and St.-Omer marched off to the sound of drums, trumpets, and bands. There was an unimaginable hubbub, uproar, and enthusiasm."

Night and day, the troops marched toward the Rhine. "We inundated cities and villages. . . . Joy was on every face and in every heart."

The Army of Boulogne crossed France asleep on their feet. As Captain Coignet told it: "One rank leaned on another so as not to fall. When some did fall, nothing could awaken them. They fell in the ditches, and blows with the flat of the sword had no effect on them. The bands played, the drums beat the charge, but nothing could conquer sleep. . . ."

The Emperor had foreseen everything, coordinated everything, and systematized everything. To P. A. Daru, who was "dumfounded with admiration," he dictated the itinerary for the seven "torrents" which would cross the north of France, marching to the rumble "of the heavy artillery rolling toward Austerlitz."

Since Napoleon had to leave 25,000 men at Boulogne and 50,000 in Italy under the command of Masséna, the forces he would have at his own disposal in the imperial "Grand Army of Germany" would consist of 186,000 Frenchmen and 33,000 Bavarians, Badeners, and Württembergers—his new allies. The enemy's forces comprised 245,000 Austrians and Russians, plus 50,000 English, Swedes, and Neapolitans who had decided to come into the war. The imbalance of forces did not frighten the Emperor. The only thing he was worried about was Prussia: if she decided to oppose him, he would have another 200,000 men facing him. Fortunately, in spite of the pressure being exerted on him by the Czar, Frederick William was hesitating. Hence the important thing was to move fast enough to outstrip him.

"We are pressed for time," Napoleon said, "and days now count for years." When he passed through St.-Cloud, his ministers noticed his enthusiasm. "Austria will be destroyed before October 12," he predicted.

Meantime, the Austrians had gone over to the offensive and attacked the Elector of Bavaria, the Emperor's ally.

On September 23 Napoleon told the Senate:

> Just a few days ago, I was hoping that the peace would not be disturbed. Outrages and threats left me unmoved. But now the Austrian army has crossed the Inn; Munich has been invaded; and the Elector of Bavaria has been driven out of his capital. All my hopes have vanished. . . . I weep to think how much European blood will be spilled. But a new luster will be added to the name of Frenchman.

And yet, as he was returning to the Tuileries from the Luxembourg, the Emperor was not hailed by crowds as he usually had been. No one was pleased with the resumption of war on the Continent, and the inevitable draft. The peace had been so brief! Had Vienna attacked Munich? But Munich had never been occupied by the French! The armchair strategists did not understand why the Austrian aggression necessarily had to bring on a conflict involving the nation. And the press, rather too openly echoing public opinion, was reproached by the Emperor for lacking in loyalty. The stock market declined, and bankruptcies increased. Moreover, as Napoleon observed with bitterness, the Bank of France itself was "having trouble." People crowded up to the tellers' windows, where one had to stand in line for an hour in order to exchange banknotes for gold. Napoleon needed money, and the Bank had to resort to inflation to meet the demand. Banknotes were devalued by 10 per cent. The cash accounts had to be built up. As the Emperor himself noted, "Nothing I can do *here* will restore order."

The same was true of the general discontent. Once again, as on the eve of Marengo (and as was to be the case for another ten years), Napoleon's empire would crumble if he were defeated in battle. He was condemned always to win—or else.

The Emperor rejoined his army at Strasbourg, and on October 1 they crossed the Rhine. The soldiers, wearing sprigs in their lapels as laurels, paraded past their demigod in a downpour of rain. He himself was so soaked that "the rainwater ran off his clothes down to his horse's underbelly, and from there to earth." His hat soon began to look like those worn by the charcoal sellers of Paris. But the troops' shouts of "Vive l'Empereur!" were heartwarming. General Karl Mack, at the head of 80,000 Austrians, had advanced through Bavaria and occupied Ulm, on the bank of the Danube. Once having crossed the Rhine, the Emperor's plan was to execute a great fanlike movement toward the south—a semicircle—in order to fall upon the enemy, turn his flank, and overrun the stronghold. In this way he would cut off all possibility of the Austrians' retreating to Vienna.

And the campaign began, at the double-quick, in incessant rain. By October 7 Napoleon had already reached Donauwörth, downstream from Ulm, where he watched the Guard cross the Danube. Despite the heavy rain falling on the grenadiers and light infantrymen, their battle dress was impeccable.

When about to pass in front of a column, Napoleon would be preceded by a clamor coming from afar: "L'Empereur! L'Empereur!" At such times, men whose backs had been bent by the weight of their field packs would straighten up, no longer feeling the fatigue of the two leagues they had just marched, and forgetting the two more leagues they had to go. With "him, a pipe, and glory," they were willing to march to the end of the world. And whenever some of them did raise their voices in complaint, the Emperor would defend them, saying: "They're right, but it's only to spare them from spilling blood that I make them undergo such fatigue."

When they heard this they would buck up, strap on their field packs, and continue the advance. Napoleon would be covered with mud, as they were; he would be marching in the rain, as they marched; and, like them, he would make sport of the snow and the wind.

Neither marches nor battles ever interfered with the *service de parade*. Whenever a halt was made, the Guard watched over the Emperor. Whether he was occupying a tent, a hut, or a château, his quarters were called "the palace." A battalion of light infantry or grenadiers served as honor guard and military police. And every day, a squadron and a picket of the Guard cavalry were ordered to serve as escorts for the Emperor and never to leave his side. On these occasions, the troops who were to watch over "him" put on "palace dress." "Caps were brushed against the grain," says Major H. Lachouque, who has described all this better than anyone else. "And then, as they formed in single file, headed by a corporal, each grenadier or light infantryman would act as a kind of hairdresser for the man in front of him. He would tie a knot in his pigtail, two inches from the end, fasten it with his 'eagle pin,' and brush out the powder with a clothes brush."

The Austrian General Mack, nestled in at Ulm, had sent word for troops from the Tyrol to come to his aid. But they had been intercepted by Murat at Wertingen and routed. On the night of October 10, Napoleon put up at the establishment of the Elector of Trier, at Augsburg. At the same time, General Mack learned to his astonishment that the three bridges over the Danube between Ulm and Donauwörth had been captured. Not only that, but Marshal Michel Ney—coming from the direction of Elchingen—was crossing the river at a point behind Ulm!

Archduke Ferdinand had managed to leave Ulm at the head of 20,000 troops, moving toward Bohemia. But Murat set out after him, caught up with him, and took 12,000 prisoners (including seven generals), plus the army's treasure.

General Mack had stayed behind in Ulm, with 30,000 men. On October 15, while the encirclement of the city was being completed, the continuing downpour had compelled Napoleon to seek shelter in the little village of Hasslach. Ségur found him on a farm, "dozing beside a stove, with a young drummer—also dozing—across from him." This unusual sight surprised Ségur. He was told that when the Emperor had made his appearance, his aides-de-camp had tried to send the young drummer away. But he had resisted stoutly, shouting: "There's enough room for everybody! I'm cold. I'm wounded. I like it here, and I'm going to stay!"

Napoleon heard him and laughed. "Let him stay there on his chair," he ordered, "since he wants to so badly."

In the morning, from a hill exposed to enemy fire, Napoleon took in the situation. Ulm was there below him, like a fine prize he would soon be able to seize. As a matter of fact, the stronghold—relatively small—was poorly defended.

The garrison attempted a last sortie. The dragoons charged, the light cavalry of the Guard and the Mamelukes unsheathed their sabers, and in a matter of moments the fighting became ferocious. In the words of Captain Krettly: "The men were fighting hand to hand on their horses, sunk up to the stirrups in mud. We were so close to each other that we could no longer use the points of our sabers. Instead, we used their heavy hilts to strike the enemy in the face."

Then the enemy cavalry drew back, and the Emperor ordered the bombardment of the city.

Finally, General Mack agreed to an unconditional surrender. On October 20, the captured garrison of Ulm—27,000 troops, 18 generals, 40 flags, and 60 horse-drawn fieldpieces—marched past Napoleon. Three thousand wounded remained in the city. Dismounting from his white horse, the Emperor took up a position in front of his generals. To the right and the left were the armies of Ney and Marmont, their weapons loaded.

The conquered general stepped forward, proffered his sword to the Emperor, and exclaimed: "Voici le malheureux Mack!"

As they marched past, the prisoners slowed their pace. Many of them shouted: "Vive l'Empereur!"

"It was a spectacle that cannot be described," wrote Marshal Marmont many years later. "And I can still feel it. Our men were drunk with joy!"

After staying a few days in Bavaria, Napoleon continued on his way toward Vienna, where the imperial family was making ready to set out through the snow and the cold, fleeing the "ogre of France." At one point a false report gave rise to the belief that the Austrians had won a victory. And a little Archduchess by the name of Marie Louise wrote:

> We have learned to our joy that Napoleon was present at the great battle he lost. May he also lose his head! Many people here are making prophecies as to his imminent death, and it is being said that the Apocalypse applies to him. They say he is fated to die this year at Cologne, in a tavern called At the Sign of the Red Crab. I don't attribute much importance to all these predictions, but how happy I would be if they came true!

On November 13, Vienna surrendered to Murat. In the words of Thiébault: "After a hundred leagues of victories, it was intoxicating to enter the enemy's capital—especially when the capital was that of the modern Caesars."

The Viennese were astonished as they watched what was happening. Their National Guard lined the streets, and their flags dipped before the French eagles. "I have never been so proud to be French!" a soldier exclaimed.

That same Wednesday evening, while the army was pursuing the Russians northward, Napoleon reached Schönbrunn—"a bit worn out," as he admitted. The noble front elevation of the palace was to his liking. Quickly, he went up the blue steps and through the stately suites of rooms where the white and gold plumpness and rotundities of the Baroque displayed themselves.

In six weeks all of Austria, from the Danube to Italy, had been conquered. Thirty thousand prisoners and eighty-six flags were on their way to France. Finally, for the first time, Napoleon was taking up lodgings in the palace of a sovereign whom he had conquered.

And that tour de force would, fortunately, take precedence over the French disaster of Trafalgar, the tragic news of which he received on November 16.

On November 20, 1805, Napoleon set out from Drünn, following the road which climbs toward Olmütz (Olomouc). He was going to choose his battlefield.

The main body of the enemy was near Olmütz, at a place called Wischau (Vyskov). Thus the battle was going to take place at an intermediate point, near Austerlitz (today called Slavkov). The road which went uphill and down again, following the gentle undulations of the terrain, would play a very important role in the next few days. On that particular day, it was used by the artillery and the huge transport train on the way to take up their positions.

When he had gone about a dozen kilometers, the Emperor noticed a rise of ground in front of the village of Schlappanitz (Lapanz). When he reached the top of the hillock, about 850 feet high, he looked over the terrain. It was here that he would defeat the enemy.

At the moment the French troops were encamped on the two eminences crowning the plateau; beyond, behind Pratzen, they were occupying the village of Krenowitz; and farther to the west they held the larger town of Austerlitz.

For a week the Emperor explored the future battlefield, the terrain of which soon became "as familiar to him as the outskirts of Paris," in the words of one of his companions. The entire slope of the knoll of Zurlan and the hollow formed by the quarries on the side of the knoll toward Olmütz were taken up by the appendages of the general headquarters. For ten days, this area was the scene of a constant bustling of couriers and dispatch riders, of aides-de-camp in multicolored, gold-trimmed uniforms, to the accompaniment of incessant tramping and stomping by men and horses.

As his horse walked slowly along, Napoleon made a close scrutiny of the terrain. Some 1,500 meters in front of the knoll of Zurlan, the road goes up the side of a hill surmounted by a wartlike eminence on which stands the Chapel of St. Mary. About a league farther on, a road branches off from the highway to Olmütz in the direction of Hungary. Napoleon followed this road, which enabled him to pass behind the plateau of Pratzen. Coming down the slope, he reached Austerlitz, which was occupied by the troops under Nicolas Soult's command.

From Austerlitz, Napoleon went on around the hill of Pratzen and reached Aujzd (Ujezd-u-Brno), the chapel of which—St. Anthony's—he had seen with his field glass from Zurlan. From there he went on to the Goldbach.

The Goldbach is a languid stream. It (and its tributaries) flow so slowly that together with the Littawa—the stream running along the eastern edge of the plateau—it long ago formed marshlands and three big ponds which at that time (in the month of Frimaire) were iced over. They have since dried up, but one can still discern their shorelines between the villages of Aujzd, Telnitz, and Moenitz—and especially before Satschan (Zatcany).

Following the western edge of the plateau, the Emperor headed north to Pratzen, which would be at the very center of the fighting.

On the evening of November 28 Napoleon once again set out on the highway leading to Olmütz. He went past his headquarters and reached a point beyond that where the road to Hungary branches off from the highway. He was now near Murat's headquarters in the post station of Posorsitz.

While the Emperor was still on his way there, a scene which was to have significant repercussions was taking place in this little building. Lannes had just arrived, and Murat and Soult gave him a very grim account of the situation. According to the last information from the advance posts, the Russian army numbered 93,000 men and had 278 pieces of artillery. The Emperor could put only 71,000 men in the field against them—provided Davout and Bernadotte joined them in time—and he had only 129 fieldpeices! They would have to retreat.

Lannes agreed; and at the request of his two comrades, he began drafting a dispatch to the Emperor.

Suddenly the door was thrown open. It was Napoleon. "Eh bien, messieurs," he said, going up to the fire, "is all well here?"

"Not to our way of thinking!" Lannes exclaimed. "I was just writing a dispatch to Your Majesty to say so."

"What's this? Lannes favors retreat? It's the first time he has done such a thing. And you, Marshal Soult—what do you think?"

"However Your Majesty makes use of the Fourth Corps," replied Soult, "it will defeat a force twice its size."

For Lannes, this amounted to betrayal. "I've only been here for a quarter of an hour!" he said angrily. "All I know about our situation is what these gentlemen have told me. I founded my opinion on what they told me, just as I was writing you at their request. Marshal Soult's answer is therefore a stupid bit of cowardice—something I was far from expecting. It offends me, and I'll make him regret it!"

The Emperor listened to all this without saying a word. Hands locked behind his back, as usual, he was pacing from one end of the room to the other. Suddenly he stopped and announced: "I, too, feel that we should retreat."

Then he opened the door and called Berthier. The marshals were smiling. Actually, Napoleon was determined to put his plan into action as soon as possible.

That plan has since become famous for its boldness. His troops were at the moment occupying Austerlitz and the entire plateau of Pratzen. He gave orders that these two key positions should be evacuated by dawn the next morning—knowing they would immediately be seized by the Austro-Russians. Meantime, he would fortify his left flank. General Claparède's artillery would be emplaced on the overlooking knoll, the top of which (then barren of the trees which now cover it) formed a regular platform. The main body of his troops would be concentrated in the center, on the left bank of the Goldbach, between the villages and the lower end of the plateau. His right flank, with reduced forces, would be pulled far back, in echelon, toward the villages of Sokolnitz, Telnitz, and Moenitz to the south.

Napoleon was himself dictating the enemy's plans. He was inciting him to occupy the hillocks of Pratzberg and Stary-Vinohrady, and then move down the plateau toward Aujzd to attack the French right flank. At this point, as soon as the plateau and its two prominences

were partially evacuated, Napoleon would attack in the center, occupy Pratzen, and then fall upon the enemy to the left and to the
right.

The next day, the Emperor again went up on the plateau; proceeding to the point where it begins to slope down toward Krenowitz, he ascertained that the Russians were beginning to take
possession of Austerlitz, which he had evacuated that day at dawn.
He smiled, and Ségur heard him exclaim: "If I wanted to block the
enemy's advance, I would take up my position right here. But in that
case it would be merely an ordinary battle. If, on the contrary, I pull
back my right flank toward Brünn, and if the Russians push on,
leaving this high ground behind them, then even though they number 300,000 they will be taken by surprise, and their situation will be
hopeless."

The next day, November 29, in order to make the enemy's deception more complete, Napoleon sent Savary to the Czar to propose a
parley "tomorrow, at whatever time is convenient for him, between
the two armies."

Alexander was convinced that Napoleon was worried—all the
more so since, upon awakening, he had learned that the imperial
troops were pulling back. "The French are refusing to fight!" he
proclaimed. "They are pulling back toward Vienna!" Napoleon's
strategic withdrawal so much resembled a retreat that Alexander
could not suspect the truth. And so he did nothing more than send
his first aide-de-camp, the youthful Prince Dolgoruky, back with
Savary.

As soon as he learned that Dolgoruky was coming, the Emperor
left his headquarters behind the knoll of Zurlan and galloped ahead
to meet him. He went so fast that his cavalry escort had difficulty
keeping up with him. The prince—a pretentious, callow youth—was
waiting for him on the Brünn-Olmütz highway, not far from where
the road to Austerlitz branches off. Coming toward him, Dolgoruky
said later, he saw "a poorly dressed, grimy little fellow." It was Napoleon.

The Emperor took the aide-de-camp aside on the highway and let
him talk. Dolgoruky immediately assumed a haughty air which irritated Napoleon. As the Emperor wrote later to the King of Württemberg: "I had a conversation with that young fop in which he
talked to me as he would have to a convict he intended to send to
Siberia."

"My sovereign," said the prince, "is fighting only for the independence of Europe, for Holland, and for the King of Sardinia."

To which Napoleon replied: "Russia should pursue an entirely different policy, and be concerned only with its own interests."

But the Emperor, though already annoyed by the arrogant manner of the "young fop," held himself in check and asked under what conditions the Czar would be willing to make peace. Dolgoruky took Napoleon's moderation "as a sign of great fear"—a misreading that the Emperor did everything he could to encourage—and disdainfully stated his sovereign's "conditions." Among other demands, the Iron Crown of Lombardy must be handed over to the King of Sardinia, along with Genoa and a portion of the other French *départements* in Italy; France must give up the left bank of the Rhine and turn over Belgium and Holland to a Russian prince or English duke.

Abandon the very conquests of the Revolution? This time the Emperor exploded: "What? Brussels, too? But you're forgetting that we're in Moravia. And even if you were on the heights of Montmartre, you'd never get Brussels!"

Dolgoruky, as if he had heard nothing, offered to let the Emperor "withdraw safe and sound behind the Danube, if he would promise immediately to evacuate Vienna and the hereditary states."

Napoleon, whose anger was mounting, exclaimed: "All right then, we'll fight! You can leave now. Go and tell your master that I'm not in the habit of letting myself be insulted like this. Leave immediately!"

Even after Dolgoruky had been escorted back to the Russian advance posts, Napoleon's rage did not subside. His officers saw him lash the ground with his riding crop as he exclaimed: *"Italy?* Just think what they would have done with France if I had been defeated! But since that's the way they want it, I wash my hands of them. And, God willing, I'll give them a rough lesson within forty-eight hours!"

Dolgoruky hadn't understood a thing. He believed—and so said to the Czar—that Napoleon was "trembling with fear." And he added with a shrug of the shoulders: "The Allied advance guard is enough to beat him."

Consequently, three days before the battle, euphoria was at its peak in the Russian camp. As for Napoleon, he now knew that fighting was inevitable. On the evening of November 30 he wrote to Tallyrand ("from my bivouac two leagues in advance of Brünn"): "There will probably be a very serious battle with the Russians tomorrow. I tried hard to avoid it, since it will mean a useless spilling of blood." And once more repeated (it was becoming a leitmotif with him) that if he was defeated, Naples and Prussia would move in to finish him off—and then would come the scramble for the spoils.

Meanwhile the financial situation at Paris had considerably worsened since Napoleon's departure. The Royalists were repeating the *mot* of La Chaise, the sycophantic prefect: "God made Bonaparte, and then rested." To which they added: "He would have done well to rest a bit sooner."

Napoleon was also well aware that his army was tired. For a native of Berry, Provence, or the Gironde—not to mention the Parisian, with his natural tendency to grumble—there was nothing very exciting about fighting in Moravia in the hail, the snow, and the freezing wind. And so, on December 1, he gave them an explanation of his tactic: "As they advance to turn my right flank, their own flank will be left open to me."

For him, victory was certain. But he did not forget to threaten his men: "I myself will direct your battalions. If, with your usual bravery, you create chaos in the enemy's ranks, I will remain at a distance. But if for a single moment victory seems uncertain, you will see your Emperor expose himself to the first volleys."

On the anniversary of his consecration, followed by a few officers, the Emperor galloped between the new lines—in an area where the Cossacks and the French scouts were within range of each other's fire. A little before four o'clock, he returned to Zurlan. Taking up his field glass—the same one he later took with him to St. Helena and bequeathed to his son—he trained it on Pratzen. The enemy was moving—a movement he himself had inspired. Already, some of the Russian and Austrian columns were leaving the plateau and moving down toward Aujzd, Satschan, and the ponds, so that the next day they could fall upon the French right flank. Ségur heard the Emperor exclaim: "It's a disgraceful movement! They're falling into the trap! They're letting themselves be taken! Before tomorrow night that army will be my prey!"

Turning to Murat, he ordered him to take a small detachment of cavalry and, by executing a hesitant movement, give the appearance of great anxiety; then deliberately pull back as though in a great panic, having ascertained that the enemy, now formed in a semicircle, intended to trap the French in a pincers movement and cut off their retreat, the road to Vienna. Napoleon laughed—relaxed in spite of the terrible weather (rain and hail) and pleased with the extraordinary *mise en scène* he was arranging. Then he returned to his nearby bivouac behind the Tatar barrow of Zurlan.

Back in his hutting, the Emperor drank a glass of Tokay and, still wrapped up in his overcoat, stretched out on a bale of hay and went to sleep. But Savary soon woke him up. Shots were being exchanged on the extreme right flank—that same right flank which, the next day, was to take the first shock. The French advance guard had even been compelled to yield some terrain.

In a matter of minutes he was at the center of the disposition, the area where, the next morning, two divisions were to move up onto the plateau and occupy Pratzen. Lieutenant Dupin and his men (from the Fourth Line Regiment) were in the same area. They had just arrived, and had had no food for three days. The young officer writes: "I had some fires built; but since this was the target of enemy shot, we had to stay 20 or 30 paces to the left or right of our fires. Every time the Russian volleys sent the embers flying up into the air, we would laugh uproariously."

Napoleon had just left Puntowitz and was heading back toward his quarters when his horse stumbled over a fallen tree. A grenadier twisted some straw together, stuck it onto the end of a branch, and in this way made a torch to light the way for his idol. The troops in the neighboring bivouac, thinking it was a signal, lighted torches of their own and shouted: "It's the anniversary of the coronation! Long live the Emperor!"

Napoleon called out: "Silence! Let all this wait until tomorrow! All you should be thinking of right now is sharpening your bayonets!"

But his words went unheeded. The soldiers of the army's twelve bivouacs abandoned their shelters, lighted torches, and started dancing a farandole. The Russians could see the seven corps of the French army—seven lines of fires in front of them. They, too, were joyous, since they naïvely believed that Napoleon's soldiers were burning their shelters in preparation for a pull-out.

When the Emperor got back to his own bivouac, touched to the heart, he exclaimed: "This is the finest night of my life!"

When day broke, a heavy fog hung over the battlefield.

After a light breakfast, the Emperor addressed his officers. "Now, gentlemen," he said, "let us begin a great day."

The weather came to his aid. The fog lifted from the top of the plateau but continued to conceal the movements and positioning of the French troops echeloned in the plain at the bottom of the hill. At about seven thirty Napoleon summoned the commanders of the army corps to Zurlan to give them their last instructions and the modifications resulting from his tour of inspection the night before.

Marshal Davout was ordered to do what he could to hold up the enemy's violent advance on the extreme right flank. For the greater part of the morning, the fighting in that sector would be hard, bitter, and heroic.

Soult, remaining by the Emperor's side after the others had left, seemed impatient to launch his attack on the plateau of Pratzen. But Napoleon held him back. The fog finally lifted. It was eight o'clock in the morning. In the distance, through a slight haze, the Emperor could see General Mikhail Kutuzov's 90,000 bayonets flashing in the sun.

Twenty-five thousand Russian grenadiers—"stout fellows all," as Coignet put it—with their weapons at the ready, had come down from the plateau and were on the point of crossing the stream.

Soult was chafing at the bit.

"How long will it take you to capture the hilltop?" Napoleon asked him.

"Ten minutes."

"All right. But wait another quarter of an hour, and then the time will be ripe."

Fifteen minutes later, divisions commanded by Vandamme and Saint-Hilaire—each ordered to take one of the hills on the plateau— began the ascent. The frost crackled under their boots.

The bands marching in the middle of each battalion were playing:

> *On va leur percer le flanc.*
> *Que nous allons rire!*

And the drums repeated:

> *Rantanplan, tirelire en plan!*

The Austro-Russian troops fell back and attacked Vandamme's men. But the French soon seized the plateau. At eleven thirty Napoleon was able to take up his post on the Stary-Vinohrady—the same post that Kutuzov had occupied a few hours earlier. From there he had an overall view of the battle, and could see that on the French left, near the hill of Santon, Lannes and Murat had thrown the Russian army into confusion and cut it off from the remainder of the enemy forces. On the French right flank the situation—after having been critical at first, since Davout was outnumbered three to one— was again in hand. Ten thousand French had stopped 35,000 Russians and Austrians. The villages of Telnitz and Sokolnitz had been recaptured. The line along the Goldbach had held.

The only place where things were going badly—for a brief time —was in the center, on the Pratzberg, where Alexander had ordered his Guard into action to retake the plateau. The cavalrymen of the Guard rushed into the fray "like madmen," said Dupin, who was in the thick of it; and in a few minutes the Fourth Line Regiment had been mowed down.

The Emperor had ordered that two squadrons of light cavalry, the corps of Mamelukes, and some mounted grenadiers set off at full speed to size up the situation. When they came within artillery range of the Pratzberg they could see the disaster: the enemy cavalrymen, dismounted, were literally strolling through the quarries and putting the French infantrymen to the saber. When they saw the French reinforcement, the enemy about-faced, and Alexander's Guard opened fire on them with four pieces of artillery. Cannonballs rained down on the French from all directions.

The French commander, Rapp, shouted to his troops: "Do you see how they are trampling on our brothers—our friends? We must avenge them—them and our flag!"

The torrent of men followed Rapp and overran the artillery. When he reached the other side of the Pratzberg, Rapp regrouped his squadrons and made another charge.

"Let's make the ladies of St. Petersburg weep!" shouted the cavalrymen, as they swung their sabers at the Czar's Horse Guard.

The Mamelukes performed brilliantly. In the words of Coignet:

> With their curved sabers, they would slice off a head with one stroke. And with their sharp stirrups, they would break a soldier's back. One of them brought three Russian standards to the Emperor, one after the other. The third time the Emperor wanted to hold him back. But he rushed into the fray again, and never returned. He remained on the field of battle.

Finally, the Russians and Austrians fled. The Czar and the Emperor of Austria, dumfounded, had witnessed the defeat of the Russian Guard, which they had believed would "wrap up" the victory.

Now that they were free to move again, Dupin, Coignet, and their comrades headed for the Chapel of St. Anthony on the far southern end of the plateau. The Russian left flank was caught in a cross fire. Soon the French were descending the slope toward Aujzd and the ponds.

Napoleon was so positioned that he had a good view of Aujzd and the ponds of Satschan and Melnitz. The routed enemy had reached the edge of these ponds when Napoleon ordered his artillery to fire on them. Thousands of men were supposed to have perished. The Emperor himself gave a figure of 20,000 men drowned, but the facts are quite different. The water was only breast high, and there weren't even a hundred who died. The miserable enemy troops came out of the water, their teeth chattering, and were only too happy to be taken prisoner. "At this sight," reports Coignet, "all our men clapped their hands, and Napoleon took out his vengeance on his snuffbox. It was total defeat."

The Russian army had been completely routed. The plateau and the plain were strewn with dead, and the villages were full of stragglers and wounded. Napoleon walked the entire length of the battlefield, and then went to pass the night at the Lecht-Auberge.

The next day he moved his quarters to the very handsome baroque château of Austerlitz. From the windows on the ground floor he could see the east slope of Pratzen—the plateau which had given him his victory. It was there, on an eighteenth century table which has been carefully preserved, that he drafted his proclamation:

> Soldiers! I am pleased with you. On the day of Austerlitz, you justified everything that I was expecting of your intrepidity. You have covered your eagles with immortal glory. In less than four hours, an army of 100,000 men, commanded by the emperors of Russia and Austria, was cut up and dispersed. Forty flags, the standards of the Imperial Guard and the Russian Guard, 120 pieces of artillery, 20 generals, and more than 30,000 men taken prisoner—such are the results of this day which will forever be famous. . . .
>
> My nation will be overjoyed to see you again. And it will be

enough for you to say, "I was at Austerlitz," to hear the reply: "There is a brave man!"

He dated his proclamation "Austerlitz." And so this little Moravian town has given its name to the battle.

On December 4, after having received Prince John of Lichtenstein, who had come to ask for an armistice, Napoleon set off in the direction of Hungary. He stopped some 15 kilometers from Austerlitz, in the valley of the Ziarochitz (Zarosice) at the "Burned Mill." It was there—"in my bivouac," as Napoleon proudly said—that he was to meet the Emperor of Austria. Not finding the mill to his liking, he chose to conduct the interview in the open air. Halfway down the slope from the mill there was "a kind of grotto" under a plane tree. His sappers built a fire in this grotto, while two light infantrymen posted on the hill kept an eye on the scene.

It was two o'clock in the afternoon. The loser of the Battle of Austerlitz had already made Napoleon wait for a considerable time, and he was growing impatient. Finally, the Emperor Francis appeared. He was accompanied by several generals, including John of Lichtenstein. The drummers of the Guard beat the general salute, and the bugles sounded the march.

Napoleon advanced along the highway, helped Francis down from his carriage, and embraced him, saying a few words that the others present could not hear. "But he certainly must have mentioned the English," Thiard reported, "because I heard the Austrian Emperor say very distinctly: 'The English are merchants of human flesh.'"

Napoleon then escorted Francis to the spot he had chosen, and the two of them held a tête-à-tête near the crackling fire. The troops of the Guard, forming an impressive array, stood silent and immobile, at parade rest.

Francis asked for a three-day cease-fire for the Russian army.

"The Czar's army is surrounded," replied Napoleon. "Not a single man can escape. But I would like to do a favor for the Emperor Alexander. I will hold up the march of my columns and let the Russian army pass. But Your Majesty must promise me that it will go back to Russia, evacuating Germany and Austrian and Prussian Poland."

"That is Emperor Alexander's intention," answered Francis. "I can assure you of it. For that matter, you can have your own officers ascertain it tonight."

At the end of the long interview, Francis exclaimed: "Good! We are agreed, then! It is only since this morning that I have been free. I told the Russian Emperor that I wanted to see you, and he replied that I was free to arrange things."

"And so Your Majesty promises not to resume the war?" Napoleon demanded.

"I swear it, and I shall keep my word."

Napoleon then escorted Francis back to his carriage, embraced him, and bowed as the equipage moved off.

As he was mounting his horse, he told the general staff: "Gentlemen, we are returning to Paris. We have made peace."

Spurring his Arabian mount to a gallop, he headed back for Austerlitz. The bands played, and the Guard's shouts of "Vive l'Empereur!" filled the air.

When she learned the news of Austerlitz, the young archduchess Marie Louise broke into sobs. In one of her letters she wrote:

> It seems to me impossible that this sad news should be true. It is as though I were dreaming. I cannot believe that such a calamity has happened to us, and yet I must believe it. But I am unwilling to doubt that God will give us victory over that hateful Napoleon, and finish him off. . . .

On January 1, 1806, by the grace of Napoleon, his ally the Elector of Bavaria became a king and gave his daughter's hand in marriage to Eugène de Beauharnais. Through his stepson's marriage, Napoleon entered into the family of kings. Decidedly, the Revolution was over!

Accordingly, on that same January 1 when Napoleon created the first of a list of kings that would in time become most impressive, the revolutionary calendar was replaced by the Gregorian, and January 1 again became New Year's Day. Napoleon had brought Time under his command.

The French approved the new state of affairs by "plebiscite." Along the way from Stuttgart to Paris there were arches of triumph, illuminated cities, and inscriptions of all sorts. "But these things," said one of the victors of Austerlitz, "were as nothing compared to the delirium of his people." Petitions were circulated, demanding that the conqueror of "Osterlitz" be accorded the "honors of triumph," as in ancient Rome.

The flags captured from the enemy were paraded through Paris amid indescribable enthusiasm. The stock market went up 13 points.

Yet there was still England, victorious at Trafalgar, and Prussia, which had avoided the war. And the King of Prussia was merely waiting for the opportunity to show that his army was still the same as that of Frederick the Great.

The Fourth Coalition was already in the making.

XIII

"THE GLORY OF MY REIGN"

In the eyes of those who found empires,
men are not men but tools.

NAPOLEON

NAPOLEON WAS DEIFIED. The 250 fieldpieces and culverins captured from the Russians and Austrians were melted down to be used in the erection of a column "built in accordance with the proportions of Trajan's Column," on the Place Vendôme. The original plan was to place atop it a statue of Charlemagne that the revolutionary armies had taken from Aachen. But this statue had such a "Gothic" look and was "so crudely executed that if exposed in a prominent place, it would provoke laughter and sarcastic remarks by the public." Therefore, said the toadying minister, what other could take the place vacated by Charlemagne if not that of "the prince cherished by all of France"? And so Napoleon agreed to be represented by a statue 45 meters high showing him as a Roman emperor (but clothed this time). He would have preferred to be shown in battle dress—as later he was.

To the victors of Austerlitz he had promised: "You will pass under arches of triumph on your way home."

Accordingly, on February 18, 1806, he ordered the construction of a monumental portal "near the site of the Bastille." But the architect Jean Chalgrin preferred another site: the crossroads of Chaillot and the Ternes, the former *carrefour de chasse* of the Place de l'Étoile —a rise of ground that Mme. de Pompadour's brother, the Marquis de Marigny, had had leveled to clear a way to the Champs-Élysées.

Jean Champagny, then the Minister of Foreign Affairs, approved:

An arch of triumph would provide a most majestic and picturesque backdrop to the superb view from the imperial château of the Tuileries. It would evoke the admiration of the traveler coming into Paris. And for those leaving the capital it would provide a deep memory of its incomparable beauty. . . . At a distance, it would always be within view of the conqueror. Your Majesty would pass under it when going to Malmaison, to St.-Germain, to St.-Cloud, and even to Versailles.

Napoleon listened to Chalgrin and Champagny. And the first stone of the Arc de Triomphe de l'Étoile was laid on August 15, 1806, for the festival of the Emperor.

During the seven months between the two coalitions Napoleon stayed in Paris, organizing his armies from his study. Everything converged on his desk. As Méneval said:

His astonishing memory took in all the details, and they remained engraved there. The result was that he was informed on the personnel and matériel of the corps as well as, or even better than, the bureaus of the Minister of War and the Minister of the Navy—even the general staffs themselves.

But there were other things besides the army. The civil affairs of his overextended empire required the same amount of attention. In his dictation (speaking of himself in the third person) he said:

It is not conquests that he is planning. He has had enough of military glory. . . . To perfect the administration—to make of it, for his people, the source of a lasting happiness, a growing prosperity and, by its acts, the example of a pure and exalted morality —such is the glory he seeks!

But for this "glory" to be realized—for orders to reach those to whom they were addressed—it was necessary above all to establish stages, post stations, and new highways; to make rivers navigable; and to build traversable roads through the mountain passes between France, Italy, and Germany.

He worked without interruption. And the work agreed so well with the conqueror of Austerlitz that he gained weight.

Napoleon applied parsimony and attention to detail in straightening out the finances of the Empire. When he returned to Paris he was of course crowned with a halo because of his victories—but also because of the 50 million francs that the Austrians had to pay France. This was a fortunate windfall, since despite the rise in the stock market, the nation's finances were still in poor condition. The shortage of metallic currency had become acute. A group called Les Négociants réunis, headed by Gabriel Ouvrard, had been "playing fast and loose" with Treasury funds. Ouvrard's wealth displeased Napoleon. "A man with thirty million," he said, "is dangerous."

Actually, Ouvrard had much more than that; and the Emperor seemed to have forgotten that he had borrowed rather large sums from him; for example, 60 million in 1805.

The housecleaning was rapidly accomplished. A few days later Napoleon told his brother Joseph: "I have made about a dozen rascals cough up. I was ready to have them shot without a trial. Thank God, I have been reimbursed!" Les Négociants réunis had to hand back 87 million to the Treasury.

His broom had swept clean, and now he could put the nation's finances on a solid footing. The main thing was to avoid the example of Louis XIV, who had gone bankrupt because he didn't know how to keep count of things or "draw up a budget."

"The budget is my law," the Emperor wrote. "It is something I must obey because, of all branches of administration, finance is the most important to me."

Without too much creaking of the machinery, the budget of 684 million francs was just about doubled in 1806. Of course the heavy tribute imposed upon the vanquished nations provided a constant flow of gold into the Treasury; but in addition, Napoleon created indirect contributions which all the succeeding governments were careful not to eliminate. As he put it:

> I want to ensure the well-being of my people, and I will not let the grumblings of taxpayers stop me. I live for posterity. France needs heavy taxation, and it will be established. . . . I want to provide my successors with reliable resources upon which they can draw in lieu of the unusual means I have had to create for myself.

Within a year, the results were evident. Banks were full to over-flowing with metallic currency, which had become abundant and even superabundant, and people now preferred banknotes!

Was there any task he would not undertake? He had tackled the Code of Civil Procedure, the Commercial Code, the university, and education in general. As in the days of the Consulate, he always presided over the sessions of the Council of State with the greatest of pleasure. As Trémont tells us:

I attended sessions of the Council of State, chaired by the Emperor, which lasted for seven hours running. His stimulating influence, the incredible penetration of his analytical turn of mind, the lucidity with which he summarized the most complex questions, his skill at strengthening personal attachment to him by means of a familiarity which enabled him to treat inferiors as equals when the occasion called for it, and the care that he took not only to support contradiction but to provoke it—all these things produced the same kind of enthusiasm he aroused in his troops. Just as men died on the field of battle for him, so we exhausted ourselves with work.

Sometimes, however, he showed signs of fatigue:

In the past, I used to tell Montesquiou several times a day: "Montesquiou, bring me a glass of lemonade." Now it's a cup of coffee or a glass of madeira that I call for, because I need it. Believe me, at the age of thirty one begins to be less fit for waging war. Alexander the Great died before he had any premonitions of his waning powers.

Waning powers? He wasn't thinking seriously of that. Early in 1806 the members of the Council heard him say: "I am sure that one of these days we shall see the 'Western Empire' come back to life, because exhausted peoples will eagerly place themselves under the yoke of that nation which is best governed."

In the same week when the news of the victory of Austerlitz reached Paris, a dispatch announced that a corps of English and Russian troops had landed at Naples. Such was the reaction of Queen Caroline (her husband did not count) to the Napoleonic victories in Austria. And yet there was a treaty of neutrality between the Kingdom of Naples and France. Napoleon moved quickly, and on December 25 he announced to the public: "General Saint-Cyr is on his way to Naples, by forced marches, to punish the treason of the Queen and to topple from the throne that criminal woman who has so shamelessly violated all that is sacred among mankind."

On February 24 the Emperor went to the Opera. There was prolonged applause for the line: "Et quel temps fut jamais si fertile en miracles?" (What age was ever so fertile in miracles?)

A few minutes later, the play was interrupted, and Talma announced from the stage that the French army had entered Naples. The enthusiasm immediately reached the point of delirium. The next day, everyone in Paris went to watch the parade on the Carrousel. The crowd applauded the victors of Austerlitz, "who had just recently settled the fate of Europe."

And Caroline? "The Queen of Naples has ceased to reign," was Napoleon's reply to someone who asked him what would be the fate of Marie Antoinette's sister.

As for the kingdom of Naples, he first offered it to Joseph: "I want to place a prince of my house on that throne. You, first of all, if it is agreeable to you. If not, then somebody else."

The year before, Joseph had refused the Kingdom of Italy so that he would not have to give up his "rights" to the French Empire. But now he accepted the throne of King Nasone, since this time he could remain his brother's heir. Moreover, Napoleon (by way of homage to the older brother) ordered that Joseph should continue to receive his salary of 333,333 francs in his capacity of Grand Elector.

Joseph left to enter upon his new duties; and immediately upon his arrival, he began to take his role as King of Naples very seriously. He tried to put the Neapolitan financial interests ahead of those of the French Empire and, insofar as he could, to exercise his "right of grace." His tolerance and mildness even earned him an imperial rebuke. For Napoleon, "la bonté n'est pas de l'humanité" in a conquered country. And he made himself quite clear to Joseph: "Mon frère, it is not by coaxing nations that you win them over; and these measures you have taken will not enable you to provide a just recompense to your army. Tax the Kingdom of Naples to the extent of 30 million francs. Incidentally, I have not heard of your having a single *lazzarone* shot."

Joseph replied sheepishly: "Your Majesty need have no cause for concern: all those who deserve it are being shot."

On March 14, less than a week after the letter of reproach he had sent to Joseph, Napoleon made another important announcement. Haunted by the idea of "reviving the Western Empire" (as he had told the Council), he had decided to elevate republican Holland—at the moment "without an executive branch"—to the status of a kingdom over which his brother Louis would reign.

But Admiral Verhuel, instructed by the Emperor to take the pulse of public opinion at The Hague, informed Napoleon that "my unbounded devotion to the Emperor obliges me to tell him frankly that the first news of His Majesty's intention provoked general consternation." And Schimmelpenninck, the Great Pensioner, who was performing the functions of stadtholder without assuming this too royal title, likewise informed Napoleon that his plan was "completely unacceptable."

The Emperor paid no more heed to him than to Admiral Verhuel. How could Holland fight? If she did not want to be purely and simply annexed, there was no question of her refusing to become a kingdom. Just look at the Batavian Republic, created under the Directory. Its budget was hopeless. It owed France 29 million francs, and its annual deficit amounted to 45 million!

So there was no choice for Holland but to yield. Better yet: the Netherlanders themselves must demand the change of regime. Napoleon then "condescended" to approve the investiture of the new sovereign "chosen" by the Batavian republics. And on June 5, 1806, an unhappy deputation of Netherlanders, presumably with a mandate "to express the will of the representatives of the Dutch people," was received in the throne room at the Tuileries.

Verhuel declared: "We beg Your Majesty to give us, as supreme executive of our Republic and King of Holland, Prince Louis, the brother of Your Majesty, to whom we consign, with entire and respectful trust, the protection of our laws, the defense of our political rights, and all the interests of our dear country."

The Emperor—who on that day must surely have been thinking of Louis XIV offering his grandson to the Spanish emissaries who had come to him asking for a king—replied after a brief silence: "Your offer of the crown to Prince Louis is in conformity with the interests of your country and with my own; and it conduces to the general repose of Europe. I proclaim Prince Louis King of Holland."

Then, turning to his brother, he added, in an imitation of the Sun King: "Prince, reign over these peoples, but at the same time never cease to be French. . . . Cultivate in your subjects feelings of union with France and love for her. Be the terror of evil men and the father of good ones. Such is the character of great kings!"

New sovereigns are scarcely ever satisfied. Louis, a king in spite of himself, had thoughts only for his rheumatism, and considered the climate of Holland much too humid and cold for his perpetual state as an invalid. As for Hortense, she was willing if absolutely necessary to become Queen of Holland provided she did not have to leave Paris. Ultimately, however, both of them gave in and left without enthusiasm for their kingdom.

They found that their reception by the Hollanders was decidedly cool. Had the spontaneous wishes of the "Batavian people" been misinterpreted?

The Emperor's rebukes soon began to rain down upon The Hague as they had on Naples: "You are behaving stupidly, and not looking to the consequences."

Before long, Napoleon was even meddling in his brother's private life: "Your quarrels with the Queen are becoming known to the public. You are treating a young woman the way one treats a regiment. You have the best and most virtuous wife in the world, and you are making her unhappy."

Italy was being transformed into a kind of Napoleonic federation. His dear Paulette—"my beloved sister Pauline"—also received a pretty trinket: the principality of Guastalla. At first "Mme. la Princesse Borghese" seemed delighted: Guastalla suggested something amusing out of an operetta. But when she learned that it consisted of only ten square kilometers with a population of 10,000, she pouted. She didn't even go to take possession of her principality. And since money seemed to her infinitely more useful than her new State, she sold it for 1,500,000 francs to the Kingdom of Italy; that is, to her brother, who had given it to her in the first place.

Another sister, Élisa, and (in his secondary role) her husband had agreed to "reign" at Lucca and Piombino. Now it was the Murats' turn to claim a crown. Sister Caroline in particular shrieked in protest at seeing Élisa—that Bacciochi!—become a reigning princess, while she herself was still "merely" an Imperial Highness! The Emperor offered them the Prussian principality of Neuchâtel, but they rejected that domain as unworthy of them. Finally—while continuing to hope for something better—they were given the Duchy of Berg (ceded by Bavaria), to which was added the Duchy of Clèves. On March 21, 1806, two French divisions occupied the states that had fallen to the lot of "Joachim, Prince and Grand Admiral of France," who had become Grand Duke of Berg and Clèves. On March 24 the new sovereign made his entry—"in the style of a Franconi circus," as Napoleon put it—into his capital of Düsseldorf. The next morning he put on the grand uniform of a Marshal of the Empire, and that evening he appeared in "a splendid Spanish costume."

The Western Empire was taking shape. Pleased with the idea of establishing these frontier domains so as to form a glacis around the French Empire, Napoleon created a number of duchies and principalities adjacent to the great fiefs. Bernadotte, Désirée's husband, became Prince of Pontecorvo, in the Kingdom of Naples; Talleyrand received the principality of Benevento, Cambacérès the Duchy of Parma, Lebrun the Duchy of Piacenza; and Berthier was offered the Principality of Neuchâtel which the Murats had rejected. Finally— and this was the great stroke, since Francis I of Austria was no longer the Emperor Francis II of Germany, and since the Holy Roman Empire had become a museum piece—why not unite the German states, which had no supreme sovereign? Perhaps the Emperor of the French could place himself at the summit of this decapitated edifice. After all, Napoleon was already the "Mediator" of the Swiss Confederation. Did the Germans of the West really want to "rush into union with the French nation, which was certainly better governed" as Napoleon (without false modesty) had affirmed? Bavaria, Württemberg, and even Baden felt that they were already sufficiently "protected." But thirteen other princes—those of Hesse-Darmstadt and Hohenzollern, for example—needed confederation, so the Emperor declared. And of course Murat, the new Grand Duke of Berg and Clèves, must also join in the new combination.

But although he considered himself to be the successor to Charlemagne, Napoleon could not yet see just how he was going to carry

out his projects. The means by which he might accomplish his ends
were, however, forthcoming, being provided by Charles of Dalberg,
Archbishop Elector of Regensburg. This prelate was presiding over
the debris of the German Empire. By way of forming this debris into
a state of sorts—and at the same time keeping his own place—he
cleverly chose the Emperor's uncle, Cardinal Fesch, as his coadjutor.
A perfect sycophant, he wrote to Napoleon, begging the master "not
to confine himself to creating the happiness of France." And he
added: "Providence bestows the superior man upon the universe.
The worthy German nation is groaning in the throes of political and
religious anarchy. Deign to be, Sire, the regenerator of the Constitution."

This "spontaneous" request induced Napoleon to agree quite
naturally to becoming the head of the late Holy Roman Empire. He
would be not the "regenerator" but the "protector" of the new
agglomeration labeled a "confederation." And its nominal head
would be Dalberg (who well deserved it) with the title of Prince
Primate and Grand Duke of Frankfurt. Actually, of course, the Emperor was sovereign of the German mosaic. From then on, the German princes and dukes were merely the superprefects of a
federative empire.

This empire, moreover, was tending to become a family property.
First, Eugène had married Augusta of Bavaria; then the Emperor's
brother Jérôme was wed to Catherine of Württemberg, and Stéphanie de la Pagerie (Josephine's cousin) to the Prince of Arenberg.

Napoleon now had no desire to go to war; and the eivdence in
support of his peaceable intentions was at no time more clear than
on the eve of the Fourth Coalition. Did not "M. de Buonaparte" (as
his enemies called him) have a free hand in whatever he wanted?
And was it not true that, without recourse to arms, he could move
frontier posts about pretty much at his own whim? But the rest of
Europe was horrified at the spectacle of an insatiable France expand-
ing (more or less indirectly and under various names) from the Hanseatic cities to Naples, and from Brest to the banks of the Elbe,
pending its extension to the Oder and eventually (some were predicting that the time was imminent) the banks of the Vistula and the
Neman. Italy, originally fragmented into Austrian (and even, to some

extent, Spanish) possessions, was another matter. But the European states could not remain impassive at the sight of German territory ceasing to be Austrian or Prussian. For them, there was no other solution but war in order to regain what had been taken from them by force of arms—arms first brandished by the French Revolution, and then by the man who had become the heir of that revolution. By contrast, what could Napoleon gain from fighting new battles? Nothing but new enemies; since as a prisoner of his own present and future conquests, he was bound to keep them—if not for himself, then for the profit of the clan or his allies and old friends, so as to recompense them for the help they had given him. Should he pursue his peaceable intentions to the point of returning the conquered domains to the vanquished? Should he voluntarily set limits to the French territory and influence? Give the English a slice of the European pie? Or at any rate let them trade freely with the Continent? That might have been wise—but dangerous. And the Emperor had no way of knowing how the fantastic adventure would end.

It was the successive gains of territory—voluntary or involuntary —of Imperial France that would compel her enemies to declare war on her. Similarly, in the future, the Emperor's perpetual victories would compel him to multiply those *casus belli* which, one day, would bring him to his ruin.

"It is impossible for me to have any real alliance with any of the great powers," the Emperor said with a sigh.

Only Austria seemed muzzled—for the time being. As for Prussia, Napoleon had given her Hanover—an English possession on the Continent—to disarm her and make her accept the creation of the Confederation of the Rhine. In exchange, the Berlin government was to accept an offensive and defensive alliance with the Emperor and close its ports and the mouths of its rivers to English shipping. It even had to break off relations with Russia. Queen Louise fulminated against the demands of the "French tyrant," and Frederick William wept. Nonetheless, the King of Prussia signed the treaty and notified England that he had been "compelled," against his will, to occupy Hanover—whereas in fact he had long coveted this prey near his frontiers. In a wheedling tone (but secretly delighted) the Prussian minister, Hardenberg, told the English: "I abhor the infamous manner in which we are making this acquisition. We could have remained Bonaparte's friends without becoming his slaves."

Needless to say, Frederick William, a master of double-dealing and duplicity—who in the words of his minister, Haugwitz, wanted to maintain "only a simulacrum of peace"—avowed to Austria that "if there had ever existed a power that Prussia wanted to deceive, it was France." And behind the scenes, the Berlin Government multiplied its gestures of friendship and loyalty toward England and Russia.

In spite of all this, Napoleon had for some time clung to his hopes of signing a peace treaty with England. William Pitt had died on January 23, 1806; and Charles Fox, the leader of the Whig party, had seemed much more accommodating than his rival and predecessor. On February 20, he had taken the trouble to write Talleyrand to warn him that a hired killer had come to him with proposals for assassinating "the leader of the French."

When apprised of it, the Emperor said: "I recognize in this the principles of honor and virtue which have always animated M. Fox." And he added that this gesture was "a presage of what one can expect from a cabinet whose principles I take pleasure in evaluating in accordance with those of M. Fox."

A few days later, on March, 2 he informed the Corps Législatif: "I want peace with England. I will always be ready to conclude it on the basis of the terms of the Treaty of Amiens."

But after attempts at reconciliation, after many talks, and after so much hope, everything collapsed: Fox died. Later, Napoleon would say: "The death of M. Fox was one of the calamities of my career. . . . If he had lived longer, we would have made peace."

In Russia, following the defeat of Austerlitz, wrath was redoubled against "that infamous Corsican smeared with the blood he has spilled to please Robespierre." But time had a mollifying effect; and in July the Czar resigned himself to the necessity of sending Baron d'Oubril to Paris to begin talks with a view to imminent peace.

Napoleon even believed that the negotiations had been completed, for on July 22 he announced to the minister Décrès: "The peace between France and Russia was signed on the twentieth of this month. . . . It is our intention that you notify all our ports that Russian vessels should be considered as friendly, and that the commanding officers of all ports, squadrons, and ships should treat them as such."

Perhaps d'Oubril had signed the peace prematurely; because the Czar, fearful of causing displeasure to England (London described the treaty as "humiliating"), refused to ratify the agreements concluded in his name. Immediately, Prussia went into spasms of joy.

The plan for having Hanover revert to England was what set fire to the powder keg. In the course of the talks with England, Napoleon had indeed proposed that Hanover, occupied by Prussia, be returned to the British royal house, provided Berlin be offered compensation. But Lord Yarmouth, who had come to Paris to try to effect a rapprochement between the two countries, felt it necessary to take Lucchesini, the Prussian envoy to France, into his confidence—without, however, mentioning compensation. As a result, Prussia felt she had been duped. This omission on Yarmouth's part—whether deliberate or not—gave Napoleon grounds for believing that "perfidious Albion" had waved a red flag in front of the Prussians to incite them to fight for Europe.

And the stupid and weak Frederick William, incited by his wife, immediately assumed the attitude of a braggart. He would defeat Napoleon with lashes of his whip—no point in using up gunpowder! The Prussian General G. L. von Blücher, too, was under great illusions. Said he: "I have no fear of meeting the French. . . . I will dig graves for all those on the banks of the Rhine." He even exclaimed: "I shall take it upon myself to get to Paris with nothing but my cavalry!"

In breaking off relations with its "ally, France," Berlin destroyed whatever hopes of a general peace—with both England and Russia —Napoleon was still entertaining. Prussia's attitude astounded the Emperor all the more in that he had seemed heretofore to have handled the Hohenzollerns with kid gloves, whereas they had gone on committing acts of deceit, duplicity, and even fraud vis-à-vis France. Frederick William misinterpreted Napoleon's amazement as fear—the fear that Bonaparte must surely feel at the mere thought of his first encounter on the battlefield with the unbeatable soldiers of Frederick William's great-uncle Frederick II.

On September 6, 1806, the Prussian King announced to the Czar: "Apparently it is I who must take the first decisive steps. My troops will march from all directions to hasten the moment."

The public witnessed Prussian officers honing their sabers on the stone steps of the French Embassy, while their colonel told them: "We won't need sabers. Cudgels will suffice for those French dogs!"

And yet Napoleon, still hoping for the impossible, wrote to the King of Prussia on September 12: "If I am compelled to take up arms in my own defense, I would employ them against Your Majesty's troops only with the greatest regret. So intertwined are the interests of our two states that I would regard it as a civil war. I want no part of it; I have demanded nothing of it."

But this letter in no way stopped Frederick William from recalling his ambassador, Lucchesini. And on September 20 Napoleon said, "Prussia has taken off the mask."

When Napoleon reviewed the Guard, with its arms and equipment ready, the public understood that war was inevitable. On the stock market "quotations dropped rapidly." In London, everyone was repeating the statement made by Lord Lauderdale, who was to have signed the unsuccessful peace treaty drawn up by Lord Yarmouth: "In case of a conflict with Prussia, a war prosecuted vigorously could bring unhoped-for results, since the French forces are scattered from Emden to the toe of the boot of Naples."

Napoleon set off for the war. He was opposed by the Fourth Coalition, which he devoutly hoped would be the last. But the war would continue for ten months—a war which, before allowing him to return to the Tuileries, would take him from Jena to Berlin, from Warsaw to Eylau, from Friedland to Tilsit. And at each stage he would be able to say, with justification: "My troops went on winning when I ordered them to stop fighting."

It was at Bamberg, on October 7, that the Emperor received the Prussian ultimatum. It was dated September 26 and, having been forwarded from Paris, had just now caught up with him. It expired the next day, October 8. The text—"the ultimate in folly and senselessness," as he put it—demanded that the French army retreat behind the Rhine.

"Does the King of Prussia think he's in Champagne?" he exclaimed.

On Sunday, October 12, he wrote his reply:

Monsieur mon Frère, I did not receive Your Majesty's letter until the 7th. . . . In it, you made an appointment for the 8th. Like a true knight, I have kept my word: I am in the middle of Saxony. Please believe that I have such troops that all your forces could not keep victory in the balance for long. . . . But why spill so much blood? To what end? . . . I set no great value on a victory which would be bought with the lives of many of my men. If I were only beginning my military career and were hence perhaps fearful of the risks of combat, this language would be quite out of place. Sire, Your Majesty will be conquered. . . . Today you are intact and can parley with me in a manner suitable to your rank. Within a month you will parley under different conditions. . . .

The next day he reached Jena on the banks of the Saale. No sooner had he arrived than he started on a climb up through the vineyards, following a path "as steep as the roof of a house," to the Landgrafenberg, a tall butte directly above the city, overlooking on one hand the deep valley of the Saale and, on the other, the plain of Weimar. From there he could see what he thought was the whole Prussian army. (Actually, it was only General Hohenlohe's 50,000 men, ready and waiting for him.)

He ordered a third of his troops—about 27,000 men—to take up their position on the hill. Then he went back down toward the city. On the way, failing to hear a French sentinel's "Who goes there?" he came within an inch of being killed.

"What's this, you rascal?" he exclaimed. "You mean you took me for a Prussian? A fellow like you doesn't waste his gunpowder on sparrows: he shoots only at emperors."

"Sorry, sir, but I had my orders. If you didn't answer the challenge, that's your fault. You should have said in the order that you didn't want to answer."

"My boy, I'm not blaming you. For a shot off the hip, it was pretty well aimed. But it will soon be daylight. Shoot more accurately, and I'll look after you."

Shortly afterward Napoleon left his bivouac. He was all smiles when he passed along the front lines. But then he stopped in amazement: 12 fieldpieces of Louis-Gabriel Suchet's division were not in their designated positions.

He himself set off to search for them, and found them at the bottom of the Landgrafenberg, so thoroughly stuck in a gorge that they could be moved neither forward nor backward.

"Where are your officers?"

"They have gone to Jena to eat."

Napoleon was once again, for this occasion, the "Captain Cannon" of the old days. He issued commands, sent men to get pickaxes and shovels, and with a lantern in his hand, he himself directed the work. Two hours later, with a regular road to follow, the batteries (pulled by a dozen horses) were brought up the hill to their positions.

Before dawn the Emperor was on his horse inspecting his troops. It was still so dark that lanterns were needed to light his way. Seeing the lights going and coming in front of their lines, the Prussians opened fire. But the Emperor continued about his business. He ordered the troops to have their arms at the ready, and the Battle of Jena began.

In his "Bulletin" on the Battle of Jena, Napoleon reported:

> In less than an hour, the action became general: from 250,000 to 300,000 men, with 700 or 800 fieldpieces, strewed death everywhere, and provided one of those spectacles rare in history. On every hand, there was constant maneuvering, as at a parade. There was never the slightest disorder among our troops, and victory was not in doubt for a moment.

Actually, there were not from 250,000 to 300,000 combatants; but in any case the Guard did not have to be committed.

The Prussians were routed and in full retreat. "By two o'clock in the afternoon," reported Von der Goltz, "the army resembled a river of runaways." The battlefield was covered with dead, and the Napoleonic legend took wing again.

Napoleon was so exhausted that as he was bending over his maps, dictating to Berthier his orders for the pursuit of the Prussian army, he fell asleep. His grenadiers noticed it and, in Ségur's words, "at a sign from Marshal Lefebvre, they silently formed a hollow square around him, thus protecting their sleeping Emperor on this plateau where he had just provided such a glorious spectacle for them to enjoy." For all his reports to Josephine that he was "in marvelous health" and had gained weight from "the fatigue, the bivouacking, and the night watches," he was in fact worn out.

That night, Napoleon believed that he had conquered the entire
Prussian army. He also believed that Davout, who had been ordered
to cut off the enemy's retreat, had succeeded in tracking down the
runaways and decimating them. His stupefaction was total when he
learned that Davout had suddenly found himself faced with 70,000
men commanded by the King of Prussia and the Duke of Brunswick
—and that he had defeated them at Auerstedt with only 26,000 men!

While Napoleon was imposing a tribute of some 160 million francs
on Prussia and her allies, his marshals were pursuing the Prussians,
who were in a state of total panic. The vanquished troops of Jena
and Auerstedt were all running away. Step by step, informed by
dispatches from his marshals, the Emperor followed the amazing
pursuit—a pursuit without letup, without respite, without pause; a
pursuit which, sword point at the enemy's back, would take his marshals from Jena to Leipzig, and from Brandenburg to Mecklenburg,
finally culminating, north of Hamburg, in the capture of Lübeck, not
far from the shores of the Baltic and the frontier of Denmark! In the
twenty-six days of the campaign the Imperial Army had captured
110,000 prisoners and 250 flags.

On October 15 the King of Prussia requested terms of armistice
from his conqueror.

Napoleon could not afford the luxury of not making his enemies
kneel. Moved by some strange sentiment, he had spared the Czar in
the days following Austerlitz. He would do the same thing, a year
later, in the days following the victory of Friedland. But for Frederick William he had no pity. On October, 24, in addition to heavy
reparations, Prussia had to cede to France all the Prussian states
between the Rhine and the Elbe. Everywhere, the French eagle
would replace the Prussian eagle; but the two nations still remained
at war.

On October 24, in a rather heightened state of emotion, Napoleon
took up quarters in the château of Sans-Souci at Potsdam. His admiration for Frederick II had always been profound. The Emperor inspected the apartments of the great Frederick, tried out his field
glass, leafed through his favorite books (annotated in his own hand),
and as trophies of war took the King's waistband, his *grands cordons*,
and his sword. "I would rather have these trophies," he said, "than

all King Frederick's treasures. I will send them to my old soldiers of Hanover; I will give them to the superintendent of Les Invalides, who will keep them as a token of the Grand Army's victories and the vengeance it took for the disasters of Rossbach."

He also appropriated the King's "alarm clock," a big silver watch that he later took with him to St. Helena.

On October 26 he went to see Frederick's grave. He made the pilgrimage on foot and stood at the graveside "immobile and silent, as though absorbed in deep meditation."

On October 27, with drums rolling and the Guard's band playing, the Emperor made his entry into Berlin through the Brandenburg Gate, where he was received by the notables headed up by the Prince of Hatzfeldt. Then Napoleon mounted a gray horse and went into the city, preceded by Mamelukes and grenadiers wearing their famous bearskin caps. The crowd was thick, and the casement windows were festooned "just as at Paris, on the day of our return home from Austerlitz," says Coignet.

Napoleon moved ahead, alone, wearing his green uniform of a Guard colonel with the *grand cordon* of the Legion of Honor across his chest. Ten paces behind him came the marshals, the generals, the aides-de-camp, and the general staff resplendent in gold, silver, and plumes. But all eyes were on him, "with his little hat and two-a-penny cockade." His eyes were flashing; and Berliners had to make a great effort (as one of them admitted in astonishment) not to bow their heads when he looked at them.

When the procession reached the statue of Frederick the Great, Napoleon galloped around it and saluted it both with his sword and with a sweep of his hat. His staff officers were obliged to follow his example.

Napoleon took up his quarters in the royal palace, leaving the Prince of Hatzfeldt in his post as governor of Berlin. But a letter from the prince to Graf Hohenlohe was intercepted—a letter containing information on the number of ammunition wagons that had entered the city. The Emperor, whose wrath can well be imagined, ordered Rapp to have the governor arrested immediately and—despite the objections of Rapp and Berthier—to have him court-martialed.

The Princess of Hatzfeldt, who was expecting a child, came and threw herself at the feet of Napoleon. She proclaimed her husband's innocence. Without replying to her, Napoleon summoned the aide-de-camp on duty and ordered that the prince's unfortunate letter be brought to him.

"Read it, Madame."

When she had read it, the Princess broke into sobs.

"Eh bien, Madame," said the Emperor, pointing toward the fireplace, "since you have in your hands the proof of the crime, destroy it! In this way you will disarm the severity of our military laws."

One hour later, having been set free, Hatzfeldt left Berlin for his estate.

In telling Josphine about this incident, Napoleon added: "So you see, I like women who are generous, unaffected, and gentle. But that's because they resemble you."

On November 22, at Berlin, Napoleon signed the famous decree ordering a Continental blockade against England, whose "intrigues," as he put it, had prompted Prussia and Russia to wage war. "What I want," he said, "is to conquer the sea by land power."

The only way to achieve this end was to bring England to the verge of ruin by cutting off her European clients. Since he had been unable to carry out his famous "invasion," he would attack in the area of trade. The British Isles were declared to be henceforth "in a state of blockade." He prohibited all trade and communication between France and her allies on the one hand, and the nation he called "perfidious Albion" on the other. In this way he would "besiege" England and reduce her to famine, like an embattled fortress. But in order to accomplish this vast project he had to be the master of the "entire" Continent, and impose upon it the deprivations resulting from the decree.

At Warsaw, the Russians had met with such a sour welcome that the Czar had ordered his troops to withdraw. This enabled Murat, on November 28, to make a grand entrance into the Polish capital. He was acclaimed. Intoxicated by this accolade, Napoleon's brother-in-law let it be known that he would willingly trade his Grand Duchy of Berg for the title of King of Poland. But on December 2, the anniversary of his coronation, Napoleon haughtily brought him back into line: "Make it plain to the Poles that I am not coming to beg a throne for one of my people. I have plenty of thrones to give to my family."

Surely, the Emperor would have liked nothing better than to confer freedom upon unhappy Poland, which had been thrice dismembered—but only under certain conditions, as he explained on December 16 to Murat:

> I shall not proclaim the independence of Poland until I am convinced the Poles really want to maintain it; until I see that they want to and *can* maintain it; until I see 30,000 or 40,000 men under arms—well organized—and the nobles on horseback, ready to pay for it with their lives.

XIV

THE POLISH WIFE

A man's private life is a mirror
in which one can read and learn
many things.

NAPOLEON

ON THE MORNING OF NEW YEAR'S DAY, 1807, as his carriage was being drawn at a gallop by four rough-shod horses along the road from Pultusk to Warsaw, Napoleon was singing—out of tune.

The day before, while still at Pultusk, he had learned that Eléonore Denuelle de la Plaigne, reader to his sister Caroline, had given birth on December 13 to a boy who, so she said, was the Emperor's child. So he *was* capable of fathering children! It was Josephine who had become sterile!

But he still had his doubts. He had a pleasant recollection of Eléonore's pretty face, her fine black eyes, and her slender, supple body. But he was quite unaware that the little coquette was telling everyone how, while the Emperor was busy with her, she would watch the clock above the bed and "manage to give the hour hand a push and set the clock a half-hour ahead." "Is it that late?" he would exclaim, raising his eyes. And he would soon leave.

He had met her in 1805, upon his return from Austerlitz. She was eighteen and already divorced—which had been easy, since her husband, one Captain Revel, had been imprisoned for fraud and larceny. Eléonore had done everything possible to make herself noticed. And she had succeeded very well, since in spite of the hour hand, she had given birth to the fruit of their affair.

As he continued on his way to Warsaw, the Emperor's face gradually darkened. *Had* the child—the future Comte Léon—been fa-

thered by him? His mother was telling the whole world that it had
been. But hadn't that little trollop also granted her favors to Murat?
From Napoleon's doubts arose the torturous question: *Could* he father a child? As for the rest, he didn't care. His casual affairs meant
little to him.

Thus, shortly before his coronation, he had been involved with
Elisabeth de Vaudey, one of Josephine's ladies-in-waiting, whom he
had dealt with very rapidly—not to say that he had "expedited" her
—in a little mezzanine located above his study. But Josephine had
sniffed out the intrigue; and one day she knocked on the door while
the Emperor was with Elizabeth. He had opened the door. The
Empress, noticing the "disorder" in the room, had no illusions as to
the nature of the reception accorded to her lady-in-waiting. To the
accompaniment of Mme. de Vaudey's sobbing, a terrible scene broke
out; and Napoleon came close to repudiating his wife. "You must
make ready to leave St.-Cloud," he said. "I've had enough of your
jealous spying on me! I've decided to give heed to political advice,
which demands that I take a wife capable of bearing children for
me!"

Afterward, things were straightened out. But only for a short
time, since Mme. Duchâtel soon appeared on the scene.

She was gorgeous. A brunette of twenty-two, she had pretty teeth
and the most beautiful eyes in the world: deep blue, with "long, silky
lashes." She had tiny feet and a charming smile; and she danced and
sang delightfully. All this was to Napoleon's liking. Her maiden name
was Marie Antoinette-Adèle Papin, and she had married Charles
Duchâtel, then director general of the Registry Office, whose chief
merit, in the view of the Emperor, was that he was thirty years older
than his wife.

Napoleon almost fell in love with this uncalculating young woman
who asked nothing of him—neither for her family nor for her friends.
He took up the habit of visiting her in a little house in the Allée des
Veuves. One night at Malmaison, Josephine surprised her husband
on his way through the paved, chilly corridors of the château to visit
his charmer, and immediately she broke into tears and complaints.
And yet the Emperor had no plans to set up a mistress as favorite:

> I have no intention of seeing my court dominated by women.
> They were harmful to Henri IV and Louis XIV. My job is a much

more serious one than that of those kings; and the French have become too serious-minded to let their sovereign get by with conspicuous liaisons and court favoritism.

Then quite suddenly, one night, Josephine found Bonaparte next to her. He was talking to her in a tone of voice that she knew well, the voice of her lover from the old days. Yes, he had been in love with Marie Antoinette Duchâtel, but the great passion had died out. "It's all over now."

Josephine felt great relief—but her husband was still talking: after telling her the intimate secrets of his affairs, the Emperor asked his wife to help him to break off his liaison!

Needless to say, Josephine put all her resources to work. And since Mme. Duchâtel was the acme of intelligence and selflessness, it went off very well.

Using Duroc as a go-between, Napoleon asked for the return of the love letters he had sent to the young woman. She complied without protest and refused the diamond necklace that he offered her. She was content merely to receive her imperial lover from time to time, when his memories prompted him to set out for the house on the Allée des Veuves.

But of this, Josephine knew nothing.

Napoleon had also been attracted by the young Stéphanie de Beauharnais, a cousin of Josephine's first husband whom Napoleon had given in marriage to the Prince of Baden. When she came to the Tuileries she was seventeen, and the Emperor found her charming. Having surmised that her "uncle" was infatuated with her, this young girl (she looked no more than fourteen) took advantage of the situation. One evening when everyone was awaiting the Emperor's appearance, Stéphanie sat down in the presence of Napoleon's sisters. Caroline ordered her to stand up. When the master arrived, he found Stéphanie in tears and asked her why she was crying. She explained.

"Oh, so that's all it is!" he exclaimed. "Well, come and sit on my lap, and you won't bother anyone."

There is no doubt that the Emperor was at first amused, and then attracted, by this child-woman; and the Empress' jealousy was soon alerted. Not only that, but Napoleon (if Mme. de Rémusat is to be believed), "always the same, made no effort to conceal his penchant from his wife; and, too sure of his power, he was annoyed that the Prince of Baden should take offense at what he saw."

The carriage was now approaching the last relay station before Warsaw. Napoleon was tired. The last campaign in the snow and freezing wind had been very trying. He had scarcely had time to think of love. And yet, while on campaign, his staff members did everything they could to provide him with a soldier's relaxation.

Thus it was that during this same year of 1806, at Berlin, he remembered a girl who, accompanied by an old lady, had brought him a petition in the course of a review.

"Constant," he told his valet, after having read the petition, "read this, and take note of the address of the women who presented it to me. Then go there and find out who they are and what they want."

"I read the petition," Constant writes, "and I saw that all the young woman wanted was an interview with Napoleon."

Constant went to the address and found a young lady of fifteen who was "strikingly beautiful." Unfortunately, he also discovered, when he "tried to talk to her, that she didn't understand a word of French or Italian." And he added: "Thinking of the 'interview' she had requested, I couldn't help laughing."

Nevertheless, Napoleon agreed to the interview; and the young lady arrived at the palace accompanied by her mother—or the old woman who passed herself off as such.

"I told the mother," Constant continues, "to wait in the study while I introduced the young lady to the Emperor. Napoleon retained her, and I withdrew. Although the conversation could not have been very interesting, since it was between two persons who could make themselves understood only by sign language, it lasted for a good part of the night."

Toward morning, Napoleon called Constant and asked him for 4,000 francs, which he himself gave to the girl. She seemed very content and went off to rejoin her "mother," who did not seem to have been the least bit upset by the "interview."

He did not really believe in love. As he had said years before, before he had met Josephine: "Love is a kind of stupidity à deux. . . . I definitely believe that love does more harm than good, and that it would be a favor to mankind if some good angel set us free of it."

And yet later, it was always Josephine, the woman he had loved the most, that he had in mind when he was talking of women's infidelities, coquetry, and tendency to run up debts. Again, it was his dear Creole he was thinking of when he established the Civil Code. And so the fact that even today—despite the modifications made in the Napoleonic Code—women do not yet enjoy equality with men can be attributed (indirectly) to Josephine.

"To grant authority to women," he declared, "is un-French!"

And that was why he had laid down what, for him, was to be the very foundation of the laws: "Women must be made to realize that when they marry and leave the tutelage of their parents, they come under that of their husbands."

He had even wanted to go further, and he suggested: "Should we not add that a woman is not free to see a person whom her husband dislikes?"

Always Josephine! Josephine, who had never hesitated to play hostess to persons of doubtful reputation, or to get involved in the shady dealings of military procurement.

"For every woman who inspires something good in us, there are a hundred who cause us to commit stupidities." And, as if to avenge himself, he added rather maliciously: "Only two things show to advantage on women: rouge and tears."

He would always be susceptible to tears. Thanks to this age-old weapon of women, his two wives, his mistresses, and his sisters could take advantage of him. A woman in great distress, her eyes brimming, her voice choked with sobs, could always make his heart beat a bit faster, because in that state she seemed to him to be "sensitive and good, unaffected and gentle." And of all the women around him, it was Josephine—with her perfect gift for *la comédie larmoyante*—who always had the greatest influence over "Bonaparte," as she never ceased to call him.

No doubt his burning passion was by now only a memory: the ardor that had consumed the heart of the young general who waged the first Italian campaign was no more. And yet, in a less ardent way, he still felt desire for his dear Creole. Between trivial affairs, he liked to come back to that supple body, reminiscent of a palm tree of her native island; to a woman who (a rare gift in that era) could manage by artifice to look ten years younger than she was. And with her, the ability to give pleasure was second nature.

Moreover, he felt great tenderness toward "the incomparable Josephine." That delightful, marvelous, and difficult woman was perhaps even more able to soften his heart through her feminine foibles —her easy virtue, the lies she told so naturally, her disarming thoughtlessness in piling up debts—than through her great kindheartedness, her natural warmth, her unfailing graciousness, and her finesse in doing good turns—a gift she possessed to the highest degree.

"Women are either much better than men or much worse," he said. "And that goes for all of them."

Josephine was unquestionably much more kindhearted than Napoleon. With him, she always "sheathed her claws," as he put it—a great virtue in the eyes of a husband, especially when that husband was Napoleon. It could not have been Josephine he had in mind when he exclaimed one day: "A man should never get angry with a woman: he should listen to her babbling in silence."

Josephine did very little babbling. This former pensionnaire of the Convent of Penthémont, this former vicomtesse (although it was only a *titre de courtoisie*), could hold court better than many a princess. She had mastered the art of playing hostess, of putting her guests at ease, of greeting them as if she had been expecting only them. She remembered faces and names and never confused them. And along with all this, she possessed the irresistible Creole charm and the elegance of the *ancien régime.*

He loved her. He had written her from Posen just the month before, emphasizing that he didn't look twice at the Polish ladies. Not that they didn't make overtures to him. But, he added, "There is only one woman for me. Do you know her? I would give you a description of her; but for you to recognize yourself, it would have to be too flattering. And yet, to tell the truth, in my heart I have only good things to say about her. The nights here are long for a lonely man. . . ."

Abruptly, the carriage pulled up. They were at the post station of Bronie, the last one before Warsaw. A whole crowd had gathered, elbowing one another out of the way to get a glimpse of him. Poland was welcoming him as a liberator. General Duroc, his companion, got out of the carriage to expedite the change of horses. Suddenly a very young woman in peasant dress tugged at the officer's sleeve, making the gesture a pretty one, and in French said to him "in a beseeching tone of voice": "Ah monsieur! Get me out of this crowd and let me talk to the Emperor for a moment—just a moment!"

Her voice was melodious, her accent charming, her features finely chiseled; and her eyes were so soft, luminous, and full of entreaty that Duroc yielded.

"With a smile, he extricated me from the throng," she says.

Holding me by the hand, he led me to the carriage of the Emperor, to whom he said (as he introduced me): "Sire, this is the young lady who braved the dangers of the crowd for you."

Napoleon raised his hat and said something I didn't catch at the moment, because I was too eager to tell him everything I had to say: "Welcome—a thousand times welcome to our country! Nothing we can do will be a sufficiently strong expression, either of our feelings of admiration for you or of our pleasure at seeing you tread the ground of our fatherland, which has awaited your arrival to rise up."

I was in a kind of transport of delirium as I let escape that tumultuous explosion of the feelings that were stirring me at the time. What with my natural shyness, I don't know how I was able to do it. I often recall that moment, but I cannot explain or define the spontaneous force that made me speak out.

Napoleon watched me attentively. Then he took a bouquet that was in the carriage and presented it to me, saying: "Keep this as a pledge of my good intentions. I hope we shall meet again in Warsaw, and if we do I shall claim a kiss from your beautiful mouth."

The change of horses had been completed. Standing there in the middle of the road clutching to her heart the bouquet that Napoleon had given her, the Polish girl watched his carriage leave, escorted by Guard cavalrymen. Through the carriage door, the Emperor waved his hat.

This pretty blond girl with a peaches-and-cream complexion was Countess Marie Walewska. (The account of the affair is from unpublished documents belonging to the Walewska family.) Her laughter, it was said, was completely enchanting. And yet for the past three years she had laughed very little. Her father had disappeared when she was still a very young girl; and immediately upon her leaving the convent (she was not yet sixteen), her mother had insisted that she choose between two suitors who were equally wealthy. One of them was young and charming, but he was the son of a Russian general. Ten years earlier, Poland had been dismembered for the third time. The three imperial black eagles of Austria, Prussia, and Russia had swooped down upon her with such voracity that Poland had disappeared from the map of Europe. The white eagle of Poland was nothing more than a memory. Marie would have preferred death to marrying the son of one of those generals of the Czar who were oppressing her country. And so she resigned herself to marrying Count Athanasius Colonna Walewski, the head of a powerful family, who was a widower twice over and almost seventy years old.

Her husband, very solicitous toward her, had tried to make her forget the great difference in their ages by giving her a son. He had succeeded. Marie adored the child, and she had only one aim in life: to make him a free man in a free Poland. Like so many other Poles in the dark hours of that nation's history, she had often dreamed that one day France would liberate her country.

Napoleon's victories over Austria and Russia in 1805—and, just recently, over Prussia—had made her thrill with hope. And that hope had grown all the greater when, at the end of December, 1806, she had learned that the battle between Napoleon and the Russians at Pultusk had been won by the French. Would those portions of Poland taken by the Austrians, the Russians, and the Prussians be united again? Would the old Polish nation be reborn from its ashes?

On the morning of January 1, 1807 (as she tells us in her memoirs), Marie learned that Napoleon was on his way to Warsaw. Unable to sit still, and "tormented more than the others with the fever of impatience," she decided to go and meet him. She had disguised herself as a peasant girl—blue dress of coarse cloth, square bonnet of black fur, and black veil—jumped into her carriage (taking her cousin along with her), and told the coachman to head for Bronie.

Napoleon had been amazed and intrigued by the peasant girl who spoke French. Such a gentle creature! And he must have been thinking of her on the way to Warsaw, because he instructed his companion: "Duroc, I want you to find her!"

As soon as they reached Warsaw, General Duroc got to work. To Prince Joseph Poniatowski, chief of the Provisional Polish Government, he supplied a detailed description of "the unknown girl of Bronie," as the Emperor called her. Thanks to the indiscretion of Marie's cousin, who had told others of the episode of the bouquet, she was identified. The moment he was informed, Napoleon ordered that Countess Walewska be invited to the reception that Poniatowski was giving in his honor. Or perhaps it was the other way around. Perhaps it was Poniatowski—urged on by Talleyrand, who was delighted to see the Emperor "busy" with an amorous adventure—who suggested to Napoleon that he invite Mme. Walewska. In any case, Poniatowski himself went to the Walewskis' palatial home.

At first, Marie refused the invitation: she had no intention of going to a ball.

"Your presence is indispensable. Napoleon insists upon it."

She still refused.

"Who knows?" murmured Poniatowski, who had surmised the Emperor's feelings. "Perhaps Heaven will make use of you to reestablish the fatherland."

Marie grew even more obstinate. At this, Poniatowski appealed for help to "statesmen whose authority was founded on public esteem and the deference due them because of their conduct and wisdom." But it was labor lost. It was not until Count Walewski himself (who was unaware of the incident at Bronie) insisted that Marie finally agreed to go to the ball at the Blacha Palace.

Who did Napoleon think she was? In a spirit of rebellion, she put on her simplest dress: a white satin sheath under a tunic of white tulle. In lieu of diamonds or pearls, her blond hair was adorned by a simple diadem of leaves. Napoleon could hardly fail to understand what was meant by this refusal to put on her finest in his honor. She was not readying herself for the sacrifice!

The moment she appeared in the ballroom, Poniatowski came forward to ask her to dance. She held him off with a gesture: "You know that I don't dance, and have no desire to."

"What? But the Emperor has spoken of you to me several times, and said he would be pleased to see you dance."

"That may be, but I don't intend to."

With the same charming obstinacy, she refused all those who asked her to dance.

Louis de Périgord, one of the Emperor's aides-de-camp, and General Bertrand were hovering around her. Napoleon noticed their stratagem. He called Berthier to him and ordered him to transfer Périgord immediately to the Sixth Corps, on the Passarge, and Bertrand to Jérôme's headquarters before Breslau.

Those present looked at one another anxiously. For the first time since the long-ago era of Josephine's love affairs, when she was openly cuckolding him with Hippolyte Charles, Napoleon was jealous. And this even before anything had happened!

But the ball was over, and the time had come for the traditional "inspection" of the guests. Napoleon seemed feverish. When he stopped in front of Marie, he looked at her as though he did not recognize her. He cast a critical eye at her dress and admired her lovely complexion. Then, in order to let it be known that he understood why she was so simply dressed, he said loudly: "Madame, white does not go well with white."

Then, in a lower voice, for her alone to hear: "This is not the welcome I was entitled to, after. . . ."

Marie did not answer, of course. But she reddened. And her uneasiness increased when she found herself, after the Emperor had passed on, the cynosure of all eyes. The ladies were talking behind their fans. What had Napoleon whispered to her? The comments quickly multiplied.

When she got back to the Walewski Palace, Marie found a bouquet waiting for her, with this note: "I saw only you. I admired only you. I desire only you. [Please favor me with] a quick reply to assuage the impatient ardor of N."

"The messenger is waiting," her maid told her.

"There is no reply!" exclaimed Marie.

Who did the Emperor think she was? But the maid came back to announce that the note had been brought by Joseph Poniatowski himself. Marie was indignant. So the chief of government had become a procurer!

To make matters worse, Poniatowski came to the very door of her room to parley with her. But he was wasting his time. Just as she had refused to dance, so now she refused to reply. And after a half-hour of arguing, he left, furious.

But everything would conspire to propel Marie into the Emperor's arms.

The next day, Count Walewski informed his wife that he had accepted, for both of them, an invitation to a great banquet being given by Napoleon. The Countess rebelled, but her husband called upon the assistance of Duroc, Prince Joseph, and the members of the Provisional Government. Marie said she was ill, lay down on her chaise lounge, and refused to appear in the salon. At this, Walewski forced the way into his wife's room for the other Poles, and one of them made bold to tell her: "Madame, everything must yield before circumstances so weighty and critical for an entire nation. We hope, therefore, that your malady will have run its course between now and the time of the banquet, from which you cannot absent yourself without seeming to be a disloyal citizen."

Once again, Marie had to yield, since the entire city was in league against her. Moreover, Prince Poniatowski sent her Mme. de Vauban, his mistress—who had been at Versailles and had lived in Warsaw since the Revolution—to teach her the secrets of court etiquette.

Mme. de Vauban possessed no scruples, prejudices, or modesty. As a woman of the eighteenth century, she regarded conjugal fidelity as a sentiment in rather bad taste. For her, "to supply a mistress to a sovereign, whether that sovereign be named Louis XV or Napoleon, is the most important service a courtesan can perform." With a disarming lack of conscience, this *personnage de comédie* kept repeating: "Everything! Everything for the sacred cause!"

In the course of her very first lessons, she slipped into the hands of Marie the following note from Napoleon:

Have you not found me to your liking, Madame? Yet I was entitled to expect the contrary. Was I mistaken? Your eagerness has abated, while mine has increased. You rob me of sleep! Please give some joy and happiness to a pitiable heart that yearns to adore you! . . . Is a reply so difficult to obtain? You owe me two of them.

N.

Marie still refused to reply, and the Emperor grew impatient. At this point the plot became rather ignoble. Members of the cabinet —with Talleyrand in the background—implored her not to be "cruel." Madame, they said in effect, small causes often produce great effects. In every age, women have had a great influence on world politics. This truth is borne out by the history of ancient times, and by that of modern times as well. So long as men are dominated by passions, you ladies will be among the most potent forces.

And they dared to add: Do you think that Esther gave herself to Ahasuerus out of love? The terror he inspired in her—so much so that she fainted under his gaze—proves that tender feelings had no part in this union, does it not? She sacrificed herself to save her nation, and she earned the glory of actually saving it. Let us hope we can say as much for your glory and our happiness. Are you not the daughter, the mother, the sister, and the wife of Polish patriots?

Once again, Marie yielded (the nerves of the nineteen-year-old girl must have been completely frayed) and agreed to go to the famous banquet.

The moment she entered the salon, the other guests hurried over toward her, seeming already to be soliciting her favor. During the meal she sat across from the Emperor, who never ceased looking at her. At one point he gestured toward the left side of his tunic. Duroc, who was seated next to Marie, understood what he meant and turned to the young woman: "What did you do, Madame, with the bouquet the Emperor gave you at Bronie?"

"I am keeping it carefully as a souvenir for my son," she replied.

"Ah, Madame! Please allow him to offer you souvenirs more worthy of you!"

Marie scented the approach of Napoleon's confidant. Did he think she was mercenary? With a lump in her throat, she looked down at her plate and said, "I like only flowers."

"In that case, we shall gather laurels on your native soil to offer them to you."

By way of making everything convenient, Count Walewski slipped away when dinner was over. As coffee was served in the salon, Napoleon looked at Marie tenderly. He had not felt so much love for anyone since the days when Josephine and her kisses "set his blood on fire."

He came up to the young woman: "Anyone with such soft, gentle eyes expressing so much kindness either yields—taking no pleasure in torturing a man—or else she is the most coquettish and cruel of women."

He left the salon, and Duroc took Marie to Mme. de Vauban's residence. There they combined their efforts.

"He had eyes only for you," Mme. de Vauban told her. "He was aflame with passion for you."

Duroc sat down beside her. "How cruel you are!" he exclaimed, taking her hand. "You are rejecting the advances of a man who has never had to endure a refusal. Believe me, his glory is tinged with sadness. Only say the word, and a bit of happiness will light up his destiny. He loves you deeply. As you saw for yourself, you were the only one he looked at throughout dinner. What great joy you could bring him!"

Marie burst into sobs. How could she resist becoming entangled in the snare? Sensing that she was weakening, Mme. de Vauban read her a new note from Napoleon:

> There are times when too much exaltation becomes a burden, and that is what I am experiencing right now. How meet the needs of a smitten soul which would like to throw itself at your feet but cannot? . . . Oh, if only you wished it! Only you can remove the obstacles which separate us. Come to me! Come! All my desires will be fulfilled. Your country will be dearer to me when you have had pity on my poor heart.

The last lines of the letter overwhelmed her. This time, she was conquered. And she murmured to the two procurers: "Do with me what you will."

And yet she still refused to reply to the Emperor. She *would* tell him viva voce of her admiration for him, and the hopes she placed in him for saving her country and retrieving it from nothingness. But she would also make it plain that he must not expect any love from her. A victim could not feel love for his persecutor.

The two cronies reassured her. Of course she could tell him everything! The main thing for these plotters was that their little bird wing her way to the eagle.

At their request (or their order) she spent the whole day at Mme. de Vauban's palatial residence, waiting for the hour when she would be taken to the torture chamber. Finally, at 10:30 P.M., she was put into a carriage and conveyed to the palace occupied by the Emperor. There, after having climbed one flight of stairs and gone through two or three salons, she suddenly found herself face to face with Napoleon. The time for the sacrifice had come.

Once again, Marie was shaken by sobs. She tried to flee. At first Napoleon failed to understand. Was she a loose woman trying to tease him? He talked to her in sweet tones, but three unfortunate words slipped out: "Your aged husband."

That didn't help at all. She only wept more. To assuage the young woman, the Emperor had to question her gently, making her acknowledge the reasons for such an ill-suited marriage. And so it was her mother who had insisted upon that unnatural union? But now, how could she have any remorse? How could she refuse to be his?

"The knot which has been tied on earth can be untied only in heaven," she explained.

He laughed—pitiless as before. And once again her tears began to flow. They disarmed him, and at last he felt sorry for her. He asked for nothing more than her presence, and his words were all kindness. He had understood that this young woman had the soul of a pure and upright girl. To take advantage of her at the moment would be inhuman. He resigned himself to being merely tender.

Little by little, Marie's weeping abated. She let him kiss her. When they parted, he made her promise him that she would come back the next day. At two o'clock in the morning, he helped her into her coat and accompanied her to the door, kissing her hands and saying, "Eh bien, my gentle and plaintive dove, dry your tears and get some rest. Have no more fear of the eagle. The only strength he can use with you is that of a passionate love—but a love that wants your heart above all. You'll end up by loving me, because it will be everything for you. Do you understand?"

Napoleon continued his pressing courtship, as is verified from the letters he wrote to Marie, which are here published for the first time. Afraid that his handwriting might be completely illegible, he dictated the following (which he merely signed and dated: "Wednesday, the 28th, 11:00 A.M."):

Madame,

You were sad at last Monday's gathering, and it pained me. . . .

I wrote to you twice, but everyone had left and my letters did not reach you. . . . Marie, I want to see you tonight at eight. Go to your friend's house—I mean the friend you told me about. A carriage will pick you up there. . . .

I hope—and need—to tell you tonight of everything that you inspire in me, and of all the vexations I have experienced. . . .

A thousand kisses on the lips of my Marie.

The next day, he wrote to her again:

Madame,

The person who will deliver this letter to you is the one I mentioned. He will tell you of all the feelings I have for you, Marie, and will let me know how you are. . . . Your letter was charming. I kiss the beautiful hand which wrote it, the heart that dictated it, and those beautiful eyes that I am mad about.

Then came another letter, no doubt written during that week when he was doing everything possible to make her yield:

Madame,

You were lovely to look at last night, but I thought you were a bit taciturn. Where were your thoughts? . . . How are you feeling this morning? . . . I shall see you tonight to tell you a thousand times over, *"vi amo."* Your heart responds to that, n'est-ce pas? A kiss on your eyes, Marie. And yet they are very wicked!

When Marie awakened the day after a meeting which was nothing but a tête-à-tête, she received from the Emperor a spray of diamonds accompanied by this note:

Marie, my sweet Marie, my first thought is for you, my first desire is to see you again. You will come back, won't you? You promised you would. If not, the eagle will fly to you! I shall see you at dinner. Our friend says so. So please accept this bouquet. And may it become a mysterious bond which will establish between us a secret rapport amid the crowd around us. Although exposed to the prying eyes of the multitude, we shall be able to make ourselves understood to each other. When I put my hand on my heart, you will know it is so full of you that you will reply by squeezing your bouquet. Love me, my gentle Marie! And may your hand remain always on your bouquet!

"There is no reply," she said once again. And she threw to the floor the red morocco case containing the jewels.

"Diamonds! I don't want them! Does he think I'm a prostitute?"

That evening at dinner the Emperor paled: Marie had not worn her gift as a corsage. The young woman feared the scene that she felt coming. With a weak smile she placed her hand where the spray should have been, and Napoleon, pacified, made the same gesture. The storm had passed—for the moment.

As soon as the dinner was over, he withdrew to a small salon and had Duroc bring in Mme. Walewska.

"Here you are at last! I had no more hopes of seeing you."

But this scene is better described by Marie Walewska:

He took off my coat and hat, and seated me in an armchair. Then he said: "Come, now! How can you clear yourself of the crimes I have charged you with? Why did you make a point of inspiring in me a feeling that you do not share? Why have you rejected even my laurels? What have you done with them? I associated so many interesting moments with them, and you have deprived me of them. My hand has not left my heart, but yours has not moved. Once only did you answer my signal. Oh, Marie! You don't love me! And yet I love you passionately. How can this be?"

And he struck his forehead in a gesture of rage. After a moment of silence that I dared not interrupt: "There's a Polish girl for you! You have confirmed the opinion I have of that nation!"

At this point I found my tongue and exclaimed: "Ah! Please, Sire, tell me what it is!"

"Well, Marie, I consider the Poles to be passionate and frivolous. I believe that they do everything out of fantasy and nothing by way of system. Their enthusiasm is impetuous, tumultuous, and instantaneous. They have no notion of how to regulate it and perpetuate it. And isn't that your own portrait, too? *Belle Polonaise!* Didn't you come running like a madwoman—at the risk of being stifled by the crowd—to see me and flatter me? I let myself be taken in by that melting look, by your passionate expression. And then you vanished. I tried in vain to seek you out; I could not find you. And when you finally did appear, all I found in you was ice, while I myself was burning! Listen, Marie! I want you to know that every time I have believed something was impossible or difficult to achieve, I have desired it ardently. Nothing discourages me. The phrase 'It can't be done!' merely spurs me on, and I continue to advance. Since I am used to seeing people yield eagerly to my wishes, your resistance subjugates me. The idea of seducing you has gone to my head, and I am set upon it. I want —and you must understand this word well—I *want* to force you to love me.

"Marie, I have revived the name of your country. It still exists, thanks to me. And I will do more than this! But just remember that, like this watch that I hold in my hands, which will shatter at your feet"— and he did throw it at my feet—"its name will perish. And so will all your hopes perish if you drive me to extremes by rejecting my heart and refusing me yours."

I fell lifeless at his feet. He was in an indescribable state of violence. . . .

The Emperor's fury had put Marie's heart to such an extreme test that she had fainted. When she revived, she understood what had happened. Napoleon had taken advantage of her fainting spell to abuse her.

There he was, on his knees, swearing that he loved her to the point of madness—that madness which was his only excuse. He said things that touched the heart of the unfortunate young woman, and Marie did not run away.

"The man who had the whole world at his feet," she continues, "was at my feet, drying my tears. He raised me up gently. 'You can be sure, Marie, that the promise I gave you will be kept.' "

She saw so much passion in Napoleon's eyes that, stirred by the violence of his love (and perhaps a bit dazzled also), she forgave him. Not only that, but she began to love him, to judge by the letter that, evidently, he sent her the next morning at five o'clock, in which he laid bare all his love:

> Madame,
>
> I am very eager to hear from you that you have not been put out of sorts, and how you slept. At no time during the night did you cease to occupy the same place in my thoughts. I will long remember last night. . . . I feel a need to tell you how dear you are to me. If you have any doubts of it, you will give me great pain. You promised me lots of things, so could you not send me that which can be done today? Remember that I love you, Marie, and that you gave me reason to hope that you share my feelings. You will be faithful, n'est-ce pas? A thousand kisses on your hands, and one on your heart, whose tranquillity I would like to disturb just a bit. As you can see, that was said in a spirit of vengeance. Adieu, mon amie. How glad I will be to see you this evening!

That same day, Marie wrote to her husband. She had decided to break with him.

> Your first thought will be to reproach me for my conduct. But you will only be accusing yourself. I did everything I could to

open your eyes. But alas! You were blinded by a vanity beyond description—and, I must admit, by your patriotism. You did not want to see the danger.

Count Walewski finally understood the situation and withdrew to Walewice. Marie's two sisters-in-law, however, served as chaperones to the Countess, who was regarded by everyone as the sovereign's mistress. No one at Warsaw found this offensive. In the matter of royal or imperial loves, morality does not exist.

This conduct may both surprise and bother the modern reader. But Napoleon, when a young Polish woman literally threw herself at him, having put on a disguise to approach him and talk to him, might very well have believed that Marie Walewska was ready to give herself to him. He was virtually uninformed of the abominable pressure being put on the young countess to become his mistress. Being afraid of causing displeasure to Napoleon, neither Prince Poniatowski nor the other members of the Polish Provisional Government kept him informed of the veritable siege they had to mount in order to achieve their ends: to make Marie yield, and to put her (for the greater good of Poland) in the Emperor's bed. They concealed from him the role of procuress that Mme. de Vauban was playing. As for him, he saw only one thing: a young woman, after a few hesitations, was keeping trysts with him at night, in full awareness of the implications. From this he concluded that she had agreed to become his mistress.

What is infinitely less excusable is the appeal to patriotism that the Emperor used in order to get Marie to relinquish her virtue, and the blackmail he employed to force her to come to those trysts—that reconstruction of the Polish State that he constantly offered as bait: "Your country will be dearer to me when you have had pity on my poor heart." When he wrote those lines, he had only one idea in mind: to come to agreement with the Czar as soon as he had conquered him. Did he not know already—and know very well—that it would be the Grand Duchy of Warsaw which would pay the bill for the reconciliation?

As for Marie, it was true that she had refused to read the notes sent by the Emperor, and she had declined to wear the jewels he had sent her. Still, it was quite understandable that Napoleon should have erred and concluded that her resistance was merely the clever strata-gem of a coquette—and a Slav at that.

Marie never reproached Napoleon for his violence, and her whole attitude proved that she did not hold it against him. Indeed, she must have written him some very loving letters, if one can judge from this reply:

Madame,

Your letter is like you—perfect—and it has made me happy. . . . I would have liked very much to talk to you yesterday. I felt that an involuntary movement was taking me to where you were, and I often had to stop along the way. . . . For some reason—just why, I don't know—I thought your ribbon was charming. Perhaps you surmise the reason? But your earrings. . . . Just three words, naughty girl. Did I likewise? No, no, not naughty: kind, beautiful, and perfect Marie. . . . You are sleeping very peacefully right now. . . . I very much want to see you tonight, if only for a moment, to hear you tell me what you wrote me and what it does me so much good to hear.. . . *Mon amie,* is your heart perhaps a bit troubled by your sin? I'm not sure, but it seemed to me yesterday that I could detect a bit of gentle melancholy in your eyes. Let me cover them with kisses to increase it still more. I kneel at your feet.

A few days later, he wrote her the following, in which one can almost hear the pounding of his heart:

You were so beautiful and so kind yesterday evening that far into the night it seemed I could still see you. There is no darkness that can prevent me from seeing you; you are like an angel.

I am angry with myself for having told you to come to the parade: it was so chilly, and you will catch cold.

I am overjoyed at the thought of seeing you dance tonight, and reading in your eyes the emotions of your heart . . . *mio dolce amore,* a sweet kiss on your charming mouth, and a thousand very respectful kisses on your hands.

"Mio dolce amore"—the same words he used to write to Jose-phine.

Now that Marie loved him, he could explain to her (at the same time assuring her that he had not forgotten his promise to restore Poland):

I have already forced Prussia to yield up the portion she usurped, and time will do the rest. This is not the moment to put everything into execution. We must be patient. Politics is a rope that parts if one strains it too hard. In the meantime, your statesmen are developing. But how many of them do you have? You have a great many good patriots; and I admit you have some good men: your heroes are bursting with honor and courage. But that is not enough: you need a great unanimity.

And then there were the interests of France to be considered:

You must bear in mind that the distances separating us [Poland and France] are too great: what I can accomplish today may be destroyed tomorrow. My first obligations are to France. I am not free to spill French blood in a cause foreign to her interests, and arm my people to come to your help whenever it is needed.

Marie had become his "Polish wife," as he called her. He loved her as much as one has time to love when one has all of Europe on one's hands. He could not do without her. After he had left at the head of his troops, he sent her a courier every day.

And yet he could not understand why Josephine wrote him that she could not do without him for such a long period of time. He laughed—with no pity—when he read a letter in which she naïvely confided to him: "I took a husband in order to be *with* him!"

And he replied (vainglorious, and quite without compunction): "In my ignorance, I had the notion that the wife was made for the husband, and the husband for the fatherland, the family, and glory. Please forgive my ignorance. One always learns something from our beautiful ladies."

Had Josephine surmised that for his "Polish wife" Napoleon had rediscovered the heart he had possessed as Bonaparte?

"As usual," he wrote later to the Empress, "you are getting excited and imagining grievous things in your little Creole head."

But the "little Creole head" remained full of anxiety. He repeated:

I don't know what you are trying to tell me about the women in contact with me. I love only my little Josephine—kindhearted, sulky, and capricious—who knows how to quarrel gracefully, as she does everything else. Because she is always amiable, except when she is jealous: then she becomes all she-devil. But to get

back to those women. If I were to take up with any of them, I
assure you I would want them to be pretty rosebuds. Do those you
mention fit this description?

A few days later, he wrote her again:

You tell me that your happiness makes your glory. That is not
generous. You should say: "The happiness of others makes my
glory." But that is not conjugal. So you should say: "The happiness
of my husband makes my glory." But that is not maternal. So you
should say: "The happiness of my children makes my glory." Now,
since neither nations, nor your husband, nor your children can be
happy without a bit of glory, you should not turn up your nose at
it the way you do. Josephine, your heart is good, but your reason
is weak. You are marvelous at feeling things, but you reason less
well. Now let's not quarrel any more. I want you to be gay and
content with your lot. And I want you to obey, not with grumbling
and tears, but of your own free will, and with a bit of happiness.

In matters of the heart, he would always be totally conscienceless.

XV

FROM THE "TROUBLE" AT EYLAU

TO THE VICTORY OF FRIEDLAND

The secret of great battles is the ability
to either extend one's forces or concentrate
them at the right time.

NAPOLEON

WHEN IT STOPPED FREEZING or snowing, the earth, swollen with water from the thaw, became all marshes.

In Napoleon's words: "For Poland, God created a fifth element: mud."

Through this thick, horrible, and incredibly deep mud, Bernadotte's army corps, on half-rations, had retreated from the 80,000 troops under Levin Bennigsen, who had become Supreme Commander of the Russian army. The Emperor was hoping that no one would budge before spring.

He was mistaken. He was also mistaken as to the bravery of the Russian troops. He had underestimated them. And yet, with that genius which enabled him to face up to any situation, he was glad of the retreat. In advancing toward the lower Vistula, Bennigsen was going to expose his flank to the Grand Army. He would be caught as in a waffle iron. The weather was turning cold, and the roads were becoming "superb," as the Emperor informed Talleyrand on January 29, 1807. Two days before, Napoleon had sent a dispatch to Bernadotte, telling him to continue his movement of withdrawal, and then victory would be assured. Unfortunately, the officer carrying the dispatch had been captured by Cossacks, and Bennigsen was forewarned. "That dispatch," the Russian general said later, "let me in on the enemy's intentions and his entire operations plan."

Bennigsen immediately ordered his 80,000 men not only to cease

322

their pursuit of Bernadotte, but to withdraw toward Eylau, where he set up his general headquarters. Even including Ney's 20,000 troops —*if* they managed to join up with the Grand Army—the total force that the Emperor could muster against Bennigsen was no more than 65,000 famished, wet, half-frozen soldiers.

The Battle of Eylau began on February 7. They were still fighting when, at 11:00 P.M., Napoleon reached Eylau, accompanied by Murat and Soult. The city was full of troops who were wounded, half-starved, and benumbed with cold. At length, the main body of the Russian army made an orderly withdrawal and occupied positions situated behind the hillocks which form a semicircle around the city.

Almost immediately after occupying these positions, the Russians began a lively artillery barrage. Was it intended to cover their withdrawal? Or, on the contrary, to prevent the French from advancing to drive the Czar's soldiers out of their bivouacs? At one point, Napoleon wanted to go in person to see what was happening on the hills. But his general staff dissuaded him. "We will find out tomorrow. His Imperial Majesty is tired, worn out, exhausted, is he not? For a whole week, now, he has not taken off his boots. Up there, it is raining cannonballs. Why should he expose himself to no purpose?"

Finally, after hesitation, Napoleon consented to "behave like an Emperor." The moment he reached the post station, he collapsed in a chair and fell asleep. At 6:00 A.M. an officer entered.

"Sire, the enemy has entered the city and is slaughtering the soldiers asleep in the houses. Flee quickly, Sire!"

Within a few minutes, the Emperor had reached the Guard's bivouac. He would have to give battle, although he could muster only 54,000 men and 200 fieldpieces against Bennigsen's 80,000 troops and 500 cannon.

It was not excessively cold, but the north wind was very strong. The snow, falling in large flakes, blinded the French, whereas the Russians had their backs to it.

To the soldiers about to go into battle, Davout shouted: "The cowards will go to die in Siberia, but the brave men will die here, with honor!"

Then the slaughter began.

The Russians had the advantage. Their cannonballs were coming down like hail on the French—"like nothing ever seen before in the history of man," said General Marbot. The destruction of life was hideous. A *biscaïen*—a large iron bullet from a can of grapeshot which had just exploded—went through the right arm of Captain Hugo. "With my left hand," he writes, "I made a grab to find out if my right arm was still there. All I found was a big hole in my sleeve."

After several hours of murderous, indecisive fighting, the Emperor realized that the enemy was trying to slice through the long French line of battle. A column of 15,000 Russian grenadiers, bayonets at the ready, without firing a shot, was advancing at the double-quick, not at all impressed by the terrible bombardment from 40 fieldpieces of the Guard positioned near the Emperor. All the while keeping his field glass fixed on that moving forest of steel, Napoleon could not help exclaiming: "How fearless! How fearless!"

"Yes," Berthier agreed. "But you haven't noticed, Your Majesty, that with all that fearlessness, you are within a hundred paces of the cannonballs!"

The Emperor disregarded the danger. "Murat!" he shouted. "Take all the cavalry you have!"

The Grand Duke of Berg and Clèves plunged ahead, followed by 70 squadrons, 20 of which had been detached from the Imperial Guard. The mass of enemy infantry abandoned its advance and formed a square to meet the avalanche. The Russian attack was almost literally nailed down, the troops lying flat on the ground "like a field of grain that has just been devastated by a terrible hurricane." But then, at about three o'clock in the afternoon, the 8,000 Prussians under General Lestocq poured onto the field of battle, and the Russians regained the upper hand. At four o'clock it was Ney's turn to appear on the terrain, with 6,000 men holding their bayonets at the ready. This time, the enemy seemed willing to begin the retreat.

The Emperor then went back to Eylau, where the fighting had been continuous since the day before. When he saw the hideous spectacle of the dead and wounded heaped all together, he wept.

That evening he ate potatoes that he himself had baked on the coals of a fire at a bivouac of the Old Guard. A half-league behind Eylau he fell asleep on a mattress, still wearing his uniform and boots. It was there that Saint-Chamans found him, "looking tired, worried, and disheartened."

"What news do you have?" he asked in a weary voice.

The officer told him in a few words that Marshal Soult had sent him to His Majesty to report that the enemy had retreated. Napoleon was radiant—Eylau was a victory, after all! Up to that moment he had doubted it.

Bennigsen had, as a matter of face, retreated. But his withdrawal had been so orderly that he had been able to inform the Czar: "The unshakable courage and bravery of the Russians have wrested from the enemy a hard-won victory."

Alexander congratulated him on "having had the glorious good luck to have conquered the one who has never been conquered." And without intending to be ironical, he added: "I must say that my only regret was to learn that you found it necessary to withdraw."

At dawn, with a two-day growth of beard (something never before seen on him), his breeches and white waistcoat still covered with mud and his buckskin gloves darkened from holding the bridles of horses successively mounted during that terrible day of February 8, Napoleon set out to survey the battlefield. He did not want to wait another minute. He had to make his appearance in the cirque of Eylau to show everyone that he was indeed the victor.

All around him was the hideous, nightmarish spectacle of the results of the battle: 12,000 Russian dead and 14,000 wounded were lying there: 14,000 wounded who would die for lack of medical attention. On the French side there were 20,000 killed and wounded. Said Saint-Chamans: "I have never seen so many dead on such a small space of terrain." Entire divisions, both Russian and French, had been exterminated on the spot. For a quarter-league, the ground was covered with heaps of corpses.

"What a massacre!" Napoleon exclaimed. "And to no purpose! A spectacle well calculated to inspire rulers with a love of peace and a horror of war."

When he returned to his headquarters, he dictated a victory bulletin acknowledging the hideous slaughter. This frankness astounded some of his aides.

"A father who loses his children," he explained with a sigh, "takes no pleasure in victory. When the heart speaks, not even glory holds any more illusions."

It was indispensable to conceal from Germany what had happened to the Grand Army. They would therefore have to remain in Poland and East Prussia. They would continue to keep the Russians at a distance; and at Osterode they would establish a camp for the

Guard: barracks surrounded with palisades. Napoleon and his "grumblers" (veterans of the Old Guard) would take up quarters in a brick
building erected in the center of the encampment.

It was there, during a period of five weeks, while frost and thaw
succeeded each other, that he learned of Europe's reaction to the
murderous battle at Eylau. Everyone realized that "Buonaparte"
had almost been beaten; and some even spoke of a defeat. He was
not invulnerable after all!

Intense diplomatic activity ensued. Prussia regarded Eylau as
revenge for Jena. She tried to tack about, and developed still closer
ties with the Czar, while at the same time sending an emissary—
Kleist—to the camp at Osterode. Kleist found Napoleon "terribly
anxious"—a bit of an exaggeration. When Alexander learned of Napoleon's anxiety, he was strengthened in his conviction that he had
the Emperor of the French where he wanted him. Finally, he was
going to bring him down! Alexander asked Austria to take up arms
again.

But the loser of the battles of Austerlitz and Ulm replied prudently, "Beat them once more."

The Austrians were wrong in hesitating. Napoleon told them as
much two years later: "You were stupid not to attack me after the
Battle of Eylau. I was in real trouble then."

Emperor Francis was not at all sure of the extent of that "trouble," and confined himself to offering his services to the belligerents
as a mediator in order "to conclude a definite and lasting peace."

But Alexander preferred to fight it out, and Napoleon had no
doubts that he would achieve a final victory over his enemy. Therefore, as he sat in the one room of his brick building, surrounded
sometimes by mud and at other times by snow, he decided not only
to bring in 14,000 troops from the replacement depots but to call up
the 80,000 men of the 1808 draft. The main thing was to build up the
morale and health of his depleted army.

When on April 1 the army had recovered its spirits and (almost)
its strength, the headquarters was shifted to the castle of Finkenstein
near the shores of the Baltic. Built in the eighteenth century, it was
the property of the Graf von Dohna, *grand-maître* of the House of
the King of Prussia.

Napoleon, while still at Osterode, on March 17, had written to
Marie Walewska the following letter:

I have received your two charming letters. The sentiments they express are the same that you inspire in me. Not a day has passed but what I have wanted to tell you this. I would like to see you; that depends on you. . . .

Never have any doubts about my feelings, Marie. That would be unfair, and unfairness is not like you.

A thousand kisses on your hands, and one on your charming mouth.

Marie had said she wanted to join him at Finkenstein. Touched by her suggestion, he replied:

Your letter gave me great pleasure. You are still the same, and you have no doubts about my feelings toward you.

And so you are willing to undergo the fatigue of the journey? You can hardly imagine how glad I would be to see you. But you must make sure not to get overly tired and undermine your health.

I have a feeling that I will soon be seeing you, Marie. Until then, a kiss on your pretty hand.

Incidentally, they tell me you have many suitors at Warsaw. And they mention one in particular who is very zealous. Is this true?

Marie set out to join him, and en route she received another letter dated April 23:

Madame,

I have received your charming letter. You have had miserable weather, and you must be very tired what with the bad roads, but the main thing is that you are in good health. I am counting on your promise. You know how glad I will be to see you. A thousand pleasurable things everywhere, Marie, and a loving kiss on your charming mouth.

Marie was soon with him; and his "Polish wife" became more attached to him every day. She now loved the great man of whom she had been so afraid: she loved him, and understood that despite his promises, he could not yet establish the Kingdom of Poland.

For more than two months, Napoleon governed the empire from his castle, 600 leagues distant from the Tuileries. Not only did he have ready at hand the portfolios containing his war plans, maps, situation reports, and the reports of the army corps—the raw materials for his

famous bulletins—but the field vans of his "cabinet," with the mass
of paperwork having to do with civil affairs, followed him wherever
he went on campaign. Exhausted couriers, asleep on their horses,
having changed mounts a hundred times since leaving Paris, were
constantly arriving at his headquarters. But it was the dispatches
brought by the express messengers that reached him most quickly.
The leather portfolio with a bronze plate on which the words
Dépêche de l'Empereur were engraved would be locked with a special key at Paris, and then passed from hand to hand, from post
station to post station, from dispatch rider to dispatch rider, until it
reached the "palace" where the Emperor was staying. The other key
was in the possession of the Emperor's secretary. If Napoleon was
absent—as would be the case during a battle—the dispatches would
be brought to him in the field. In the very midst of battle he would
seize upon them eagerly.

At least once every week an *auditeur* from the Council of State
would set out from Paris, bringing the portfolios of all the ministers,
and come to where the Emperor had his headquarters. Although at
first these officials were horrified at the thought of having to dash
along the post roads in the dead of winter, little by little they got to
the point where they thought it the simplest thing in the world to
endure the frightful fatigue of going clear across Europe without
stopping.

Every day, from his headquarters at Finkenstein, Napoleon sent
out orders which were taken by courier to Paris, Amsterdam, or
Naples. It is amazing—and an instance unique in history—that the
Emperor, thousands of kilometers from Paris, and despite the demands of a hard-fought war, could have the flexibility of mind to
dictate four orders at once on different subjects.

Together with directing civil affairs, he had to continue with his
métier as a commanding general; and he made constant tours of
inspection. In addition to the cohort of generals, officers of the general staff, aides-de-camp, masters of the horse, orderly officers, and
pages, the duty picket—consisting of an officer and twenty light
cavalrymen—was always waiting in front of the "palace," since the
Emperor's departures were made with the speed of lightning.

A "brigade" of saddle horses (there were ten such brigades) was
always held in readiness, to be mounted by the Emperor and his
retinue. For him there were two chargers and a pacer: three mounts

"of the rank of His Majesty." The other horses were for the use of the grand master of the horse; for the duty master of the horse; for the Mameluke Ali, who had in his care the Emperor's greatcoat, his dress coat, and a flask of brandy; for the surgeon, who took with him "an assortment of everything required to dress wounds"; for the outrider, in charge of a canteen and the (cavalryman's) valise; for the two valets, who brought along the lint for dressing wounds, the salt, the Madeira wine, and surgical instruments; for the three stewards; and for their canteen—a more important kind of canteen than the for-mer. Finally, the portfolios and maps were carried by the grooms. A page was in charge of "the field glass on the saddlebow, the satchels containing a handkerchief and a pair of gloves for His Majesty, and a little desk assortment consisting of paper, pens, ink, pencils, a compass, and sealing wax—all in conformity to 'List B.' On the back of the Emperor's saddle was a little case with his personal weapons." When the Emperor leaped on his horse, all these men rushed off—not so much merely following him as in pursuit of him.

At the end of May, on the same day when he received the Turkish ambassador, Napoleon learned of the capture of Danzig, the last Prussian stronghold. Fourteen thousand men had surrendered, and a large quantity of supplies had been captured by the Imperial Army, on the very eve of launching a new campaign. Immediately, the Emperor called for his carriage and set out toward the Baltic. And the entire imperial apparatus likewise got under way.

In the Emperor's traveling carriage, drawn by six horses, com-partments had been arranged for papers and maps. Napoleon would dictate letters, reports, and notes for Duroc and Berthier. The orders would be sent out from the next relay station. When he wasn't writ-ing, the Emperor would read a book from his "traveling library," a book of small format printed especially for him. If he did not find it interesting, he would throw it out the window. In another car-riage behind him was his portable field desk (one of these has been preserved in the museum at Malmaison), an armchair, and a table.

Then came the general service wagons, the field kitchens, and, in the form of a one-horse chaise, the "wine cellar" with fine wine for the staff officers and Chambertin for the Emperor, each bottle marked with an N.

A complete set of kitchen utensils was carried under the tilt; and sometimes the Emperor would call a halt in the open country, sit down under a tree, and order lunch. Roustam and the footmen would get out the table service (kept in leather cases) and the little silver casseroles in which the food was already prepared. Everyone would eat on his knees. "They would light a fire to warm up the coffee," Constant tells us, "and less than a half-hour later, everything would have vanished, and the vehicles would be rolling along in the same order as before." The full complement included 52 vehicles and 630 horses and mules.

With the return of good weather, the enemy resumed the offensive and attacked the forces commanded by Soult, together with those of Ney and Bernadotte. At dawn of June 5, Ney had been so violently set upon by 50,000 Russians that his corps, which consisted of only 25,000 men, had to withdraw toward Guttstadt.

Although the general staff was anxious, Napoleon was delighted. On Saturday, June 6, he wrote to Fouché from Finkenstein: "Eight days after you have received this letter, it will all be over." And in fact, one week after writing this, the Emperor attacked.

Once again the victory had to be total and decisive. If not, the Austrians would join forces with the Russians, and then would come the kill.

Four days before the battle, on June 10, the Emperor set out from Guttstadt for Heilsberg, in an already blazing sun. Suddenly he noticed a rise of ground overlooking the countryside. He headed for it, followed by the staff and the Horse Guard. When he reached the summit, he reined in his horse: "Berthier, my maps!"

Immediately Caulaincourt, the Grand Master of the Horse, called over the orderly officer in charge of the map case, opened it, and gave it to the chief of staff, who bent over and spread out on the ground a huge map. The Emperor at first got down on his knees to look at the map, then down on all fours; finally he sprawled out flat on it, marking it with a little pencil. He remained in that position for a full half-hour, not saying a word. The two high-ranking officers remained standing, motionless, in front of him, waiting for a gesture or a command. In spite of the blazing sun of the northern summer, they kept their caps off. The tableau was framed by the cavalrymen of the Guard. . . .

Abruptly, Napoleon stood up, "laughing and showing his good-looking teeth." He had just hit upon the tactics he would use to defeat the Russians. He had to take immediate advantage of the mistake made by the enemy, whose offensive had been "a stupid move." Ney was to continue his retreat in order to draw the enemy's troops after him. Meantime, Napoleon would congregate his forces and maneuver the Russians onto the terrain he himself had chosen.

"I will engage them in battle in order to have done with it!"

This time he would not let them escape. The mousetrap was ready; it was as though they were already caught. He climbed on his horse and set out at full gallop on the road that would lead to Friedland.

While the main body of the French army was moving toward Königsberg, the enemy's base of operations and the middle of its line of resistance, it was learned that Bennigsen was heading north. As a matter of fact, he was taking all his forces up the right bank of the Alle, a river which for the most part winds through the bottom of a narrow valley. Well protected by this natural defense, the Russian general had no fear of his flank's being threatened. But suddenly he was informed that a French advance guard had entered Friedland, situated on the right bank between two bends of the Alle. These were Lannes' troops, who had gone on ahead of the Imperial Army.

At this point Bennigsen made a mistake that he would regret for the rest of his life: in order to wipe out the enemy, he ordered the main body of his troops to cross the river, and then he moved on Friedland. Lannes, who had only 10,000 men, had to abandon his position—all the more so since the Russian artillery had been emplaced on the hills of the right bank overlooking the city.

Bennigsen had no idea that the Emperor was only a few leagues away, and that the entire French army was making ready to pounce on him—at a moment when his only means of retreat was to cross the narrow bridges over the Alle, whose banks are steep at this point. To make things even worse, the outskirts of Friedland were rendered almost inaccessible by two more natural obstacles: a lake and a stream called the Mühlenbach (the millstream), a tributary of the Alle, which meandered through a ravine.

But Bennigsen still did not realize the danger. He continued to build up his forces on the left bank—that left bank which would spell his ruin. He even rejoiced when he learned that another French force (the one commanded by Oudinot) had appeared. And the battle—the first Battle of Friedland—began.

It was a very hard battle for the French, who were numerically inferior—26,000 men against 70,000. But the imperial troops fought with fierce vigor, certain that they would soon see Napoleon arrive at the head of 50,000 men.

And the Emperor? At this very moment—having learned that Bennigsen had fallen into the trap he had set for him and now had his back to the river—he set out from Eylau, "radiant with joy." As soon as he came within view of the battlefield, at noon, Napoleon went up on the plateau, sat down in his armchair a short distance away from a mill, and began to lunch off a loaf of black bread "in the shape of a brick" and wrapped in straw. Relaxed and in good spirits, he laughed and asked the page on duty to hand him his field glass.

He could see that the enemy's force was grouped around the city, which served as its center. That force, formed of two flanks, was moving down the Alle, and therefore constituted an echelon bent slightly backward.

The Emperor's plan was to let the Russians become further entrapped on the left bank. Meantime, using the bridges that his engineers had rapidly built upstream, he would move a maximum of troops to the right bank, between the two bends of the Alle. And a short while later, in accordance with the classic and habitual maneuver, he would smash the enemy's center and then destroy the two flanks separately. "That is the whole idea," he explained to Ney. "Move ahead without looking around you. Drive into that thick mass, at whatever cost. Get into Friedland, capture the bridges, and don't worry about what is happening to the right, to the left, or behind you. The army and I will be keeping an eye on things."

Why didn't the Emperor launch a decisive attack immediately? Because the French army was not actually assembled in force until 5:00 P.M. Was it not too late to give battle? Would it not be better to wait until tomorrow?

The Emperor shook his head in the negative. He could see that the Russian general staff had not been able to overcome the forces under Lannes, Oudinot, and Mortier—and that it had made the foolish mistake of constantly sending new reserves across the river.

"No!" he exclaimed. "You can't catch the enemy making that kind of mistake twice over!"

There was plenty of time. Around the Baltic, in the month of June, twilight (or rather, "white night") does not come until 11:00 P.M. "Lashing at the tall grass and laying it low with his riding crop," the Emperor asked Marshal Berthier: "'What day is it?'"

"The fourteenth of June, Sire."

"The day of Marengo! A day of victory!" the Emperor exclaimed.

And Napoleon "went on playing his battle as if it were a game of chess." At 5:30 a French battery of twenty fieldpieces began to thunder. It was the signal for the attack. By this time, all the imperial forces were ready at hand. The troops rose up shouting: "Long live the Emperor! To Friedland! Forward!"

And once again, everything happened as he had said it would.

Ney gave the order to advance, weapons at the ready, while the enemy's artillery—still emplaced on the hills of the right bank—deluged the French with a hail of grapeshot.

Levasseur, sent by Ney, came on the gallop and shouted to a colonel: "Move to the left!"

"But just as I shouted at him" continues Levasseur, "he was killed by a cannonball. Without hesitating, a major stuck his cap on the end of his sword and shouted: 'Long live the Emperor! Forward!' Then came another volley, and the major fell, with both legs shorn off. A captain took his place and executed the same movement with great difficulty."

But now the French artillery was thundering. In three hours—an impressive figure for that era—the imperial artillery fired 2,600 volleys, first silencing the enemy's batteries, then demolishing his hollow squares one by one.

Next came the French infantry, advancing at the double-quick with platoon firing. This was the *coup de grace.* While the Guard remained with their arms at the ready, not having been ordered into action, the enemy's forces broke up as Napoleon watched in delight. Before the sun went down, a headlong stampede was already in progress. The pontoon bridges, which were too narrow, hindered the enemy's retreat. The Russians jumped into the river so as to reach the other bank more quickly. But the Alle is deep, and many drowned. The soldiers in flight did not take the time to find a ford, though there was one, downstream, near the tileworks of Klochenen.

This time, the defeat of the Russians was total, which did not prevent Bennigsen from explaining to the Czar: "The French had the advantage, since prudence demanded that I should not try to gain the battlefield from them." But before long, astounded and pitiable, he had to admit the frightful reality and the "slaughter" of his army at Friedland.

To be convinced of the fact, it would have sufficed to inspect, the next day, in the company of the Emperor, the corpse-covered battlefield. The odor of decay was overpowering in the terrible heat. Any notion of burying the dead was abandoned. Something had to be done quickly; and the order was given to drag the dead, both men and horses, to the banks of the Alle. This operation, rapidly accomplished, ended with the guffaws of the soliders, delighted with the spectacle of corpses tumbling down the slope of the ravine before disappearing in the river.

Seven thousand French had also perished. But every effort was made not to think too much about them.

Only one thing bedazzled the Emperor. On June 19 Murat, who had set out in pursuit of the vanquished troops, had reached the border of the Russian Empire. Thus Napoleon could write proudly to Fouché: "My eagles have been unfurled on the banks of the Neman."

On June 18, 1807, Talleyrand, who was at Danzig, wrote the Emperor to tell him that he considered the victory of Friedland as "a harbinger of peace." He even stipulated: "That is why I value it so much. For, fine as it is, I must admit that in my view it would be diminished more than I can say, if Your Majesty were to go on to new battles."

But Talleyrand had no reason for anxiety. Napoleon wanted to get back to Paris after his long absence. For him—as he wrote on June 20—Friedland was a "denouement." The Russians had admitted their defeat and were shouting at the top of their voices: "Peace!"

And yet, some of the "old Russians" wanted the Czar to let the victor of Friedland cross the frontier. They maintained that "the army of M. Buonaparte," far from its bases and harassed and weakened by guerrilla warfare, would at the first great battle perish like the army of Charles XII. Bennigsen seemed to be forgetting that he had just been thoroughly beaten. For him, the rout of Friedland was nothing more than a strategic withdrawal. Said he: "Our reinforcements will soon enable us to be more formidable than ever in the eyes of Bonaparte."

But Alexander still meditated. What if Napoleon reestablished the Kingdom of Poland? If the French entered Russia, that Poland would surely go along with the invader. For Holy Russia, peace was preferable.

And so on Friday, June 19, refusing to listen to Bennigsen, the Czar sent Prince Lobanov to Napoleon to ask for an armistice. The demands of the Emperor of the French would certainly be radically modified. Moreover, having been either minimally aided or abandoned completely by his allies, Alexander was now beginning to admire Napoleon. He declared that the union of France and Russia seemed to him the only guarantee for "the happiness and tranquillity of the universe."

Apparently, Napoleon was of the same opinion. For on June 22, pointing to the Vistula on a map, he told Prince Lobanov (who had again been received at Tilsit): "Here is the boundary line between our two empires. Your sovereign should reign on one side of it, and I on the other."

It was urgent that the two emperors meet as soon as possible. At first Napoleon was only mildly interested in such an interview, and he said as much in a letter to Talleyrand written on the very eve of the meeting. But then an idea came to him: why not make peace by abandoning, with magnanimity, the advantages that the victory of Friedland entitled him to demand of the Czar? Instead of creating a vast Polish State threatening Russia, would it not be better to settle for an advance post on the Vistula consisting of the old Prussian Poland? Why not give Alexander a free hand: in the north, to seize Finland; and in the south, to take over a considerable part of the Ottoman Empire, which was breaking down? True, Napoleon had recently signed an alliance with the sultan Selim, his old enemy of the Egyptian campaign (who, as a matter of fact, had been an ex-sultan since May 27). And true again, in failing to reassemble the fragments of Poland he would horribly disappoint those Polish magnates who had put their trust in him. And Marie! But the partition of the world was well worth a sacrifice on the banks of the Neman and the Vistula.

Massed on the banks of the Neman, the spectators looked toward the raft in the middle of the river, on which the pontoniers were busy putting up a kind of cottage consisting of an entrance hall and a living room. The whole structure was adorned with garlands of flowers and greenery.

On Thursday, July 7, Alexander—in black tunic, white breeches, and cap with white and black plumes—got into a barge and headed for the raft, where Napoleon was already waiting for him, garbed with his customary simplicity. At the Emperor's side were Berthier, Duroc, Caulaincourt, and Bessières.

The two emperors embraced.

Alexander misread Napoleon's motives in not treating his adversary as one vanquished. He took this moderation and disinterestedness to be nothing more than the pride of a parvenu named Buonaparte who was bold enough to converse with a czar on terms of equality. To his mother he wrote: "With all his genius, he has a vulnerable spot: his vanity. I have decided to sacrifice my own *amour-propre* for the well-being of the Empire."

Napoleon considered Alexander "a very handsome, kind young man with more intelligence than is commonly supposed." And he even remarked: "He is like a hero out of a novel. He has all the style of a cultivated man of Paris."

After a second interview the next day, they felt it would be difficult to continue the talks on the raft. Therefore, it was decided that the two emperors, their general staffs, and their guards should shift to the town of Tilsit (which would be neutralized in order to spare Alexander's tender sense of dignity). No other troops would be quartered in the town.

After having welcomed his guest with all possible honors—salutes fired by his cannon, and the presentation of troops—Napoleon escorted Alexander to his quarters. "Here is Your Majesty's house," he said.

"Sire," replied the Czar, "allow me to take a walk as far as the end of the street to see your Guard, which I find superb!"

It almost appeared that a flirtation had developed between the two sovereigns engaged in dividing up Europe. In the evening they could be seen walking arm in arm. And the Czar wrote: "Here I am, spending my days with Bonaparte—spending entire hours with him. I ask you: Is it not like a dream?"

The air was full of plans. Russia would have the East, and France the West. They even talked of an alliance.

For the Czar, the terms of the armistice were astoundingly favorable. True, the King of Saxony was to get the Duchy of Warsaw. But Alexander got himself out of a fix when he abandoned his possessions in the Mediterranean—possessions that Napoleon was coveting, since he wanted to make the Mediterranean an entirely French sea. Provision was made for a treaty of alliance with Napoleon; and most important, the Czar undertook to serve as mediator between France and England. If nothing came of his arbitration, Russia would declare war on England and adhere to the Continental blockade. Finally, Alexander recognized the Confederation of the Rhine and the Napoleonic kingdoms, and approved the planned mutilation of Prussia.

Finally, the Czar had managed to have Frederick William come to Tilsit. The unfortunate fellow arrived looking thin, wretched, and pitiable. "What a shabby sovereign!" Coignet exclaimed.

When the three monarchs went horseback riding, the two emperors, who were better riders, would leave the King behind. Pitilessly, Napoleon said of him: "He is a man of no scope whatsoever—without character and without resources. A real booby! A numskull! And a bore!"

To the unfortunate sovereign who had come to beg for a piece of his crown, the Czar acknowledged that he could do nothing. One last hope remained to the King: he would arrange for his wife—the lovely, intelligent, and sentimental Queen Louise—to come to Tilsit. Frederick William was counting on his wife's beauty to soften the conqueror's heart.

Although she entertained a Platonic love for Alexander, whom she considered a god, Louise was a model wife. "The terms are frightful," her husband wrote her, in begging her to come to Tilsit. Louise broke into tears. But in obedience to her husband's wishes, she bravely set out to confront "the monster."

On July 6, dressed all in white (the mourning of queens), Louise arrived at her husband's "palace," a ramshackle building that had formerly served as a mill.

When Napoleon was ushered in, he wasted few words asking the Queen how her trip had been. He considered her solely responsible for the war that had been imposed on him, and he attacked without delay: "How did you dare declare war on me?"

"Sire, we were blinded by the glory of the Great Frederick. It was so brilliant that our mistake was quite understandable."

Then she grew bolder and asked: "Won't you leave us Magdeburg and Westphalia?"

"You are asking for a lot, but I promise you I'll think about it. That's a very pretty dress you are wearing. Is it crepe or Italian gauze?"

Louise interrupted him, with tears in her eyes: "Sire, should we be talking of dresses at such a solemn moment?"

At dinner that evening she was seated next to the conqueror and did everything possible to charm him. After all, was she not the most beautiful queen of her day? But Napoleon's only response was to ask her: "Why are you wearing a turban? Surely not to flirt with the Emperor Alexander, because he is at war with the Turks."

Flirt with Alexander? By no means! He had disappointed her— disappointed her terribly. Conquered by Napoleon, and even infatuated with him, the Czar had come to terms with the common enemy! And she told him as much, speaking straight out: "You have betrayed me most cruelly."

After dinner, Napoleon offered the Queen a rose. "I accept it," she murmured, "but only along with Magdeburg, at the least."

He promised nothing.

To Josephine he wrote: "The Queen of Prussia is really charming. She is very flirtatious with me, but don't be jealous. For me, it is like water running off a duck's back. And it would cost us a great deal if I were to play the ladies' man with her."

When they parted company, Louise once again begged him: "Now that I have seen the man of the century at close quarters, is it possible that he will not let me have the satisfaction of assuring him that he has attached me to him for life?"

"I am to be pitied, Madame. It all comes from my unlucky star."

Prussia was demolished. The treaty stipulated that Napoleon, "out of regard for His Majesty the Emperor of All the Russias, and wishing to give proof of his sincere desire to unite the two nations with bonds of unalterable trust and friendship," simply condescended to take from Frederick William only his strongholds (including Magdeburg), the territories to the west between the Rhine and the Elbe, and all that portion of the Polish cake that had been sliced off at the time of the famous partitions. And that was not all: Prussia found herself compelled to enter into the French alliance; and the provinces that had been taken from her were used to form a new kingdom for Jérôme.

"You have been recognized as King of Westphalia," Napoleon wrote to his brother. "The kingdom comprises all the states listed in the enclosed document." Kassel was to be the capital of this kingdom of 7,000 square kilometers in which the Prussian provinces were combined with the Duchy of Brunswick and a few duchies of Hesse taken from their owner "because of his treachery." Apart from the common language there was no unity, either historical or geographic, in this mosaic. Westphalia had neither the Rhine nor the sea as a border.

The new king must be made a wiser and more settled man than he was. He must, therefore, be made to marry the young lady who had been his fiancée since late 1806. This was the plump little Catherine of Württemberg, daughter of the potbellied King of Württemberg. King Frederick I of Württemberg was so potbellied, in fact, that before he could sit down at a table, a special indentation had to be carved out for him. "God created him," Napoleon used to say, "to show how far human skin can be stretched."

His Württembergerian Majesty seemed delighted at the idea of becoming the father-in-law of Napoleon's brother. Or so he pretended, at any rate. But the Pope, some years before, had refused to annul the marriage between Jérôme and Elizabeth Patterson. He had not found, he said at the time, "any grounds" which might authorize him to nullify the bonds uniting the pair who had been married in Baltimore.

The Emperor therefore addressed himself to the Ecclesiastical Court of Paris, which made haste to comply, and merely notified the Pope of his action. Pius VII, who had put up with so many indignities since 1805, resigned himself to thanking "His Majesty for his gracious letter, full of the liveliest expressions of his filial piety." Imperturbable beyond belief, he wished the newlyweds "not only the greatest but the purest consolations."

On July 29, 1807, twenty-four hours after his return from Prussia, Napoleon was holding his levee at the Tuileries, beginning at eight o'clock in the morning.

> I can still see him [Chancellor Pasquier writes] as he was that day, wearing his ceremonial uniform. . . . The features of his calm, serious face reminded one of the cameos representing the Roman emperors. He was short; and yet the totality of his person was in

harmony with the role he was called upon to maintain. The habit
of command and the awareness of his strength seemed to endow
him with greater physical stature. A sword encrusted with glittering jewels hung at his side. Its hilt was formed of the famous
diamond known as the "Regent." Its brilliance forcibly reminded
one that this sword was the most violent and victorious one that
had appeared in the world since those of Alexander the Great and
Caesar.

"I give you leave to refrain from comparing me to God," he wrote
to the minister Décrès. "I would like to believe that you had not
thought seriously about what you were writing to me."

And yet Décrès was not wrong: the Emperor could have been
taken for a divine emanation. He who had once been the little
Nabulio had humiliated emperors, trimmed the claws of kings, and
clipped the wings of the Russian, German, and Austrian eagles. Now,
after ten months of campaigns, he was glad to become Emperor
again.

He allowed himself to assume a lofty, even slightly arrogant, manner toward Louis XVIII, who because of the Czar's policy had had
to leave Mitau and seek asylum in England.

More bedazzled and fascinated by himself than ever, the Emperor was losing his sense of proportion. He reigned as a despot.

"I have had enough of being a general," he declared. "I am going
to take up the métier of prime minister again. It is high time that
grand reviews of armies be supplanted by grand reviews of domestic
business, and I am going to resume the latter."

Undoubtedly, the Emperor was again thinking of a successor—
and thinking twice as hard since his triumph at Tilsit. The death of
the young Napoleon Charles, the son of Louis and Hortense, had
provided him with an opportunity to speak to Josephine "of the need
he might some day have of taking a wife who could give him children."

> If such a thing should happen, Josephine, it would be up to you
> to help me make such a sacrifice. I would count on your friendship
> for me to spare me the hateful business of a forced break between
> us. You would take the initiative, *n'est-ce pas?* And, putting your-
> self in my place, you would have the courage to withdraw volun-
> tarily, would you not?

"I will obey your orders," she had replied, resigned.

Then, adroitly, she had added: "But I will never anticipate any order."

Sometime afterward, Josephine suggested to her husband (he told the story at St. Helena) that he "get some demoiselle with child, and then pass it off as hers." But Napoleon refused to act out a comedy incompatible with his dignity.

Yet all the decrees issued early in 1808 tended toward one goal: to forge a hereditary empire. Thus after having created sovereigns, he decided to create an imperial nobility. At first, as their rightful due, the great dignitaries were given the title of prince; the ministers, archbishops, and councillors of state received the title of count; and the bishops, prefects, and mayors were created barons.

His Serene Highness, Talleyrand, the Prince of Benevento, was named vice-grand elector. When Fouché learned of the new distinction conferred upon his old enemy, he snickered: "That was the only vice he lacked."

But for all this, Napoleon remained faithful to his principle that none of his ministers should at the same time be a great dignitary. Accordingly, early in August he made a decision which would have grave consequences for the future: he took the Ministry of Foreign Affairs out of the hands of the Prince of Benevento and entrusted it to Champagny. There is no doubt that Talleyrand was hoping the Emperor would make an exception in his case. And when things turned out otherwise, he showed symptoms of a rancor ill concealed by his air of detachment.

Actually, it was only "officially" that Talleyrand gave over his functions. The Emperor continued to make use of his talents as a diplomat, keeping him informed of things and entrusting him with very delicate negotiations. But by dismissing him from the ministry —by touching his pride—he had "provided him with grounds for betrayal." No later than the next summer, he would effect that betrayal con brio.

Once having made his decision on the Continental blockade, Napoleon assumed as a matter of course that the Papal States would join the federative system. He looked upon His Holiness as a chief customs officer.

"As a temporal prince," the Emperor explained to Talleyrand, "the Pope belongs to my confederation, whether he wants to or not. If he makes an arrangement with me, I will not disturb his sovereignty. If he doesn't, I will take possession of all his coastlines."

Pius VII felt there was no good reason why he should consider himself the ally of the one he had crowned. The successor of St. Peter did not arrogate unto himself the right to expel the English from Rome and close his ports to British trade. In his view, a trader from the banks of the Thames and his counterpart from the Seine were both Christians, and that was all there was to it. But for Napoleon, the fact that the Pope regarded himself at one and the same time as the father of the faithful and the "King of Rome" meant that he was not following the path that "Jesus Christ, dying on the cross" had laid out for him.

"If the Pope does not do what I want," he declared to the papal nuncio, Monsignor Arezzo, "I will suppress his temporal domain, but I shall always respect him as head of the Church. There is no good reason why the Pope should be sovereign of Rome. The holiest of the popes were not sovereigns of Rome. . . ."

> Your Majesty [replied Monsignor Arezzo] will permit me to repeat what he has already heard many times. The Pope, being the common father of the faithful, cannot break off from some of them to attach himself to others. Since his ministry is one of peace, he cannot make war on anyone; nor can he declare himself the enemy of anyone whatsoever without abandoning his responsibilities and compromising his sacred character.

At this the Emperor exclaimed:

> I'm not asking that he wage war on anyone! What I want is that he should close his ports to the English, that he should not receive them in his states, and that since he cannot defend either his ports or his fortresses, he let me defend them. You may be assured that they have lost their heads at Rome. . . . I want everything in safekeeping in my own domain. All of Italy belongs to me by right of conquest. The Pope did not crown me king but Emperor of France: and I have inherited not the right of kings but the rights of Charlemagne. . . . If the Pope does not yield, I will take away his states. Excommunications are out of fashion, and my soldiers will not hesitate to march where I tell them to go. . . .

When these words were conveyed to Pius VII, he said:

> You are stronger than I. You can become the master of my states whenever you want to. If His Majesty so desires, he can carry out his threats and take from me all I possess. I am resigned to everything and am prepared, if His Majesty so wishes, to withdraw to a monastery or the catacombs of Rome. . . . If the Emperor throws us down, his successor will raise us up again.

The honeymoon between the Pope and the Emperor was decidedly over. The drama was building up. In his rage, Napoleon went so far as to say that he was considering following, for his own benefit, the example set by Henry VIII: "I would have no qualms about assembling the Gallican, Italian, German, and Polish churches at a council to conduct my affairs without the Pope, and to shelter my peoples from the claims of the Roman priests. . . . This is the last time I will discuss things with that clerical crew."

Frightened at the thought of seeing a schism arise under his pontificate, Pius VII agreed (much against his will) to close his ports to the English. But Napoleon demanded more: Rome must make common cause with the Empire and declare itself the "enemy" of all the enemies of France. This position was unacceptable to God's vicar on earth. And this time the Pope refused to yield. The result was that on January 10, 1808, General Miollis was ordered to march on the Eternal City.

> There will be no military resistance [said Pius VII]. But we will order the gates of Rome to be closed. We shall retire to the Castel Sant'Angelo with whoever wishes to accompany us. Not one shot will be fired, since we abhor the spilling of blood; but your general will have to break down the doors. We shall place ourselves at the entrance of the fort. The troops will have to pass over our body, and the Christian world will learn that the Emperor has caused to be trampled underfoot the one who anointed him.

The cardinals, less courageous, explained to the Holy Father that martyrdom did not solve anything. The wisest choice was to yield to force.

While waiting for the tragedy to come to an end, Pius VII patiently endured the yoke of the occupying forces and their annoyances, which were carried to such a point that his mail was delivered to him after having been opened.

And yet it was the Pope—that shadow of a man—who had the last word. As Napoleon said one day: "There are only two forces in the world: the sword and the spirit. . . . In the long run, the sword is always defeated by the spirit."

XVI

THE AMBUSH OF BAYONNE

The Spanish expedition was
the greatest mistake I made.

NAPOLEON

THE HOLY FATHER HAD BEEN COMPELLED to go along with the Continental blockade; and in the spring of 1808 Napoleon had just chalked up a new score in the conflict between France and England. On the other hand, far in the west, the English had accomplished much more than merely "trading" with the European continent: they had secured a foothold there, thanks to the complaisance of Portugal, which had become a kind of British colony.

At Fontainebleau, on October 15, 1807, Napoleon had told the ambassador from Lisbon: "I will not tolerate the presence of an English envoy in Europe! If Portugal doesn't do what I want, the House of Braganza will cease to reign in Europe within two months' time!"

The Lisbon government, by agreement with London, made a pretense of declaring war on England; but Napoleon was not taken in by this farce. Accordingly, on October 27, 1807, he ordered Junot, commanding a pathetic army of conscripts, to invade Portugal. But in order to reach Portugal the French troops had to cross several Spanish provinces. And thus it was that the Portuguese affair—which turned out to be nothing more than a military parade, despite the mediocrity of Junot's army—became the "Spanish affair." Not at all because Charles IV offered any resistance to the French invasion (this Bourbon king's servility toward Napoleon ultimately became nauseating), but because the King of Spain, who coveted a portion of the Portuguese cake, became the Emperor's ally by virtue of signing a treaty of partition with him on that same October 27, 1807. Thus it was quite natural that when a family conflict (which would soon degenerate into a national conflict) broke out at Madrid, the descendant of Louis XIV would appeal to Napoleon for help.

History knows no personages more unfortunate than the members of the Spanish royal family. The Comtesse d'Albany described them as "morons without flesh, without soul, and without feelings"; and one look at Goya's pitiless painting will convince anyone that the countess was not exaggerating in the slightest. Three degenerates with pronounced prognathism: Charles IV, his wife Marie Louise, and their son, the Prince of the Asturias. And hovering over all of them was Manuel de Godoy, a kind of bull become prime minister who for twenty years had been the Queen's lover and a favorite of the King, who had named "his dear Manuel" Prince of the Peace.

Charles IV remembered that he belonged to the Bourbon family only when the outcome of the Napoleonic battles obliged his minister to seek closer ties with Moscow, Vienna, or Berlin. Napoleon had even found, at Potsdam, a letter from Charles IV to Frederick William (left behind by the latter when he fled) in which the King of Spain said he would attack the French from the back while Napoleon was still on the banks of the Elbe!

One must remember this proposal in order to understand why the Emperor took such a disdainful attitude toward these puppets. It was that disdain, together with Napoleon's underestimating the Spaniards' attachment to their monarchy, which would lead him astray and prompt him to intervene in the affairs of Spain. Thus the Spanish adventure would prove to be, so to speak, the first crack in the edifice. Later, the man exiled to St. Helena admitted: "I started that business off very badly."

While Junot was winning the victory that would bring him the title of Duc d'Abrantès and was occupying Lisbon, and while the royal family of Braganza was fleeing to Brazil, Murat, the Grand Duke of Berg and of Clèves, who had become his brother-in-law's *lieutenant-général*, crossed the Pyrenees. His mission was to frighten Charles IV by his mere presence, compelling him to abandon his throne and, like the Braganzas, flee to the Americas.

The Spanish people, believing that the French had come to liberate the country and the king from the dictatorship of Godoy, did not receive the French too badly. And Napoleon had been right about

Charles IV. At Aranjuez, a melancholy château sprawling above the Tagus, Charles was thinking of leaving his kingdom—now that it had been partially occupied by Napoleon's troops—and going to the New World. Was he not also "King of the West and East Indies"? But this plan was opposed by his son, Ferdinand, Prince of the Asturias, a man "with the heart of a tiger and the head of a mule," as his mother amiably expressed it. Ferdinand threatened that if need be, he would use force to block any such plan.

In Madrid, ten leagues away, things immediately came to the boiling point. The demonstrators, led by a few grandees loyal to the heir to the throne, marched to Aranjuez, where they pounded on the gates of the château and then invaded Godoy's residence. That much-loathed personage was taken prisoner.

The same grandees who had fomented the riot besieged the king, telling him over and over that the fall of his favorite would not be enough to turn away the wrath of the people, and that only his abdication in favor of Ferdinand would avert the revolution whose rumblings could already be heard.

So it was that Ferdinand VII became King of All the Spains. But on March 12 Charles IV, in order to save that dear man, his wife's lover, wrote to Murat (who was at El Molar, just outside of Madrid):

> I have a favor to ask of you. Would you please inform the Emperor that I beg him to set free the poor Prince of the Peace, who is suffering only because he has been a friend to France. I also request that we be allowed to go to a country suitable to us, in the company of the aforesaid prince.

Murat, who had refused to recognize Ferdinand VII, occupied Madrid the next day. Furthermore, he suggested to Charles IV that he take back the crown—for the time being—and that he write Napoleon as follows:

> I have been forced to abdicate. But still having complete trust in the magnanimity and genius of the great man who has always shown himself to be my friend, I have decided to abide by whatever that great man decides with respect to the fate of myself, the Queen, and the Prince of the Peace.

Unquestionably, Murat was hoping that thanks to this imbroglio he would receive the crown of Spain from the hands of his imperial brother-in-law. But Napoleon had very different ideas on the subject, as he reminded the Grand Duke of Berg and of Clèves: "I will take care of your personal interests; you yourself need not bother to think about them. . . . Your attention must not be absorbed, or your conduct guided, by any plan whatsoever. This would be prejudicial to me, and even more so to you."

In the Emperor's judgment, his brother-in-law did not have the slightest understanding of the problem, and he told him so: "Monsieur le Grand Duc de Berg, I fear you are deceived as to the situation in Spain, and that you are deceiving yourself. . . . Never believe that you are attacking an unarmed nation, or that you can subjugate Spain merely by a display of troops."

And the pseudo-Ferdinand VII? "The Prince of the Asturias," the Emperor added, "has none of the capacities required of a chief of state."

Napoleon's plans had not yet been fully worked out. He believed it was necessary to drive the Bourbons out of Spain "in order to make sure of the throne of France." But what would he then do with this country that seemed to be breaking up more and more from one day to the next?

> I have two choices open to me. One is to take over all of Spain and give it a ruler from my own family, under the pretext of avenging the rebellion of a son against his father—of a subject against his king. The other is to seize and annex to France the northern province of Spain, negotiating with Ferdinand VII and recognizing him—provided he give up that province—as King of Spain and the Indies.

The first alternative—the annexation of all of Spain—was the less prudent of the two; but it was the one he chose. He then wrote the following lines to his brother Louis, King of Holland:

> The King of Spain has just abdicated, and the Prince of the Peace has been imprisoned. . . . I have decided to place a French ruler on the Spanish throne. The climate of Holland does not agree with you. I am thinking of you for the Spanish throne. Answer me categorically: If I name you King of Spain, will you accept?

Annoyed at the idea of being transferred like a subprefect—even "indignant," as he was bold enough to put it—Louis refused. Then the order went out to Joseph to exchange his throne of Naples for that of Madrid.

Napoleon never forgot that he was a Corsican; and he made the mistake of trying to associate the clan with his own success—a success that transcended human values. It was not simply that his brothers were in no sense qualified for the tasks assigned to them: they considered themselves kings "by right." (Except, of course, for the intelligent Lucien, who still refused to become a part of the system without his wife.)

"A man doesn't become king just to follow orders," Murat said.

Louis, Jérôme, Joseph, and (shortly thereafter) Murat spoke of their "nations." In the Emperor's view, the sovereigns of Holland, of Naples, of Westphalia—and soon, of Spain—were nothing more than viceroys whose first duty was to serve France and reign over kingdoms that were merely enfeoffed.

However, these kings were actually no longer even allies that could be counted upon by the brother to whom they owed everything. Joseph, in Naples, had shown himself to be a wretched sovereign. Surrounding himself with nothing but idealogues, he had effected no reforms whatsoever. As a military leader, he had proven equally incompetent. With an army of 45,000 men, he had not even attempted a landing in Sicily. Even worse, he had let the island of Capri be captured by the English, who therefore thumbed their noses at him all the more insolently.

And yet it was to Joseph that Napoleon offered the Spanish throne. True, the Emperor had not yet taken possession of the crown that had once belonged to Charles IV, but he had no doubts as to the success of the operation.

In order to achieve his goal, Napoleon planned a rather shady deal. The *deus ex machina* who would lead the Bourbons into the ambush of Bayonne, who would compel Ferdinand VII to vanish, who would make Charles IV abdicate in favor of Joseph Bonaparte, was General Savary, the new Duke of Rovigo.

The first object of his mission was to make a fool of Canon Escoï-quiz, the former tutor and confessor of the new sovereign. With apparent candor, Savary described Napoleon's astonishment at the abdication and immediate retraction of his ally Charles IV. Spain could not have two kings! The situation had to be clarified. If Ferdinand wanted to dispel this ambiguity and have himself recognized by the Emperor as the sovereign of Spain, why did he not come in person to plead his cause before His Imperial Majesty?

Ferdinand, upon receiving a report of this interview from Escoï-quiz, asked Savary to come and see him. Savary stressed the danger of Ferdinand's position, and added that the Emperor was on his way toward the Spanish frontier.

Ferdinand reflected, insofar as his limited intelligence made that possible. Would it not be better to get to the Emperor before the old king did? This seemed all the more desirable since Savary had indicated that his master would not raise any serious objections to a change of regime. "What happened," says Thiers very accurately, "was what usually happens in interviews of this kind. The general believed he had promised nothing in giving Ferdinand everything to hope for, and Ferdinand believed that everything he had been led to hope for amounted to a promise."

"Like a schoolboy," as Savary put it, the unfortunate sovereign entreated the general to take him to Napoleon. Bayonne was the place to which Ferdinand had to be taken, whether he was willing to go there or not. It was at Bayonne that the Emperor was already beginning to spin "the spider's web in which the wretched royal prey would be caught."

When they reached Burgos, Ferdinand, who had believed that Napoleon was coming to meet him, was dumfounded at not finding the Emperor there waiting for him. Savary then went into a new scene from his repertory. Surely His Majesty was waiting for "the king" at Vitoria. And the procession got under way again.

But of course the Emperor was not at Vitoria, either. This time Ferdinand's resistance became vigorous. He declared firmly that he would wait for the French sovereign at Vitoria. He would not leave his own territory at any price!

Savary set off for Bayonne, in order to ascertain what his master's intentions were at this point. He located the Emperor at the château of Marracq. After listening to the account given by his faithful aide-de-camp, Napoleon decided to follow Savary's lead along the path of deceit. He wrote to Ferdinand:

> I declare to Your Highness, to the Spanish people, and to the entire world: if the abdication of King Charles was purely voluntary—if he was not coerced into it by the insurrection and the

rioting at Aranjuez—I will not hesitate to acknowledge it, and I will recognize Your Highness as the King of Spain. I therefore want to discuss this matter with Your Highness. . . .

Napoleon did not intend to "recognize" anyone but his brother Joseph I, and with a distressing lack of good faith, he added slyly:

All my thoughts on the subject have been laid bare to Your Royal Highness. You can see that I am vacillating among various ideas which need to be clarified. And you can be certain that in any case, I will treat you in the same way as your father, the King. You may be sure that I am anxious to reconcile everything.

When he read this letter, in which he was addressed merely as a prince, Ferdinand rebelled.

Savary then began his great performance, a performance that does little honor to his memory. He told Ferdinand firmly:

I will wager my head that within a quarter-hour after Your Majesty's arrival at Bayonne, the Emperor will recognize you as King of Spain and the Indies. He may start out by calling you Your Highness, but he will soon be calling you Your Majesty. All will be settled, and Your Majesty can immediately return to Spain!

This time, on April 19, Ferdinand agreed to set out.

They stopped for the night at Iruna. The next day, to Savary's great pleasure, the carriages reached the bank of the Bidassoa and headed over the bridge. Duroc and Berthier were there, having been sent to meet "the prisoner." In inviting him, on the Emperor's behalf, to dinner at the château of Marracq, they too addressed him merely as "Your Royal Highness." Ferdinand frowned. He was being treated as a prince instead of a king!

The dinner went off without incident, but no one had yet called Ferdinand "Sire." Hardly had the unfortunate prince returned to his quarters than he received a visit from Savary. This time the scales fell from the eyes of the Prince of the Asturias. The general had been entrusted by the Emperor with a mission that anyone other than himself would have refused; but the Duke of Rovigo did not even consider such a possibility. That mission was to inform his "prisoner" that His Imperial Majesty had recognized Charles IV as King of Spain and was offering him, Ferdinand—provided he yield gracefully—the crown of Etruria, a little state manufactured out of Italian Tuscany.

Ferdinand choked with rage. He rushed out onto the balcony, shouting, "Yo soy [estoy] traido!"

He had indeed been grossly betrayed—both by the Emperor and by the man who had taken him to Napoleon.

Meantime, at Madrid, Charles IV and his wife were living in terror that their son might reach an agreement with the Emperor and thwart their beloved Godoy. So they, too, set out for Bayonne.

Napoleon believed that the whole thing would soon be over. "Unless I am mistaken," he wrote to Talleyrand on April 25, "we are now into the fifth act of this tragedy. The denouement will come soon."

Five days later, Charles IV and Queen Marie Louise reached Bayonne, flanked by Godoy.

The Emperor wrote to Josephine: "With her sallow complexion, the Queen looks like a mummy. She has about her an air of evil and falsity, and you can't imagine anything more ridiculous than she is."

When he saw his son, the King literally pounced on him. "Haven't you had enough of committing outrages on my gray head? Go away! I never want to see you again!"

Then, turning to Napoleon, he said with a sigh: "Your Majesty doesn't know what it is to have an ungrateful son!"

Napoleon could have replied that his brothers and sisters had amply provided him with family troubles. But, as can well be imagined, the atmosphere was not conducive to joking—neither then nor during the dinner that followed. The mood of the guests could not be brightened even by the astonishing performance of the Spanish King, who had three carafes of water placed in front of him—one with ice water, one with hot water, and one with water at room temperature—and then mixed their contents very carefully and expertly until the temperature was just what he wanted. But along with his drinking water, there was another thing that very much concerned him that evening: his dear Godoy had been seated at a *table de service*. His equanimity was not restored until the Prince of the Peace was seated not far from him.

The descendants of Louis XIV were now at the mercy of Napoleon.

Two days later, Charles IV wrote his son a note informing him that his crimes made it impossible for him to succeed to the throne, and that "Spain could now be saved only by the Emperor." Accordingly, on that same day of May 2, Napoleon posed this singular problem for Murat: "I intend for the King of Naples to reign at Madrid, and I want to give you either the Kingdom of Naples or the Kingdom of Portugal. Tell me right now what you think of this, because it has to be done in one day."

"Sire," Murat replied, "I shall not hesitate. I opt for the country where I have already commanded, and where I can better serve Your Majesty. I prefer Naples. And I can assure Your Majesty that I would not accept the crown of Portugal at any price."

So the Kingdom of Naples was taken care of. As for Lisbon, Napoleon would see about that later. But, fearful that Joseph would be upset at having to trade Naples for Madrid, he made much of this Spanish gift to his brother: "It is something quite different from the Kingdom of Naples. It has 11 million inhabitants and more than 50 million in revenue, not to mention the possession and the great revenues of the Americas."

Joseph yielded, as had Murat. As Chateaubriand described it: "With one move of the hand, the Emperor stuck these bonnets on the heads of the new kings, and they went marching off, each in his own direction, like two recruits who had just traded shakos."

And yet, on that May 2 when Napoleon was making his kings play musical chairs, Charles IV had not yet abdicated. This matter was settled, however, on May 5, when the King of Spain ceded his states to Napoleon, stipulating only that "the territorial integrity of the kingdom be respected, and that no other religion than Catholicism be tolerated there." In exchange, Charles and Marie Louise received Compiègne, Chambord, and an annual stipend of 6 million francs. Only Ferdinand continued to resist and could, legally, still consider himself King of all the Spains.

Suddenly, on that same day of May 5, the news reached Bayonne of the new and bloody insurrection in Madrid on May 2—the famous "dos de mayo"—sternly put down by Murat's Mamelukes, who charged on the crowd at the Puerta del Sol. On that day, the Spaniards could well believe they were back in the age of the wars against the Moors! This event enabled Napoleon skillfully to play out the last act of the dramatic "ambush of Bayonne." Actually, Ferdinand had been of no importance in the unleashing of the insurrection, which had been caused by the departure of the Infantas—or rather, by their kidnapping. But the Emperor nonetheless had a good pretext to work with.

When he heard the news of the rioting, he was out horseback

riding. Immediately, he galloped back to Bayonne. After summoning the Prince of the Asturias to his father's quarters, Napoleon accused him of having fomented the revolt. And Charles IV approved.

"The blood of my subjects has been spilled!" roared Charles. "Yes, and the blood of my great friend Napoleon's soldiers! You had a hand in the slaughter!"

Then the Queen, like a Fury, heaped abuse on her son, calling him a "bastard" and demanding that he "go to the gallows." Napoleon's demands were more moderate. To "Ferdinand VII" he declared: "If between now and midnight, you have not recognized your father as the legitimate king and sent word of that recognition to Madrid, you willl be treated by me as a rebel."

Ferdinand, frightened out of his wits, finally yielded. From that time on he would be nothing more than a prisoner immured behind the gilded gates of the château of Valençay, with Talleyrand as his jailer. "You might bring Mme. de Talleyrand to the château with four or five other ladies," Napoleon suggested to his vice-grand elector. "If the Prince of the Asturias became infatuated with some pretty woman, it wouldn't do any harm."

Napoleon did not yet realize that the adventure in Spain had been unwisely undertaken. He considered the matter as settled, and remained at Marracq. Once the curtain had fallen on the tragic days of Bayonne, he became very pleasantly disposed; and with Josephine he indulged in the playfulness of a new husband. He went bathing in the ocean, each of these dips being preceded by "an aquatic reconnaissance to prevent any surprise move by the English." While Napoleon was paddling about, a detachment of the Horse Guard would "reconnoiter the sea, going as far as possible without running too much risk." Once back on the beach, the Emperor would chase his wife, pushing her under the waves and taking off her shoes, which he would throw far away. Josephine would laugh. She was happy, and could well have believed they were back in the days of the Consulate.

On June 7, Napoleon received the new King of Spain, who in all seriousness was going to have himself proclaimed "Don José I, by the Grace of God King of Castile, Aragon, the Two Sicilies, Jerusalem, and Navarre." Joseph did not neglect to mention his sovereignty over the Canary Islands and the East and West Indies. Moreover, his impetus unabated, he styled himself "Archduke of Austria, Duke of Burgundy, Brabant, and Milan, and Count Hapsburg." Finally, he found it quite natural that he should receive the following lines of congratulation from his predecessor, Ferdinand: "I beg Your Catholic Majesty to accept the oath of loyalty that I owe you, along with that of the Spaniards of my entourage." The weakness of the predecessor was equaled only by the vacuity of the successor.

A hundred and twenty deputies were supposed to assemble at Bayonne to proclaim "Don José I" King of Spain. Eighty of them failed to appear, but this by no means discouraged the Emperor, who was already thinking of reaching Morocco by way of Spain and, from there, of occupying Algiers and Tunis. He did not suspect that, for the Spanish priests, Bonaparte was the man of the Revolution—the Antichrist in person: he would have dared lay hands on their sovereigns, that is to say, their gods. As soon as the details of the ambush became known, all of Spain exploded.

Tens and tens of thousands of men rose up at the shout of "Death to the Infidel!" And the war that followed was one of the most hideous ever. For the first time, the soldiers of the Revolution had to fight not against kings but against a people struggling for its freedom, falling on the invader at every bend in the road and slaughtering him not only with rage but with the most horrible cruelty.

But Napoleon remained obstinate; he sent reinforcements across the Pyrenees, enabling Joseph (after the Battle of Medina del Rio Seco) to enter his capital on July 20. Two days later came the news of General Dupont's surrender at Baylen: 17,242 untried soldiers, exhausted by heat and thirst and laden with booty, were taken prisoner by the 30,000 soldiers of General Castaños' "Army of Andalusia."

The Emperor was at Bordeaux when he learned of the catastrophe. His rage was immense. *"Une ignominie!"* he shouted.

He had scarcely left Bordeaux when a courier arrived with the news that the insurrection was triumphing everywhere on the other side of the Pyrenees. In his fury, the Emperor smashed a large earthenware bowl that had just been brought to him so that he could bathe his feet. The situation was in fact so bad that the day after Baylen, "Don José I" had been obliged to depart from his capital with his soldiers. And Junot's capitulation had compelled him to retreat toward the Pyrenees so rapidly that Napoleon wrote him on August 16: "The army would appear to be commanded not by generals but by postal inspectors. How can you evacuate Spain without reason— without even knowing what the enemy is doing?"

The Emperor was ready to weep for shame. "I have a stain there," he said to Josephine, putting his hand on the lapel of his coat.

The Emperor had the impression that his little "flirtation" with the Czar had started to cool a bit. Was the ardor of Tilsit, which had been almost amorous, dying out already? True, as soon as he had heard the news of Baylen, Alexander declared to Caulaincourt: "It is when things are difficult that Napoleon will be able to count on me." But he nonetheless advised the Hapsburgs—speaking through Kurakin, his ambassador at Vienna: "It seems to me that the most prudent policy for Austria is to remain a peaceable spectator of the war that Napoleon will have to fight in Spain. There will always be time, later on, to adopt the policy suggested by the circumstances."

The last part of his statement revealed the double game that the Czar was playing. For the moment, the important thing was to lull the watchfulness of the French Emperor. As for the future, they would see about that when it came! And Alexander would be perfectly happy, when his friend of Tilsit was in danger, to adopt the "policy" suggested by "the circumstances."

Vaguely sensing that the "young and good emperor" had grown lukewarm in his feelings, and anxious to keep a free hand on the other side of the Pyrenees, Napoleon suggested a meeting. Alexander agreed eagerly. For his part, he wanted carte blanche from France so that he himself could have a free hand in and around the Danubian provinces. In exchange, he would approve the conquest of Spain.

The site chosen for the talks was Erfurt, in the heart of Germany. It was also decided to summon (for late September, 1808) the kings of Bavaria, Saxony, and Württemberg, and the princes of the Confederation of the Rhine. "Before we even begin," said Napoleon, "I want Alexander to be dazzled by the spectacle of my power!"

The Emperor was thinking that he might some day ask Alexander for the hand of his sister, the Grand Duchess Catherine, and he sent Talleyrand to the Czar to lay the ground for the talks. "Mon cher

Talleyrand," he instructed him, "I want you to be at Erfurt a day or two before us. . . . You know the Emperor Alexander well, and can talk the right kind of language to him."

But now that Talleyrand's interests no longer coincided with those of his master, just what kind of language did he think was "right" for Napoleon's purposes?

> "Sire," Talleyrand said to the Czar, "what are you doing here? It is up to you to save Europe, and you can succeed in that only by standing up to Napoleon. The French people are civilized, but their sovereign is not. The sovereign of Russia is civilized, but his people are not. It is therefore fitting that the sovereign of Russia be the ally of the French people. The Rhine, the Alps, and the Pyrenees are acquisitions of France. The rest represents acquisitions by the Emperor. France does not want to keep them!"

And this was said as early as the autumn of 1808!

M. de Talleyrand, the Prince of Benevento, had decided to betray his master. Of all the irreparable errors of the past year—the creation of the Kingdom of Westphalia, to be ruled by Jérôme, that charming and amusing buffoon of a king; the appointment of the incompetent and morbidly hot-headed Junot to the Lisbon command; the occupation of Rome; and the ambush of Bayonne, followed by the ridiculous game of kings' musical chairs played at Madrid and Naples—sending Talleyrand to Erfurt on a diplomatic mission was certainly the one error that would weigh most heavily on the future of the Empire.

As Alexander listened to Napoleon's emissary in the act of revealing everything that was on his mind, he was delighted.

But Talleyrand had not finished. He proceeded to tell the Czar quite plainly that, far from keeping Austria calm, he should on the contrary urge Vienna to arm, so that Alexander might one day have with him a powerful ally—which would enable him to conquer the troublemaker of Europe.

From the very outset of the talks between the two emperors, Napoleon was astonished to find that his friend the Czar was no longer "so compliant" as he had been at Tilsit. "He has grown wary," Napoleon confided to Caulaincourt. Talleyrand had done his work.

Outwardly, harmony reigned. The crowd of kings and princes squeezed close "to come near to the one who dispensed everything: thrones, calamities, fears, hopes."

The talks lagged, and even bogged down. "A week had gone by," says Caulaincourt, "and each of them was still feeling his way, trying to ascertain the extent of his adversary's demands without being able to grasp them entirely."

The rub between the Czar and the Emperor had to do with the question of the Danubian provinces (which Alexander wanted to invade) and Napoleon's refusal to evacuate his strongholds along the Oder.

As Napoleon tried to explain to Alexander: "How can I abandon my position in Prussia—in short, weaken myself in Germany—at a time when Austria, taking advantage of my troubles in Spain, is threatening me?"

But for all that, the Czar would have preferred to see France less far advanced into the heart of Europe.

Napoleon went on: "Does my ally and my friend suggest that I abandon the only position from which I can threaten the flanks of Austria if she attacks me while my troops are in southern Europe, four hundred leagues from her?"

The Czar was reluctant to yield. Napoleon sensed that he was becoming more and more reserved. One day the Emperor lost all self-control and threw his hat on the ground.

"You are violent, and I am stubborn," Alexander said calmly. "With me, anger avails nothing. Either we talk reasonably, or I leave."

Napoleon persuaded him to stay on. But to Talleyrand, who must surely have laughed up his sleeve, he confided: "I haven't accomplished a thing! I have turned him every which way, but he has a limited mind. I simply cannot make any progress!"

"Sire," replied Talleyrand with great gravity, "I would say that Your Majesty has accomplished a great deal since coming here, because the Emperor Alexander is completely spellbound!"

"He has duped you," was Napoleon's answer. "If he is so fond of me, why doesn't he sign?"

And Caulaincourt heard his master sigh: "That Emperor Alexander of yours is stubborn as a mule! He plays deaf whenever anyone mentions things he doesn't want to hear. That damned business in Spain is costing me a lot!"

Finally, however, both Napoleon and Alexander yielded, and a treaty was signed. Russia could take over Finland and the Danubian provinces, and France was free to conquer Spain. As for Austria, if she objected to this partition, or if she dared attack the French Empire, the Czar and Napoleon would join forces against her. "Everything is going well," Napoleon wrote to Josephine, "and I am satisfied with Alexander. For that matter, he should be satisfied with me! If he were a woman, I think I would take him as a mistress. I will be with you soon. Be well. I want to see you plump and blooming."

Napoleon had tried his best to talk to the Czar about a possible marriage with the Grand Duchess Catherine; but, suddenly shy, he had not dared venture further. It was Talleyrand who received Alexander's reply to this delicate question: "If it were up to me alone, I would gladly give my consent. But my consent is not the only one that must be obtained."

There was no doubt that Catherine detested "Buonaparte." But in that age no one bothered to ask the opinion of young ladies as to their marriage—and especially not when it involved a princess. Above all, it was the Empress Mother who would never permit such a union with the "Corsican adventurer."

On October 14, "satisfied with their arrangements but dissatisfied with each other," the two emperors took leave of each other on the road to Weimar, after having embraced before their general staffs. They would never see each other again.

The Austrian Chancellor, Count Stadion, received Baron Vincent, who had been sent to Erfurt as an "informer." Vincent summarized the talks that had just been concluded: "Although war may not play a part in Napoleon's calculations, it definitely must play a part in ours." One should not always look in the same direction when trying to find out who was responsible for the Napoleonic wars.

As for Austria, there would be another encounter at Wagram. But in the meantime "Don José I" had to be put back on his throne.

And yet the war in Spain was extremely unpopular in France. The soldiers of the Grand Army—those soldiers whose lack the Emperor would feel so acutely in his wars of 1809 and 1812 against Austria and Russia—had no enthusiasm for the fighting beyond the Pyrenees. They were not spilling their blood for a French cause, but in order to save the crown of the incompetent Joseph. Discipline began to break down during this frightful campaign.

Napoleon insisted that his brother not budge until Madrid had been recaptured from "that vile mob of braggarts" guilty of loyalty to their legitimate monarchy. But Joseph's lesson—his headlong flight the day after Baylen—had taught him nothing. He thought of himself as a great captain, and no longer spoke of his "grave." In a matter of days, following his tactic, Napoleon destroyed the Anglo-Spanish left flank commanded by Blake, annihilated the enemy's right flank commanded by Palafox, and then drove toward the center, where Count Belvedere was in command of the Army of Estremadura. Bessières, Mouton, and Lasalle made the breakthrough, and the Spaniards fled toward Madrid. Once having crossed the wild Sierra de Guadarrama, Napoleon reached the capital; and on December 3, in a tent pitched outside the gates of the city, he accepted the capitulation of Madrid.

But what was he going to do with Joseph, who had been authorized to rejoin his brother?

Joseph proposed that he abdicate—a renunciation that the Emperor should never have refused. Later, Napoleon would regret it bitterly: "He was the most incompetent man imaginable, and just the opposite of what was needed!" And so Joseph became king again. But the majority of his people regarded him as "king by the grace of the devil" and treated him as a "crowned slave."

For the moment, Napoleon had decided to drive the English out of the Peninsula. Coming from Portugal, Sir John Moore had sent 30,000 men into Spain, and 5,000 redcoats had landed at La Coruña. At the moment of his rapid departure from the château of Chamartin on December 22, 1808, Napoleon wrote to Josephine: "They are pretending to be brave so as to hide their fear." In order to forestall the enemy's marching on Madrid, to make him retreat, and force him back to the sea, Napoleon had to cross the Sierra once again.

It was a frightful march. When Napoleon reached the foot of the Guadarrama he learned that the battalions of the advance guard, repulsed by the torrents and blinded by the snow, had fallen back. The Emperor ordered that all men in the same platoon should hang on to each other's arms so as not to be blown away by the wind. The cavalry had to dismount and march in the same way, leading their horses by the bridle. Halfway up the slope, Napoleon straddled a cannon, and his staff officers did likewise. "We marched ahead in this grotesque array," says Marbot, "and finally we reached the monastery on the summit of the mountain."

The senseless, inhuman struggle through the raging elements

went on for the next few days. Napoleon forged ahead, straining himself and suffering like his men, and pretending not to hear their curses.

By December 28 he was galloping toward Valderas, leaving all the troops behind him. The cavalry had a hard time keeping up with his headlong pace. Napoleon was a poor horseman, and the cavalrymen of his retinue always had to bring along five or six spare mounts for him; whenever he took a fall, they would bring up another horse, already saddled.

On January 2, 1809, shortly before reaching Astorga, the Emperor received numerous dispatches: Austria was rearming more heavily than ever, and the Czar's lack of cordiality had become evident. And he heard an even more serious piece of news, that Talleyrand and Fouché had become reconciled. They had been seen walking arm in arm and chatting in the most friendly way. What were they plotting?

Fouché affirms in his memoirs that he had warned Napoleon about the hornets' nest of Spain. But now he was having thoughts about the possible death of the Emperor—an emperor without an heir. A new war with Austria seemed inevitable. And yet Napoleon still seemed insistent upon postponing the repudiation of Josephine. Were the two cronies, reconciled by their common interests, thinking of Murat or Bernadotte as Napoleon's successor? Were they already (in late 1808) thinking of the demigod's fall?

The Emperor sensed the danger and decided to return to Paris immediately, leaving Soult to pursue the English—which, as it turned out, he failed to do with any real vigor, since instead of crushing them he let them escape and take ship at La Coruña.

Napoleon had left behind him the best of his soldiers: men who had fought at Austerlitz, Jena, and Friedland—men he would sorely miss at Wagram. In Spain, those ill-fated troops would experience the most atrocious of wars.

Captain François tells us:

> I saw French officers, soldiers, and even women disembow-
> eled. The women were eviscerated from the womb to the stom-
> ach, and their breasts were cut off. Some of the men were placed
> between two boards and sawed in two; others had their genitals
> cut off and put in their mouths; others were buried alive up to the

shoulders; and still others were hung up by the feet in fireplaces, and their heads burned.

The survivors, in their turn, adopted the methods of this inhuman warfare.

"What a war!" said Lannes sadly. "To have to kill so many brave, impetuous men! Victory brings only sorrow!"

In this struggle beyond the Pyrenees, victories were soon followed by defeats. As Napoleon admitted later: "This miserable war has ruined me. All my disasters can be traced back to that fatal cause. It has complicated my troubles, divided my forces, and destroyed French morale in Europe."

Fouché was the first to be summoned to the Tuileries (on January 27, 1809), where, cringing, he took a browbeating. And yet the Emperor did not cashier him. He had too much need of Fouché, and so refused to apply to him his own formula: "Those whom one can no longer reward should be dismissed."

The next day, it was Talleyrand's turn. Cambacérès, Lebrun, Montesquiou, Décrès, and Fouché witnessed the terrible scene.

After declaring that his ministers must "cease to give free rein to their thoughts and expressions," Napoleon made it plain that they must consider themselves as reflections of their master. If they "doubted" him, they were betraying him! Then, in a violent rage, the Emperor began pacing back and forth between the fireplace and the console against which Talleyrand was leaning, "pale as death" and afraid to say a word in reply.

Talleyrand had claimed he had "not been involved" in the murder of the Duc d'Enghien. Suddenly the Emperor bethought himself of the man killed at Vincennes, and his rage mounted still higher:

> That poor, hapless man! And who was it that notified me where he was living? Who urged me to deal harshly with him? "Not involved" in the murder of the Duc d'Enghien, you say? But aren't you forgetting that you advised me—in writing—to have him killed? "Not involved" in the Spanish war, either? But aren't you forgetting that you advised me to go back to the policy of Louis XIV? Aren't you forgetting that you were the intermediary in all the negotiations that resulted in the present war? What are your schemes? What is it you want? What are you hoping for? Do

you dare tell me? After what you have done, I should break you into a thousand pieces. And I have the power to do it. But I despise you too much to take the trouble! Do you know what you are? You're a turd in a silk stocking!

Talleyrand blanched, but still said nothing. He merely watched while Napoleon insulted him for three frightful hours. Until the Emperor fired a last broadside: "You never told me that the Duke of San Carlos was your wife's lover."

This time, Talleyrand replied: "As a matter of fact, Sire, it never occurred to me that such a report could have any bearing on Your Majesty's pride or my own!"

Napoleon was finally at a loss for words. He went to the door. Then, looking at both Talleyrand and Fouché, he said threateningly: "Remember this! If there should be a revolution, you would be the first to be crushed by it, whatever the role you might have played!"

The next day Talleyrand went to see Metternich. He told him: "The time has come. . . . I feel it is my duty to enter into direct relations with Austria."

As a starter, he asked Metternich for a few hundred thousand francs. The diplomat placed a value of no more than 400,000 francs on Talleyrand's treason.

Fouché, too, went to see Metternich, but he was not so bold as to ask for a subsidy. He contented himself with remarking ironically: "When 'one' has made war on you, there will still be Russia. . . . and then China."

Since the Grand Army was confined in the Spanish weir, the Emperor had to forge a new army. The princes of the Confederation of the Rhine promised to supply their Protector with 100,000 men. But how much could be expected of these Saxons, Bavarians, and Württembergers? By calling up the 1810 age-class in advance, by putting in uniform some of the Frenchmen favored by the lottery in the course of the past three years, and by recalling the few units left in Germany, plus the Guard from Spain, the Emperor was able to muster from 250,000 to 280,000 troops, most of whom had never smelled gunpowder. At the same time, he had to send troops to Prince Eugène, who would surely have to face an Austrian army.

In Austria, the government, the army, and the people were eager for war. The Austrian Emperor had been able to assemble 300,000 men who were infinitely more enthusiastic about fighting than were the French draftees and those called back to the colors.

On Wednesday, April 12, a courier sent by Berthier reached the Tuileries: the Austrians had crossed the Inn and occupied Munich.

"The war has begun," the Emperor observed.

He decided to leave before dawn, saying, "I'm going off to Vienna with nothing but my little draftees, my name, and my big boots."

XVII

THE MIRACLE OF WAGRAM

In war, one must bear down on the obstacle
in order to overcome it.

NAPOLEON

IN EACH DIVISION, a twenty-one-gun salute was fired to announce the Emperor's arrival; and the following message was read, between two rolls of the drums, to the front lines of the regiments:

> Soldiers, the territory of the Confederation has been violated. The Austrian general is hoping that we will flee at the sight of his weapons—that we will abandon our allies. I have moved with the speed of lightning.
>
> Soldiers! You were with me when the sovereign of Austria came to my bivouac in Moravia; you heard him beg mercy of me and swear eternal friendship to me. Austria owed everything to our generosity when we were victorious in three wars; and three times she has gone back on her word! Our victories in the past are a sure pledge of the triumph that awaits us. Forward! And at the sight of us, let the enemy recognize his conquerors!

The "four-day campaign" was about to begin—four days during which Napoleon once again became General Bonaparte.

By Wednesday the nineteenth he was at Ingolstadt. There at the confluence of the Danube and the Abens, he surveyed what would become, the next day, the battlefield of Abensberg. Sitting exhausted in an armchair that a baker had offered him, he watched his troops file past. They acclaimed him with cheers.

That night Marshal Lannes, who had come from Spain, reached the château of Vohburg, which had become the "palace." Napoleon greeted him affectionately. Lannes was the only one of his old com-

panions-at-arms that he still addressed with the familiar *tu*, as in the
old days.

The field marshal was discouraged. The siege of Saragossa, which
had lasted fifty-two days, had been hideous. Fifty-four thousand inhabitants had perished, and the city was a heap of ruins.

"I don't know whether it's a political war," Lannes admitted, "but
it's an inhuman war and an irrational one, because in order to win
a crown you have first to kill off a nation defending itself—a sad
business and a lengthy one. Conscience is mightier than force."

Napoleon tried to justify himself. Was it he who had started the
war?

"Sire, they are comparing you to Ghengis Khan, and the French
to the Mongols."

To hell with Spain! It was Austria that mattered now. "You will
accomplish great things," Napoleon told Lannes by way of assuaging
his feelings. "No one knows the road to Vienna better than you. At
Vienna we shall discuss the conditions of a peace that Austria will
never be able to violate!"

But Lannes had lost heart. It seemed to him that it would be
impossible to achieve peace in Europe so long as French soldiers
were mounting guard at Warsaw and Madrid. He would not agree
to take a new command until the Emperor had given him the best
troops of the army.

"Sire," he finally said in a low voice, "I shall do everything you
order me to."

The next day, April 20, Lannes was the chief architect of the
Battle of Abensberg, which split the Austrian army into two fragments. In forty-eight hours the archduke lost more than 13,000 men.

The Austrians had retreated across the swampy plain to Regensburg, but Napoleon did not pursue them until the next day. Why the
delay? Was he oppressed by an ever more hideous vision of war? Was
it because of the heaps of dead men on the ground? Was it fatigue?
Although he always gave unstintingly of himself to accomplish his
work (which, as he often said, was his element), he had come to know
fatigue in his body and legs.

On April 23 he resumed the march and advanced on Regensburg.
He was seen to make boldly for the high ramparts of the city, which
were strongly defended. Was he himself going to set up a ladder
against the wall, as Lannes had just done? At that moment, a bullet

fired from the top of the wall wounded him in the heel, "grazing" the Achilles tendon, as he told Josephine. Dr. Yvan ran up to him.

"That could have been a Tyrolese," he said to the doctor. "Those people shoot very straight."

The Emperor refused to leave the spot. He sat down on a drum and had his wound dressed. Then, disregarding everyone's protests, he got up on his horse and, without putting his boot back on, headed for Lannes' corps to show himself to the soldiers.

The soldiers, who had heard of the incident, cheered him at length. Galvanized, the troops rushed to storm the city, which was soon aflame.

And so the fourth day of the campaign came to a close—"in the sorrowful brightness of fires."

The enemy, retreating toward Bohemia, crossed the Danube, leaving the right bank to the Emperor, and headed for Wagram, a village situated in the north and almost at the gates of Vienna. Thus the road to the capital was open—a road that battles would leave strewn with corpses.

The imperial family was fleeing from the *Krampus,* the Austrians' word for a horned devil. The most appalled of them was the Archduchess Marie Louise. This time she was no longer of an age to burn her dolls, saying that she was "roasting the Corsican," as she had done the day after Austerlitz. But she declared that the French were "waging war like the Huns." What a sad thing for her when she learned that the "Antichrist" was besieging Vienna for the second time, and had again taken up quarters in her dear palace of Schönbrunn!

Vienna capitulated on May 13; and that same day, accompanied by Lannes, Napoleon made a reconnaissance along the Danube. Downstream from the city, the river—dotted with islets—divided into several arms. One of these formed the shore of a rather large island measuring four by six kilometers. This was the island of Lobau, which would find a place in history.

The Austrians, who had massed 150,000 troops on the left bank, had neglected to occupy the island in force. The Emperor therefore (who seemed in this case to be defending Vienna) chose this site for crossing the river and attacking the archduke.

On May 18, General Molitor's division, consisting of 45,000 men, crossed the main arm of the river and easily drove from the island the few Austrian troops who were there. They immediately set about building two pontoon bridges which would enable the army, first, to reach the Lobau by crossing the main arm and, second, to pass over to the left bank of the river.

That same day, Napoleon left Schönbrunn and took up quarters in the village of Ebersdorf, from where he himself could supervise the building of the bridges. On the night of May 20 the first bridge was completed, and the Emperor crossed the Danube at the head of his general staff. At the head of the bridge across the main arm of the river, he set up his headquarters.

When Napoleon crossed this bridge, he came to "a superb plain." It was in fact a vast expanse of flat fields ending, to the north, in a kind of embankment: "the plateau of Wagram." A good thousand meters distant from the riverbank, where the French were standing, two steeples indicated the center of two villages, Aspern and Essling, then occupied by the enemy.

Masséna was commanding the left wing, toward Aspern, and Lannes the right wing, toward Essling. About half the troops had to be left behind as a rear guard. To bring 80,000 men into the area over two bridges—and under fire from the Austrians at that—seemed insane. And Napoleon admitted later: "It was a mistake to throw only one bridge over the small arm of the river."

Sunday, May 21, 90,000 Austrians rushed forward to meet the French as they emerged onto the plain after crossing the small bridge. "Thunderbolts struck our troops," one of the participants said. It was out-and-out carnage. The villages were taken and retaken five times. There was bloody fighting in the cemetery of Aspern beside the little church, whose belfry was being used as an observation post by Masséna. In Essling there was equally hard fighting before the long façade of a farmhouse belonging to the Hapsburgs. At the far end of the farmyard, in the direction of the open country, along the road to Gross-Enzersdorf, was the old imperial granary, which the infantrymen of Boudet's division had taken cover. The dents made by Austrian bullets can still be seen on the two iron doors of the building.

Enemy troops were continuing to flow onto the battlefield, while the French troops (because of the bottleneck of the one small bridge) were not so much flowing as trickling onto the plain. As a result, the

Emperor could not employ his usual tactic: to crush the enemy's center, and then attack the two flanks. For the moment, owing to a lack of reinforcements, his troops were fighting in a ratio of one to four under the downpour of shot from the archduke's 300 fieldpieces.

The butchery went on for hours. When night fell, the two flaming villages cast a glare of light over the plain, where the artillery had ceased firing. On the morning of May 22 the Emperor still had only 34,000 combat-ready troops to use against the Archduke Charles's 90,000 men. Yet the day's fighting began brilliantly. The Austrians gave evidence of wanting to abandon the battle—before the villages, at any rate—and under cover of an artillery barrage withdrew toward Wagram. The archduke had already conceded the battle, when suddenly he was astonished to see the French attack slow down, falter, and then stop.

The little bridge had been damaged. Not only that, but the big bridge—700 meters in length—linking the island to the right bank had been swept away. The Austrians had delivered regular battering-ram blows against the structure, using large boats loaded with rocks and tree trunks, which were launched upstream and then borne rapidly along by the fast current of the Danube.

The day before, the bridge had been hit and breached, but it had been possible to patch up the gap rather quickly. This time, however, the damage was irreparable: the big bridge had been swept away in its entirety, at a moment when both infantry and artillery were running short of ammunition. Even though the battle might go on, the artillery would undoubtedly have to cease firing. Hence it was necessary to withdraw to the island and dig in, before giving battle again later on.

As the withdrawal began, Lannes was ordered to contain the enemy drive, holding (temporarily) the line along the ditch between Aspern and Essling. The Austrians, who had learned the reason for the halt in the French offensive, exulted and furiously attacked the French forces calmly pulling back to the Danube.

Shot was falling thickly around the Emperor, his staff, and the Guard, thinning out the ranks. Impassive, he observed the movements of the various units with his field glass. Two battalions consisting entirely of wounded men who had just come from the front lines passed in front of him. Among them was the hapless Dupin, his elbow seriously wounded by a bullet. Like his comrades, he was done in by fatigue, suffering, and hunger—since, as he said, "all I had had to eat or drink for three days was water from the Danube."

When an able man was noticed among the wounded, he would be sent back into battle.

Napoleon's horse whinnied: it had been hit. A shout went up: "Lay down arms unless the Emperor withdraws immediately!"

He obeyed. But a few minutes later he was back—near the little bridge, which had by this time been repaired, and over which the retreat was being effected in orderly fashion. But alas! On the left bank they had left 16,000 dead—almost one soldier out of two. Although the archduke had lost 27,000 men, he was the official victor, since he occupied the same positions as before the battle.

Suddenly, Napoleon paled: there on a stretcher was Lannes, seriously wounded by a cannonball which had smashed both of his legs.

The Emperor dismounted from his horse, ordered the stretcher placed on the ground, and rushed over to it. He got down on his knees and tearfully embraced his old comrade.

"Montebello, do you recognize me?"

"Yes, Sire. You are losing your best friend."

"No! You'll live!"

When Napoleon got to his feet, his waistband stained with his friend's blood, he said: "They'll pay dearly for this!"

While the retreat was being completed under the command of Masséna, the Emperor was in a boat heading for the right bank of the Danube. Throughout the crossing, he remained standing in the bow of the boat, saying nothing. The night was dark, and the only sound that could be heard was that of the oars' rhythmic strokes in the water. The handful of officers making the crossing with the Emperor respected his grief and exchanged only a few words in a whisper.

Lannes was going to die. And the whole army—or rather, what troops had survived after the carnage of Aspern and Essling—was stuck on the island. Lights began to show from the fires at the bivouacs—those bivouacs where sorrow reigned.

When he reached the right bank the Emperor took Savary's arm and, leaning heavily on it, set out along a sunken road through the woods toward the village of Kaiser-Ebersdorf, where his headquarters had again been established.

The next day, his first care was to have a boat sent to the island of Lobau so that Marshal Lannes could be brought to Kaiser-Ebersdorf. The quarters to which they carried him were on the second floor of an old brick building. Lannes' leg was amputated, and soon thereafter so was the other. For a few days there was hope of saving the great soldier's life; but on the night of May 27, gangrene set in and the patient became delirious.

Napoleon came hurrying from the nearby château where he had taken up quarters for some two weeks.

"There is no need to ask you to look after my wife and children," Lannes told him. "Since I am dying for you, your pride makes it your duty to protect them."

Then (Constant tells us) he heaped violent reproaches on the Emperor.

"Lannes shouted at me," Napoleon later told Metternich. "And I instantly told myself: 'Lannes is going to die,' because he was scolding me the way an atheist scolds God, without having believed in him once in his life."

"That has the ring of truth," said Metternich (from whose correspondence this account is taken). "But what exactly did Lannes say?"

" 'You have made a great mistake; but even though it is costing you your best friend, it will not teach you anything. Your ambition is insatiable, and it will be the end of you. Unsparingly, and unnecessarily, you sacrifice the men who serve you best; and when they die, you feel no sense of loss.' "

Lannes lived three days more. On May 31, Napoleon wrote to the Duchesse de Montebello (Mme. Lannes):

Ma cousine,

The marshal died this morning from wounds received on the field of honor. My grief is the same as yours. I have lost the most distinguished general of all my armies, my comrade-at-arms for sixteen years, and the man I regarded as my best friend. . . .

On May 17, four days before the Battle of Essling, Napoleon had issued from Schönbrunn a decree annexing Rome and the Papal States to the Empire. A short time before that, he had dictated his wishes in the matter:

The following ultimatum is to be delivered to the Pope: "Either the Pontiff agrees to join an offensive and defensive league against the enemies of France, or we shall break off relations." If the Pope refuses, it will mean he wants war; and the first result of conquest is a change of government.

The Pope refused.

On the morning of June 10, the French troops patrolling the Eternal City seemed to be even more martial than usual. Dispatch riders went by at a gallop. An artillery volley rattled the window-panes. At the Castel Sant'Angelo the pontifical standard was lowered; then the French tricolor was hoisted.

The Pope could hear, from a distance, the shouts of the heralds:

> Romans, you are invited to join in the triumph without having shared the dangers. . . . Run through the annals of your victories: for a long time, now, they have been merely those of your misfortunes. . . . Today, joined together with France, you are made strong by her. The troubles resulting from your weakness are at an end. . . . Romans, you have not been conquered but brought into the fold. . . .

The decree issued from Schönbrunn had gone into effect: Rome had become a French city.

Pius VII would defend himself with his own weapons. He signed the text pronouncing major excommunication against Napoleon.

The news of the annexation of Rome to the French Empire perhaps caused Europe to look upon Napoleon as a greater threat than ever; but it did help to offset somewhat the news of the setback at Essling. A man who, with one stroke of the pen, could downgrade the Eternal City to the rank of a prefecture was by no means vanquished! All the more so, since the tricolor was flying over Vienna.

But Essling *had* been a defeat. (The Austrians call it the victory of Aspern.) The news of that battle brought hope to the Faubourg St.-Germain in France, and to the Emperor's enemies elsewhere in Europe. England considered invading the Continent, and could already imagine the Bourbons back in Paris. Scharnhorst, the Prussian Minister of War, wrote to his king:

> I should not like to go to my grave dishonored, and I would be doing just that if I did not advise Your Majesty to take advantage of the present situation and make war on France. Do you want a victorious Austria to hand your states back to you like alms to a beggar?

To which Frederick William replied cautiously: "One more Austrian victory, and I shall join in."

During the days that followed Essling, the Czar firmly decided not to keep faith with the Treaty of Erfurt. Was he not obliged to take up arms against Austria, in view of the undoubted fact that the Emperor Francis was responsible for the aggression that had unleashed the new war? But no! He would not budge. He, too, was waiting for "one more victory."

"That isn't much of an alliance that I have with him!" Napoleon remarked bitterly.

All of them were hoping for a quick kill and sharing of the spoils. As Napoleon said, "They have all made an appointment to meet on my grave, but they are afraid to keep it!"

They were waiting for Wagram.

Archduke Charles had assumed that the Emperor would repeat the piece of folly that had spelled his defeat at Aspern and Essling: to send an army across a broad river—an army that would once again be fighting with its back to the Danube. But instead of attacking—and an Austrian "victory of Lobau" might have been decisive—the archduke too preferred to wait things out. Both armies had to lick their wounds. But the delay would nonetheless mean defeat for Austria.

To fortify the island, which would be the staging area for the next offensive, Napoleon ordered the pontoon bridges replaced by bridges built on pilings. Batteries were positioned not only on the Lobau but on the right bank of the Danube and on the islands in midstream. The fortifications built at the point where the big bridge abuts on Lobau Island were so extensive and well built that they have resisted the ravages of time. The site is now overgrown with trees; but the remains of this imposing fortress are still to be seen. Elsewhere, the Emperor ordered the construction of three redans on the left bank, leading out from the smaller bridge.

On the island there was a constant buildup of ammunition, matériel, weapons, and stores, including wine.

With the arrival of the Italians commanded by Eugène and by Jacques Étienne Macdonald (who had just defeated Archduke John), and that of Marmont's corps from Dalmatia, Napoleon now had 150,-000 troops and 600 fieldpieces. On the enemy side Archduke Charles, whose artillery had also grown to large proportions, had mustered

160,000 men before Wagram. Then, too, he was expecting from one day to the next the arrival of his brother John, who still had 20,000 troops despite the losses inflicted by Macdonald. But Archduke John was slow in getting there. The Emperor decided to forestall him and go over to the attack.

"Woe to the man who comes to the battlefield with a system," Napoleon once said.

The archduke, misled by the construction of the three redans, expected that the French forces would emerge onto the plain before Aspern and Essling. (As Napoleon said, "He thought the mouse would come out of the same hole it had run into.") Accordingly, the Austrian generalissimo, in his turn, built "a maze of redoubts," linking Aspern and Essling by means of fortifications which he thought would enable him to stand up to the attack and win the victory. Still other breastworks, more isolated, were thrown up between Essling and Gross-Enzersdorf.

At this point Napoleon decided to cross the small arm of the Danube much farther downstream (using three or four bridges this time), so as to bring the main body of his forces around behind Aspern and Essling, with their strong defenses. He would attack the enemy's left and drive toward the plateau of Wagram, which was relatively unfortified—or so he hoped, at any rate. What he had in mind was, in short, to effect a vast flanking movement, more or less pivoting around Essling, Aspern, and Gross-Enzersdorf.

The pivot—the French left flank—would be under the command of Masséna. But the plan involved a certain risk: if the archduke's forces were not strictly contained in the villages and if he went over to the offensive, he could move down the riverbank, seize the bridges, and cut the French army off from its base on Lobau.

On Tuesday, July 4, Masséna's corps was built up by a constant influx of troops. They were so closely packed together on the island that they bumped into one another "on all sides." That same day, the archduke learned that he was opposed not merely by Masséna's forces but by the entire French army concentrated on the island of Lobau. And he ordered the bombardment of the French positions.

Toward three o'clock in the afternoon, a heavy rainstorm poured down on the army. Should the attack—scheduled for July 5 and 6— be postponed?

"No," the Emperor decided. "If we delay one more day, we'll have Archduke John on our hands!"

The French troops were as wet as if they had swum across the Danube. In his unpublished account, Corniquet, a warrant officer of the Guard, says: "The heavy rain soon soaked us to the bone. Thunder was rumbling everywhere. Shells and bullets were falling like hail. . . ." When night came down over the island, the cloudburst was still unabated. But in spite of it, six new bridges were thrown across the small arm of the Danube. And in the deep of night, under a downpour of rain, the army began to cross the river via the new bridges, and to overrun the Austrian left flank.

The Battle of Gross-Enzersdorf, which preceded the Battle of Wagram, took place on Wednesday, July 5.

The army continued its movement, and the battalions flowed onto the plain—precisely at the point where the enemy was not expecting them. "In grain up to the neck," as Corniquet says, the army marched and countermarched, and took up its positions. By nine o'clock, 150,000 men were in line of battle. Once again, the next two days would decide the fate of the Empire.

By now, a bright July sun was shining, drying out uniforms. More than 300,000 soldiers were facing one another. As Captain Tascher put it: "Three hundred thousand men who did not hate one another —who might have become friends if they had known one another— were crowded into the narrow space of three square leagues, ready to kill one another the moment the signal was given." The vast flanking movement began—an implacable movement that has been compared very accurately to "a gigantic scythe with Masséna's troops as the handle."

The plan was carried out brilliantly. The fortified village of Gross-Enzersdorf was the first to be captured. Under the artillery barrages, the archduke pulled back. By the end of the afternoon, his army was in danger of being cut in two. The center seemed to be cracking. It was then that the Emperor ordered the Saxons, commanded by Bernadotte, to storm the plateau of Wagram, at the foot of which flows the Rüssbach.

With his eye to his field glass, the Emperor watched the Saxons move ahead without difficulty. Surely it would all be over before nightfall! The Saxons were followed by the Italians under Macdonald.

But Macdonald's troops, seeing strange uniforms on the "crest," took the Saxons for Austrians and fired on them.

With this, Bernadotte's troops were caught in a cross fire and they panicked. They headed back toward the Italians, who, believing this was a charge, about-faced and fled in disorder. The Austrians, mouths agape at this sudden rout, witnessed a stampede which swept everything along with it and even compelled Oudinot, who had been holding his position, to pull back and form a new line. The day ended with this bit of bad luck.

That night, in his tent pitched in the middle of the plain between Raschdorf and Grosshöfen, Napoleon gave vent to his wrath. And yet it was he himself who deserved the blame. If he had had the army of Friedland with him, instead of Saxons and Italians, the battle would have been over. But he had preferred to leave the veterans of Friedland squirming in the hornets' nest of Spain.

He calmed down, however, at the thought that he had managed in twenty-four hours to amass his entire army before Wagram. Victory would come tomorrow. At one in the morning he went to sleep. But at four, on that morning of July 6, he was awakened by a heavy barrage: the Austrians had gone over to the offensive, coming down from the plateau and attacking Davout's corps.

The Emperor leaped on his mount. The battle—the Battle of Wagram this time—was soon raging. Over a front of some 15 kilometers, 1,100 fieldpieces were unleashing a hurricane of iron.

The extreme French left flank, under the command of Masséna, gave way—18,000 men were being attacked by 60,000!

"Sire," an aide-de-camp reported, "the enemy is moving down the Danube and threatening our rear. All the artillery of Boudet's division has been captured."

The Austrians now seemed to be defending Vienna, while the French seemed intent on attacking the left bank of the Danube. Between the river and the villages, the Austrian army bogged down.

"Just hold firm," Napoleon shouted to Masséna, "and the battle is won!"

There were those who thought he was mad. But he was right. In pulling back on the left, and drawing the enemy toward the Danube, he would free his right flank, which could then drive toward Wagram and make the final breakthrough.

In order to cut the Austrian army in two and hence be able to drive toward the "plateau," the Emperor amassed a formidable concentration of artillery over a front of 1,400 meters: some 100 pieces, lined up as though for a parade. This was the famous battery of Wagram which, as it thundered, rained fire down on the Austrians.

The enemy's center gave way. Into the breach charged Macdonald's cavalry, banners waving, with drummers in the lead. To the left, Masséna had not merely held the line: he had driven the enemy back to the village of Breitenlee. To the right—at the other end of the scythe—Davout and Oudinot were going up the gradual slope of the plateau, routing the enemy. Davout was the first to reach Wagram.

While all this was happening the weary Emperor, certain of victory, stretched out on a bearskin rug. In spite of the terrible noise, he napped for twenty minutes, protected by a pyramid of drums.

On every hand, the fragments of the Austrian army were in retreat, pursued by the victors. The miracle of Wagram had been accomplished. And it *was* a miracle—one that had come within a hair's breadth of being a catastrophe.

Wagram was the last great victory of Napoleon's reign. But at what a cost! What a horrible butchery! Of the two armies, more than 50,000 killed and wounded were left lying on the battlefield.

The Emperor went back to his tent and slept for two hours.

While he was sleeping, some hundreds of leagues away at Rome the Pope had retired for the night. But he was awakened by shouts of "Help! Treason!" And a bell was ringing furiously. General Radet and his gendarmes had been ordered to arrest Pius VII, and were trying to break into the Quirinal.

When he had been informed of the excommunication pronounced against him by the Pope, the Emperor had exclaimed: "I have just now learned that the Pope has excommunicated all of us. Actually, it is an excommunication he has pronounced against himself. No more kid gloves: he is a raving maniac who must be locked up. Have Cardinal Pacca and the Pope's other followers arrested!"

Those who had received the orders did not hesitate. Using an ax, Radet tried to break down the heavy door of the palace. One of his officers managed to get in through a low window and opened the door from inside. Then came the stampede. The gendarmes scarred the parquet floors with their heavy boots and broke up furniture with the butt ends of their rifles.

As the looting began, Radet asked for instructions from Miollis, commanding general of the French troops. Miollis replied that the Pope must be made to leave, whether or not he was willing to. Radet then made his way to the door of the Pontiff's apartments. He once again had to use his ax before the door would yield.

"What do you want of me?" the Pope asked Radet, who was still holding his ax. "Why do you come at this hour to disturb me in my dwelling?"

"Most Holy Father," replied the gendarme, "I come in the name of the French Government to reiterate to Your Holiness the proposal that you officially yield up your temporal powers."

"We cannot yield," the successor of St. Peter stated with dignity. "Nor can we abandon what is not ours. The temporal power belongs to the Church, and we are only its administrator."

Radet slowly replied: "I have orders to take Your Holiness away."

There was a silence. At length the Pope said:

> In truth, my son, those orders will hardly bring down divine blessings upon you. . . . So this is the reward for my long compliance with the Emperor and the Gallican Church? But perhaps in this respect I have been guilty in the eyes of God, and it is he who is now punishing me. I shall submit with humility. Am I to leave alone? When one does not cling to life, one clings even less to one's possessions.

The Holy Father was not even given time to go and get his breviary. A few minutes later, Radet put his prisoner in a carriage. It was the first stage on the road to captivity.

Napoleon disapproved, in spite of the orders he had given. "It was a great piece of folly," he wrote to Fouché.

The Austrian Emperor had asked for peace. The conditions laid down by the victor were frightful: they amounted to a partition. During the prolonged negotiations (Napoleon stayed three months at Schönbrunn) Francis I tried to struggle. He was astounded by the proposed terms and maintained quite rightly that Wagram had not been equivalent to Austerlitz. But Napoleon, more uncompromising in 1809 than in 1805, wanted to let Europe know that he had trounced

Austria even more thoroughly than before, and he threatened to force Francis to abdicate. He wrote to Champagny:

> You can tell M. Metternich that if the Emperor Francis wants to abdicate in favor of the Grand Duke of Würzburg, I will hand over to the latter the country just as it is, with its present independence, and will make an alliance with him enabling us to straighten out the affairs of the Continent.

If Francis wanted to save his throne, rather than to sacrifice himself for Austria, he would have to yield and sign the terrible Treaty of Vienna. He did. Bavaria received the district of Salzburg, and northern Galicia was added to the Duchy of Warsaw. The Czar, an honorary combatant who had done nothing, got 400,000 Galicians as a kind of tip—and was furious at seeing the Duchy of Warsaw expand. Thus Austria had to give up 300,000 square kilometers and 3,500,000 inhabitants. Trieste, Carniola, a part of Carinthia and of Croatia, Istria, and Fiume were annexed to the French Empire, and together with Dalmatia (taken from Austria in 1805) made up the "French" Illyrian Provinces. In this way, Francis lost all his holdings along the Adriatic. "We want to control the Mediterranean," Napoleon explained. "We want to maintain the independence of Turkey."

He thought that these frightful conditions, along with the arrest of the Pope, would intimidate Europe. He was deluding himself. All those he had conquered during these past few years, arming themselves with patience, were awaiting the inevitable halloo signaling the death of the stag and "the end of all this," as he would one day tell Talleyrand. After all, had not Wagram been a kind of miracle? Was not Portugal lost? And were not things going from bad to worse in Spain? As for the sovereign superprefects that Napoleon had put on their thrones, with each passing day they were succumbing further to the illusion that they were real kings, and were kicking over the traces. With utter solemnity, Napoleon reproached Louis with having become a Hollander (Louis had refused to apply the blockade) and Joseph with having become a Spaniard.

"The sovereign of Spain must be a complete Spaniard," was the constant reply of "Don José I."

In the days following Wagram, Jérôme had gone back to Kassel, after having been defeated by the Austrian general Kienmeyer. Not only that, but he was furious that his brother the Emperor had not placed Junot under his orders. Napoleon therefore wrote to him:

> You wage war like a satrap. Stop being ridiculous. . . . You had better get it into your head that, as a soldier, I have no brother. None of your futile or ridiculous pretexts will ever conceal from me the motives for your conduct. I am very much afraid there is nothing to be expected from you.

Even Élisa, Princess of Lucca, was given an imperial scolding: "You are a subject; and like all the other French, you must obey the orders of the ministers. A writ of arrest issued by the Ministry of Police would easily suffice not only for your own arrest but for that of the first prince of the blood."

Austria, now dismembered, had become a second-rate power. It was being said that Napoleon would go to see the imperial family, who had taken refuge at Erlau. The Archduchess Marie Louise quivered at the thought. "I assure you," she wrote, "that seeing that person would be a worse torture than all the martyrdoms."

Every morning, at ten o'clock, the Emperor viewed the parade held in the park of Schönbrunn, filing past the horseshoe-shaped stairs, or in the courtyard of the "imperial palace" at whose entrance stood two obelisks surmounted by Napoleonic eagles.

On the morning of Thursday, October 12, when the Emperor was reviewing the Guard as usual, Rapp was disconcerted by the strange attitude of a young German with a face like a girl's who had managed to get close to Napoleon. Several times he was heard to repeat that he wanted to talk to the Emperor. He kept his right hand in his coat pocket. "He looked at me," Rapp said later, "with a disturbing gaze." The young man's eyes were light blue. He was pale; and yet his effeminate features seemed to give no cause for anxiety.

Nonetheless, Rapp signaled to a gendarme officer, and the stranger was arrested. When he was frisked, he was found to be carrying a big butcher knife wrapped in several sheets of gray paper. His name was Frederick Staps.

"Why did you want to kill me?" the Emperor asked him.

"To kill you is not a crime. On the contrary, it is the duty of every good German. I wanted to kill you because you are the oppressor of Germany."

"I wasn't the one who started the war."

The Emperor had his would-be assassin shot. He failed utterly to learn from this attempted assassination that he was a despot who was oppressing Europe. He learned only one thing: that he and his gigantic empire might be destroyed by the dagger of a fanatic. Consequently, he had to have an heir!

His desire to forge the first link in a dynasty was perhaps never so urgent as it was during these days following Wagram. The mere thought that some day one of his brothers—or even one of his nephews—might succeed him and rule France threw him into a nervous fit. For that matter, he had recently come to judge the clan at their true worth. One day when the whole family was together, he told them:

> I don't believe there is any other man in the world as unlucky as I am when it comes to family matters. To sum it up: Lucien is an ingrate; Joseph is a Sardanapalus; Louis is a legless cripple; and Jérôme is a wretch. As for you, mesdames, you know what you are.

The Emperor sighed and continued, "Eugène does not bear my name. And, for all the trouble I have taken to ensure the security of France, my death would be followed by total anarchy. Only a son of mine could establish harmony throughout the country."

And then in that month of October, 1809, Marie Walewska, who the month before had come to Schönbrunn, and who had taken up residence in the charming village of Moëdling, gave him a piece of news that overjoyed him: she was pregnant by him!

Every day, he sent Constant—in a carriage with no armorial bearings—to pick up his beloved Marie. The road was bad. Full of anxiety that she might have an accident, he would tell his valet: "Be very careful tonight, Constant. It rained today, and the road must be difficult. Are you sure of your coachman? Is the carriage in good condition?"

And so he could procreate! Sterility was not (as he had come to think it must be) the price of his genius. From now on, he could have no doubts as to his ability to engender an heir. No such doubts were possible with his Marie, his Polish wife. Now he must do everything possible to provide himself with a successor.

In order to do that, he obviously had to repudiate Josephine and break off that sterile union.

"Throughout my life," he used to say, "I have sacrificed every-thing—serenity, self-interest, and happiness—to my destiny!"

This time it was a great love that he had to sacrifice: for he still loved his dear Creole. "I advise you to be careful at night," he wrote to her from Schönbrunn, "because one of these nights you are going to hear a loud noise. . . ."

And Josephine loved him more than ever. For years, now, she had adored him; for years she had trembled with anxiety; for years she had known that some day she would have to give him up. But it was not the thought of leaving the Tuileries that made her break out into sobs so often: it was the thought of no longer seeing "Bonaparte," as she still called him. She missed the man, not the Emperor.

She realized full well the hold she had on her husband. But she also realized (as he had told her over and over) that for him "politics has no heart." The moment she saw him at Fontainebleau (he had reached the palace on November 26), she knew that her sentence had been pronounced.

The communicating door between the two apartments had been sealed on orders from the Emperor—orders issued from Schön-brunn. And no sooner had he arrived than he summoned Cam-bacérès to tell him where things stood: "I want to marry a womb!"

XVIII

THE MINOTAUR

I am marrying a womb.

NAPOLEON

NAPOLEON HAD NOT YET WARNED HIS WIFE. It was not until November 30 that he dared take the step. Josephine had surmised that the sentence was to be pronounced that same evening.

Silence reigned during dinner—"such a silence as I had never experienced before," says Constant. The Empress had wept all day. And by way of concealing as best she could her pale cheeks and red eyes, she had put on a big white hat tied under the chin.

The Emperor's eyes were almost continuously downcast. Whenever he did manage to raise his eyes, it was merely to steal a glance at the Empress "with a very evident feeling of great grief."

The officers of the household observed this gloomy and painful scene with anxiety. And throughout the meal—a meal served merely *pro forma*—all that could be heard was the sound of dishes being brought in and taken away, the monotonous voices of the waiters announcing the courses, and the clinking sound made by Napoleon as he kept tapping his knife inside his glass. Only once did he speak up. Sighing heavily, he asked one of his officers: "How is the weather?"

It was a rhetorical question, and he did not hear the answer: it was raining, and the thermometer was close to freezing.

Finally, he got up from the table. The Empress followed him, walking slowly and holding her handkerchief over her mouth "as if to keep back her sobs." Coffee was served; and a page offered the tray to the Empress, as was the custom. But the Emperor himself took the cup, poured the coffee, and added sugar, meantime keeping an eye on Josephine, who remained standing "as though in a stupor."

Napoleon gulped down the coffee and handed the cup back to the page. Then he made a gesture. He wanted to be alone with the Empress. The others left, and the door to the salon was closed.

In a pitiable voice she asked: "So then it's all over?"

He tried to explain the situation to her: "Unless I have a child, there will be nothing solid in my dynasty."

Of course. But didn't he have nephews?

"Nephews could not take my place: the nation would not understand. For the nation and the people, a child born to the purple, on the throne, in the Tuileries, is something quite different from a nephew."

The unfortunate woman—"a woman in the fullest sense of the word," as the Emperor often said—seemed to lose consciousness.

"You are squeezing me too hard," she murmured a few moments later, as the chamberlain Bausset was helping Napoleon carry the "unconscious" Josephine to her apartments.

She would have to give up everything. Napoleon had just offered her the "principality" of Rome. But she had no desire to leave France and him. It was decided that she should retire to Malmaison, retaining her rank, her house, and her pension as Empress. In addition, Napoleon would give her the rather unpleasant château of Navarre, at the gates of Évreux.

At two o'clock on December 15, the lady who was no longer anything but a name to the State got into her carriage, the Opale. The blinds were lowered, and the carriage set off at full speed toward St.-Germain. It was cold, the southwest wind was blowing, and it rained heavily during the entire trip of the repudiated Empress to Malmaison.

Two hours later, the rain—"very heavy," according to the Observatory—was still coming down when Napoleon left the Tuileries for the Trianon, after reviewing a parade in the courtyard.

Did it occur to him that in repudiating Josephine he was going to lose his lucky star? That star that had started to shine in the days after Vendémiaire, when he met her? That evening (December 15, 1809) at the Trianon, he tried instead to disperse his memories. Immediately upon his arrival, he ordered that the apartments other than his bedroom be redone. That same night he had the conservator and attendants of the palace of Versailles awakened so that he could

THE MINOTAUR

385

immediately choose and hang new pictures on the walls and make new arrangements. Perhaps he was already thinking of his future bride, who would be all the more pleased with the Trianon if nothing in it reminded her of the "modern" setting—the heritage of Josephine.

Apart from this decorator's work, the Emperor did very little for the next ten days. The life of the gigantic empire seemed suspended. He went to Malmaison to call on Josephine, who was still tearful. Pauline, being rather more obliging than was proper for a sister, brought the blond Mme. de Mathis to him. But what he called *de la petite amitie* with the Piedmontese lady was hardly satisfying—she was, he said, "lacking in desire."

A much more important preoccupation did him far better service as an antidote: Whom was he going to marry? Would it be Marie Walewska, his "Polish wife," who was already pregnant by him? Only she could replace Josephine in his affections. But such a marriage would add nothing to his glory. For a Napoleon, it is out of the question to legitimize a situation of that kind—or to marry a divorcee.

He still had hopes of marrying one of the Czar's sisters. Catherine was now married to the Duke of Oldenburg; but there was still Grand Duchess Anna, who had just turned sixteen. Her "suitor" was almost forty, but Napoleon had not been put off by the age difference. On November 4—more than three weeks before he announced to Josephine that he had made his decision—he had sent a formal proposal to St. Petersburg, with Caulaincourt acting as intermediary. The Czar was appalled, although he had actually been expecting the proposal ever since Erfurt. But he must have been even more appalled now, in thinking of the future. A refusal would entail war between the two empires sooner or later. Not only that, but it would oblige Napoleon to turn to Austria for a wife. The Hapsburgs, who always had an abundant reserve supply of archduchesses, would certainly agree to hand over one of them, and the alliance which would inevitably ensue might well be prejudicial to Russia.

So Alexander decided to stall. His sister's tender years would give him a plausible pretext for postponing the project. Napoleon had only to wait a little while. But this kind of thinking showed very little understanding of the Emperor.

Already prepared for a refusal by the Czar's long silence (the courier had been delayed by the snow, and Alexander had just left St. Petersburg), Napoleon finally received, on January 27, 1810, Ambassador Caulaincourt's first reply describing the Czar's hesitation. The ambassador maintained that Alexander had not refused to give his sister's hand in marriage to Napoleon, but that he did not know how to go about overcoming the resistance of the Empress Mother, the widow of Paul I. Displaying once again that remarkable second sight which characterized all his thoughts and actions, Napoleon surmised that Alexander would never agree to his marrying the young grand duchess. And so, without waiting for the final answer, he decided to marry the young lady whose hand had already been offered to him. For—incredibly enough—Metternich, now Austrian chancellor, had already offered his master's daughter to the "Corsican ogre" as a "sacrificial victim," in the words of the Russian Empress Mother.

Some members of the Council of State, however, were troubled at the idea of Napoleon's marrying a young lady who was, on both sides of her family, the grand-niece of Marie Antoinette.

Someone exclaimed: "Austria is no longer a great power!"

"Monsieur," said Napoleon, "it is plain to see that you were not at Wagram!"

At this point, nothing had yet been finally decided. Six days later, new dispatches from Caulaincourt reached the Tuileries. There was no question about it: the Czar was still playing for time. For Napoleon, it was essential not to be exposed to a final refusal. On February 5, therefore, he sent word to Schwarzenberg, the Austrian ambassador—conveying it by way of Eugène, in order to make it plain that Josephine was in agreement with him. He instructed his son-in-law to tell the ambassador that he was ready to marry the daughter of the Austrian Emperor. Fearful that the dispatch announcing the Czar's final refusal might arrive at any moment, he demanded that the hand of Archduchess Marie Louise be granted him immediately without waiting to hear from Vienna.

Schwarzenberg was in a terrible quandary. As Eugène described the scene: "No ambassador was ever in a more painful position. He fidgeted, perspired heavily, and offered futile objections." But he had to yield. "If I had hesitated," he explained to Metternich, "Napoleon would have made a deal with Russia or Saxony."

Josephine's son returned to the Tuileries, where Napoleon was waiting for him in a feverish state. "As soon as I had uttered the word 'yes,'" says Eugène, "the great man was overwhelmed with a joy so impetuous and insane that I remained stupefied."

That same evening, without waiting any longer, an announcement was made to the French people:

> Nuptials will be celebrated between His Majesty the Emperor Napoleon, King of Italy, Protector of the Confederation of the Rhine, and Mediator of the Swiss Confederation, and Her Imperial and Royal Highness Madame the Archduchess Marie Louise, daughter of His Majesty the Emperor Francis, King of Bohemia and Hungary.

Now Napoleon had to play out the comedy with the Czar. He dictated two dispatches, one dated twenty-four hours after the other. In the first he informed Alexander that he had abandoned his intentions of marrying Grand Duchess Anna, in view of her tender years (as though he had just discovered her age!). In the second, sent out the next day, he informed the Czar of his imminent marriage to Archduchess Marie Louise.

"You will inform him," he told Champagny, "that I have chosen the Austrian."

On the highway, the two couriers carrying these two dispatches crossed a third courier coming from the other direction: he had been sent by Caulaincourt and carried word of the Czar's final refusal.

But the main items in this astonishing matrimonial comedy still remained to be done: notifying the Emperor Francis, and announcing to the fiancée that she was to wed the man she still called the Antichrist or the *Krampus.*

> I shall leave the decision up to my daughter [said Francis I]. I shall not exert any pressure on her. Before throwing my duties as a monarch into the scales, I want to know what her feelings are. Go and see her [he told Metternich], then come back and tell me what she tells you. I would rather not notify her myself, so as to avoid seeming to influence her decision.

When Metternich came to Marie Louise to request her agreement to the extravagant project he had championed, the young lady replied nobly: "I wish only that which my duty commands me to wish. When the interest of the State is in question, I must follow it rather than my own feelings. Please entreat my father to consult his duties as Emperor and not subjugate them to considerations of my personal interest."

Berthier, "Prince of Wagram," was the man designated by Napoleon to go to Vienna and there present the official proposal to Emperor Francis. He was advised, however, to use only his title as Prince of Neuchâtel! Everyone was in a state of near-delirium. Archduke Charles, the victor of Aspern, would stand in for Napoleon and lead his niece to the altar at the wedding by proxy.

The Prince de Ligne exclaimed: "Austria is making the gift of a fine heifer to the Minotaur!" Some of the Viennese accepted the whole thing philosophically. "It's better for an archduchess to be f———ed than the monarchy," said they. But persons of a more serious cast of mind maintained that what was about to take place was the consummation of an act of adultery and the blessing of a bigamous union. Was not Napoleon still married to Josephine in the eyes of God? Had not Cardinal Fesch blessed their union on the eve of Napoleon's consecration as Emperor? And Metternich had written to the Austrian ambassador at Paris: "His Majesty—Emperor Francis —would never give his consent to a marriage which was not in conformity with the precepts of our religion."

Cambacérès was instructed to settle this thorny question. After summoning the Minister of Religion, the two ecclesiastical judges of the archdiocese of Paris, and the archiepiscopal and diocesan *promoteurs,* he told them:

> The Emperor cannot possibly have a child by the Empress Josephine. On the other hand, in founding a new dynasty he cannot abandon the hope of leaving an heir who would ensure the tranquillity, the glory, and the integrity of the Empire he has founded. He intends to remarry; and he wants to wed a Catholic. But first, his marriage to the Empress Josephine must be annulled; and it is my intention to submit the matter to the ecclesiastical court for examination and decision.

Since Pius VII was a prisoner, the ecclesiastical court, whether willingly or not, had to yield and take up the matter. But what pretexts would the Emperor and Empress invoke in requesting the annulment of their marriage? At this point Cambacérès explained: "On Saturday, December 1, 1804, the day before his consecration, His Majesty . . . worn out by the Empress' insistence, told Cardinal Fesch to give them the nuptial blessing, and the cardinal did so right there in the Empress' chambers, without witnesses and without a parish priest."

One can imagine the stupefaction of the prelates. So the master of Europe wanted them to believe that he had been constrained and forced to marry Josephine! Napoleon "ravished"! This was the usual grounds on which shy young ladies asked for annulments from the ecclesiastical court.

In any case, the court had to buckle under and declare that "the marriage between Their Majesties must be regarded as null and not validly contracted and null *quoad foedus*, owing to the absence of the competent priest and that of the witnesses required by the Council of Trent and the statutes."

On Tuesday, March 27, 1810, in a torrential rain, a carriage without armorial bearings was on its way from Compiègne to Soissons. Despite the downpour, it was making good time. In it were two men: Napoleon and his brother-in-law King Murat. They were going to meet the cortege bringing Marie Louise from Vienna. Napoleon had not had the patience to wait until the next day when, at Soissons, the new Empress was to throw herself at the feet of the Emperor and recite a little compliment. Rather than go through this ceremony scrupulously prepared by the diplomats of the two empires, Napoleon had preferred to jump into a carriage and set off to meet his wife.

All during the week beginning on Monday, March 19, when he arrived at Compiègne, Napoleon had been like a drunk man: "drunk with impatience" (although Mme. de Mathis had kept him busy at night) and "drunk with happiness." Apparently, Austerlitz and Wagram had not gone to his head so much as this marriage with the granddaughter of Charles V.

"I am providing myself with ancestors," he said arrogantly.

He was also providing himself with a family that included Louis XVI and Marie Antoinette, who by means of this strange alliance became the bridegroom's great-uncle and great-aunt. Already, even before he had made the acquaintance of his bride, he was planning the empire of the son that she "had" to give him. By the *senatus consultum* of January 30, 1810, Italy was taken back from Eugène, and the apanages of his brothers and their descendants were abolished to the advantage of the Emperor's direct heirs.

"I must now learn how to be charming," he told Hortense, his stepdaughter and sister-in-law. "My serious, stern manner would not be pleasing to a young woman. She is no doubt fond of the pleasures of youth. Come, Hortense! You are our Terpsichore—teach me to waltz!"

Josephine's daughter burst out laughing. But the Emperor insisted, and she had to do what he said. Napoleon probably hadn't danced since he had been at military school.

He couldn't sit still. He kept going to look over the apartments prepared for the new Empress, where dresses, lingerie, and shoes made after models sent from Vienna were awaiting her.

One day he picked up an especially tiny shoe and "by way of a caress" slapped it across the face of his valet. "Look, Constant!" he said. "This shoe is a good portent. Have you ever seen feet that small? You could take one of them in your hand!"

On that Tuesday when he raced through Soissons in his carriage, he was like a lover running to his first tryst.

Under the same downpour, Marie Louise's cortege, coming from Strasbourg, was rolling along toward Soissons. Seated in the carriage sent by her imperial fiancé, and having as her companion the unbearable Caroline Murat, who kept trying to lord it over "that snip of a girl," Marie Louise was on her way to meet the "ogre." Time and again, since that Tuesday of March 13 when she had left Vienna, the tears from her light blue eyes had rolled down her plump pink cheeks. So as not to break out in sobs, she kept her mouth tightly pursed—that mouth whose lower lip hung down rather prettily.

The "remise"—copied after that of Marie Antoinette—took place at Braunau, on the frontier of the Confederation of the Rhine. The Emperor had heaped jewels and dresses on his new wife. But neither his gifts nor his passionate letters had got the better of her fears or assuaged her despair: she was about to take her place on a throne from which her grand-aunt had come down to go to the scaffold. And she was the bride of the man who symbolized the Revolution: the man who, having twice entered Vienna as a conqueror, had twice dismembered the Hapsburg Empire with great strokes of the sword.

Surely, as she traveled through the rain toward Soissons, she must have been thinking of how great a sacrifice she was making.

Suddenly, the hussars riding ahead of the carriage signaled for it to stop. They were just outside the little church of Courcelles. A footman hurriedly opened the carriage door and lowered the step. Marie Louise did not even have the time to ask what was happening. At that same moment the chamberlain on duty—M. de Seyssel—called out: "The Emperor!"

There in front of her was Napoleon: Napoleon in his rain-soaked gray greatcoat—the one he had worn at Wagram and had put on again *par une coquetterie de gloire,* since he was going to capture Vienna once again. He embraced her.

The whole schedule had been upset by the Emperor's haste—the haste of a schoolboy. He sat down across from the two ladies: "Madame, it is a great pleasure for me to see you."

In spite of the silly toque trimmed with macaw feathers that Marie Louise was wearing, the first impression was excellent: she was indeed the "fine slip of a girl" he had been expecting. Her eyes were too prominent, but they were a pretty light blue; her nose was too long, but it gave her features a touch of nobility; her chin was a bit too heavy. Her breasts were high and full, as the fashion demanded. All this combined to give an impression, if not of grace, at any rate of pink and blond freshness.

For her part, the young lady was pleasantly surprised. The bridegroom-to-be was infinitely charming—especially when he smiled and was ingratiating.

Soissons! They careened along the road. The Emperor was in a hurry to reach Compiègne.

It was night. The courtiers had quickly formed into a crowd on the outside steps, in the stairway, and in the grand salons. Suddenly the drums rolled. The carriage had entered the vast courtyard illuminated by torches carried by servants. A rather pathetic band was playing. Marie Louise stepped out of the carriage, helped down by her bridegroom. Quickly, he called out the names of the kings and queens, and she embraced them. But the Emperor was in no mood to brook delay.

It was not so much a wedding as an abduction. Abruptly interrupting the introductions and curtsies, Napoleon suggested to the

Empress that she go to her apartments. She was guided by her lady-in-waiting, Mme. de Montebello, to whom she said: "For such a formidable warrior, the Emperor is very charming and gentle. I'm beginning to think I'll like him very much."

As she entered her apartments, Marie Louise found additional reasons for regarding the Emperor as charming: the canary she had left behind at Vienna, her little dog, and a tapestry she had left unfinished in her room at the Hofburg.

A table had been set for three; and the Emperor, Marie Louise, and Caroline dined in good spirits. Meantime, the courtesans were making comments on the arrival of the new Empress and criticizing her rather reserved and constrained attitude.

Later, while the ladies were still chattering behind their fans and making ironical remarks, a farce was being played out on the floor above. Napoleon was interrogating his uncle, Cardinal Fesch. Was he really married? Certainly, in accordance with the civil laws, but perhaps not completely married in accordance with the canonical laws. Would it be possible to receive the sacrament by proxy? Well, it might be discussed.

Napoleon, however, had no intention of convening a council. And that same night, without waiting for the religious ceremony, which was to be celebrated on the following Monday in Paris, he decided to go into action. He was not of a mind to go and spend the night at the Chancellery, as etiquette demanded.

An account of the ensuing scene has been related by Gaspard Gourgaud, to whom Napoleon described it at St. Helena on August 30, 1817.

He asked Marie Louise what her father had advised her to do.

"He told me that the moment I was alone with you, I should do absolutely everything you told me to, and should obey you in whatever you asked."

"Well, I want to sleep with you tonight."

"Very well," she replied.

"She was very eager to get to it," the Emperor added, in his account.

Caroline had been given the responsibility of providing the customary advice to the bride, but "she had already been told everything at Vienna." Then Napoleon, soaked in eau de Cologne, came back to join Marie Louise. "I came to her," he told Gourgaud, "and she did the whole thing with a laugh."

The next morning, he went around tweaking everyone by the ear. And he told his aide-de-camp: "My good man, be sure to marry a German girl. They are the best women in the world: gentle, kind, naïve, and fresh as roses."

And Marie Louise wrote to her father:

Ever since my arrival I have been with him constantly, and he loves me very much. I am very grateful to him and respond to his love sincerely. I find he becomes much more likable upon closer acquaintance. There is something very fetching and very eager about him that is impossible to resist. . . .

The religious ceremony was to take place in the Salon Carré of the Louvre. On April 2, dazzled by his incredible good fortune, he advanced toward the altar to a flourish of trumpets. The guests were struck by the triumphal air of the bride and groom. Napoleon was radiant with happiness. The ceremony, celebrated by Cardinal Fesch, followed the traditional forms, including the blessing of the thirteen gold pieces symbolizing the redemption of the bride. But those guests who had remained in the Galerie were amazed when they noticed, as the couple returned, that the Emperor's face—so joyous a few moments ago—was now dark and menacing. What had happened?

When he came into the Salon Carré, Napoleon had noticed that out of twenty-seven cardinals who had been invited, only twelve were present. The Italian prelates, in compulsory residence in Paris at the time, had preferred to stay home, in this way showing their disapproval of the rulings made by the Ecclesiastical Court of Paris. For them, the Emperor's second marriage was a kind of sacrilege. Napoleon had become a bigamist, and the future heir would be a bastard. Moreover, since the groom was excommunicated, he was not entitled to receive the sacrament of marriage.

"Oh, those fools!" muttered the Emperor. "I see what they're aiming at! They want to protest the legitimacy of my race and undermine my dynasty! Oh, the fools!"

The next day, on the occasion of the reception, Napoleon did no more than to drive the recalcitrants out of the Tuileries. The prelates' carriages having disappeared, one could see the cardinals, wearing their red garb, wandering through the courtyard of the Carrousel. In the eyes of the Emperor, this outrage was not harsh enough, and he wanted to have them brought to trial. But he never carried out his threats.

The attitude of the Italian cardinals (it would be the Vatican's attitude four years later), would eventually simplify things for Metternich, who would be able to convince the daughter of his master that her marriage to Napoleon was not valid. But on this day of April 2, 1810, Austria's interests were something very different: it was essential to exploit the sacrifice and please the Emperor. That night, while Paris was illuminated with a thousand lights under clearing skies, the Chancellor, who had come from Vienna for the wedding, stepped out (champagne glass in hand) onto the balcony of one of the salons of the Council of State where the banquet had been held, and called out like a herald: "I drink to the King of Rome!"

This toast was surprising to say the least, coming as it did from the mouth of the prime minister of the ex-Emperor of the Germanic Holy Roman Empire—that Emperor who, before having been crowned Francis I of Austria, had (like his fathers before him) borne the title of King of the Romans.

In the month of April, 1810, Victoire de Poutet, a childhood friend of Marie Louise, informed the new Empress of her impending marriage to the Comte de Crenneville. Marie Louise wrote her in return: "May you soon enjoy a happiness like that which I am experiencing!" Not only did she thank Heaven "for the great felicity" it had granted her; she also thanked her father "for not having given her Archduke Francis as a husband."

And yet Napoleon's behavior with her was that of an Oriental Sovereign. He wanted no man to be able to boast that he had been alone with the Empress for as much as two minutes. A lady-in-waiting was given a sharp tongue-lashing by the Emperor for having thought it proper to leave the room while her mistress was taking her music lesson with M. Paër. Does not Mohammed assure us that a woman left alone with a man for the length of time it takes to cook an egg must be considered an adulteress?

Napoleon was full of kindness for his wife. He even gave her horseback riding lessons himself, and reassured her when she cried out in fright, saying: "Allons, Louise! Be brave. What is there to be

afraid of? I'm right here." And how anxious he was about her the
night when a fire started during a ball at the Austrian embassy!

The following year, when the Emperor was far away, Marie
Louise again wrote to Victoire de Crenneville: "I can only be happy
when I am near him." And she went on to tell her friend that she
"could not bear" being separated from her husband for any length
of time. Or again: "One day without getting a letter from him is
enough to drive me to despair."

There was no doubt that the new Empress loved the man to
whom she had been married as the result of her country's defeat.
Perhaps the sensuous Marie Louise (one of her friends said after her
death that she had died "from an excess of sensual pleasures") appreciated above all else the physical love to which her husband had
introduced her during the "fetching" night at Compiègne. Yet how
good was the Emperor at love-making? Obviously, it was impossible
for the young lady to be a competent judge of such matters in the
days before she had become the mistress of Neipperg.

She nicknamed her husband "Napo" or "Popo"—which is rather
amusing in the case of Napoleon—and fretted when her *très mechant
galant,* as she called him, was away from her for only a few hours.
In the presence of the Court, Marie Louise would put her hand on
her husband's shoulder and "fondle" him when she wanted something from him and these displays would put the Emperor out of
countenance.

Unquestionably, he appreciated her as a "charming child." But
above all, his vanity as a man, and as a parvenu, was pleasantly
flattered. He was surprised and emotionally stirred by the desire for
him manifested by this young lady of nineteen, "naïve and fresh,"
who might have been his daughter. He laughed with her, almost
stupidly. They were like those young newlyweds who, in the presence of others, seem always to be sharing secrets.

One evening at St. Helena he said: "For that matter, she was very
fond of trying to stir up my senses—with her breasts or otherwise."

And with her there was none of that play-acting that Josephine
had indulged in. Napoleon's pride could only have been flattered
when he saw how much he, a former lieutenant of artillery, was loved
by this archduchess, the great-granddaughter of Marie Thérèse and
the grand-niece of Marie Antoinette. But this unexpected success
certainly did not make him strut and swagger. On the contrary, it

rather put him in a state of inferiority vis-à-vis the new Empress. "I'm not afraid of Napoleon," she told Metternich, "but I'm beginning to think he's afraid of me."

The Emperor took pleasure in doing everything he could for his young wife, and tried to dazzle her with gifts which, in his words, would make her "the most richly adorned person of old Europe." He would not leave her side. He was forgetting his empire for her. He came late to Council meetings. But there was something else far more serious: being unwilling to leave her, he would not make the decision to go to Spain and put an end to the frightful hemorrhage that was continuing unabated beyond the Pyrenees. He persisted "in his project to subjugate that country at the price of all the blood of his own." Three different times he announced his departure; and three different times the servants, horses, and transport wagons set out for Bayonne. But when he saw Marie Louise's pale blue eyes fill with tears, he changed his mind. Was he a Hercules sitting at the feet of Omphale and spinning? But Marie Louise was no Queen of Lydia (her brain was incapable of conceiving the slightest calculated act), and in that respect Napoleon was even less of a Hercules. He was not blinded; but he seemed blissfully complacent, relishing his domestic happiness.

He explained it himself: "A young, pretty woman with a sweet disposition came into my life. Was I not entitled to express my joy at this? Could I not devote a few moments to her without incurring blame? Was it not permissible for me, too, to give myself over to a few moments of happiness?"

And yet he never spent the whole night with Marie Louise as he had done with Josephine. As he said:

> The Empress did not like to be awakened at night—not even for *la petite affaire*. She had a mania about never keeping the fire going in her fireplace. Since I got up every night, this was an inconvenience for me. That may have been the reason why, on more than twenty occasions, I refrained from going down to the Empress' apartments.

He was consumed with pride. He was intoxicated by the incense that kept swirling up toward him. He himself had remarked, when he saw his statue atop the Vendôme column: "How can you help feeling dizzy when you see yourself raised up so high?"

Hence it was quite natural for him to write to Talleyrand, who had been put in charge of the dethroned Ferdinand VII: "Prince Ferdinand addresses me as 'My cousin' in his letters. Make it plain to the minister, San Carlos, that that is ridiculous, and that he should simply call me 'Sire.' " He was no longer content to "royalize" himself. "Why," he asked, "do *my ministers* abroad, and even *my consuls,* wear *my livery?* If I recall correctly, I authorized it only for my ambassadors." True, in 1808 he had told Décrès: "I give you leave to refrain from comparing me to God." But it was also true that he had authorized the inscription *Ego sum qui sum* above his throne at the Hôtel de Ville.

And the Court! "It was a regular galley in which everyone plied his oar according to the regulations," said Chaptal.

Time and again, guests at the imperial table were able to eat no more than a half-plate of soup, because the Emperor had got up a few moments after sitting down. As Talleyrand remarked amusingly: "The Emperor doesn't trifle: he wants everyone to enjoy himself!"

But the press had never before been so muzzled. There were only four authorized newspapers—the *Moniteur,* the *Journal de l'Empire,* the *Gazette de France,* and the *Journal de Paris*—and a very strict watch was kept over them. The prisons of the State, which in the preceding eleven years had had only 1,500 to 1,000 "guests," took in 2,000 of them between 1811 and 1814. The immense empire was in the grip of a hand of iron.

Everything was regulated and covered by laws. Despotism was unleashed. As early as 1807 Napoleon had admitted that he loved power as a musician loves his violin. He wanted to enjoy that power without limitation; and he wanted to enjoy it alone. His ministers were no longer anything but puppets; nor should they be anything else! Gathered around the council table they were all like instruments: instruments of Napoleon's will.

Orders continued to flow out from the Tuileries in a torrent. He still gave his attention to the tiniest details. Thus he sent a notice to Clarke, the Minister of War: "The vast ignorance of the officers commanding the coastal batteries renders useless the cannon entrusted to them. The projectiles do not reach the target because, with the vessels beyond point-blank range, they have not removed the bushings."

And what was his work?

He had not achieved the aim he had been pursuing since the Peace of Amiens: to bring England to her knees, to starve her out by means of the blockade, and then to secure that peace which had been eluding him and which he would not find until July 15, 1815, when he climbed up the sea ladder of the *Bellerophon*. The wisest thing would have been to end the atrocity-ridden war in Spain. "It requires the head and arms of a Hercules," Kellermann told Berthier. "Only he, by dint of strength and skill, could bring this great conflict to an end—if it can be brought to an end."

But Hercules had now given way to Jupiter; and Jupiter was thinking only of the gigantic blockade. Europe must be converted into a citadel that was inaccessible to English goods. And the empire must be expanded still farther. Since February 8, 1810, Catalonia, Aragon, Navarre, and Biscay had been "*French* military provinces." The French ambassador at Madrid was simply notified of the fact in instructions from his minister. Napoleon had merely added with that arrogance which by now had become habitual: "You will instruct him to inform the King that such is my will."

Although Joseph no longer dared shout that he was the successor of Charles V, Louis still regarded himself as the successor of the stadtholders, and was obviously reluctant to enforce the blockade. The subjects of King Louis no longer used sugar in their coffee every day, and they lacked English cotton for their textiles and English salt for curing meats; but the fact was that since the autumn of 1809 the blockade applied to the Low Countries had been nothing more than an empty word. Napoleon was hardly exaggerating when he wrote to Louis that Holland and the British Isles were trading "as they had in time of peace." Therefore, the Emperor issued a deadly decree: henceforth, all commercial relations between Holland and his vast empire were cut off, since Louis' kingdom—a regular "British colony"—was no longer anything but an obstacle to the liberty of the empire. Napoleon intended going even further, and said so straight out to his brother: "I'll make a meal of Holland!"

For the moment, however, he contented himself with devouring only a morsel of it: he ordered the occupation of Breda and Bergen op Zoom.

"It is the English," he explained to Louis, "who have compelled me to expand constantly. If they keep it up, they will oblige me to annex Holland."

But Louis (on whom Paris was keeping a strict watch) refused to let his territories be nibbled away, and wrote to his Minister of War that "the impending advance of the French troops into the kingdom must be resisted." It began to appear that the Bonapartes were going to declare themselves each other's enemies, as the Bourbons of France and Spain had done in the past century. The ministers were frightened.

"We shall not resist them with naked force," said Louis in his instructions, "but we shall make formal protests."

The town governor of Bergen op Zoom refused to hand the fortress over to Oudinot. Napoleon sent his Minister of War to Louis to warn him: "Your Majesty will be responsible for whatever blood is spilled."

The King of Holland replied that he did not intend "to discuss the matter with the Minister of War of a *foreign nation*, even though that nation be friendly."

"Does this mean," asked the Duke of Feltro, "that Your Majesty is declaring war on France and the Emperor?"

The sovereign shrugged. "Let's have no feeble jokes, please! A prisoner does not declare war! If the Emperor will just leave me alone, he can do as he likes."

Louis yielded, of course, and Oudinot took possession of Bergen op Zoom.

Napoleon obviously no longer wanted his brother on a throne, and he told him as much without subterfuge: "I have already told you several times that I want you to abdicate. Once more I say: be a French prince again, and you can live a pleasant and carefree life."

Louis replied sharply: "You can dethrone me, since I do not have the means to prevent it. But when I have ceased to be King of Holland, you will never be able to make me remain a French prince."

A treaty between France and Holland, signed on March 16, 1810, sanctioned Napoleon's annexation of Brabant, Zeeland, and part of Gelderland. But the great irony was that the soldiers and customs officers responsible for enforcing the blockade throughout the territory of the Netherlands were to be paid and maintained by Holland.

Louis considered resisting the invasion of his kingdom by French customs officers: "I have the same kind of attachment for Holland that one has for one's family; and the greater her misfortunes, the more I feel obligated to devote myself entirely to her. She has only me as an intercessor. I shall not abandon a duty of this kind."

Accordingly, he prohibited the Duke of Reggio from occupying Haarlem. Napoleon's response was to order Marshal Oudinot to advance toward Amsterdam.

Louis' ministers advised him to yield, but he refused, saying: "This is too much! I have made up my mind! I shall back the Emperor up against the wall and force him to reveal to the eyes of Europe and France the secret of his policy toward Holland and myself for the past five years. I shall put my son in my place."

And on July 1, Louis abdicated in favor of his son and vanished. Whatever other results it had, his flight liberated his wife, Hortense. Now that she was "emancipated" (as the Emperor put it), she took advantage of her freedom to get herself with child—the future Duc de Morny—by the handsome Flahaut, the natural son of Talleyrand.

Needless to say, Napoleon entertained no thoughts whatsoever of having his brother's oldest son crowned. To have Louis I succeeded by Louis II was out of the question. And so, on July 9, 1810, the former Kingdom of Holland was cut up into eight French *départements*. A few days later, on July 23, the former consul Lebrun, who had become Duke of Piacenza, was named Napoleon's *lieutenant-général* at Amsterdam. Whereupon he addressed the following words to his former colleague of the Consulate: "Sire, the territory and the waters of Holland are yours."

On August 15, the Emperor received the deputies of Holland, and informed them of his decision:

> I have just brought to an end the painful uncertainty in which you were living, and have halted an agony which was on the verge of exhausting your strength and your resources. I have just now opened up the Continent to your industry. The day will come when you will fly my eagles over the seas that made your ancestors illustrious.

The oversized, hybrid, insane, monstrous empire was being built. It took two weeks for couriers to cross it. It was an empire that would devour nationalities, provinces, and kingdoms.

For Holland was not enough. On August 18, 1810, the Emperor informed Jérôme: "I have just ordered my troops to occupy the whole country from Holstein to Holland. . . . I request that you withdraw your troops from this area."

On November 30 of that same year of 1810, the Emperor annexed the Republic of Valais, which became the Département de Simplon, under the pretext that (as Napoleon said) "this wretched population was separating Italy from France *to my detriment.*" Thirteen days later it was the turn of the old Hanseatic cities—Bremen, Hamburg, and Lübeck—to become *chefs-lieux* of French *départements.*

"It was not my territory that I wanted to expand," he explained, "but my maritime resources."

Always England!

There were 130 *départements* comprising 45 million "Frenchmen," to which must be added the 40 million inhabitants of the vassal states: Italy, Spain, Naples, the Grand Duchy of Warsaw, the Confederation of the Rhine, and the Swiss Confederation. The Neman, Gibraltar, Messina, Hamburg, and Zadar—these were certainly strange "French" frontiers!

In this way, as he went on toward the inevitable catastrophe, he was forging the empire of his heir. For Marie Louise was now expecting a child; and that child, Napoleon affirmed, would unquestionably be a boy. He was completely convinced of it. This newborn would find a crown in his silver cradle. He would not be a prince: he would be the King of Rome. He would be called "Sire" and "Your Majesty." He would be surrounded by an entire court—titled, gilded, and plumed.

The Emperor Napoleon II? Rather, the master of a federative empire! And the Emperor was by no means talking nonsense when he predicted: "My son must be the champion of the new ideas and the cause I have made victorious everywhere—to unite Europe with indissoluble federative ties."

But that wasn't all: the European dream had taken possession of him: "My destiny is not yet accomplished. I want to complete what has only been sketched out. I want a European Code, a European Court of Appeals, the same currency, the same weights and measures, the same laws. I must make all the nations of Europe one nation, and Paris the capital of the world."

In this year of 1810, even a country then at the other end of the world, a country over which he exerted no influence—Sweden— asked the Emperor to provide her with one of his lieutenants as a king. Bernadotte was chosen, the same Bernadotte who had married Désirée, the ex-fiancée of General Bonaparte.

There is little doubt that secretly Napoleon was furious at the idea that, without his intervention, one of his marshals could become a "legitimate prince"—a title neither he nor any of his brothers could ever claim. But he disclosed his thoughts to Metternich in these words: "I could not turn down the offer, because a French marshal on the throne of Gustavus Adolphus is one of the best tricks one could play on England."

His yearning to fight it out to a finish with "perfidious Albion" would bring him into conflict once again with the Pope, would make him prolong the Spanish war until the final defeat, and would then plunge him into the frightful Russian adventure.

Already, in late 1811, Décrès was prophesying: "Do you want me to tell you the truth and unveil the future for you? The Emperor is mad—completely mad. He will throw all of us, such as we are, head over heels, and the whole thing will end in a catastrophe."

XIX

THE FUTURE BELONGS TO ME

Great men are meteors destined
to burn up the earth.

NAPOLEON

ON WEDNESDAY, MARCH 20, a light fog lay over Paris. The cannon began to thunder, and the capital held its breath. If 21 shots were fired, it would mean the birth of a Princess of Venice; 101 volleys would mean that the King of Rome was born.

There was a pause after the twenty-first volley, apparently in order to prolong the pleasure—a kind of tradition among the artillerymen. Then the twenty-second shot rang out. Hats flew into the air. There was a tremendous explosion of enthusiasm—"a wild joy," says an eyewitness—and a prolonged cry of love rose up from the city. It was a "knockout blow" for the Royalists, since it seemed to them that the imperial batteries had just "killed off the race of Bourbons."

The inhabitants left their houses and shops and ran toward the Tuileries. From his windows, Napoleon saw the gardens fill with a crowd that was shouting, singing, and cheering. He feasted his eyes on the extraordinary spectacle. That day certainly marked the high point of his incredible good fortune.

A few moments after the first cry uttered by the heir to the empire (whose delivery had been painful and difficult) the Emperor, drunk with joy, had seen his son carried into the salon—crowded with courtiers—by Mme. de Montesquiou, his governess, followed by the colonel general of the Guard and the imperial officers and ladies-in-waiting. The crier of the court stepped forward and announced in a loud voice: "The King of Rome!"

On the great staircase, the grenadiers (one on each step) presented arms. "They had been ordered not to move a muscle," a witness tells us. "But their manly faces expressed great emotion, and I could see tears of joy in their eyes." After the ceremony, the noncommissioned officers of the Guard cut off their mustaches in order to make a pillow for the imperial heir.

During the next few days, as couriers and the telegraph carried the astounding news to the confines of the immense empire, there were explosions of joy everywhere. From the Atlantic to the Neman one saw and heard only fireworks, balls, fountains of wine, buffets alfresco, salvos of artillery, and theatrical shows improvised for the occasion. In the Eternal City, all the bells rang out to celebrate the birth of the King of Rome.

"I envy him," Napoleon said, leaning over the sumptuous and clumsy cradle offered by the city of Paris. "Glory awaits him, but I had to pursue it. I was Philip; he will be Alexander. He has only to reach out his arms to seize the world."

On June 9, 1811, the carriage used for the consecration took the Emperor and Empress to Notre Dame for the "dynastic enthronement"—that baptism of the King of Rome which may have seemed, to the eyes of the master, a more important celebration than that of December 2, 1804. Was he not forging, on that day, the first link in his dynasty? He had once again donned his tasteless imperial uniform, the livery of his greatness: a livery of purple, white, and gold. How far all this was removed—in only ten years!—from the Bonaparte of Marengo! He was "sallow, obese, and bloated," his head already sunken down between his shoulders. He was growing stout —and he was disappointing. "I didn't see the hero I had imagined," someone said. "I was expecting a god, and all I saw was a fat man."

The spectators missed Josephine's charming smile. Marie Louise, all aglitter with diamonds, was notably devoid of graciousness.

When, later on, Napoleon was asked when he was the happiest, he hesitated between Tilsit and this day of baptism, then finally settled on the day after Friedland, admitting that in 1811 he felt "out of sorts."

Out of sorts? It is hard to believe that, in spite of his intoxication, he had doubts about the future; but he was already aware, on every hand, of the growing lassitude of the nation. Unquestionably, the birth of the little king had unleashed enthusiasm; but this great joy at Napoleon's good fortune was already beginning to die down. Dazzlement no longer dazzled anyone. People had been intoxicated by glory so often that glory had become insipid—as it had already been for Napoleon in 1798. What did it matter that some Spaniards, Dutch, Germans, or Illyrians had become French? All that seemed like a *vue de l'esprit*. Who cared about the European or Carolingian dream of the new Emperor of the West? And besides, that glory was so dearly bought—at the price of so much spilled blood.

Once the Chinese lanterns had been extinguished, would the birth of the King of Rome bring peace? A vague anxiety was on the rise. Nothing seemed stable or sacred. It looked as if Napoleon wanted to shatter his own edifice.

The censorship, the inquisition of the government agents, the dark suspicion of the customs officials which affected the entire empire, and the iron hand weighing heavily on the whole country made for a painful malaise.

Besides, there were religious problems which made the atmosphere oppressive. The Pope, still a prisoner, had refused to bless the King of Rome—that king to whom the heritage of St. Peter had just been assigned. In short, Napoleon had taken from the Pope—in order to give it to a newborn child—the most visible part of his temporal power: that temporal power that belonged not to His Holiness but to the Church.

Moreover, the Pope refused to give the investiture to the bishops so long as he was not at liberty; and the drama between the Pope and the Emperor continued to build up.

Another drama was making Napoleon feel "out of sorts": the drama with Russia had begun to develop with the Czar's refusal to give his sister's hand in marriage to the former lieutenant of artillery. Taking his revenge, the Emperor was more than willing to display his bad humor by wrecking the loan that Russia was about to make in France. And the ruble was seriously weakened as a result of the enforcement of the blockade, an enforcement often violated but still sufficient to harm Russian trade to a considerable extent.

At the same time the problem of the future of Poland came to life again, and this bone of contention made relations between the two countries still cooler. Napoleon refused to sign the convention whereby he was to pledge himself to "prevent forever and always the reconstruction of Poland."

"That would be prejudicial to my dignity and my honor," he said. "I would have to be God to decide that there should never be a Poland!"

In the autumn of 1810, a huge convoy of 1,200 British merchant ships—flying a neutral flag, of course, but escorted as far as the Sound by 20 British naval vessels—passed through the Baltic in search of a port to unload the merchandise cramming their holds. Denmark, Prussia, and Sweden were either unwilling—or unable—to incur Napoleon's displeasure. Elsewhere, imperial customs officers, protected by Davout's bayonets, were guarding the coast from Danzig to Memel. And so the 1,200 allegedly neutral ships began to wander from port to port—"like the vestiges of a routed army." Would the Czar agree to receive them?

> If Your Majesty gives them entry [the Emperor wrote to Alexander on October 23, 1810] the war will continue. If, on the other hand, you sequester them and confiscate their cargoes, it will be a terrible counterblow to England. All this merchandise means a profit for the English. It is up to Your Majesty whether we shall have peace or a continuation of the war.

The Czar opened his ports. Napoleon was informed of the fact on November 11, and the next day—still with a view to keeping England shut up in her island—he made a serious decision: together with the annexation of the Hanseatic cities, he gave orders to seize the Duchy of Oldenburg, situated between Bremen and the North Sea. The duke did not accept the territorial compensation offered him by the Emperor. He took refuge at St. Petersburg, since not only had he married the Czar's sister Catherine, but he had received his duchy from his cousin, the Emperor Paul I, Alexander's father. This development provided Alexander with the grievance he had been looking for.

Napoleon was certainly in the wrong when he signed the decree annexing the Duchy of Oldenburg—as a result of which the Elbe became a "French" frontier. The Czar, taking as a pretext the drop in the value of the ruble (a result of the partial blockade), on the last day of the year 1810 closed his ports to ships carrying French merchandise, all the while maintaining that he was "doing everything possible to keep peace."

"No more commercial relations between the two empires? Is that a state of peace and alliance?" exclaimed Napoleon.

The Czar's response was one of astonishment. Only "economic necessity," he affirmed, had "compelled" him to take such a step.

At St. Petersburg, Caulaincourt, who was a naïve ambassador and very much under the spell of Alexander, was still trusting in the good faith of the sovereign to whom he was accredited—this at a time when Russia was moving closer to England and had even begun negotiations with her. In this respect, the Czar was far more responsible than Napoleon for the new conflict: it is plain to see that he was skillfully preparing to break off relations with France and looking for new allies. He held out a hand to Austria; and on February 13, 1811, suggested to Emperor Francis an offensive and defensive alliance: "I propose to Your Majesty that if Poland should fall to my lot by the fortunes of war, I will immediately cede you Wallachia, Moldavia as far as the Sereth, . . . and Serbia in addition."

Fortunately for Napoleon, Metternich was wary (wrongly so, as it turned out) and exclaimed: "The offer is too attractive to be genuine!"

Napoleon was not informed of the double game being played by Russia, but he surmised it.

Nonetheless, he wrote to Alexander expressing his trust and friendship: "These feelings will not change, although I can no longer conceal from myself that Your Majesty's friendship for me is a thing of the past. . . ." Napoleon went on to list his grievances. Why the refusal of the compensation he had offered the Czar's brother-in-law for the seizure of the Duchy of Oldenburg? Why that ukase directed against France? Why those fortifications "built at ten places along the Dvina"?

The Czar did not reply; but up until the very moment of Caulaincourt's departure for Paris, he continued to reassure the French ambassador of his peaceable intentions. Immediately upon Caulaincourt's return, Napoleon told him straight out: "I tell you he wants to make war on me. . . ."

This was about the same thing the Czar had told him, Caulaincourt reported to Napoleon.

If the Emperor Napoleon makes war on me [Alexander had said], and if we decide to fight back, it is possible—and even probable—that he will defeat us. But that will not secure peace for him. The Spaniards have often been defeated, but they are neither vanquished nor subdued. And yet they are not as remote from Paris as we are; and they have neither our climate nor our resources. We shall not compromise ourselves. We have plenty of territory, and we shall keep a well-organized army.

War was now inevitable.

On December 5, 1811, Jérôme alerted his brother: "The fermentation is at its highest point. The wildest hopes are being entertained and nurtured with enthusiasm."

The French "observation" armies were built up from 50,000 to 80,000 men. Issuing this order was easier, however, than transforming the Emperor of Austria, the King of Prussia, and the King of Sweden into French allies. Metternich agreed to furnish a contingent of 34,000 men to Napoleon, but apologized to the Czar for this move, saying that these troops would be nothing more than "auxiliaries." Alexander thanked him, and assured him that the Austrian soldiers would not receive so much as a scratch. (As it turned out, the freezing weather took care of matters.) The King of Prussia had to resign himself to sending 20,000 troops against his friend Alexander, meantime informing him sub rosa: "If war should break out, we shall do you only such harm as is absolutely necessary. We shall always remember that we are united and are to become allies again some day."

Bernadotte indulged himself in sending Napoleon great protestations of affection. Take sides with the Czar? The very thought that he might do so was an insult to him! Fight against the Emperor—his former comrade-at-arms? The ex-sergeant from Gascony declared that he would never do anything so infamous. He would rather "throw himself headfirst into the sea" or "straddle a barrel of gunpowder and be blown high into the air."

Yet in Pomerania the Swedes were doing so little to enforce the blockade that Napoleon occupied the province (which had been given to Sweden by France in 1810). Bernadotte's reaction to this move—justified but brutal—was to swing over toward Alexander. The alliance between the two cronies was signed on April 5, 1812. And Désirée's husband, who was holding off and would not enter the conflict until the stag was at bay, offered this piece of advice to the Czar on April 24:

> The important thing is to avoid big battles; to worry the enemy's flanks, thereby compelling him to form separate detachments; and to harass him with marches and countermarches: this is what annoys the French soldier most, and what will give you the greatest advantage over him. Be sure there are plenty of Cossacks everywhere!

Orders went out by the thousands, and the Grand Army began to take shape. Two hundred thousand men remained in Germany and in the Grand Duchy of Warsaw, while nine army corps consisting of nearly 400,000 troops marched toward the Russian frontier. They included Frenchmen, Netherlanders, Belgians, Germans, Italians, and Illyrians, plus the unwilling allies (20,000 Prussians and 34,000 Austrians)—not to mention a Spanish regiment and the 130 battalions still stationed at the replacement depots scattered throughout the vast empire.

"My absence will be immense," said the Emperor.

But the balls went on at the Tuileries, despite the troubled times. Those troubles, the peace that kept eluding him, and the double game being played by Alexander made Napoleon anxious and so preoccupied that one night the entire court saw him stop in the center of the salon, cross his arms, and stare at the floor six feet in front of him. The kings then at Paris, the princes, and the Empress drew away. Others stepped up, and a circle formed in silence around the mute and immobile Emperor.

They looked at each other questioningly, then lowered their glances. All they could do now was wait. After some seven or eight minutes, to everyone's consternation, Masséna—the old veteran of Italy—left his place, passed through the circle "that an evil genius seemed to have formed," and slowly approached the Emperor. He had scarcely uttered a few words in a low voice when Napoleon roared: "What do you mean breaking in on me?"

Without a word, Masséna "back-pedaled" to his place. "Never," says an eyewitness, "had the despot in Napoleon shown himself with so much arrogance and impudence."

When he finally came out of his reverie, the Emperor raised his head, unfolded his arms, and walked out of the salon, followed by Marie Louise, whom he had imperiously ordered: "Venez, Madame!"

Having seen that (in his own words) "everything had become a problem," and having realized that in order to secure the peace that was still eluding him he would have to open a new campaign—and what a campaign!—Napoleon, vexed beyond all limits, had some justification for letting the others see how heavily his thoughts were weighing upon him.

Alexander was already at Vilna, expecting Napoleon's attack. The attack was inevitable, since on April 8 the Russian government had sent an ultimatum to the Emperor of the French demanding the total evacuation of Prussia, Swedish Pomerania, and all the points beyond the Elbe occupied by the French.

Faced with such demands, the Emperor had no choice but to fight. And yet he still delayed setting out after his army. He was waiting for the results of vague negotiations being conducted with England. These negotiations, if successful, would above all have permitted him to bring an end to the bloody conflict in Spain and to the imbroglio of the command, which in the peninsula had been entrusted entirely to the incompetent Joseph. "Don José I" was reigning over a kingdom now unaware of his existence. And henceforth he would be in supreme command of an army comprising 230,000 men, fine troops which Napoleon would sorely miss.

On May 9, 1812, the following announcement appeared in the *Moniteur:*

> The Emperor left today to make a tour of inspection of the Grand Army, now encamped on the Vistula. Her Majesty the Empress will accompany His Majesty as far as Dresden, where she hopes to have the pleasure of seeing her august family.

Before pulling on his combat boots, the Emperor was going to play once more (and for the last time) his role as Emperor of the West. He had hopes that this "triumph" would prompt Alexander to negotiate. Also, it would appear that in order to recover his famous aplomb, he needed to preside once again over a court of kings and overawe his brother-in-law and ally.

Along the master's route—at each stage between Paris and Dresden, and even at each relay station—German princes stood at attention. On May 11, Napoleon and Marie Louise left Metz at two in the morning; and by the end of their third day of travel they had reached Mainz, where they were saluted by the princes of Hesse-Darmstadt and Anhalt. The next day, they left at dawn. At Würtzburg they were greeted by the grand duke, the King of Württemberg, and the Grand Duke of Baden. The next day, at the relay station of Bamberg, Princes William and Pius of Bavaria bowed low before the Emperor. On May 16, coming from Plauen, the Emperor and Empress were welcomed to the frontier of Saxony by the King and Queen. That same evening the four of them made their entrance into Dresden (illuminated for the occasion), where the Emperor and Empress of Austria came to join them.

Inside the palace, it was difficult to get anywhere near the master. "I got into a crowd of kings," said Narbonne to Napoleon, "and had a hard time getting through it." Sovereigns intermingled with high dignitaries elbowed one another aside so as to be present at the levee.

Francis of Austria, astonished, saw Napoleon take precedence over him, go to the table first, keep the sovereigns at a respectful distance, and preside at table still wearing his hat, while he, Francis —a Hapsburg!—was uncovered. *"Das ist ein ganzer Kerl!"*—That's quite a fellow!—he exclaimed.

On June 23 a huge army—400,000 men speaking ten different languages: "a Tower of Babel on the march"—made ready to cross the Neman at Kovno. The river was hidden from view by its high banks and the forest of Pilwisky. On that day Count Roman Soltykx, a major in command of a squadron of Polish lancers bivouacked not far from the banks of the Neman, saw a big carriage pulled by six horses arrive at full gallop. It stopped, and Napoleon stepped out, preoccupied and exhausted by his trip.

The Emperor decided to inspect the banks of the river. In order not to be recognized by the Russian scouts known to be on the right bank, he put on the uniform of a Polish officer. His staff officers did the same. When they reached the bank of the broad river, a major who had swum across it came to report to the Emperor that the Russian army seemed to have pulled back.

That same night, toward midnight, Napoleon returned to the riverbank and rode along it at a gallop. He was barely able to discern the other bank (the Russian side) through the darkness. Suddenly his horse shied—a hare had dashed between his legs—and the Emperor took a fall.

He got up immediately. As he did, a voice exclaimed: "That's a bad omen! A Roman would draw back!"

But he was not the man to draw back.

The next day, from a hill overlooking the river and the three bridges thrown across it "as if by magic," Napoleon gazed upon a most unusual spectacle:

> All the hills, their slopes, and the valleys were covered with men and horses. The moment the sun rose upon all those mobile masses with their sparkling weapons, the signal was given and the multitude forthwith started to flow in three columns toward the three bridges. You could see them wind their way down the narrow, sloping plain between them and the Neman, come up to it, reach the three bridges, stretch out and then contract to cross them, and finally reach that foreign soil which they would devastate, and which they would soon cover with their debris.

When they reached the Russian side, where they had thought they would be greeted by gunfire, the soldiers stopped in bewilderment. "We thought we were in a cemetery," one of them said later. "There was not a single living creature on the horizon; not one inhabitant in the villages." In the distance, black clouds of smoke swirled up from the burning villages. When the first troops reached them, the huts were nothing but ashes. And still there was not a single inhabitant to be seen.

Impatiently, Napoleon set off at a gallop through the silent forest along the river, covering more than a league.

Suddenly, a hollow, rumbling sound was heard. It was not artillery, but the beginning of a terrible storm. The sky darkened, thunderclaps and flashes of lightning followed one another, then everything was inundated by a downpour.

There were those who considered that, too, as a bad omen.

The Czar's Minister of Police, Balachov, stood in the room that the Russian Emperor had occupied a few days earlier in Vilna. Now, however, it was not Alexander who was facing him, but Napoleon. He had come to the Emperor with a note from his master. Alexander was offering to negotiate with the invader, on condition that the

Grand Army countermarch and go back across the Neman. It was impossible. Napoleon had not come all that way merely to go back to his staging areas—especially since he had not been defeated. And yet in the course of only one week after having crossed the Neman, the Grand Army had sustained heavy losses without once having been engaged in combat.

The numerical weakness of the Czar's forces—the delayed junction between Mikhail Barclay de Tolly's armies (100,000 men) and those of Pëtr Bagration (50,000)—had compelled the Russian High Command to order a retreat. The scorched-earth tactic had become imperative.

On the French side the wagons carrying rations and fodder bogged down in the mud and were left behind by an army that often covered 15 leagues in one day. Some 50,000 marauders who left their formations to go out and look for food became stragglers. The troops who remained in formation around the Napoleonic eagles marched on with empty bellies to the sound of the drums—sometimes under a lashing rain, sometimes under an oppressive sun and clouds of dust. When they bivouacked—exhausted, famished, and parched with thirst—they slept on the wet ground.

Shortly after crossing the Neman, a stupid mistake had been made: the horses had been fed green grain mixed with straw taken from the roofs of huts. Within a week, 10,000 mounts and draft horses had died of dysentery.

For the moment, the terrible climate was the Czar's most reliable auxiliary.

When Balachov was brought to see the Emperor, his itinerary was carefully calculated so that he would not realize the extent to which the French army was disorganized.

Alexander's envoy had not come to propose to Napoleon the opening of negotiations. His master had prohibited it: "So long as one armed soldier remains on Russian territory, I swear that I will not utter or listen to a single word about peace."

Since no negotiation was possible, Napoleon paced from one wall of the room to the other, taking the Russian general along with him:

> Alexander is making sport of me. Does he think I came to Vilna to negotiate trade agreements? I came to have done, once and for all, with the barbarous colossus of the North. The sword

has been unsheathed. They [the Russians] must be driven back to
their ice fields so that they won't meddle in the affairs of civilized
Europe for another twenty-five years. Alexander now realizes
that the situation is serious, and that his army has been cut off. He
is afraid and would like to come to terms. But when I sign an
armistice, it will be at Moscow.

It would seem, however, that Napoleon was not yet thinking of
pushing on as far as Moscow. His plan was to defeat the Russian
armies quickly. Once again, what he needed was a victory. But now
he was no more the Bonaparte of Rivoli than he was the Emperor
of Austerlitz. And the first thing he did was to lose precious time by
remaining twenty days at Vilna waiting for Jérôme and Eugène, both
of whom were late in joining up with the main body of the army.

Actually, the Emperor was expecting a good deal of the 84,000
men that he had imprudently (to put it mildly) placed under the
command of the King of Westphalia. Napoleon assumed that his
brother would bring his troops to bear against the army of Prince
Bagration. Attacked at the same time by the 72,000 men under Davout, Bagration would be caught in a cross fire.

"I've got them where I want them," he kept saying.

But Jérôme failed to send any word to headquarters. Not only
that: he had remained at Grodno, strutting about. He had added
Napoleon's first name to his own, and apparently felt that this promotion conferred military genius upon him.

"You are jeopardizing the success of the entire campaign," the
Emperor wrote him. "It is impossible to wage war in this way."

Bagration managed to avoid being trapped, and Napoleon sent an
order to Davout: "The Emperor orders His Majesty, the King of
Westphalia, to recognize the Prince of Eckmühl as supreme commander so long as the two army corps are combined." At this, Napo-
léon-Jérôme, in a rage, put himself at the head of his Royal Guard,
ordered a countermarch, and set off for Westphalia.

Faced with this kind of desertion, Napoleon simply gave up and
exclaimed: "What a stupid blunder!"

With the enemy everywhere retreating, Napoleon decided to set
out for Vitebsk, hoping to prevent the junction between Bagration
and Barclay.

Hunger, thirst, rain, and a suffocating heat contributed to the disintegration of the Grand Army. The units lost from 25 to 50 per cent of their effective forces. Even the Guard—the least exposed to hardships—had only 28,000 men left out of 37,000.

Finally they reached Vitebsk—on July 27. It was already night when Napoleon pulled up short on a hilltop: the whole of Barclay's army was there before him, their campfires glowing in the darkness. Now, at last, there would be a battle!

"Tomorrow we will see the sun of Austerlitz!" he announced.

But Barclay had learned that Bagration was moving toward Smolensk; and he chose to slip away once more and vanish into the night.

With ill-concealed disappointment, Napoleon made his entrance into Vitebsk. He would stay there until August 15, always hoping that the Russians would come to attack him. Once again, disorder and looting reigned, and the wounded went untended.

By this time, 150,000 men had already disappeared. The Russian tactic, whether intentional or inadvertive, had proven effective. The Grand Army now comprised no more than 250,000 men—not to mention that garrisons had to be left here and there to assure communications. At Vitebsk, as at Vilna, Napoleon tried to regroup his forces: to bring in stragglers and assemble supplies. But the wheels of the great machine were squeaking.

Some of his officers thought it better to remain at Vitebsk. But on August 12 the army set out on the march again—toward Smolensk. Surely, Napoleon hoped, the Russians would defend that important crossroads, especially since it was the sanctuary of the Miraculous Virgin!

But the same scenes were played over again. For the Russians, this was a true holy war. The peasants burned their harvests and their huts. Mobile units had to be sent out to loot villages far from the main highway. Some of these "commandos" formed into groups, chose a leader, and became deserters. And the soldiers who remained under their banners had no choice but to become marauders in their turn. Most of the time they returned empty-handed.

On August 15, Napoleon called a halt in front of Smolensk. That city, located on the rather steep right bank of the Dnieper, was well defended by a long, wide, massive wall topped by twenty-nine red-brick towers with white battlements, some of which still exist. The fortifications had been built long ago by Boris Godunov in the Tatar style. From his advance post, the Emperor noticed many troop movements. Were the Russians going to abandon the city?

"If such is the case," he declared, "in giving me Smolensk, one of their sacred cities, the Russian generals are dishonoring their arms in the eyes of their own subjects!"

But the next day Ney took the Emperor through the brushwood to a hilltop. From there, through a cloud of dust in which the glitter of weapons could be discerned, he could see 120,000 troops assembled. "Carried away by joy," Napoleon uttered his familiar exclamation: "Finally I've got them!"

On August 17 the Emperor awoke at dawn with the hope of seeing the Russian army lined up on the battlefield that he had virtually picked out. But the main body of the enemy forces had taken refuge on the heights, behind the strong walls of the city.

The battle began with intense fighting in the outskirts of the city, where the houses were built in tiers above three ravines just in front of the earthwork fortifications. Having captured the fortifications with heavy losses, the imperial troops ran up against the strong walls which, though bombarded, held out against the fire from twenty-six fieldpieces spitting out big projectiles in an attempt (vain, as it turned out) at opening a breach. The attack columns left "a long, wide trail of blood from the wounded and dead," says Ségur.

Would they have to begin a siege? The Russians were already confident of victory. Nonetheless, Barclay once again ordered his troops to resume the retreat—in spite of Bagration, whose anger never subsided. Bagration wrote to his friend Yermolov, Barclay's chief of staff:

> I have the honor of wearing the uniform, and by God, it's killing me! They sent us to the frontier, then they scattered us around, putting us just about anywhere, like pawns. Then we stayed there, gaping, and after f———ing up the frontier, we took to our heels. I swear I am so disgusted it is driving me mad! God keep you. As for me, I plan to trade in my uniform for a peasant's blouse.

Smolensk was aflame. Before withdrawing, Barclay had ordered that the city be burned in order to cover his new getaway.

Those houses spared by the flames were given over to looting. "There was nothing left with which to dress wounds," wrote Ségur.

"There was no more linen, and they had to use paper from the archives. Parchment was used for splints and bandages, and for lint they had to use waste cotton and birchbark strips. . . ."

Would it not be more reasonable, now, to halt the pursuit and spend the winter at Smolensk? But Napoleon thought otherwise: "I must have a great victory! A battle in front of Moscow! I must capture Moscow and amaze the world!"

And so, on August 24, the pursuit was resumed. As he left Smolensk, Napoleon kept repeating: "Peril is pushing us toward Moscow!"

The road to Moscow was broad. The infantry and the cavalry proceeded in two columns along the sides, while the artillery and the transport kept to the middle. As Napoleon came abreast of each unit, it would halt and draw up in battle array. The drums would beat the general salute, the eagles of the Grand Army would dip, and long cheers would ring out. Only the Guard had orders not to greet the Emperor with cheers, since because they constantly accompanied him, "the cheering would become too frequent and, so to speak, banal." There were constant outbursts of enthusiasm, despite the fires that raged on every hand.

On August 28, Napoleon reached Vyazma, which had also been destroyed by flames. The army was still suffering from exhaustion, hunger, and thirst. "They were fighting over a few puddles," Ségur wrote. "They would fight over the springs, which soon become muddied and clogged. The Emperor himself had to settle for a kind of liquid mud."

On August 31, at the château of Velichego, where Napoleon was staying, a captured Cossack reported that since Barclay had committed "one stupidity after another," the Czar had transferred the supreme command of his army to the old and fat Prince Mikhail Kutuzov—the man Catherine the Great had called "my Kutuzov"— the "too passive, too fatalistic" loser at Austerlitz, as Tolstoi has described him. Both in St. Petersburg and in Moscow, the Czar had been pressured to appoint the man he called disdainfully "that old, one-eyed satyr."

"I had no choice but to yield," Alexander said.

When the appointment was announced, the joy of the Russian troops was beyond description. Kutuzov refused to have his soldiers slapped or flogged—both practices being routine in the Russian army

of those days. And everyone made ready for the battle upon which
the fate of Moscow would hang.

For Kutuzov, "Moscow is not all of Russia." And he said further:
"It is better to lose Moscow than the army and Russia." Yet, as he
knew very well, it was impossible to abandon the city to its fate. He
had to give battle, although the Russian army was also in a pitiable
state; it was numerically inferior to the enemy's army, and most of
it had been retreating since the first days on the Neman. His men
were suffering from hunger. In the words of one veteran of the
campaign, "The cavalry was scarcely alive."

Still and all, they had to give battle. And the Russians' joy at the
thought that they were finally going to fight it out was equaled only
by the joy of Napoleon.

"A battle at last!" he exclaimed. "In two weeks Alexander won't
have either his army or his capital. Then we'll make peace."

The next day, however, the climate gave the Emperor another
warning sign: the army was soaked by a cloudburst. The cannon were
bogged down, the transport was immobilized, and the horses were
up to the hocks in the famous Russian mud which one had to have
seen—and "navigated" through—to have believed.

That same day King Murat, commanding the advance guard,
informed Napoleon that Kutuzov apparently intended to fight and
was strongly fortifying the position in front of the villages of
Borodino, Gorki, and Semenovskaya 130 kilometers from Moscow.
The terrain bristled with trenches and redoubts jammed with big
guns. The Russians were sure that in this way they could stop the
invader from reaching Moscow, whereas the Emperor was convinced that this time he would gain his needed victory.

But the Russian army was literally stuck to the earth. Then the sun
began to shine, partially drying up the swamplike earth, and the
troops were able to continue the advance.

By September 5 the two armies were face to face, and this time
it was the Russians who had chosen the terrain. There were 112,000
of them positioned over a convex front four kilometers in length and
possessing an artillery park of 640 pieces which fired heavier projectiles than did the French cannon.

Fifteen hundred meters in front of Bagration's "three redans,"
atop a small rise of ground, was the redoubt of Shevardino, an extreme advance post of the Russian disposition. It was this position

that—on September 5, 1812—Napoleon ordered General J. D. Compans to capture from the enemy.

Its defenders greeted the French troops with shouts of "Hurrah!" —the Russian battle cry. Not one of them yielded ground when the terrible charge came. The artillerymen were killed where they stood by their guns. This operation cost the French 5,000 men.

The Emperor set up his command post on top of the redoubt. Says Corniquet: "We passed the night in a hollow square formation, with the four fieldpieces at the four corners. The first rank would keep watch standing up, while the second and third sat on their fieldpacks." Napoleon retired to his tent close by the redoubt.

He was very pleased at having captured this "handsome hillock." The position "overlooked everything." In his own words, he would now be able to launch an attack on the main battlefield, "taking it by the horns."

When he awoke at dawn on September 6, he was very satisfied to learn that the Russian army was still entrenched in its positions. Bayonets glittered on the hillsides, as they had the day before. Napoleon was heard to repeat almost greedily: "I need a great battle!"

This time he no longer feared that the enemy would slip away, and there was "general rejoicing," as Ségur reported. But of all those soldiers who had come *on foot* from France, the Low Countries, Germany, and Italy, how many would be alive the next day?

On the Russian side there was the same kind of enthusiasm as they worked away with ardor at strengthening the "great redoubt."

The waiting period—that oppressive *veillée d'armes*—lasted throughout the day. On "the other side," on that Sunday, September 6, Russian priests crowded around the Icon of the Holy Virgin, which had been rescued from Smolensk on August 17. All this while, Napoleon was drawing up his plans. At dawn the next day, with troops commanded by Eugène, he would simulate an attack in force on the Russian right flank; that is, on the village of Borodino. This movement was one of deception: Eugène had orders to stop as soon as he had reached a point from which his batteries could bombard the "great redoubt" on his right. It was against this strong enemy fortification that the successive cavalry charges would be made—from all directions, and over a terrain much rougher than historians have generally noted. Elsewhere, in a movement that would take them around a wooded area, the French would attempt to turn the Russian *left* flank—the "three redans." This role fell to Poniatowski.

When he got back to his headquarters some three kilometers back from Borodino, Napoleon had the chills and thought he had caught cold. But in his tent he found waiting for him a crate containing the portrait of the King of Rome painted by François Gérard, which Bausset had just brought from Paris. This was enough to make him forget his fever. He could not conceal his impatience while the portrait was being unpacked. When he finally got a look at it, he instantly declared that it was "a masterpiece."

"My son is the handsomest child in Europe," he told Rapp.

All that day, the portrait remained propped up on a chair. "Messieurs," Napoleon would say to the officers who came to get their orders, "if my son were fifteen years old he would be here in person and not just on canvas."

That evening, the grenadiers of the Guard filed past the King of Rome. Before making the rounds of the bivouacs, as was his custom on the eve of a battle, Napoleon took one last look at the portrait of his son and then ordered: "Put it away. He is getting a look at a battlefield too early in life."

Napoleon could not sleep that night. Time and again he got up to go and see for himself that the campfires of Kutuzov's troops were still glowing through the darkness. The last time he stepped out of his tent it was five in the morning. One quick glance showed him that the Russians were still in their positions.

"At last we have them! Forward! We'll open the gates of Moscow!"

At 5:30 A.M. he went to a point somewhat beyond the redoubt and sat down on the grass. The terrain he viewed was dotted with birch groves and thickets. On the far horizon were the "three redans." The enemy was at a distance of 1,500 meters. The Old Guard, commanded by Lefebvre, formed a hollow square around the Emperor. The Young Guard and the Horse Guard were massed nearby, a short distance behind the redoubt of Shevardino. Wearing their dress uniforms—retrieved from their knapsacks—they were standing at parade rest. The officers had on the same uniforms they wore at the Tuileries. Murat was caracoling in front of the cavalry, decked out in one of those uniforms the secret of which was known to him alone.

Then the sun rose on that day of September 7, 1812, abruptly dissipating the mist. "There is the sun of Austerlitz!" shouted Napoleon.

He made a gesture, and from a point not far away, a fieldpiece of the Guards Artillery thundered. It was the signal. The hideous slaughter of Borodino—the carnage of the Moskva—had begun.

Twelve hundred pieces of artillery spewed forth fire, iron, and death. Eugène had difficulty getting through the deep ravine of the Kolocha but managed to occupy Borodino, while the French right flank made eight successive attacks on Bagration's "three redans." Some detachments charged to the strains of the "Marseillaise," as in the days when they "were fighting for Liberty." In the attempt to take the triple redoubts, assaults, counterassaults, frightful melees, murderous charges, and hand-to-hand encounters followed one upon another. Under clouds of smoke that darkened the sky, with bullets and cannonballs flying thick and fast, they fought. They fought with muskets, bayonets, and sabers. Some even used "their fists and their sticks." But the "three redans" still held out. To get it over with, the Emperor had the fire of 400 fieldpieces directed against Bagration's position. And finally, one after another, the three redans were taken by Murat and Ney.

"It was then," says a Russian who took part in that day's fighting, "that the great event took place." Bagration had surmised Napoleon's intent: to crush the enemy's left flank and then attack the center. Accordingly, he undertook a magnificent exploit: "One command, and the entire left flank charged with fixed bayonets."

They were beaten back: by the unrelenting fire from Napoleon's artillery; by Murat's cavalry, sweeping the plain with their charges; and especially by a report that went through the whole Russian left flank like a powder train: Bagration had been mortally wounded. "The soldiers' arms fell to their sides."

It was noon.

As the ill-fated Bagration was borne away in a carriage, the three redans were occupied by French troops. There was hard fighting beside Semenovskaya Creek and before the flaming huts of the village bearing the same name. Napoleon's artillery was brought up to the front line to blast the defenders of the village. The charges of both the French and the Russian cavalry became a prodigious movement of flux and reflux. Farther to the right, General Raevski's "great redoubt" was lost from view in the smoke from the frightful artillery duel.

Napoleon, on his white horse, had ridden up to the edge of a ravine. From there he could get a better idea of how the battle was going to develop. This was at a moment when, to the rear of the three redans, which had changed masters, the Russian left flank (a veritable dead limb) had formed a hollow square; when there was hard fighting on the slopes of Kurganskaya Hill; when the "great redoubt" was on the point of being recaptured by the enemy; when Eugène's Italians would have to stand up to a violent counterattack by Matvei Platov's Cossacks and Uvarov's cavalry.

Napoleon then returned to the base of the Shevardino redoubt, dismounted, and remained there—curiously passive. Was it because of his poor health that he was so unassertive and resigned to his fate? And yet the blood of his soldiers—the survivors of the Grand Army —was being spilled everywhere on the vast field of battle.

When he was not sitting down, he walked slowly back and forth in front of the redoubt. The big Russian cannonballs passed over his head. Some of them came rolling up to his feet, and he kicked them aside "like stones in his way when he was taking a walk." He watched the battle through his field glass. Those who did not know that he was quite ill were astonished to see that the Emperor was no longer behaving like a general, no longer electrifying the fighting with his presence. One after another, the deaths of his best generals were announced to him. Twelve generals killed and twenty-seven seriously wounded! At this news, he made a gesture of sorrowful resignation.

One after another, marshals, generals, and aides-de-camp begged him to send in the Guard "to get it over with." Every time he shook his head. Every time he replied: "It will be a long day. We must be patient."

When they insisted, the Emperor would come back at them: "And if there is another battle tomorrow? What would I fight it with?"

And yet they kept hoping that he would come out of it—that he would yield to their entreaties and give the famous command: "Send in the Guard!" Among those around him, there was some grumbling. He silenced it: "We are eight hundred leagues away from Paris and near the gates of Moscow."

At length his facial expression took on some life. But the most he did was to send 60 fieldpieces of the Guards Artillery into the fiery furnace. And throughout the battle he refused to let his beloved "grumblers" plunge into the horrible melee.

Amid whirlwinds of fire and smoke, under a thick hail of grape-shot, Kutuzov's troops—"dug into the earth"—fought with a courage and ferocity that Napoleon could not help but admire. "When a Russian soldier has been killed," he said, "you still have to push him to make him fall down."

On St. Helena, when recollecting the Battle of Borodino, he said: "The Russians showed they were worthy of remaining invincible."

Eyewitnesses had seen Bibikov, aide-de-camp to General Miloradovich, raise his arm in the midst of battle to show the Prince of Württemberg where his general was. At this moment, his arm was torn off by a cannonball. "As he fell from his horse, Bibikov raised his other arm and again pointed in the same direction."

And the "great redoubt" was still holding out.

Not only corpses but the bodies of the wounded formed a regular wall protecting the redoubt. It was not until four o'clock in the afternoon that Raevski's batteries were silenced. Three-fourths of the defenders had been killed on the spot.

Finally, the cannon stopped spewing forth death.

The most murderous battle in Napoleonic history was over. They had fought for twelve hours to a tempo of 140 artillery salvos per minute—a record never before attained. With nightfall, silence came over the battlefield where 60,000 lay dead (of whom 40,000 were Russians). A great moaning, uttered by the 35,000 wounded, rose up from the hills and the plain. Of those wounded, 13,000 Russians would not survive. And of the 10,000 French, German, and Italian wounded, how many would die far from their native land! The Grand Army, which on the morning of September 7 still comprised 130,000 men, now had only slightly more than 100,000. The survivors were hungry, thirsty, and shivering with cold. Toward each campfire glowing in the darkness came wounded men in agony, crawling and looking like ghosts. Captain François wrote: "Among all the rest, I saw one who had dragged himself along the edge of the road. His fractured leg was held together with rags; and he had crawled halfway into the belly of a horse whose flesh he was devouring like a dog."

The next day, Napoleon wrote to Marie Louise: "Ma bonne amie, I am writing you from the battlefield of Borodino. Yesterday I beat the Russians. . . ."

At the same time, Kutuzov was writing to his wife: "I am well, mon amie, and I was not beaten. I won the battle."

Borodino was perhaps a "moral" victory for the Russians. As the Soviet historian Tarlé has accurately said:

> The Russian army, half of which had fallen on the field of Borodino, did not regard itself as defeated. Nor did the Russian people regard themselves as defeated. And they will always remember Borodino not as a defeat, but as a proof of their resistance against the most formidable of attacks on their national independence.

There are those who still feel that Borodino was a victory for Russia. The leaflet handed out to the large number of people who visit the "Panorama of Borodino" which can be viewed on Kutuzov Avenue in Moscow goes so far as to state: "The field of battle was won by the Russians." True, the artillery had ceased firing; and that first night, the Russian survivors bivouacked on the plain behind the hills which had served to mark their forward defenses. But the French, pending the opening up of the road to Moscow (an undeniable result of their victory), had occupied Borodino, Semenovskaya, and the redoubts. Moreover, at ten o'clock in the morning of the next day, the Russians turned their backs on the field of battle and retreated toward Mozhaisk.

It was Kutuzov's turn to ask the question: "What do we do now?" With 50,000 men—half the number he had had the day before—it was impossible to resume combat. The prince therefore ordered a retreat; and four days later he took up a position at the gates of Moscow. The marshal (the Czar had given him this title following the "victory" of Borodino) had just taken up quarters in the isba of the peasant Serastyanov in the village of Fili when he got word of the approach of the French advance guard. The generals surrounding him—Barclay, Bennigsen, Platov, and Uvarov—expressed their opinions. In the view of some of them the battle had not been decisive for either of the two armies.

If the Holy City was abandoned, how would it be possible to make people believe that the French had suffered a defeat? Kutuzov answered the question by saying, very slowly, "You are afraid of a retreat through Moscow. But I consider it a gift of Providence, because it saves the army. Napoleon is like a torrent that we have not yet been able to stop. Moscow is the sponge that will absorb him."

A heavy silence fell over the isba, and the marshal concluded: "In any case I shall be responsible vis-à-vis the Emperor, the fatherland, and the army."

Kutuzov spent that night in the wretched isba in Fili—a night during which he could be heard sobbing.

The army retreated in silence through the city, dumb with stupefaction. Already the French could be seen on the hills which, in the west, form a semicircle around the city.

X X

MOSCOW

In warfare a great disaster
always points to a great culprit.

NAPOLEON

IN THE OLD DAYS, every Russian traveler bowed low and crossed himself when he first saw Moscow from the top of the hill over which the road from Mozhaisk passes. Therefore the spot was named Poklonnaya Gora, the "Hill Obeisance." This was the place where, on the afternoon of September 14, Napoleon stopped and looked about, "ecstatic with joy." Before him lay Moscow with its domes, its onion-shaped, gold and multicolored cupolas, glittering in the sun. In the heart of the city, on the banks of the Moskva River, rose the twenty towers and the warm, reddish-brown crenelated walls of the gigantic citadel encircling an entire hill covered with palaces, towers, and churches: the Kremlin—two syllables that contained a strange evocative power. "So here is that famous city!" he exclaimed. "It's high time!"

The troops, upon reaching that point, stopped as if paralyzed, forgetting all the hardships they had gone through since the crossing of the Neman. "Moscow! Moscow!"

Napoleon had entered Cairo, Milan, Vienna, Venice, Madrid, Berlin, and Warsaw, but he had never enjoyed his triumph so much as this. The suffering of the terrible march, the bloodbath on the Moskva River, were forgotten. What more could he desire? Peace? It could not be too far away. Was not the Czar forced to his knees?

Then came a rolling of the Guards' drums: it was the signal to enter Moscow. With the band in the lead, the troops descended toward the city.

Not a sound was heard. The Emperor, first astonished and then anxious that not a single boyar (to use his expression) had come to meet him, crossed the Moskva River and approached the Dorogomilov Gate. The white walls surrounding the city had disappeared. A path was there instead—the path that has since become the tree-shaded Sadovoye Koltso. Napoleon stopped in front of the gate—but it was not necessary. Nobody was before him; nor was there anybody on the famous Arbat leading into the city toward the Kremlin. The surprising news was then announced to him: "Moscow is deserted."

He was dumfounded: "What an incredible event! We have to march in. Go, bring me the boyars!"

He had to face up to the fact: the 300,000 inhabitants of the Russian capital—except for a handful of Moscovites, some domestics or vagabonds, some deserters, and of course the foreign colonies—had left Moscow, following the army. The staff officers begged Napoleon not to enter Moscow immediately, pointing out that in the suburb of Dorogomilov, not far from the main road, there was an inn where His Imperial Majesty could take lodgings. The room where Napoleon spent his first night was frightfully dirty and foul-smelling. The servants boiled vinegar, but to no avail.

Meanwhile disturbing rumors started to circulate: in some places —especially in the Great Bazaar—fires had broken out, and hoodlums were already looting the deserted houses. During the night the fires multiplied, and it was no longer possible to keep them under control, since the Russian governor had given the order to "remove all fire engines from the city and take them to Ryazan." He had ordered even more than that: the burning of the city!

On the night of November 14 a blaze erupted in the Yauza quarter and awoke its inhabitants. One house had already fallen prey to the fire; on the opposite side, near Peter's Bridge, the big brandy warehouse that belonged to the Crown was on fire. About eleven o'clock the fire swept through the shops close to the stock exchange: shops full of oil and tallow were burning like torches. Kitai-Gorod, the Chinese district, was one big blaze.

It was still impossible to find the city fire engines. But the fires all around did not hinder the Emperor from mounting his horse in the dawn of November 15 and heading for the heart of the city. He took the Arbat, the street that was usually the busiest in Moscow but which on that morning was hopelessly empty, just like the night

before. The tricolor was waving above the Kremlin. The Emperor
rode around the long brick walls that were built by Duke Daniel six
centuries before. He entered the citadel through the Kutafya Gate,
which was crowned by the Tower of the Holy Trinity, and took
lodgings in the apartments that were usually occupied by Czar Alexander when he resided in Moscow. There were salons, banquet halls,
and a ceremonial room with windows facing the Moskva River.

"Here I am in Moscow," Napoleon kept reassuring himself. "I am
in the ancient palace of the czars—in the Kremlin." But he could not
help feeling uneasy after having gone through those streets with the
dead-silent, deserted houses that the inhabitants had fled just as they
had when they escaped from the approaching Tatars. Caulaincourt
noticed the "changed expression" on Napoleon's face. These fires,
breaking out for no apparent reason, depressed him. Disdaining the
Czar's sumptuous bed, he stretched out on his small iron cot, which
was surrounded by green curtains. It had been set up at each overnight stop since the crossing of the Neman River.

Napoleon was abruptly awakened by his valet. His entire room
was lighted by the blazing red sky of Moscow. The fire had spread
in frightening dimensions as the whole city fell prey to the flames.
Followed by Montesquiou and Caulaincourt, the Emperor climbed
the bell tower, called Ivan the Great by the Russians, which stood
directly opposite the faceted palace. The sight from the highest observation point of Moscow was Dantean: a sea of fire covered the
capital—a sea of which the Kremlin seemed to form the center, like
an island still intact. At first Napoleon was thunderstruck and speechless. Then he gritted his teeth, and his companions heard him mutter:
"This is unbelievable! Those barbarians, those savages! To burn down
their own city! What worse could an enemy do? They draw upon
themselves the curse of posterity."

There was some question whether the Guards, who occupied the
citadel of the Kremlin, could protect this core of the city, where an
artillery depot had just been set up. The Emperor nevertheless left
the tower, returned to his living quarters, and tried to work.

When the sun set, the Kremlin seemed to be almost surrounded
and besieged by the fire. There was no choice but to escape. Begged
by Eugène and Murat, the Emperor finally consented to give the
order to depart. The citadel gate leading to the city and Red Square
—"the Beautiful Square"—was already being licked by the flames

and could not be opened. At last a postern was discovered on the side next to the Moskva River. Napoleon, leaning on Caulaincourt's arm, crossed a wooden bridge over the Neglinnaya—the stream that once encircled this part of the Kremlin like a moat. They reached the quay along the Moskva, crossed the river, and found themselves in the merchants' quarter. Covering his face with a handkerchief, Napoleon followed a narrow, winding street, walking between crackling fires. Burning beams were collapsing around the small group, and they were afraid they had lost their way. The smoke blinded them.

At last the fugitive found one of his grooms. He mounted a horse, took the road toward St. Petersburg, and set up quarters in the ugly Petrovsky Palace where Alexander had spent the night preceding his coronation before he entered the city.

Soon the Guard picket took up its post again. Quite a number of bearskin caps were scorched. The general staff watched the terrifying spectacle. "One could see a wall of fire more than a mile long: it resembled a volcano with several craters." The following morning the city was still burning. It looked like a huge fiery tornado with its funnel whirling to the sky. After a moment of gloomy silence the Emperor exclaimed, "This is an omen of great misfortunes."

Despite all, nearly a third of the city remained intact. But what was spared by the fire was destroyed by the plunderers in an absurd, grotesque, and insane orgy of looting.

Napoleon himself also pillaged—but in his own style. He gave the order to dismount the huge golden cross from the tower of Ivan the Great. The cross was destined to adorn the dome of Les Invalides. The emperor watched the difficult operation, carried out by the sappers of the Guard. When a cable broke, the cross dropped—and "the earth trembled under the impact of its enormous weight." It was a useless trophy: the cross disappeared during the retreat— where to, nobody knows.

Napoleon obstinately believed he could obtain a peace because he was occupying the Russian capital. But the Czar in no way wanted an end to the war: he was waiting for "General Winter" to arrive. His sister Catherine, the wife of the Duke of Oldenburg, had told him: "No peace, and you can hope to regain your honor."

"Be assured," the Czar said, "that my resolution to fight is more firm than ever. I prefer to cease being what I am rather than compromise with the monster who has brought misfortune over the entire world."

On October 5 Napoleon sent the French ambassador Lauriston to the Russian outposts. In spite of the opposition of the English military observer, Kutuzov received the French envoy. The semiofficial plenipotentiary tried to convince the marshal that the friendship that had existed between the two emperors had been disrupted "in a regrettable manner owing to purely exterior circumstances." Was this not a good occasion to resume the friendship?

"Shall this peculiar war," he continued, "shall this outrageous war last forever? The Emperor, my master, sincerely desires to end this conflict between two great and noble nations—to end it forever."

"I have no instructions concerning this matter," Kutuzov answered coldly. "When I left to take up my command, the word 'peace' was not mentioned once!"

Disdainfully, the Russian marshal declared that he had no intention to communicate anything whatsoever to his sovereign: "Posterity would curse me if I were thought to have been the first to have initiated any kind of settlement—for such is the spirit of my nation today."

The marshal graciously added: "For the Russian people the French are the same as Genghis Khan's Tatars."

"Oh, but there is still a difference!" Lauriston protested.

"The Russian people don't see any," Kutuzov replied implacably.

The French emissary nevertheless delivered a letter that Napoleon had addressed to Alexander. Then he returned to the Emperor to give a report on his encounter.

Deluded, Napoleon exclaimed, "Upon receipt of my letter one will see Petersburg light fireworks of joy!"

But when he learned about the report that Kutuzov had sent him in spite of what he had said, the Czar exclaimed: "Peace? But we haven't had war yet! My campaign has only started!"

The Emperor was in a very bad mood, since he had not received an answer from the Czar. It has been reported that for entire nights he paced the halls of the Kremlin or read a pretty little book bound in morocco leather: *The History of Charles XII*, by Voltaire.

To keep in touch with Paris became difficult. The couriers (who took only 13 to 18 days to make their way from one capital to the other

—almost a record in those times) were too often intercepted. The supplying of provisions was not easy. General de Fezensac reported that the army could hardly get even black bread and beer. In order to find meat, strong detachments had to be sent into the countryside to catch the cattle in the forests where the peasants had taken refuge. There was plenty of liquor and jam, but no meat and bread. The soldiers covered themselves with furs, but they needed ordinary clothes and shoes. The occupying forces had an abundance of diamonds, other precious stones, and all the luxurious things imaginable, but they were nevertheless on the verge of starvation. The Russian army formed a circle around Moscow and foraging became a heroic task for the cavalry. Sometimes a sheaf of straw had to be paid for "with one's own blood." Future events would prove it: the enemy would not allow the Grand Army to pass except to the west. The question was: Should one think of departure?

"Our departure would look like flight," Napoleon cut the question short. "It would have repercussions in Europe."

Then he repeated: "Moscow is not a military position, but a political one. In politics one must never sound retreat or admit one's own errors. That way you lose esteem."

On October 6 he wrote Marie Louise: "The weather here is very good, just like Paris. It is like a beautiful day in Fontainebleau."

On October 13, however, the first snow fell over Moscow. It melted during the day. "But with these first flakes," as the Comte de Ségur expressed it, "all the illusions with which the emperor had tried to surround himself disappeared."

For Napoleon the old question was still unresolved: What should he do? Stay in Moscow? "What would they say in Paris?" he asked. "The effect of six months without communication is unforeseeable! No, France could not get used to my absence. Prussia and Austria would take advantage of it."

The decision was made abruptly: retreat to Smolensk. They could pass the winter there, and in the spring march on St. Petersburg.

"This is in no case a withdrawal but a strategic move," Napoleon said explicitly. "My army is not defeated as far as I know."

From then on, the only thing the Emperor had in mind was withdrawal—although he did not dare employ this word, which he had stopped using since Acre. He merely declared that "within twenty days the army must be in its winter quarters." He urged the departure of his wounded men. He was too proud to consent to leave anything behind voluntarily. His artillery did not have enough horses; besides it was too big for an army that was reduced to 100,000 men. But he became angry at the suggestion that part of it be left in Moscow: "No, the enemy would take it as a trophy! Everything will come with me!"

Absent-mindedly (unless he did not want to face facts) he ordered the purchase of 20,000 horses—just as if he had been at the Tuileries. He demanded that the cavalry procure supplies "for two months," even though for several days the detachments sent to forage for one day's food supply had returned with empty bags. In order to avoid admitting defeat, he passed those last few days (to the stupefaction of his aides-de-camp) "discussing the merits of some new poems he had just received, or the rules and regulations of the Comédie Française of Paris, which took him three evenings. Then," Ségur continues his report, "they saw him become dull and pass long hours sitting up in his bed as if benumbed—awaiting, a novel in his hand, the outcome of his horrible adventure."

Napoleon was nevertheless working out the plan for the retreat. Then he would hesitate, change his mind, and a moment later dictate a different itinerary. He gave Junot the order to burn all the muskets of the wounded men and to blow up superfluous ammunition wagons. And—as a last attempt at peace—on October 16 he once more sent Lauriston to the Russian outposts. But the envoy returned the following morning without an answer from Kutuzov.

On Sunday, October 18, Napoleon inspected Ney's corps in the courtyard of the Kremlin. In the distance one could hear cannon thundering. Suddenly Béranger, Murat's young aide-de-camp, arrived at a gallop: the front lines of the King of Naples had been routed by 80,000 men under Bennigsen's command. "Twelve cannons, twenty ammunition wagons, and thirty other vehicles have been taken; two generals were killed, and three or four thousand men lost." Fortunately Poniatowsky, who was in the vanguard, had been able to offer resistance and stop the enemy from advancing.

"We have to wipe out the affront of this surprise attack," exclaimed the Emperor, sending out a multitude of general and detailed instructions. "And above all we have to see to it that people cannot say a setback has forced us to retreat!"

Therefore the southern route was to be taken to Smolensk: "Let's march on Kaluga, and woe to those who cross my way!"

The following morning, October 19, under a beautiful sunny sky, he made his exit from the Kremlin through the Gate of the Savior. A quarter-hour later he had left Moscow—his most distant and last conquest. He had ordered the Duke of Treviso to guard the Kremlin with a division, a brigade, two sapper companies of the artillery, and 500 cavalrymen. To guard it—but also to set it on fire and blow it up after the French troops had left the citadel.

Still more than 100,000 strong—50,000 of them on horseback or in carriages—the army followed their leader. The Guard brought up the rear of the huge column.

Many officers possessed several servants who were following their masters. Women marched along with the soldiers—an infinitely larger number of them than has commonly been assumed. The regiments were accompanied by emaciated steers and cows, which soon died without having to be killed. Loaded not only with everything that was necessary to eat, set up camp, and clothe the troops, but also with stolen goods, thousands of vehicles of every kind rolled behind the army in an immense disorderly mass.

"Fatigue and the first raid by the Cossacks will take care of all this," Napoleon said, giving the order to burn the wagons that were not indispensable. But everybody found that his vehicle was necessary. The Emperor shrugged his shoulders and pursued his way.

Moscow had conquered Napoleon's obstinacy. The destruction that the Emperor had ordered was not total: the rain had dampened the fuses—which is why the Tower of Ivan the Great was preserved. What was destroyed by the fire, however—the arsenal, part of the towers and walls of the Kremlin—was enough to nourish feelings of hatred among the Moscovites.

The intelligence service functioned as badly on one side as the other. Kutuzov learned about the retreat only on the morning of October 23. The marshal was awakened, and the duty officer found him sitting majestically on his bed, dressed in a tunic decorated with all his orders. His one eye was beaming, but he could not believe that the 100,000 Frenchmen had departed:

"Tell me, my friend," he said, "has Napoleon really left Moscow? Quick, tell me, don't keep me in suspense."

The officer repeated his report, and the old man turned "to the icon of the Savior" and exclaimed: "God, my Creator, you have at last heard my prayers! From now on Russia will be saved!"

Kutuzov had reason to thank the Savior. Napoleon had stayed 32 days in the Kremlin. During this time the marshal had managed to muster 85,000 foot soldiers and 35,000 horse—not to speak of the 200,000 militiamen in reserve. Having belatedly learned that Napoleon was heading for Kaluga to take the road to Smolensk, where he would doubtless go into winter quarters, Kutuzov decided to block the Grand Army's way. He would do this with only part of his forces, since he did not have the time to muster more. He chose a strong position behind Maloyaroslavets. It was his hope that the mere presence of the Russian army might suffice to throw Napoleon back on the old Smolensk road—the same route the emperor had taken on his way eastward—which, since it was now despoiled of all provisions, would spell the ruin of the Grand Army. It was no longer Napoleon who imposed his will on his enemies.

On October 24 the emperor stopped two kilometers from Maloyaroslavets. He set up quarters in a termite-ridden isba. As in all isbas its only room, which was dirty and dark, was divided by a sheet. This was the place where at eleven o'clock at night Bessières entered. He had carefully surveyed the front of the Russian position and concluded: "It is unassailable." One could perhaps at best occupy Maloyaroslavets, but after that the way out would be blocked.

"Are you sure?" asked the Emperor. "Can this be true? Do I have your word for it?"

Bessières was firm: "Three hundred grenadiers would be enough to stop an army there!"

Ségur saw Napoleon fold his arms in dismay and lower his head. He was crushed: his army was victorious, and yet he was defeated. His way was cut off, his maneuver was frustrated. Kutuzov, an old man, a Scythian, had thwarted his plans! And he could not even blame his star for it. Had the road to Maloyaroslavets not been free only the day before? So his luck had not failed him! Was it he who had failed his luck?

Nevertheless the city of Maloyaroslavets was taken and retaken. In the end Eugène held it. But the fighting—the Battle of Kaluga—had cost 700 lives. The Emperor hesitated. Should he go on? Should he attempt to take the "unassailable" position? For the first time he felt defeated before the fight had begun. The Battle of Kaluga was definitely not a victory, whatever his bulletin had said. The Russians themselves certainly considered it as the defeat of the enemy; for the battle had hindered the French from taking the position held by Kutuzov and from proceeding to the fertile provinces where the Grand Army could have found provisions and continued its march on Smolensk. For Kutuzov the event was a landmark on the way to victory.

A last time Napoleon asked himself what he should do. He still hesitated. Then on the morning of October 26 he decided to go north and take the highway running from Moscow to Smolensk. Although this road was still guarded by numerous French posts, one would find no food there for either men or horses.

Kutuzov had foreseen it.

The horrible retreat really started on October 27 as the army moved north. That morning the troops woke up under a thick blanket of snow.

On the twenty-eighth, Napoleon's soldiers—who carried with them food supplies for only two weeks—camped in the poor wooden houses of Mozhaisk. On Thursday, October 29, the Emperor crossed the battlefield on the Moskva River, where many dead had been left unburied. The sight was infernal: huge flocks of ravens had taken possession of the terrain. All of a sudden the Emperor stopped in horror: a wounded French soldier had survived amid all the putrefaction. As soon as he noticed Napoleon he crawled toward him on all fours, blaming him "for all he had suffered after he had been abandoned so cruelly. He went on cursing war and glory, predicting that the Emperor himself would sometime be abandoned and forgotten." Napoleon merely turned to his officers and said, "Put this unfortunate man on a wagon and give him all the care he needs."

The army marched along the Smolensk road where, on its way east, it had cleaned up everything to the last straw on the roofs of the isbas. The twenty regiments of Platov's Cossacks started to harass the imperial troops. They were following a parallel route—the one the Emperor had intended to take, where they found food and forage in abundance—and conducting constant raids on the Grand Army. This was the famous "parallel march" planned by Kutuzov. All around, the peasants had taken up arms and supported the regular army. Every night the Emperor's cot was set up behind small fortified palisades in a kind of a relay station built for the post. The Cossacks, the fatigue, the hunger, the snowstorms, the icy wind, the frozen, slippery roads—and the fact that the unroughed horses could not keep their footing on these roads—had already taken their toll, not only of the unusual baggage train that the "tribe" dragged behind, but also of numerous soldiers. And the real winter had not yet started.

"The foe is fleeing," wrote Raevski in an unpublished letter, which is preserved in the Moscow Museum of History. "The road is covered with bodies and people who are dying of starvation. The enemy troops are being killed off. Generals and other officers are taken prisoner every day, but not many enlisted men, since they are slaughtered. After all the atrocities that have been committed, humanity has lost its rights. . . . " According to the defender of the "grand redoubt" of Borodino, from this point on, the Russian army could relax: "the job" was going to be finished "by the Cossacks alone. . . . "

Already entire cavalry units were walking. Misery overtook the army. The war was ruthless, for nothing counted but survival. One could see men killing each other over a morsel of horse meat. Weakened by malnutrition, the Russian prisoners could not keep walking. Their guards simply slaughtered them, breaking the skulls of some, and shooting others. When there was an attack, the survivors had to throw themselves face down into the snow; for if they raised their heads they were killed without mercy.

The army had long ago rid itself of the amputees and the wounded of Borodino. Those poor, useless human bundles had been piled on wagons or gun carriages, and some of the drivers intentionally drove the horses into deep ruts in the road. The unfortunate wounded men—most of them amputees—who fell from the vehicles were left behind.

On November 6 the sky darkened, the thick black clouds hung low over the earth. A storm broke out, and huge snow flakes started to fall thickly on the frozen ground.

The Russian winter made its grand entrance.

The temperature fell to 22 degrees below zero. "Our lips stuck together," said Sergeant Bourgogne. "Our nostrils—or rather our brains—froze. We seemed to be marching in a world of ice." On November 10, after having laboriously crossed a tributary of the Dnieper, Napoleon saw (through his field glass) hordes of Cossacks come up to French soldiers whom they had just taken prisoner, undress them, and leave them to die naked in the snow.

The survivors—the word was already being used—marched toward Smolensk as if they were approaching the Promised Land. There they would find warm houses. There they would be able to sleep, eat, wash, and dress properly.

Finally they reached the city. With the exception of the Guard, who stayed in formation, all the others ran to the high red walls of Smolensk, which was occupied by a small French garrison. But the gates remained closed. This disorderly crowd—these emaciated faces smudged with dirt and smoke, these tattered uniforms, these bizarre clothes, these men dressed in pink or purple satin coats— looked frightening. After waiting for a long time on the shores of the Dnieper, the wretched crowd could at last enter the city. The quartermasters gave rations only to those officers whose units had remained organized. The rest—the two-thirds of the army who did not have officers anymore, and who did not even know where their regiments were, as well as the numerous servants who followed the troops—dispersed in the streets hoping to find something to plunder in the city.

> But everywhere [Ségur wrote] the sight of dead horses whose flesh had been eaten down to the bone, signaled famine. Everywhere, the doors and windows of the houses had been broken and torn off, to be used as fuel for the bivouacs. Here they could find no refuge, no winter quarters ready for them, and no wood. The sick and wounded were left in the streets on the carts which had brought them.

The Emperor stayed five days in a beautiful house on New Square. He was "furious" at the supply officers who had been instructed to store provisions in the city. But the spectacle he experienced was not yet enough. He was beset by bad news: Vitebsk was in Russian hands, Eugène had lost two-thirds of his artillery, and recently Augereau's brigade had been wiped out. Ludwigsberg Wittgenstein's Russian-Swedish army seemed intent upon joining forces with General Chichakov to cut off the retreat of the Grand Army, which no one dared called by that name any longer. Napoleon concluded that he had to leave Smolensk and make the long march to Vilna—not via Vitebsk, as on the way to Moscow, but via Orsha and

Bobr to avoid facing the two armies of the enemy. (Both—one of
them 45,000 men strong, the other with 35,000—were still kept under check by Victor's and Oudinot's corps.) Besides, there were
Kutuzov's 60,000 troops, who were still close on Napoleon's heels and
could have completed his encirclement. On the new route he had
chosen he would, however, have to cross the Berezina, a tributary of
the Dnieper. It was more than 500 kilometers long, and had become
famous because of the crossing made by Charles XII. But he had no
choice: this was the only hope for survival.

In the morning of November 14 the Emperor prepared to leave
Smolensk. The thermometer showed 20 degrees below zero. It was
still dark. Napoleon had exchanged his legendary uniform for a Polish coat trimmed with marten. On his head he wore a green velvet
cap trimmed with fur and a golden tassel. This headdress was tied in
a strange way under his chin with two black ribbons.

On Wednesday, November 17, not far from Krasnoye Kutuzov's
troops almost wrecked everything. But the Old Guard prevented
30,000 to 40,000 Russians from closing their vise on the survivors of
the Grand Army.

Marching in a goose-step, the "grumblers" of the Guard followed
Napoleon, who walked on foot, an iron-tipped staff in his hand. That
evening they entered Orsha, the band leading the way. By now,
there were no more than 6,000 of them. Eugène had no more than
1,800 men left out of 40,000. Of the army of 70,000 troops under
Davout's command, 4,000 remained.

And the terrible march went on. The temperature had gone
down to 28 degrees below zero. Every morning they left behind
them, around the bivouacs, frozen corpses covered with snow. Every
morning the survivors would lag as the march began again, expand-
ing the number of stragglers—a horde that increased with the addition of remnants of units from which officers and noncommissioned
officers had completely disappeared. "The most horrible thing," one
of the soldiers said later, "was having to spend sixteen-hour nights in
bivouacs in the snow, usually without either food or fire." As they
broke camp, they would see men get up on shaky legs, lean forward,
and then fall—never to rise again. Another witness recounts:

> The men who were about to die showed strange symptoms.
> One of them would come up to you with a beaming face, his eyes

full of gaiety, and grasp your hand enthusiastically. You would know he was a goner. Another would look at you darkly, rapidly uttering words of indignation and despair. And you would know that he, too, was done for.

Many of them had to throw away their muskets, since they could not touch the freezing-cold metal "without feeling an intense pain, as from a hot coal."

On November 20, at Baranoye, Napoleon learned that the bridge over the Berezina at Borisov, guarded by 1,200 Poles, had been captured by the Russians. Their retreat was cut off! They had to prepare to rout the enemy.

> This time [he told Caulaincourt] there will be no salvation except for the brave. If we can cross the Berezina, I will be master of the situation; because together with the Guard the two fresh corps we will join up with there—those of Victor and Oudinot—will be enough to beat the Russians. If we are unable to cross the river, we'll break ranks and fight individually. Take Duroc, and find out how much we can carry with us if we have to make a break for it across the fields without vehicles. We must be prepared in advance to destroy everything so as not to leave any trophies for the enemy. I would rather eat with my fingers for the rest of the campaign than leave the Russians one fork with my crest on it.

In order to hitch as many well horses as possible to the cannon and caissons, they burned those vehicles which could no longer be pulled, including some of the imperial transport—even the vans containing the archives.

On November 23 the eagles—those emblems that the Emperor had handed out to his soldiers at the camp of Boulogne—were thrown into the flames.

Lined up along the right side of the road leading to Borisov, a town on the banks of the Berezina, the 20,000 men under Marshal Victor were waiting for the Grand Army. Victor's reserve corps (the Second Corps), like Oudinot's (the Ninth Corps), had not advanced to Moscow. Napoleon had arranged to rendezvous with them on the banks of the Berezina, so as to cover the retreat while they crossed the river via the bridge at Borisov.

Victor's troops were in good condition. True, they had fought engagements (with varying degrees of success) with the Russians under Wittgenstein; and after a brief letup in the weather, they had been exposed to extreme cold. But they had eaten well at Smolensk, and since then the supplies of rations had not been too bad.

They waited.

Abruptly, to their horror and stupefaction, a bedraggled line of wraiths in rags and indescribable uniforms came within view. Their faces were emaciated and bearded; their eyes stared fixedly; their feet were wrapped in straw tied with rags. They moved along in silence, like captives. Among them, staff in hand, was the Emperor. Behind them came some motley vehicles loaded with wounded and dragged along by horses that were nothing but skin and bones.

This horde was the Grand Army.

Heavy-hearted, with tears in their eyes, Victor's troops watched as these emblems of the horrible disaster filed past them.

From positions on both the right bank of the Berezina and the left (where Napoleon was), 120,000 Russians were preparing to join forces and make the kill. Needless to say, the armies of Chichakov, Wittgenstein, and Kutuzov had also suffered from the terrible cold. But their march had not been encumbered with stragglers, and it had been orderly. Napoleon, on the other hand, could count on only the 5,000 or 6,000 men of the Guard, the 20,000 troops brought up by Victor and Oudinot, and the handful of Poles under Jan Dombrowski who had fallen back after the capture of Borisov. It is difficult to ascertain how many men in the Grand Army (apart from the Guard) were capable of holding a musket: certainly not more than 3,000 armed and disciplined troops under the command of Ney and Davout. As for King Murat, who had been in command of 50,000 cavalrymen when the campaign began, most of his horses had long ago been eaten or hitched up to fieldpieces.

Thus there were 120,000 men ready to fall upon 26,000 to 30,000 starved, half-frozen combat troops, and 40,000 half-dead stragglers—40,000 sick and wounded with frozen limbs. For the Grand Army, crowded into an area of 15 square leagues, escape seemed impossible.

"I doubt that this monster Napoleon can escape either death or captivity!" exclaimed Count Mikhail Vorontsov.

On the evening of November 25 the Emperor took up quarters

on a farm which was the residence of Baron Korsach, the overseer of the Radziwill family.

Accompanied by Caulaincourt, the Emperor went to the bridge at Borisov and stepped out on that part of it which had not been blown up. It had been blasted at three points.

The two men stopped at the first breach. Beneath them flowed the black waters of the Berezina (it was not yet frozen over) carrying huge ice floes. Low islands divided the river into numerous branches, and owing to the swampy nature of the banks, the distance to be crossed amounted to more than 700 meters. Opposite them, on the right bank (near the road which now leads to the railroad station of Borisov), Admiral Chichakov's batteries were trained on the site of the former bridge. If Ségur is to be believed, the artillery of the Guard could have neutralized them; but an artillery duel would have made for new losses and hampered the work of the pontoon soldiers. So it was impossible to rebuild the bridge and cross the river at this point. They would have to look for a ford, meantime "scouting" around Borisov itself and farther downstream, toward Uksholda, so as to make the Russians believe they were intending, simultaneously, to repair the destroyed bridge and find another crossing by going downstream toward the Dnieper.

They had to find a ford! And they had to find one quickly, because time was pressing. Whereas Admiral Chichakov was content to keep an eye on the French, Wittgenstein could at any moment launch a violent attack on Victor's corps, and Kutuzov could easily attack—at one and the same time—the rear guard and the left flank of the Grand Army (or rather, what was left of it).

And then came a miraculous bit of luck. General J. B. Corbineau, when he found Borisov occupied by the Russians, took his phantom brigade upstream through the wooded banks of the river and hid in the forest. There he came across a Lithuanian peasant whose horse was wet up to the breast. This meant there was a ford somewhere in the vicinity. The peasant, willy-nilly, agreed to guide the general to a place five leagues upstream from Borisov—to the village of Studyanka, whose isbas stood on the bank of the river opposite the hamlet of Bychi. At this point, too, the river was divided into several branches dotted with swampy islands, and flowed between low, wooded hills.

As it turned out, one could wade across the river at this point,

where the water came only up to one's armpits. Corbineau coura-
geously plunged into the icy water. He lost 70 cavalrymen, who were
carried off by the rapid current, but most of his brigade managed to
reach the right bank. This proved that a trestle bridge could be built
here. Napoleon immediately commanded the engineers to get to
work, while the other troops continued to "entertain" the Russians
at Borisov.

During the night of November 25, 400 pioneer troops arrived on
the scene and, completely naked, in water up to their shoulders, set
about building the trestles and fixing them in the muddy bottom of
the Berezina—paying no attention to the ice floes borne along by the
river. "Some of them," says the grenadier Pils, "fell dead and were
carried away by the current. But the spectacle of their tragic end in
no way diminished the energy of their comrades."

On the other side of the river they could see the campfires of the
Russian army. This was the division commanded by Chuplits, consisting of 6,000 men.

When dawn came, the French saw that the Russian bivouacs had
been abandoned. And on the heights they could see thirty fieldpieces
being pulled back. In the words of Ségur: "Just one of their cannonballs would have been enough to destroy the single escape bridge we
were about to put up from one bank to the other. But their artillery
was withdrawing while ours was being positioned."

To the amazement of the French, the Russians, believing the
whole thing was a snare, had pulled up stakes so as to mass all their
forces opposite Borisov—and, farther downstream, opposite Uksholda!

The French shouted for joy. Rapp and Oudinot rushed off to tell
the Emperor: "Sire, the Russian army has just pulled up stakes and
left its position."

"Impossible!"

Napoleon stepped out of his headquarters and dashed to the river's edge. He arrived just in time to see the tail of Chuplits' column
disappearing.

"I have fooled the admiral!"

Shortly thereafter the capture of a prisoner enabled him to discover that Chichakov had been so far deceived as to pull back Chuplits' troops and not leave a single observer opposite the village of
Studyanka. He had been doubly deceived, since he had no doubt
been informed that the French were active in the area of Studyanka,

but he had taken this to be a feint, and believed that the crossing would be made at Borisov. And so he kept his force of 27,000 men at Borisov.

Napoleon had to make sure of the right bank. Accordingly, he ordered 50 cavalrymen of the Seventh Light Cavalry Regiment—each of them carrying a light infantryman behind him—to cross the Berezina so as to reinforce Corbineau's brigade and establish a bridgehead. In spite of the ice floes that bloodied the breasts and flanks of their horses, the cavalrymen managed to reach the other bank. After several such crossings, both on horseback and on rapidly built rafts, 400 men occupied the opposite bank.

Meantime, to the north, on the left bank, Marshal Victor's corps was keeping Wittgenstein at a respectful distance. As for Kutuzov, he had apparently succumbed to lethargy. He had given up all pursuit for the past four days, and seemed not at all to realize that if he were to push on toward the Berezina (some 115 kilometers away) he would be able to win a total victory.

By the morning of November 26 the first bridge was completed and the 9,300 men of Oudinot's corps crossed the river. Another bridge, intended for the artillery, the wagons, and what carriages were left, was completed by four o'clock in the afternoon. But that same evening the rising waters carried away part of it; and the same thing happened twice on the following day. Both times the pontoniers jumped into the water—which soon attained a depth of more than 5 feet—and went at their work amid the ice floes.

The 40,000 stragglers camped on the bank and fought with one another over a few pieces of bread. The houses of Studyanka and the neighboring forest had provided them with wood. For the first time in several days they were warm; and they therefore refused, despite orders from the officers sent by Napoleon, to cross the river on the night of the twenty-sixth. The officers tried to get at least a few of these wretches to pass over to the right bank, but in vain: they preferred to spend the night squatting before the embers of a weak campfire.

But with the coming dawn, on November 27, the stragglers began a rush for the bridge—a spectacle witnessed by the Emperor.

> The worst moment came [writes Ségur] when the Guard, from whom the stragglers were taking their cue, started to move off.

The departure of the Guard was like a signal: the others came running from all directions, piling on top of one another along the riverbank. In a matter of moments the narrow approaches to the bridges were jammed to overflowing with a broad, dense, confused mass of men, horses, and vehicles. Those in front—being shoved by those behind them, then forced back by the Guards and pontoniers, or stopping at the edge of the water—were crushed, trampled underfoot, or pushed into the Berezina amid the ice floes. From this immense and horrible crush of people there arose at times a kind of dull, humming sound, at other times a great clamor, intermingled with moans and frightful curses.

Throughout the day, with the temperature at 20 degrees below zero, the army continued to inch its way along. Napoleon came to the river several times to observe the crossing. The next night, with the temperature down to 30 degrees below zero, the bridges were again free, since the men had returned to the campfires.

On that November 28, Marshal Victor had Wittgenstein's entire army to cope with. Not only did he manage to contain it, but in order to save the last units crossing the two bridges he went over to the attack, driving the enemy back and inflicting heavy losses on him. In one of the ravines, Wittgenstein's 5,000 horse were routed by General Fournier's 800 cavalry. On the right bank Oudinot, Ney, and Mortier were holding in check the 27,000 men under Chichakov, who had finally realized what the situation was. Meantime, on the left bank, Victor managed to hold his ground until nightfall. Then, however, the enemy attacked with reinforcements, and on the Emperor's orders, Marshal Victor retreated. With great difficulty, two companies of the Guard were keeping open the approaches to the two bridges toward which the Second Corps was heading, using force to get through the mass of stragglers. Hardly had Victor's army got across when the huge throng made a rush for the bridge, causing the platform to collapse once again. As before, the pontoniers jumped into the water, and two hours later the crossing was resumed.

The widow of a colonel who had been killed a few days earlier, holding her four-year-old daughter in her arms, was vainly trying to reach the bridge. The surgeon Huber heard her exclaim: "Oh, God! How sad for me that I can't even pray!"

A few moments later her horse was hit by a musketball, and another shot broke her left leg just above the knee.

With the composure of silent despair she picked up her crying child, kissed her several times, and then, with the bloodied garter she had taken off her own broken leg, she strangled the poor little thing. Still holding her child in her arms, and squeezing her tightly against her, she sat down beside her fallen horse and waited for the end, without saying a word. She was soon crushed under the horses of those crowding toward the bridge.

When Eblé, the French engineer general, received his orders to burn the bridges, there were still some 12,000 stragglers on the left bank. It was then seven o'clock in the morning. The officer commanding the pontoniers waited until nine o'clock to carry out the order, and did not set fire to the bridges until he saw some Cossacks coming down the hill toward the bank. There were still 8,000 people on the left bank. Says Ségur: "We could see them wandering in desolate groups along the edge of the river. Some of them jumped in and tried to swim; others risked climbing onto the ice floes; while still others rushed, with lowered heads, straight into the flames on the bridge, which collapsed under them." And he adds: "Their bodies piled up and, along with ice floes, beat against the trestles." The survivors sat down in the snow, resigned to their fate, and waited for the Russians to come.

The spectacle that greeted the eyes of the enemy troops when they reached the bank of the Berezina has been described by an engineering officer, Martosa: "Imagine a wide, winding river whose surface, as far as the eye could see, was covered with corpses, some of which were beginning to freeze. It was the reign of death, resplendent in all its destructive might. . . ." Although the 8,000 stragglers were massacred by Wittgenstein's Cossacks, the remnants of the Grand Army had managed somehow to cross the river.

The most horrible ordeal yet experienced by the soldiers began the day after that twenty-ninth of November.

It was sheer terror. In three days the 25,000 soldiers who had fought on the Berezina, intermingled with the horde, which had become "a crowd in flight," marched pell-mell, strewing the way with discarded weapons and cannon—those trophies that today ornament so many Soviet museums. Only the remnant of the Guard still preserved a martial appearance. "The old campaigners," says Caulaincourt, "brightened up as soon as they caught sight of the Em-

peror. And every day, the battalion of the Guard on escort duty kept
up an astonishing standard of smartness."

The imperial equipage, which at the time of departure from
Moscow comprised 630 horses and 52 vehicles, now consisted of only
the Emperor's carriage and some 20 other vehicles. Yet every day
Napoleon had his fresh linen, white bread, Chambertin, beef or mutton, and his favorite rice with beans or lentils.

The temperature was 21 degrees—and on some days, 31 degrees
—below zero. Ravens froze in midflight and fell to the ground. Ex-
haled breath froze when it came into contact with the air, making
a sharp little popping sound. A horrible detail is given by Sergeant
Corniquet in his unpublished memoirs. "Many of the survivors were
walking barefoot, using pieces of wood as canes, but their feet were
frozen so hard that the sound they made on the road was like that
of wooden clogs."

Whenever a person collapsed, the horde would rush at him and,
without waiting for him to breathe his last, strip off his clothes. The
last of the horses were dying of starvation. The moment one of them
fell, a gang of famished people would throw themselves on it. The
first to get there would go for the animal's flank and get the liver.
"The whole thing would take place without anyone's thinking of
killing the poor beast—so anxious were they to resume the march."

On December 3 Napoleon reached Molodechno, where there
were some food supplies and relatively abundant forage. It was a fine
day, with a bright sun, and the cold seemed bearable. Finally, all at
the same time, the couriers arrived at the imperial headquarters.

Up until then, the Emperor seems not to have planned to leave
his army. But toward noon that day he suddenly announced that he
had decided to leave for France immediately. His mind had constantly been occupied by the Malet affair, a plot very well carried out
on October 23, at Paris, by Brigadier General C. F. de Malet, who had
announced the Emperor's death at Moscow and had very nearly
succeeded in taking his place. To be sure, the whole thing had not
lasted for more than a few hours, but Napoleon nonetheless believed
he had to get back. He felt the survivors of the catastrophe could
reach Vilna without him; and once there, they could get both food
and rest while waiting for spring to come.

The command of the army was entrusted to King Murat rather

than to Eugène. And at 10:00 P.M. on December 5, traveling under the name of his Grand Equerry, the Emperor left Smorgonie for Paris. His journey—which would take him across Poland and Germany in thirteen days and fourteen nights—was one long, wild ride: first in a traveling carriage, then in a sleigh, and finally in a cabriolet.

As Napoleon approached the Neman he became more optimistic: "With plenty of supplies at Vilna, order will be restored. There is more than enough there to enable us to resist the enemy. The Russians are at least as exhausted as we are. And since they too are suffering from the cold, they will go into winter quarters."

And yet he was worried about the way he would be received at Paris: "Our disasters will create a great sensation in Paris, but my return will cancel out the negative effects."

On December 16 they crossed the Rhine in a boat and reached Mainz. Finally, Napoleon was in France.

On that day the *Moniteur* published that famous and terrifying bulletin which (as Marshal Oudinot said) would "confound France":

> Until November 6 the weather was perfect, and the army's movements were executed with the greatest success. The cold wave set in on the 7th. From then on, every night, we lost several hundred horses which died in the encampment. . . . This army, which had been so splendid on the 6th, was in very different condition by the 14th: without artillery, without a supply train, and almost without cavalry. . . . This difficulty, together with a sudden and severe cold wave, made our position very trying. Those men whom Nature had not molded strongly enough to remain unaffected by the hazards of fate and fortune seemed to be shaken: they lost their lively spirits and good humor; their thoughts dwelled only upon misfortunes and catastrophes. . . . The enemy, having observed along the roadsides the traces of this frightful calamity which had overwhelmed the French army, tried to take advantage of it. . . .

Now that they were getting close to their destination, the Emperor brought up the Malet affair again:

> Among all those military men and civilian officials to whom my death was announced, not a single one thought of my son!
> And yet when I reach Paris everyone will make much of his devotion to me. I must make an example of someone, because fidelity is a sacred duty for the magistrate—probably more sacred

than for the military man, since the latter has only to obey the orders he receives without reasoning about them. . . . The fact of becoming accustomed to change, and the ideas of the Revolution, had left their marks. It took a man of action like me—a man who knew the French as I did—to even hope for those things which by now have been accomplished. France needs me for another ten years. I can see now that if I should die, everything would become a chaos. If my son's throne were to collapse, all other thrones would fall; for it is plain to me now that everything I have accomplished thus far is very fragile.

On December 17 he took a late evening meal at Verdun. Once back on the road, he was overtaken by dispatch riders who had left Russia sixty hours after his own departure. Feverishly, he broke open the seals on the dispatches: the army was completely disorganized, but was nonetheless approaching Vilna.

It was a quarter-hour before midnight on Friday, December 18, when the post chaise drove into the courtyard of the Tuileries.

"Good night, Caulaincourt," Napoleon said to his companion. "You need rest, too." Then he went into the apartments of Marie Louise.

A few days later the Emperor, who had assumed that the survivors of the rout on the Berezina had been recuperating in Lithuania, learned that Murat had abandoned the "broken skeleton" of the Grand Army. It was the *coup de grace.*

After setting out from Vilna on the road to Kovno, the artillery of the Guard and the last imperial field wagons had been unable to get up the icy slope of the narrow pass of Ponari. They had to abandon the cannon and empty the treasure bags. In the words of Ségur, who was horrified by the spectacle: "The troops of the rear guard who came upon this scene of disorder threw down their arms in order to plunder. They went at it so frantically that they no longer heard the whistling of the musketballs or the shouts of the Cossacks behind them."

Henceforth, there was no more artillery: Ney, who had been keeping guard over the last few cannon, had to abandon them. Marshal Victor was seen marching toward Kovno "alone," since the rear guard under his command had simply left him.

Marshal Berthier's final report to the Emperor read:

I must inform Your Majesty that the regular army is in complete disorder, as is the Guard, which now comprises no more than 400 or 500 men. The generals and other officers have lost all they owned, and most of them have some parts of their bodies frostbitten. The roads are littered with corpses, and the houses are packed full of dying men. The entire army now consists of nothing more than a column stretched out over a distance of a few leagues, which sets out in the morning and halts in the evening without receiving any orders. The marshals are walking along with everyone else. . . .

The army no longer exists. . . .

XXI

THE KILL

My star was fading. I felt the reins
slipping out of my grasp,
and could do nothing to stop it.

NAPOLEON

NAPOLEON HAD VIRTUALLY LEAPED FROM his post chaise to seat
himself on his throne. The very day after his return, anxious and
exhausted, he summoned his ministers.

Messieurs, I was bedazzled by Fortune. I let myself be carried
away, rather than follow the plan I had conceived. I was in Moscow, and intended to sign the peace there, but I stayed there too
long. I thought I could manage in one year what can be accomplished only in two campaigns.

At this time he was still unaware of the almost total destruction
of the Grand Army. He fondly believed that the survivors were
regrouping on the banks of the Neman, and that his forces still numbered 150,000.

"I made a great mistake," he added, "but I have the means to
retrieve it."

With this, he considered that he had gone far enough in confess-
ing his sins to his civilian aides-de-camp. It was now their turn to be
abashed; and without further ado he took up the Malet affair: "Your
oaths of loyalty! Your principles! Your doctrines! You make me tremble for the future!"

It was his hope that, at his death, following the example of the old
shout for royalty, the people would cry out: "The Emperor is dead!
Long live the Emperor!" In that hope, he had made it his business

450

scrupulously to follow the usages of the *ancien régime* in regard to the birth of his son and the child's education and the composition of his household. And he had gone even further. He had made of his son not a dauphin but a king: a sovereign like the King of the Romans —a title that was borne not only by the Emperor of the West before his coronation, but by the recognized successor of that same Emperor. To that end he had revoked, with one stroke of the pen, the donation that his "predecessor," Charlemagne, had made to His Holiness. He had ordered a baptism at Notre Dame—a ceremony which, to his way of thinking, would demonstrate by its splendor and pomp the definitive establishment of the Napoleonic dynasty reigning over a homogeneous empire in which the various peoples, having become inhabitants of French *départements*, would gradually lose their awareness of once having been Netherlanders, Italians, or Germans.

And all this had been to no purpose! People had given no more thought to Napoleon II than to the "Empress Queen." Once Napoleon was dead—and during the terrible retreat this was by no means a remote possibility—once the Emperor was gone, the empire would collapse of itself. Napoleon had to face the fact: he was reigning over an "empire for life." There was no assured succession. He had bedded down with the daughter of the Caesars and given ancestors to his son, but to no purpose: the little king would not succeed him.

One thing was therefore indispensable (and it had to be done quickly, since the war would soon be resumed): to find a way somehow to associate the little King of Rome with the governing of the empire, and thus confirm his right of succession. The successor of Napoleon I would have to be crowned while his father was still alive. And of course he would have to be anointed by the Pope. But before bringing up the matter of anointing the little king and placing the crown on his brow, it was imperative to put an end to the quarrel between the Emperor and the Pope, who was now a prisoner at Fontainebleau.

Napoleon decided to handle the matter himself. On January 19, 1813 he went to Fontainebleau, where for the past year the Pope had been under the guard of a captain of the gendarmerie disguised as a chamberlain. The first interview was reminiscent of the hours spent in that same palace on the eve of the coronation. The two men embraced.

"Father!"

"My son!"

But beginning the next day, the interviews became less cordial.
During a period of five days, one quarrel followed another. Napoleon's point of view was simple: Rome was the second city of the
empire and no longer belonged to the Pope. Why didn't His Holiness
take up residence at Avignon? This would in no way prevent him
from keeping—as a kind of second residence—the Vatican, which
the French troops had never occupied.

But Pius VII was so obstinate about preserving the sovereignty of
the heritage of St. Peter that the Emperor could not keep his anger
in check.

"One day," the Pope recounted, "in the heat of a discussion about
renouncing the Papal States, Napoleon—in a gesture that had become a habit with him—took hold of a button on my cassock and
shook me so hard, as he pulled at it, that his whole body went into
the effort."

One main point remained to be settled: the eternal one of ap-
pointing bishops. This time, Pius VII had to yield. If, after the lapse
of six months, the Pope refused to appoint a new bishop, he would
be appointed by either the archbishop or the senior prelate of the
ecclesiastical province. And it was not specified that the appointment
would be made "in the name of the Pope."

On January 25, in the presence of the Emperor, the treaty was
presented to Pius VII. The prisoner of Fontainebleau cast an implor-
ing glance at the cardinals witnessing the scene; but the cardinals,
when they saw the implacable expression on Napoleon's face, lowered their eyes. At this, the Sovereign Pontiff heaved a heavy sigh,
took the pen, and signed. Napoleon then signed the new Concordat
in his illegible hand.

After this kind of abdication, Pius VII felt no great concern at
promising to crown the King of Rome and the Empress; and Napoleon went back to Paris as a victor. But a few days later Cardinal
Pacca, who had been set free, came to Fontainebleau. The cardinal
was under no illusions: he had surmised the reactions of the Pope,
exhausted by illness and the painfulness of a long captivity. "I knew,"
Pacca said, "that he was surrounded by persons who had sold themselves to the Emperor. . . . From that moment I realized that the
struggle between the former monk Luigi Barnaba Chiaramonti and

Napoleon Bonaparte would be unequal, and I knew who would emerge victorious."

He went toward the Pope. He scarcely recognized his master— this shadow of a man with an anguished expression who stepped forward to greet him.

"We have ended in degradation, alas!" lamented Pius VII. "Those cardinals dragged me to the table and made me sign. Ah, my friend, I can sleep neither night nor day! I fear I shall die mad like Clement the Fourteenth."

"It's not a question of dying," exclaimed the prelate, "but of repairing the damage done!"

"Do you believe it can be repaired?"

"Yes, Holy Father. There is a remedy for almost every evil."

The "remedy" would be the retraction of March 24, 1813. On that day, the Pope declared that he could not carry out the Concordat, a "vicious and badly composed" document. And he added: "Such being the case, with God's help we desire that it be revised so that it will cause no damage to the Church and no prejudice to our soul."

Napoleon's wrath was unrestrained. The spectacular reconciliation of January 25 was henceforth a dead letter. But for the public, it must continue to exist.

The Ministre des Cultes [dictated the Emperor] will keep strictly secret the Pope's letter of March 24, the receipt of which I may or may not acknowledge, as circumstances dictate. . . . The Concordat of Fontainebleau is henceforth a law of the State. His Majesty regards it as the most sacred of treaties.

As it turned out, the King of Rome and the Empress were never crowned. As for Pius VII, he remained a prisoner until "the beginning of the end" liberated him and enabled him to return to Rome, which by then was threatened with confiscation by Murat, who had become the ally of Austria.

In the opinion of a great many people, Napoleon was now on his way toward that "beginning of the end." During the months preceding the Austrian declaration of war on France, Metternich was about to come into his own. First of all, the Emperor Francis was to become arbitrator of the situation, posing as a mediator. Metternich was completely surprised when he learned, on December 31, that Napoleon took the whole thing quite seriously.

"Let us make peace," he declared to the Austrian minister. "I would be very glad to see your Emperor speak out plainly to Russia. I am delighted that he had decided to become the mediator."

The day before, something had happened of which Napoleon was not yet informed: the Prussian General Yorck, the Graf von Wartenburg, had signed with the Russians the capitulation of Tauroggen. The Prussian corps of the Grand Army had become "neutral"—until such time, naturally, as they should turn against Napoleon. Königsberg was immediately evacuated; and the French imperial forces, consisting of Heudelet's division (which had come from Berlin) and a Polish division, had to withdraw to the Vistula.

Schwarzenberg, commanding the Austrian corps, had already abandoned Volynia and, instead of joining up with Eugène, had headed for Vienna. Napoleon did not conceal his displeasure from Metternich. And to Talleyrand he said: "You go around telling everybody we must make peace. But how can it be done?"

"Your Majesty still possesses negotiable securities," replied the Prince of Benevento. "If you wait any longer and lose them, you will have lost the opportunity to negotiate."

By "negotiable securities" Talleyrand meant the Papal States, the Piedmont, Tuscany, Holland, the Hanseatic cities, and the Duchy of Warsaw—territories that Napoleon refused to give up, knowing full well that a first concession would lead to a second, then a third, and so on until his abdication. He no more wanted to give up his mediation over the Rhenish Confederation than that over the Swiss cantons. The very most the Emperor would have agreed to was to give up what he no longer possessed: Portugal or Sicily (which he had never even occupied). He was also prepared to offer the Czar Russian Poland, Lithuania, Volynia, Podolia, and the Ukraine—territories that had at no time ceased to belong to the Emperor of Russia.

Under these conditions, how could peace be secured—that peace that the future Allies had no intention of making with Napoleon?

The Austrian Government had no desire to make the slightest concession. On the one hand, Metternich and his Emperor assured the Czar that they would never again let Napoleon have so much as one soldier. On the other, they declared at Paris that the alliance between France and Austria seemed to them so indispensable that "if you broke it today, we would propose tomorrow that it be reestablished under conditions absolutely the same."

Actually, Francis I was eager for only one thing: to shake off the alliance and, once having acquired his "independence," to declare war on his son-in-law. He envied the King of Prussia, who was on the point of finally being able to become a turncoat quite openly. The Prussian army, which on paper numbered only 30,000 men, would soon comprise (thanks to an influx of volunteers and clandestine rearming) a body of 134,000 troops ready to attack France.

On February 27, 1813, a treaty of alliance (still secret) was signed between King Frederick William and Czar Alexander, who could still muster 190,000 survivors of the terrible pursuit. Prussian enthusiasm was at its height. The long-awaited revenge was imminent! The married women exchanged their wedding rings for an iron ring with the inscription: "I have given gold for iron."

On March 16, Prussia notified France that the alliance had been broken off; and on the following day the King declared war on Napoleon. The joy at Berlin was beyond description: a holy war was in the making! On March 19 General Yorck entered Berlin; and on March 22, the King returned to his beloved city. Everyone was delirious, and hatred of France reached the stage of a paroxysm.

Metternich now offered some "advice" to Napoleon:

> Only peace can prevent the calamities that threaten us. But so long as you refuse to reestablish the states in their rights, to recognize that everyone is master in his own house, and to allow free trade so that some money can come back into circulation, peace itself will remain a chimera.

But in that spring of 1813 the situation still appeared in no way dramatic to the Emperor—this despite the fact that Bernadotte, on March 3, had signed a treaty with England promising to provide 30,000 men to help dismember his former fatherland; that the British had entered Madrid; and that Murat had begun to waver and was thinking of becoming the Bernadotte of southern Europe.

On January 26, the Emperor wrote to Murat:

> I trust you are not among those who think that the lion is dead. If so, you are wrong. From the time I left Vilna, you have done all you could to damage me. The title of king has made you lose your head. If you want to keep it—the title, I mean—you will have to behave otherwise than you have up to now.

Murat's reaction, when he received this browbeating, was not to get back in line. That magnificent soldier began to make overtures to the enemies of his brother-in-law. At the first opportunity—the Austrian declaration of war on Napoleon—the King of Naples offered his services to Austria, provided he could keep the Kingdom of Naples.

On April 15, entrusting the regency to Marie Louise, the Emperor left St.-Cloud. On the way to Mainz, he made his count of human lives and concluded that he could soon reinforce the army so as to bring his troops up to the number of 400,000. He even had hopes of mustering 600,000 by calling up the old age classes!

When he reached Mainz, forty hours after leaving Paris, he had to face up to the facts. He had been deceived by his optimism: the greatest number of combat troops he could muster was somewhere between 230,000 and 250,000. Most of this army, moreover, consisted of Germans, Italians, Swiss, Hollanders, and even Illyrians—troops who would go over to the enemy the moment things began to look doubtful. As for the Frenchmen, most of them were minimally trained, and the age of the recruits ranged from eighteen to twenty years. True, these young soldiers of 1813 were courageous enough. But as one of their officers said, "They have only the instincts and strength of children."

The army had 600 cannon; but to the Emperor's great distress, there was a severe shortage of cavalry for all the different corps—a fact whose importance cannot be overemphasized. Between Moscow and the Vistula, 60,000 horses had perished. And Napoleon's tactics —the pursuit of a defeated army in retreat from the battlefield— required a strong cavalry. But in 1813 he had only 15,000 horse as against 27,000 cavalrymen on the enemy side. Moreover, many of these troops, though they may have known how to ride a horse, were totally untrained in their specialty.

By April 28 Napoleon was at Weimar, and the German campaign began. Ney crossed the Saale and defeated the Russians: the link-up between Eugène's army and that of the Emperor was completed. As they saw Napoleon ride past their ranks, the recruits cheered and hoisted their shakos on the ends of their bayonets. Their youthful enthusiasm was heartwarming for him, and compensated for the glum expressions of the marshals, who did not dissimulate their weariness.

He marched his army toward the plain of Lützen. From there, thanks to one of those movements that he alone knew how to execute, they pivoted around the flanks and backed the enemy up against the mountains of Bohemia.

The Battle of Lützen began on May 2. The Allies attacked two days earlier than had been expected and routed General Souham's forces. The recruits, who were getting their first smell of gunpowder, gave way several times. The French line was broken, and Blücher, the Prussian general, was sure he had already won a victory. But Napoleon unsheathed his sword, put himself at the head of the Young Guard, and as in the days of the Italian campaign, dashed forward between two columns, leading the assault. Meantime, from the hillsides of Starsiedel, the French batteries were spewing forth a murderous barrage, and the battle "changed complexion." By evening, as the village of Kaja burned (it had been constantly taken and retaken during the day), Napoleon was able to announce: "We have won the battle!"

Twenty thousand Russians and Prussians were left lying on the field of battle; but the number of dead from the ranks of the Grand Army was almost as great: 18,000. The enemy was withdrawing toward the Elbe, and they could not pursue, owing to the lack of cavalry.

On May 7 Napoleon crossed the Elbe, and the next day he made his entrance into Dresden. The civil officials, who had welcomed the Russians warmly, looked sheepish; and Napoleon did not conceal how he felt about them. "Out of love for their King," however, he decided not to treat Saxony as a conquered country. That night at the royal palace of Dresden, before going to bed, he wrote to the King of Saxony (who had prudently betaken himself close to the Austrian frontier), inviting him to return to his "liberated" capital.

Ten thousand Saxon soldiers were incorporated into the Grand Army. "Things are going well," Napoleon wrote to Marie Louise. "They are trying to deceive Papa Francis and involve him in some bad business. Metternich is nothing but an intriguer."

He became all the more certain of this when, on May 16, he received General Ferdinand von Bubna. The Austrian general informed him of the three points proposed by Metternich to establish a general peace: the Grand Duchy of Warsaw was to be given up; France would yield up those territories which had been annexed to

the empire in 1811; and she would return Illyria to Austria. But the
Emperor was perfectly well aware that if he accepted these reasonable conditions, it would only mean the beginning of other concessions, of which Metternich would take advantage to crush him. The
rest would follow until he was run to ground. Napoleon therefore
rejected the Allied proposals:

> I want nothing to do with your armed mediation. You are
> merely confusing things. You say you cannot do anything for me:
> that means you are strong only when acting against me. . . . I will
> not yield up a single village which is constitutionally a part of
> France. You are trying to snatch Italy and Germany away from
> me! . . . What I am really concerned about is the fate of the King
> of Rome. You begin demanding Illyria; next you will demand
> Venetia, then the Duchy of Milan, then Tuscany—and you will
> compel me to fight you. It's better to begin by fighting.

But "in order to avoid a useless spilling of blood," he sent Caulaincourt to Alexander's headquarters:

> If I have to make sacrifices, I would rather they be made to the
> advantage of the Emperor Alexander, who is fighting a fair kind
> of war against me, and of the King of Prussia—a country in which
> Russia is interested—than to the advantage of Austria, who has
> betrayed the alliance and who, under the title of mediator, wants
> to arrogate unto herself the right to decide everything, after
> having taken what share she deems suitable.

The Czar interpreted this request as a clear proof of his enemy's
weakness. He was not even willing to receive Caulaincourt. There
must be no letup until the death of the stag.

And so the war continued. After their victory of Bautzen, Napoleon's forces tried to pursue the Allied troops, who were in retreat
toward the Oder. But once again the lack of cavalry prevented them
from carving up the enemy. True, the next day the infantry was close
on the heels of the Prussians and the Russians. But the foot soldiers
ran out of breath trying to perform a role for which they were not
suited. They began to mutter: "When are we going to get this over
with? Where is the Emperor going to stop? We have to make peace
at any price!"

The Allies, still lacking munitions, kept retreating in great haste.
Glogau was soon evacuated, and Napoleon's army reached the Oder.

It had taken him less than a month to drive the enemy back over a distance of 350 kilometers.

As Metternich wrote in his *Memoirs:* "Napoleon's advance had to be stopped." Therefore, the Russians and the Prussians asked the Emperor what his peace terms were—a move that Napoleon looked at with a jaundiced eye. Did he surmise that this desiderated truce was only a "curtain" behind which the pack of hounds could deliberately re-form, then join forces with the armies of Austria and Sweden so as to attack him again?

As early as May 10, the Prussian minister Hardenburg had written: "War will certainly break out between Austria and France when Bonaparte rejects—as he will undoubtedly do—the proposals that will be made jointly to him by Russia, Prussia, and Austria."

Despite the victory of Bautzen, Napoleon was terribly distressed. He could see that the marshals around him were weary and incapable of initiative. And he knew that it would be folly to continue the war without reinforcing his cavalry. So it was that he agreed to the truce while realizing full well the risk he was taking: "If the Allies are not sincere in their desire for peace, this armistice could be disastrous for us."

In order to demonstrate his own "sincerity," Napoleon agreed to pull back his troops. He abandoned the line of the Oder. "I intend to set up my headquarters at Dresden," he explained to Murat, "since there I will be closer to my territories."

The Allied demands had merely increased with their defeats. In addition to the terms already proposed by Bubna, they demanded the reestablishment of the Hanseatic cities, the dissolution of the Rhenish Confederation, and the restoration of Prussia to the kingdom's "status quo ante 1806." Incidentally, these last two clauses were not to be communicated to the Emperor unless he agreed to the others. Moreover, the Russians and the Prussians had just signed an agreement with England stipulating that no peace could be concluded without the consent of Great Britain. And London, of course, would never consent to the presence of the French at Anvers.

When Metternich was informed of all this, he declared to the Allies that if Napoleon rejected the new proposals, Austria would declare war on him. Then the Chancellor set out for the French General Headquarters, "like a veritable man of God bearing the burden of the world," as he modestly expressed it.

On June 26 the Emperor crossed swords with this strange "arbitrator":

> It would appear, Monsieur, that it no longer suits your purposes to guarantee the integrity of the French Empire. But why didn't you say so sooner? . . . In letting me exhaust myself with new efforts, you were no doubt not counting on such rapid developments. I win two battles, and you come to me to discuss truces and arbitration! Had it not been for your disastrous intervention, I would have made peace with the Allies by now. You may as well own up to the fact that since Austria assumed the title of mediator, she has ceased to be on my side. Nor is she impartial: she has become my enemy!

When Metternich tried to protest that he had never entertained such evil designs, Napoleon relented somewhat:

> All right, so be it! I'm willing to negotiate. But what do you want? Let's speak out more plainly and get to the point. But don't forget I'm a soldier who is better at breaking than bending. I have offered you Illyria if you will remain neutral. Does that suit you? My army is more than adequate to make the Russians and the Prussians come around, and your neutrality is all I am asking for.

Metternich, a hypocrite to the core, exclaimed:

> Oh, sire! Why should Your Majesty carry on this struggle alone? Why not double your forces? Just say the word, Sire, and ours will be entirely at your disposal. Yes, things have come to a point where we can no longer remain neutral. We must either be for you or against you.

The Emperor was not duped. He knew very well that Austria was going to throw herself into the arms of his enemies: "I have heard talk of a treaty with another power. . . ."

Finally, he laid his cards on the table: "Do you want peace or war?"

And he did not give the Austrian minister the time to reply:

> So you want war? Well, that's what you'll get. I destroyed the Prussian army at Lützen, and I beat the Russians at Bautzen. If you want to take your turn, I'll meet you at Vienna. Human beings are incorrigible; experience is lost on them. I put the Emperor Francis back on his throne, and I promised to remain

at peace with him all my life. I married his daughter. I told myself at the time that I was making a stupid mistake, but I did it anyway. Now I am sorry I did.

A few minutes before, Berthier had ventured to tell Metternich: "Don't forget that Europe needs peace, and France needs it especially. . . ." Now Metternich talked of peace. The Emperor asked:

What do you mean by peace? Do you want to despoil me? Do you want Italy, Brabant, Lorraine? I will not yield up one inch of terrain! I'll make peace in accordance with the "status quo ante bellum. . . ." I'll even give some of the Duchy of Warsaw to Russia. But I won't give you anything, because you have not defeated me. I won't give anything to Prussia, because she betrayed me. If you want Western Galicia, and if Prussia wants some of her former possessions, I might agree—but only with compensations. In that case you would have to indemnify my allies. The conquest of Illyria cost me 200,000 men. If you want it, you will have to spend (as the Czar puts it) an equal number of men. . . .

Actually you want Italy, Russia wants Poland, Prussia wants Saxony, and England wants Holland and Belgium. And all of you want one thing: the dismemberment of the French Empire. . . . That's right! You want me to evacuate Europe (half of which I still possess), pull my supposedly defeated legions back across the Rhine, the Alps, and the Pyrenees, and entrust my doubtful future to the generosity of those whose conqueror I am today! . . . What kind of position do you want to put me in vis-à-vis the French people? The Emperor Francis is laboring under a strange illusion if he thinks that in France a mutilated throne can serve as a refuge for his daughter and his grandson. . . . Ah, Metternich! How much did England pay you to persuade you to play this role against me?

The Emperor showed the Chancellor his maps in an attempt to demonstrate his strength: "I'll make another appointment with you: I'll meet you in Vienna next October."

"I have seen your troops," Metternich said, unruffled. "You have nothing but children. You have caused an entire generation to be wiped out. What will you do when these, too, have disappeared?"

The Emperor replied indignantly, "Monsieur, you are not a soldier. You don't know what goes on in the heart of a soldier. I came of age on the battlefield, and I don't give a damn for a million lives."

He threw his hat on the floor and started pacing back and forth, exasperated by the cold irony of Metternich, who kept looking at the hat on the floor.

Abruptly, Napoleon picked up the hat and walked over to the Chancellor. "Tell me, Metternich," he said. "Wasn't I stupid to marry an Austrian princess?"

"Well, since you ask for my opinion, I must say that Napoleon, the great conqueror, made a mistake."

"And the Emperor Francis is willing to drive his daughter off the throne of France?"

"Sire, the Emperor of Austria is concerned only with the well-being of his empire and will be guided only by its needs, regardless of his daughter's fate. He is first and foremost a sovereign, and will not hesitate to sacrifice his family for the good of his empire."

There was silence. Then Napoleon said:

What you have told me is by no means surprising, and merely shows me the immensity of my mistake. When I married the Austrian archduchess I thought I could revitalize the past by merging it with the new era—by merging the prejudices of the old Goths with the enlightenment of the present century. I was mistaken; and now I see how great my mistake was. It may cost me my throne, but I will drag the whole world down in its ruins!

The scene was over. Napoleon escorted the minister to the door. There he paused and, placing his hand on Metternich's shoulder, said, "You're not really going to make war on me again, are you?"

Metternich said, "Sire, you are finished! I suspected it when I was on the way here, and now I know it!"

After his departure, Metternich wrote, "It's all over with Bonaparte." The day following the terrible scene, the Emperor wrote nothing more to Marie Louise than: "I talked a long time with Metternich. It wore me out."

In spite of the victory of Bautzen, it was now clearly the beginning of the end for Napoleon. He learned that as a result of the defeat of Vitoria, Spain was definitely lost. "The misfortunes in Spain," he wrote to Savary, "are all the greater in that they are ridiculous."

On August 5 the Emperor, in Dresden, sent a letter to Caulaincourt, his representative at the Allied conference at Prague, telling him to communicate the Allied proposals without delay. Caulaincourt received the letter on the sixth. On the seventh, Metternich finally conveyed to him the famous conditions laid down by the Allies. Napoleon received Caulaincourt's report on the ninth, at 3:00 P.M., and replied with counterproposals, but they did not reach Prague until the morning of the eleventh. Meantime, the talks had been broken off at midnight on the tenth, and the Emperor of Austria had declared war on his son-in-law.

Upon hearing this news, Napoleon sent Caulaincourt new proposals. This time he was willing to give up the Confederation of the Rhine, Illyria (except for Trieste), and the northern part of Germany (except for Hamburg and Lübeck). But it was too late. Metternich, who in his own words was "placed in the most frightful dilemma a minister had ever been in," even refused to pass on the communication. The Allies would not lay down their arms until France had been shrunk to its former size and Napoleon rendered harmless.

On that same day, the Emperor Francis wrote to his daughter: "Don't worry. The war we are waging is quite different from the others. It is purely political. I shall never be your husband's enemy, and I hope he will never be mine."

Marie Louise replied: "The Emperor would not respect me if he were not reassured as to the feelings I have for you. Nor would you respect me if I were not primarily concerned with the happiness of the Emperor and my son."

General Moreau, at the enemy's general headquarters, offered this advice:

> You must expect to be defeated wherever the Emperor himself is in the field. Insofar as possible, avoid direct combat with him. . . . But attack his lieutenants wherever you can engage them in combat. Finally, when his lieutenants are defeated and weakened, build up your existing forces with all the troops you can muster, advance on him, snatch victory from him, and give him no respite.

On Thursday, August 26, Napoleon rushed to the aid of Gouvion Saint-Cyr, whose 20,000 troops had been attacked at Dresden by 250,000 men. Followed by Marmont's corps and the Old Guard, the Emperor galloped across the "Bridge of Augustus" which linked Neustadt to Dresden. The Russians, who were occupying the heights on the other side of the city, were already shouting: "To Paris! To Paris!" And the troops under Saint-Cyr had been driven back behind the palisades of the suburbs. But Dresden had not yet been captured by the enemy. The road to France had not yet been cut off. As the Baron de Peyrusse said, the Emperor's presence alone gave new life and hope to the terrorized inhabitants. "They crowded around him and greeted him as a liberator. This enthusiasm was shared by all the columns His Majesty ordered to file past him at the double-quick." To every colonel who filed past him with his unit, he would call out the position of the regiment. He seemed to know Dresden as well as Paris. He even remembered the name of the Dippodiswalde Gate.

In the enemy ranks, the terrible name was repeated: "Napoleon! Napoleon!" The French regimental bands struck up their music. The redoubts and trenches that Saint-Cyr had been compelled to abandon were retaken. The Allies withdrew, and soon the French were pursuing them, hard on their heels.

All that night the Emperor dictated orders while pacing back and forth in his room. At dawn on August 27, the fog enabled Murat to take up a position without being seen by the enemy. The battle for Dresden resumed even more violently under a heavy rain. From a point not far from the Dippodiswalde Gate, near a big campfire, the Emperor directed the battle.

And victory finally came—a victory that was dearly bought. The Czar, the Emperor of Austria, and the King of Prussia were defeated, leaving 12,000 prisoners in the hands of their enemy and 27,000 dead on the field of battle.

One hundred thousand French had defeated 250,000 Allies! Totally exhausted, the Emperor left to his lieutenants the task of pursuing the retreating enemy, and returned to Dresden at eight o'clock in the evening. He was so soaked by the rain that "the back part of his hat was drooping down on his neck." Constant tells us that "the water ran down from his uniform and entirely filled his boots."

Such was his condition when he was embraced by the King of Saxony. Then Napoleon, shivering with fever, jumped into a steaming bath. He started vomiting. But by five o'clock the next morning he was ready to go again: he mounted his horse and went to take up a position on a hillside. The third day of the battle of Dresden was given over to pursuing the retreating enemy. That evening, the

Emperor again felt ill. He returned to Dresden in a carriage and went to bed.

The next day, fully recovered, he wrote to Marie Louise:

> I have trounced the Prince von Schwarzenberg and the Emperor Alexander. The troops of Papa Francis have never been in such bad shape: they are poorly dressed or naked. I have taken 25,000 Austrian prisoners, along with 30 flags and many cannon. . . .

On 3 September the Emperor left Dresden to give battle to Blücher, who had defeated Marshal Jacques Étienne Macdonald. But the Prussian general, too, followed Bernadotte's advice and slipped away.

On the way back to Dresden, Napoleon learned that Marshal Ney had been defeated by Bernadotte at Dennewitz—a defeat aggravated by the fact that some of the Saxons and a division of Bavarians had gone over to the enemy.

"Wherever I am not physically present," he exclaimed, "they do nothing but commit stupidities!"

Ney, who felt crushed, begged the Emperor to let him leave "this inferno."

"Commanding under these conditions," he said, "is only half-commanding. I would rather be a grenadier!"

By Sunday, September 12, the Emperor was back at Dresden. His marshals—who were now being defeated whenever Napoleon was not with them—were becoming increasingly sour and depressed. But the Emperor went ahead with his plan: to concentrate his armies. He needed men and more men! And so he signed a decree calling up 300,000 new recruits who would be combat-ready—or so he thought—by the spring of 1814.

The great—and final—battle was imminent.

All Germany was aswarm with French regiments marching to join the Emperor. Napoleon even entertained the idea of pulling out the 30,000 men occupying Dresden and taking them along with him; but at the last moment he decided to do without that force—which he would sorely miss at the Battle of the Nations. He also dispensed with the aid of the 25,000 soldiers at Hamburg, the 15,000 immobilized at Magdeburg, and the 10,000 others scattered through different German provinces. He had at best no more than 185,000 French and allies to put in the field against 360,000 Coalition troops. In the face of this desperate situation, he managed to preserve his sang-froid. But the marshals and generals almost rebelled when he announced to them his intention of going over to the attack and marching on Berlin.

On October 12 a last demoralizing piece of news reached the general headquarters at Düben: Bavaria had dropped out of the Rhenish Confederation and gone over to the enemy.

The marshals, taking advantage of the Bavarian volte-face, tried to persuade Napoleon to modify his plan. They maintained that instead of marching on Berlin he should force the barrier of the Elbe, which would enable him to get back to the Rhine—and to France. Murat, who had already signed a secret agreement with the Allies to abandon the cause of his brother-in-law, was unwilling to give battle anywhere except in the direction of Mainz. And on October 14, Napoleon yielded.

Marching orders for Leipzig were issued to his army—that army with which he still hoped to defeat the Allied forces, which after the defection of Bavaria were more than twice the size of his own.

On the first, terrible day of the Battle of Leipzig—the Battle of the Nations—the fighting took place at Wachau. Napoleon directed his forces from the top of a little hill not far from the town. Positions were taken and retaken. Napoleon threw all his cavalry into the action, but the Czar's Cossacks and Hussars repulsed Murat.

On the next day, a Sunday, the action was confined to an intense barrage. But on the following day, Napoleon found himself confronted by an additional 110,000 men. The enemy had 320,000 troops, or three for every one Frenchman.

In the predawn darkness of October 18, Napoleon set up his field headquarters on a knoll near Probstheyda. The general staff was quartered in a tobacco barn nearby. Soon 15,000 Allied cannon opened fire, and their armies enveloped the imperial forces on three sides. For the first time Bernadotte, an ex-marshal of France and the brother-in-law of King Joseph, was fighting the Emperor. The attack was even more violent than two days before. The French began to run short of ammunition, and the Saxons, predictably, defected to the enemy.

The Old Guard rushed in to close the breach. The Emperor— "cool, collected, and purposeful," as Macdonald wrote, "but looking discouraged"—put himself at the head of 5,000 cavalry and charged the Swedes and the Saxons, who fell back in terror. Then, in their turn, the Württembergers went over to the enemy and turned their weapons against the French.

On that one day alone, Napoleon lost 20,000 dead, wounded, or taken prisoner. He decided to abandon Leipzig and order a retreat. As 1,500 cannon thundered, the French moved out under enemy fire. There was fierce fighting in the suburbs: 450,000 men, almost breast to breast, struggled in an area of seven or eight square kilometers.

Then the imperial army was shaken by a new catastrophe. The Hessians, supposedly Napoleon's allies, climbed up on the ramparts and began firing on the French.

In incredible disorder, the imperial army moved toward the bridge over the Elster. Then came the final disaster: panicking at the sight of enemy troops far down the main street, the sappers of the engineering corps blew up the bridge. A great shout of despair rose above the sound of battle: from 12,000 to 15,000 men of the rear guard were still in the city. Some jumped in the river and tried to swim across, but most were drowned before the eyes of their comrades.

This new loss marked the end of the Battle of the Nations, in which ten nations were fighting under the command of three emperors and a king. The "holy cause" had triumphed, as Metternich announced happily.

The explosion at the bridge had not awakened the Emperor, who had fallen asleep at his headquarters. Murat and Augereau came to give him the terrible news.

"There was nothing left to do but fight," Napoleon said later. "And every day, through one fatality or another, our chances grew smaller and smaller."

Napoleon set out for Erfurt. His marshals came behind him, grumbling.

With the 110,000 men who had got out of the inferno of Leipzig —a third of whom were fleeing in disorder—Napoleon headed for Mainz. The enemy was close behind, but dared not attack.

At the same time, the Allies were palavering at Frankfurt and formulating their terms. Should France be allowed to keep her frontier on the Rhine, or merely her old boundaries of 1792? Bernadotte had a precise, personal point of view:

> Bonaparte is a blackguard. He must be killed. As long as he is alive, he'll be the scourge of the earth. There mustn't be any more Emperor. That title is not French. France needs a king, but a soldier-king. The race of the Bourbons is a worn-out race which will never be any good again. What man is more suitable for France than I?

On 7 November, after a week's stay in Mainz, Napoleon left the city and turned his back on the Rhine for the last time.

Everything was breaking up. The Hollanders were rebelling to shouts of: "Long live the Allies! Long live the House of Orange!" The French forces, numbering only 2,000 men, evacuated the country upon the arrival of Prussian General Friedrich von Bülow's corps.

A few days later, Napoleon (back at St.-Cloud), restored Spain to Ferdinand—provided the Cortes would agree. They did.

Murat, after receiving an ultimatum from Metternich (an ultimatum brought by Count Adam von Neipperg, the future husband of Marie Louise), and after four days of temporizing, agreed to sign a treaty marking the end of a full year of secret negotiations with Austria. According to this treaty, the King of Naples agreed to provide the Allies with a contingent of 50,000 men and pledged that he would make peace only with approval of Austria.

When Napoleon learned of this, he "started to pace rapidly back and forth in his salon."

> Murat! My brother-in-law! This is rank treason! I knew very well that Murat was hot-headed, but I thought he loved me. It's his wife who made him defect. . . . Caroline, my own sister, has betrayed me! The idea of Murat firing his cannon at Frenchmen! It's abominable! It's odious! He's the Bernadotte of the Midi!·

By late December, the Allied armies were moving in on France.

On January 23, 1814—a snowy Sunday two days before Napoleon's departure from Paris to resume command in the field—800 officers of the Paris National Guard assembled, at the Emperor's summons, in the great Salle des Maréchaux. The Emperor entered, carrying the

King of Rome in his arms, and said: "Messieurs, a part of the territory of France has been invaded. I am going to place myself at the head of my army, and with God's help I hope to push the enemy back beyond the frontiers. . . .

"If the enemy approaches the capital," he continued, "I shall entrust the Empress and the King of Rome—my wife and son—to the courage of the National Guard."

A few officers stepped forward to kiss the hand of the Emperor and the little King.

The Emperor retired to his study and looked over his reports. He studied his maps. With a mere 60,000 men, how could he simultaneously stop Blücher and Schwarzenberg? Blücher, with his Silesian army numbering 80,000, had already crossed the Rhine and was advancing in Lorraine; Schwarzenberg, with his Bohemian army of 140,000, had crossed Switzerland and was marching toward the plateau of Langres. Not to mention a second Austrian army! And not to mention the two renegades: Bernadotte with his Swedes and Murat with his Neapolitans!

Some 460,000 men were about to attack France. But on this particular evening the Emperor was thinking only of the 220,000 troops who had already invaded France—they were being met by a paltry 60,000 French troops.

The next day he told Marie Louise, who could not stop weeping: "I'm going to beat Papa Francis!"

The scene took place after dinner. The Empress and Hortense were warming themselves at the hearth. Fuel for the fire was provided by the bundles of papers that Napoleon kept throwing on it. Each time he came up to the fireplace he would kiss his young wife. "Don't be sad," he said. "Just trust in me!"

Early in the morning of January 25, before getting into his carriage, the Emperor tiptoed in to take a look at his sleeping son, the little king without a kingdom whom he would never see again.

The France across which the Emperor traveled all during that day was a country in a state of both anxiety and stupefaction. At the relay stations, women and children crowded around the carriage, while men hastily transformed into National Guardsmen kept watch along the roads, expecting at every moment to see the Cossacks appear.

Napoleon had been able to muster only 33,000 men at Châlons, and their morale was as low as their level of physical energy.

When he had routed and defeated one Russian division left at St.-Dizier by Blücher, the Emperor learned that the Prussian general was heading toward Brienne with 30,000 men. Napoleon decided to engage him in combat with only 10,000 soldiers of his own. The rest of his forces could join up with him later.

Thanks to a strong counterassault by the imperial forces, Blücher had to abandon the field in haste and withdraw toward Bar-sur-Aube, where the Prussians hoped to find Schwarzenberg.

Napoleon entered the Château des Loménie—that handsome residence where he had been a guest as a youth, and where he had spent a night before leaving for Italy to be crowned.

From the terrace, he took in the view that he knew so well. Tomorrow's field of battle was there before him: "Who would have thought, in the old days, that I would be fighting the Russians and the Prussians in this spot!"

He had been joined by Marmont and Gerard, and now had his 33,000 men at hand. But Blücher had also received reinforcements: he now had 150,000 troops and was able to attack.

The Battle of La Rothière took place on February 1 in a blizzard. The ratio between the forces was so unequal that the French soon had to retreat. Four thousand of the Emperor's soldiers were killed, and the enemy took 2,000 prisoners.

Night fell. From his room Napoleon saw that the Allied campfires embraced, in a vast semicircle, the bivouacs of the little French army.

The French troops left their fires burning, even stirring up the embers. Then, very quietly, they packed up and left. At dawn, Blücher saw that the 27,000 French troops had vanished.

Unrecognizable and spattered with mud, Napoleon entered Troyes and took up quarters in the Rue du Temple at the home of the mayor, Duchâtel-Berthelin. There were no acclamations, no shouts. But before setting out again on the icy, wind-swept roads, he tried to calm the fears of those in the capital, who had been confounded by the defeat of La Rothière.

After their victory at La Rothière, the Allies believed that the campaign was over. The way to Paris was now open for them, and they made the grave mistake of dividing their forces. Blücher and his

Silesian army went along the Marne, while Schwarzenberg and his Bohemian army moved along both banks of the Seine. The Emperor wasted no time in making his decision: driving first toward the Austro-Russians, then toward the Germans, he would beat the Austrians, the Prussians, and the troops of the Czar. He would put on his boots of '93 and ornament history with his finest campaign!

Blücher had split his forces up into four groups. Thus the Emperor should attack them successively. Could he manage it?

He had written to Joseph: "If I should lose the battle and if my death should be reported, you will be informed of it before the ministers are. If so, have the Empress and the King of Rome sent to Rambouillet." Finally, he added, prophetically, "I would rather my son were killed than reared at Vienna as an Austrian prince; and I have a good enough opinion of the Empress to be convinced that she is of the same persuasion—as much as a wife and mother can be."

On February 10, Blücher joyously wrote to his wife: "We are only 15 miles from Paris. In a week we shall certainly be under the walls of the capital, and Napoleon will no doubt lose his crown."

But the Emperor, followed by his handful of mud-spattered men, had joined up with Marmont before St.-Gond and then assaulted the Russians. The moment they saw the tall fur caps of Napoleon's troops on the heights of Champaubert, the Czar's soldiers hesitated and gave ground. The dragoons of the Guard charged and cut the enemy into two segments. Alexander's soldiers threw down their arms and escaped into the woods, where the peasants did their bit to help the little imperial army.

With him, the Emperor had about 5,000 veterans of the Old Guard, 4,700 cavalry, and fewer than 1,800 young recruits, called "the Marie Louises." At nine in the morning of February 11, at Montmirail, Napoleon's 14,000 men encountered the Pomeranian General Sacken at the head of a Russian army corps numbering 30,000. The Guard and Ricard's division showed so much fighting spirit in taking the farm of La Cour d'Airain that Napoleon immediately distributed 1,750 crosses of the Legion of Honor.

Napoleon did take the plateau of Nesle. But the retreating enemy had burned the bridges over the Marne, and he could not pursue. When he entered Château-Thierry at three o'clock on the afternoon of Sunday the thirteenth, he found that Yorck's Prussians had ruthlessly sacked the town. But there was one consolation: the atrocities committed by the Cossacks would make the peasants take up arms. And they were soon waging their own kind of war, with scythes and even knives.

On the night of February 13 Napoleon learned that Blücher was continuing his march toward Montmirail, as if he had no inkling of the defeat of two days before. The Emperor moved on him rapidly, and the Battle of Vauchamps took place on Monday the fourteenth. The Guard attacked to shouts of "Vive l'Empereur!" and Emmanuel de Grouchy charged at the head of 3,500 cavalry. It was a total victory for the French: Blücher left 6,000 men on the field.

Napoleon, intoxicated with joy, watched the 8,000 prisoners file past. Those soldiers who brought him a flag or a cannon were awarded a cross. At Montereau, mindful of his legend, Napoleon personally aimed a cannon on the battlefield. His staff officers were justifiably frightened. "Allez, mes amis," he said. "There's nothing to fear. The ball that can kill me has not yet been cast."

In Paris everyone was saying: "The French are fighting with the odds three to one against them!"

Napoleon continued his campaign. But his marshals, once again exhausted and demoralized, were demanding peace. Although he objected violently, he realized they were right. And on February 21, from Nogent, he wrote to his father-in-law proposing peace.

Actually, talks had been in progress at Châtillon since February 4, but without success. Caulaincourt, speaking for Napoleon, had offered to negotiate on the basis of the Frankfurt clauses, with France keeping "the French *pré carre*"; that is, the entire left bank of the Rhine.

The Allies, however, felt that their enemy should not be allowed to keep anything more than the prerevolutionary boundaries, and that France "should be prohibited from taking part in the arrangements that would be made for the organization of Europe."

Caulaincourt, the Grand Equerry, was incredulous. This was a far cry from the terms of Frankfurt.

"If I accepted your proposals," he asked, "would you sign immediately and stop the spilling of blood right now?"

The Allies hedged, and Caulaincourt wrote to Napoleon: "What I know with certainty is that I am dealing here with men who are anything but sincere; to make quick concessions to them is merely to encourage them to demand more concessions, without being able to see how far they will go, and without obtaining any results."

Europe had no desire for peace. Like the Congress of Prague the year before, the Congress of Châtillon was a farce. The Allies wanted only one thing: to finish off "Buonaparte."

"The important thing," declared Metternich, "is to deal a decisive blow to the existence of Napoleon."

All those whom Napoleon had crushed since the first Italian campaign—and whom he had routed ten times since the ill-fated Battle of La Rothière—were thinking only of gaining time. Sooner or later, superiority of numbers would prevail over the Emperor's strategy!

Napoleon, blinded by illusions, still believed that his genius could overcome that numerical superiority; and he therefore did not urge Caulaincourt to make terms. He wanted to issue his own ultimatum.

On Thursday, February 24, the Emperor entered a liberated Troyes. The enthusiasm stirred up by the sight of him was beyond description. People kissed his boots. The three foreign sovereigns barely had time to flee.

The Allied sovereigns held a conference. What should they do? Schwarzenberg, with 120,000 men under his command, favored retreating, whereas the Czar wanted to go on fighting. With the forces at their disposal, it was unthinkable that the Allies could not overwhelm 74,000 Frenchmen! Finally they decided to have the army of Bohemia withdraw to the plateau of Langres. On March 1, at Chaumont, the Allied sovereigns and ministers signed a treaty—the prelude to the Holy Alliance—which bound Napoleon's enemies to one another for the next twenty years and obliged Russia, Austria, and Prussia each to furnish 150,000 men to the Coalition. Lord Castlereagh opened his purse wide and offered England's allies 150 million francs to be shared among them.

Blücher had been left free to do as he liked. With 48,000 men he made ready to advance toward Paris in a flanking movement. Napoleon set out after him. His plan was to crush (he even said "exterminate") the army of Silesia, then to reach out a hand toward the garrisons occupying the strongholds of the northeast. This done, he would turn and attack the Austrians and Russians.

But as early as March 1 he found himself checkmated. He couldn't cross the Marne: Blücher, in his retreat, had had the bridges destroyed.

The French set about repairing them. Meanwhile, the Russians and the Prussians were heading for Soissons, which was occupied by the French. With one of the bridges repaired, Napoleon resumed his drive at two o'clock on the morning of March 2, leaving La Ferté-sous-Jouarre for Château-Thierry. Surely Soissons would hold, and Blücher, trapped in the bends of the Aisne, would be finally defeated.

But on the evening of the fourth the Emperor learned that Soissons had capitulated the day before. Brigadier General Moreau, commanding 1,320 men, had been attacked by sizable forces of Russians and Prussians. After the surrender, as he watched the little garrison file past the enemy's general staff with drums rolling, General Ferdinand von Winzingerode asked Moreau: "Why didn't you have your entire division leave with your advance guard?"

"Because," answered Moreau, "those troops there are all I had."

Moreau could undoubtedly have held out longer in obedience to his orders; but he surrendered after the first few assaults. There are those who maintain that, "next to the Battle of Waterloo, the capitulation of Soissons is the most disastrous event in our history."

The Emperor could not get over his anger. Now Blücher could use the bridge at Soissons and cross the Aisne. The army of Silesia was out of trouble. Napoleon had to give up all thoughts of catching it in the trap he had set.

It was a hard blow, and the Emperor was profoundly distressed. At Fismes, on the morning of March 5, he signed the decree ordering a mass draft; but he knew there was no more hope. He could not be everywhere at the same time; and he now realized that wherever he was not leading the army the imperial troops would be defeated.

On Sunday, March 6, after setting out from the presbytery of Berry-au-Bac (where he vainly tried to get some sleep), he crossed the Aisne and headed for Laon along the frozen road. His plan was to anticipate Blücher and defeat him on a battlefield chosen by himself. But the day after the capture of Soissons, the field marshal's forces had been swelled by the addition of the 18,000 Russians under Winzingerode. Disconcerted by Napoleon's movement, the Prussian modified the disposition of his troops and decided to occupy the plateau of Craonne so as to threaten the flank of the Emperor's army.

That evening, back in his hotel in Corbeny, Napoleon bent over his maps and studied them for a long time, making ready for the next day's battle—the Battle of Craonne.

According to Napoleon's *Correspondence* and the *Moniteur*, this battle was a decisive French victory. If Thiers is to be believed, 30,000 Frenchmen took an impregnable position occupied by 50,000 men. For the Russian historians, it was a "brilliant victory" won by the Czar's troops, who numbered only 15,000 against 30,000. Actually, the opposing forces were substantially equal: 20,000 Frenchmen against 22,000 Austrians and Russians.

In any case, Napoleon remained master of the plateau—a plateau where 5,400 Frenchmen and 5,000 enemy soldiers were left lying fraternally integrated in death. But it was a Pyrrhic victory and by no means decisive.

On the afternoon of March 10 the Emperor learned that Soissons had been retaken. He decided to abandon the Battle of Laon (which had begun the day before) and take refuge in the recaptured city. On all other fronts the imperial armies were retreating. The English and Spanish had crossed the Pyrenees.

Happily, Reims had been reoccupied by the French. It was a complete success—the last twinkle of the imperial star. Napoleon entered the city after midnight, and as soon as they learned of the Emperor's arrival, the inhabitants illuminated the town.

Discouraged by the recapture of Soissons and the victory of Reims, the Allied troops—who had again gone over to the offensive —halted everywhere. Blücher and Schwarzenberg were immobilized. Everyone was sure that Napoleon, upon leaving Reims, would join up with the garrisons of his strongholds. Andrault Langeron, commanding a corps of the army of Silesia, said later: "That terrible Napoleon! We thought we could see him everywhere. He had trounced all of us, one after the other. We were in constant fear of the boldness of his moves, the rapidity of his marches, and his skillful schemes. No sooner had we concocted a plan than he would frustrate it."

During the two days he spent at Reims, the Emperor learned of the defeatist spirit prevailing in the capital and wrote to his minister:

> You tell me nothing of what is happening in Paris. There is talk of petitions, of a regency, and all kinds of intrigues—as stupid as they are absurd. These people must be made to realize that I am the same man I was at Wagram and at Austerlitz. There is no other authority than my own!

Napoleon left Reims on Thursday, March 17, with 23,000 men intending to attack the 100,000 troops of Schwarzenberg, who had been contained (with some difficulty) by Macdonald and his 30,000 men. When the Emperor joined up with Macdonald, the ratio would be one Frenchman against two of the enemy. But this imbalance was not so terrible, since, as the Emperor liked to repeat, "50,000 men plus myself makes 150,000."

As cowardly and fickle as ever, Schwarzenberg slipped away (he effected a very hasty retreat), and the Emperor was convinced he would be able to "occupy his positions in no time."

The Austrian field marshal halted his retreat at Arcis-sur-Aube. He was to be saved by a last impulse of fear—"an itch of energy," as someone said. More or less by accident, his forces—consisting of 100,000 Allied troops—were concentrated around him. He decided to attack Napoleon, since the Emperor as yet had only 23,000 men with him.

On Sunday, March 30, the Emperor was at Torcy-le-Grand when he heard a heavy barrage. He left at full gallop and found himself in the thick of a battle. The wind of defeat was already blowing. Sword in hand, he took refuge in a hollow square formed by the Battalion of the Vistula. A few moments later, he could be seen stopping runaways on the bridge with the words: "Which one of you dares cross before me?"

The Guard, coming up at the double-quick, managed to contain the flood; and when night fell, the French still held the town—which was burning. The Emperor later told Caulaincourt: "I did my best to get killed at Arcis."

During the night, thanks to Oudinot's arrival, Napoleon had managed to muster 30,000 men; and he wanted to give battle. But when day broke he could see, from his observation post on a hill, that he was faced by some 100,000 Württembergers, Bavarians, and Russians. Moreover, Schwarzenberg's troops were supported by 400 cannon.

The imperial army had no choice but to retreat across the Aube while the rear guard contained the entire thrust of the enemy forces. The Emperor stood near a bridge, wearing a "dismayed and pensive expression." Night was falling when he crossed the river with the last corps. His entourage was in a state of torpor. The demoralization was total.

But this by no means prevented Napoleon from drawing up a new plan: to lure the Austro-Russians toward himself and the frontier, then get back to the Aube. "I'll go and spend the night in the enemy's own bed," he remarked.

And he wrote to Marie Louise: "I have decided to head for the Marne in order to draw the enemy away from Paris and get back closer to my strongholds."

Unfortunately, the courier was captured by the Cossacks. Blücher had the letter translated and sent a copy to Schwarzenberg. In a gallant gesture, he forwarded the original note to the Empress, along with a bouquet of flowers.

The Prussian general could well afford to send a bouquet to Marie Louise. The captured letter made him fully cognizant of Napoleon's intentions: to attack the enemy in the rear and in that way cut off his communication lines. Without delay, the Allies decided to assemble at Châlons and march on St.-Dizier, where they would overwhelm the little French army.

On Thursday, March 24, a letter from Savary to Napoleon was likewise intercepted by the Allies. In it, the Duke of Rovigo begged his master to return to Paris, where Royalist intrigues were rampant.

At Sommepuis, in a small town hall where he had spent the night, the Czar convened a council of war.

"Now that we have reestablished communications with Blücher, should we follow Napoleon and attack him with superior forces, or should we march directly on Paris?" he asked his officers.

General Toll offered the best advice: "Under the present circumstances, there is only one course of action. We must move on Paris by forced marches with our entire army, except for 10,000 cavalrymen who should be detached and sent against the Emperor Napoleon in order to mask our movement."

All that remained, that day, was to convince Schwarzenberg and the King of Prussia. Both agreed enthusiastically with the Czar. The Allied armies were overjoyed. Finally there would be an end to these recrudescent battles in which 100,000 troops would pursue 20,000 or 30,000 elusive Frenchmen, finally engage them, and then be forced to retreat.

At St.-Dizier, Napoleon was issuing a flood of directives. But all the faces he saw around him were either impassive or desperate.

"You're all poltroons—as bad as Quakers!" he shouted at them.

Napoleon had no notion of the enemy armies' movements. On March 26 he fought the Russians at St.-Dizier. It was a victory for him —his last—but it still left him with some anxiety. The corps he had defeated was one attached to Blücher's command, whereas he had thought he was fighting Schwarzenberg's cavalry. The explanation was forthcoming the next day, when at Vitry he received a big batch of intercepted dispatches. As he feverishly read though a mass of enemy bulletins and mail, the harsh fact emerged: the Allied forces were marching on Paris. He had been dealing only with a few Prussian and Russian troops sent to deceive him and carry out reconnaissance.

Perhaps the best thing would be to follow his plan—even to expand it—and be no more concerned about Paris than the Czar had been about Moscow in 1812. If he stayed in Lorraine he could muster all the garrisons in Germany, proclaim a mass levy, destroy the enemy's supply columns, and retake the big cities occupied by the Austrians and the Russians. But, on the other hand, he had repeated over and over: "If the enemy reaches Paris, there is no more hope." And he had often promised: "So long as I am alive, Paris will never be occupied!"

As late as Monday, March 28, he had not yet made his decision. Then, at St.-Dizier, he received an enciphered note from Lavalette: "The Emperor's presence is necessary, if he wants to prevent his capital from being handed over to the enemy. There is not a moment to lose."

He issued the order: "To Paris!"

But the Emperor did not dare gallop across a Cossack-infested country with only his regular picket accompanying him. He had to wait for the Guard.

That same Monday evening the Council of State assembled at the Tuileries. What decision would be made by the Empress Marie Louise? Could she perhaps avoid the worst by throwing herself into the arms of her father and welcoming the Czar and the King of Prussia to the Tuileries? Would the reign of Napoleon II be considered the only possible solution?

The discussion dragged on. With the exception of King Joseph, everyone thought that it would be a great mistake to leave Paris and give the Bourbons a free hand. A vote was taken, and it was almost unanimous: the Empress and the Government should remain. At this point Joseph read the letter—already several weeks old—in which Napoleon ordered a general evacuation to the Loire region "in the event of a lost battle."

The master had spoken, and everyone yielded. But they all knew that in leaving Paris, the Empress was losing her crown.

It was three in the morning. As Talleyrand got into his carriage in the courtyard of the Carrousel, he remarked: "So we've come to the end of all this. I must say he held good cards in this game that he lost!"

XXII

THE AGONY OF FONTAINEBLEAU

Great Powers die of indigestion.

NAPOLEON

THE DAWN OF TUESDAY, March 29, 1814, had not yet broken over Paris when Marmont, commanding the garrison of the city, sent a note from the outposts: "The enemy is gaining ground; we may be surrounded by this evening." Surely, the city could not be held for more than twenty-four hours.

Panic broke out. The exodus began at nine in the morning, under a rainy sky. The Parisians watched in silence as a long cortege went up the Champs-Élysées and set out on the road for Rambouillet. A squadron of grenadiers and chasseurs preceded the green carriages with the imperial crest into which were crowded the Empress, the King of Rome, Madame Letizia, the Queen of Westphalia, Cambacérès, the ladies-in-waiting, and the ministers.

The King of Rome's pages were riding in huge "gondolas" pulled by eight horses. Next, with lancers of the Guard as their escort, came the heavy coronation carriages with their gilt gleaming in the morning mist. Inside, tossed in a heap on the satin cushions, were the ceremonial harnesses and saddles. Finally, bringing up the rear, came the wagons carrying the crown jewels, the coronation costumes, the imperial sword, the silver service, the vermeil ware, and the treasure, thirty-two little barrels of gold.

Of the whole gigantic empire, there remained only this parody of the epic—this caravan dragging gilded bric-a-brac behind it.

At dawn of the next day, March 30, Napoleon abandoned the Guard and left on horseback with an ordinary escort. At Villeneuve-l'Archevêque he left even his escort and, with Caulaincourt, got into

480

a wicker cabriolet lent him by a butcher. Followed only by Gourgaud and Marshal Lefebvre, they set out for Paris.

Napoleon lunched at Sens, changed vehicles, and toward 10:30 P.M. reached the place called La Cour de France, just beyond Juvisy.

It was a cloudy night, and a light fog hung over the countryside. The thermometer at the Observatory registered 8 degrees. The relay station was crowded with cavalrymen and infantry. Napoleon climbed out of his carriage, and an officer emerged from the fog.

"Who are you?" the Emperor asked.

"General Belliard, Sire."

"Eh bien, Belliard! What's going on? Why are you here with your cavalry? Where is the enemy?"

"At the gates of Paris, Sire."

"And the army?"

"It is following me."

"And who is guarding Paris?"

"It has been evacuated. The enemy is to enter the city tomorrow at nine o'clock."

"And my wife and son—what has happened to them? Where is Mortier? Where is Marmont?"

"The Empress, your son, and the whole Court left for Rambouillet yesterday morning. Marshals Mortier and Marmont are surely still in Paris to terminate all the arrangements for the capitulation."

The Emperor flew into a rage, forgetting that he himself had ordered Joseph to remove Marie Louise and the Government from Paris if the city were threatened by the enemy. He shouted at the top of his voice: "So everybody has lost his head! That's what comes of employing men who don't have either common sense or energy. . . . That swine of a Joseph, who thinks he can lead an army as well as I can! . . . And that bastard Clarke, who can't do a thing once you take him away from his office routine!"

The defeated troops continued to file past, but not one of them saluted the Emperor.

"What cowardice! Capitulating! Joseph has ruined everything! Four hours too late! If I had come four hours sooner, everything would have been saved!"

His voice seemed choked with grief. But abruptly his vigor returned: "In a few hours, the courage and devotion of my good Pari-

sians can save everything. Caulaincourt, my carriage! We are going
to Paris! I'll put myself at the head of the National Guard and the
regular troops. We'll make things right again. . . . General Belliard,
order your troops to turn around."

But Belliard pointed out that since the capitulation had been
signed, he had to abide by it; that the Emperor would find no more
troops in Paris; and that therefore he should not go there in person.

Napoleon swept away these objections with one gesture. "Caulaincourt, my carriage! And you, Belliard, follow me with your cavalry! What is this agreement you're talking about? By what right was
it concluded?"

Then, struck by an idea, he abruptly came back toward the relay
station and spread out his maps.

"The Emperor Alexander is going to be all puffed up with pride
in Paris! He'll review his army in formation along both banks of the
Seine! And I don't even have mine at hand."

"In four days it will be here, Sire."

"Four days! But just think how many people have abandoned me
in only two days! The Empress herself!"

Suddenly he recalled the orders he had given. "Yes, I wanted her
to leave, because God knows what her inexperience would have got
her into!"

Then he bent over his maps again, and was heard to exclaim: "Yes,
I've got them! God is handing them over to me! But I must have four
days. You can get me those four days by negotiating."

And he dictated the following to Caulaincourt:

> We order the Duke of Vicenza, our Grand Equerry and Minis-
> ter of Foreign Affairs, to present himself to the Allied sovereigns
> and the commanding general of their armies to appeal to their
> kindness vis-à-vis our faithful subjects in the capital. We hereby
> invest him with full powers to negotiate and conclude peace,
> promising to ratify whatever he does for the good of our service.

And to Caulaincourt he said:

> Allons, Caulaincourt, you'd better be leaving. Go and save
> France and your Emperor. Do what you can. They will surely
> impose harsh terms on us. But under these circumstances, I rely
> on your honor as a Frenchman, and on your proven fidelity and
> devotion.

It was now three in the morning. The Emperor got back into his carriage: "The road to Fontainebleau!"

He arrived at six o'clock and took up quarters in his apartments on the second floor. After a few hours' rest he went to inspect the positions held by Marmont's 11,000 men, who had slipped out of Paris and formed the advance guard of the imperial army before Essonnes. The weather was very cloudy. Toward the end of the afternoon it thundered, and rain began to fall. When he got back to the palace, Napoleon learned that new regiments had joined his forces. In three days, all the troops the Emperor could muster—some 60,000 men— would be there, ready to resume fighting.

For the Parisians, the fall of Paris meant the fall of the empire. The Senate—a rump Senate of 64 members appointed by Napoleon —met at three o'clock in the afternoon of that Friday, April 1, and elected a Provisional government.

On April 2, the Emperor viewed the parade of the Guard and was cheered. His courage returned. To resume fighting did not seem impossible. And yet peace would be better.

Caulaincourt came from Paris. He had seen the Czar and told him of his master's wishes.

"Peace with Napoleon would only be a truce," Alexander had said.

"And Napoleon the Second?" the Grand Equerry had asked.

"But then what would we do with the Emperor? The father is an insurmountable obstacle to the recognition of his son."

That evening as he went to bed, Napoleon was hoping that "Papa Francis" would not dethrone his daughter and grandson. Would the Austrian Emperor be able to stand up to Metternich—who, as Napoleon knew, wanted to ruin him? An archduchess as the Regent of France! Would that not be a fine stroke for Vienna? The conquered man clung to that thought as night enveloped the château.

At Fontainebleau, on April 4, after the parade of the relieving guard, the soldiers once again cheered the Emperor and wanted to set out for Paris. But the marshals had their role to play. They had been rather relieved by the defeat, but were not yet thinking in terms of a Bourbon restoration. For them, the enthronement of the King of Rome seemed the sole means of saving the empire and their

own holdings, since the Senate had just voted Napoleon's dethronement.

They walked along behind the Emperor with the ringing step of
conquerors and followed him into his study without being invited.

"Affecting a self-confidence he did not really possess," as one
witness put it, Napoleon set forth his plans. "The Allies! I'll crush
them in Paris! We must march on the capital at once!"

"We can't expose Paris to the fate of Moscow," Macdonald said.
"We have made up our minds. We are resolved to have done with
it."

"I'll appeal to the army!" the Emperor almost shouted.

"The army won't march!" Ney warned him.

"The army will obey me!" Napoleon riposted.

"Sire, the army obeys its generals."

There was a silence. Crushed, he asked them: "Well, then, what
is it you want, Messieurs?"

"Abdication."

So far as can be determined, it was Oudinot and Ney who uttered
the terrible word. And Lefebvre added: "That's what you get for not
following the advice of a friend when he begged you to make peace."

The Emperor shrugged. Taking up a piece of paper, he wrote his
conditional abdication:

> The foreign Powers having declared that the Emperor Napo-
> leon was an obstacle to the restoration of peace and the integrity
> of the French territory, the Emperor Napoleon, faithful to his
> principles and to his oaths to do all possible for the happiness and
> glory of the French people, declares that he is ready to abdicate
> in favor of his son, and to submit the Act to the Senate in due form
> by a message as soon as Napoleon II has been recognized by the
> Powers, together with the recognition of the constitutional re-
> gency of the Empress. If these conditions are met, the Emperor
> will immediately withdraw to a place which shall be agreed upon.
> Done at our palace of Fontainebleau this fourth day of April, 1814.
>   [Signed] Napoleon

When the marshals had left, the Emperor called Caulaincourt
into his study and ordered: "Leave for Paris at once. You know my
intentions and my plans. If I win, we'll get an honorable peace.
. . . If I lose the battle, poor France will be left to fate. As for me, I
repeat what I have told you before: I don't need anything."

But after a moment of silence he asked pensively: "Do you think they'll accept my son?"

Certainly they would pretend to accept the son in order to get rid of the father more easily; and Napoleon hardly entertained any illusions.

At 4:30 P.M., accompanied by Ney and Macdonald, the Grand Equerry left for Paris, while the Guard and the Emperor's little regular army—sheltered behind Marmont's corps—made ready to fight for Napoleon II. En route, the plenipotentiaries stopped off at Marmont's headquarters and told him of the decision just made by Napoleon.

"The Emperor has abdicated?" exclaimed General Bordesoulle, Marmont's cavalry commander. "Now that, Monsieur le Maréchal, gets us out of a fix!"

Ney, Macdonald, and Caulaincourt were astonished. What did the general mean? At this point Marmont was obliged to admit that, upon receiving an envoy from Schwarzenberg, he had told him that he was "ready to leave the army of the Emperor Napoleon and take his troops along with him," provided he be allowed to retire to Normandy. He also demanded, by way of exchange, that a suitable situation be provided for the Emperor "in a circumscribed region." Having sent off this message to Schwarzenberg, the marshal had called in his generals to settle the details of their defection. Souham, the general in command of the most important division, had agreed enthusiastically, and with one exception the others had yielded with more or less good grace. Bordesoulle was the one who objected most: "What's this, monsieur le maréchal? You mean you would open up the way to Fontainebleau? You would leave the Emperor at the mercy of the enemy?"

But Marmont (as he admitted to the Emperor's two envoys) had nonetheless stuck by his decision: the troop movement was to be effected that same evening.

"Did you sign?" asked Caulaincourt, dumfounded.

"Not yet."

"Then you can come with us! When we go through Chevilly, you can tell Schwarzenberg that your talks have been broken off."

Marmont agreed. Before leaving, he delegated the command of the Sixth Corps to General Souham, instructing him not to effect any movement during his absence. But he added: "As soon as I leave, you will muster the troops and inform them of the Emperor's abdication."

He took care not to tell them that it was a conditional abdication in favor of Napoleon II. Moreover, Napoleon's decision was supposed to remain a secret so long as the Allies had not accepted it.

Everything seemed to start off well at Talleyrand's town house, where Alexander was staying. The first question that the Czar put to the four plenipotentiaries was whether the Emperor had agreed to abdicate.

"Yes, Sire, in favor of his son."

Alexander seemed to be listening attentively. "He chatted, talked about everything, objected only to trifles," and finally said: "I am by no means a partisan of the Bourbons. I am not acquainted with them. I shall inform my allies of your proposals, and I shall give those proposals my support. I, too, want to complete this as quickly as possible."

He dismissed his interlocutors, telling them to come back the next day at noon. "By that time," he said, "I shall have conferred with the King of Prussia and the Allied ministers."

The next day, as they lunched at Ney's residence, the Emperor's four plenipotentiaries still had some hope—although they had no illusions as to the difficulties confronting them. Just when Caulaincourt and the marshals were on the point of going to the audience granted them by the Czar, an officer entered and asked for Marshal Marmont. Marmont went out with him, and returned a few moments later. During the night, Marmont's corps, under orders from General Souham, had crossed the Austrian outposts and gone over to the enemy.

"I have been dishonored!" exclaimed Marmont. "Souham has disobeyed orders and been unfaithful to his duty. He has defected with the entire Sixth Corps. I'd rather have lost an arm than to see that happen!"

What had happened was that in the absence of his superior, Souham had opened a message from general headquarters addressed to Marmont. It read: "Monsieur le Maréchal, the Emperor wishes you to report to the Palace of Fontainebleau at 10:00 P.M." A few minutes later Gourgaud arrived and confirmed the order. Souham and the other generals were in a panic. Actually, Napoleon—who knew nothing of their plans—had summoned all the army corps commanders to Fontainebleau with a view to preparing for a possible resumption of hostilities. But Marmont's division commanders believed the Emperor had been informed of the planned defection to which Marmont had agreed.

"The marshal has fled!" Souham exclaimed. "I'm taller than he is, but I don't want to become a head shorter on the guillotine!"

The only way to escape the Emperor was to go over to the enemy. Even Bordesoulle was convinced of this. So the orders went out through the encampments; and by dawn the Sixth Corps, passing between two lines of enemy troops presenting arms, was in the Russian camp. The road to Fontainebleau was open! Napoleon was no longer in a position to bargain.

Marmont was livid. "What a dishonor! All is lost! I'm going to go to my troops and try to patch up everything."

Despite what had happened, Ney, Macdonald, and Caulaincourt —sick at heart—went to keep their appointment with the Czar. Apparently he had not yet heard anything. He declared (as he had the day before): "I repeat, the sovereigns are far from wishing to impose an unsuitable government upon France."

The discussion got under way, and once again Caulaincourt felt that the Czar, who had no great love for the Bourbons, favored the candidacy of the King of Rome.

Suddenly the door opened and an aide-de-camp announced the arrival of one of the commanding general's staff officers.

"What does he want?" Alexander asked.

"To inform you, Sire, that the corps commanded by Marshal Marmont defected to us this morning and is now in our camp."

The aide-de-camp had spoken in Russian. But Caulaincourt, who had served as ambassador to St. Petersburg, had understood him. And as the Czar took the aide-de-camp aside, Caulaincourt whispered to Macdonald: "Bad news! We are done for! He knows everything!"

And everything was, in fact, lost. The Czar immediately informed Napoleon's envoys that he "would negotiate neither with the Emperor nor with any member of his family." All Napoleon could do now was to abdicate unconditionally. Marmont and Souham had finished off the regime.

At two o'clock in the morning of April 6 the envoys reached Fontainebleau and, despite the late hour, were immediately received by the Emperor. Gourgaud had told Napoleon of the defection of Marmont's corps, and the Emperor was now clinging to the hope that the Czar would remember their former friendship. In an uncertain voice, he asked his envoys: "Did you succeed?"

The officers told him just how great the castastrophe really was.

Instantly, "General Bonaparte" came back to life. "I'll find brave men willing to die with me! War offers nothing worse than peace! We can still save everything!"

But an hour later he realized the folly of this, and called in Caulaincourt. "What can I do? If I resist, it will mean civil war in France. And I love France too much for that! All I have ever wanted was her glory. I will not be the cause of misery for her. I will not have this beautiful country ravaged because of me! So they want me to abdicate? Well, I *will* abdicate!"

At dawn he called in the marshals. Napoleon's hair was unkempt and his uniform coat unbuttoned. He made one last attempt to fight. Couldn't they seek refuge in the Rhône Valley and reach out a hand toward Italy?

But the Emperor's lieutenants didn't even reply. Then Napoleon exclaimed: "So you want repose? All right, you'll have it!" He wrote the following brief lines:

> The Powers having declared that the Emperor Napoleon was the sole obstacle to the restoration of peace in Europe, the Emperor Napoleon, faithful to his vows, declares that he renounces —for himself and his children—the thrones of France and Italy, and that there is no sacrifice—not even that of life itself—which he is not prepared to make in the interests of France.

A huge blob of ink fell from his pen and made a splotch in the center of the document, rendering it even more illegible than his handwriting had.

The *Moniteur* for April 6 published letters from a number of Napoleon's generals declaring their loyalty to King Louis XVIII. "I am humiliated," said Napoleon as he read the list, "to see that men I raised so high should have fallen so low. What will the sovereigns think of all the illustrious men of my reign? Everything that deflowers France is like a personal affront to me. I had identified myself with her so much!"

That same day the senators and deputies assembled jointly "to call to the throne, of their own free will, Louis Stanislaus Xavier de France, brother of the last King"—that last King whom some of those senators had sent to the guillotine. Thus "the French nation" was directly involved. But, as Chateaubriand emphasized, "the French nation" was virtually unaware of the existence of that "Louis Stanislaus Xavier" who had been imposed on it. And even if it had called him, it would have been in vain, since the King—still in England—was bedridden with a bad case of gout.

The next day, Thursday, April 7, "Les commissaires de la Pitié," as Caulaincourt had nicknamed his two companions, Ney and Macdonald, were received (along with Caulaincourt) by the Czar, who now spoke of Napoleon sadly—even compassionately.

The negotiations began. And Alexander proved to be the strongest supporter of the wounded eagle. It was he who first suggested the overlordship of the island of Elba for his friend from the days of Tilsit; and it was he who set the figure of two million francs for the stipend that Louis XVIII was to pay to "the King of the Island of Elba."

Everything was collapsing around the conquered master. His marshals, his generals, and even his servants fled in haste. When the Comte de Plancy, the Prefect of Seine et Oise, came to Fontainebleau, there was not even a servant to meet him. He went through one door, then another, and found himself in the presence of the Emperor, "all alone, and sadly leaning against the embrasure of a window." In the words of General Petit: "It was as though His Majesty were already buried."

In the same palace where he had received the Pope and six kings, Napoleon wandered about like a ghost. His valet tells us that "he fell into a kind of apathy—to the point where he did not even see things that were near him." When spoken to, he did not answer. There was only one consolation for him. That evening, the regiments of the Guard emerged from their quarters and, carrying torches, ran through the streets of the town cheering the Emperor—"their" Emperor—and shouting: "Down with the traitors! To Paris! To Paris!"

But Paris was being flooded with anti-Napoleon broadsheets. The vanquished leader was being called a "villain, an assassin, and a tyrant." He had become Cromwell, Attila, and Robespierre rolled into one! Couplets were being composed:

Enfin! grace a Napoléon
On ne parle plus de Néron!

[Finally, thanks to Napoleon,
There is no more talk of Nero.]

Marie Louise, at Blois, was still unaware of how extensive the
collapse had been. An enforced silence reigned around her. She had
only one desire: to rejoin her husband. She wrote to him that she
would be "more courageous and less anxious" if she could be near
him, sharing his fate and consoling him for his setbacks. She even
hoped she could be useful to him "in some way." For that matter, it
is plain that by having his wife and son come to be with him, the
Emperor could have established a kind of power base. If the King of
Rome and his mother had been with Napoleon on April 2, the enthronement of Napoleon II would have been much more feasible.
The presence of the Austrian Emperor's daughter and grandson at
Fontainebleau would have been a strong card in Caulaincourt's
hand.

But Napoleon apparently wanted to leave the decision up to
Marie Louise. He was not stopping her from coming to join him at
Fontainebleau, but he certainly did not order her to do so.

She was waiting for precise instructions. Instead, he wrote to her:
"I gather you were at Orléans this morning. You can stay there, if you
are traveling with your own horses. If you had post horses and can
come here, you can do it. . . ."

Considering the vagueness of his intentions, can she be blamed
for having decided to go *first* to see the Emperor Francis before
setting out for Fontainebleau or the island of Elba? By way of explaining her decision, she wrote Napoleon: "If you want to let me go and
see my father, I am sure—almost certain—that I will obtain Tuscany." And the same evening she wrote again: "He is kind. He will
be moved by my tears, and you will come out better, because while
you will go to stay on the island of Elba, you will also reign over the
possessions that may be given to us: I mean Tuscany."

What amazes one the most is that Napoleon, too, seemed to believe in the urgent necessity for a meeting between the father, the
daughter, and the grandson. How could he have failed to realize that
Francis would not let them join the exile?

As for Francis' giving Tuscany to his daughter and grandson, it was out of the question. That territory was to be given back to her brother, Ferdinand, Grand Duke of Würtzburg and godfather of the King of Rome, who had been dispossessed of it and who would thus be able to resume his title of Grossherzog von Toscana. And Parma, too, was out of the question. There was only one thing for Mme. the Archduchess to do: to come back to Vienna with her son.

Thanks, however, to the Czar, who was disgusted by the Austrian attitude, Caulaincourt was able to include the following clause in the Treaty of Paris:

> The Duchies of Parma, Piacenza, and Guastalla will be conveyed in fee simple and complete sovereignty to Her Majesty the Empress Marie Louise and her direct descendants. Effective immediately, the Prince, her son, will assume the title of Prince of Parma, Piacenza, and Guastalla.

Marie Louise left Orléans on the evening of April 12. The Emperor Francis had sent Prince Esterhazy and Prince Lichtenstein to meet her and accompany her to Rambouillet.

When she had talked to her father's two envoys, she began to have doubts. Would she be allowed to join her husband later? She wrote to him:

> It would be most barbarous to prevent me from it. And if they wanted to, I assure you, they could not do it. I want to share your unhappiness. I want to take care of you, console you, be useful to you, and assuage your sorrow. I feel I need that in order to live —in order not to succumb to this last blow.

But as soon as the carriage set out, Marie Louise—accompanied by the two princes—knew that she and her son were prisoners. In the middle of the night, en route between Orléans and Rambouillet, she managed to scribble this note in pencil: "There are orders to stop me from joining you, even by means of force. Be on guard, mon cher ami. We are being tricked. . . ."

On that night of the twelfth, Napoleon had not yet received her last two letters, but he had surmised everything. Shortly before noon on that same day he had learned that the Comte d'Artois, Louis XVIII's brother, had made his entrance into Paris flying the Bourbon white, and had taken up residence in the Tuileries. The crowd had hugged his boots and even the neck and chest of his horse. At the

Bondy Gate, the future Charles X had been welcomed by Marshals
Ney and Moncey!

Late in the evening, in that bedroom each wall of which was
ornamented with a golden *N*, while above the fireplace was an Austrian eagle (that of Marie Antoinette and Marie Louise), the Emperor
—in Louis Madelin's accurate phrase—"passed in review all the acts
of treason and desertion." Then he dismissed Caulaincourt. The
Grand Equerry went to his own room "strongly affected" by the brief
phrase that Napoleon had kept repeating like a leitmotif: "Life is
unbearable for me . . . unbearable!"

At three o'clock in the morning, a valet came to get Caulaincourt:
the Emperor wanted him to come quickly.

When the Grand Equerry entered Napoleon's bedroom, he saw
his master lying on the bed. A night lamp cast a feeble glow over the
gold fixtures in the room.

"Come here and sit down."

His voice was very weak. Napoleon had tried to commit suicide.
Between hiccups he told Caulaincourt he had taken some poison
made up by Dr. Yvan—poison that he had carried on his person since
the Russian "Hurrah!" at Maloyaroslavets, shortly after the departure
from Moscow.

As for his motive, he explained it to Caulaincourt, but with frequent pauses, "like a person experiencing great pain that paralyzes
the faculties."

> I can see that they are going to separate me from the Empress
> and my son. They will practice all kinds of humiliations upon me.
> They will surely try to assassinate me—or at any rate insult me,
> which for me is worse than death. . . . They won't let me reach
> the island of Elba. I have thought long and hard about my situa-
> tion, and given much thought to my position.

With some difficulty, he retrieved a letter from under his pillow.
It was intended for the Empress: "I love you more than anything in
the world. My misfortunes trouble me only because of the pain they
bring you. . . . Kiss my son for me. Adieu, chère Louise. Tout à
toi."

Caulaincourt wept unrestrainedly.

"Give me your hand," said the Emperor. "Embrace me. In a short time, I'll be dead. Take my letter to the Empress. . . . Tell her that I died knowing she had given me all the happiness that was hers to give."

A hiccup forced him to break off. Caulaincourt wanted to call for help, but the Emperor stopped him: "I want no one here but you, Caulaincourt. Don't try to prolong my agony. What I have been going through during the past two weeks has been much more painful than the present moment."

> I tried in vain to get away [writes Caulaincourt] and call in someone else, but he held on to me with irresistible force. The doors were closed, and his valet didn't hear me. His hiccups increased; his limbs began to stiffen; his stomach and body arched up. A cold sweat was followed by a raging fever, then a cold chill. . . . He seemed to be making every effort not to vomit; his teeth were clenched.

"How hard it is to die! How unlucky I am to have a constitution that puts off the end of a life I would so much like to have done with!"

But he soon began to vomit. He was suffering terribly. "His face was profoundly altered, as though the contracted features had been distorted." By morning "he had changed frightfully." But Caulaincourt managed, not without difficulty, to move him to an open window. Little by little, the specter of death receded.

"I have made up my mind. . . . I shall live until death shows the same indifference to me when I am in bed as when I am on the field of battle. And it will take courage to endure life after such events."

A few hours later he agreed to sign the treaty which conferred upon the man who had reigned from Hamburg to Rome the overlordship of the island of Elba—that little rock whose outline he had discerned on the horizon, in days gone by, from his native Corsica.

That same morning, the valet Hubert knocked softly on the door and announced the Countess Walewska. But Napoleon scarcely heard him. He was prostrate, exhausted by the agonies of the night before; and his thoughts never left the Empress and the King of Rome who, that same night, had become the "prisoners" of Austria. He completely forgot that his beloved Marie was close by him.

She stayed throughout the day and the following night, in the antechamber, waiting for the Emperor's door to open. Finally, at dawn, sorrowful and exhausted, she left the château and got back into her carriage.

Shortly after her departure Napoleon collected himself. "The poor woman!" he said with a sigh. "She'll think I forgot her!"

No sooner had she returned home than she sent a note to her former lover. This time he responded immediately: "The feelings that stir you touch me to the quick. They are worthy of your beautiful soul and the kindness of your heart. . . . Be well, repent of nothing, think of me with pleasure, and never doubt me."

To Marie Louise, who had just reached Rambouillet, he wrote: "I am so disgusted with men that I am no longer willing to let my happiness depend on them. Only you can do something about it. Adieu, mon amie. Kiss the little King for me. Regards to your father. Entreat him to be good to us."

"Good to us!" Two days later he received the following letter from Marie Louise:

> My father arrived two hours ago. I saw him immediately. He was very tender and very good to me, but it was all wiped out by the most frightful blow he could have struck at me. He will not let me come to you or see you; and he is unwilling to let me make the voyage with you. I pointed out that it was my duty to follow you, but in vain: he said he would have none of it, and wanted me to spend two months in Austria and then go to Parma, whence I shall come to see you. This last blow will be the death of me. All I want is that you should be happy without me; as for me, I can never be happy without you. I will write you every day, and I will always think of you. . . . I am so sad I don't know what to tell you. Once again I beg you to believe that I am most unhappy. I kiss you, and I love you with all my heart.
>
> Ta fidèle amie Louise

And so the Emperor lost his wife and son.

Only one consolation remained for Napoleon: by the terms of the treaty, he was authorized to designate 400 men to accompany him in his exile. But how could he choose? The requests were so numerous that the number was raised to 600. Under the orders of General Cambronne the splendid phalange, headed by the standard-bearer, left the château, preceded by the band: four clarinetists, a flutist, a French horn player, and a few drummers. They served as escort for four cannons, the Emperor's twenty-seven carriages, and his favorite mounts.

The Allied observers ("commissioners") who were to accompany the fallen Emperor to Elba—an Englishman, Sir Neil Campbell; two Austrians, Field Marshal Koller and General Clam-Martinic; a Russian, General Shuvalov; and a Prussian, General von Waldburg-Truchsess—arrived at Fontainebleau April 17–19. The jailers, decked out in gold braid and plumes, presented themselves before their "prisoner." The spectacle left them dumfounded. "He showed all the signs of a very disturbed mind," said Koller, "rubbing his forehead with his hands, then putting his fingers in his mouth and chewing on them in the most agitated manner."

Then it was Sir Neil Campbell's turn to be presented to the fallen Emperor:

> I experienced a strange kind of embarrassment when the aide-de-camp, after having announced me, withdrew and closed the door after him, leaving me suddenly alone with that extraordinary man whose name had for many years been the touchstone of my feelings, both as an Englishman and as a military man, and whose face I had imagined in every form that exaggeration and caricature could make most striking. I saw before me a little man of vigorous appearance who was pacing rapidly back and forth in his room, like a wild animal in a cage. He was wearing an old green uniform coat with gold epaulets, blue breeches, and boots with red tops. His beard had not been trimmed, and his hair was uncombed. There were particles of snuff on his upper lip and his waistcoat. When notified of my presence, he turned quickly toward me with a courteous smile, obviously trying to conceal his anxiety and indignation under an affectation of calm.

On Wednesday, April 20, the time came for Napoleon's departure. The moment "the King of the Island of Elba" appeared at the top of the winding staircase, General Antoine Drouot announced in a voice heard at the far end of the courtyard: "The Emperor!"

What remained of the Guard—the First Regiment of Foot Grenadiers and the sailors of the Young Guard—were drawn up in two files. The entire population of the town had formed into a crowd visible in the distance, beyond the gates.

At first there was complete silence; then came a roll of the drums. But Napoleon broke it off with a quick gesture.

Followed by the foreign observers and the last of his faithful followers, he came down the steps. When he reached the bottom, he paused; and in a clear voice said:

> Officers, noncommissioned officers, and soldiers of the Old Guard, this is my farewell to you. In twenty years you have never once strayed from the path of honor and glory. With men like you, our cause was not lost. But war was interminable: it would have meant civil war, and France would have suffered more as a result. I therefore sacrificed my own interests to those of the fatherland.

His voice choked. After a silence, he went on:

> I am leaving. But you, my friends, must continue to serve France. . . . Do not grieve over my fate. . . . I agreed to go on living only for the sake of your glory. . . . Adieu, mes enfants! I would like to press all of you close to my heart. Let me at least embrace your general and your banner!

With tears in his eyes, General Petit stepped forward. The Emperor opened his arms. The atmosphere was charged with emotion.

"Bring me the eagle!"

The honor guard stepped forward, carrying the banner of the First Regiment of Grenadiers. Napoleon went up to the banner and kissed it: "Dear eagle, let this last kiss resonate in the hearts of all my soldiers!"

Sobs were heard. The Emperor made an effort and said in a firm voice: "Farewell, once again, my old comrades. Let this last kiss enter into your hearts!"

The Emperor walked rapidly to his carriage, where Bertrand was awaiting him. General Petit followed him, weeping. The door slammed shut, the coachman touched up the six horses, and the berlin passed in front of the Guard and out through the gates. When it reached the square, it headed to the left, taking the road toward the forest. The Emperor was on his way to his exile.

"As soon as the carriage had disappeared from view," says Captain Parquin, "the soldiers, in a single spontaneous and unanimous movement, burned the eagles. And some, unwilling to be separated from them, ate the ashes."

Four days later Napoleon reached Provence: the drama was about to begin.

Toward seven o'clock on the evening of April 24 (a Sunday), the imperial carriage stopped in front of the Hôtel de la Poste in Montélimar. The Emperor was apprehensive, and asked M. Chabeaud, proprietor of the hotel, if it was true that the inhabitants of Provence were enraged at him. Had they really dragged a bust of him through the mud?

Later that same evening, as they were passing through Donzère, a Royalist town, the Emperor was recognized. The inhabitants tried to stop his carriage, demanding that "the Corsican" be handed over to them. For the first time in his life, as he scrunched down in the back of the carriage, Napoleon heard shouts of "Down with the tyrant!" and "Long live the King!" The equipage moved on at full speed.

At dawn on Monday, April 25, they approached Avignon. Did Napoleon remember that it was here—more than twenty years ago, when he was an undernourished captain of artillery quartered at the home of the pharmacist Renaudet on the Rue Haute—that he had written the radical *Souper de Beaucaire?* By way of precaution, the exchange of horses had been scheduled to take place outside the city. But there was a crowd on hand anyway, muttering and offering threats. As soon as the "ogre's" carriage came into view, the shout could be heard: "Napoleon to the gallows!"

The imperial carriage changed horses again at Orgon and set off. But it could not pass through the public square, where the local inhabitants, who were rioting, raised up a great clamor when they saw it.

Napoleon put his head out of the window, and what he saw horrified him. Directly in front of him was a gallows, and from it was hanging a bloodstained mannequin. Around the mannequin's neck was hung a placard on which was written in red letters: "Bonaparte." As the shouts redoubled, the grotesque figure was set on fire. The Emperor, staring fixedly, witnessed the execution—the burning of himself in effigy.

Some of the crowd rushed toward the carriage shouting, "Die, tyrant!" And there were women crying out, "Give me back my son!" The carriage was heavily pelted by rocks, and some windows were broken. The Emperor paled. What humiliation!

Orgon was finally left behind. Other towns were awaiting the exile, but Napoleon had no desire to live through the nightmare again. The foreign observers, seeing how frightened he was, agreed to his proposal that he should play the role of his own courier and ride one hour ahead of his carriage. As the generals watched, he donned a shabby blue greatcoat and a round hat with a white plume. Then he climbed on a sorry post horse and, followed by a groom, galloped off, leaving the observers behind. For the first time in fifteen years, Napoleon was taking a ride on horseback without being followed by a squadron of aides-de-camp.

At St.-Cannat, where he was not recognized, he quickly changed horses and set out again without taking a moment's rest. The mistral was blowing, raising up clouds of dust and bending the cypresses. Without slowing his pace, he raced through the villages. He knew this route well. Twenty-four years earlier, he had traveled it often as a poor second lieutenant wearing the chiffon wristbands and the blue uniform of an artillery officer of the Régiment de la Fère.

Three hours after leaving the cortege, with a few kilometers still to go before reaching Aix, he stopped in front of the long, gray façade of a wretched wagoners' tavern called La Calade. He got off his horse and went into the dining room, where he introduced himself as Colonel Campbell, an English officer from Napoleon's escort, and asked that a dinner be quickly prepared "for the ex-Emperor and his suite."

The Proprietress replied "that she would be much put out at preparing a dinner for such a monster." Then she began whetting a knife on a grindstone, and asked the Emperor to touch its point.

"Isn't it well sharpened?" she asked. "If somebody wanted to use it to stab the Emperor, I'd gladly lend it to him."

"You have a good deal of hate for the Emperor. What did he do to you?"

"*What did he do?* Ah, the monster! It was because of him that my son is dead—and my nephew, and so many other young people!"

And the conversation went on in that vein. When the foreign observers reached La Calade an hour later, they found "the former sovereign of the world deep in meditation, his head in his hands."

The Prussian observer wrote:

At first I did not recognize him, and I came up to him. Hearing footsteps, he started and jumped up, enabling me to see his tear-stained face. He signaled to me to keep quiet and take a seat next to him. As long as the proprietress was in the room, he talked only of trivial things. . . . We sat down at the dinner table; but since the dinner had not been prepared by his own cooks, he was afraid of being poisoned and was unwilling to eat anything. However, when he saw us eating with a good appetite, he felt ashamed to let us see how terrified he was, and took everything that was offered to him. He made a pretense of nibbling at it, but he sent the dishes back without really eating anything. Sometimes, after taking a dish of something, he would throw it under the table to make us believe he had eaten it. His dinner consisted of a bit of bread and a flask of wine which he had brought from his carriage, and which he even shared with us. . . .

He was also trying to think up ways of tricking the population of Aix, since he had been warned that a very large crowd was waiting for him at the post station there. Accordingly, he told us that he thought the best thing would be to return to Lyons and, from there, take another road to the point of embarkation for Italy.

We could not have agreed to this plan in any case, and so we tried to persuade him to go directly to Toulon, or to go to Fréjus via Digne. We tried to convince him that the French Government could not possibly have such perfidious intentions toward him, and that the local inhabitants—in spite of their unruly behavior—would never be guilty of such a crime. . . .

How could he "trick the people of Aix," who were surely on notice that he would be passing through, and would be waiting for him at the next relay station? To his way of thinking, the foreign observers had by no means realized the seriousness of the situation. Napoleon therefore told them what the proprietress had asked him: "They're going to drown Bonaparte, aren't they?" And he added: "You can see the kind of danger I'm exposed to!"

Little by little, a crowd from the neighboring hamlets had gathered in front of the tavern. The Emperor decided to leave La Calade at midnight. He put on General Koller's uniform, donned the Order of St. Theresa worn by the Austrian officer, set on his head the cap worn by the Graf von Waldburg-Truchsess, and wrapped himself in the cloak of the Russian observer. General Shuvalov's aide-de-camp put on the blue greatcoat and the round hat that Napoleon had been wearing upon his arrival.

The carriages were brought up. Preceded by General Drouot, the false Napoleon left the tavern. He was followed by another aide-de-camp and the foreign observers, with whom walked the Emperor, disguised in his strange assortment of enemy uniforms, with his cap shoved down to his eyebrows. "In this way we passed through the bewildered crowd of people, who were trying in every way they could to find out which of us was the one they called their 'tyrant.' "

The Emperor spent the night of April 26 at Luc, at the château of Bouilledou, where he found his sister Pauline. The "little pagan" was horrified when she saw her brother still wearing his curious garb. Rumor has it that she said: "I can't embrace you while you're wearing that Austrian uniform."

With a feeble smile, he went to change.

On Wednesday, April 27, still accompanied by his "guardians," the Emperor reached Fréjus and put up at an inn called Le Chapeau Rouge. From there he wrote to Marie Louise: "My health is good, and my spirits surmount everything. The only thing that could weaken them is the thought that you no longer love me. Kiss my son for me. . . ."

The next day, he was ready to embark; but there was no wind and he therefore remained in his room at Le Chapeau Rouge. That evening he went to St.-Raphaël, where the *Undaunted* was waiting for him, and boarded the ship at a point near the present-day customs house. As he came aboard, he was accorded the honors due a sovereign.

At eleven o'clock on the morning of Friday, April 29, with the return of the wind, the British frigate got under way. The Emperor remained on the bridge as the shoreline receded—that same shoreline he had seen take shape from the sea on 17 Vendémiaire, Year VIII, upon his return from Egypt fifteen years ago.

The whole, prodigious epic had taken place in fifteen years. The man who was now nothing more than the King of the Island of Elba continued to stare at the horizon as if he could still discern the contours of the French coast, which were gradually being blurred by the mist. Field Marshal Koller was standing near him. The Emperor thought of that terrible day of April 25 and avoided the jeering look directed at him by his father-in-law's general.

"I showed them a clean pair of heels," he admitted to Koller.

Napoleon had known fear. The man who had never quaked on the field of battle, had trembled in the face of a raging crowd. He dreaded riots, and was horrified by the unleashed "human beast." The agony of Fontainebleau, the impression of being "among the wolves," and that death which had refused to take him had shaken his nerves. Panic had made him gallop along the rocky roads of Provence; and in the gloomy dining room of La Calade, anguish had constricted his heart.

For that matter, he would much have preferred death. It should not be forgotten that he was the one who said: "I am a man who can be killed but not insulted."

On May 1 the *Undaunted,* well off shore, sailed past Ajaccio. On May 2 the frigate remained becalmed off Calvi. How many memories it, too, held for him! Did he catch the scent of Corsica—a scent he used to claim he could detect three leagues from his native land?

On that same day the King of Rome and his mother, accompanied by Austrian horsemen, crossed the French border. Marie Louise had just learned of the scenes that had taken place in Provence; and in her *Intimate Journal* she wrote: "How cruelly his soul must have been affected! I blame myself for not having followed him. Am I, too, abandoning him? Oh, my God! What will he think of me? But I will go to be with him, even though it means being eternally unhappy. . . ."

On the evening of Tuesday, May 3, having sailed past the island of Capraia, with the coast of Corsica behind him and that of Tuscany to his left, Napoleon saw a lofty island emerging from the Tyrrhenian Sea, taking up most of the horizon. The arm of the sea which separated it from Piombino (where his sister Élisa had been reigning only a few months before) was only six miles wide.

The Emperor looked at the chain of rocky mountains which, on that side, reached an altitude of 3,300 feet; some 60 feet above them rose Monte Capanne. The coast seemed to have been cut, slashed, and eaten away by the sea. But the profile of the island, which at this hour stood out squarely against the setting sun, was nonetheless dazzling because of the granite embedded in the ferruginous soil. Hence the name given by the Ancients to this island with the broken coastline: "Aethalia the Gleaming."

But now it was nothing more than the Island of Elba, forming part of the "Département Français de la Méditerranée, chef-lieu Li-

vourne, sous-préfecture Porto-Ferñajo"—the capital of a toy kingdom granted by the Allies to the man who had so often humiliated
them.

While the Emperor was sailing to his little island, Louis XVIII was
making his *joyeuse entrée* into Paris. He was riding in a carriage
pulled by eight white horses from the imperial stables led by outriders wearing the Emperor's livery. The carriage was accompanied by
the Imperial Guard. Some of the old veterans of the Guard had
pulled their fur caps down over their eyes: they preferred not to
witness the spectacle. "Their jaws were set with impotent rage.
. . . When they presented arms, their movements were angry, and
the sound made by their weapons made one tremble. . . ."

What was being celebrated was not the entrance of Louis XVIII
but the fall of Napoleon.

XXIII

THE KINGLET OF ELBA

After making a mistake or suffering
a misfortune, the man of genius always
gets back on his feet.

NAPOLEON

NAPOLEON HAD TAKEN WITH HIM from the library at Fontainebleau a little book titled *Notice sur l'Île d'Elbe.* He was therefore not overly surprised when from the bridge of the *Undaunted,* all he could see on the hilltop above Portoferraio was two forts with a few huts in between. It was not, in fact, until one had entered the little harbor that one could see the town of Portoferraio, whose buildings rose in tiers up the hill between the forts. The town, with its back curiously turned to the sea, is built on a peninsula. In 1814, the peninsula itself was separated from the rest of the island by a moat, and the capital was surrounded by salt water.

To enter the port the *Undaunted* first had to pass through the narrows, heading for the far end of the bay. Then she sailed past La Linguella, where a squat, round tower was used as a prison in the days of Cosimo de' Medici. Finally, the frigate came completely about and dropped anchor in the small "lake" before the town.

Napoleon remained on board while Bertrand, Drouot, and Campbell went ashore in a longboat. They were greeted on the dock by General Dalesme, to whom they handed the following note from the Emperor:

General:
I have sacrificed my rights to the interests of our country, and *have reserved for myself* the overlordship and ownership of the Island of Elba—an arrangement to which all the Powers have

503

agreed. Please be so kind as to inform the inhabitants of this new state of affairs, and of my *choice* of their island as a dwelling place, because of the climate and their gentle ways.

Everyone went along with this deception. The generals, the sub-prefect, and the mayor set about making preparations for the entrance, on the following day, of the Emperor (since the "King of Elba" was still retaining his imperial title).

The first thing was to haul down Louis XVIII's white flag from atop the two forts—Il Falcone and La Stella—and hoist the new banner in its place. Napoleon, who always thought of every detail, had had the new emblem designed and made up on board the frigate.

The next morning, the flag of Elba was hoisted over the forts; and the guns of the *Undaunted,* along with the batteries of the forts, thundered a salute to Napoleon as he left the frigate. The British sailors presented arms and, with drawn swords, gave out with the regulation cheers.

As the longboat with its twenty-four oarsmen was approaching the dock, the Emperor saw a crowd assembled on the waterfront. It was the kind of crowd he had known in his youth in Corsica, with everyone wearing bright-colored clothing. As the bells rang out and the drums rolled, the crowd shouted: "Evviva il Imperatore!"

As the longboat reached the dock, Mayor Pietro Traditi stepped forward, bearing on a silver tray the keys to the Gateway of the Sea. (Actually, they were the keys to the cellar of his house: they had been quickly gilded for the occasion, since the real keys had been lost.) The Gateway of the Sea, the only means of entry into the town, was a triumphal arch erected by the Grand Duke Ferdinand II in the seventeenth century; in it was a high door with nail-studded leaves.

Napoleon responded to the mayor's gesture with the traditional phrase: "Take back the keys, Monsieur le Maire. They could not be in better hands."

The soldiers and the National Guardsmen stood at attention. The Emperor was about to walk toward the Gateway of the Sea when the vicar general, a Corsican named Arrighi (like so many other Corsicans, he claimed to be a cousin of Napoleon), gestured. Astounded, the Emperor saw four stout fellows in holiday costume coming toward him, carrying a throne with a canopy of gilded paper decorated with cardboard bees gleaming in the sunshine. This honor, customarily reserved for the Holy Sacrament, was not one that he could refuse; so he went and took his place under the strange canopy. Behind him came the local authorities, his own officers, and the Allied observers. With the drums beating out march time, the cortege—a veritable carnival procession—passed through the Gateway of the Sea and entered the Emperor's new capital.

It was only a few paces from the triumphal arch to the simple parish church, whose three portals opened onto the parade ground. When the ceremony was over, Napoleon again took his place under his canopy and they set out for the town hall, which was located nearby, in a recessed area on the other side of the esplanade. The "Imperatore" entered the town hall to the accompaniment of a little chamber orchestra. Before going to the quarters that had been hastily prepared for him, he gave audience—in the "Grand Salon"—to the important personages of Elba.

The day after his arrival, Napoleon expressed his wish to pay a visit to the village of Capoliveri (the Summit of Liberty), which was built like an eagle's aerie on top of a vineyard-covered hill. The inhabitants were proud. (The time would come when they would refuse to pay the tax demanded by Napoleon; and he would have to send two companies of troops to give them a better understanding of their duties.) From Capoliveri he had a panoramic view of three bodies of water. To the west lay Corsica and the island of Pianosa. On a clear day one could even see beyond them to the island of Montecristo. At Capoliveri, Elba is no more than a league in breadth, as the crow flies.

On the way back to Portoferraio, Napoleon stopped off at the old Etruscan fortress of Volterraio, which from its height of some 1,300 feet overlooks the Gulf of Portoferraio. While he was visiting Volterraio, his attention was caught—as it had been the day before, while he was still aboard the *Undaunted,* and would be again a short time later as he was returning via boat to Portoferraio—by a complex of structures which overlooked the capital from between the two forts, offering a view of both the bay and the sea at once. This group of buildings, erected under Jean-Gaston de Médicis to serve as a courthouse and prison, had been converted into a residence for the gardener. The residence had been named I Mulini because of two

windmills which had been on the premises. A few years before the
Emperor's arrival the windmills had been demolished, and the
French officers commanding the artillery and engineering troops
had expanded the buildings of I Mulini and established quarters
there.

Napoleon decided to established his "palace" on this site—the
most handsome in the vicinity of Portoferraio. He had the ground
floor rebuilt, combined the two existing wings into one building, and
had one story added.

Today, this house looks rather gay from the outside, with its pink
walls and green shutters; inside, the walls are painted white, and the
floors consist of red tiling. The building was so narrow that no hallway
could be built; the rooms abut upon one another and look out upon
either the town or the garden and the sea. The monotony of this floor
plan is broken only by the two salons of the ground floor and the
second floor.

For his "interior," as he called it, the Emperor reserved four little
rooms for himself: on the side facing the garden, his study and a small
salon; and on the side facing the town, a library and a bedroom. The
big salon on the second floor (later occupied by Pauline) took in all
the space above these four rooms.

For all its noble proportions, however, this salon was not large
enough for the "miniature court" of Elba. And so the Emperor had
an additional wing constructed by converting the former flour warehouse into a long "ballroom" with seven French windows overlooking the garden.

To obtain furniture for his palace, Napoleon quite brazenly seized
plunder from his own family. He sent a sailing vessel to Piombino,
the location of the palace that Élisa—Grand Duchess of Tuscany and
Princess of Piombino—had been compelled to abandon despite the
pact between her and Murat. Its current occupant, the Austrian
General Starhembert, protested strenuously when he saw the officers
of the "King of Elba" taking away the furniture, the draperies, and
even the floors of his dwelling, leaving only a receipt in exchange.
Thus it was that Napoleon came into possession of Élisa's heavy,
awkward, gilded bed: that sculptured bed with candelabra at the
corners, its canopy supported by swans and surmounted with a lyre,
in which "La Bacciocha" (as her Tuscan subjects called her) had
spent some rather unchaste hours.

"I have punished my sister and robbed Austria, which succeeded her," the Emperor said with a laugh.

With the same lack of scruple, he unburdened his brother-in-law Borghese of a few possessions *au passage*. Pauline's puppet-husband was having his luggage sent to Rome via ship. When a storm compelled the vessel to put in at Portolongone, Napoleon had the cargo requisitioned. Were not his sisters and brothers-in-law indebted to him for everything they owned? And besides, it all stayed in the family!

The garden around the palace was charming. There was a view of the sea some 100 feet below, and the Italian coast was visible in the distance.

The semblance of etiquette which held sway at I Mulini was the characteristic sign of the fall of the Titan. Those present must have had the impression of a cruel pastiche of the imperial residences. On Sundays, there was a levee, "as at the Tuileries." A visitor could be admitted only "when introduced by the Grand Marshal or a chamberlain." There were four chamberlains, garbed in purple and silver. And there were ministers to govern the island. The former sub-prefect was given the portfolio of Justice; and the other ministries were divided up among Bertrand, Drouot, and Peyrusse, the treasurer. The seven aides-de-camp, all Elbans, wore green uniforms; their tunics and breeches had red piping, there were bees on the facings, and the epaulets and shoulder knots were of silver. The household also included two doctors, a chaplain, and a pharmacist. The three prefects of the palace, who were French, had sixty-five servants under their orders.

In the stables there were 10 saddle horses, 48 draft horses, and 17 vehicles: berlins, calashes, landaus, carts, and wagons. When the Emperor went out for a ride the postilions had to have on "a round hat with gold braid, a green frock coat with gold buttons, and a red laced jacket." Eight outriders sounding flourishes on their trumpets rode ahead of the carriage. Officers rode on either side of it, and the escort brought up the rear. Napoleon also required that "on every day of duty, five mounted men with carbines and loaded pistols" should follow his carriage.

For the Emperor had troops. The arrival of the "grumblers" (veterans of the Old Guard) from Fontainebleau had delighted him. "Now that you're here," he said, "all is forgotten!"

To these 607 Guardsmen, commanded by Cambronne, were added 43 gunners, 118 Polish light cavalrymen and lancers, a rather mediocre battalion of 400 men recruited on Elba and Corsica, and a dozen noncommissioned officers of the elite gendarmerie. The "navy" consisted of two or three small vessels like the *Abeille* and the *Mouche*, with a crew of eight, and one sailboat, the *Étoile*, whose crew numbered sixteen. In addition, Louis XVIII had given Napoleon a genuine warship. The Treaty of Fontainebleau had called for a corvette, but the King had sent only a brig, the *Inconstant*, with ten guns and a crew of sixty-four commanded by Lieutenant Taillade.

Like the officers, the functionaries and servants maintained the appearances of an illusory court. Napoleon went on playing at being a chief of state. This activity was indispensable to him.

And yet he also devoted himself to a more effective kind of activity. In slightly more than ten months the face of the island was so radically changed that the Emperor's handiwork can still be discerned today: roads, bridges, irrigation, hygiene, communications, and the establishment of agriculture (previously very feeble), including the addition of olive trees and mulberry trees. He was constantly on the move, inspecting his domain. One day, with Colonel Campbell watching, he walked from five in the morning until three in the afternoon, under a broiling sun; and then, after inspecting his "fleet," he took a three-hour ride on horseback—"to untire myself," he explained to the amazed Englishman.

It has been said with good reason that this tireless bustling of the "kinglet" concealed an intense secret activity. Had Napoleon begun preparations for his escape and return to France immediately upon his arrival at Elba? It would seem that the flight of the eagle, in March, 1815, could not have taken place without certain agreements, certain promises, and even certain compromises. And yet there does not seem to have been any real plot. If Louis XVIII had paid him the pension called for in the treaty, and if Marie Louise, holding her son by the hand, had come to be with the exile, perhaps Napoleon would have accepted his banishment.

The Emperor was eager to be kept accurately informed on current events; and for that purpose he employed at least as many spies as the Allies were using to keep an eye on their former conqueror. It was not merely that his "fleet," under whatever pretexts, kept visiting Leghorn and Genoa. The accounts of the Emperor's privy purse are quite astounding. At the same time that he was pinching his pennies at Portoferraio—keeping a close watch on his laundry and on the candles used in the kitchens; renting grazing lands on the neighboring island of Pianosa, and even half-starving his horses—the Emperor was paying his aides 136,000 francs. Surely it was in exchange for some unusual services that Napoleon paid out such considerable sums.

One source of Napoleon's revenue was the purse of his mother, who had come to be with her son, bearing a passport made out in the name of "Mme. Veuve Bonaparte."

Pauline's visit to "the Isle of Repose" also helped him out. Paoletta first spent only two or three nights at Portoferraio; then she returned, on November 1, to take up permanent residence on the island. She was greatly distressed by the lack of comfort at I Mulini, and by the oppressive heat. In her opinion, it was imperative that the Emperor get out of town during the summer months.

In the course of his excursions, Napoleon had noticed a cluster of small houses prettily situated on the slope of a hill among the vineyards in the valley of San Martino, a league and a half from Portoferraio. From there, one had an admirable view of the port, the town, and the fortress of Volterraio. Unfortunately, the owner was asking 180,000 francs for his property. But Pauline, in a sentimental gesture, opened her jewel box, and Napoleon was able to buy the property of San Martino.

Ostentation seems to have been the keynote for this house. The grand salon, with a marble floor, is ornamented by a work (obviously in the trompe-l'oeil style) executed by Signore Ravelli, which in its own mediocre way represents the Nile, the desert, camels, the columns of Thebes, and the hieroglyphs. Worked into the center, at Napoleon's request, is "an octagonal basin with a little fountain, in the Egyptian manner." The ceiling of the Salle de Conseil is an imitation of the sky. Two doves, each holding in its beak the end of a ribbon, "the knot of which tightens as they draw farther away from each other," symbolically represent Napoleon and Marie Louise separated by circumstances.

On August 25, the Emperor put his mother up for a few days in one of his occasional residences, a modest little house situated on the outskirts of the hamlet of Marciana Alta belonging to the Sieur Cerbona Vadi, the deputy mayor.

The invitation to his mother to come and join him was the cover-up for a romantic little plot: the Emperor was looking for a discreet place where his impending meeting with Marie Walewska could be kept private.

At the same time, he made sure that the Countess was warned that she should use all possible discretion in disembarking at Elba. Every care must be taken so that no report of his Polish lady's escapade reached the ears of the Empress Marie Louise. After all, he was waiting, from one day to the next, for the arrival at Elba of his legitimate wife and the King of Rome. This is why the Emperor had gone to Marciana Alta. There, perhaps, he would experience the joy of embracing (as a substitute for the little King?) the young Alexander.

On the day of Marie's arrival, Napoleon left the village to climb to a more secluded spot. Behind the Emperor came a few men, including his valets: Marchand (loyalty incarnate) and the pseudo-Mameluke Ali, who was really named Saint-Denis and had been born at Versailles. The others sweating under the hot sun included Bernotti, an aide-de-camp recruited on Elba, and Captain Paoli, a Corsican, who commanded the gendarmerie of the island. Paoli felt awkward in his new role of courtier.

"What time is it?" the Emperor asked him.

"Whatever time is most pleasing to Your Majesty," Paoli replied.

There was also a Captain Mellini, an Elban. How low the Emperor had fallen! Now he was surrounded by Paolis, Bernottis, and Mellinis, rather than Talleyrands, Caulaincourts, or Ségurs.

He had put on a great deal of weight. And even though he had made the climb on foot that day, the ascent via flagstones between which the intervals became wider and wider as the goal was neared must have seemed atrocious to him. Finally, halfway up the slope, they came to the hermitage, overlooking a little grove of chestnut trees whose fruits, in this time of late August, were yellow-green and ready to burst open. It was there, in the five wretched rooms that usually served as cells for monks, that the Emperor would receive Marie.

He wandered off and sat down to meditate on a rock which looked down directly on the sea. From there, he could see a good part of his kingdom.

What he was gazing at from the heights of this rock was not the island that had become his prison—that island spread out before him. It was the shoreline and the mountains of Corsica that he stared at for hours on end, that Corsica where he was born.

Now he could not openly play host to a woman for whom he no longer felt anything but a warm affection.

On Thursday, September 1, from the terrace of Cerbona Vadi's house, he watched the approach of the sailing vessel which was carrying Marie, her brother and sister, and the little Alexander. At nine that evening the brig dropped anchor in front of the hamlet of San Giovanni in the far end of the gulf, directly across from Portoferraio, whose lights were sparkling in the night. Grand Marshal Bertrand and Captain Bernotti were there to meet them. The party set off at a fast trot, but the carriage soon pulled up unexpectedly near Marciana Marina, where three horsemen with torches were waiting on the road.

"The Emperor!"

The King of Elba kissed Marie's hand and embraced Alexander. Then they set off again. At Marciana Alta they got out of the carriage and, without stopping by to see Madame Mère, continued the climb on foot. Little Alexander was carried, sometimes by Napoleon and sometimes by one of his officers.

It was one in the morning when they reached the hermitage. A late supper was awaiting—a supper during which the little Alexander was heard to say: "Let me eat, Papa Emperor!"

Marie reproached her lover with having forgotten her at Fontainebleau, when she was in the antechamber.

"I had so much on my mind, then," he said.

Two monk's cells had been fixed up in the hermitage for Marie and her sister. Leaving the ladies there, Napoleon went to spend the night in a tent pitched downhill, under the chestnut trees. Hardly had he gone to bed when, at two thirty in the morning, there was a violent thunderclap. Napoleon got up quickly and went to Marie's room, still in his dressing gown. Was it because his *belle Polonaise* was afraid of thunder?

Meantime, at Portoferraio the news was rapidly spreading that

the Emperor was being visited by a blond lady accompanied by an
equally blond little boy; and no one doubted that the Empress had
finally come to be with her husband on Elba. The Emperor's physician, Dr. Foureau de Beauregard, put on his finest clothes, mounted
his horse, and galloped toward Marciana Alta. The first person he saw
under a chestnut tree was Napoleon, seated on a chair in front of his
tent and holding in his lap the little Alexander.

"Well, Foureau," said the Emperor as he saw his physician approaching, "what do you think of him?"

"Why, Sire, it seems to me that the King has grown a great deal!"

Actually, as the Emperor's valet was to observe later, the two
half-brothers did resemble each other: each had the Emperor's forehead and a head a bit too large for his body.

Napoleon broke out laughing. He asked the child: "What are you
going to do when you grow up?"

"I'm going to make war, like Napoleon."

The physician's blunder made the Emperor realize that he could
not for any length of time maintain the deception that the Empress
was with him. Marie Louise might very well learn that Marie and the
young bastard son were with Napoleon, and immediately seize upon
this as a pretext for not coming to join him.

And so, in the course of a walk he asked his "Polish wife" to leave
the island. Marie yielded, agreeing to leave on the evening of the
next day, September 3.

On the evening of the following day, Napoleon accompanied
Mme. Walewska as far as Marciana Alta. It was already time to part.
Marie offered to leave her jewels with him, saying, "You need
money."

But Napoleon declined. After a last farewell, the Countess went
down the hillside toward the brig which was lying at anchor.

Suddenly, a storm broke and rain came down in torrents. Napoleon immediately sent an officer to Marie with orders that she should
not embark. But Bernotti, who was escorting the Countess, having
noticed the dangerous swell of the sea, had already ordered the brig
to anchor on the other side of the island, in the more sheltered harbor
of Portolongone.

As soon as he heard of this change of itinerary, Napoleon jumped
on his horse and galloped toward Portolongone. He reached it before

daybreak, only to learn that Marie—in obedience to his wishes—had left the island.

All the scheming and precautions by way of dissimulating Mme. Walewska's arrival had been in vain: on the evening before Marie saw Napoleon again, Marie Louise had given her father her "word of honor" that she would not go back to her husband.

Napoleon was still counting on her coming, as is proven by the commissioning of the ceiling for the council chamber at San Martino. But Marie Louise had left Austria to take the waters at Aix-les-Bains. She was accompanied to France by the Austrian General Adam von Neipperg, who had received the following precise instructions from Metternich:

> Employing all the tact required, the Graf von Neipperg will try to dissuade the Duchess of Colorno [Marie Louise] from any thought of making a voyage to Elba—a voyage which would deeply afflict the paternal heart of His Majesty, who entertains the tenderest wishes for the well-being of his beloved daughter. In the worst eventuality, if all persuasion proves vain, the General will follow the Duchess of Colorno to the island of Elba.

Neipperg behaved with the requisite tact, and Marie Louise had no inkling of the aim being pursued by this handsome officer. He was blind in one eye, but the black patch he wore over that eye gave him a rather piratical appearance that pleased the ladies. Marie Louise wrote to her husband:

> I am very pleased with General Neuperg, whom my father assigned to me as an escort. He speaks of you in a proper manner, and in the way my heart desires, for I feel a need to speak of you during this cruel separation. When shall I finally be able to see you again and kiss you? I so much want to. . . .

It was then that Napoleon sent an envoy to his wife to ask her to come to Elba.

And Neipperg attacked. Probably he had not yet become Marie Louise's lover; but he already exerted enough influence over her to prevent her flight.

Napoleon sent another envoy to Aix with the message: "Your home is ready, and I am expecting you in the month of September to reap the harvest. No one has any right to oppose your making the voyage. I have already written to you about that. So please come. I am awaiting you eagerly."

But Neipperg had achieved his ends; and on August 31 the Empress wrote to her father:

> Three days ago I received a visit from one of the Emperor's officers, bearing a letter in which [the Emperor] told me to come right away—and all alone—to Elba, where he was awaiting me, pining away with love. . . . Please rest assured, my very dear papa, that now I have less desire than ever to undertake such a voyage, and I give you my word of honor that I will never try to undertake it without having asked your permission.

A few days later, on the way back to Austria, at an inn at Righi called The Golden Sun, the erotically inclined Marie Louise, having dismissed the servant assigned to guard her bedroom door, gave herself to Neipperg.

Upon reaching Vienna she wrote to her counselor, Mme. de Montebello, in a flippant tone most unusual for her:

> Just imagine! During the last few days of my stay at Aix the Emperor sent me one message after another asking me to come and join him, to go on a lark with M. Hurault unaccompanied by anyone else! I was told to leave my son at Vienna; that he was there already, and that he [Napoleon] had no need of him. I found that a bit excessive, and I answered frankly that I could not come at present. . . . I will not go to Elba at present, and I will never go there (for you know better than anyone that I have no desire to). But the Emperor is really so inconsistent, so frivolous!

It was all over. Marie Louise had become an Austrian again, and she would never again belong to Napoleon.

XXIV

THE FLIGHT OF THE EAGLE

Calculations are useful when one
has a choice of means. When one
has no such choice, it is bold
moves that bring success.

NAPOLEON

IF COLONEL NEIL CAMPBELL, who was officially responsible for the
surveillance of Napoleon on Elba, had not fallen madly in love, the
imperial exile would never have managed to get away from Portoferraio. In that case, several generations of dealers in engravings would
not have made a fortune selling the legendary "flight of the eagle"
from steeple to steeple, "as far as the towers of Notre Dame." But,
on the other hand, the treaty of 1815 would not have deprived France
of those territories left her in 1814; and—most significant—the bloodbath of Waterloo would not have taken place.

Colonel Campbell had a cold, penetrating glance. He was always
listening to what was being said, and his smile was always forced. He
spoke "only to make others speak." In the words of Pons de l'Herault,
"Taken all in all, he was the perfection of the British type." That
perfection, of course, stopped short at the portals of love: the Englishman in love lost his equanimity, his phlegm, and his self-control. The
colonel's heart (according to Hyde de Neuville) was pounding furiously for love of his mistress, the very pretty and very worldly Contessa Miniaci, who spoke three languages, Italian, English, and
French—all of them poorly. This ravishing creature did not make a
practice of coming to Elba to be with her lover; she preferred meeting him at Leghorn, Florence, or Lucca.

Consequently, during the nine months and twenty-two days of

the Emperor's exile, his guardian Campbell made numerous quick trips to the Continent. Every month, for a period ranging from a week to two weeks, he would absent himself from Elba so as to be with his beautiful Contessa. In his diary, these were put down as trips for his "health and amusement."

So it was that on February 14, 1815, he boarded his frigate, the *Partridge*, and set sail for Leghorn and his lady love. When he returned to Portoferraio—at noon on Tuesday, February 28—Napoleon had already taken flight.

The Allies had never intended to put the fallen Emperor in the custody of a jailer: Napoleon was to reign on his island as an independent ruler. At the end of the month of May, 1814, the Prussian, Russian, and Austrian observers who had accompanied Napoleon from Fontainebleau to his new kingdom had come to make their farewells. It was only then that Campbell offered to remain on Elba. Napoleon eagerly accepted the offer: Campbell would have all the appearance of an accredited ambassador whose presence alone would demonstrate the Emperor's sovereignty; and besides, he might prove useful in a possible resumption of the dialogue with the Allies.

One can easily imagine the warm approval forthcoming from Lord Castlereagh, the British Minister of Foreign Affairs. It was an unhoped-for bit of luck! Not only would a British officer be openly spying on the dangerous exile with all the advantage of day-to-day circumstances, but Campbell's British frigate would hence have Portoferraio as a home port.

Campbell had very little understanding of the Emperor's genius. To the astonished Lord Holland he said in a tone of superiority: "Napoleon's talents do not strike me as being any greater than those one would require of a subprefect." Without blinking an eye, he had completely believed an avowal made to him by Napoleon in September, 1814, when Campbell had just returned from a lover's journey to Lucca: "I no longer exist for the world at large. I have told you before, and I repeat it now: I am as good as dead. All I am concerned with now is my family and my retirement; my house, my cattle, and my mules."

And yet Colonel Campbell's optimism was a bit shaken on February 17 when he reached Leghorn and, as usual, before heading for

Florence, had a meeting with the French consul. At the time, this office was held by the Chevalier Mariotti, an ardent anti-Bonapartist. (This attitude was rather surprising in a Corsican—especially one who had been among the first to be named an officer of the Legion of Honor by the Emperor.)

As early as September, 1814, Mariotti had proposed to Talleyrand that he, Mariotti, become the moving spirit of a plot to kidnap Napoleon during one of his trips to La Pianosa and take him as a captive to the prison of Le Masque de Fer on Sainte-Marguerite Island. Mariotti had a very clever agent on Elba: an "oil merchant" (this is the only name he is known by) who was much harder to deceive than the colonel. And that agent had reported one very precise fact: to a few veterans of the Old Guard, Napoleon had hinted at a change: "Be patient! We'll get through this short winter the best way we can. Then we'll make plans for a different kind of life come spring."

According to the "oil merchant," Napoleon was planning to land in Italy and appeal for help to Murat, who was still on his throne. Campbell had immediately forwarded this information to the foreign minister, adding, "I nonetheless persist in my opinion that if Napoleon receives the income stipulated in the treaties, he will remain quite tranquil here, unless there should be some extraordinary development in Italy or France."

On this point, Campbell had made an accurate appraisal: if the King of France continued to refuse to pay the King of Elba the annual income of two million francs stipulated in the Treaty of Paris, hunger might make the wolf come out of the woods.

The colonel was also aware that Napoleon had learned there had been some question, at the Congress of Vienna, of seizing him and deporting him far from Europe. As a matter of fact, shortly after his arrival in Vienna, Talleyrand had written to Louis XVIII: "There is evidence of a rather firm intention to remove Bonaparte from the island of Elba. But no one yet has any precise notion of the place to which he might be taken. I suggested one of the Azores. This island is 500 leagues distant from any country."

To the King this idea had seemed "excellent." And he declared: "It is high time that the Powers reach an understanding so as to pull up the last root of evil."

But by November, the Azores were regarded as too near; and for the first time, the name of St. Helena was mentioned. It was the King of Bavaria (he owed his crown to a whim of Napoleon) who announced it to a member of the Genoese delegation, even adding: "At this very moment, as I am speaking to you, the thing is supposed to have been done. And as for me, I am delighted, because I never had any peace of mind so long as that devil of a man was so near the Continent."

The Emperor *seemed* to be completely uninformed—putting into practice his own maxim: "One can undo a great many things by pretending not to see them." Actually, however, nothing had escaped his attention. As already mentioned, the Emperor had a good many observers. It is well established that Cipriani, a "jack-of-all-trades employed at the office and by the police," made several trips to the Continent, and even to Vienna. Through him and his "colleagues," the Emperor knew what was being schemed against him. For that matter, he didn't even need an informer at Vienna. All he had to do was look at the *Journal des Débats* for November 19, which stated: "It is said that several agents or emissaries of Bonaparte have been arrested in Italy, and that as a result he will be transferred to the island of St. Helena."

> I cannot believe [exclaimed the Emperor] that Europe wants to take up arms against me! In any case, I would not advise anyone to come and attack me here. He might pay dearly for it. I have provisions for six months, good artillery, and brave soldiers to defend me. The overlordship of Elba was guaranteed to me. This is my castle, and I would not advise anyone to come here and disturb me.

On February 10, in secret session, the Congress of Vienna took the last step and decided on deportation. Campbell, despite the resignation avowed by his "prisoner," sniffed the danger. These plans for a kidnapping might force the Emperor to go over to the attack. As soon as he reached the Continent, therefore, Campbell voiced his fears to Cooke, the British Under-Secretary of State, who had just returned from the Congress of Vienna.

Cooke shrugged his shoulders and said: "Tell Bonaparte that he is completely forgotten—as if he had never existed."

When Louis XVIII's soldiers were compelled to shout "Long live the King!" they added in a whisper: "of Rome!" As Thibaudeau

writes: "People pitied Napoleon for his sad fate. They grew sentimental, and wept for him." Napoleon did not fail to hear the heart-
beat of the nation: he decided to go back to France.

On February 16, nobody suspected anything. But no sooner was
Campbell's frigate lost to sight beyond the horizon than Napoleon
ordered Drouot to refit the *Inconstant* (the only ship of any size that
he possessed) and "give it a paint job that will make it look like a
British ship." In order to ward off any suspicions on the part of
Drouot himself, Napoleon added: "The brig will be provisioned for
three months for one hundred and twenty men."

Three months? It would take only three days to reach France.
Was Napoleon thinking of going to the United States?

The first preparations that aroused the suspicions of the "oil merchant" were made on February 21: that night, artillery, muskets, and
cases of ammunition were loaded on the *Inconstant* and the *Étoile*.

The next day, provisions were brought aboard the two ships.
"During these last days," says Marchand, "a big map of France was
spread out on the rug in the Emperor's salon. Kneeling on it, he
traced out the route he proposed to follow."

On February 24, the coming of daylight revealed that the *Partridge* had returned and dropped anchor in front of Portoferraio.
Campbell was not on board—he was still in Florence—and the skipper had merely come to introduce six English tourists to the Emperor. Napoleon received them, and when the "exhibit" was over,
the *Partridge* hoisted its sails again and headed for Leghorn.

Immediately, an embargo was placed on all vessels: not even
fishing smacks could leave their anchorages. The troops were inspected at a general review.

On the evening of February 25, Napoleon led Mme. Letizia out
to the garden of I Mulini. "Ma mère, I have something to tell you.
It is something you must not repeat to anyone—not even to Pauline.
I am leaving tomorrow night."

"Where are you going?"

"To Paris. What do you think of the idea?"

Mme. Letizia is said to have replied: "My son, it has not been
God's will that you should die in an idleness unworthy of you, and if
you must die now, I hope it is God's will that it not be by poison but
with sword in hand."

As he was going to bed that night, he instructed Marchand to get two uniforms ready: "A chasseur's uniform, a grenadier's uniform, some shirts, and nothing else."

His loyal valet noted: "I made sure to bring along a tricolor cockade to hand to him when the time came and he asked for it."

On Sunday, February 26, Cambronne issued an order to the "army": they would embark at five o'clock.

This time the news spread through the town. Everyone shouted: "The Emperor is leaving!" The weather was splendid. All the inhabitants of Portoferraio were in the streets, heading either for I Mulini or for the waterfront to gaze upon the magnificent imperial fleet.

But how could the *Inconstant*, a single-masted, flat-bottomed sailing vessel, the *Caroline*, and the two xebecs, the *Étoile* and the *Saint-Joseph*, transport the 1,000 men who made up the imperial army? The 90-ton *Saint-Esprit*, lying at anchor in the harbor, was simply requisitioned.

Now the soldiers marched down from their barracks. As the embarkation began, making the port the scene of intense activity, the Emperor received the notables of Elba at his "palace": "I am entrusting you with the defense of the city. I can give you no greater proof of my trust in you than to leave my mother and sister in your care."

He then spent a few minutes alone with Madame Mère and Pauline. Marchand, who had been waiting in the next room, saw the door open suddenly, and Pauline came in. With a sob, she handed him her diamond necklace. "Here, the Emperor told me to give you this necklace. He may have need of it." And she held out her hand for him to kiss.

At seven o'clock that evening, having donned his legendary uniform, the Emperor got into his carriage. It moved quickly down through the crowd toward the entrance to the tunnel that the Emperor had had built on the hillside below I Mulini in order to reach the town more conveniently. When he reached the esplanade, he stopped in front of the Gateway of the Sea and got out of his carriage. Silencing the shouts of "Evviva Napoleone!" with a gesture, he said in a ringing voice:

Elbans, I render homage to your conduct. At a time when it was fashionable to heap bitterness upon me, you gave me your love and devotion. I thank you for that. Elbans, I am incapable of being ungrateful: you can count on my gratitude. I shall always cherish the memory of you. Farewell, Elbans! . . . I love you. You are the brave men of Tuscany! . . .

The Emperor was now surrounded by the crowd. Everyone was talking at once.

"Sire, be happy, and count on the Elbans!"

"Sire, our wishes go with you. Let us hear from you soon."

Not without difficulty, he tore himself away from the hands clinging to him. He boarded the *Caroline*, which, using oar power, took him to the *Inconstant*.

A shot rang out from a cannon on the brig. It was the signal for departure. When a southeast wind sprang up, the Emperor ordered the vessels to set sail—proceeding separately—for the Gulf of Juan, keeping as far offshore from Italy and Corsica as possible.

On February 27, as they came abreast of the island of Capraia, they sighted the *Partridge* in the distance. The frigate, with Campbell on board, was returning to Portoferraio. The colonel had cut short his amorous escapade, in view of the most recent dispatches that the "oil merchant" had sent to Leghorn. There was no doubt about it: something portentous was happening on Elba. But the *Partridge* had been held up by the same calm that had delayed Napoleon's departure; and now the southeast wind compelled it to tack. Moreover, the sun, now low on the horizon, prevented the British from seeing the flotilla which was carrying Napoleon and his destiny.

The next day, when the frigate entered the port, Campbell was dumfounded: the *Inconstant* had vanished! And a short time later he discovered, to his consternation, that the soldiers standing guard at the entrance to the inner basin and the Gateway were grenadiers of the Guard, who had replaced the National Guard of Elba.

After vainly questioning General Bertrand's wife and subjecting Pauline to an interrogation, Campbell put to sea again in pursuit of Napoleon. He knew only one thing: the flotilla was heading for either the French coast or Piedmont.

Campbell's negligence seemed so extraordinary that some persons accused the Foreign Office of having instructed him to let his so-called prisoner escape so as to create an opportunity either to wage war on the Bourbons (this is what the "oil merchant" said in one of his reports) or to conquer Napoleon once and for all and send him to St. Helena.

Others declared that in 1815 Austria had agreed to let Napoleon get his throne back. For this legend, the Emperor himself is responsible. To abate the qualms of the ill-fated Ney, who had come to join him at Auxerre, Napoleon argued that his father-in-law was looking after the interest of his daughter and grandson, and that interest demanded that they be returned to the throne of France.

As the sun rose on Wednesday, March 1, 1815, it revealed the outlines of the Cap d'Antibes and the Lerins Islands. The imperial flotilla entered the Gulf of Juan. Napoleon, wearing his tricolor cockade, appeared on the bridge of the *Inconstant*.

The soldiers immediately threw away their white and red cockades (the Elban colors), and the French ensign was hoisted to the gaff of the vessel's mizzen mast.

The day before, Napoleon had dictated con fuoco his proclamations to the French people and the army, datelining them "Gulf of Juan, March 1."

"Electrified" (as his valet described him), and stressing the phrases that rang out in the little stateroom of the *Inconstant*, he had declared:

> Français! In my exile I heard your laments and your prayers. You demand that government of your choosing which alone is legitimate. You were objecting to my prolonged idleness. You were reproaching me with having sacrificed the great interests of the nation to my own leisure.
>
> I have crossed the sea amid all kinds of perils. I come to you to reassert my rights, which are also yours. . . . Soldiers! In my exile I have heard your voices! I have surmounted all obstacles and all perils to come here. Victory will march at the double-quick! The eagle, bearing the national colors, will fly from steeple to steeple as far as the towers of Notre Dame!

These were the words that would create the legend of the Eagle and make people forget how disastrous this reckless adventure was for France.

It was one o'clock in the afternoon when *Inconstant* and the other vessels dropped anchor. The "army" disembarked immediately.

When they left their ships, the detachments of troops passed in front of Napoleon. By five o'clock they had all disembarked. The Emperor summoned Cambronne and sent him to Cannes with some forty grenadiers and chasseurs, instructing him to requisition provisions and (making payment for them) horses and mules.

"Cambronne," he added, "I am entrusting you with the advance guard of my finest campaign. You are not to fire a single shot. Please bear in mind that I want to regain my crown without spilling one drop of blood."

The general found Cannes in a state of effervescence. The firing of the flotilla's cannon to herald the Emperor's disembarkment had been taken to be a bombardment by Algerian corsairs, and the inhabitants of Cannes had barricaded themselves. The fur caps of the grenadiers had helped to calm their fears; but the crowd nonetheless showed more anxiety than sympathy as they gathered around the soldiers. Some of the inhabitants were already thinking of the spectre of war hovering behind the Emperor.

Meantime, the "grumblers" of the Old Guard had lighted their campfire in the dunes which then existed near the chapel of Notre-Dame du Bon-Voyage. Nearby, wrapped up in the old blue greatcoat he had worn at Marengo, the Emperor was sitting in his camp chair. While waiting for his dinner, he chatted with the passersby. The mayor of Cannes had not put in an appearance, but the mayor of a neighboring commune came up to Napoleon and said, "We were just beginning to be happy and at ease, and now you're going to disturb everything."

Later, Napoleon said: "I can't tell you how I was shaken up by his words—how much they hurt me."

He had decided to cross the Alps to reach Grenoble and Lyons. It was a decision he had made several days before, never having forgotten the horrors he experienced when crossing Royalist Provence in late April, 1814: the insults, the curses, the hail of rocks thrown at his carriage, and the burning of himself in effigy.

Shortly after five o'clock in the morning, the Elbans set out for Grasse. But Cambronne, still with the advance guard, had no luck: the mayor of Grasse—the Marquis de Gourdon—was an ardent Royalist.

"In the name of what sovereign are you making your requisitions?" he asked.

"In the name of the Emperor Napoleon."

"We have our own sovereign, and we love him."

"Monsieur le Maire," replied Cambronne, "I have not come here to play politics with you, but to demand rations, because my column will be here any moment."

The mayor complied. But when the Emperor, at Mouans, learned of the strong current of feeling at Grasse, he decided not to enter the town. He detoured around it.

There was no road between Grasse and Digne, the point at which they were to get on the road to Grenoble. As a result, they had to abandon the "artillery" (four fieldpieces) and go in single file along the snow-covered mountain paths.

Night had already fallen when Napoleon, staggering with fatigue, reached the hamlet of Seramon, whose few houses are built in tiers on the slope of a magnificent valley between rocky mountains.

It was essential to move faster than Masséna (loyal to Louis XVIII) and reach Sisteron ahead of the Marseille garrison, though it was not until that same day (March 3) that the news of the Emperor's landing reached Marseille. And so, setting out at dawn, the Elbans continued along the mountain paths—climbing from deep valleys up to crests, from cols down into gorges, and from narrow transversal valleys up steep rock faces—that would take them to Digne.

They got there early in the afternoon of the next day, and were met by a curious but not enthusiastic crowd. Sunday, March 5, found them in Volonne. After taking lunch at the Hôtel du Poisson d'Or, the Emperor continued on toward the extraordinary village of Sisteron, nestled at the foot of its famous fortress. When they reached the village, its mayor came to meet the Emperor wearing, prominently displayed on his chest, the Bourbon fleur-de-lis. "You'd better not wear that while I'm here," Napoleon advised him. "My soldiers might not take it kindly."

A room had been prepared for the Emperor at the wretched Auberge du Bras d'Or. It was there, while taking refreshment, that Napoleon got into a conversation with the subprefect.

"What impression will my return to France make?"

"People are more surprised than anything else."

"But will they be pleased to see me back on the throne?"

"I think they would, if they weren't afraid that conscription and all the other calamities were coming back with you."

"I realize," the Emperor admitted, "that a lot of stupid mistakes have been made. But I have come back to patch everything up. My people will be happy."

At two in the afternoon, the column resumed its march toward Grenoble, as the inhabitants of Sisteron shouted "Vive l'Empereur!" The Elbans were now preceded by a tricolor flag improvised from a few rags and surmounted by an eagle "taken from some curtain rod or bedpost."

Owing to his rapid march, Napoleon had outdistanced the troops that Masséna had sent in pursuit of his former chief. As soon as he had learned of the King of Elba's landing, Masséna had sent off a message to the Baron de Vitrolles, the Secretary of State. But since at that time, Chappe's Paris semaphore telegraph system did not extend any farther than Lyons, Masséna had to use a courier to carry his message to Lyons, from where it was sent via telegraph to Paris. Consequently, it was not until March 5—at the same hour when Napoelon was lunching at the Bras d'Or in Sisteron—that Chappe delivered the message to the Baron de Vitrolles.

Vitrolles left immediately for the Tuileries and handed the dispatch to the King. With his gouty fingers, Louis XVIII had trouble opening the envelope. He finally torn it open, unfolded the sheet of paper, and stared at it for a long time. Then he threw it on the table and asked calmly: "You don't know what this message says?"

"No, Sire, I do not."

Louis XVIII said: "Bonaparte has landed on the coast of Provence."

Then, in a detached tone, he dismissed Vitrolles: "You must take this dispatch to the Minister of War. He will decide what he has to do."

The Minister of War was now Marshal Soult, Duke of Dalmatia by the grace of Napoleon. It did not occur to him to blow up a single bridge or cut down a single tree. In fact, he did nothing at all to impede the progress of Napoleon, "whom the inhabitants of the towns were neither resisting nor following." Marshal Soult was not taking sides with his former chief. He referred to "Buonaparte" as "the lowest of the low," and talked in all sincerity of running him through with his sword. For him, as for the *Moniteur*, the Emperor's landing was "an act of madness, the punishment for which could be handled by a few village policemen."

Only the Baron de Vitrolles saw the danger. He counted heavily on the Comte d'Artois. He was convinced that the future Charles X could win the support of the troops "with his charm and his knightly eloquence." But when he went to seek out the Comte d'Artois at his residence of Marsan, he was astounded to learn that he was attending vespers.

Why was he in church at a time like this? There surely could have been only one explanation for this surprising fact: Louis XVIII distrusted his brother and had not informed him of the developments. When Vitrolles entered his study, the Comte d'Artois seemed totally unaware of what had happened.

The Secretary of State therefore violated etiquette and made bold to ask: "Has Monsieur not seen the King since Mass?"

"Why, yes, I saw him." Then, as if mentioning an event of no importance, he added: "By the way, what do you think of the report of the landing?"

With considerable difficulty, Vitrolles tried to explain the seriousness of the situation.

"Eh bien," said the Prince, "I suppose you are right. We'll have to grease our boots and get ready."

"Non, Monsieur," the breathless minister insisted. "You'll have to leave without taking time to grease your boots."

That same evening the Comte d'Artois set out for Lyons in order —as the royal command expressed it—"to fall upon Bonaparte, the traitor and rebel, for having made an armed incursion into the Département du Var." He was followed a few hours later by the Duc d'Orléans, the future King Louis Philippe.

The next day the newspapers outdid themselves. The *Journal des Débats* stigmatized "that man besmeared with the blood of generations." And it added: "God grant that the cowardly warrior of Fontainebleau die the death of a traitor!" During the next few days the Emperor's former comrades joined in the outcry—until it came time to throw themselves into the arms of Napoleon!

The Emperor spent the night of Monday, March 6, in the mountain village of Corps, where the stoops of the houses remain buried under the snow during the winter. The next morning he was awakened by a courier with a message from Cambronne—who was still with the advance guard—telling him the long-feared moment had come. The Elbans were about to encounter the troops under General Marchand, who was defending the stronghold of Grenoble for Louis XVIII and had orders to stop the advance of "Buonaparte's brigands."

The heights of La Pontine, not far from La Mure, were occupied by a battalion commanded by one Major Delessart, a Royalist. When warned of Napoleon's approach, Delessart assembled his troops. Followed by a company of engineers, they withdrew toward Laffrey, a little town situated in beautiful countryside some three leagues from La Mure.

Delessart took up his position in front of the village, on the edge of one of Laffrey's three lakes. Soon he could discern, in the distance, the Emperor's open calash and the famous gray greatcoat. Napoleon seemed apprehensive. Delessart saw him get out of the carriage, walk out on the promontory overlooking the lake, and study the "enemy" on the prairie through his field glass. Then one of the Emperor's staff officers—Colonel Raoul—set off at a gallop toward the major.

"The Emperor is going to advance toward you," he announced. "If you open fire, the first shot will be at him. You will answer for it to France."

Delessart interrupted him: "I am determined to do my duty. And if you do not withdraw immediately, I'll have you arrested."

"What I want to know is: Are you going to open fire?"

"I will do my duty."

The soldiers of the Fifth Line Battalion listened impassively. Suddenly, the Polish lancers advanced toward them. Delessart's men could see, behind the cavalry, the bearskin caps and long blue greatcoats of the Guard. A shiver went through the ranks, and the major shouted: "Battalion! About-face! March!"

With the lancers on their heels, Louis XVIII's soldiers—pale, with set jaws—obeyed the command and marched off in good order.

Beside Delessart was the young Captain Randon, General Marchand's nephew and aide-de-camp, who would one day be a Marshal of France. Delessart remarked to him: "How can you give battle when your men are trembling all over and pale as death?"

But the lances of the Poles were so close to the backs of the major's men that he shouted: "Halt! About-face!"

The battalion obeyed; and the lancers, who had been ordered not to charge, fell back toward the Emperor.

Then came the famous scene.

"Colonel Mallet," ordered Napoleon, "have your men trail their muskets and unfurl the flag!"

Then, as the little Elban band played the "Marseillaise," the Emperor stepped forward. Behind him came Drouot, Cambronne, and Bertrand.

"There he is! Fire!" shouted Randon.

The muskets trembled, but not a single man dared raise his weapon to his shoulder.

The Emperor stopped and called out in a loud voice: "Soldiers of the Fifth, I am your Emperor. Recognize me!"

He took two or three more steps, opened his gray greatcoat, and shouted: "If there is one soldier among you who wants to kill his Emperor, here I am!"

The response was a tremendous shout of "Vive l'Empereur!" The troops broke ranks immediately. Tossing their shakos on the ends of their bayonets, they ran toward their Emperor—crowding around him, cheering him, kneeling at his feet, and worshipfully touching his boots, his sword, and the skirts of his greatcoat.

In an instant, the tricolor cockades that the soldiers had been keeping in their knapsacks since the year before replaced their white cockades.

General Marchand, still loyal to Louis XVIII, had ordered the Seventh and Eleventh Regiments of the Line, which were at Chambéry, to march to Grenoble. The two colonels had obeyed. The officer commanding the Seventh was named La Bedoyère. A former aide-de-camp of Lannes, he was one of the most brilliant officers of the imperial army. One can well imagine the emotion that was gripping him on that Tuesday of March 7, 1815.

After reviewing the two regiments, General Marchand moved them into position on the ramparts facing the road to La Mure. What would the soldiers do when they had Napoleon in their line of sight?

It was at this point that La Bedoyère made the move that would bring him a death sentence later. Drawing his sword, he shouted:

"Follow me, soldiers of the Seventh! Follow me! I will show you the way. Forward! Let those who love me follow me!"

The Seventh marched off, shouting "Vive l'Empereur!"—a shout that was soon being echoed by the greater part of the garrison. Once through the suburbs, La Bedoyère pulled the regiment's old eagle out of his pocket and affixed it to the end of a willow branch, which thus became the staff of the new flag. An hour later, between Grenoble and Vizille, the Emperor embraced the eagle and the colonel who had in this way brought him reinforcements amounting to 1,800 men.

Toward nine in the evening General Marchand, whose window looked out over the ramparts, saw the "Usurper" followed by his little army and surrounded by some 2,000 peasants brandishing pitchforks and rusty muskets, and carrying torches "of burning straw." When they reached the Bonne Gate, Colonel Raoul ordered it opened "in the name of the Emperor." But Colonel Roussille, in command at the gate, refused.

General Marchand then harangued his troops—2,000 infantrymen and a strong artillery detachment—and ordered them to load their weapons. But not a single infantryman obeyed.

A few moments later the wheelwrights of the Faubourg St.-Joseph broke down the gates to shouts of "Vive l'Empereur!" General Marchand, with only 200 or 300 men, galloped through the St.-Laurent Gate and out of the city.

To Napoleon, who had put up at the Hôtel des Trois Dauphins, a delegation brought the panels of the Bonne Gate in lieu of the keys to the city.

The next day, he reviewed his troops. As they filed past him, the men showed him their cockades, shouting: "This one is from Austerlitz! This one is from Friedland! I had this one at Marengo!"

And the Emperor exclaimed: "Before reaching Grenoble I was an adventurer. At Grenoble I was a prince!"

On Friday, March 10, Napoleon was moving on from Bourgoin, after spending the night there. Meantime, the Comte d'Artois had managed to muster, at Lyons, no more than three regiments and 1,500 National Guards. The 30,000 men promised by Soult had not yet arrived.

On the Place Bellecour, before the regiments formed into a

square, Marshal Macdonald made a speech ending with the words: "The only pledge I ask of you is to shout 'Vive le Roi!' "

Not a single voice replied. All that could be heard was the splashing of the raindrops. The Comte d'Artois was next to speak. His ambitions were more modest. A *single* shout uttered by a *single* soldier would suffice for his happiness. He went up to an old dragoon "and spoke to him kindly, praising him for his courage, the proof of which he wore on his breast." Then he asked him to join him in shouting "Vive le Roi!" But the dragoon, "mouth agape and eyes staring," remained "immobile and impassive." Macdonald, the colonel commanding the Thirteenth Dragoons, and the other officers "shouted, exhorted him, and urged him." But all in vain. The man remained "unshakable."

The scene began to take on a ridiculous aspect. "Flushed with anger," Artois returned to the archbishop's palace. The crowd did not even greet him. True, the Lyonnais were massed along the Rhône; but they had gathered there to see Napoleon, who (so it was said) was already at the gates of the city. By eleven in the morning Artois had no choice but to leave—following the example of his cousin, Orléans, who had headed back to Paris a good two hours before.

After entering Lyons, Napoleon took up quarters at the archbishopric palace, in the apartments left him by the Comte d'Artois; and for three days he resumed the life style of a sovereign. He received *corps constitués,* drafted decrees, and wrote to his wife:

> My advance guard is at Chalon-sur-Saône, and I am leaving tonight to catch up with it. Crowds are coming on the run to greet me. Entire regiments are leaving everything to join up with me. . . . By the time you get this letter, I will be in Paris. . . . Come and join me there, and bring my son. I hope that before the end of the month, I shall be able to kiss you.

This note was never delivered to the Empress. Instead, it was taken to the Congress of Vienna, where the Allied ministers tried "to interpret a scrawl that no one could read." Each of them, however, managed to decipher a word here and there; and soon all of them were faced with the tragic certainty that the Emperor would be back in Paris.

A few days before, Talleyrand had managed to secure his colleagues' approval of a text he had drawn up. It depicted Bonaparte's escape as "an attack on the social order." And it stated plainly: "By returning to France with plans for causing disturbance and upheaval, he has forfeited the protection of the law and demonstrated to the whole universe that with him there can be neither peace nor a truce. . . . "

In the concluding paragraph, the criminal who had escaped was outlawed: "Consequently, the Powers declare that Napoleon Bonaparte has debarred himself from civil and social relations; and that, as the enemy and disturber of the peace of the world, he has made himself liable to public prosecution."

Talleyrand the traitor must have rejoiced inwardly as he watched the Emperor of Austria debase himself to the point of calmly signing this document, which was a slap in the face of his daughter's husband and his grandson's father.

"The important thing," Talleyrand explained, "was to get him to sign a civil death sentence rather than a declaration of war. One can always negotiate with an enemy; but one does not remarry a convict."

On Monday, March 13, the Emperor left Lyons for Mâcon. At Paris, the King had lost hope in everyone but Ney. Since March 10, the Marshal had been blocking the road to Paris, constantly repeating that he would bring Bonaparte back in an iron cage.

"It would be a better idea to bring him back dead in a tumbrel," remarked the subprefect of Poligny, an advocate of efficient methods.

"No," replied Ney, "you don't know Paris. The Parisians must see him."

On March 11, the proclamation written by the Emperor when he sighted the Gulf of Juan was brought to Ney. He sighed audibly, and then exclaimed: "Nobody writes like that any more! . . . The King should write like that! That's the way to talk to soldiers and stir them up!"

Then, pacing back and forth in his office, he repeated aloud: "Victory will march at the double-quick. The eagle, with the national colors, will fly from steeple to steeple, as far as the towers of Notre Dame!"

Ney was firm in his determination to give battle. But he had no more than 6,000 reliable men under his command, echeloned from Besançon to Bourg, whereas the Emperor now had 14,000 troops.

A short time later, Marshal Ney received a note from Napoleon: "Come and join me at Chalon. I will greet you as I did the day after the Moskowa." Next he learned that tricolor flags were flying everywhere. Finally, it was reported to him (falsely, at that time) that Louis XVIII was making ready to leave Paris. Also, he was confidentially (and inaccurately) informed that England was in on the plot; and that Metternich had been tipped off before the departure from Elba but had feigned ignorance so as to make things difficult for the Czar (which was quite plausible at the time). At a time when French blood had not been spilled, was Ney going to set off a civil war by giving battle to his former chief?

"What do you expect? I can't stop the flow of the tide with my hand."

The affronts he had undergone in the past few months, the contemptuous attitude of the Bourbon Court, came crowding into his mind. "I don't want to be dishonored any more! I don't want to see my wife come home in tears because of the humiliations she has gone through during the day! It's plain to see that the King wants no part of us!"

On March 14 (the Emperor spent that night at Dijon), the Marshal assembled his troops and gazed at their mournful faces. Ney was going to lose his head.

"I was caught up in the storm," he said later to the royal tribunal that sent him to the firing squad.

As his soldiers watched, he unsheathed his sword and raised it high. "Officers, noncommissioned officers, and soldiers!" he shouted. "The Bourbon cause is forever lost!"

His voice was drowned out in a great shout of "Vive l'Empereur!" as the soldiers threw their arms around each other. The Marshal himself ran through the ranks "like a man delirious," embracing even the fifers and drummers.

Two days later, when the news reached Paris, a placard was hung on the grating around the Vendôme column: "Napoleon to Louis XVIII: Mon frère, you needn't bother sending me any more soldiers. I have enough."

THE FLIGHT OF THE EAGLE

The King's admirable serenity—not to mention his unawareness —was beginning to be disturbed.

On March 18 the Sixth Lancers, occupying an outpost at the bridge of Montereau, about-faced and declared they were the Emperor's advance guard. The King was informed immediately. The next morning, Palm Sunday, a courier reported that Napoleon had left Auxerre and was continuing his march on Paris. He might reach Fontainebleau by that evening!

Actually, he spent the night of the nineteenth at Pont-sur-Yonne. That same night the royal carriages began forming a line in the courtyard of the Tuileries.

Louis XVIII's carriage drew up in front of the entrance to the Pavillon de Flore. Immediately, the bodyguards and National Guards emerged unarmed from the guardroom and crowded the stairway and the antechamber, mingling with the courtiers and duty officers. All eyes were on the door to the King's apartments.

A few moments later he emerged and, after a brief speech, made his way with some difficulty through the crowd of the faithful to his carriage. As he took his seat in the back, he waved farewell; and the carriage, with bodyguards riding before and behind it, set out for the St. Martin's Gate—the road to Varennes. A few service vehicles followed it. The entire royal personnel had left the Tuileries, and for a few hours a heavy silence reigned over the abandoned palace.

The next morning—the famous Monday of March 20, 1815—the Parisians were keeping a watchful eye on the long, gray façade of the château. The white flag had been hauled down. "The crowd wandered first in one direction, then in another," one witness said. "People accosted one another distrustfully, scarcely daring to whisper." Suddenly, from the direction of the quay, a horseman appeared carrying the tricolor.

The herald of the Emperor's arrival—scheduled for that same evening—was General Remi Exelmans, who had come at a gallop from Fontainebleau. A few moments after he had reached the Tuileries the tricolor was flying from the balcony of the Salle des Maréchaux. The National Guards on sentry duty around the palace had taken off their white cockades that morning; now they got their tricolor cockades out of their knapsacks. Little by little, Napoleon's officers and former servants took up their old positions in the palace, as though their master were merely returning there from another of his residences. The imperial uniforms and the green livery made their appearance. The ushers resumed their duties at the doors, and saw to it that the imperial protocol was followed. People embraced and congratulated one another. The ladies, wearing court dress, got down on the rugs and, working feverishly, removed the fleurs-de-lis that had been sewn on them, making place for the Napoleonic bees.

La Valette had sent a courier to Napoleon to notify him that the coast was clear. The moment he got this word, the Emperor left Fontainebleau in a post chaise. At nine in the evening he entered the courtyard of the Tuileries. He was greeted not only by shouts of "Vive l'Empereur!" but by roars of joy; and he was literally snatched out of his carriage.

"The explosion of feelings was irresistible," writes Baron Thiébault. "Only three hours before, as a soldier serving the Bourbons, I had my cannons aimed at him. But now it seemed that I had become French again. . . ."

Through this incredible throng, Napoleon was escorted toward his apartments. "For God's sake!" shouted Caulaincourt to La Valette. "Go ahead of him!"

La Valette did so, climbing the stairway backwards and constantly repeating: "It's you! It's you!"

And the Emperor let himself be carried along, his eyes half-closed, intoxicated with happiness.

XXV

THE ONE HUNDRED DAYS

I felt that Fortune was abandoning me.
I no longer had the feeling that I was sure
to succeed. . . . When a man does not act boldly,
he never does anything at just the right moment;
and a man does not act boldly unless he is convinced
that luck is on his side.

NAPOLEON

WHEN HE LOOKED OUT HIS WINDOW the next morning at the still-wintry park, the Emperor saw—at the point where the long tree-shaded walk begins—a solitary chestnut tree in flower. It was as though Paris had prepared a gigantic bouquet for the hero.

A cheering crowd had assembled in the park, over which a light mist still lay.

"Bah!" exclaimed Napoleon, already disenchanted. "The time for compliments and flattery is past! They let me enter, just as they let others leave!"

A short time later he held his first review of the troops. The Englishman John Cam Hobhouse thought he looked pale.

His paunch protrudes so far that one can see his linen beneath his waistcoat. He generally keeps his hands clasped behind his back or in front, but sometimes he unclasps them in order to rub his nose, take a few pinches of snuff, and look at his watch. Sighing often, and swallowing his saliva, he seems to be feeling some pain in his chest. . . .

The bands were playing tunes that had often been prohibited in Paris at the time of the Napoleonic dictatorship:

535

Veillons au salut de l'Empire
Veillons au maintien de nos drotis.
Si le despotisme conspire,
Conjurons la perte des rois.

Let us look to the welfare of the Empire,
Let us look to the maintenance of our rights.
If despotism conspires,
Let us plot the downfall of kings.

Now the Emperor spoke: "Soldiers, I came to France with six hundred men because I was counting on the love of the people and the memories of the old soldiers. I have not been deceived in my expectations."

That evening the crowd, exhilarated from shouting and cheering, dispersed homeward—and it began to rain.

Napoleon's former followers were showing up at the Tuileries, sometimes rather belatedly.

"You must admit, Sire," Rapp told him, "that our position was painful. You abdicate, you leave, you tell us to serve the King, and then you return. Despite all the potency of memories, we could have no illusions."

"What? What do you mean?"

And once again he tried to maintain the impossible fable. "Do you think I returned without alliances and agreements? For that matter, I have changed my system. No more wars, no more conquests. I want to reign in peace and bring happiness to my subjects."

The most urgent thing was to get money. The imperial coffers had to be filled—and they were, in a most unexpected manner: by England and Holland.

"When I returned from Elba," the Emperor told Las Cases, "the banks of London and Amsterdam secretly opened credit accounts for me totaling one hundred million, at an interest rate of a mere eight per cent."

For the bankers, money came before patriotism.

But the Emperor was nonetheless "alone against Europe," as he himself realized. He knew very well that the Allies would not passively accept the impressive flight of the eagle—not even if he agreed to the frontiers imposed on France the year before.

He first attempted, though without entertaining any great illusions of success, to arouse the sympathies of the Emperor Francis by playing on his feelings as a grandfather. He wrote to Francis that everything he was going to undertake by way of consolidating and strengthening his throne would be made with a view to assuring that, one day, "the child whom Your Majesty has treated with so much paternal kindness" would come into his heritage. In order to achieve this "sacred goal," he needed peace. He went on to say that he was too familiar with the "principles" of his "dear brother and dear father-in-law" to have any doubts that Francis would "be eager to cooperate in hastening the reunion of a woman with her husband and a son with his father." And his concluding lines to Francis spoke of "that longed-for reunion no less impatiently awaited by that virtuous Princess."

But the "virtuous Princess," atremble with fear, had thrown herself into the arms of her lover, Neipperg, officially repudiating the man whom, a few months before, she had claimed to adore. Marie Louise declared that she was "angry at that individual" who, in leaving Elba, had jeopardized the future of her son. She assured the Emperor Francis that henceforth she would recognize no will but his own. After having betrayed the father, she agreed to hand the son over to the Austrian police. "Prince Charles Francis" was to be hastily transferred to Schönbrunn, where surveillance of him would be infinitely easier than at the Hofburg, some of whose buildings were almost adjacent to an entire district of the city.

The Emperor had also sent a circular letter to the sovereigns of Russia, Prussia, and England in an attempt to explain to them that the Bourbon Restoration—that dynasty whose return had been "forced on the people"—was no longer suitable to the French nation. He emphasized: "The Bourbons were never willing to associate themselves with the nation's sentiments or way of life. France had to separate herself from them. She called for a Liberator." And that Liberator could be none other than Napoleon.

Napoleon had informed London that he was "prepared to hear any proposal from the British Government which would ensure a firm and lasting peace." He was in fact betting on Great Britain. And in this entente where long-enslaved nations were giving full vent to their hatred, the most moderate words would certainly come from

England. True, the British Government had not deigned to reply to
the overtures made by the ghost from Elba. True again, the *Times*
had called Napoleon "the bloody Corsican" and had condemned his
"companions in villainy" who had dared to "recall this brigand—this
monster charged with so many crimes and horrors." But on the other
hand, in the House of Commons the opposition had declared: "Bonaparte has been received in France as a liberator. The Bourbons lost
their throne through their own fault. It would be a monstrous thing
to make war on a nation in order to foist upon it a government of
which it wants no part."

In the view of the *Morning Chronicle,* "it was of no importance
whether a Bonaparte or a Bourbon was on the throne of France."
And the paper took the liberty of posing the following questions to
Lord Castlereagh:

> Did the Allies faithfully comply with the terms of the Treaty
> of Fontainebleau? Were Bonaparte and his family paid even a
> portion of the pension that had been guaranteed to them? Were
> there not plans to deport him? . . . English patriots are of the
> opinion that the potentates of the Continent are uniting not so
> much against Bonaparte as against the spirit of liberty.

Napoleon was aware of this viewpoint; and it undoubtedly influenced him, three months later, when he decided to go and "sit at
the hearth of the British nation."

The French Royalists realized very well that it was the son of the
Revolution who had landed in the Gulf of Juan and the adherents of
Louis XVIII were fierce in their abuse of "M. de Buonaparte." The
Emperor had the impression that the clock had been put back
twenty years, and said so bitterly: "I can see that the hatred felt by
the priests and the nobility is as widespread and violent as it was at
the beginning of the Revolution."

And so Napoleon had no choice: he had to make the gambit that
was more or less forced upon him. This is indicated by his first proclamations:

> I have come to deliver France from the émigrés. . . . I am a
> product of the Revolution. . . . I have come to liberate the French
> from the slavery to which the priests and the nobles were trying
> to reduce them. . . . Let them beware! I'll send them to the
> gallows. . . .

THE ONE HUNDRED DAYS

He wanted to create a liberal empire. Beginning in late March, the *Moniteur* published official speeches indicative of his state of mind:

> The Council of State affirms that the Emperor has pledged himself to guarantee liberal principles, the freedom of the individual, the freedom of the press, the abolition of censorship, the voting of taxes and laws by the representatives of the nation, and the responsibility of ministers and all government officials. . . .

It was all a lot of foolishness, wrote Mme. de Staël. They should have given Bonaparte dictatorial powers the moment they took him back. Otherwise, the terror that he inspired, and the power that resulted from that terror, would cease to exist.

Later, Napoleon himself acknowledged he had made a mistake in not seizing "all" power. The people had offered him that power with their shouts of "Down with the priests!" and "Down with the nobles!" But he had not dared to seize it: he was frightened by his youthful memories.

He even dealt sparingly with the Royalists, despite the insults they continued to heap upon him. Out of 87 royal prefects, 61 were dismissed. Most of the mayors left in office were partisans of Louis XVIII who had been selected "from the clan of the old nobility." New elections were fixed for May; but two-thirds of the "bad mayors" were reelected.

By way of veering to the left, Napoleon called upon Benjamin Constant, the liberal writer, to draw up a new constitution. He explained to Constant his views on the subject:

> For the past twelve years the nation has rested from all political agitation, and for the past year it has rested from war. This twofold repose has resulted in a new need for activity. The nation wants, or thinks it wants, a tribune and assemblies. . . . I am no enemy to freedom. I set it aside when it was in my way; but I understand it, and was brought up on ideas of it. . . .

But Constant had the audacity to draw up his draft constitution with no mention of the Empire.

> That's not what I had in mind [exclaimed Napoleon]. You are depriving me of my past, but I want to preserve it. What have you

done with the eleven years of my reign? I should think I have some right to them. The new Constitution must be linked to the old one. It will have the sanction of glory.

The text of the "Additional Act" (a reworking of Louis XVIII's Charter, with a touch of liberalism added) was submitted to the Emperor. He angrily protested when the suppression of confiscation of property (a real constitutional yoke) was proposed to him:

I am being pushed in a direction that is not right for me. I am being weakened and put into chains. France looks for me and can no longer find me. Public opinion was excellent, now it is execrable. France is wondering what has become of the Emperor's old arm—that arm she needs to tame Europe.

Before that raised and threatening arm, Benjamin Constant yielded. The question was passed over in silence in the final draft, which provided for an Emperor flanked by two chambers—the Chambre des Pairs and the Chambre des Représentants—with prerogatives copied from those granted by Louis XVIII. The press would be free, censorship abolished, and the imperial dynasty legitimate. Finally, *la Benjamine* (as the new Constitution was called) abolished, once and for all time, the tithe and the old privileges.

La Benjamine was criticized. The liberals felt that the Emperor had not moved far enough in the direction of their demands. Had he not kept for himself the right to appoint peers and magistrates? And did he not also have the right to propose laws? Above all, confidence was lacking. There was good reason for skepticism.

On the occasion of the plebiscite on the "Additional Act" and Napoleon's "reenthronement," the number of people abstaining was greater than the number of voters. At the end of April, Napoleon was obliged to convene the two chambers. The new Assemblée des Représentants was elected in May. Out of 629 members, it had 80 Bonapartists, 30 or 40 Jacobins, and 500 Liberals.

The first session was held on June 3. Jean Denis Lanjuinais, who in April, 1814, had signed the proposal for the Emperor's dethronement, was elected president.

Napoleon was furious. "They chose my enemy in order to insult me!"

But, once again, the dictator showed his true character: "If that's the way things stand, I'll dissolve the Assembly. I'll appeal to France, who knows only me. . . . Because now the Revolution must be defended by cannon shots. And which one of them knows how to fire one?"

And as a matter of fact, things would be settled be cannon shots.

At Vienna, toward the end of March, the Allies had signed a treaty of alliance "having as its purpose the maintenance of peace"; in other words, the resumption of hostilities. The contracting parties each pledged to keep 150,000 men in the field "until such time as Bonaparte is rendered absolutely incapable of stirring up trouble, of making new attempts to seize supreme power in France, or of threatening the security of Europe." The army of Waterloo would soon be ready to take the field.

At the same time, Napoleon was taking steps which would enable him to muster an army. The royal forces numbered only 85,000 men. Every day, he pondered the means he would employ to improve the situation.

It was in the bosom of his army that he found consolation. His old comrades-at-arms—especially the lowest ranks—restored his confidence. True, in the Midi and the west there were many desertions among the conscripts and the men called back to duty. But elsewhere in the country the results were so encouraging that the Allies were apprehensive.

An English spy wrote to the Duke of Wellington:

> To give an accurate idea of the army's enthusiasm, I need only draw a parallel between the year '92 and the present army. And even then, the balance would be in favor of Bonaparte, because today it is no longer enthusiasm, it is frenzy. . . . The struggle will be bloody and bitterly contested.

The last imperial festival was a regular *veillée d'armes*. The gathering, called the Champ de Mai, was held on the Champ de Mars, on June 1. All of the authorities, the dignitaries, and the imperial family took their seats on the viewing stands. The standard-bearers, the Guard, the garrison, and the legions of the National Guard—45,000 men in all—covered the plain. Two hundred thousand Parisians attended the ceremony at which the new Empire attempted to regain its pomp.

The Duc de Broglie, who would later be a minister under Louis

Philippe, wrote: "I saw the imperial party pass by in ceremonial dress: plumes waving in the wind, hats cocked, little Spanish cloaks, white satin breeches, shoes adorned with rosettes, and all the rest."

Napoleon had, in fact, made the mistake of again donning the coronation robes. People had been expecting to see the Little Corporal of the "flight of the eagle," and all they saw was a freak. "It was a masquerade," says Broglie, "that provoked as much indignation as scorn."

Nor was it only the Royalists who were shocked. As Fleury de Chaboulon has accurately put it, the imperial pomp also "offended the eyes" of "the old patriots he had deceived"—people with memories that it was unwise to stir up.

The Grand Chamberlain had a little gilded table placed in front of the Emperor. On it was the Constitution. Napoleon signed it, and then spoke: "Français! My will is that of the people; my rights are the people's; my honor, my glory, and my happiness cannot be other than the honor, the glory, and the happiness of France!"

The Archbishop of Bourges, the Chief Almoner, kneeled and presented the New Testament, upon which the Emperor swore to uphold the Constitution. After the Te Deum, Napoleon took off his imperial mantle and jumped quickly down from his throne. The drums rolled, and the ceremony of the distribution of the eagles began.

Rather than waiting for the avalanche that was about to descend upon France, Napoleon decided to forestall it and attack the enemy. The French army was already massed on the Belgian border. On Sunday, June 11, he attended the last Mass at the Tuileries. Thiébault was struck by the change that had come over him:

> His glance, which in the old days was so formidable because of its penetration, had lost its power and even its fixity. . . his tight-lipped mouth had none of its former magic; even the way he held his head no longer suggested the ruler of the world. . . . Everything about him seemed disfigured and distorted; his complexion, ordinarily pale, was now distinctly greenish. . . .

That evening, after the dinner *en famille*, he was in a melancholy mood as he sat there holding in his lap the little Louis, Hortense's son

—the boy he called "Oui-oui," who would one day be the Emperor Napoleon III.

The torrent of men was flowing toward the border. Across the frontier, the enemy did not yet suspect anything. Blücher, who was on hand with his army of 120,000 men, had written to his wife on June 13: "We shall soon enter France, although it would be perfectly possible to stay right here for another year, because Bonaparte will not attack us."

Wellington, too, had assembled 100,000 men in front of Brussels. On June 14 he notified the Czar that he would attack the French at the end of the month. Neither of these generals could foresee an attack by Napoleon on Charleroi, which was strongly held by the Prussian advance guard. Hence the surprise was total.

Napoleon reached Charleroi toward noon on June 15, and received Ney four hours later, saying:

> I am very glad to see you. You will take command of the First and Second Army Corps. In addition, I'll give you the Light Horse of my Guard. Tomorrow you will be joined by Kellermann's cuirassiers. Meantime, throw the enemy back toward the Brussels road, and take up your position at Quatre Bras.

But Ney had grown old. Seeing Quatre Bras occupied (actually, there were only a few units there, virtually without ammunition), he did not take the risk of attacking the Allied advance guard—an operation which would have made him master of the situation.

Napoleon consoled himself with the thought that Ney would take Quatre Bras the next morning, and from there march on to Brussels.

That same evening of the fifteenth, although he now knew that Napoleon was at Charleroi, Wellington enjoyed a *souper* and dancing at a ball given by the Duchess of Richmond at Brussels. This was not negligence on his part. To Karl von Müffling, the Prussian liaison officer, he explained: "My troops will be on the march. But Napoleon's followers are starting to rear their heads here. We must reassure our friends. We shall mount our horses at three in the morning."

Some of the officers did not even have the time to change clothes and, as Lady Lenox tells us, "went off to battle in their evening dress."

Early in the morning of June 16, Napoleon sent Ney a message again urging him to establish his position at Quatre Bras: "Such a prompt and rapid movement would isolate the British army from Mons and Ostende; and it is my intention that your dispositions be such that, upon receiving the first order, your eight divisions can march rapidly and unimpeded on Brussels. . . ."

Ney was slow in setting out—so slow that Wellington, acting more promptly, had Quatre Bras strongly occupied by the Prince of Orange.

Meantime, the Battle of Ligny and Fleurus was beginning. It was about 3:30 P.M. The slaughter was vicious on both sides. Each soldier fought as if he were settling a personal score—mercilessly and giving no quarter. "It was not a battle," said Coignet, "it was a butchery. The charge was sounded from all sides. And there was only one shout: 'Forward!' "

A half-hour before the battle began, Soult (who had succeeded Berthier as chief of staff), sent the following message to Ney:

> At this moment the fighting is very intense. His Majesty has instructed me to tell you that you should maneuver on the field of battle so as to envelop the enemy's right wing and fall upon his rear with all available forces. If you act vigorously, his army will be routed. The fate of France is in your hands.

But Ney, "stricken with paralysis," refused to "maneuver on the field of battle." Napoleon himself had to lead the Old Guard into battle before Ligny was taken. Blücher, unseated from his horse, escaped capture only by a miracle. As therapy for this accident, he soaked his feet in brandy, taking advantage of the situation to drink a good bumperful of it. He was soon back on his horse.

But the Prussians had to pull back in haste. With their uniforms in tatters, they were unrecognizable. They had been "given a damned good spanking," said Wellington. But it had not really been all that good, since Ney's failure to act had prevented Napoleon from mopping up the defeated troops. Beyond containing the English at Quatre Bras, the marshal had done nothing.

The Emperor decided to stay at Fleurus overnight. Later, he would say: "My mistake was in spending the night at Fleurus. [But for that] the Battle of Waterloo would have taken place twenty-four hours earlier, and Wellington and Blücher would never have joined forces. . . ."

In the future, he would refight that battle a hundred times.

When he awoke on Saturday, June 17, at Fleurus, Napoleon decided to go himself to Quatre Bras. Had not the Prussians been routed? They would not be able to take part in any engagements for at least three days. Or so the Emperor thought, at any rate. At 11:00 A.M., after passing in front of the bivouacs of Ligny and St.-Amand, he ordered Grouchy:

> While I am marching on the English, you will set out in pursuit of the Prussians. You will have under your orders the two corps commanded by Gérard and Vandamme, Teste's division, and the cavalry corps of Pajol, Exelmans, and Milhaud: 33,000 men in all.

These were the 33,000 men Napoleon would have needed the next day to make Waterloo a French victory.

When toward 1:30 Napoleon reached Quatre Bras, he learned from a captured Englishman that Wellington, having learned of Blücher's defeat, had pulled back to Mont St.-Jean to enable the Prussians to join up with him. Napoleon ordered a pursuit, and the French cavalry came fast on the heels of the English rear guard, commanded by General Uxbridge, who panted: "Faster! Faster! For the love of God! Gallop, or you'll be captured!"

In the heavy rain, the Emperor too was galloping along—on his white mare, named Désirée. His gray greatcoat was soaked. As evening fell, the torrential, never-ending rain became a downpour. The heavens seemed intent upon drowning out human folly. Both soldiers and horses were wading in mud.

The forces on both sides came to a halt, the pursuit coming to an end at the foot of a little hill, Mont St.-Jean.

The "redcoats" dug in on the plateau and in the positions just before it. These can still be seen today: the château, the farm, and the orchard of Hougoumont, not far from the Nivelles highway in front of the French left wing; then the farm of La Haye Sainte in the center of the disposition; and, finally, the farm of Papelotte, facing the French right flank.

Through the thick fog that was beginning to settle over the ter-

rain, the British cannon, as a prelude to the battle, began to spit out
their shot, accompanied by spurts of mud. In the twilight—wading
through the mire, his uniform scarcely dried out—Napoleon made a
reconnaissance as far as the foot of Mont St.-Jean.

To him, victory seemed assured. In the morning he would crush
the enemy's center and then, employing his usual tactic, fall upon the
two wings.

He returned to the farm of Gros-Caillou with its whitewashed
buildings (which still stands at the edge of the highway), where he
established his headquarters. He studied his maps, then took a quick
meal. In spite of the wind and rain, he made two other reconnais-
sances in the dark of the night. At 1:00 A.M. on June 18 he held a
council of war before leaving on a third reconnaissance to the outposts.

Meantime, an officer was galloping through the night on his way
to find Grouchy and give him orders to return urgently with his corps
—the bulk of the imperial army.

All the forces Wellington had ready at hand were 17,000 men
positioned on his right (for fear of being outflanked) and 67,000 on
the rise of ground before Mont St.-Jean, well dug in and echeloned
—a total of 84,000 men and 270 cannon. Opposing him were 74,000
French. But the French—and their 240 cannon—were commanded
by Napoleon. Wellington, therefore, was counting heavily on Blücher's 88,000 troops who—still pursued by Grouchy—were retreating toward Wavre.

Blücher, who had fallen off his horse the day before, had promised
Wellington: "I will come, not just with two corps, but with my entire
army."

And, very sure of himself, he stipulated: "I beg you to inform the
Duke of Wellington that, despite my injury, I will put myself at the
head of my troops and fall on the enemy's right wing as soon as
Napoleon has given battle."

He could not, however, advance on Napoleon's right flank with
his entire army, since he had to leave Thielmann's corps at Wavre
to contain Grouchy.

"They are all moving toward Wavre," Grouchy informed the
Emperor. He was quite content to defeat 88,000 retreating troops
with the 33,000 men Napoleon had given him.

"Toward Wavre and *toward Brussels,"* where—or so the Marshal was convinced—he would certainly find Wellington. It was at Brussels, too, that he intended to rejoin the Emperor, who would by then have thrown back the British army.

On that dawn of June 18, Napoleon was still sleeping in his room on the ground floor of the farmhouse at Gros-Caillou. On his last reconnaissance he had found the terrain soggy and the fog still thick. Besides, he had to wait for Grouchy, to whom he had sent an officer with these orders: "Bring him to me, and don't leave his side until his army corps reaches our line of battle."

It had stopped raining, and little by little the sunlight revealed the lines of the troops. At ten or eleven o'clock the Emperor left Gros-Caillou and, led by his guide, a Fleming named de Coster, went to the farm of Belle-Alliance, with a tavern situated on the highway to Charleroi, three kilometers to the north, facing Mont St.-Jean. He chose his observation post: a rise of ground near the farm of Rossomme. From there he had a view of the famous valley with the plateau occupied by the enemy just across from him.

Waterloo was not Austerlitz. At Waterloo, as at Wagram, words like "rise," "plateau," "valley," and "hill" are quite relative terms. Waterloo is in fact a "dismal plain," in Victor Hugo's phrase, and the "slopes"—the undulations in the terrain—would soon be crossed at full gallop.

The two armies looked at each other. The fate of Europe was about to be decided.

> It was a most magnificent spectacle [a Lieutenant Martin tells us]. The bayonets, the helmets, and the cuirasses glittered; the flags, the guidons, and the lancers' pennants, with their three colors, fluttered in the wind; the drums rolled, the bugles sounded, and all the regimental bands struck up "Veillons au salut de l'Empire"; for at that very moment, Napoleon was reviewing his army on the field of battle for the last time. Never had he heard "Vive l'Empereur!" shouted with more enthusiasm; never had more absolute devotion been expressed on the faces, in the gestures, and in the voices of his soldiers. It was a kind of frenzy. . . . And what rendered this scene even more solemn and moving was that across from us—at some thousand paces—we could clearly discern the dark red line of the British army.

Wellington's troops were also making ready. At 11:30 the heavy battery of the Imperial Guard, positioned a little forward of Belle-Alliance, fired three volleys. *Les trois coups* had been sounded.

The battle began with an infantry assault—intended to deceive Wellington—by the division under the command of the former King Jérôme, who fought heroically all that day. It was directed at the château of Hougoumont, toward the English right flank, but was thrown back twice. Scarcely had this happened (at about one o'clock) when Napoleon, looking to his right from his observation post, caught sight of some 5,000 to 6,000 men in the distance, coming from the direction of St.-Lambert and Wavre.

"It's probably one of Grouchy's detachments," said Soult.

The staff officers had differing opinions. It was still foggy, and some declared that what the Emperor had seen was "trees," others "columns in position." But a captured Prussian dispatch rider soon brought them to agreement: "Those troops are General von Bülow's advance guard. Our whole army spent the night at Wavre. We did not see any French, and we assumed they had marched on Plancenoit."

Napoleon felt less apprehensive. If Grouchy had marched toward Plancenoit—somewhat to the rear of the Emperor's right—he would arrive in time to fall upon the Prussian advance guard; and Blücher, caught between two armies, would be crushed.

Even so, the most urgent thing had to be dealt with first; and the Emperor sent 10,000 men—Lobau's corps—to oppose Bülow. At the same time a dispatch rider was sent off to tell Grouchy to draw near to the Emperor and effect a junction with him in order to crush Bülow's advance guard.

Soult observed: "If Grouchy makes up for the horrible mistake he committed by wasting his time at Gembloux, and moves fast, the victory will be more decisive, because Bülow's corps will be entirely destroyed."

It was already 1:30. The imperial artillery first opened fire on Mont St.-Jean. Then Drouet d'Erlon's infantry launched an assault, succeeding in gaining a foothold on the road to Ohain and reaching the crest of the hill, where the rye and wheat grew thick. But the English and Scots, sheltered behind the walls of the farm of La Haye Sainte, managed with their accurate fire to check the attack of the imperial forces. Seeing the French line hesitate, Wellington put in his Scotch dragoons against them, and the famous gray Scots easily broke the French ranks. The battalions fell back in disorder. The cavalrymen drove forward, reaching the batteries. They put the gunners to the saber, overturned the guns, and drove off the horses. Then, continuing their "unbridled dash," they broke through the whole French line of battle and did not pull up until they were facing the imperial heavy cavalry.

Napoleon had to intervene personally to stop the enemy's breakthrough. Everything had to be started again from scratch. And 4,000 men had been lost.

While this was happening, Grouchy was north of Gembloux. He heard the barrage announcing the start of the battle as he was finishing a plate of strawberries in the notary Hollërt's green summerhouse. But he went calmly on with his lunch before resuming his march on Wavre.

At two o'clock, however, General Gérard told Grouchy: "Monsieur le Maréchal, we should march to the sound of the guns!"

"We must march to the Emperor!" another officer repeated.

Grouchy was annoyed (as he himself admitted). To his division commanders he explained:

> The Emperor told me yesterday that it was his intention to attack the British army if Wellington accepted battle. I am therefore by no means surprised by the engagement taking place at this moment. If the Emperor had wanted me to take part in it, he would not have detached my forces just when he was attacking the English. Moreover, since it would be necessary to march along bad side roads made soggy by the rain which fell yesterday and this morning, I would not reach the scene of battle in time to be of any use.

It was not until 3:30 or 4:00 P.M. that Grouchy received the message from Soult written at 10:00 A.M.—the dispatch rider had lost his way for a time. It must be assumed that this message was not a call for help, since after reading it Grouchy declared that he "was pleased with himself for having carried out the Emperor's orders so well in marching on Wavre instead of listening to General's Gérard's advice."

And yet the dispatch also mentioned "making communication with the bulk of the army."

As for the first messenger, sent off on Saturday night, nothing more was heard of him. Somewhat later, now in the throes of anguish, Napoleon asked Soult how many officers he had sent to Grouchy on the night of the seventeenth with the categorical command to join up with him.

"I sent one," replied the chief of staff.

"Ah!" exclaimed the Emperor. "Ah! Monsieur! Berthier would have sent a hundred!"

Meantime Grouchy, his brain still clouded by the Emperor's orders to pursue Blücher, still intended to march on Wavre. Nor did he give up that intention.

But Soult had sent another dispatch at 1:30 P.M. on the eighteenth —a dispatch that Grouchy received at 5:00 P.M. at Wavre. This time the text was precise:

> At the present moment the battle is engaged along the line of Waterloo and in front of the forest of Soignes. Maneuver so as to join up with our right wing. We believe we have sighted Bülow's corps on the heights of St.-Lambert. Therefore, do not lose a moment in drawing near to us and crushing Bülow, whom you will catch red-handed.

It matters little whether the Marshal—as some have maintained —misread *"la bataille est engagée"* (the battle is engaged) as *"la bataille est gagnée"* (the battle is won). The conclusion to be drawn from the order was nonetheless clear and precise: Grouchy was to join forces with the Emperor without losing a moment. But it was already five o'clock. Even if Grouchy had finally understood and obeyed this new order, he would have reached Mont St.-Jean too late.

It was a frightful drama: the battle was "getting away" from the Emperor's control. Ney's furious and legendary charges were about to begin, in order to "sweep" the plateau "clean."

With his cavalrymen in their steel helmets and breastplates, he charged. Sabers and lances glittered through the dust raised up by thousands of hoofs. A rumble like that of thunder moved along the earth, drowning out the bugle calls. It was admirable, but in no way decisive. The English sharpshooters in the first line were overrun by the wave of iron and horses. But those of the second line resisted, and 5,000 enemy dragoons, hussars, and lancers managed to "show Ney the way" back to the bottom of the hill.

Napoleon (who by this time had taken up a new observation post on the hill of La Belle-Alliance) realized the great error committed by Ney, who on that day seemed so excited that there was talk of his having gone mad. "It was a premature move, and may make this day a disastrous one!"

And a few minutes later the Emperor was heard to sigh: "The wretch! This is the second time since yesterday that he has jeopardized the fate of France!"

As "Congreve rockets" streaked through the sky, frightening the soldiers and making the horses rear and shy, the battle degenerated into a senseless series of charges. Ten times, under the blazing sun, the heavy masses of horses, cuirasses, and raised sabers rushed the English at a frenzied gallop and, despite the precision of the enemy's fire, reached the rows of bristling bayonets, which sliced open the horse's breasts and unseated the riders. Ten times the cuirassiers re-formed around a little grove (their number reduced each time) and on their panting horses again assaulted the English lines, trying to open the famous breach. The buglers blew themselves out, and the whinnies of pain could be heard among the shouts of the men and the crackling of the firearms. Each time the heroic charge of the steel-clad centaurs was thrown back on the plain.

> I was more moved than I can say [wrote a Colonel Trefcon]. And despite the danger I was in myself, I had tears in my eyes and was shouting my admiration for them. I was particularly impressed by the carbineers. I saw their gilded cuirasses and their helmets glitter in the sun. Then they passed by me, and I never saw them again.

Meantime, the Guard had taken Plancenoit. There, it was the enemy's turn to flee, "as though stricken by fear." They threw down their arms and equipment so as to reach the English left flank as quickly as possible. Of the 4,000 men making up the British Fifth Division, only 500 were left.

"There is nothing that I can do for them," said Wellington calmly. "Like me, they will have to defend their position to the last man. Let us pray to God for the coming of night—or of Blücher."

It was Blücher who reached the spot first.

The French had occupied the hills beyond Plancenoit, as the routed English "for a few moments spread their own terror" among the ranks of Bülow's Prussians. The entire enemy left wavered. But the Emperor could not send reinforcements to exploit this success; and the Guard, once their task was completed, went back to Napoleon's position. The moment they arrived, the Emperor put himself at their head and marched them toward the plateau.

It was at this moment that the bulk of Blücher's army—30,000 men—debouched from the farm of Papelotte onto the field of battle. Soon they would engulf it. Napoleon sent a part of his forces in their direction. And he sent another part to Ney, who claimed that with some infantry he could "take everything." But the first French wave was cut down, as though by a gigantic scythe, by the fire from the English soldiers lying flat in the rye and wheat. The second line wavered, and a great shout went across the battlefield like a train of powder: "We've been betrayed!"

Napoleon had stationed himself near La Haye Sainte, a few paces behind the two artillery batteries of the Guard. Here the enemy grapeshot was decimating the gunners, but the survivors nonetheless kept up their steady fire.

Although worn out by their hard march, Blücher's Prussians repulsed the French and compelled the Emperor to pull back to Belle-Alliance, while the English cavalry charged with as much spirit as Ney—and with more effectiveness.

And now, from mouth to mouth, came another shout never heard before: "The Guard is retreating!"

And in fact the eight battalions of the Old Guard—who had formed up to advance toward the plateau of Mont St.-Jean and had reached the bottom of the valley—had effected a change of front so as to oppose the Prussians who were coming down in a constant stream from the English left flank. There was only one thing to do: form a square and retreat.

Everywhere from Hougoumont to Plancenoit, the French army was routed, crushed, and broken. Everywhere it wavered, fell back, and fled. It was the end.

One last cry—the most terrible of all—resounded over "the dismal plain": "*Sauve qui peut!*"

"Come, my friends, and see how a French marshal dies!" shouted

Ney, trying in vain to rally a few squads to make a last charge: that of death.

Night fell on the battlefield. The Emperor had taken refuge in one of the squares formed by the First Grenadiers of the Guard. Napoleon had stepped upon the stage of history by sounding *les trois coups* of Toulon, of Vendémiaire, and of Arcole. What a beautiful ending to his legend if he were to leave history sword in hand, struck down by an enemy bullet! He sought death, but death did not take him. And he returned to France protected by a triple row of bayonets.

The enemy did not succeed in breaking the squares of the Guard. Cambronne, with the Second Battalion of the First Chasseurs, uttered his immortal words: "The Guard is dying but not surrendering!"

Then came the retreat from Waterloo.

Five hundred musicians marched in front of the Guard, playing —for the last time—the triumphant tunes of the Carrousel. The "furcaps" marched in good order as the English shells and grapeshot continued to rain down on them. Behind them, around them, ahead of them, panic-stricken troops stampeded toward France, with the enemy cavalry cutting down the stragglers. The road was so jammed with fleeing soldiers that the Emperor, moving like an automaton, had to go cross-country.

With the coming of night, a few grenadiers had built a fire some distance back from Quatre Bras. Stopping nearby, the Emperor watched, powerless to do anything, as the horrible debacle continued. An eyewitness saw him "standing motionless, his arms folded on his chest, gazing toward Waterloo."

Suddenly, he had an idea: he would try to get a few troops into position in Quatre Bras. "It's already late," he told Colonel de Baulus. "If the enemy finds this position occupied when he reaches it, he will probably call off his pursuit." "I set off at a gallop," wrote Colonel de Baulus. "But as I drew near to the houses I was greeted by gunfire. I came back to warn the Emperor; and I urged him to move on, since he was no longer covered by anyone. A few tears fell from his eyes."

It was with those few tears that both the battle and the epic came to an end. The empire was about to perish, once and for all time.

The atrocious bloodbath of Waterloo—the result of the heady

NAPOLEON

fumes of vainglory that had intoxicated Napoleon—was a page in the history of France that could never be forgotten, for all the mad heroism of Ney or the Rabelaisian panache of Cambronne. The One Hundred Days left the country weakened, mutilated, and bankrupt. Few ventures have proven more disastrous for France. And yet there are many today who refuse to face up to this tragic result. Some of them refuse to remember anything but the belated liberties the Emperor was obliged to grant to the French. For others, all that counts is the marvelous adventure and those turns of fortune which forged the legend culminating in St. Helena.

XXVI

THE END OF THE EMPIRE

One cannot repair a throne.

NAPOLEON

WHEN HE REACHED THE ÉLYSÉE at 7:00 A.M. on Wednesday, June 21, the Emperor explained to Caulaincourt with a sigh: "The army performed miracles. But it was overcome by panic, and all was lost. I'm completely exhausted. I need two hours of rest before I can get back to business."

And putting his hand over his heart, he said: "I feel a tightening there."

He ordered a steaming-hot bath and soaked in it for a full hour while the Council was assembling.

Early in the session of the Council, the question of Napoleon's continuing in office was posed by Carnot, who advised him to have the Chambre des Représentants offer him full powers.

The Emperor approved. "In order to save the country, I need a temporary dictatorship. I could simply seize it; but it would be useful, and more democratic, if it were granted to me by the Chambers."

Regnault Saint-Jean d'Angély, the Minister of State, shook his head sadly. He liked Napoleon; and it was with feelings of great distress that he told him: "I doubt that the representatives will go along with the Emperor's views. They are apparently convinced that he is no longer capable of saving the country. I fear that a great sacrifice is required."

There was a silence.

"Speak plainly, Regnault," said Napoleon. "Is it my abdication that they want?"

"I'm afraid it is, Sire. And painful as it may be for me, it is my duty

555

NAPOLEON

to so inform Your Majesty. I would even go so far as to say that there is a possibility, if the Emperor did not decide to abdicate of his own free will, that the Chamber would demand it of him."

Lucien was indignant. The Emperor should by-pass the Chamber, name himself dictator, and declare the whole territory in a state of siege.

Napoleon's eyes flashed. "To reject me when I was landing at Cannes would have made sense. But now that I am a part of what the enemy is attacking, I am a part of what France should defend. In handing me over to the enemy, she is handing over herself. She is admitting defeat, and encouraging the audacity of the victor. It is not liberty which is deposing me, it is fear!"

And he went on talking, enumerating his forces and outlining the defense of the territory. Everything could still be saved. But if he abdicated, there would be no more armies.

The ministers remained silent—at first subdued, then won over. Fouché alone felt beads of sweat forming on his brow. "To tell the truth," he said later, "that devil gave me a scare that morning. As I listened to him, I had the feeling that everything was going to begin all over again."

Abruptly, the door opened and an emissary from the Chamber brought a message: "The Chamber declares itself in permanent session. Any attempt to dissolve it constitutes high treason. Whosoever is guilty of such an attempt is a traitor to the fatherland, and will be treated as such."

Napoleon paced back and forth in the room, as was his habit. He declared that a company of grenadiers should be sent to deal with these troublemakers, as had been done at St.-Cloud on the evening of 19 Brumaire.

At this point Davout, the Minister of War, raised his voice: "It is too late to act. The resolution of the representatives is unconstitutional, but it is a consummated act. Under the present circumstances, we cannot expect to repeat the performance of 18 Brumaire. As for me, I would refuse to take part in it!"

Everyone, downcast, watched the master.

"I can see," he said, "that Regnault did not deceive me. I will abdicate if necessary."

When the deputies assembled the next morning, they seemed like so many braggarts. They had dared openly to attack the master, who had ordered no disruption by armed force. They had gone as far as anyone could.

"Tell your brother," said the Marquis de Lafayette to Lucien, "to send us his abdication. If not, we will notify him of his dethronement."

The first reaction of the wounded lion was to bare his claws. He would expel those Jacobins—those hotheads!

But Regnault told him: "By abdicating, Your Majesty would preserve the throne of your son, which would be destroyed by dethronement."

"My son! My son!" Napoleon riposted. "What a chimera! I am not abdicating in favor of my son, but in favor of the Bourbons. At any rate *they* are not prisoners in Vienna!"

It was 12:30 P.M. when the Emperor ordered: "Prince Lucien, take this down: 'I am offering myself as a sacrifice to the hatred of France's enemies. Let it be hoped that they are sincere in their declarations, and that their resentment is confined to my person.' "

For the second time, the dream of 1811 had come to naught. The Emperor no longer had faith in anything—not even in the possible reign of his son. It was only at the insistence of Lucien and Carnot that he added these lines to his declaration of abdication: "My political life is over, and I proclaim my son Emperor of the French, under the name of Napoleon II."

It was only because of their hatred of the Bourbons that, on June 23, the representatives agreed to proclaim the young Emperor "Prince of Parma."

The accession of the new Emperor had no great effect on the French. Says Labretonnière: "There was no ceremony or ostentation to announce it. The Chamber voted for the accession of the poor little King of Rome with the same solemnity as for an amendment to a bill dealing with tobacco or potash."

And a new kind of night fell on Paris. There was a decision to be made; Napoleon had to leave the Élysée. But where could he go? He asked Hortense if she could receive him the next day at Malmaison, where Josephine had died the year before.

Fouché's hour of triumph had come. On the second day of the "reign" of the new Emperor, the Duke of Otranto, who had become president of the Governmental Commission, arranged for the release from prison of the Baron de Vitrolles (Louis XVIII's former minister) and explained his plans to him:

> You will go and seek out the King. You will tell him that we are working only to serve him; and that even though we may proceed indirectly, we shall ultimately restore him to power. For the moment, we have to put up with Napoleon II, but when all is said and done we shall restore him to power.

It had rained on the morning of June 25. But the sky cleared, and from the windows of the Élysée Napoleon could see several thousand Parisians crowding the Rue du Faubourg St.-Honoré. They were shouting: "Long live the Emperor! Don't abandon us!"

Napoleon had decided to go to Malmaison, where he would wait for the passports that would enable him to reach America. Since he was afraid that the crowd would oppose his departure, he had ordered his carriage to leave by the main entrance, while he himself was crossing the park on foot. At the gate opening onto the Champs-Élysées, he waited for Grand Marshal Bertrand's carriage. For the last time, Napoleon rode up the Champs-Élysées. He went past the unfinished Arc de Triomphe, where the workmen were still busy, then took the highway leading to Neuilly.

Malmaison was all abloom. The day after his arrival, Napoleon received the Countess Walewska and little Alexander. Held close in his arms, she wept for a long time. She offered to follow him into exile. He promised to send for her if developments allowed it. But —as she knew very well—developments would compel the Emperor to weave his legend, to depict himself as a martyr for posterity, and in this way to provide a throne for the King of Rome, rather than to end his days in a bourgeois fashion with one of his mistresses: even though that mistress be the gentle Marie.

At Malmaison the memory of his beloved Creole obsessed him. He said to Hortense:

> Poor Josephine: I just can't get used to being here without her! It seems to me that I can still see her coming toward me from one of those shaded walks and gathering those plants she loved so much! Poor Josephine! But for that matter, she would be very unhappy now! The only thing we ever quarreled about was her debts, and I certainly scolded her enough! No doubt about it: she

was the most gracious person I have ever seen. She was a woman in the strongest sense of the word: animated, vivacious, and with the best heart. Please have another portrait of her painted for me. I would like to have it in the form of a medallion.

Hortense promised to do so.

General Béker had been appointed by the Provisional Government as a kind of jailer to watch over Napoleon. On the morning of June 29, quite oblivious of this role, he was about to leave for Paris, taking to the Provisional Government a proposal from "General Bonaparte."

In their haste to occupy Paris, the Prussians had advanced incautiously. With their vanguard already on the Basse-Seine, they were in a position to be "hewed to pieces." And Napoleon, studying his map, had immediately seen their mistake. He was heard to mutter: "France must not be subjugated by a handful of Prussians!"

In a matter of moments, he had donned his Guards uniform. Then, booted and spurred, he summoned Béker.

Let them appoint me general, and I will command the army. Go to Paris: a carriage is ready for you. Explain to the Provisional Government that I have no intention of taking power again. I want to defeat the enemy, to crush him, and compel him by means of a victory to give a favorable turn to the negotiations. . . . Then I shall leave.

When Fouché learned the nature of Béker's mission, he exclaimed: "Is he making fun of us? Even if his proposals were acceptable, don't we know how he would keep his promises?"

And the Emperor's former minister, in a rage, demanded of Béker: "Why did you take on such a mission, when you should have been urging the Emperor to leave as soon as possible?" Actually Fouché had done everything to sabotage the Emperor's plans: first denying him a passport (thereby putting him at the mercy of a village mayor), and then making the departure of the frigates from Rochefort dependent on his request to the British for a safe-conduct for "Napoleon Bonaparte"—a safe-conduct at a time when the Allies had only one thing in mind: to "arrest the troublemaker of the world." Blücher even wanted to have Napoleon executed in front of his troops. He had ordered Major de Colomb to march on Malmaison with his troops and seize the dethroned Emperor.

Fouché was aware of all this. He was so well aware of it, in fact, that the French envoys sent by the Provisional Government to Wellington for the signing of an armistice had been given secret instructions to offer to hand Napoleon over to England.

But upon thinking it over, the Duke of Otranto had changed his mind. He no longer wanted the operation to be carried out at the gates of Paris. The arrest would be so much more easily managed, and so much more discreet, at Rochefort or in the harbor of the island of Aix. The passport had been entrusted to Béker, and the frigates had been ordered to set sail as soon as the Emperor and his suite were on board. There was no point in waiting for the safe-conducts, since Fouché intended to notify the British squadron, which would then simply pick up the fugitive.

"Tell the Emperor," the Chief of the Provisional Government added, "that his offers cannot be accepted, and that it is most urgent that he leave immediately for Rochefort, where he will be safer than in the environs of Paris."

As soon as Napoleon learned of the government's reply, he yielded: "Those people have no notion of public opinion. They'll be sorry they refused my offer!"

Yet for a moment, he clung to one hope. "Did you tell them exactly what I said, and the oath I swore to?"

Pathetically, Béker murmured: "Yes, Sire."

"Bien, alors. All I can do is leave. Give the orders. When they have been carried out, let me know!"

Walking slowly, he left the library and, using the little secret staircase, went up to his bedroom. He took off his uniform, put down his sword, and donned a brown frock coat. With his round hat in hand, he went to Josephine's bedroom. He wanted to be alone there. In that domed room, beside the bed where two swans with outspread wings kept guard, he gave himself over to daydreams.

His eyes were tear-stained when he left the room.

He went back to the library. Queen Hortense made him accept a belt into which she had sewn a necklace of big diamonds.

Madame Mère was there, too. She would never see her Napoleone again. She knew it, and wept.

The officers of the Malmaison "garrison" came into the room. "It is plain to see," stammered one of them, "that we will not have the good fortune to die in your service!"

The imperial carriages were lined up in the courtyard. An impressive suite of officers, servants, and baggage would rejoin Napoleon at Rochefort. He himself would travel incognito, along with Béker, the Duke of Rovigo, and Grand Marshal Bertrand. No one noticed a yellow calash without armorial bearings and drawn by four horses that the Mameluke Ali had waiting for him on the road of Celle-St.-Cloud.

Shortly after five o'clock, followed by his companions, he went out on the drawbridge and headed for the gate. Then he turned and took one last look at the château. "How beautiful Malmaison is!"

But to dally any longer would be imprudent. The Prussians were nearby—he could hear the sounds made by the approaching artillery and the explosions as bridges were blown up to impede the enemy's march. At that moment, the Emperor may have recalled a recent conversation with Fleury de Chaboulon:

"Your Majesty is not the kind of a man who escapes."

"Where would I escape to?"

"It would be splendid if Napoleon the Great—after having removed the crown placed on his head, and after twenty years of glory—offered himself as a sacrifice to obtain the fatherland's independence."

Surrender to the enemy? Yes, perhaps.

"It would be a fine denouement!"

But he had not agreed. And yet the notion remained with him, tenacious and obstinate.

Abruptly, he tore himself away from his memories and jumped into the calash, where according to the passport provided by Fouché, he was to play the role of Béker's secretary. And thus began the first stage of the journey toward St. Helena.

He reached Niort on Saturday, July 1, at 10:00 P.M., after having traveled for thirty-eight hours. The Emperor told the postilions to pull up at an inn called La Boule d'Or, on the Place de la Brèche, where he had decided to spend the night.

When he woke the next morning he looked out his window at some cavalrymen who were grooming their horses. One of them recognized him, and the word soon spread through the town. The prefect came on the run and begged the Emperor to come and stay at the prefecture. Napoleon accepted his invitation.

Later, carriages which had set out from Paris and Malmaison

reached Niort. By now the Emperor was surrounded by a regular
court, including generals, other officers, and chamberlains. There
were even two ladies: the Comtesse de Montholon and the Comtesse
Bertrand. Next came twenty carriages crowded with servants and
baggage. Even King Joseph showed up, provided with French and
American passports.

Early in the afternoon the Emperor was handed a message from
the maritime prefect of Rochefort—the Capitaine de Vaisseau,
Baron de Bonnefoux—stating that the harbor was tightly blockaded
by a British squadron.

And the Capitaine de Vaisseau went on to say: "In my opinion,
it would be very dangerous for our frigates and their cargo to try to
force the passage."

Actually, the "squadron" guarding the narrows of Antioche,
Breton, and Maumusson consisted of only one ship of the line, the
Bellerophon, plus one or two small vessels of the corvette or sloop
type. But the Emperor took the maritime prefect at his word and
again thought of his legend. Going to America to "plow the earth,
live off the produce of his fields, and end up where man had begun"
was not the way to prepare for his son's throne and his own transfigu-
ration. The *Bellerophon* actually seemed to attract him. And the next
day, he left for Rochefort.

As soon as he arrived, a discussion began. The prefect advised
against trying to break the blockade. Instead, why not get aboard the
corvette, *Bayadère,* which had hove to off Royan? Its skipper, Captain Baudin, replied the moment he was alerted that he would take
the responsibility for getting the Emperor to America. Napoleon did
not reject this plan; but he could not make up his mind. It would be
so much more decorous to surrender on board a British vessel than
to flee like a culprit on a cockleshell.

For the same reason, he turned down the proposal of Lieutenant
Bresson, the skipper of a little sloop, who conceived the notion of
hiding the Emperor in a big barrel—"well padded and provided with
air holes." Imagine leaving the country with only his valet when he
could go to the English with a retinue of some fifteen officers in dress
uniform, plus sixty servants—not to mention his sumptuous plate and
dishes and his vast amount of luggage.

After spending the night on board the frigate *Saâle,* the Emperor
paid a visit to the island of Aix.

Today this little piece of land, relatively high above sea level, has fewer than a hundred inhabitants. In 1815, however, it was a regular stronghold where the Fourteenth Naval Regiment was garrisoned. As the Emperor inspected the island's numerous fortifications, the inhabitants shouted: "To the Army of the Loire!"

An hour after he had returned to the *Saâle,* the prefect Bonnefoux brought dispatches from the Provisional Government written on the eve of Louis XVIII's entry into Paris. Fouché authorized the Emperor to embark on a dispatch boat, if the fugitive thought he could more easily slip through the enemy's net that way. But at the same time he forbade him to return to the Continent, and advised him to turn himself over to the English squadron "immediately."

Napoleon gave serious thought only to the last part of Fouché's dispatch. Accordingly, the next day (July 10), he sent Savary and Las Cases—formerly a Councilor of State and now a chamberlain—as emissaries to the *Bellerophon.*

The British captain, Maitland, a thin, pallid man, gulled them with the skill of a master. He pretended to be totally ignorant of what was going on. One might have believed he was just taking a pleasure cruise off the coast of France. Waterloo? It was the first time he had heard the name of the place. The Emperor had abdicated? He was on the island of Aix? And he was asking if his safe-conducts had arrived?

"I know nothing," he stated. "I would like to be in a position to give you what you want. I shall report the matter to my admiral, who is in the Bay of Queberon."

Actually, Maitland was informed of everything. On July 7 he had learned from Admiral Henry Hotham that Napoleon was on his way to Rochefort to try to embark for America. Also, Maitland had been notified that the British Government had refused to grant Napoleon the safe-conduct he had asked for. Not only that, but he had received explicit orders "to do his utmost to prevent Bonaparte from escaping." Fouché had done his job well.

But Maitland was most polite to the two emissaries. While they were at lunch, a corvette, the *Falmouth,* arrived from England with dispatches. The captain read them and then said with a smile, "There is not a word in here of what you have just told me. I see that even at the moment of this vessel's departure no one there knew anything of what you have just imparted to me."

As a matter of fact, however, the text of the dispatch that Maitland had just read without batting an eye said:

> You are enjoined to conduct the strictest search of all vessels you encounter. If you are fortunate enough to take Buonaparte, you will have him transferred to the vessel you command, to keep him there under strong guard, and to return with all possible speed to the nearest English port.

As Admiral Hotham instructed him in another dispatch, the captain was to employ "all means to intercept the fugitive, upon whose capture the repose of Europe would appear to depend."

And so, becoming more and more polite, Maitland told Savary and Las Cases: "The Emperor is well advised to ask for safe-conducts in order to avoid any new unpleasantness at sea." Then he inquired, "But what objection could he have to coming to England? In that way he could remove all the obstacles."

The two emissaries returned to the *Saâle* and gave the Emperor an account of the interview. Napoleon decided—in order to make it plain that he had abandoned any notions of trying to slip past the blockade—to disembark from the *Saâle* and take up quarters on land.

He chose the new house built in 1808 for the commandant of Aix, who had been absent for several days. His room on the second floor offered a view of the Rade des Basques, where the *Bellerophon* now lay at anchor. The Emperor immediately lay down to sleep.

The next day there was more talk of running the blockade in a shallop that some midshipmen offered to crew, and Napoleon seemed tempted. But Gourgaud told him:

> You would be better advised to go to England. This noble choice is the one most suitable for you. You cannot play the role of an adventurer. History would one day reproach you for having abdicated out of fear, since you had not made the total sacrifice. . . . A gambler kills himself. A brave man faces up to adversity.

There was a silence. Then the Emperor replied: "Yesterday I entertained the idea of betaking myself to the English squadron, and calling to them upon my arrival: 'Like Themistocles, unwilling to have anything to do with the mutilation of my country, I come to ask asylum of you.' "

At the same moment, a little bird flew in the window.

"A sign of good luck!" Gourgaud shouted.

He took the bird in his hand, but Napoleon exclaimed, "There are enough wretched creatures in the world as it is! Let it go free!"

Gourgaud obeyed, and the Emperor said, "Let's see what its flight portends."

The bird flew off, and Gourgaud exclaimed, "Sire, he is flying toward the British squadron!"

At 4:00 A.M. on July 14 Las Cases and General Frédéric Lallemand went aboard the *Bellerophon*. Maitland, imperturbable, told them he had received no reply from Admiral Hotham, but that he was expecting a corvette to arrive at any moment. Then he added:

> If the Emperor wants to embark for England immediately, I have the authority to receive him on board and take him there. In my private opinion, there is no doubt that England would accord to Napoleon all the respect and hospitality to which he can lay claim. In my country, the Prince and the ministers do not exercise the kind of arbitrary authority that is exercised on the Continent. The English people possess a generosity of sentiment and a liberality of opinion superior to sovereignty itself.

Las Cases replied that he would inform the Emperor of the captain's offer, and added: "I believe I know the Emperor Napoleon well enough to assume that he would not be unwilling to go England in complete trust, so as to find means there of continuing his voyage to the United States."

For the rest of his life, Maitland insisted he had made no promises to the Emperor's two envoys. To Lord Keith he explained:

> I can assure Your Lordship that I neither made nor accepted any conditions concerning the treatment that General Bonaparte was to receive, and that at the time it had not even been definitely settled that he would come aboard the *Bellerophon*. In the course of the conversation M. Las Cases asked me if I thought that Bonaparte would be well received in England. I gave him the only reply I could possibly make in my situation; namely, that I had no notion whatsoever of the intentions of the British Government, but that I had no reason to suppose that he would not be well received.

At about two o'clock on that same day, the Emperor called a last meeting of his faithful followers and asked, "Should I try to embark on the *Bayadère* tonight, or try to slip through the English squadron, either on Lieutenant Bresson's sloop or on the midshipman's shallop? Or would it not be preferable to ask for the hospitality of England?"

Charles Montholon, Napoleon's aide-de-camp at Waterloo, later claimed he had told the Emperor that it was "a thousand times preferable to take the risk offered by Captain Baudin, captain of the *Bayadère*, who (so he said) had pledged himself to take the Emperor anywhere in the world."

And he is reported to have added: "Actually, if you don't succeed in slipping through the squadron and reaching America, you could always go to England as a second choice."

It was on that July 14 that the Emperor finally made his decision. Las Cases and Gourgaud were instructed to go aboard the *Bellerophon* to inform Captain Maitland of their master's intentions. Gourgaud was to ask Maitland's permission to embark in a small vessel and proceed to London without delay, taking with him the following letter addressed to the Prince Regent—a letter the Emperor had written the day before:

Rochefort, 13 July

Your Royal Highness:

Defenseless against the factions which are dividing my country, and the enmity of the greatest Powers of Europe, I have reached the end of my political career, and I come, like Themistocles, to sit at the hearth of the English nation. I put myself under the protection of its laws—something I claim from Your Royal Highness as the most powerful, the most unwavering, and the most generous of my enemies.

"What do you think of this text?" he asked Gourgaud.

"Sire, it brings tears to my eyes."

Then the Emperor dictated a letter addressed to Maitland: "If I am to go to England, I would like to reside in a country house some ten or twelve leagues from London, where I would like to arrive as much incognito as possible."

That same day, the prefect Bonnefoux received the new prefect of La Charente-Inférieure, who brought a dispatch from the Comte de Jaucourt, Minister of Justice of His Majesty Louis XVIII. The captain of the *Saâle* was ordered to "hand over Napoleon Bonaparte to the English captain as soon as the latter should request it."

The text of the dispatch further stipulated that the summons would not be issued only in the name of His Britannic Majesty: "It will be issued in the name of the King, your legitimate sovereign. . . . If you are sufficiently vicious or blind to resist what you have been ordered to do, you will be guilty of open rebellion."

Louis XVIII was giving himself the pleasure of personally handing Napoleon over to England.

Frightened at the idea of having to carry out such an order, Bonnefoux contrived not to leave Rochefort until 10:00 P.M., and did not get to the *Saâle* until one in the morning. There he learned that the Emperor was to go aboard the *Bellerophon* at dawn. Bonnefoux preferred not to take part in the ignominy of arresting Napoleon and delivering him to the British vessel. He pretended he had arrived too late to carry out the orders of the Royal Government.

It was Saturday, July 15, 1815, and the sun was about to rise. Napoleon donned the green uniform of a colonel of Light Horse of the Imperial Guard. From among his decorations, he chose the Grand Cross of the Legion of Honor and the Order of the Iron Crown. He put on his legendary two-cornered hat. Then, followed by his officers (all in dress uniform, as at the Tuileries), he embarked on the *Epervier*, an armed brig which was to take him to the *Bellerophon*, where Maitland was waiting for him.

The *Epervier*, flying the tricolor, moved slowly away from shore. Through the field glass he had used at Austerlitz, Napoleon looked out toward the open sea, where he could discern the profile of the *Bellerophon* in the light of the rising sun. A whaleboat had already left the side of the vessel and was being rowed rapidly toward the brig. It was six o'clock in the morning.

Napoleon would not set foot on land again until three months and two days later. And this time it would be on another island: that "little island" the name of which he had written, twenty-seven years before, at Auxonne, on the top of a page in the notebook he was using for his courses as a lieutenant of artillery: a page that had been left blank.

Captain Maitland was standing on the bridge of his ship, spyglass to his eye, trying to make out the legendary profile of the Emperor. Then he discerned him, sitting in the stern sheets of the English whaleboat which had gone to meet the *Epervier*. The prolonged cheer of "Vive l'Empereur!" shouted by the sailors on the brig could be heard by the captain of the *Bellerophon*.

Maitland was so doubtful that the stout man in uniform was actually "Boney" that he asked Lieutenant Mott (the first to come up to the bridge of the *Bellerophon*) in anxiety: "Do you have him?"

At that same moment Bertrand, who had come behind Mott, saluted Maitland and announced: "The Emperor is in the longboat."

Everything was silent, except for the sound of the wind in the rigging. Maitland started down from the bridge to greet his prisoner, but Napoleon was suddenly there in front of him, saying in a strong voice: "I come to put myself under the protection of your Prince and your laws."

There was considerable emotion as the Emperor, still mindful of history and his legend, continued: "The fortunes of war have brought me to my cruelest enemy, but I count on his fairness."

Before going to have breakfast, the Emperor wanted to inspect the *Bellerophon*. As usual, he asked all kinds of questions, which the captain was obliged to answer.

At nine o'clock it was announced that the *Superb*, a seventy-two-gun vessel flying the pennant of Admiral Henry Hotham, had just dropped anchor. Maitland was anxious, and for good reason. There was no doubt that he had acted out a farce with Napoleon's emissaries. According to his orders, he was to take up a position offshore from Rochefort "so as to prevent Bonaparte from escaping." But he had exceeded his authority somewhat in declaring that England would accord to Napoleon "all the respect and hospitality to which he can lay claim."

To his superior, Hotham, Maitland explained, "I believe that I acted wisely, and that the Government will approve my conduct, because I felt it was of great importance to prevent Bonaparte's fleeing to America, and to obtain possession of his person."

To this Sir Henry Hotham replied, "To have taken custody of him under just any conditions would have been most imprudent. But since you stipulated no conditions, there is not the slightest doubt but what you will obtain the approval of His Majesty's Government."

The admiral came to dinner on the *Bellerophon* that evening and invited the Emperor and his retinue to take their repast, the next day, on the *Superb*.

On the flagship, Napoleon adopted the attitude that he was on a vessel of an ally of France. He had his camp bed set up and dismounted for Sir Henry, just as he had done for Alexander at Tilsit. He put his guard through their motions. And, needless to say, when they went in to dinner—at a table set with his own plate and dishes —he entered the wardroom first, indicating with a wave of the hand that the admiral should sit at his right. His servants stood behind him just as they had at the Tuileries.

Maitland, who was speechless, reports that Napoleon conducted himself "like a royal personage." But how else should he have behaved, when he had been received on board the *Superb* as a sovereign? The staff officers were standing at attention in dress uniforms, while a band played and the crew, likewise in dress uniform, trimmed the yards and riggings. True, everyone but Maitland called him "Monsieur." But is that not the translation of "sir," which is used only when addressing a superior?

The Emperor still had a kind of court around him: some fifteen officers—including the generals Savary, Lallemand, Montholon, and Gourgaud—plus Grand Marshal Bertrand and Mmes. Bertrand and Montholon. Also, his retinue comprised some sixty servants, some of whom were carried on the *Bellerophon* and some on the *Myrmidon*, a veteran of Abukir which had been ordered to sail as consort to the ship commanded by Maitland.

While the *Bellerophon* was sailing slowly toward England (it would take her more than a week to reach Torbay), the British Government, the press, and the lawyers were debating. What should be done with the man whom the *Times,* the *Morning Post,* and the *Courier* called "the Corsican ogre"? The conservative papers gave full vent to their fury. He who had trustingly come to "sit at the hearth of the British nation" was being described as "a bloody good-for-nothing" and a "knave with a coronet." Some declared that this "scourge of humanity" should be fairly hanged. The most peaceable talked of putting him in a cage of iron; and the *Sun* went so far as to state that the incarceration would take place in the fortress of Sharness. Contrary to the Tory press, the liberal papers—including the *Morning Chronicle*—considered the imperial exile as nothing more than an "uninvited guest" of England. In their opinion, he must be treated with forbearance; that is, with magnanimity.

The famous letter addressed to His Royal Highness the Prince

Regent (who had replaced George III, the poor demented King) in no way prompted the sovereign to take a hand in the fate of Napoleon. This was a matter for the Government—a government with which, according to the English Constitution, he could not interfere. It was up to the Chief of Government, Lord Liverpool, to make the appropriate decision. In the view of His Britannic Majesty's Prime Minister, Napoleon was a leper "whose existence was the greatest disgrace of modern history." What mattered above all was to make it impossible for "this man without a law or a fatherland" to attempt a second return from Elba. The solution that Blücher was clamoring for—execution by firing squad—would never be approved by that great lord the Duke of Wellington. What, then, could be done with this "independent belligerent"? Lord Liverpool opined: "The easiest solution would be to hand him over to the King of France, who would have him treated as a rebel. But in such a case he must be sentenced in a manner that will prevent any chance of his escaping."

Louis XVIII had pronounced "Napoleon Bonaparte a traitor and rebel for having made an armed incursion into the Département du Var." One can easily imagine what Louis would be obliged to do, now that the ghost from Elba, still armed, had made an incursion even into the Tuileries. But the trial and execution—or even the imprisonment—of the Emperor would certainly have unleashed a civil war in France that might very well have threatened the throne (scarcely reestablished) of the former Comte de Provence.

In the face of history, it seemed difficult to hand over to the Bourbons a man who considered England "the most generous" of his enemies. Thus the only solution was to keep this individual under guard—a strong guard. Napoleon himself was to say, at St. Helena: "If I had gone to the United States, I could have come back two or three months later."

In the view of the British Cabinet, it seemed best to take up the scheme that had already been mooted at the Congress of Vienna: to incarcerate the troublemaker. Not in a jail in England, since such a decision would not have been worthy of true gentlemen, but on an island where "one day his tombstone would be reared." There he would be treated humanely; and he could keep some of his officers and servants with him. Rapidly, and for different reasons, the islands of Maurice, St. Lucia, and Trinity were rejected. St. Helena, isolated

in the middle of the South Atlantic, seemed to be the ideal place—
for the jailers, of course. The island did not belong to the Crown but
to the East India Company. But this detail was of no importance: the
Company would be indemnified. Only one thing mattered: this former volcano was a fortress on a suitable scale for a Titan. Its cliffs
plunged down to the sea from vertiginous heights. And when one
went from the island's only port into its only "town," one seemed to
be entering a medieval citadel. The troublemaker may have returned from Elba, but he would not return from St. Helena.

This was the same island that Napoleon almost decided (on September 30, 1804) to have occupied by a French squadron, noting that
"this object would require from 1,200 to 1,500 men." By an astounding
trick of fate, "this object" was to become his prison.

Moreover, the British Government declared—quite sincerely—
that the climate on the island was excellent. These gentlemen seem
not to have been informed that there were several climates on the
island, depending upon where one's residence was located; and depending, too, upon the seasons—which for that matter were the
reverse of those in the Northern Hemisphere.

But for the time being the Emperor hadn't the slightest inkling
of the decisions that had just been made. True, the question of his
deportation to St. Helena had already been raised before his escape
from Elba; but Napoleon thought that his having surrendered in
good faith would make it necessary to reconsider everything.

For a week—first in Torbay and then in Plymouth Harbor—Napoleon waited for his fate to be decided. Finally, at 10:00 A.M. on July
31, a longboat was seen to be approaching the *Bellerophon,* carrying
Admiral Lord Keith and Sir Henry Bunburry, the Under-Secretary
of State. Maitland met them at the gangway. Without delay, he took
them to Napoleon, who was waiting for them, with Bertrand at his
side. Bunburry saluted with a cold kind of dignity. Keith felt the need
to say a few words of regret: he was obliged to perform a painful
mission. Then Bunburry handed the Emperor a communication
from the British Government to "General Buonaparte."

The document was in English, and the "prisoner" did not understand it. Lord Keith and Bertrand set about putting it into French,
and their words—rather disjointed as a result of the translating—
resounded in the small stateroom:

It would hardly be compatible with our duties toward our country and the Allies of His Majesty if General Buonaparte were left with the means or the occasion to again disturb the peace of Europe. For this reason it becomes absolutely necessary that he be restrained in his physical freedom, to whatever extent may be necessary for securing that first and paramount object. The island of St. Helena has been chosen for his future residence. Its climate is healthful, and its geographic situation is such that he can be treated with more indulgence there than would be possible elsewhere, in view of the indispensable precautions that would have to be taken to restrain him.

The Emperor was quivering with indignation; his teeth were clenched, and his brows knit in a dark frown; but he managed to keep his self-control as he waited to hear the rest of the communication.

General Buonaparte will be permitted to choose, from among those persons who have accompanied him to England—with the exception of Generals Savary and Lallemand—three officers, who together with his surgeon will have permission to accompany him to St. Helena but may not leave the island without the sanction of the British Government.

The Emperor's features were distorted by rage as he took the document and put it on the table. Virtually choking, he launched into a lengthy protest.

Lord Keith and Sir Henry Bunburry remained impassive. There was no question of beginning a discussion. They had not come to hear the "general's" objections but to convey to him the intentions of their Government. They silently saluted and withdrew.

Then Napoleon exploded, giving full vent to his rage:

To St. Helena! The very thought of it horrifies me! To be confined for life on a tropical island at an immense distance from any continent, deprived of all communication with the world and all it holds that is dear to me! . . . It's worse than Tamerlane's cage of iron! I'd rather be handed over to the Bourbons! And among other insults—but it's only a trifle, a very secondary thing—they call me "general."

Abruptly, the storm passed and the flow of words stopped. With astounding self-control after that first outburst of rage, the Emperor recovered his equanimity. Says Marchand:

A little later I went to his stateroom. As I entered, I found the window curtains hermetically sealed. They were of red silk, and lent a mysterious cast to the atmosphere of the room. The Emperor had already taken off his uniform, saying he wanted to rest for a bit. As he went on undressing, he told me to continue reading to him from *La Vie des Hommes illustres* [Plutarch's *Lives*].

On Saturday, August 5, the *Bellerophon* rendezvoused with the *Northumberland,* which had been designated to take the prisoner to St. Helena. There was a strong wind, and the sea was rough. As the storm rose, Napoleon addressed the following words to the world and to history:

> I hereby solemnly protest, before God and mankind, against the violence that has been done upon me, and against the violation of my most sacred rights, in dealing forcibly with my person and my liberty. I came on board the *Bellerophon* of my own free will. I am not a prisoner; I am the guest of England. I came, moreover, at the instigation of the captain, who said he had instructions from the Government to receive me and to take me to England with my retinue, if that was agreeable to me. I presented myself in good faith to come and put myself under the protection of the laws of England. Once on board the *Bellerophon,* I was at the hearth of the British nation.
>
> If the Government, in instructing the captain of the *Bellerophon* to receive me and my retinue, merely intended to set a trap for me, it has forfeited its honor and disgraced its flag. If this act is consummated, it will be futile for the British to tell Europe of their fairness, their laws, and their liberties. British honor will have been lost in the hospitality of the *Bellerophon.*
>
> I appeal to History: it will say that an enemy who was at war with the English nation for twenty years came voluntarily—in his misfortune—to seek asylum under its laws. What more striking proof could he have offered of his esteem and trust? But does England respond to such magnanimity? She pretended to reach out a hospitable hand to that enemy, and when he had handed himself over in good faith, she immolated him!

Who would accompany the exile? Savary and Lallemand had been ruled out by the British Government, since both of them were on a proscription list drawn up by Louis XVIII: Savary because of his role in the abduction of the Duc d'Enghien, and Lallemand because

in 1815, at the time of the flight "from steeple to steeple," he and his
division had taken sides with Napoleon.

The choice was difficult. Finally it fell upon Grand Marshal Henri
Bertrand (despite the tears of Mme. Bertrand) and Generals Montholon and Gourgaud. Mmes. Bertrand and Montholon, together with
their children, were to go along too. In addition, Napoleon succeeded
in having Las Cases accepted as "Secrétaire du Cabinet." His son
would accompany him. There were also eleven servants, headed up
by the loyal Marchand, the chief *valet de chambre*.

Then too, Napoleon had the "right" to designate a physician. He
asked an Irishman, Barry O'Meara, surgeon of the *Bellerophon*, if he
would like to accompany him. After consulting with his superiors, Dr.
O'Meara accepted. Lord Keith was delighted to see a British officer
in the exile's entourage, and hoped that O'Meara would not invoke
the principle of privileged communication to reject his superiors'
requests for information.

On the morning of Sunday, August 6, the *Northumberland*—a
large ship of seventy-four guns—dropped anchor not far from the
Bellerophon. Other vessels would make the long voyage as well: two
troop transports, a frigate, five brigs, and two store ships.

Lord Keith came on board the *Bellerophon* to introduce Admiral
George Cockburn, the jailer, to his prisoner. Napoleon was awaiting
them on the bridge.

"How do you do, General Buonaparte?" asked the admiral.

The Emperor frowned at the title.

Cockburn had come to read his Government's instructions to the
"general." Immediately incensed and offended, Napoleon listened to
the decisions that had been made with regard to him. His luggage
was to be inventoried without delay, and his weapons confiscated. At
St. Helena, he could go out for a ride or a walk only within a certain
area. If he wished to go beyond it, he would have to be accompanied
by a British officer. The correspondence of the "general" and of those
in his retinue would be censored. There was even a mention of the
decisions that would be taken in the event of his death; and His
Britannic Majesty pledged himself to respect the exile's testamentary
arrangements.

Napoleon burst out indignantly: "I never expected anything like
this! I simply do not see how anyone can reasonably object to my

spending the rest of my life peaceably in England!"

In his exasperation, he again brought up the argument that had become a kind of mania with him. "You sent ambassadors to me, as to a potentate! You recognized me as First Consul!"

Cockburn merely responded with another question; and in asking it, he apparently thought he was showing great respect. "At what time should I come tomorrow morning, General, and when may I receive you on board the *Northumberland?*"

The Emperor's rage left him. Impotent, vanquished, and resigned, he murmured: "At ten o'clock."

The distressing procedure of taking an inventory of the countless crates and pieces of baggage embarked on the *Bellerophon* from the island of Aix took place the next morning (Monday, August 7). Napoleon had succeeded in concealing the bulk of his fortune by entrusting it to his companions. The British seized only 5,500 napoléons, of which they returned 1,500 to the Emperor so that he could pay his servants' salaries.

When the procedure was completed, the British officer bowed to the "general," saying: "England demands your sword."

Napoleon put his hand on the hilt of his sword and glared so fiercely that the Englishman dared not insist. He stepped back sheepishly.

It was not until eleven o'clock that Admiral Cockburn and Lord Keith came aboard the *Bellerophon* to take charge of their prisoner. Since they had come late, Napoleon gave himself the pleasure of making them wait. Cockburn grew impatient, but Keith placated him: "He has made men much more important than you and I wait longer than this. Let him take his time."

At length Napoleon appeared, looking disheartened. The condemned man walked up to Maitland and took off his hat, saying: "Posterity will not hold you responsible for any part of what has happened. You were deceived as I was."

He next went over to the crew, mustered for the occasion. Then, still looking profoundly dejected, he came up to the little group of French officers headed by Savary and Lallemand. All of them wept unrestrainedly.

"As you can see, my lord," Las Cases whispered to Lord Keith, "those who are weeping are the ones who are staying behind."

As he was about to leave the ship, Napoleon turned one last time toward the officers of the *Bellerophon*, who were standing on the quarter-deck, and sadly waved good-by. Then he grasped the man-ropes of the gangway and climbed down the sea ladder to the long-boat of the *Northumberland*, where he took his seat between Lord Keith and Admiral Cockburn.

Bertrand was the first to go aboard the *Northumberland*, and he made one more attempt to assert his chief's rights by announcing in a loud voice: "The Emperor!"

But this time no honors were rendered to the exile. It was for Lord Keith that the drums rolled and the guard presented arms. Sourly, Napoleon raised his hat and said to Cockburn, "Monsieur, I am at your orders!"

Those orders were strict: henceforth, the prisoner was to be treated as "a general on the reserve list." In the wardroom, the admiral introduced the prisoner to his officers, who included Captain Ross, commanding the *Northumberland*, and Colonel Bingham, whose regiment (the Fifty-Third Infantry) was being taken to St. Helena to guard Napoleon.

The wardroom, which was of fine proportions, struck the Emperor as just what he needed as a study during the long voyage. But Cockburn refused: the wardroom belonged to all the officers in common. And "General Buonaparte" had no choice but to content himself with a small stateroom. Later the admiral claimed that his prisoner yielded "docilely, and with good grace." But actually, Napoleon's pride had made him dissemble: he was completely crushed.

Marchand had already set up the famous camp bed with the green curtains in the stateroom assigned to his master. It was there, between walks on deck, that for more than two months he would live, read, and begin to dictate his memoirs to Las Cases.

It was the Emperor who presided over the wardroom table. Cockburn did not object, but he was shocked when Napoleon, fatigued by the length of the meal, would leave the wardroom immediately after coffee, abandoning his table companions, who (following the English custom) liked to stay at the table and chat, passing the traditional flask of port from hand to hand. The first evening, the admiral gave a start. "I gather," he said, "that the general has not read Lord Chesterfield."

"Don't forget, Admiral," riposted Bertrand, "that you are speaking to a man who has been the ruler of the world, and that kings disputed the honor of being invited to his table."

Seventeen days after their departure, far out at sea, the *Northumberland* met up with a Neapolitan ship. The Emperor cupped his hands and called out in Italian: "Where do you come from?"

"Madeira," replied the captain.

"Where are you bound to?"

"Naples."

"Well, send word to Rome that on August the twenty-second, at sea, you met up with Napoleon, proscribed and deported to St. Helena."

XXVII

THE DRAMA OF ST. HELENA

. . . languished under Hudson Lowe.

HEINRICH HEINE

IN THE ARCHIVES OF THE CASTLE of Jamestown, St. Helena, one can still read these words in the Record Book:

> . . . *Northumberland* arrived Sunday the 15th, coming from England flying the pennant of Rear Admiral Sir George Cockburn and having on board General Napoleon Buonaparte and certain individuals as prisoners of the Crown. . . .

On that Sunday, October 15, 1815, standing on the bridge of the *Northumberland* with his eye to his field glass, the "prisoner of the Crown" gazed at that overwhelming red and brown wall which, from the dizzy height of 1,000 to 2,500 feet, falls in one solid mass into the sea.

It had taken seventy-two days to reach that Cyclops' cave of about 47 square miles. During those days the exiles had been exposed to frightful storms and torrential rains, plus a maddening dead calm lasting twenty long days during which the *Northumberland*, immobilized, seemed to be floating on a pond. It had taken seventy-two days to reach "the most isolated, the most inaccessible, the least attackable, and the most unsocial place in the world"—as it was described a few months later by the Marquis de Montchenu, who had been sent by Louis XVIII to keep watch on the troublemaker of Europe and his jailers.

The Emperor kept his gaze fixed. In a fault between two gigantic faces of red-ocher lava, crowned with a poor growth of yellowish grass, he could make out a kind of village. A steeple, tarred roofs, a few palms and, finally, a sinister, ramshackle structure called a castle: this was Jamestown, the capital of the island. And everywhere (as he could see through his field glass)—emplaced in the rock faces, bristling on the crests, overlooking the abyss, and nestled beneath crags —were the muzzles of cannon.

From a few paces away, those "individuals" mentioned in the Record Book—the Emperor's companions—dejected, frightened, and throats tight with anguish, watched their master's face. But he, unapproachable and disdainful, went down to his stateroom without saying a word. Nor did he confide his impressions to Las Cases, who had come (as he did every morning) to work with him. He may well have been distressed to see that his pride—and his desire to supply a good ending to his legend—had brought his loyal followers to such a dwelling place.

At noon the ship drew near the island. At the time Napoleon was with Gourgaud. He looked through the porthole at the gigantic rock which now filled the entire horizon.

"It's not exactly a nice place to live!" he exclaimed. "I would have done better to stay in Egypt. If I had, I would now be the Emperor of the whole Middle East."

There was no port, no pier—merely a wretched landing, a few slippery steps carved into the rock leading to an embankment along which some fig trees grew. When he went ashore Napoleon would go along this embankment to the postern in the rampart—a sally port which served as the main means of access to the town, passing as it did through the crenelated enceinte. This "capital" had only two or three "streets" lined with houses in the "colonial style."

But for the moment he was still an inmate of his floating prison. He had to stay there all that Sunday and throughout the next day, while Admiral Cockburn and the governor of St. Helena, Colonel Wilks, explored the rock in search of a suitable residence "for the general and his family."

Finally, the admiral returned to the ship and announced, almost gaily, that he had found a "very pretty house" up in the hills. While it was being made ready, he said, everyone would stay with Mr. William Porteous, who had a furnished house in Jamestown itself, on the edge of the park.

The next evening, the Emperor and his companions arrived at the Porteous house, where they were crowded into little rooms. One

can imagine their low state of morale in these miserable surroundings. The admiral himself went to stay at the manor house, but did
not think it proper to invite the Emperor there.

All night long, Napoleon could hear the crowd stirring about
beneath his windows. He got up and tried to read. It was almost dawn
when he finally fell asleep.

At six o'clock on the morning of Wednesday, October 18, the
admiral came to take him on a visit to Longwood, "the country house
which would later be the general's residence." Napoleon was not
ready, and Cockburn grew impatient.

Horses had been brought for them. Napoleon leaped on his
mount, and without waiting for his companions—the admiral, the
grand marshal, and Ali, the Mameluke—he went up the main street
at a fast gallop. But he soon had to stop and wait for Cockburn, since
he had come to a fork in the road.

The admiral indicated the street leading off to the left, which
before long became a steep, narrow path leading up the flank of a
basaltic mountain. Along one side of it ran a low wall, separating it
from the crevasse in which Jamestown lay nestled. Before reaching
the plateau, they came to a last hairpin turn in the path—"the turn
where you have to put on your coat," as they said on the island, since
here the temperature dropped abruptly and it became almost cold.
The vegetation was no longer tropical. The path was bordered by
Chilean pines, araucarias, and tamarisk, bent low by the wind. The
Emperor might well have imagined that he was back in the days of
his youth, except that this was a "Corsica" where volcanic eruptions
and earthquakes had produced upheavals and broken the rock into
debris.

The narrow road—a veritable isthmus—followed a sharp crest. To
the right was a green valley with a few houses, and to the left loomed
a gigantic crater called the Devil's Punch Bowl—a fitting name!
Black, rocky debris was strewn down the declivity, through a great
many ravines thick with pines, to the bottom of the abyss and the
edge of the sea. Behind them loomed the mountain chain from which
reared the conical peaks of Diana and Acteon.

The admiral announced, "This is Longwood."

"The long wood"! But the wood was nothing more than a small
clump of trees offering no shade.

They had covered more than eight kilometers since leaving

Jamestown. Leaving the road, they passed between two pavilions flanking the entrance to an *allée* of mulberry trees. At last, some shade! At the far end of the tree-lined drive was the house: an old farmhouse with a low façade, walls of pinkish ocher, green shutters, and a roof covered with tarpaper.

Desolation was undisputed master of the place; and yet Napoleon's first reaction upon viewing his "prison" was not unfavorable. He did not realize that this arid plateau was often exposed to very strong winds. Nor was he aware that the difference in temperature between Jamestown and Longwood was often as much as 14 degrees, whereas the climate of the western and southern parts of St. Helena was comparable to that of the Canary Islands.

That morning the sun was shining brightly, and the occupants of Longwood—Lieutenant Governor Skelton and his wife, who spent the warm season there—welcomed their guests most hospitably. Napoleon looked over the dwelling—five small rooms and numerous annexes into which his officers and servants would one day be crowded—and he listened as the admiral told him of the improvements he had planned.

And yet the Emperor was puzzled. Why hadn't his residence been fixed at Plantation House, a manor house with some twenty rooms? Plantation House had a beautiful reception room which was luxuriously appointed, and it was surrounded by a handsome, large park of some 220 acres. But it was the Governor's residence; and the admiral considered (as Sir Hudson Lowe did later) that it was not fitting that the prisoner should occupy better quarters than his jailer. Moreoever (although Napoleon was as yet unaware of the fact) the southeastern part of the island around Blue Mountain was scenically admirable, varying from a kind of magnificent wilderness to green valleys reminiscent of the smaller Jura Mountains. But Longwood, situated on an arid plateau hemmed in by ravines, and close to the military camp, could be easily watched; and that was the major concern of the English.

As they were returning to Jamestown, Napoleon noticed—to his right, halfway down the slope of the mountain and not far from a waterfall—a charming house with a red roof, nestled in among cypresses, banana palms, pomegranate trees, and laurels. The garden seemed full of flowers. In answer to the question put by his prisoner, Cockburn replied that this was "The Briars." The Emperor expressed a desire to visit the estate, and he and his party rode up the long drive lined with fig trees and eucalyptus, leading to the house.

The Briars was the property of Mr. Balcombe, an agent of the East India Company for the ships which put in at St. Helena. When the introductions had been made, Napoleon went out to admire the lovely flower garden. Across from the house, a short, winding, rocky road, bordered with geraniums, led to a little pavilion on a rise of ground. Its double roof gave it the appearance of a Chinese pagoda. This was the children's playhouse, and the whole family took tea there on rainy days.

Instead of returning to the noisy Porteous house to wait until Longwood was ready for his occupancy, why should not the Emperor stay in this bungalow? Mrs. Balcombe objected that it had only one main room with a garret above it—an objection quickly overcome when Napoleon remarked that he had occupied much worse quarters when on campaign. And the admiral gave his consent.

Napoleon's seven-week stay at The Briars is an odd chapter in the history of his captivity. His accommodations were almost primitive in this pavilion which lacked even shutters and was furnished only with his famous camp bed, his silver washbowl, a chest of drawers, a table, and a few chairs. He was deprived of the hot baths he believed to be good for his health. And as Las Cases said:

> His companions and servants were quartered two miles away from him. They had to be accompanied by a soldier when they came to be with him. They were not allowed to carry their weapons. And if they returned to Jamestown too late, or if there was a garbling of the password—which happened almost every day— they had to spend the night in the guardhouse.

He was also guarded by an officer and two sergeants of the Fifty-Third, who pitched their tent in the garden. But for the first time in many years he was no longer obliged to live up to his role as Emperor —not even a captive Emperor, as on the *Northumberland*. Perhaps some of his happiest days were spent at The Briars.

And yet it was there that Napoleon realized for the first time that St. Helena was a prison. In taking over his job as jailer, Admiral Cockburn had issued very strict orders. The islanders were not allowed to speak to the "general" or the members of his retinue without the governor's authorization. Patrols constantly ranged over the island, arresting everyone who did not know the password. All the ships had to be back at their moorings by 9:00 P.M. Night and day, two brigs were on patrol around the island, one sailing before the wind and the other into it. Every individual who sighted and reported a suspect vessel was awarded one piaster. And anyone reporting a violation of the regulations received a reward which might go as high as 25 pounds. The government's instructions to the admiral stipulated that all letters written by the prisoners had to be submitted "open" to the governor, who was authorized to subjoin, to any demands that the "general" might formulate, "whatever observations he deemed suitable." And he had categorical orders to throw the Emperor in prison if he made any attempt to escape.

When Napoleon learned of these regulations, he exclaimed:

> This is the agony of death! To injustice and duress they have added outrage and prolonged torture! If I was so noxious to them, why didn't they simply do away with me? A few bullets in the heart or the head would have sufficed. And it would at least have been a *vigorous* kind of crime. . . . Make your protests, Messieurs, and may Europe learn of them and be made indignant! Any protest from me would be beneath my dignity and my character.

And he added a phrase which bears his own trademark: "I either give orders or I remain silent."

Then he dictated the following note, which Bertrand was to sign:

> The Emperor wishes to have news of his wife and son by the next boat, and to learn whether the latter is still alive.
> He takes advantage of this opportunity to reiterate and bring to the attention of the British Government those protests he has already registered against the strange measures taken against him. The Government has declared that he is a prisoner of war. The Emperor is not a prisoner of war. . . .

Cockburn replied:

> You compel me to declare to you officially that I am not aware that there is now an emperor on this island, or that any person with that title came here with me on the *Northumberland*, as you have indicated to me. I have taken, and shall continue to take, every care to make your position—yours and that of the other distinguished officers who have accompanied you here—as devoid of unpleasantness and painfulness as is possible under the

circumstances. I can assure you that I sincerely regret that my efforts to this end have not yet been crowned with success. . . .

This matter of the imperial "title" would poison the rest of Napoleon's life at St. Helena. For a Frenchman, a sovereign who has abdicated continues to be addressed as "Sire" and "Your Majesty"— as was the case with Charles X, Louis Philippe, and Napoleon III. In Napoleon's case, although the British had recognized "the First Consul, General Bonaparte," they had continued to ignore the existence of an "Emperor Napoleon" even though he had been anointed by the Pope and crowned King of Italy—not to mention his other titles, by virtue of which he reigned over some three-fourths of Europe. But the British simply canceled out some twenty years of history: for them, the exile was merely "General Buonaparte." At the very most, they condescended to eliminate the *u* from his name.

Everything might have been straightened out if the British had accepted their prisoner's proposal that he take a different name, such as "Colonel Duroc" or the "Comte de Lyon"—although the latter title had been borne by canons of the Church. It is a privilege of sovereigns to change their civil status, but this was precisely why the governors refused this proposal. For them, "the Emperor Napoleon" did not exist.

Napoleon had hopes that his tether would be lengthened when he was at Longwood. But Las Cases, who had been there to see how the improvements were getting on, told him: "Sire, here we are in a cage. There, we'll be penned up."

And as a matter of fact, the day would come when the Emperor would look back on The Briars as a kind of Eden. On the other hand, at Longwood it would be easier for him to weave his legend with consummate art.

On Sunday, December 10, Cockburn came to get his prisoner: Longwood was ready for his occupancy.

It was raining when the little cortege climbed up toward the wind-swept plateau. But then the sun came out between two clouds and greeted the Emperor on the threshold of his prison—that prison he would leave only when lying in his coffin.

Napoleon lived four years and five months of his life in a T-shaped building in this foggy climate. As for the furniture: "I have managed," wrote Cockburn to London, "to procure all the indispens-able articles at the lowest bargain prices." The room was adorned by two maps of the world. For the antechamber, the governor provided a big, ugly billiard table. Napoleon seldom played billiards on it, preferring to push the balls around with his hands. But he did use it as a place to spread out his maps. And it was on this same billiard table that the autopsy on his body would be performed.

Beyond the salon was the dining room, likewise poorly furnished, with two other doors. The one on the left led to the library, and that on the right to the Emperor's study and bedroom. In each of these little rooms, hung in cream-colored nankeen with borders of red roses, was one of the Emperor's camp beds. During his long, sleepless nights, the prisoner liked to go from one bed to the other. Or he would stretch out on a couch.

Marchand did as well as anyone could have done in arranging what Napoleon called, out of old habit, his "interior." In it he placed a portrait of Marie Louise holding the King of Rome in her arms, another portrait of the little King painted by Isabey, Frederick the Great's silver dressing case, and a few miniatures.

Had it not been for the small size of the rooms and their poor arrangement (the Emperor had to pass through the dining room in order to go to the salon from his bedroom), the general accommoda-tions would not have been particularly bad.

The two sash windows faced the north (directly into the sun of the Southern Hemisphere), and looked out over the little garden where the Emperor felt almost at home. During the day he could walk there at leisure—there, and elsewhere within the pale, which was seven kilometers in length and enclosed by a low wall. Along this wall, at fifty paces from one another, stood the sentinels. At night they left these posts and took up positions around the house.

When he wished, Napoleon could go horseback riding beyond these limits in a second enclosed area called "the twelve-mile enclo-sure." At each bend in the road, the presence of the patrols reminded him that he was a prisoner. If he wanted to visit any other part of the island beyond the fortified areas, he had to notify the British officer stationed at Longwood, who would then accompany "General Buonaparte."

At Longwood, the exiles lived like so many sardines in a can. The occupants included the three generals, Mmes. Bertrand and Montho-

lon and their children, Las Cases and his wife, Dr. O'Meara, twelve
servants, and some dozen sailors from the *Northumberland* who had
become domestics in the household. On December 29, their number
was increased by the arrival of a Polish officer, one Piontkowski, who
had somehow reached St. Helena. The Emperor and his companions
declared they had never seen him before, and the historians know
no more about him than they did. In any case, this gentleman—a
braggart and a bit of an adventurer—left the island a year later.

The Emperor tried to keep up his morale by maintaining the
customs of the Tuileries on St. Helena. Shielded by protocol, he felt
that he was still the Emperor. In the evening Cipriani, the butler,
wearing a green uniform trimmed in silver, would announce: "His
Majesty is served." The officers in full dress uniform and the ladies
in décolleté dresses would gather around the table, which was brilliantly illuminated and served by footmen wearing the uniforms of
the Tuileries. All the serving dishes were of silver, the plate of silver
gilt, and the famous "headquarters" service would make its appearance at dessert. The meal included soup, a remove, two entrées, a
roast, two side dishes, and sweets prepared by Pierron. They forgot
that the dining room was tiny and wretched; they forgot the rain
beating on the tarpaper roof; they forgot that "redcoats" were on
guard all around the house; that 500 officers and 2,500 soldiers, with
their eyes fixed on this ramshackle dwelling, were watching and
spying on the fallen ruler; that a guard was posted at every "hole in
the fence" between the coast and the interior; that two warships
were constantly patrolling around the island; that 500 cannon were
pointed out toward sea; that the island was bristling with signaling
apparatus to transmit the slightest news item about the prisoners;
that at night, not a single inhabitant of the island dared step outside
his home without knowing the famous password.

After dinner the exiles found that killing time was difficult. They
would play reversi or chess; Mme. de Montholon would play the
piano and sing; or the Emperor would read—aloud and very badly
—a tragedy. Toward ten o'clock, he would stand up and sigh: "Another day has gone by."

On Sunday, April 14, 1816, the Emperor's calash, drawn by six
horses with the Archambault brothers as postilions, drew up before
the little perron of Longwood. General Gourgaud and the Polish

officer, Piontkowski, were standing beside their horses. In accordance with the custom, they were to gallop alongside the carriage— not without difficulty, since the narrow roads on St. Helena almost always went along the brinks of precipices.

On that Easter Sunday the Emperor had called for his carriage so that he could go up to the crest. From there, through his field glass, he could see the harbor and watch the frigate *Phaeton* enter it and drop anchor.

On board that frigate was the new governor general, Sir Hudson Lowe.

Lowe did not even wait until his first interview with the Emperor to give himself the trouble—or the pleasure—of conveying the instructions of Lord Bathurst (the British Minister of War and Colonial Secretary). That very same day he transmitted them to Bertrand. Napoleon's officers and servants were to pledge, in writing, that they would abide by "all the restrictions it is necessary to impose upon Napoleon Bonaparte personally." Those who refused would be shipped off to Europe via the Cape.

Instantly, the whole household was in an uproar.

"Eh bien," said Napoleon to General Gourgaud, "have you heard the news? You must either go to the Cape or promise to share my fate in perpetuity."

"That was all we needed to complete the horror of our situation!" exclaimed the young aide-de-camp. "Do you mean to rob us of the hope of ever seeing our families again?"

And in his diary he noted: "It was a most melancholy dinner."

Napoleon ordered his entourage not to sign the statement demanded by Lord Bathurst. He dictated a new text:

> We, the undersigned, desirous of continuing in the service of *the Emperor Napoleon*, agree to remain on St. Helena, however frightful our sojourn there, abiding by the restrictions imposed upon His Majesty and the persons in his service, even though those restrictions are unjust and arbitrary.

They all agreed to sign. But a conflict—the first between the prisoner and his jailer—was brewing. Following the admiral's example, Lowe refused to allow the use of the imperial title in the statement. After considerable grumbling and protesting, and a vain attempt at negotiating with the governor, the French finally signed a text in which the prisoner was referred to as "Napoleon Bonaparte."

Then came the second conflict. Astonished by the unanimous loyalty manifested by the members of the Emperor's suite, Lowe made a point of interrogating the servants personally to find out if any of them had signed under coercion. He was convinced that Montholon—the chief of the household—had influenced them. But he had to yield before the facts. As he left Longwood, he stated: "I am now satisfied. I can inform my Government that they all signed of their own accord and free will."

Meantime, Napoleon had finally received a copy of the agreement signed among the Allied Powers on "the measures most suitable to render impossible any attempt" on the part of "Napoleon Bonaparte against the repose of Europe." The man who had been defeated at Waterloo was declared to be a prisoner of the Powers, and his custody was "specially entrusted to the British Sovereign," but Austria, Russia, and even France were each to send an observer to the island.

"It is being said that the sovereigns have restrained me physically by a treaty. By what right? I am their equal, and I was often their master! I am not their prisoner!"

This protest was made to Lowe, and the governor nodded his approval. He, too, considered that "General Bonaparte" was the prisoner of England alone.

For a week, a combination of bad weather and Napoleon's lassitude had prevented him from going outside. At their second interview, the Emperor received Lowe in a dressing gown, lying on the couch in his bedroom.

"I came to seek asylum in a country whose laws were believed to be all-powerful—a nation whose greatest enemy I had been for twenty years. But what did your people do?"

He got up from his couch and began to pace as was his habit. The wind was blowing in strong gusts, shaking the house; and the rain was lashing at the panes in the two sash windows.

I was put in the most unhealthful part of the island, where it is always windy and foggy. The climate is not like ours: it has neither our sun nor our seasons. An atmosphere of deadly boredom reigns here. This location is unpleasant and unhealthful.

There is no water. This part of the island is deserted—it has repelled its own inhabitants!

Lowe meekly observed that his Government was doing all it could to alleviate the situation of "the general," and the prisoner exclaimed:

> Those efforts amount to very little. I requested subscriptions to the *Morning Chronicle* and the *Statesman* so that I might read about "the question" in the least unpleasant phraseology. Nothing was done. I asked for books—my only consolation. Nine months have gone by, and I have not received them. I asked for news of my son and my wife, but no one gave me any.

When the governor could find nothing to say, the Emperor went on to talk about his wretched dwelling.

Lowe tried to interrupt the flow of words, but without success:

> You and I are soldiers, Monsieur. We appreciate those things, know what they are worth. You have been in the town where I was born, perhaps in my house. Although it is not the poorest house on the island, and is not one to be ashamed of, you saw that it was not much. And I tell you that though I may have sat on a throne and handed out crowns, I never forgot my early living conditions. My couch and my camp bed, there, are enough for me!

During this second interview, Lowe had been clumsy and stupid, but he had not committed any breach of good manners. And yet Napoleon maintained Lowe was capable of poisoning him: "If a man like that has been near your cup of coffee for as much as a moment, you had better not drink it."

Ten days later there was another scene. The governor had come to convey his Government's instructions to the prisoner. "The general" had to be viewed every day by a British officer; "the general" could not leave his compound without a guard. And Napoleon exploded:

> In the month that you have been here, you have destroyed all my trust in you. When I learned of your arrival, I was glad that I would be dealing with an infantry general who, having been involved in the important affairs of the Continent, would understand that he should employ vis-à-vis me only those measures

dictated by suitability. But I was grossly deceived. You say that you offer me the whole of the island's interior for horseback riding; but you know very well that your offer is only a joke, since I must be accompanied by one of your officers. Soldiers who have smelled gunpowder are all the same in my eyes, whatever the color of their uniforms. It is not the red uniform of your officers that annoys me. It is simply that I refuse to acknowledge, by any of my behavior, that I am your prisoner.

It must be said in Lowe's favor that he had informed his superiors of Napoleon's "repugnance" at being accompanied by a British officer when going beyond the limits that had been fixed for him. But Lord Bathurst had replied: "Not only must General Bonaparte be accompanied by a British officer when he goes outside the limits, but that officer must be ordered to prevent, insofar as possible, any intercourse that General Bonaparte might seem disposed to maintain with the inhabitants."

Unquestionably, Lowe was far from being the horrible hangman depicted by the Napoleonic legend. In reading the accounts of the eyewitnesses, one realizes that the blame must often be laid at the door of Longwood. For the sake of history, Napoleon had to be persecuted. As he was heard to say one day: "Jesus Christ would not still be God were it not for his crown of thorns. It was his martyrdom that stirred up the imagination of the masses. If instead of being here I were in America, like Joseph, I would be forgotten and my cause would be lost. Voilà les hommes!"

And Gourgaud said frankly: "In my opinion, Hudson Lowe rendered a great service to the Emperor by means of his ill-advised procedures: with anyone else, there would have been no grounds for complaints."

Or, as Montholon put it: "Even if the governor of St. Helena had been an angel from heaven, he could not have pleased us."

Sir Hudson Lowe was far from being an angel. In fact, his tactlessness was extraordinary. Thus a few days after this second interview he had the temerity to invite (with kind of disarming innocence) "General Bonaparte" to dine at Plantation House so that he could meet Lady Loudon-Moïra, who was visiting the island on her way back from the East Indies.

"No reply!" exclaimed Napoleon. "It's just too stupid!"

"It seemed quite natural to me," Lowe explained later. "I was going beyond my instructions, since in accepting a dinner invitation, General Bonaparte could have had the impression of being free."

There was another scene between the two of them on July 16. After greeting the governor, Napoleon burst out: "Every day brings more needless annoyances! Las Cases sent Mr. Balcombe a shoe so that he could have a pair of boots made for him in England. You had the shoe returned, saying it should have been sent to you directly. I fail to see why old shoes have to be sent to you, as though keeping you informed were not enough!"

"My intentions were maliciously interpreted."

"Your conduct will bring reproach upon your nation and your Government. . . . Shall I tell you what we think of you? We think you are capable of anything, and would even make us drink hemlock. The Grand Marshal [Bertrand] used to be allowed to issue passes. But now he can't. The result is that I cannot invite anyone to dinner. And if I had a mistress, I couldn't even send for her."

"You don't have a mistress."

"But I may have one."

"Oh? I shall report that to the Government."

"But that's not the question. It wasn't a corporal that the Government sent here. It was a lieutenant general that England sent here; and it's up to him to behave properly. You are a man with a score to settle against us here."

And, once again, Napoleon enumerated all his grievances against his jailer, concluding with an apt metaphor: "You are sticking pins in our backs!"

Another drama (a latent one) was being played out on St. Helena, and it would bring the conflict to the point of paroxysm. It had to do with expenses, which at Longwood were extravagant. The servants, apparently believing they were still at the Tuileries, were reselling a portion of the provisions. The governor therefore issued orders that henceforth "daily" deliveries for the ten masters and twenty servants should not exceed 70 pounds of beef and mutton and 7 chickens. Also, the monthly provisions were to consist of 22 roasts, 9 hams, 9 salted tongues, and 45 pounds of bacon, not to mention vegetables, other groceries, and dairy products. Finally, Longwood would receive, every month, 210 bottles of Bordeaux, 26 bottles of champagne, 23 bottles of Madeira, 60 bottles of Graves, and 11 bottles of

Constance. Each of the servants would receive one bottle *vin or-dinaire* per day. This was not exactly a life style of poverty. But the prisoners pleaded poverty anyway.

Moreover, when the governor requested that the empty bottles be returned to him (the wine was brought in from the Cape, and the supply problem was not simple), the servants made haste to break them.

The heap of broken bottles—placed ostentatiously in front of the outbuildings at Longwood—was a most distressing sight for the governor. Lowe, in his attempts to economize, was taking measures that his prisoners would exploit cleverly, measures which would soon enable Napoleon to order the spectacular sale of his silver plate in order "to provide for" his needs.

This waste was the subject of a violent argument between Bertrand and the governor. Then two days later, on Sunday, August 18, Lowe came hurrying to Longwood to protest to Napoleon himself. This scene took place in the garden, which consisted simply of a flower bed surrounded by a circular walk on which one could stroll while chatting. Admiral Malcolm, now commanding the naval forces based on the island, was present. The Emperor said:

> Eh bien, Grand Marshal Bertrand wants nothing more to do with you. It is very simple. He has been a high-ranking officer of the Crown; he fought, as commander of his own army corps, against the army in which you yourself were a colonel attached to headquarters staff. But you write to him, and speak to him, not even as to a corporal of brave regular troops, but as you did to the corporals of the Corsican soldiers you commanded, all of whom were deserters and traitors to their country. He has taken offense at this and no longer wants to have anything to do with you. For that matter, no one wants to see any more of you. Everyone wants to avoid you. There is not a single one of these gentlemen who, if he had a choice between four days on bread and water in his room and a talk with you, would not prefer the former.

Lowe tried to bring the problem down to a simpler level, and again brought up the subject of expenses. But Napoleon could not be stopped:

> You really don't know me at all. My body is captive to evil men, but my soul is independent. It is as proud here as if I were

at the head of 600,000 troops and were still on my throne, creating kings and handing out crowns. You are always telling me about your instructions. But none of them compels you to do what you are doing. For that matter, this is no excuse. I have ruled, and I know that there are missions and instructions that one gives only to dishonored men.

"You are staining my name in the eyes of Europe," said Lowe. "That is unfair. I have instructions which—"

"But the hangman, too, has his instructions," interrupted the prisoner. "He carries them out, and it's all very simple. But at least one isn't asked to live under the same roof with him. You have your instructions: carry them out and leave me in peace. If you don't want to give us food, then don't. As long as we have the Fifty-Third Regiment as neighbors, they won't let us starve."

"For me, all that goes in one ear and out the other," said Lowe.

"To be sure, the hangman laughs when his victims cry out."

Such is the scene as described by Bertrand, who witnessed it from a distance and based *his* account on what the Emperor told him. In view of this, it seems only fair to let Sir Hudson Lowe have his say.

According to him, the scene began with a long silence—"so long," he wrote to Lord Bathurst, "that I concluded he was resolved not to speak at all." Finally, "in a tone of annoyance," the Emperor began to speak, ignoring the presence of the governor and addressing himself only to the admiral: "There are two sorts of men that governments make use of: those they value and those they hold in contempt. *He* is among the latter. The position they gave *him* is that of a hangman."

Lowe replied, "I understand this kind of tactics perfectly. When you have no other weapons with which to attack a man, try to dishonor him with infamy. I am quite indifferent to all that. I did not ask for my present position, but when it was offered to me I felt that I had a sacred duty to accept it."

"And so if you were given an order to assassinate me, you would carry it out?"

"No, Sir."

Napoleon then went on talking to the admiral [Lowe continues], telling him that I had made his situation forty times worse than it was before my arrival. . . . He said I had no sensitivity, that the soldiers of the Fifty-Third, when they passed near him, looked at him with compassion and wept. Then he told the admiral: *"He kept a book that had been sent to me by a Member of Parliament, and then boasted of it."*

"What? I boasted of it?"

"Yes Monsieur, you boasted of it to the Governor of Bourbon [Réunion] Island. He told me so."

The tension was increasing. "My body is in your power," the Emperor repeated, "but my soul is free. You are treating me like a Botany Bay convict—and Europe will hear about it."

Once again, the governor defended his position. "I should be most glad if everything relative to my conduct were published, not only in the English newspapers but in all those on the Continent as well."

He complained of our addressing him as "General" [Lowe continues], and said he was "the Emperor." [He said] that when England and Europe no longer existed and no one remembered the name of Lord Bathurst, he would still be "the Emperor." He told me that he was doing everything possible to avoid me, and that twice he had pretended to be in his bath so that he would not have to see me.

The three men went on walking around the flower bed, as Napoleon told Lowe: "You want money, but I don't have any except for what is in the possession of my friends. But I am not allowed to send letters. You have never commanded armies. You were nothing more than staff clerk. I had imagined that I would be well received by the English, but you are not an Englishman."

If he had dared, Lowe would have shrugged his shoulders. Instead he merely said: "Sir, you make me smile."

"What? I make you smile, Monsieur? I am merely saying what I think."

"Yes, Sir, you make me smile. The false opinion that you have formed of my character and the rudeness of your manners arouse my pity. I wish you good day."

Lowe turned on his heel without taking formal leave of his prisoner. The admiral raised his hat, bowed, and then went to join Lowe, who while waiting for his horse exclaimed to Bertrand: "General Bonaparte treated me very offensively. I left him rather abruptly, telling him, 'Sir, you are rude!' "

The Emperor admitted later that he had treated the Governor very badly, and concluded: "I must not receive that officer any more. He makes me angry, and that is beneath my dignity. When he is here, I say things which would have been unpardonable at the Tuileries. If there is any excuse for them here, it is that I am in his hands and in his power."

Napoleon's jailer, Sir Hudson Lowe, was choleric, irritable, vainglorious, pedantic, niggling, and terrified by his responsibilities. But above all, he was clumsy.

M. de Balmain, the Russian observer at St. Helena, said of him: "He is a narrow-minded person—a man who is overwhelmed and frightened by the responsibility he bears. He is alarmed by the slightest thing, racks his brain over trifles, and must make a great effort and fuss-and-bother to accomplish what another man could do while scarcely stirring."

Certainly, Lowe was "lacking in education and judgment," as Wellington remarked, adding that he was "a damned fool."

After their argument, not a single week went by in which the jailer did not torment his prisoner. The limits within which Napoleon could go horseback riding without being under guard were reduced by one-third; and Lord Bathurst demanded "categorically" that the British orderly officer verify the presence of "the general" twice a day. On the other hand, not a single week went by in which the prisoner did not do his utmost to be martyred: "Oppression and insults add to my fame. I shall be indebted to England for the radiance of my glory."

Napoleon kept his word: he never met with Sir Hudson Lowe again. When the governor again came to Longwood, his prisoner watched him, with the field glass he had used at Austerlitz, through holes he had had drilled in the shutters of the antechamber.

The governor did not see the Emperor again until Napoleon was laid out on his deathbed, that little iron bed he had carried about with him on all his campaigns.

Except for the boy who had now become the Duke of Reichstadt (the former King of Rome), and the impoverished "grumblers" on half-pay who would get together to talk about their idol, nearly everyone had forgotten Napoleon. Of all the high dignitaries of the

Empire who owed their success to him, not one tried to send him a single word. As for the members of the "clan"—apart from Pauline —their chief concern was to court oblivion and be tolerated by the new masters of Europe; or else, like Joseph, to live out a life of gilded exile in the New World.

Napoleon himself, however, thought long and often about his past grandeur and what he had become since. He could not sleep at night: memories assailed and overwhelmed him.

He was perfectly aware of everything he had contributed to the world; and his companions once heard him argue his case in a voice that might have come from beyond the grave:

> For all the attempts at curtailment, suppression, and mutila-tion, it will be hard to make me disappear completely. French historians will have to deal with the Empire; and if they have any spirit, they will have to restore something to me and give me my rightful due. And the task will be easy, because the facts speak for themselves—they shine like the sun. . . . I closed up the abyss of anarchy and brought order out of chaos. I inspired emulation in everyone, rewarded merit wherever I found it, and advanced the frontiers of glory. . . . What charges can be brought against me that a historian could not refute? . . . My despotism? But the historian will prove that dictatorship was urgently necessary. Shall I be accused of having been too fond of war? He will show that I was always attacked. Of having tried to set up a universal monarchy? He will make it plain that this was only the fortuitous product of circumstances; that it was our enemies themselves who brought me to it, step by step. . . .

He had frequent fits of anger. They were not due to pride or cruelty (as his warders maintained) but to his rage at realizing how low he had fallen and to what extent others had often "failed him," as he put it. He tyrannized over his companions. When he could not sleep, he would call for one of his unfortunate officers in the middle of the night (and they had to report in uniform, as at the Tuileries) to dictate an endless protest addressed to the world or an equally interminable explanation of the Battle of Waterloo.

"You are no longer anything but a little handful of people at the other end of the world," he told his companions on the morning of New Year's Day, 1816. "You should at least enjoy the consolation of loving one another."

Actually, they didn't like one another at all; and their mutual envy was bitter. Under their crowded living conditions, the men quarreled over precedence and functions, and the two ladies called each other "whore."

One and the same thought preoccupied all of them: to get off that horrid rock called St. Helena. Las Cases was the first to go, although he had been the best treated. He was followed by Gourgaud, an irritable and oversensitive fellow.

Then it was Dr. O'Meara's turn to leave St. Helena: he had refused to report the gossip of Longwood to Lowe. He had not always been so recalcitrant. But of late the governor had managed to make himself detested by the doctor, who henceforth refused to spy on the prisoners. The conflict between the two men grew sharp. Lowe went so far as to restrain O'Meara from traveling between Longwood and Jamestown; and this attitude provoked the Emperor's physician to abandon his patient and go back to Europe.

Napoleon felt that it was wrong to have foisted upon him a physician whom Lowe had chosen—one who, in Napoleon's opinion, would become a kind of spy placed at his bedside by the governor. The result was that for the next six months the Emperor had no medical care except that provided by his companions in accordance with O'Meara's instructions.

In January, 1819, the Emperor's health was so bad (repeated fainting spells and complaints of a sharp pain in the right side) that he agreed to an examination by one of Dr. O'Meara's friends, Dr. Stokoe, the surgeon of the *Conqueror*. The diagnosis was chronic hepatitis.

"How long can a person live with that kind of illness?" Napoleon asked Dr. Stokoe.

"Why, there are some people with it who live to a very old age!"

"Yes, but are the chances the same in a tropical climate?"

"No."

"What is the thing most to be feared?"

"That the hepatitis becomes acute."

Stokoe repeated the conversation to Lowe. If those words had been spread through Europe, they would have shown conclusively that the climate on the plateau of Longwood was unhealthful. But their only effect on the governor was to throw him into a mortal terror. As a result, he made things very rough for Stokoe; and he, too, asked to be sent back to England.

But Lowe, who had called the doctor a "great culprit," had him court-martialed, accusing him, *inter alia*, of having used the word "the patient" in referring to "the general," and of having written "alarming medical reports." The unfortunate man was retired with a pension of 100 pounds.

And for the next seven months, the Emperor was again without a physician—pending the arrival of the mediocre Dr. Francesco Antommarchi.

Early in March, 1819, Napoleon learned that the sovereigns and ministers meeting in congress at Aachen had decided to keep Europe's prisoner—that "power of the Revolution concentrated in one individual"—on St. Helena until his death. Thus was he "put beyond the law of the nations," as Russia had demanded. Until he learned of that decision, Napoleon had hoped that some day he could leave his prison. Now he knew the rocky island would be his burial site. And he was not yet fifty years old.

His disillusionment was frightful and total. He locked himself in his room and refused to come out. His insomnia became interminable. And whenever he did manage a brief, leaden sleep, he would awaken in a sweat to the mediocrity of his "toy court" and—as always—that plateau swept by the incessant trade winds.

After Las Cases, Gourgaud, O'Meara, and Stokoe, it was Mme. de Montholon's turn to leave the island. She was exhausted after her labor in giving birth to her baby daughter, Napoléone. (Born in 1817, Napoléone lived until 1907—the last survivor of the captivity. Some of her grandchildren, who would rather be descendants of Napoleon than of Tristan de Montholon, say she was the Emperor's daughter, but of course with no proof.) Besides, she had to think of the two children she had left in France. Montholon was supposed to accompany his wife. But thanks to splendid testamentary promises, Napoleon persuaded him to stay on for two more years.

On July 1, 1819, Albine de Montholon and her children, tearful, left Longwood forever. The Emperor, who had feelings of both gratitude and affection for her (it is not known just how far things had gone between them), watched the little group recede into the distance and wept—"perhaps for the first time in his life," Montholon wrote to his wife.

Napoleon then went to see Mme. Bertrand, who was rather ill that evening. As he came outside, he saw the guards, already drawing near to the building. He gave up the idea of taking the air, and went back to his quarters, where he stumbled and almost fell: two rats had run between his feet.

Once again, the Emperor was feeling ill. For the first time, he wrote his will; and he refused to leave his room. Fearing an escape, Lowe rushed to Longwood and insisted that the orderly officer, Captain Nicholls, stationed in an outbuilding of the Emperor's house, must be able to fulfill his mission: he must make sure of the prisoner's presence. One day the captain even climbed up to the window of the little room where Napoleon was taking his bath and (as he wrote in his report) saw the Emperor *in naturalibus*. But that wasn't enough for Sir Hudson, who kept prowling around the house, sent an officer to knock on the door, summoned the servants, asked to speak to Montholon or Bertrand, and finally ordered Nicholls to view "the general," by force if necessary.

At this, Napoleon had his windows barred, and muskets and pistols placed beside his bed. "He swore," Ali tells us, "that if anyone dared to cross his threshold, he would stretch him out there. And he added that no one would come into his room until he, Napoleon, was a corpse."

The Emperor, living in virtual solitude, would receive no more strangers. Montholon had been near to a feeling of panic when he let his wife leave. He had told Lowe that "he would not stay on the island for more than six months after the departure of his wife." The Bertrands, too, were thinking only of being relieved of their duties.

Napoleon could not forget Albine de Montholon. The distress caused by her departure stayed with him, and imparted a gloomy cast to his thoughts. "Your wife used to strew flowers on my burial plot," he told Montholon. "Since she left, only brambles grow there."

Perhaps, when Napoleon mentioned brambles, he was thinking of Mme. Bertrand (Fanny). She no longer came to Longwood. Since Mme. Montholon had left, the undeniable charm of Bertrand's wife had had its effect on Napoleon. He had come to like her "drawing-room bosom." Fanny was a tall, slender, elegant blonde with blue eyes. Her unpleasantly prominent nose was the only flaw in her face. Napoleon gave her to understand that there was a vacancy.

"She is so stupid that she doesn't come to see me," he complained. "And yet I could give her a diamond locket."

But Fanny wrapped herself in the cloak of her dignity: she could not possibly betray the Grand Marshal!

On the other hand, Dr. Antommarchi (recently arrived from Italy) was received by the Bertrands every day; and Napoleon evinced his envy of this intimacy. Embittered and angry at the doctor, he exclaimed: "I will never forgive him for having taken care of a woman who did not want to be his mistress, and for having urged her to it."

But then he decided to make use of the relationship between the doctor and Fanny. Incredibly, he asked Antommarchi to plead his cause with the "cruel fair."

As he admitted to the lady's husband: "I wanted Antommarchi to act as my 'Mercury' and persuade Madame Bertrand to be my mistress." (This statement is actually recorded in the journal kept by the Grand Marshal.)

That same day, Napoleon told him: "You should have prostituted your wife. It was your duty to persuade her."

"For that matter," Bertrand adds humorously in his journal (speaking of himself in the third person), "the Grand Marshal always agreed with the Emperor and never complained!"

Understandably enough, the Grand Marshal wanted to leave the island. But Napoleon didn't want to let him leave unless he found a replacement. One day Marchand noticed in his master's desk a list of names written in pencil: Caulaincourt, Rovigo, Ségur, Montesquiou, Daru, Drouot, Turenne, Arnaud, Denon. The Emperor was unwilling to entertain the prospect of no longer having with him, in the presence of the English, a *grand-officier de la Couronne*—a title which Montholon did not possess. But those *grands-officiers* the Emperor was thinking of—would they agree to leave everything and go off to be buried alive on that rock?

Silence was the only response to the Emperor. And so one day he told Montholon to inform Lowe ". . . that he would abide entirely by the choice made by King Louis XVIII and his ministers, and would gladly receive anyone who might have been employed in his civil or military household, or in the Council of State. . . ."

So that was what things had come to! Asking Louis XVIII to choose his companions in captivity! As he said sadly to Marchand one day, "The two of us will soon be alone!"

The Emperor's health was deteriorating from day to day, and the two generals were henceforth tied down. On December 5, 1820, Montholon wrote to his wife: "The Emperor's illness has taken a turn for the worse. His chronic disease has been complicated by a well-defined lingering illness. He is so weak that he cannot perform any vital function without experiencing extreme fatigue, and often losing consciousness. . . ."

By this time it was not just a question of great fatigue: he was in terrible pain: "I don't know what's wrong with my stomach. I have a pain there, as if someone had stuck a knife in it and kept moving it around."

In the early part of this austral summer, he would still go outside in the morning in his dressing gown and sit down heavily on his folding chair in the garden or on the little front stoop. "Ah!" he would sigh. "Poor me!"

By way of combating his listlessness, he had a seesaw built in the living room. Montholon, holding a bag of lead, would sit on one end of it, and the Emperor on the other. Such were his last rides, in the company of his last officer.

He soon lost his appetite, "except for a few thin slices of bread dipped in mutton gravy, a few spoonfuls of aspic, and a few slices of fried potato. He would drink only half a glass of wine diluted by the same amount of water. A few drops of coffee ended the meal." Then he would stretch out on his couch, where he would remain for an hour before going to bed.

Beginning in early March, 1821, he became extremely weak. On March 5 Montholon wrote to Albine: "Today he is a corpse animated by a breath of life—physically and psychologically. This damned St. Helena has killed him."

On March 16, he was unable to rise from his bed.

"Just look what I have come to! I was so active and alert! And now I can hardly raise an eyelash! But I'm no longer Napoleon!"

By this time his complexion was "so sallow it was frightening." As he lay prostrate in a quasi-torpor, his sleep was nothing more than a long reverie—or, rather, a state of depression.

His autopsy was to reveal that "the internal surface of the stomach, throughout almost all its extent, was a solid mass of cancerous affections or of scirrhous areas on the point of becoming cancerous: this was especially pronounced in the vicinity of the pylorus." The liver, though not hypertrophied, was somewhat larger than normal. But the medical report stated that "the convex surface of the left lobe of the liver was adhering to the diaphragm. With the exception of the adhesions caused by the diseased condition of the stomach, no pathological alteration was apparent in the liver."

Finally, he agreed to be treated by the British physician Dr. Arnott. But it was too late.

Napoleon was about to fight his last battle. Gnawed at by cancer, his body constantly shaken by vomiting, in such terrible pain that he could take no other nourishment than aspic, he asked Dr. Arnott in a feeble voice "whether one could die of weakness, and how long one could live when taking as little nourishment as he was." This dying prisoner was going first to dictate and then to write (making an effort to render his dreadful handwriting legible) a text that one cannot read without being moved.

Longwood, St. Helena, April 15, 1821

The following is my last will and testament.

I die in the apostolical and Roman religion, in the bosom of which I was born more than fifty years ago.

It is my wish that my ashes repose on the banks of the Seine, amid the French people whom I have loved so well.

He was quite aware that Marie Louise had forgotten him—although he did not suspect to what extent—and he wrote accordingly:

I have always been pleased with my very dear wife, Marie Louise, for whom I continue to have the greatest affection as my life draws to its close. I ask her to be vigilant in securing my son against the snares by which his youth is still beset.

I should wish my son never to forget that he was born a French prince, and never to allow himself to become an instrument in the hands of the triumvirs who are oppressing the peoples of Europe. He must never take up arms against France, or act against her in any way. He must adopt my motto: "Everything for the French people."

I die prematurely, murdered by the English oligarchy and its hired assassin. But the English people will not delay in avenging me.

The two most unfortunate outcomes of the invasions of France, at a time when she had so many resources, are due to the

treason of Marmont, Augereau, Talleyrand, and Lafayette. I forgive them. May future generations in France forgive them as I
have. . . .

All those remnants of his glory that he had so often gazed at
nostalgically during his exile were left to his son:

> My arms; to wit, the sword that I wore at Austerlitz, my dag-
> ger, my glaive, my hunting knife, and my two braces of pistols
> from Versailles. My golden dressing case that I used on the morn-
> ings of Ulm, Austerlitz, Jena, Eylau, Friedland, Lobau, La Mos-
> kowa, and Montmirail. . . .

There in that wretched little wooden house, while the wind blew
outside, the whole epic was lived over:

> My field glass, the French one, my orders, my camp beds, my
> uniforms, the *grand collier* of the Legion of Honor, my spurs, my
> Consul's glaive, the gold chain of the Order of the Golden Fleece,
> the three silver brandy flasks carried by my chasseurs in the field,
> the "alarm clock" belonging to Frederick the Great that I took at
> Potsdam, Sobieski's saber.

And the last trophy was ". . . four boxes found on the table of Louis
XVIII in the Tuileries on March 20, 1815. . . ."

Throughout these lines, the Alexandrine verse of nine words
recurs like a leitmotif: *"les remettre à mon fils quand il aura seize
ans"* [to be given to my son when he is sixteen].

With his remarkable prescience, Napoleon had foreseen that the
boy who had been fitted out with the title of Duke of Reichstadt—
and with a whole batch of titles from Czech seigniories un-
pronounceable even by an Austrian—would come into his brilliant
heritage. But Metternich was keeping an eye on things: the executors
of the will would not be authorized to pass on the relics of St. Helena
to the eagle's son.

And the prisoner in the Hofburg had given up the fight. He had
become an Austrian prince, thinking and writing in German, who in
his homework referred to his father as "M. de Buonaparte" and to
France as "the enemy." Just before he turned sixteen, the reading of
Napoleon's will (found in Montholon's *Mémoires*, which had appeared in 1825) would be, for him, like the rending of a veil.

On April 20, for the last time, Napoleon addressed himself to the British Government—although his immediate audience was Dr. Arnott:

> I came to sit at the hearth of the British nation, asking for honest hospitality; and against all the rights on earth, I was put in chains. I would certainly have been better received by Alexander, the Emperor Francis, or even the King of Prussia. Those sovereigns would have been more generous. But England won them over to her views, and provided the world with the unprecedented spectacle of four great powers hurling themselves against one man. It was your ministry which chose this loathsome rock where Europeans wear out their lives in just a few years, to finish mine off with an assassination. How have I been treated since I have been here? There is not a single indignity which has not been heaped upon me by my captors, to their own great delight. The most ordinary family communications have been denied me. I have not been permitted to have any news whatsoever of my wife and son. My dwelling place was fixed in the least habitable spot, where the murderous tropical climate is at its worst. I, who used to range over all Europe on horseback, was compelled to remain within four walls, in an unhealthful atmosphere. Such, Doctor, is the hospitality I have received from your Government! I have been done to death—slowly, deliberately, step by step; and the infamous Hudson Lowe is your Government's executioner. You shall come to the same end as the haughty Republic of Venice. And I, perishing on this loathsome rock, bequeath the shame of my death to the Ruling House of England.

He was speaking for posterity.

The next day he asked Father Vignali, an ignorant priest sent to St. Helena by Madame Mère and Fesch, "Do you know what a mortuary chapel is?"

"Yes, Sire."

"Have you ever officiated in one?"

"No, Sire."

"Well," continued Napoleon, "you will officiate in mine, when I am in the throes of death. You will set up an altar in the next room, you will display the Host, and you will say the prayers for the dying. I was born in the Catholic religion. I want to go through the rites it prescribes, and receive the comforts it dispenses."

On April 27 he was carried into the salon, where he could be cared for more easily. One of the little camp beds was set up in front of the black fireplace between the two sash windows.

It was not yet the end. On the night of April 28 he called in Marchand for a last codicil. The loyal valet could not find a piece of paper, so he picked up a playing card, on which he wrote:

> I bequeath to my son my dwelling house at Ajaccio, together with its outbuildings; the two houses in the vicinity of the salt marshes, with their gardens; and all my possessions in the territory of Ajaccio, capable of providing him with an annual income of 50,000 livres . . . I bequeath to my son.

He stopped, gasping: "I'm very tired. We'll continue tomorrow."

On May 2, the Emperor was like a docile, gentle child. Dr. Arnott gave him some wine with sugar. After each swallow he repeated, in English: "Good. Very good."

> They changed the flannel undervest [wrote Bertrand] and changed the dressing on his stomach. He almost fainted. Very weak, with glazed eyes, he gave Marchand a look that inspired pity and seemed to say: "You are cruel to make me suffer like this!" Throughout the day, he lacked the strength to refuse anything. He took everything offered him, and did everything he was told, without saying a word. Except on two occasions, he spoke only with his eyes. His hiccups became frequent, and he was given a teaspoonful of ether, which quieted him and brought him a few minutes' sleep. The second time he said, "That rogue, Marchand!" At 11:30 they changed his top sheet. To the Grand Marshal, who was sweating profusely as he held his hand, he said: "You are very warm." And again: "Mon ami, chase the flies away."

At the governor's request, a consultation was held among several physicians. They decided to rub down the small of his back with eau de Cologne.

When the Emperor was informed of the doctors' decision, he came abruptly out of his torpor and found the strength to exclaim: "What a scientific conclusion! What a consultation! Rub down the small of the back with eau de Cologne? Fine! As to the rest, I want none of it."

He was referring to the dose of calomel that they had given him without his noticing it. Or rather, by the time he did notice, it was too late, and he merely sighed, "Ah, Marchand! You too are deceiving me!"

The result was a stool "which looked like pitch or tar." The sheets had to be changed again—for the last time. Ali was supporting him. Napoleon gave him a tap in the side with his fist and moaned, "Ah, you scoundrel! You're hurting me!"

That evening the dying man called for Father Vignali. When he came out of the room, the priest said to Marchand, "I have just administered the last sacrament to the Emperor. The condition of his stomach does not permit any other rites."

> I went into the Emperor's room [writes Marchand], and found him with his eyes closed, and one arm extended along the edge of the bed. I got down on one knee and touched my lips to his hand, but his eyes did not open. Then I notified Saint-Denis. He did the same, but still the Emperor did not open his eyes. I stayed there alone, standing at the Emperor's bedside. I held back my sobs but not my tears.

But the Emperor came out of his torpor sufficiently to ask Marchand in a faint voice, "What is my son's name?"

"Napoleon."

On Friday, May 4, the day before his death, it rained without a letup, and the wind was violently strong. The willow beneath which the Emperor had liked to sit was torn up by the roots. Throughout the day the dying man, growing steadily weaker, lay prostrate and apparently senseless. The moment he had taken a bit of sugared water, he would throw it up.

Toward two in the morning Montholon thought he heard him utter the words: "*France, armée, tête d'armée, Josephine. . . .*"

Others maintained he had also said: "*Mon fils.*"

Saturday, May 5, dawned clear. A signal was hoisted, announcing to Plantation House: "General Bonaparte is in imminent danger."

Lowe came on the run: he wanted to wait out the denouement at Longwood. When he arrived, he was told that his prisoner was totally unconscious.

The salon was flooded with sunlight. The Emperor was motionless, not even lifting his hand to drive off the flies which had so much annoyed him these past few days.

One or two at a time, all the French came into the room to watch Napoleon die. His face was livid. With dull, half-closed eyes he stared at the foot of the bed. His right hand lay on top of the sheet, inert and clammy. There was nothing left of him but a dying man whose gasps were broken by the dull, wheezing moans of his agony.

At 7:30 he fainted, but life returned. At 8:00 a tear formed in his left eye and ran gently down his cheek. Bertrand wiped it off.

Throughout the day the last of his faithful followers and attendants—sixteen persons in all—kept their eyes fixed on that waxen face, now emaciated, whose features were gradually coming to resemble those of the young General Bonaparte. The silence was broken only by the ticking of the clock.

Toward the end of the afternoon, his breathing became labored and gasping. Napoleon was giving himself up slowly, very slowly, and slipping into death. At the moment when the sun sank into the sea, his breathing stopped. Antommarchi touched the jugular vein and bowed his head. Someone got up and stopped the clock.

It was 5:49.

Weeping unrestrainedly, they went one by one to kiss the dead man's hand.

Lowe, his staff officers, and the useless Montchenu (the other observers had left the island) bowed stiffly before the corpse, lying between the two windows of the salon where Napoleon had died.

"Do you recognize him?" the governor asked Montchenu in a whisper.

"Yes, I recognize him."

When the autopsy had been performed and the plaster death mask made (rather ineptly), the body—in the legendary uniform of a colonel of the light cavalry, with a crucifix on the breast—was laid out on one of the camp beds. The face was surprisingly beautiful. "In death," said the English doctor Shortt, "his face was the most splendid I have ever seen. It seemed to have been formed for conquest." All day long, the islanders and the officers and troops of the garrison filed past. Quite a few of them kneeled and, with the thumb, made the sign of the cross on the Emperor's forehead. One noncommissioned officer came up, leading a child by the hand, and said: "Come. Come and see the great man—the great Napoleon."

When Napoleon's death was announced in Vienna, stocks went up by two thalers. The prisoner of the English—the little corporal brought low by cancer in his bed of iron—was still making the world tremble.

At a time when death was already stalking the plateau of Longwood and Napoleon had made his will, he had called for Montholon, to dictate a letter. What the general took down from the dying man on that occasion is certainly the most extraordinary text among the hundreds of thousands of the Emperor's communications.

"Montholon, take this down. Here is the letter I want you to send to Hudson Lowe when I am dead."

Monsieur le Gouverneur,
    The Emperor Napoleon died on—you can fill in the date, Montholon—after a long and painful illness. I have the honor to inform you of the fact. He authorized me to convey to you, if you should so desire, his last wishes. Please let me know what arrangements your Government has ordered for the conveyance of his body to Europe; also, those relative to the persons in his suite.

With the Emperor dead, Montholon—who had been named by Napoleon as first executor of his will—anticir ted the Grand Marshal and filled in the blank left in the text of the letter, then had it taken to the Governor, informing him of the Emperor's wish to be buried in France.

The Governor replied to him that the matter had already been settled in September, 1817, by the British Governmer and confirmed by Lord Bathurst in 1820: the body of "General Bonaparte" was not to be taken off the island. The choice of a burial plot was left to the executors.

At this point, Bertrand intervened. He recalled that one day he and the Emperor had gone down into the valley which would later be named Geranium Valley, a fold in the terrain which formed a part of the vast Devil's Punch Bowl. Climbing down a steep path among the pines, the two men had reached a little valley from which, looking down the slope, one could see the ocean. Three weeping willows lent their shade to this tranquil spot. A spring flowed from a fissure in a rock, filling a small stone basin.

Napoleon had stooped down and drunk from the spring. He had liked the water so much that every morning since, the outrider Archambault had come with two silver bottles to get some of it for the Emperor's personal use.

As they left the little valley the Emperor had told his companion: "Bertrand, if after my death my body remains in the possession of my enemies, you will have it buried here."

Hence there need be no hesitation: that was the place where Napoleon would be buried.

"I should think that you would not want any inscription on the gravestone," Lowe had said, "since you would want to use titles that I cannot allow."

"No, all we want is the words: 'Napoleon. Born in 1769, died in 1821.' "

"I cannot permit you to use 'Napoleon' alone. It must read: 'Napoleon Bonaparte.' "

Bertrand and Montholon refused—and the slab over the grave remained without a name.

On Thursday, May 10, the heavy coffin—loaded into the Emperor's former carriage transformed into a hearse—was taken down the road to the valley. The entire garrison stood at attention along the roadside. Salvos were fired by the forts and the naval vessels; and military bands played as the funeral cortege went by.

The procession was headed by Father Vignali, accompanied by the little Henri Bertrand, who served as choirboy. The pall was carried by the three executors: Bertrand, Montholon, and Marchand, together with the young Napoleon Bertrand. They were followed by a dozen unarmed grenadiers, who carried the coffin when the path broke off from the road so that the carriage could no longer follow it. Behind them came the Emperor's horse, led by Archambault; then all the servants of Longwood; and finally a vehicle carrying Mme. Bertrand, her daughter, and her youngest son. Lowe walked along behind his prisoner's coffin, accompanied by his officers and Montchenu, who was now representing Austria as well as France— and who, when all is said and done, had come to St. Helena only to witness the burial of "the Usurper," since the Emperor had never agreed to receive him.

When the prayers had been said, the coffin was lowered into the grave. Then the heavy slab was put in place; and the last loyal followers had the sudden feeling of an overwhelming solitude.

A detail of a dozen British soldiers would remain on guard at the grave for nineteen years. Thus, among the geraniums planted by Mme. Bertrand, a sentinel in his red uniform would keep watch over the body which had remained a prisoner of its implacable enemy.

Nineteen years after Napoleon's death King Louis Philippe asked England to be kind enough to return Napoleon's remains to France. The Prince de Joinville—the King's son—went to bring back the Emperor's coffin; and on December 14, 1840, the body was brought up the Seine to Neuilly, at the gates of Paris.

Twenty-one salvos signaled the arrival. All the troops in Paris marched ahead of the cortege or stood at attention along the roadside, holding back with difficulty the huge crowd of people who were gazing—through shakos and fur caps—at the unusual spectacle. Then came the Emperor's war-horse, bearing the saddle and trappings of the First Consul. (Actually, it was a mount obtained from the royal stables.)

Eighty-seven noncommissioned officers on horseback held aloft the banners on which were written the names of the 86 *départements,* plus Algeria. At the top of each standard was an eagle with outstretched wings. Next came the Prince de Joinville, mounted, wearing the full-dress uniform of a naval captain. The 400 sailors of the frigate *Belle Poule* marched in two columns beside the hearse. To its right and left, the four corners of the imperial pall were held up by Marshal Oudinot, Marshal Molitor, Admiral Roussin, and General Bertrand. They were followed by the Emperor's former aides-de-camp and the civil and military officers of his household.

> The cannon thundered [wrote Valérie Masuyer, goddaughter of the Empress Josephine], the bells rang, and the flags dipped. As the bells rang the hour of noon—in a freezing cold which recalled the retreat from Russia, but under a sun recalling that of Austerlitz—the hearse moved along, pulled by sixteen horses in violet velvet with the armorial bearings of the Empire. Under the golden dome formed by the emblems, the garlands, and the trophies supporting the crown of glory and thorns, the hidden Em-

peror was yet visible! Yes, one could still see him as a poor officer, as general, as Consul, as conqueror, as the vanquished man and the captive, but still great. With its devout murmur the crowd seemed to be acclaiming him again—in ecstasy, yet gently, so as not to disturb his repose: his last conquest.

The Emperor in his hearse, wearing his legendary uniform of a colonel of the chasseurs of the Guard and surrounded by personifications of Victory, passed through the Arc de Triomphe de l'Étoile— that arch commensurate with his glory that he had offered to Paris. To the strains of a funeral march, he went down the most beautiful avenue in the world—an avenue sketched out one day, with one stroke of the pen, by the royal gardener of the Sun King.

On St. Helena, the Emperor had predicted to his companions: "You will still hear Paris shout 'Vive l'Empereur!' "

Grenadiers, chasseurs of the Old Guard, the Empress' Dragoons, Red Lancers, the Dragons de la Mort—all filed past, swaggering and holding their heads high for this last parade—for this procession of phantoms. And the hearts of these ghosts pounded to the breaking point as they escorted their Emperor toward the gilded dome which would henceforth preserve his eternal sleep.

Marshal Moncey, officer in charge of Les Invalides, who was eighty-seven years old, had had himself carried to the foot of the catafalque in his chair. For the past week he had been begging his physician: "Doctor, let me live just a little while longer! I want to receive the Emperor!"

At the entrance to the Dome, Louis Philippe came to meet the cortege. At his request, Bertrand placed Napoleon's sword on the coffin. Gourgaud did the same with the legendary hat.

When the long religious service was over, Moncey was heard to murmur: "And now let's go home to die."

INDEX